Praise for On Writing: A Process Reader

"I think that *The Process Reader* will help students become better writers, readers, and thinkers."

—ANN K. DEPREY, UNIVERSITY OF WISCONSIN, GREEN BAY

"I am unbelievably impressed with the reader."

—M. TODD HARPER, KENNESAW STATE UNIVERSITY

"This book is critically astute and also fun, written and edited with a poet's love for language, as well as with a teacher's awareness that students and other readers are real people, not statistics. It is a book that encourages students to take responsibility for and invest themselves in their learning."

—CORNELIA WELLS, WILLIAM PATTERSON UNIVERSITY

"As with all of her other work in composition, Wendy Bishop here demonstrates a keen awareness of the thoughts, feeling and situations of today's composition students and teachers. [. . .] *On Writing* helps demystify the many challenging concepts presented to students in college writing courses."

—RANDALL MCCLURE, MINNESOTA STATE UNIVERSITY, MANKATO

"On Writing is a smart, ambitious text that keeps its focus on writing and writers—even in its reading selections. The text invites students to see themselves in the company of writers: to explore their own literacy history as they read others' histories; to become aware of their rhetorical choices as they plan, draft, collaborate, and edit, and to acquire a sense of authorship as they revise in response to their own readers, whether peers or instructors."

—DONA J. HICKEY, UNIVERSITY OF RICHMOND

"What makes this text different is the way in which it approaches students. It deems them writers right from the start and seeks to hone or reveal their skills rather than create them where there was presumably nothing before."

—JENNIFER E. BRADNER, VIRGINIA COMMONWEALTH UNIVERSITY

"I loved the material at the end of the chapters. Loved it. Rarely do I see in textbooks this quality of writing activities and reflective work. [. . .] The text's greatest strength? I can't choose [just] one."

—MICHELLE PAYNE, BOISE STATE UNIVERSITY

"Bishop demonstrates a genuine respect for student writers, and her introductions are fine examples of learning-centered writing. [. . .] The 'Consider This' sections are splendid, and the prompts go beyond the generic 'pre-reading' exercises I find in so many other readers."

—JAMES BROCK, FLORIDA GULF COAST UNIVERSITY

"The introductions are lively and thought-provoking. Confronting students with the fact that they are already writers and rhetoricians is an ingenious approach. [. . .] The 'Connection to Reading' prompts are well conceived and offer a variety of activities that will be fun (yes!) for students."

—ED MORITZ, INDIANA UNIVERSITY AND PURDUE UNIVERSITY

"Here's a reader that allows a composition instructor to teach the writing process while involving the student in a wide range of readings that allow for varying methods and assignments."

—KATHRYN M. HAMILTON, COLUMBUS STATE UNIVERSITY

"On Writing sheds new light on an old approach."

—ANNE GERVASI, DEVRY INSTITUTE OF TECHNOLOGY

On Writing

A Process Reader

Wendy Bishop
Florida State University

Boston Burr Ridge, IL Dubuque, IA Madison, WI New York
San Francisco St. Louis Bangkok Bogotá Caracas Kuala Lumpur
Lisbon London Madrid Mexico City Milan Montreal New Delhi
Santiago Seoul Singapore Sydney Taipei Toronto

ON WRITING: A PROCESS READER
Published by McGraw-Hill, a business unit of The McGraw-Hill Companies, Inc., 1221 Avenue of the Americas, New York, NY, 10020.
Some ancillaries, including electronic and print components, may not be available to customers outside the United States.

This book is printed on acid-free paper.

1 2 3 4 5 6 7 8 9 0 FGR/FGR 0 9 8 7 6 5 4 3

ISBN 0-07-237939-1

President of McGraw-Hill Humanities/Social Sciences: *Steve Debow*
Senior sponsoring editor: *Alexis Walker*
Executive marketing manager: *David S. Patterson*
Project manager: *Ruth Smith*
Lead production supervisor: *Randy L. Hurst*
Senior designer: *Gino Cieslik*
Supplement producer: *Kathleen Boylan*
Permissions: *Marty Granahan*
Cover image: *Paul Klee*
Interior design: *Gino Cieslik*
Typeface: *10/12 Palatino*
Compositor: *GAC Indianapolis*
Printer: *Quebecor World Fairfield Inc.*

Library of Congress Cataloging-in-Publication Data

Bishop, Wendy, 1953-
On writing: a process reader/Wendy Bishop.
p. cm.
Includes index.
ISBN 0-07-237939-1 (acid-free paper)
1. English language—Rhetoric. 2. College readers. 3. Report writing. I. Title.
PE1408.B5125 2004
808'.0427—dc22

2003061417

www.mhhe.com

To my family—Dean, Morgan, & Tait;
Jesse, Andrea, Amelia & Katie; Jeremy, Jen, Payton & Jacob;
Eowyn, Julian, & Tyler; Dean & Andrea

I am so composed that nothing is real unless I write it.
—Virginia Woolf

Brief Contents

Contents

About the Author

WENDY BISHOP, Kellogg W. Hunt Professor of English, teaches writing at Florida State University. She is the author or editor of a number of books in composition as well as several chapbooks of poetry. She lives in Tallahassee, Florida.

Introductions

To the Writing Student

How wonderful the struggle with language is.

—THEODORE ROETHKE, POET

You're in a writing class. You're assigned an anthology to read. It is this one, *On Writing: A Process Reader.* You may be wondering how you'll put this collection to use. While your teacher will assign certain chapters and particular readings and activities, I hope, too, that you'll explore and make use of this reader as you compose. Say you come home with an assignment. You go to the keyboard, but your hands aren't moving. At that moment, this reader has a place beside the computer. Open it to Chapter 3, "Considering Community and Audience"; or Chapter 4, "Writing to Find Your Topic: Inventing, Exploring, Discovering"; or Chapter 6, "Drafting, Responding, and Revising." Whenever you write, you can consult selections in this book for ideas about how to start—and continue—your work. And at the end of each chapter, you'll find a number of writing projects to help you launch yourself into your draft or improve a draft you've already begun.

Now it's another day. You look at the words glowing on the computer screen and think you'd rather do anything than continue. Writers whose work is shared in *On Writing: A Process Reader* understand that feeling. Do the housework and think about your writing. Go to a coffee shop, go for a run, write an e-mail to a friend, or do other things that allow you to place your writing on the meditative back burner (*Hint:* watching TV is rarely the best choice since it seems to put thought entirely off the stove). In any case, after a short break, return to *On Writing: A Process Reader* and read Gail Godwin's essay. It can give you ideas about what is stopping you and make suggestions for getting going again. Psychiatrist Thomas Szasz claims, "As the swimmer depends on water, so the writer depends on language," and poet and essayist Adrienne Rich explains that "Language is as real, as tangible, in our lives as streets, pipelines, telephone switchboards, microwaves, radioactivity, cloning laboratories, nuclear power stations." Workers in words with two distinctly different professions, Szasz and Rich agree that language matters, and you'll find similar testimony when you turn to literacy narratives like those found in Chapter 2 of *On Writing: A Process Reader.* When a section of these narratives pulls you in, compare your own writing background to that author's background.

I encourage you to write back to the authors in this anthology, saving your responses in a journal entry. Better yet, consider how you might incorporate their experiences or advice into your own drafts. Writers regularly turn to other writers because sharing thoughts on processes and techniques can prime the pump. *On Writing: A Process Reader* provides such counsel in a fairly compact form. Instead of a shelf of books containing writers commenting on writing, you have this collection. It's an oasis, a reservoir, a cache, a compendium of insights and exercises. Enter as directed for your class, but be bold and join these conversations for yourself.

Thinking like and with writers inclines you to reconsider your own essay on local elections, or the history of the scientific method, or contemporary literature. For instance, you can use the index to help you find Kurt Vonnegut's essay that offers direct advice for your writing. You realize he's a writer you've heard about before, so you go to the Internet, as one end-of-chapter writing project suggests, and create your own, extended, author's biography for him from the many biographical resources you find there. Then you compose your own author's introduction. Or perhaps you decide to look up other works by Vonnegut using the on-line search engine at your library or consulting an on-line bookstore. By checking out or purchasing some of his other writings, or by borrowing a friend's copy of his books, you find ideas for your own writing life. Writers often undertake tangential yet text-related wanderings and wondering of this sort.

Still writing? Still waiting to write? Perhaps it will help to read all the poems on writing in this book and write your own poem. Perhaps you wish you were done with your draft so you look at the chapters on revising to see if you can safely say that's so, or, if you can't, to get some ideas for continuing and finishing. Perhaps you simply feel disengaged from your essay: it seems . . . the same. . . . That's when you should remember that I've provided some stylistic jump starts. Look at suggestions for undertaking a radical revision of your own essay draft (Chapter 6), and consider how each of the contributors to this reader writes with style and voice—aspects of texts that can be analyzed, imitated, and incorporated into your own style kit. While all the selections collected in *On Writing: A Process Reader* offer ideas for improving your writing, the style discussions and samples in Chapters 5 and 9 do so pointedly, providing a number of options to explore as you polish and prepare to present your paper.

Poet Derek Walcott reminds us that "the English language is nobody's special property. It is the property of the imagination: it is the property of the language itself," and essayist Bell Hooks explains, "Like desire, language disrupts, refuses to be contained within boundaries." Writers rise to the challenge of language work. They strive to organize and make sense of their worlds using the words at their command. In each chapter of this reader, I've included drafts by both undergraduate and graduate students who were enrolled in my writing courses and were meeting writing challenges similar to the ones you are meeting. Some of these classroom authors were required to take these courses, some elected to take them. Some had extensive writing experience, some very little. With several of their essays, I've included the writer's process narrative. These offer detailed composing stories and provide insights into writing decisions, the normally *hidden* work of writing. And, of course, I encourage you to keep similar composing notes of your own to tell your stories of writing.

In compiling this book, I assume you are in charge. You have needs as a writer. I know that writers have to hazard a draft and then all else comes to them. Remember, writing is not a 1 + 1 = 2 math problem or we'd all have arrived at the same solution by now. Sometimes you'll forget what you learned, sometimes you'll learn what you can't yet use. Some days you're hot and some cold, but the net progress is forward. I trust this collection of readings can support your forward movement, and that you'll make this collection yours: underline, highlight, doubt, believe, journal, draft. The goal here is to create your own best writing.

A Few Words on How Writing and Reading Work Together

Writers need readers. Writers are readers. Let's examine these two claims by considering this student's scene of writing:

> I live in a loud dorm, so I constantly have people running in and out of my room. I share my ideas with them and see how they react. If I see an interest in a certain part of the story, I go back to the computer and expand on it.

Like most authors, this writer is already immersed in a composing process. As you'll (re)learn in Chapter 1, writers engage in a complex, interactive cycle of idea generation, drafting (trying out those ideas), revision after response (gained when they reread their own texts or other readers review them), editing, and sharing. Writers and readers construct texts together: they need each other. The two activities create a dialogue, a conversation, a dance, a game, a compact, a contract.

The writer has aims and she enacts them in a text to the best of her abilities, and the reader responds to that text, bringing to bear on each rendering of text a complex history as a reader of other texts. In describing this interaction, teacher Jeanette Harris explains that each writer constructs his version of a *mental text,* which is the physical text—generally words on a page but also text on a Web page or visual and other media texts—and a reader creates her "mental text" from the physical text. Much can happen along the way: herein rests the oxymoronic "wonderful struggle" with language that poet Theodore Roethke mentions in the quote that opens this introduction.

Consider the reader you were of *Alice's Adventures in Wonderland,* the classic children's text, at age 10 (substitute *your* favorite children's book to make this example work). Perhaps you enjoyed the outlandish cast of characters—the White Rabbit, the Caterpillar, and the Mad Hatter—or your reading was informed by your viewing of the Disney animated feature, or you were influenced in how you visualized each character by the original John Tenniel drawings that accompany the text. Perhaps all three influences shaped your initial and subsequent readings of this book. If a parent or sibling or baby-sitter read all or part of the book with you or aloud to you, you may have been informed, too, by any shared discussions of the book. You may have been asked in school to write a poem like "The Jabberwocky" or watched a scene from *Alice's Adventures in Wonderland* illustrated or parodied on a TV show. Then, you may have returned to the book privately, poured over the pictures, daydreamed across the text: imagined your family members as characters in that world or escaped to that world (and to the worlds of Lewis Carroll's other books).

By the time you left the book, the TV screen, the computer game based on these or related characters and moved on to other texts, you had particular ideas of what the book was all about. Rereading *Alice's Adventures in Wonderland* in your children's literature course in college will prove dramatically different, familiar yet strange. In that class, you may read the *Annotated Alice* by Martin Gardner, which offers historical information and asides about the life of the author Lewis Carroll, in real life Charles Dodson (1831–1898), an eccentric lecturer in mathematics at Oxford University whose stutter disappeared in the presence of the young girls whose company he preferred, and whose images he captured in photographs and in his imaginative writing. You will find the book less enchanting, perhaps, but more interesting as you realize the author was working at several levels: to entertain Alice Liddell, the original Alice, but also to find an outlet for Dodson's witty and complicated language play, math puzzles, and commentary. You'll marvel at the number of Web discussion groups on the Internet and find biographies and any number of informative (and silly) links and even full-text versions of Carroll's classic.

One physical text written by Charles Dodson. A number of mental texts, including your own, changing over time. And, of course, your early reading and pleasure (or bemusement) with the book will inform your later readings, even as you gain new insight. Jeannette Harris claims, "By understanding the process by which writers and readers construct texts, you will become a better writer and reader." I agree. But more exactly, how does that happen? If you don't consider yourself much of a reader, how do you become more proficient at reading to aid your writing?

Think about a successful child who reads as outlined above. He picks (or is offered) texts that interest him and challenge him (*Alice's Adventures in Wonderland* is not simple reading). He rereads, reads aloud, talks to others about his reading, imagines, rehearses, practices, draws pictures, writes back to the text. Later, in college, aiming to be a successful adult who reads, he studies, investigates the historical time period, gathers biographical data about Charles Dodson, studies Dodson's photographs, forms his own, more complicated version of how and why *Alice's Adventures in Wonderland* was composed, and writes back to it again, converses with the text in the form of a critical written response (which can still be admiring). All the activities I've mentioned are advocated by reading experts and writing experts. They are methods for situating yourself actively in the textual processes and usefully inform your reading, writing, and thinking. Let me in this case replace the term you've often heard—critical thinking—with some other useful terms: active thinking, reflective thinking, systematic thinking, engaged thinking (and, finally, reading and writing). Then, when you're ready for a further discussion on this subject, turn to Chapter 3, where Deborah Coxwell Teague offers you advice about reading and rereading in college by reviewing selective underlining, making marginal comments, and keeping a reading response journal or double-entry notebook.

To explore your own feeling about reading, consider the following strong statements generated by one first-year writing class. Circle those you believe in and place a check beside those you would challenge:

Strong Statements About Reading

(Truths, Myths or . . . ?)

1. If it's in a book it's true.
2. Women are better readers than men.
3. Reading is a linear process.
4. Good writers have to read a lot.
5. Reading is a solitary activity.
6. The teacher's interpretation (reading) is always right.
7. English majors love to read.
8. Reading is to gain information.
9. Faster reading is better reading.
10. Reading is all about printed texts.
11. Always highlight key points in what you read.
12. It's the writer's fault if a reader can't understand.
13. Reading is exploration.
14. Reading is a learnable process.
15. Reading is a waste of time.
16. Reading is escape.
17. One is born to be a good reader.
18. There is no such thing as a nonreader.

Add two statements of your own or your peers.

19.

20.

During discussions, classroom authors offered the following advice to each other:

> Eat something before you read, otherwise hunger preoccupies your thoughts. • Keep a pen and paper near to write down important things. • Take a short nap before you read. Or stop reading, nap, and wake up refreshed and ready to read. • Use your dictionary. Be comfortable but not too comfortable. • If highlighting is distracting, outline and read more than once. • Research the author. Make a schedule and stick to it. • Carry the book with you since you'll never know when you'll have some free time. • Don't be overly critical; go into reading with an open mind. • Clean your room before you read. • When reading something that is not interesting, sit up. • When reading a textbook, look at pictures, headings, extra comments, to get a full idea of what you will be reading before actually doing it. • Ask others for their input about the book you are reading.

Does this advice sound familiar? Useful? Problematic? In what ways? Now, transfer these observations about reading to writing. Which provide sound advice for you as you compose? For instance, isn't it important when rereading your own writing to use a dictionary, to be comfortable, to not be over critical, and sometimes even to clean your room so as not to be distracted or in order to focus your procrastination? In addition, consider two informal writings by classroom authors. What advice could you now offer them for connecting reading and writing processes?

> For me, the process of reading factual texts is a struggle. I find my mind drifting off to another place. I feel as if it's being forced upon me and that I have no choice but to read it. The process of reading imaginative texts is much easier. It's not something you have to think about; it's something you enjoy. I can't really see it as a process, because it just flows much easier. I read student writing as something I could have written myself. So at first, I am very easy on it. I pick out only the good points. But then I get more critical with it and think of ways it could be different. Yet, as a whole, I like reading students' works because they are something I can closely relate to.

> For me, factual material is like putting a stew together—if you read or skip over something, everything is messed up or will fall apart. For me, reading imaginative material is like a bird gliding over the ocean. For me, reading my own writing is like cleaning up my room. I have to make sure nothing is wrong and everything is in the right place.

This term, you'll add your own investigations to this developing conversation. You can do so by composing a literacy narrative (Chapter 2); by considering the role of audience (readers) for writers (Chapters 3 and 8); and by investigating the relationship of fact-based to imaginative-based texts or pleasure to academic reading. You'll notice that in the course of this introduction I've begun to list all the chapters of this reader since nearly all the authors included make some mention of reading in relation to writing. As you join in, as you read your peers' work, I trust you'll keep in mind, too, the delight of shared texts:

> "I read for pleasure and to find out things, learn about things and worlds, people I don't know and am curious about."

And that you'll continue on to become a similar sort of writer for the readers of your own work.

To the Writing Teacher

> All essays should be, not trials, but celebrations.
>
> —THEODORE ROETHKE

It seems to me that practicing, professional, publishing writers do two things that the students in my writing classes often don't. First, professional writers write often and a lot even if "a lot" consists of rewriting the same opening paragraph 15 times. They spend hours on a task; they are committed. Writing is not a trial but a celebration of craft. Commitment is something we know student writers often don't have in similar quantities, but they don't have it for many different reasons. Some have never received positive responses to their writing, making it hard to return to a writing task. Some do not allow for (or have) many spaces in their lives that support productive drafting sessions. They may not yet see themselves as writers, so returning to writing is difficult. Second, professional writers are interested in writing as a subject; they live in that territory, they speak that language. They read professional journals and participate in live readings; they attend conferences and panel discussions. Their houses and offices are filled with texts, in many genres, not only in the genre they perform best in or write in most often. They love the trappings of and technologies of communication (pen, paper, notebooks, note cards, notebook computers, the Web). Writers are interested, too, in the wide world—culture and nature—the people and environments that they encounter, that they actively seek out.

Most writing classroom readers provide writing students with models: examples of good writing by good writers. Potentially, this type of collection will help an interested student become engaged in a craft conversation. The theory is, beginning writers read exciting work and in response produce excellent works of their own. This may happen sometimes, but not often enough; perhaps because a models-oriented anthology doesn't help classroom authors with the *whys* and *hows* of their own composing process. It doesn't always get them in dialogue with writers or explain the inner workings of text-making from a writer's point of view, which is so often the view our writing students need to adopt.

The selections in *On Writing: A Process Reader* help your students to talk more expertly about composing and to produce engaging and effective written products. Consider using *On Writing: A Process Reader* in one of several ways. It can function as a rhetoric when you assign reading selections and the three types of chapter exercises ("Connecting to Reading," "Connecting to Writing," and "Writing Projects") in a manner that supports your own, current class plan. I've offered suggestions for how these invitations and activities can work to encourage reflection in a writing process journal, prepare an author for small- or large-group discussions, and lead to collaborative writing (through e-mail exchanges with class partners or by posting to a class on-line discussion board), and so on. Most of the end-of-chapter activities, in fact, can be adapted to any of these modes and methods.

Early in the term, for a first draft of a paper, you might choose selections from Chapter 4, "Writing to Find Your Topic: Inventing, Exploring, Discovering" to help classroom authors generate topics. You might also choose to assign the literacy narrative as a first paper, using samples in Chapter 2, or you can begin by focusing on readings in Chapter 1, "Writers and Ways of Writing" to help students begin a review of their own writing history as part of their literacy narrative or to set the scene for their term-long writing activities. *The Instructor's Manual for On Writing: A Process Reader* offers additional advice on course design.

Equally, you can use *On Writing: A Process Reader* for a course themed to literacy and cultural study since there are many essays that delight but also instruct. For instance, Lorrie Moore's "How to Become a Writer" offers models of parody and humor and illuminates the how-to form. Fan Shen's "The Classroom and the Wider Culture: Identity as a Key to Learning English Composition," Gerald Graff's "Disliking Books at an Early Age," and Haunani-Kay Trask's "Tourist, Stay Home" are all, different, yet teachable versions of the essay: the kind of essays we and our classroom authors want to, need to, and are often asked to write. A course might begin by examining essays like these. Read selectively, *On Writing: A Process Reader* can also support a number of term-long themes. Using this text, you can shape a course around issues of memory, language, access, writers' worlds, and other literacy and writing topics.

For each chapter in *On Writing: A Process Reader,* you'll find a brief overview of the readings and an explanation of how these readings connect to the chapter's theme. You'll notice that I don't provide the traditional author's biography for each reading; rather, I've mixed together biographical information, invitations to read the style of an essay (suggestions for rhetorical analysis), discussions of theme, and pre- and post-reading activities in a headnote titled "Consider This."

Despite numerous drawbacks (among them, unjuried posting of information which makes all sites look equally valuable and appealing), the World Wide Web allows writing students to become more active as researchers. For instance, before reading work by Mike Rose, your students might be encouraged to consult a useful search engine such as google.com, finding 6,109 hits for "mike rose" in an 0.87 second search (as I just did). Several of those hits will be valuable, an interview with Mike Rose, a homepage, discussion groups commenting on his writings; on the other hand, a researcher will have to sort out the Mike Rose

Soccer Complex, Mike Rose Hobbies (another Mike Rose), and so on. Only about every tenth listing on this search is potentially useful for learning more about this author (for Lorrie Moore, I found 4,070 hits, for Gerald Graff, 1,170, for Richard Rodriguez 6,060). In fact, you and your students may be writing in a computer-supported classroom where materials like these can be accessed immediately, or you may still ask your no-doubt-networked students to perform this type of pre- or post-reading exercise at any time during the term. Doing this creates an opportunity to talk about the strengths and weaknesses of web-based research.

The fact that *On Writing: A Process Reader* asks students to be active co-creators of their writing process knowledge illustrates how this collection of writings on writing does—intentionally—represent a very different theory of textbook design. I've collected here the most student-friendly selections I could find but also selections that are united by their rendering of writers' actual experiences, thoughts, reflections, and practices, and I've included numerous examples of undergraduate *and* graduate writing. I've chosen to include graduate writing because these drafts demonstrate the rich possibility of student work and challenge undergraduates to become better writers (and in several cases, the graduate writers whose work I share began as undergraduate writing students in my courses). Classroom-generated texts are printed in a typewriter font to indicate that they developed out of the same assignments that are shared before or after readings.

This is a textbook of textbooks, an anthology that compiles the best writing on writing from other anthologies. I've surveyed collections to see what essays seemed to endure and I've gone into my own teaching files and those of friends to gather additional materials in order to compile the best advice I could find concerning writing. In a way, I've tried to make orderly the normal, disorderly collections all teachers and writers keep in a big file called memorable and practical advice. *On Writing: A Process Reader* shares voices that can substitute for your teacher's voice when your student is away from class and in need of a quick instructional pick-me-up. For the new teacher or for the seasoned teacher who wants a bit more discussion of the teaching theory that informs this collection, again, consider the *Instructor's Manual.*

Acknowledgments

Teacher: one who carries on his [and her] education in public.

—THEODORE ROETHKE

My deep gratitude to the many classroom and professional authors who have allowed me to showcase their work here (and to their publishers). I've learned from every piece I've read and, hopefully, these authors' fine examples have informed my prose style. Lisa Moore, Katherine Glynn, Alexis Walker, and the McGraw Hill editorial and production staff all deserve tremendous thanks for their insights, patience, and support for this project. I also hope this collection pleases my family who have watched it develop, page after page.

Chapter 1

Writers and Ways of Writing

Thinking About Definitions of Writer *and the Processes Writers Choose and Use*

Classroom authors on writing

- Writing is like painting a picture with words and lots of details.
- Writing is like giving birth: conception of an idea, delivery of the idea onto paper (strain, stress, pain, and anxiety) and completion (relief and joy), leaving one empty and exhausted, yet elated with the product and anxious for its future.
- Writing is like talking; it should be entertaining.

Writing teachers on writing—

- Writing is like running. It's hard to get motivated, but once I get going, it picks up momentum until I reach that "high."
- Writing is like spelunking with no light. I bump my head really hard, then change directions. Sometimes I draw a little map of what the cave is supposed to look like, but I always lose it a few feet into the darkness.

Think about "scenes" of writing that you have read in books or seen in movies or on TV. If the writer is scribbling furiously, surely he must be composing a masterpiece. Is the hollow-eyed writer sitting in a small, shabby room, pecking at a typewriter with two fingers and blowing cigarette smoke into the air? Then surely he is a dedicated artist. Most of us have vivid media images of writers. Consider the writers you meet in movies such as *Misery, Wonder Boys,* and *Orange County:* boys and men touched by madness, obsession, discouragement. Look for the few good women in *His Girl Friday* and *Dash and Lilly:* scrappy, pushy, often bucking the male-dominated system.

Late into the last century, writers seemed always to work late at night before typewriters, cursing and crushing paper. And now, less glamorously, they peer into computer screens. Often, we seem to love our authors best when they are most outrageous in their behaviors. Popular images of loneliness and eccentric behaviors dominate, and many authors become as well known for personal characteristics and habits as for their writing. Writers smoke and drink (Lillian Hellman, Raymond Carver). They fight or deploy ironic wit (Dorothy Parker, Lorrie Moore). They're hip and intellectual (T. C. Boyle, Susan Sontag, Henry Lois Gates, Jr.). They're wild men and women (Jack Keroac, Jane Gallop); they're expansive and wise (Walt Whitman, Toni Morrison); they're famous suicides (Ernest Hemingway, Anne Sexton, Sylvia Plath); they're mysteries (Weldon Kees); they're keen observers of the human psyche (Lynna Williams, Brent Staples); and they're renowned for their insights into the every day (William Stafford, Charles Baxter, Anne Tyler). Actually, most writers I know exhibit many of these behaviors, and more. And generally, they're less concerned with image and more aware of their own fallibility. They are interesting and dedicated individuals. And they write in moving ways—different ways.

For some of us, this persistent image of the lone writer is troubling; perhaps that is why Lorrie Moore composed her tongue-in-cheek yet also rather serious directions on how (not?) to become one of these culturally constructed stereotypes. As you read her work, remember also the images that aren't regularly portrayed in the media yet still exist in great variety. Consider a young female wiggan vegetarian who writes plays in collaboration with her sister; a dreadlocked poet who performs his poetry to jazz and composes and presents his work on video; a once-heterosexual, now-gay, older woman who shapes her best-selling romance novels on the PC screen. For many, the romantic "scene" of writing has been illuminated with new light, new knowledge, new images like these. Writers are people who write, varied in personality and process.

How do you write? How do professionals write? How do successful and unsuccessful authors compose, and what are the differences between their writing processes? To investigate, you could begin by responding to the prompts: "For me, writing is like. . . . " "For me, revising is like. . . . " "For me, the best 'scene' of writing is. . . . " "For me, sharing my writing is like. . . . "

As you'll see, authors seek to develop new understandings of how they write:

> After spending this semester learning about composing as a process, I am more apt to see similarities between "art" and regular writing. Similarities exist in the process itself. The stages are the same whether you are writing a sonnet or an essay, prewriting, writing, and revision. It happens over and over no matter what the outlet. The stages may vary but by and large they remain similar. By learning about the composing process a writer can become more fluent in the language of writing.
>
> —Classroom Author

It's easy to forget the way in which we are like our favorite authors and those authors are much like us, travelers (Barry Lopez, Diane Ackerman) and dog and horse lovers (Vicki Hearne, Jane Smiley). Real writers represent diverse home cultures (Jamaica Kincaid, Langston Hughes, Richard Rodriguez, Paule Marshall, Sherman Alexie, Terry Tempest Williams); they hold other jobs, as many of us do or will (Oliver Sachs, Spike Lee, Domitila De Chungara, Stanley Witkin). For many writers, a number of whom you'll read in this book, composing is only part of their active, often activist, lives. For others, it is the center of everything they do. Because of this diversity, it's worth investigating how writers actually create their texts.

Early researchers in composition studies in the 1960s and 1970s began to do this by studying writers' drafts and final written products and developed a model of writing that included three stages: prewriting, writing, and rewriting.

By the 1980s and 1990s though, researchers realized this model still remains relatively linear, which is no surprise since it was derived from written products. Over time, we've learned a great deal about the complicated nature of composing, exploring the ways in which writers use planning in the prewriting *and* in the writing stages. "It's crucial to stress the process of draft, critique, and revision" explains Kelley Cherry.

When writing researchers began to focus on revision, they found that expert writers use many strategies to improve their work—adding and deleting material, for example, but also reordering a text and thinking about its structure and meaning in general. Inexpert writers, on the other hand, speak primarily of cleaning up their writing; they have few strategies for revision; and often, they just don't revise enough.

Ask classroom authors about their previous experiences with writing and you'll find that some can't say much and some say a lot. Some keep their heads down in English classes and methodically turn in assigned themes and essays. For many, it seems ludicrous to consider what they do a process: they are happy if they just get a paper turned in on time. In some cases, classroom authors experience a disjunction between what their teachers say and what they actually seem to expect.

Others know about their processes of writing and have learned to think through writing assignments systematically, to bring in a rough draft for peer and/or teacher response, and to take those responses and use them to help revise writing. Some consider their audience—and places where writing like theirs might be published—and learn to edit texts to conform to standard publishing conventions and common usage.

Such self-knowledge leads to improved abilities. I believe you are a writer every time you write. I also know you become a better writer by drafting and revising; by studying writers' lives in the fullest sense; by learning about their interests and beliefs, work habits and rituals, writing processes and techniques. You'll also want to read nonfiction, essays, poems, stories, dramas, screenplays, and novels to extend your knowledge of form and craft.

As a writer, you are yourself composed of your beliefs, and no two writers will view the world in exactly the same way; you have to find your way. That's a good thing, actually, for as you do this you develop self-knowledge and you also develop self-trust. Research and writers' practices show that writing is about choices, large and small—choices that can't always be discovered by looking at the finished text. Everything we've learned about writing suggests that more writing leads to improved writing. Although hers is an unusual scene of writing for most of us, what we've reviewed here about writers' processes makes Maya Angelou's process more understandable. She says, "I go to work everyday about 6:30 in the morning. I keep a hotel room and I go to the same room each day." You don't need a hotel room, though, to analyze your rituals and habits and improve your processes and skills.

> I found this fantastic old drafting table at a rummage sale. . . . This is where I work, with my laptop . . . live in a house with 2 other women. They make me crazy about once a month. I can hear the television in the other room right now. I have to wear headphones. Listen to music when I work: Garth Brooks, Sarah McLaughlin, Diana Krall, Cowboy Junkies. I have to wear comfy clothes, cotton shorts, a t-shirt . . . I usually write lyrically, with much focus on setting and details, dialogue, creating portraits of people. This is my strength—to create a sense of place and time. . . . My drafts [on this paper] came slowly. . . . I know I went through: 3 pots of coffee, 2 bags of popcorn, 2 bottles of Coke, 4 gallons of water, 1 container of Reese's Peanut Butter Cup Ice Cream, 1 glass of chocolate milk, a handful of strawberries in whipped cream (low fat), 2 green apples, 2 flat raspberry seltzer waters, 3 bananas, 2 granola bars. I think that's about it.
>
> —CLASSROOM AUTHOR

What happens, then, when you consider writing as a process that offers chances to learn from mistakes, when you're allowed to conduct writing experiments, when your class creates a common language for talking about writing? I find, again and again, that this is when you'll learn most about yourself, and others, as writers.

> The members of our [writing group] are surprisingly similar with respect to the way we write. Almost all of us do some form or formal categorizing. Some of us outline, some brainstorm, some write lists, and some of us just write. One thing remains constant among all six of us—we all procrastinate. I used to think I was a horrible individual for waiting until the last minute, but now I realize that everyone procrastinates—maybe we do it to actually "psych" ourselves up. We all preferred to write straight through with breaks only for their nutritional value. Most of us need quiet in order to keep up our train of thought but one of us (surprisingly) preferred lots of loud music. With regard to writer's block we all agreed that the only way to beat it is to keep working. We all seemed to have a lot in common—at least where writing is concerned.
>
> —MINUTES OF A WRITING GROUP

To repeat, you are a writer every time you write. More attention given to your writing and writing process results in more certainty about and skill at what you're doing. And finally, yes, there is much to study as well—essays and sentence style, invention and revision, working with other writers and imagining multiple audiences:

> A well-known writer got collared by a university student who asked, "do you think I could be a writer?"
>
> "Well," the writer said, "I don't know . . . Do you like sentences?"
>
> The writer could see the student's amazement.
>
> "Sentences? Do I like sentences? I am twenty years old, do I like sentences?"
>
> —ANNIE DILLARD

You, as a writer, face the challenge of making all available information about writing relevant to your own writing life. Because writing is both serious and humorous, in this chapter I ask you to tap your images of writers by reading a short story, a memoir, and a poem that create three distinct images of these individuals. Lorrie Moore's narrative lets you examine, in humorous detail, the romantic idea of being an author with all the dysfunctional elements highlighted. Paule Marshal describes how her mother and her mother's friends taught her what it means to be a writer. Richard Wilbur's poem captures his feelings about his daughter; in doing this, he reviews his love for her and projects his fears and hopes on her act of composing. You'll find Jane Yolen's short, writing self-analysis, which is followed in turn by an essay by Winston Weathers, a writing teacher, who explores his writing process using alternate styles of writing (discussed again in later chapters). Weathers's work provides a useful sampler of self-conscious stylistic experimentation. Next, Terry Tempest Williams answers the question "why write?" in a lyric list, a poetic meditation. Finally, you'll read essays by two classroom authors—Debbie Olander and Brian Overcast. Their writing process narratives illustrate how writers can productively pause and consider why they make the drafting choices they make.

Some of the material in this chapter will be old news and some will be new. Taken together, these readings offer a brief (re)introduction to current thinking about how writers compose and recompose their thoughts into pleasing and effective written texts. Although you'll certainly hear much more about composing in other chapters, these authors' works invite you directly into the subject.

5

Chapter Readings

LORRIE MOORE (b. 1957)

How to Become a Writer

CONSIDER THIS:

Laurie Moore was born in Glens Falls, New York and studied at St. Lawrence University and Cornell. While still a teenager, Moore won *Seventeen* magazine's contest for her short story "Raspberries." She is currently an English professor at the University of Wisconsin Madison, specializing in creative writing. Moore's work is celebrated for its humor, which sometimes can take wide turns. She told *Salon,* "I am a sucker for silliness sometimes. And when someone says something silly to me, I find it wildly funny. So I'm often given to having my characters say completely silly things and I think this is wonderful."

A persona is a character created by an author, similar to them perhaps in some degree, but not identical with the actual author. When we create a persona, we create an opportunity to investigate an alternate life. While the narrator of "How to Become a Writer" is named Francie, it's easy to imagine she was created—to a degree—out of Moore's own experiences of becoming a writer. As you read, note any telling details that let you begin to visualize Moore's narrator, Francie. "You are great with kids," Francie says in one section, talking about herself in the unusual, second person singular point of view. "You spend too much time slouched and demoralized, " she says in another. Where visual details aren't given, derive them from what you've read. For instance, given what you know about Francie, would that slouching take place in an old sweatshirt? What would be printed on that sweatshirt? Try describing Francie's wallet and address book. Since details such as these weren't provided, explore with others what associations of your own lead you to assign characteristics to a textual character. To follow up, create a persona who is like but not like you, who could narrate the story you might write of how to become (or how you became) a writer.

One thing that Moore resists, her interviewers find, is the idea that her work blends genres. Basically, she says her fiction is fiction: "Fiction can come from real-life events and still be fiction. It can still have that connection, that germ. It came from something that happened to you. That doesn't mean it's straddling a line between nonfiction and fiction." Having completed your persona-sketching and having read Moore's work, what do you make of that remark when considering a story with a title that starts with the words "How to"? What uses can you imagine in your own writing for a how-to format or one that uses a similar narrative perspective?

First, try to be something, anything, else. A movie star/astronaut. A movie star/missionary. A movie star/kindergarten teacher. President of the World. Fail miserably. It is best if you fail at an early age—say, fourteen. Early, critical disillusionment is necessary so that at fifteen you can write long haiku sequences about thwarted desire. It is a pond, a cherry blossom, a wind brushing against sparrow wing leaving for mountain. Count the syllables. Show it to your mom. She is tough and practical. She has a son in Vietnam and a husband who may be having an affair. She believes in wearing brown because it hides spots. She'll look briefly at your writing, then back up at you with a face blank as a donut. She'll say: "How about emptying the dishwasher?" Look away. Shove the forks in the fork drawer. Accidentally break one of the freebie gas station glasses. This is the required pain and suffering. This is only for starters.

In your high school English class look at Mr. Killian's face. Decide faces are important. Write a villanelle about pores. Struggle. Write a sonnet. Count the syllables: nine, ten, eleven, thirteen. Decide to experiment with fiction. Here you don't have to count syllables. Write a short story about an elderly man and woman who accidentally shoot each other in the head, the result of an inexplicable malfunction of a shotgun which appears mysteriously in their living room one night. Give it to Mr. Killian as your final project. When you get it back, he has written on it: "Some of your images are quite nice, but you have no sense of plot." When you are home, in the privacy of your own room, faintly scrawl in pencil beneath his black-inked comments: "Plots are for dead people, pore-face."

Take all the babysitting jobs you can get. You are great with kids. They love you. You tell them stories about old people who die idiot deaths. You sing them songs like "Blue Bells of Scotland," which is their favorite. And when they are in their pajamas and have finally stopped pinching each other, when they are fast asleep, you read every sex manual in the house, and wonder how on earth anyone could ever do those things with someone they truly loved. Fall asleep in a chair reading Mr. McMurphy's *Playboy.* When the McMurphys come home, they will tap you on the shoulder, look at the magazine in your lap, and grin. You will want to die. They will ask you if Tracey took her medicine all right. Explain, yes, she did, that you promised her a story if she would take it like a big girl and that seemed to work out just fine. "Oh, marvelous," they will exclaim.

Try to smile proudly.

Apply to college as a child psychology major.

As a child psychology major, you have some electives. You've always liked birds. Sign up for something called "The Ornithological Field Trip." It meets Tuesdays and Thursdays at two. When you arrive at Room 134 on the first day of class, everyone is sitting around a seminar table talking about metaphors. You've heard of these. After a short, excruciating while, raise your hand and say diffidently, "Excuse me, isn't this Birdwatching One-oh-one?" The class stops and turns to look at you. They seem to all have one face—giant and blank as a vandalized clock. Someone with a beard booms out, "No, this is Creative Writing."

Say: "Oh—right," as if perhaps you knew all along. Look down at your schedule. Wonder how the hell you ended up here. The computer, apparently, has made an error. You start to get up to leave and then don't. The lines at the registrar this week are huge. Perhaps you should stick with this mistake. Perhaps your creative writing isn't all that bad. Perhaps it is fate. Perhaps this is what your dad meant when he said, "It's the age of computers, Francie, it's the age of computers."

Decide that you like college life. In your dorm you meet many nice people. Some are smarter than you. And some, you notice, are dumber than you. You will continue, unfortunately, to view the world in exactly these terms for the rest of your life.

The assignment this week in creative writing is to narrate a violent happening. Turn in a story about driving with your Uncle Gordon and another one about two old people who are accidentally electrocuted when they go to turn on a badly wired desk lamp. The teacher will hand them back to you with comments: "Much of your writing is smooth and energetic. You have, however, a ludicrous notion of plot." Write another story about a man and a woman who, in the very first paragraph, have their lower torsos accidentally blitzed away by dynamite. In the second paragraph, with the insurance money, they buy a frozen yogurt stand together. There are six more paragraphs. You read the whole thing out loud in class. No one likes it. They say your sense of plot is outrageous and incompetent. After class someone asks you if you are crazy.

Decide that perhaps you should stick to comedies. Start dating someone who is funny, someone who has what in high school you called a "really great sense of humor" and what now your creative writing class calls "self-contempt giving rise to comic form." Write down all of his jokes, but don't tell him you are doing this. Make up anagrams of his old girlfriend's name and name all of your socially handicapped characters with them. Tell him his old girlfriend is in all of your stories and then watch how funny he can be, see what a really great sense of humor he can have.

Your child psychology advisor tells you you are neglecting courses in your major. What you spend the most time on should be what you're majoring in. Say yes, you understand.

In creative writing seminars over the next two years, everyone continues to smoke cigarettes and ask the same things: "But does it work?" "Why should we care about this character?" "Have you earned this cliché?" These seem like important questions.

On days when it is your turn, you look at the class hopefully as they scour your mimeographs for a plot. They look back up at you, drag deeply, and then smile in a sweet sort of way.

You spend too much time slouched and demoralized. Your boyfriend suggests bicycling. Your roommate suggests a new boyfriend. You are said to be self-mutilating and losing weight, but you continue writing. The only happiness you have is writing something new, in the middle of the night, armpits damp, heart pounding, something no one has yet seen. You have only those brief, fragile, untested moments of exhilaration when you know: you are a genius. Understand what you must do. Switch majors. The kids in your nursery project will be disappointed, but you have a calling, an urge, a delusion, an unfortunate habit. You have, as your mother would say, fallen in with a bad crowd.

Why write? Where does writing come from? These are questions to ask yourself. They are like: Where does dust come from? Or: Why is there war? Or: If there's a God, then why is my brother now a cripple?

These are questions that you keep in your wallet, like calling cards. These are questions, your creative writing teacher says, that are good to address in your journals but rarely in your fiction.

The writing professor this fall is stressing the Power of the Imagination. Which means he doesn't want long descriptive stories about your camping trip last July. He wants you to start in a realistic context but then to alter it. Like recombinant DNA. He wants you to let your imagination sail, to let it grow big-bellied in the wind. This is a quote from Shakespeare.

Tell your roommate your great idea, your great exercise of imaginative power: a transformation of Melville to contemporary life. It will be about monomania and the fish-eat-fish world of life insurance in Rochester, New York. The first line will be "Call me Fishmeal," and it will feature a menopausal suburban husband named Richard, who because he is so depressed all the time is called "Mopey Dick" by his witty wife Elaine. Say to your roommate: "Mopey Dick, get it?" Your roommate looks at you, her face blank as a large Kleenex. She comes up to you, like a buddy, and puts an arm around your burdened shoulders. "Listen, Francie," she says, slow as speech therapy. "Let's go out and get a big beer."

The seminar doesn't like this one either. You suspect they are beginning to feel sorry for you. They say: "You have to think about what is happening. Where is the story here?"

The next semester the writing professor is obsessed with writing from personal experience. You must write from what you know, from what has happened to you. He wants deaths, he wants camping trips. Think about what has happened to you. In three years there have been three things: you lost your virginity; your parents got divorced; and your brother came home from a forest ten miles from the Cambodian border with only half a thigh, a permanent smirk nestled into one corner of his mouth.

About the first you write: "It created a new space, which hurt and cried in a voice that wasn't mine, 'I'm not the same anymore, but I'll be okay.'"

About the second you write an elaborate story of an old married couple who stumble upon an unknown land mine in their kitchen and accidentally blow themselves up. You call it: "For Better or for Liverwurst."

About the last you write nothing. There are no words for this. Your typewriter hums. You can find no words.

At undergraduate cocktail parties, people say, "Oh, you write? What do you write about?" Your roommate, who has consumed too much wine, too little cheese, and no crackers at all, blurts: "Oh, my god, she always writes about her dumb boyfriend."

Later on in life you will learn that writers are merely open, helpless texts with no real understanding of what they have written and therefore must half-believe anything and everything that is said of them. You, however, have not yet reached this stage of literary criticism. You stiffen and say, "I do not," the same way you said it when someone in the fourth grade accused you of really liking oboe lessons and your parents really weren't just making you take them.

Insist you are not very interested in any one subject at all, that you are interested in the music of language, that you are interested in—in—syllables, because they are the atoms of poetry, the cells of the mind, the breath of the soul. Begin to feel woozy. Stare into your plastic wine cup.

"Syllables?" you will hear someone ask, voice trailing off, as they glide slowly toward the reassuring white of the dip.

Begin to wonder what you do write about. Or if you have anything to say. Or if there even is such a thing as a thing to say. Limit these thoughts to no more than ten minutes a day; like sit-ups, they can make you thin.

You will read somewhere that all writing has to do with one's genitals. Don't dwell on this. It will make you nervous.

Your mother will come visit you. She will look at the circles under your eyes and hand you a brown book with a brown briefcase on the cover. It is entitled: *How to Become a Business Executive.* She has also brought the *Names for Baby* encyclopedia you asked for; one of your characters, the aging clown–school teacher, needs a new name. Your mother will shake her head and say: "Francie, Francie, remember when you were going to be a child psychology major?"

Say: "Mom, I like to write."

She'll say: "Sure you like to write. Of course. Sure you like to write."

Write a story about a confused music student and title it: "Schubert Was the One with the Glasses, Right?" It's not a big hit, although your roommate likes the part where the two violinists accidentally blow themselves up in a recital room. "I went out with a violinist once," she says, snapping her gum.

Thank god you are taking other courses. You can find sanctuary in nineteenth-century ontological snags and invertebrate courting rituals. Certain globular mollusks have what is called "Sex by the Arm." The male octopus, for instance, loses the end of one arm when placing it inside the female body during intercourse. Marine biologists call it "Seven Heaven." Be glad you know these things. Be glad you are not just a writer. Apply to law school.

From here on in, many things can happen. But the main one will be this: you decide not to go to law school after all, and, instead, you spend a good, big chunk of your adult life telling people how you decided not to go to law school after all. Somehow you end up writing again. Perhaps you go to graduate school. Perhaps you work odd jobs and take writing courses at night. Perhaps you are working on a novel and writing down all the clever remarks and intimate personal confessions you hear during the day. Perhaps you are losing your pals, your acquaintances, your balance.

You have broken up with your boyfriend. You now go out with men who, instead of whispering "I love you," shout: "Do it to me, baby." This is good for your writing.

Sooner or later you have a finished manuscript more or less. People look at it in a vaguely troubled sort of way and say, "I'll bet becoming a writer was always a fantasy of yours, wasn't it?" Your lips dry to salt. Say that of all the fantasies possible in the world, you can't imagine being a writer even making the top twenty. Tell them you were going to be a child psychology major. "I bet," they always sigh, "you'd be great with kids." Scowl fiercely. Tell them you're a walking blade.

Quit classes. Quit jobs. Cash in old savings bonds. Now you have time like warts on your hands. Slowly copy all of your friends' addresses into a new address book.

Vacuum. Chew cough drops. Keep a folder full of fragments.

An eyelid darkening sideways.
World as conspiracy.
Possible plot? A woman gets on a bus.
Suppose you threw a love affair and nobody came.

At home drink a lot of coffee. At Howard Johnson's order the cole slaw. Consider how it looks like the soggy confetti of a map: where you've been, where you're going—"You Are Here," says the red star on the back of the menu.

Occasionally a date with a face blank as a sheet of paper asks you whether writers often become discouraged. Say that sometimes they do and sometimes they do. Say it's a lot like having polio.

"Interesting," smiles your date, and then he looks down at his arm hairs and starts to smooth them, all, always, in the same direction.

PAULE MARSHALL (b. 1929)

The Poets in the Kitchen

CONSIDER THIS:

Paule Marshall was born in Brooklyn to recent immigrants from Barbados. She earned a degree from Brooklyn College; worked as a librarian and as a staff writer for *Our World* magazine; and lectured about literature at Columbia, Yale, and Oxford. She has been awarded Guggenheim, National Endowment for the Arts, and MacArthur fellowships, and is currently an English professor at New York University. Central to Marshall's work is its connection to a specific oral tradition to which she was exposed while growing up. Speaking of her mentors—poets in the kitchen—for an interview in *New Letters* she said, "It wasn't only what the women talked about, the content; but the way they put things, the style. The insight, irony, wit and their own special force which they brought to everything they discussed; above all, the poet's skill with words." Marshall speaks of the importance of this cultural heritage as she continues the interview: "They had taken a language imposed upon them, and infused it with their own incisive rhythms and syntax, brought to bear upon it the few African words and sounds that had been retained." This Caribbean-American influence would have a profound effect on her life and work.

Before you begin reading, you might want to make a list of your own mentors. From whom do you derive your style? How have these individuals nourished you? Where is your "kitchen"—that is, explore the scenes where teaching and mentoring and oral wit took center stage and influenced you. Whose voices do you remember and what are (were) they saying? After you read, consider how your own assumptions about "poets" were confirmed or challenged by Marshall's essay. What is your cultural heritage and who are the "poets"—public or private—who you draw on most proudly? Testify. Tell one story from these memories to your group.

Some years ago, when I was teaching a graduate seminar in fiction at Columbia University, a well known male novelist visited my class to speak on his development as a writer. In discussing his formative years, he didn't realize it but he seriously endangered his life by remarking that women writers are luckier than those of his sex because they usually spend so much time as children around their mothers and their mothers' friends in the kitchen.

What did he say that for? The women students immediately forgot about being in awe of him and began readying their attack for the question and answer period later on. Even I bristled. There again was that awful image of women locked away from the world in the kitchen with only each other to talk to, and their daughters locked in with them.

But my guest wasn't really being sexist or trying to be provocative or even spoiling for a fight. What he meant—when he got around to explaining himself more fully—was that, given the way children are (or were) raised in our society, with little girls kept closer to home and their mothers, the woman writer stands a better chance of being exposed, while growing up, to the kind of talk that goes on among women, more often than not in the kitchen; and that this experience gives her an edge over her male counterpart by instilling in her an appreciation for ordinary speech.

It was clear that my guest lecturer attached great importance to this, which is understandable. Common speech and the plain, workaday words that make it up are, after all, the stock in trade of some of the best fiction writers. They are the principal means by which characters in a novel or story reveal themselves and give voice sometimes to profound feelings and complex ideals about themselves and the world. Perhaps the proper measure of a writer's talent is skill in rendering everyday speech—when it is appropriate to the story—as well as the ability to tap, to exploit, the beauty, poetry and wisdom it often contains.

"If you say what's on your mind in the language that comes to you from your parents and your street and friends you'll probably say something beautiful." Grace Paley tells this, she says, to her students at the beginning of every writing course.

It's all a matter of exposure and a training of the ear for the would-be writer in those early years of apprenticeship. And, according to my guest lecturer, this training, the best of it, often takes place in as unglamorous a setting as the kitchen.

He didn't know it, but he was essentially describing my experience as a little girl. I grew up among poets. Now they didn't look like poets—whatever that breed is supposed to look like. Nothing about them suggested that poetry was their calling. They were just a group of ordinary housewives and mothers, my mother included, who dressed in a way (shapeless housedresses, dowdy felt hats and long, dark, solemn coats) that made it impossible for me to imagine they had ever been young.

Nor did they do what poets were supposed to do—spend their days in an attic room writing verses. They never put pen to paper except to write occasionally to their relatives in Barbados. "I take my pen in hand hoping these few lines will find you in health as they leave me fair for the time being," was the way their letters invariably began. Rather, their day was spent "scrubbing floor," as they described the work they did.

Several mornings a week these unknown bards would put an apron and a pair of old house shoes in a shopping bag and take the train or streetcar from our section of Brooklyn out to Flatbush. There, those who didn't have steady jobs would wait on certain designated corners for the white housewives in the neighborhood to come along and bargain with them over pay for a day's work cleaning their houses. This was the ritual even in the winter.

Later, armed with the few dollars they had earned, which in their vocabulary became "a few raw-mouth pennies," they made their way back to our neighborhood, where they would sometimes stop off to have a cup of tea or cocoa together before going home to cook dinner for their husbands and children.

The basement kitchen of the brownstone house where my family lived was the usual gathering place. Once inside the warm safety of its walls the women threw off the drab coats and hats, seated themselves at the large center table, drank their cups of tea or cocoa and talked. While my sister and I sat at a smaller table over in a corner doing our homework, they talked—endlessly, passionately, poetically, and with impressive range. No subject was beyond them. True, they would indulge in the usual gossip: whose husband was running with whom, whose daughter looked slightly "in the way" (pregnant) under her bridal gown as she walked down the aisle. That sort of thing. But they also tackled the great issues of the time. They were always, for example, discussing the state of the economy. It was the mid and late 30's then, and the aftershock of the Depression, with its soup lines and suicides on Wall Street, was still being felt.

Some people, they declared, didn't know how to deal with adversity. They didn't know that you had to "tie up your belly" (hold in the pain, that is) when things got rough and go on with life. They took their image from the bellyband that is tied around the stomach of a newborn baby to keep the navel pressed in.

They talked politics. Roosevelt was their hero. He had come along and rescued the country with relief and jobs, and in gratitude they christened their sons Franklin and Delano and hoped they would live up to the names.

If F.D.R. was their hero, Marcus Garvey was their God. The name of the fiery, Jamaican-born black nationalist of the 20s was constantly invoked around the table. For he had been their leader when they first came to the United States from the West Indies shortly after World War I. They had contributed to his organization, the United Negro Improvement Association (UNIA), out of their meager salaries, bought shares in his ill-fated Black Star Shipping Line, and at the height of the movement they had marched as members of his "nurses' brigade" in their white uniforms up Seventh Avenue in Harlem during the great Garvey Day parades. Garvey: He lived on through the power of their memories.

And their talk was of war and rumors of wars. They raged against World War II when it broke out in Europe, blaming it on the politicians. "It's these politicians. They're the ones always starting up all this lot of war. But what they care? It's the poor people got to suffer and mothers with their sons." If it was *their* sons, they swore they would keep them out of the Army by giving them soap to eat each day to make their hearts sound defective. Hitler? He was for them "the devil incarnate."

Then there was home. They reminisced often and at length about home. The old country. Barbados—or Bimshire, as they affectionately called it. The little Caribbean island in the sun they loved but had to leave. "Poor—poor but sweet" was the way they remembered it.

And naturally they discussed their adopted home. America came in for both good and bad marks. They lashed out at it for the racism they encountered. They took to task some of the people they worked for, especially those who gave them only a hard-boiled egg and a few spoonfuls of cottage cheese for lunch. "As if anybody can scrub floor on an egg and some cheese that don't have no taste to it!"

Yet although they caught H in "this man country," as they called America, it was nonetheless a place where "you could at least see your way to make a dollar." That much they acknowledged. They might even one day accumulate enough dollars, with both them and their husbands working, to buy the brownstone houses which, like my family, they were only leasing at that period. This was their consuming ambition: to "buy house" and to see the children through.

There was no way for me to understand it at the time, but the talk that filled the kitchen those afternoons was highly functional. It served as therapy, the cheapest kind available to my mother and her friends. Not only did it help them recover from the long wait on the corner that morning and the bargaining over their labor, it restored them to a sense of themselves and reaffirmed their self-worth. Through language they were able to overcome the humiliations of the work-day.

But more than therapy, that freewheeling, wide-ranging, exuberant talk functioned as an outlet for the tremendous creative energy they possessed. They were women in whom the need for self-expression was strong, and since language was the only vehicle readily available to them they made of it an art form that—in keeping with the African tradition in which art and life are one—was an integral part of their lives.

And their talk was a refuge. They never really ceased being baffled and overwhelmed by America—its vastness, complexity and power. Its strange customs and laws. At a level beyond words they remained fearful and in awe. Their uneasiness and fear were even reflected in their attitude toward the children they had given birth to in this country. They referred to those like myself, the little Brooklyn-born Bajans (Barbadians), as "these New York children" and complained that they couldn't discipline us properly because of the laws here. "You can't beat these children as you would like, you know, because the authorities in this place will dash you in jail for them. After all, these is New York children." Not only were we different, American, we had, as they saw it, escaped their ultimate authority.

Confronted therefore by a world they could not encompass, which even limited their rights as parents, and at the same time finding themselves permanently separated from the world they had known, they took refuge in language. "Language is the only homeland," Czeslaw Milosz, the emigré Polish writer and Nobel Laureate, has said. This is what it became for the women at the kitchen table.

It served another purpose also, I suspect. My mother and her friends were after all the female counterpart of Ralph Ellison's invisible man. Indeed, you might say they suffered a triple invisibility, being black, female and foreigners. They really didn't count in American society except as a source of cheap labor. But given the kind of women they were, they couldn't tolerate the fact of their invisibility, their powerlessness. And they fought back, using the only weapon at their command: the spoken word.

Those late afternoon conversations on a wide range of topics were a way for them to feel they exercised some measure of control over their lives and the events that shaped them. "Soully-gal, talk yuh talk!" they were always exhorting each other. "In this man world you got to take yuh mouth and make a gun!" They were in control, if only verbally and if only for the two hours or so that they remained in our house.

For me, sitting over in the corner, being seen but not heard, which was the rule for children in those days, it wasn't only what the women talked about—the content—but the way they put things—their style. The insight, irony, wit and humor they brought to their stories and discussions and their poet's inventiveness and daring with language—which of course I could only sense but not define back then.

They had taken the standard English taught them in the primary schools of Barbados and transformed it into an idiom, an instrument that more adequately described them—changing around the syntax and imposing their own rhythm and accent so that the sentences were more pleasing to their ears. They added the few African sounds and words that had survived, such as the derisive suck-teeth sound and the word "yam," meaning to eat. And to make it more vivid, more in keeping with their expressive quality, they brought to bear a raft of metaphors, parables, Biblical quotations, sayings and the like:

"The sea ain' got no back door," they would say, meaning that it wasn't like a house where if there was a fire you could run out the back. Meaning that it was not to be trifled with. And meaning perhaps in a larger sense that man should treat all of nature with caution and respect.

"I has read hell by heart and called every generation blessed!" They sometimes went in for hyperbole.

A woman expecting a baby was never said to be pregnant. They never used that word. Rather, she was "in the way" or, better yet, "tumbling big." "Guess who I butt up on in the market the other day tumbling big again!"

And a woman with a reputation of being too free with her sexual favors was known in their book as a "thoroughfare"—the sense of men like a steady stream of cars moving up and down the road of her life. Or she might be dubbed "a free-bee," which was my favorite of the two. I liked the image it conjured up of a woman scandalous perhaps but independent, who flitted from one flower to another in a garden of male beauties, sampling their nectar, taking her pleasure at will, the roles reversed.

And nothing, no matter how beautiful, was ever described as simply beautiful. It was always "beautiful-ugly": the beautiful-ugly dress, the beautiful-ugly house, the beautiful-ugly car. Why the word "ugly," I used to wonder, when the thing they were referring to was beautiful, and they knew it. Why the antonym, the contradiction, the linking of opposites? It used to puzzle me greatly as a child.

There is the theory in linguistics which states that the idiom of a people, the way they use language, reflects not only the most fundamental views they hold of themselves and the world but their very conception of reality. Perhaps in using the term "beautiful-ugly" to describe nearly everything, my mother and her friends were expressing what they believed to be a fundamental dualism in life: the idea that a thing is at the same time its opposite, and that these opposites, these contradictions make up the whole. But theirs was not a Manichaean brand of dualism that sees matter, flesh, the body, as inherently evil, because they constantly addressed each other as "soully-gal"—soul: spirit: gal: the body, flesh, the visible self. And it was clear from their tone that they gave one as much weight and importance as the other. They had never heard of the mind/body split.

As for God, they summed up His essential attitude in a phrase. "God," they would say, "don' love ugly and He ain' stuck on pretty."

Using everyday speech, the simple commonplace words—but always with imagination and skill—they gave voice to the most complex ideas. Flannery O'Connor would have approved of how they made ordinary language work, as she put it, "doubletime," stretching, shading, deepening its meaning. Like Joseph Conrad they were always trying to infuse new life in the "old old words worn thin . . . by . . . careless usage." And the goals of their oral art were the same as his: "to make you hear, to make you feel . . . to make you *see*." This was their guiding esthetic.

By the time I was 8 or 9, I graduated from the corner of the kitchen to the neighborhood library, and thus from the spoken to the written word. The Macon Street Branch of the Brooklyn Public Library was an imposing half block long edifice of heavy gray masonry, with glass-paneled doors at the front and two tall metal torches symbolizing the light that comes of learning flanking the wide steps outside.

The inside was just as impressive. More steps—of pale marble with gleaming brass railings at the center and sides—led up to the circulation desk, and a great pendulum clock gazed down from the balcony stacks that faced the entrance. Usually stationed at the top of the steps like the guards outside Buckingham Palace was the custodian, a stern-faced West Indian type who for years, until I was old enough to obtain an adult card, would immediately shoo me with one hand into the Children's Room and with the other threaten me into silence, a finger to his lips. You would have thought he was the chief librarian and not just someone whose job it was to keep the brass polished and the clock wound. I put him in a story called "Barbados" years later and had terrible things happen to him at the end.

I sheltered from the storm of adolescence in the Macon Street library, reading voraciously, indiscriminately, everything from Jane Austen to Zane Grey, but with a special passion for the long, full-blown, richly detailed 18th- and 19th-century picaresque tales: "Tom Jones," "Great Expectations," "Vanity Fair."

But although I loved nearly everything I read and would enter fully into the lives of the characters—indeed, would cease being myself and become them—I sensed a lack after a time. Something I couldn't quite define was missing. And then one day, browsing in the poetry section, I came across a book by someone called Paul Laurence Dunbar, and opening it I found the photograph of a wistful, sad-eyed poet who to my surprise was black. I turned to a poem at random. "Little brown-baby wif spa'klin' / eyes / Come to yo' pappy an' set on his knee." Although I had a little difficulty at first with the words in dialect, the poem spoke to me as nothing I had read before of the closeness, the special relationship I had had with my father, who by then had become an ardent believer in Father Divine and gone to live in Father's "kingdom" in Harlem. Reading it helped to ease somewhat the tight knot of sorrow and longing I carried in my chest that refused to go away. I read another poem. " 'Lias! 'Lias! Bless de Lawd! / Don' you know de day's / erbroad? / Ef you don' get up, you scamp / Dey'll be trouble in dis camp." I laughed. It reminded me of the way my mother sometimes yelled at my sister and me to get out of bed in the mornings.

And another: "Seen my lady home las' night / Jump back, honey, jump back. / Hel' huh han' an' sque'z it tight . . . "About love between a black man and a black woman. I had never seen that written about before and it roused in me all kinds of delicious feelings and hopes.

And I began to search then for books and stories and poems about "The Race" (as it was put back then), about my people. While not abandoning

Thackeray, Fielding, Dickens and the others. I started asking the reference librarian, who was white, for books by Negro writers, although I must admit I did so at first with a feeling of shame—the shame I and many others used to experience in those days whenever the word "Negro" or "colored" came up.

No grade school literature teacher of mine had ever mentioned Dunbar or James Weldon Johnson or Langston Hughes. I didn't know that Zora Neale Hurston existed and was busy writing and being published during those years. Nor was I made aware of people like Frederick Douglass and Harriet Tubman—their spirit and example—or the great 19th-century abolitionist and feminist Sojourner Truth. There wasn't even Negro History Week when I attended P.S. 35 on Decatur Street!

What I needed, what all the kids—West Indian and native black American alike—with whom I grew up needed, was an equivalent of the Jewish shul, someplace where we could go after school—the schools that were shortchanging us—and read works by those like ourselves and learn about our history.

It was around that time also that I began harboring the dangerous thought of someday trying to write myself. Perhaps a poem about an apple tree, although I had never seen one. Or the story of a girl who could magically transplant herself to wherever she wanted to be in the world—such as Father Divine's kingdom in Harlem. Dunbar—his dark, eloquent face, his large volume of poems—permitted me to dream that I might someday write, and with something of the power with words my mother and her friends possessed.

When people at readings and writers' conferences ask me who my major influences were, they are sometimes a little disappointed when I don't immediately name the usual literary giants. True, I am indebted to those writers, white and black, whom I read during my formative years and still read for instruction and pleasure. But they were preceded in my life by another set of giants whom I always acknowledge before all others: the group of women around the table long ago. They taught me my first lessons in the narrative art. They trained my ear. They set a standard of excellence. This is why the best of my work must be attributed to them; it stands as testimony to the rich legacy of language and culture they so freely passed on to me in the wordshop of the kitchen.

RICHARD WILBUR (b. 1921)

The Writer

CONSIDER THIS:

Richard Wilbur was born in New York City, the son of a painter. He has taught at Harvard, Wellesley, and Smith, and was Poet Laureate of the United States from 1987–1988. Among his numerous honors, Wilbur has won the National Book Award and the Pulitzer Prize twice for his poetry. Wilbur recalls his experiences as a soldier as profoundly affecting his work. In an interview for *Voice of America,* he said, "My first poems were written in answer to the inner and outer disorders of the Second World War, and they helped me, as poems should, to take a hold of raw events and convert them, provisionally, into experience."

Although initially inspired by the chaos of the war, Wilbur tends to write poems rich in telling detail that are full of positive energy and high spirits. He told *Image* that when he writes he strives "for poetry of close observation, for poetry that acknowledges the importance of things however small, poetry that aims to fuse moral and other thought with the creatures of this world." Apply Wilbur's explanation to his poem "The Writer." Has he observed closely, acknowledged important small things, explored a moral issue? Be specific about lines, words, images, and metaphors as you make your case. Also, you might want to follow your reading of the poem with an informal freewrite to your imagined (or real) child. What would you tell that child about writing, about maturing? Express some of your wishes for the next generation.

In her room at the prow of the house
Where light breaks, and the windows are tossed with linden,
My daughter is writing a story.

I pause in the stairwell, hearing
From her shut door a commotion of typewriter-keys
Like a chain hauled over a gunwale.

Young as she is, the stuff
Of her life is a great cargo, and some of it heavy:
I wish her a lucky passage.

But now it is she who pauses,
As if to reject my thought and its easy figure.
As stillness greatens, in which

The whole house seems to be thinking,
And then she is at it again with a bunched clamor
Of strokes, and again is silent

I remember the dazed starling
Which was trapped in that very room, two years ago,
How we stole in, lifted a sash

And retreated, not to affright it;
And how for a helpless hour, through the crack of the door,
We watched the sleek, wild, dark

And iridescent creature
Batter against the brilliance, drop like a glove
To the hard floor, or the desk-top,

And wait then, humped and bloody,
For the wits to try it again; and how our spirits
Rose when, suddenly sure,

It lifted off from a chair-back,
Beating a smooth course for the right window
And clearing the sill of the world.

It is always a matter, my darling,
Of life or death, as I had forgotten. I wish
What I wished you before, but harder.

JANE YOLEN (b. 1939)

Interview Excerpt: "I find out that a story isn't working or isn't good enough in two ways."

CONSIDER THIS:

Are you a saver or a spender? Think of this question across a range of options: money, time, love, friendship, and so on. Do you find that you are a careful spender but profligate with your emotions (or perhaps, the reverse)? Now, if you didn't already, think in an analogous manner about yourself as a writer—are you a single-drafter or a multiple-drafter? Do you hoard words or spin them out? Complete this inventory and then enjoy Jane Yolen's discussion of her own work habits.

Jane Yolen, called "America's Hans Christian Andersen" by *Newsweek,* was born in New York City. She has written more than 200 books, and among her many honors are two Nebula Awards and the Jewish Book Council Award. She has also been a journalist and an editor, and has taught children's literature at Smith College.

Yolen counts as strong early influences both folktales and music. She writes in many genres including fantasy and science fiction, and for all age ranges. Her flexibility is evident in a comment, one of her *rules* for writing, that she shared at a conference for the Society of Children's Book Writers and Illustrators: "Write for the child inside of you. (Or the adult, if you are writing adult books.)" If this incredibly prolific and popular author has a credo it just might be "We write not just to show off, to tell, or only to have written. We write to know ourselves." If you were to have lunch with this author what question would you ask her? What story about yourself would you tell her?

I find out that a story isn't working or isn't good enough in two ways. I might send it to my publishers and get many rejections letters, all of which say the same thing so the weakness must be there. The other way comes from my own self-filtering system. It's important to be critical of my own work. I then keep working away each day at the story, or I put it aside and come back to it a long time later with a new way of looking at it.

I never throw anything out. Sometimes a piece of writing that I think is disgusting and horrible and awful might (a day or a week or a year from now) seem different, because I will be different. I can look at the writing differently later on and perhaps see how to change it.

The book that took nineteen-and-a-half years to write, I wrote five totally separate ways. It was a short novel for teenagers, and I had a terrible time chipping away until I found the story I wanted to tell. In the first drafts of the story I killed off the mother; I tried it with the father dead; I wrote it as complete fantasy; I wrote it as part-fantasy; then I wrote it as totally realistic. Each time I was telling a slightly different story, but it wasn't until the very last time that I found the story that I wanted to tell.

It used to bother me that when I put my story down on paper it always fails. It's never the story that's in my head. I keep reminding myself that the story I've written down has its own beauty, and that it may be the one story which really touches someone and be important to them.

WINSTON WEATHERS (b. 1926)

The Winston Weathers Writing Way: A Self-Examination

CONSIDER THIS:

Winston Weathers was born in Pawhuska, Oklahoma, earned his degrees from the University of Oklahoma, and is emeritus professor of English at the University of Tulsa where he began teaching in 1957. Weathers proposes a fairly radical view of the writing process in his *An Alternate Style: Options in Composition:* "*Another* way of writing that offers yet more options and offers us yet further possibilities for rhetorical adaptations and adjustments. It is not just another style—way out on the periphery of our concerns—but is an altogether different 'grammar' of style, an alternate grammar, Grammar B." Grammar B, then, rejects the traditional approach in favor of one that is more verbal and intuitive. Putting it another way, Weathers compares the conventional approach to putting one's ideas into a rectangular box and then questions whether using "a round box or oval box or tubular box" might work better.

Consider Weathers's essay: what sorts of boxes is he using (that is, stylistic techniques): ones that jump out are, of course, the sidebars, including a self Question and Answer session. As you list Weathers's techniques, think of others he might have used to increase the number of boxes. For this, you might think of magazine article layouts, hypertext design, and so on. How has desktop publishing increased a writer's stylistic options? Do you think his essay would be usefully mounted on a Winston Weathers's website?

Weathers's approach to writing and style suggests a comparison with Edward Corbett and Robert Connors's views as found in their article in Chapter 3. Whereas we could read Corbett and Connors's call to return to classical rhetoric and its dependence upon the logic and rules of the more traditional Grammar A as reacting more formally to style issues than does Weathers, the three style experts may hold some beliefs in common. Where do they appear to differ and where do they appear to agree?

A great deal of my writing time is spent building a storehouse of writing material. I squirrel away passages of writing, anything from a short sentence to a long character sketch. Not generated by particular projects, these writings are, rather, "savings" put aside for the future.

Intro: How do I write? (Let me count the ways.) Various ways, actually. (As in most of our affairs.) Various scenarios for "the forthcoming movie *Writer at Work*."

(Just as I have various styles in which to write any given composition, so I have various processes, methods of getting words down on paper, of making my journey toward the completed composition.)

(Invention: Often I turn to literary invention as a way to begin. Not to *passive* invention (waiting for the Muse to strike, q.v.)—but *active* invention—playing word games, doodling, a host of other tricks and devices to unlock the unconscious and start the creative juices flowing. Invention is an important part of the pre-writing process for me: If my attempt to write a sentence with the words in alphabetical order—"After Bill caught David eating fresh grapes . . . "—starts me down a rewarding path of thought I'm certainly willing to play the game. Yes, invention has to do with games, tricks, artificialities, exercises—see Raymond Queneau's *Exercises in Style.* The immediate invention product may eventually be discarded, but the process may have generated thoughts, even copy, that may lead to a finished text. Invention is the game I play to get from "nothing to say" to "something to say" to "something more to say" to "something said." I call it game/writing. And it works for me.)

Writing Instruments: Pencils first, of course. Well-sharpened. No. 2 lead. A good eraser. For notes, rough designs, ideas, lines of poetry. But also pen and ink. (I've always enjoyed black ink on white paper; something sharp and visual.) But pen and ink are for shorter things even so. Poems, sketches, miniature essays. For longer things, obviously the typewriter. I've typed nearly all my life. And it makes sense to me to move to the electric, correcting typewriter: It opens a door to more extended production, greater sweeps of narrative, the longer flow of ideas, several pages of writing at one sitting. And now, in recent years, I've discovered the word processor, the miracles of which continue to amaze me, making more revision possible, making a dreamed-of perfection more feasible. Now I find the word processor absolutely necessary for final or near-final drafts. (And the computer will proofread my writing for me, will check my spelling, will—via the *Quintilian Analysis*—analyze my prose style, and do a lot of other time-saving tasks.) I actually like to play one writing instrument against the other. Moving a particular composition from pencil, to pen, to typewriter, to word processor makes the composition seem always new to me, permits me to be more objective than I would be otherwise; I understand my writing better; the writing seems more serious.

(This very article has been written with (a) lead pencil, in my University of Tulsa office; (b) ball-point, on a Delta Airlines flight; (c) an IBM Selectric at Texas Woman's University in Denton, (d) my TRS80-Mod III, 48K, two disk drives, here in my Tulsa apartment.)

Outlines: I'm not too keen on formal outlines, the kind I learned in school. I do, however, find value in a kind of rough outline, at least a list of matters to be dealt with in a composition. If I am writing in Grammar A (q.v.), the rough list of topics guides me as I move from one idea to the next. If I am writing in Grammar B (q.v.), I think of the list more as a map whereon I have tried to locate parts of a composition. In either case, I use the list, or rough outline, or map simply as tentative guide. If in the process of composition I find the outline not working, I drop it; if I find it in need of change, I alter it.

Actual Writing: I distinguish between pre-writing and actual writing, between preparatory writing and the actual task of putting ideas into sustained discourse, into sentences and paragraphs, etc. That is, I do a lot of bits-and-pieces writing before I come to the actual preparation of a draft.

Draft writing is always linear (q.v.), even if I'm only drafting a block of writing (q.v.) to be included in a larger composition. In draft writing, I let some "inner pilot" take over, some inner awareness that moves ideas into words, sentences, paragraphs. In draft writing, I try not to think; rather I let my mind, unimpeded by too much conscious decision making, do the work. My general rule is: Think *before* preparing a draft, think about the draft *after* it is prepared, but while in the actual throes of composition, try to be uncritical, put down what seems necessary at the time, what seems to connect, what is being drawn up to the conscious mind from the unconscious at the very moment you're busy putting words on paper.

The Muse/Imagination: Yes, Virginia, there is a Muse. And she does visit writers. And she does a lot of the writing for which human writers receive the credit. She has certainly done a lot of writing for me. And yes, she comes at odd hours, at the most unexpected times. She can just suddenly appear, carrying her great quill pen and her set of matched luggage full of wit and wisdom. I have discovered, however, that when she does show up her visit is much more pleasant if I am prepared to work with her. I've learned not to tell her I don't feel like working today or that I'm not ready or that I haven't done my homework. I've known her to leave a message something like this: "I'm not coming back until you're ready to play." Which means: Try to be ready, any time of the day, with your writing instruments ready to go, with your desire to write alive and afflame. If you aren't ready, she'll simply depart—and she may wait a long time before she returns. She certainly deplores getting all dressed up and making the trip if, when she gets to the writer's studio, the writer's vocabulary is no larger than it was her last visit; the writer's journal is no thicker than it was before; the writer's wastepaper basket is as empty of writing efforts as always.

And one last point: I know, of course, that all goddesses and muses and fairy princesses love gifts, little tokens from their supplicants. And I know that what the Muse likes best of all is a nice stack of words on paper, evidence that I have worked on my own. The Muse loves to see that I'm doing my part, that I'm a serious courtier. She once told me that she really hates frivolous little writers who can't get their act together and who expect her to do every bit of the work. She also hates writers who simply stare out the window all the time. A little window staring, O.K. A little wool gathering, O.K. A little meditation O.K. But I know that my relationship with the Muse depends primarily on my having some words on paper, on the desk in front of me, at all times. I know I must give her proof that I want to write, that I *am* writing. Otherwise, she doesn't seem to be of much help at all.

Polishing: Yes, I have to give every text I create a final polishing. No matter which scenario I have used, I must polish—after revision—all the joints, cracks, connections. I must edit to ensure consistency of tone and style. I don't really mind editing; in fact, I find it one of the more pleasant parts of composition. Not that it isn't sometimes laborious; yet, by the time I get to the editing, I know I have a composition with which to work. By the time I get to the editing, I know that the bulk of writing work is behind me.

Building: I use the building metaphor a great deal of the time to describe my own writing processes. Writing, for me, is a kind of building, building a text—even a linear text—out of words, sometimes out of blocks and pieces and hunks and incomplete passages. I figure I spend at least two-thirds of my time in the construction business.

Building blocks, frames, connections, fasteners. And even though the final composition may be read sequentially, viewed sequentially, its sequentiality is probably one of the last things it has achieved.

An Interview:

Q. Do you listen to music while you write?

A. No. I find it a distraction.

Q. Do you write in the morning or evening or when?

A. Whenever I can find the time. I believe, of course, in having a set time for writing, a schedule to follow. But sometimes circumstances deny me a schedule—and I have to write whenever the opportunity presents itself. If I have my wishes, I write in the morning from eight until noon.

Q. Do you ever ask anyone—friends, family, colleagues—to read your work while you are in the process of writing it?

A. No. I suppose every writer would like some kindly reader on hand to respond instantaneously to the words, yet responses midst process don't really help. Anyway, why impose on people? I believe a writer should be his own worst/ best critic. Besides, I'd rather make my own mistakes than the mistakes that someone else has advised me to make.

Q. Do you read very much?

A. Not as must as I should.

Q. When you were a student in college what course or courses did you find most helpful to you *in re* writing and composition?

A. Classical Greek.

The Situation: So much depends. Each writing situation is special, unique. Those ancient determinants of rhetorical situations still play their part. (Let me see if I remember: subject, audience, occasion, purpose, authorial identity, the rhetorical profile . . .)

But other determinants, too: How much time do I have? What's the state of my mind? my mood? What equipment do I have on hand? Pencil, typewriter, word processor? What resources are available? A lot of books on the shelves in this room? How far am I from a decent library? No books at all, only memory? is this going to be published? Am I getting paid for this? In other words, what's going on? what's the deal?

Grammars of Style: One of the most important decisions I try to make, early on, is whether I shall write in Grammar A or Grammar B. Grammar A is, of course, the syndrome of style I use when I'm planning to be very orthodox, rational, logical, orderly, coherent in my composition. Grammar B, on the other hand, is the syndrome of style I use when I wish to create a verbal experience just as much as I want to transmit information; when I'm trying to be disjunctive, provocative, synchronic, etc. Often I decide to use one grammar or the other on the basis of the material itself: This very article, for instance, dealing as it does with my own writing process, is being written more in Grammar B than in Grammar A—since I'm not sure my writing process (or anyone's writing process for that matter) is as orderly and reasonable as Grammar A would suggest. I think Grammar B gives a better idea of the synchronic relationships that exist in composition, the complexities, etc. Grammar B (or as I also call it, *An Alternate Style: Options in Composition*) permits me to speak more appropriately about the mysteries of writing.

Basic Writing Methods: Usually, I follow one of three basic writing scenarios, realizing as I do that I may have to make minor adjustments. But most of the time I can tell—once I have determined the writing situation—which of the three scenarios will serve me best. Sometimes I make a mistake and have to start over again. But I never really deplore this. So much of writing is a kind of trial-and-error experience; one learns even by false starts, false paths. Which path first? Well, usually,

THE SHORT LINEAR ROMANCE CO-STARRING THE MUSE AND THE INSPIRED AUTHOR

One word after another. Don't look up until you're done. Like floating down the rive, rapids and all. You either make it or you don't. Or, to mix a metaphor: You turn on the mind, say "go," let it take hold of the topic, the subject, the thesis, and run. When most people say "writing," I think they usually mean linear activity; writing words in the same sequence that will be read.

I, like everyone else, write a great deal in this linear mode. I find it works fairly well for briefer compositions—letters, short essays, short statements, even for blocks of writing (q.v.) that may eventually be incorporated into longer works. The linear method draws upon knowledge and skill already in place, already functional in the mind. And when all goes well, linear writing is a beautiful demonstration of the mind's ability to search, integrate, synthesize, articulate quickly and smoothly: the microcomputer of the brain purring away with a flawless program up in the head. But I have found that the linear run can only last so long. After so many words, it peters out. At least it frequently does for me. I come to an abrupt halt. And either I have to sit back and wait for some renewed inspiration or I have to abandon linear method altogether. The linear method is rarely a successful method for composing long texts: Only for a brief time can I row the boat, hold my breath, court the Muse—all at the same time! Yes I write letters home, brief reports, brief reviews, mini-essays, essay examinations, and the like in a generally linear way. But I realize I'm flirting with danger if I continue on the linear path after about the fourth or fifth page.

One problem with extended linear writing is that it becomes difficult to see the "whole." And certainly this ongoing, down-the-line method has a way of breaking down in the middle of chapters, in the middle of books. It has a tendency to break down cross-country.

A second way to write is

THE EXTENDED ENGAGEMENT CO-STARRING LEFTY CEREBRUM AND THE METHODIC AUTHOR

A lot of my own writing involves something other than linear activity (q.v.). A lot of my writing has to do with research, getting material, gathering and organizing material, ordering material, constructing a composition, building and rebuilding. It certainly isn't a matter of sitting down and writing from first word to last.

For nearly all nonfiction pieces (articles, papers, reviews, reports), especially if careful reasoning is involved, I have developed the habit of writing down incidental thoughts, ideas, expressions, observations on pieces of paper (or cards, or what have you) that can later be organized into categories, into a sensible sequence, and incorporated into a finished text.

Usually this kind of composition is identified well in advance of writing—and it isn't usually written overnight. Many times I write toward a deadline—a week away, preferably a month away, perhaps even a year away. And in the time between knowing that I have the task to perform and the completion of the task, I proceed steadily, somewhat methodically, gathering appropriate material—some drawn from my own thinking, some arrived at in traditional research ways. I accumulate a stack of cards or slips of paper—all of them related, some way or other, to the topic at hand.

What I really do is tack up the "theme" or "topic" or "thesis" on a wall in my mind. I start walking around it, pondering, thinking. This is a ritual of gestation for me. And as ideas, images, words, sentences come to mind I jot them down. Sometimes I become very physical about it all—I write out the topic on a piece of paper and place the paper at the center of a table; then I literally lay cards all around the topic, watching the raw material grow. Admittedly, at some time during this "collection" process, an outline (q.v.) also begins to appear, but the outline is always tentative until the "research" is done, until all the evidence is gathered and my basic thoughts have been articulated. During this gathering process, I keep checking evidence against outline, outline against evidence. And at some propitious moment, the "outline" jells. I then begin to write a draft (q.v.). I simply set the cards or slips of paper by my word processor and begin to write copy, incorporating card or slip, one by one, into a text. If some card or slip seems obdurate and cannot be incorporated easily or effectively, I set it aside for later evaluation.

Finally a draft is produced. In all likelihood it is a rough piece of writing, with some rather finished sections, but with a good many sections, paragraphs, passages suffering either from overwriting or undue brevity. This draft must now be submitted to careful revision (q.v.).

I consider this kind of writing to be very much an act of construction. Though it involves at certain points "actual writing" (q.v.) (linear, perhaps even inspired), it is not the outgrowth of spontaneous, flowing articulation. It is a writing that pieces together, then polishes.

A third kind of writing is

THE MIRACULOUS POT LUCK PAYOFF CO-STARRING FORTUNA AND THE DON'T-THROW-ANYTHING-AWAY AUTHOR

This kind of writing is more speculative, a kind of "tomorrow" writing, not done on special assignment. This is writing done without knowing, at the time, exactly where or when the writing will be used. It's writing in advance of specific need. A great deal of my writing time is spent building a storehouse of writing material. I squirrel away passages of writing, anything from a short sentence to a long character sketch. Not generated by particular projects, these writings are, rather, "savings" put aside for the future.

I try to have a good supply of such material always on hand. And it is from this supply of already written material that I often turn to build a composition. I know that if sometime in the future I need to write on a particular topic or thesis, I may well find in my storage closet a good deal of writing already in existence related to this thesis/theme. I may have a poem, a chapter, a sentence. I dig these out and ponder how I might integrate them into the composition I want to build. I know, of course, that what has been saved as a poem may well have to be rewritten as prose. I know that a list of this or that may have to be transformed into a serial sentence.

Sometimes I go through my "saved" writings and simply look for some common denominator that will bind some of the savings together. New composition ideas are generated this way. And I have had happy success with this method: piecing and patching, bringing together diverse pieces of writing, done over a long period of time, tacking them onto a common idea. This kind of potluck writing depends, of course, upon what's in the cupboard when I go to fix supper. That's why I never worry about writing something that turns out not to work; I save it. Maybe tomorrow it can become a part of a greater whole.

Revision: Revision for me involves a very careful reading of a draft, noting in particular (a) the structure and arrangement of the material and (b) the flow and sound of the words.

Looking first at structure, I edit toward design and form. Ideas usually appear to me, in the first place, as structure—in structured sentences, in balances, tricola, tetracola. I'm eager to find patterns and designs in my work.

I look first to the overall structure, the form in general. Timing and spacing are important to me at this point. A composition should have its own kind of balance, its own kind of structural stability. I look at the big sections: Are they equally treated? Are there disproportions anywhere?

After dealing with the big picture, I turn to smaller things. I turn to the actual phrasing of the material. In general, I have a tendency to overwrite, so I'm on the lookout for places to cut. And I keep an eye out for the usual editorial matters—usage, spelling, punctuation, ambiguities, etc. Especially important to me is the conclusion of a piece of writing. I fear abrupt endings; I don't want to write compositions that just "stop." I work hard for closure, for some sort of rhythm, cadence, denouement, descent. My mind goes into slow motion when I come to the final sentences. And I probably spend more time on the last few words of a text than I do on any other similar quantity of words.

Another important aspect of revision to me is the auricular aspect of the composition—that is, the way it sounds. And I spend a great deal of time reading a draft, giving full attention to the sound of it. I listen. I listen again. Sound is very important to me—and it involves all such things as rhythm, fluidity of sentences, sequences of sounds, the readability of the text in general. As I read—not aloud (though I might read a text aloud on some occasions) but silently—I mark those parts of the text (a word, a sentence, a transition) where I find a rough auricular spot. I then go back and try to polish each such place. Then, of course, I must listen again to the text. Sometimes I have repeated "listenings" before a manuscript sounds just right. Even if a text will never be read aloud, the text should be written so that it *would* read out loud very well.

I have one rule as far as my "listening" to the text is concerned. It must be an uninterrupted listening. If I am interrupted, I always start the listening process all over again; I go back to page one and start over. So much of the sound of a text depends upon all that has come before; the sound of one sentence depends upon the sound of all previous sentences. Because listening is so important to me, I am more concerned about my privacy as a writer when I'm doing this listening than I am at any other time in composition. Even the actual writing (q.v.), when I'm in the throes of composition, requires no greater privacy.

Structure and sound. Paying attention to those two things in particular, I sometimes revise a manuscript, one way or the other, twenty to thirty times.

In Conclusion: Any description I might give of the writing process will be incomplete, partially false, perhaps misleading. Whatever I say about writing—whatever anyone says about writing—always misses the mark to some degree or other.

Writing is, alas, more mysterious, miraculous, unpredictable than we pedagogically say it is. Yet, on the other hand, writing is far simpler actually than pedagogy would often have it be. A paradox? Yes, it is.

Writing, on the one hand, is a skill, craft, art that one can indeed learn from others; in fact, writing is an "unnatural" activity in comparison with the naturalness of language and speech: children do not have to be taught "speaking" very often; at a certain age, children begin speaking, without much tutoring, their "native tongue." But they do have to be taught writing/reading. One learns writing from others. One learns writing from formal education—in elementary school, in middle school, whenever it is one first learns about sentences and paragraphs.

But, on the other hand, writing is a skill that can only be learned through one's own practice. As with so many skills—riding a horse, flying an airplane—formal instruction only goes so far. The rest of the skill must be learned solo: the writing facing the page by himself.

That's why, in my own writing life, so much attention is given to my own trial/error activities, my own dry runs, my own dry holes, my own experimentations, my own playing with words to see "what if . . . ". I've found that actually I never write the same thing twice, at least rarely so. Every writing task draws upon prior knowledge, prior skill—yet every writing task also calls for a certain amount of "learning on the job," the job that this particular writing task happens to be. I think I usually know more about writing at the end of each new composition than I did before. That is, I not only write any given composition for the usual reasons—to communicate, to entertain, to reach others, to reveal myself, etc.—but I write to learn about writing. What I have learned in writing this very article, I will carry over to the next writing task I may face—next week, next month, yet this evening perhaps. And in that new writing task—later on—I will use this knowledge, but if I am lucky I will also generate new knowledge about writing that, in its own turn, will be carried over . . . .

So it goes. Learn. Write. Learn. Write. A circle.

Now let me see. I think I'm about ready now to go back to the beginning of this text and start reading it with an eye and ear toward revision (q.v.) . . . .

TERRY TEMPEST WILLIAMS (b. 1955)

Why I Write

CONSIDER THIS:

Terry Tempest Williams is the author of *Refuge: An Unnatural History of Family and Place* and a number of other books, including two collections of essays, two children's books and, most recently, *Leap,* a spiritual meditation on the work of Hieronymus Bosch and *Red: Patience and Passion in the Desert.* A conservation activist and spokesperson, Williams serves on the Governing Council of the Wilderness Society. *The Utne Reader* named her as one of their "*Utne* 100 Visionaries," that is, "a person who could change your life." Formerly, naturalist-in-residence at the Utah Museum of Natural History, she lives in Castle Valley, Utah.

In an interview, Williams notes: "Each of us writes out of our own biases. I am a Mormon woman who grew up in the Great Basin and now lives in the Colorado Plateau. These are the lens of culture, gender, and geography that I see out of," and explains her own writing aims in this manner: "I wanted to try and write out of the body, not out of the head. I wanted to create a circular text, not a linear one. I wanted to play with the elemental movements of Earth, Fire, Water, and Air, and bow to the desert, a landscape I love. I wanted to see if I could create on the page a dialogue with the heart-open wildness." Keep these aims in mind as you read Williams's explanation of why she writes. Read more of her biography and interviews by searching the Web and see how that information allows you to understand and connect to the striking claims she makes in this brief lyric essay.

It is just after 4:00 A.M. I was dreaming about Moab, Brooke and I walking around the block just before dawn. I threw a red silk scarf around my shoulders and then I began reciting in my sleep why I write:

I write to make peace with the things I cannot control. I write to create fabric in a world that often appears black and white. I write to discover. I write to uncover. I write to meet my ghosts. I write to begin a dialogue. I write to imagine things differently and in imagining things differently perhaps the world will change. I write to honor beauty. I write to correspond with my friends. I write as a daily act of improvisation. I write because it creates my composure. I write against power and for democracy. I write myself out of my nightmares and into my dreams. I write in a solitude born out of community. I write to the questions that shatter my sleep. I write to the answers that keep me complacent. I write to remember. I write to forget. I write to the music that opens my heart. I write to quell the pain. I write to migrating birds with the hubris of language. I write as a form of translation. I write with the patience of melancholy in winter. I write because it allows me to confront that which I do not know. I write as an act of faith. I write as an act of slowness. I write to record what I love in the face of loss. I write because it makes me less fearful of death. I write as an exercise in pure joy. I write as one who walks on the surface of a frozen river beginning to melt. I write out of my anger and into my passion. I write from the stillness of night anticipating—always anticipating. I write to listen. I write out of silence. I write to soothe the voices shouting inside me, outside me, all around. I write because of the humor of our condition as humans. I write because I believe in words. I write because I do not believe in words. I write because it is a dance with paradox. I write because you can play on the page like a child left alone in sand. I write because it belongs to the force of the moon: high tide, low tide. I write because it is the way I take long walks. I write as a bow to wilderness. I write because I believe it can create a path in darkness. I write because as a child I spoke a different language. I write with a knife carving each word through the generosity of trees. I write as ritual. I write because I am not employable. I write out of my inconsistencies. I write because then I do not have to speak. I write with the colors of memory. I write as a witness to what I have seen. I write as a witness to what I imagine. I write by grace and grit. I write out of indigestion. I write when I am starving. I write when I am full. I write to the dead. I write out of the body. I write to put food on the table. I write on the other side of procrastination. I write for the children we never had. I write for the love of ideas. I write for the surprise of a sentence. I write with the belief of alchemists. I write knowing I will always fail. I write knowing words always fall short. I write knowing I can be killed by my own words, stabbed by syntax, crucified by both understanding and misunderstanding. I write out of ignorance. I write by accident. I write past the embarrassment of exposure. I keep writing and suddenly, I am overcome by the sheer indulgence, (the madness,) the meaninglessness, the ridiculousness of this list. I trust nothing especially myself and slide head first into the familiar abyss of doubt and humiliation and threaten to push the delete button on my way down, or madly erase each line, pick up the paper and rip it into shreds—and then I realize, it doesn't matter, words are always a gamble, words are splinters from cut glass. I write because it is dangerous, a bloody risk, like love, to form the words, to say the words, to touch the source, to be touched, to reveal how vulnerable we are, how transient.

I write as though I am whispering in the ear of the one I love.

Classroom Authors

DEBBIE OLANDER

The Fortunes

CONSIDER THIS:

Who can resist breaking open a fortune cookie and reading? Even people who don't like to eat the cookie seem to find fortunes riding home with them in their purses or pockets. Debbie Olander was a Master's student in English and a Ph.D. student in Musicology when she composed her essay. She borrowed Winston Weathers's discussion of Grammar B and chose to write in crots. The idea of a "crot" is derived from the Old English word for a bit or a fragment or an independent unit of thought. Debbie analyzes the types of fortunes she has collected and discusses each type in a different section of her essay. After reading Debbie's draft, list other topics that would lend themselves to a similar analysis and method of presentation. For instance, a discussion of movies (or other art), or an analysis of ads and signage are two such possibilities. How might using short, subtitled sections like these help you organize your observations for a reader? Finally, consider *other* ways Debbie might have approached an essay on fortune cookie fortunes. Suggest two or three alternate formats for an investigation of this topic, and outline the possibilities and limits of each approach.

WRITING PROCESS NARRATIVE FOR THE FORTUNES

This essay proceeds from the in-class free-write exercise, "Listing and Memory," on things we save: lists of what's in the junk drawer, or what items are in my wallet. The original invention is 3½ pages long, and I am satisfied with the work, not envisioning taking the matter further. I prefer to move on to a different subject. When it undergoes peer review in small group on September 14th, however, the reviewers clearly want more, more, more. They suggest directions in which I might take this piece. Also in this class, we discuss "revising out."

So I try to revise out. And fail. I feel stuck with this stupid piece of writing about fortunes, and fortune cookies. But in straightening out my house, I come upon what amounts to a pile of these fortunes—so I just start putting them into little groups according to theme or type, and the invention grows to 8 pages. It undergoes small peer-group review as an expanded draft on Sept. 21st. The group still wants more, more, more.

In response to the in-class discussion of fat drafts and full-breath drafts, I again return to "The Fortunes," and decide to make it my essay for the first Full Class Peer Workshop on October 5th. Again I scrounge around my house for more fortunes. By the end of the scrounging, I have 65 fortunes, and I believe I have teased every last fortune from its hiding place in my house, car, purse, wherever. I also have an eleven-page essay which has essentially written itself. In other words, its content is self-generated. All I do is dig around for fortunes, organize them into piles, and type what they say.

The discussion in the Peer Workshop is spirited, as the "great fortune cookie debate" ensues. Each reviewer has his or her own (apparently strong) opinion about what is good or bad about "The Fortunes." Views are at such variance that I can make no consensus of them. Phrases and sections are singled out for being awful or awesome. The same phrases or sections. My readers have a love/hate relationship with them.

In general, though, I make the following observations:

- There is a shift in tone on page 7 which is bothersome to readers. Half of the group prefers the wry, humorous tone of the first six pages; the other half of the group prefers the introspective tone of pp. 7–11.
- There are contradictory statements in the essay which should be clarified or omitted outright.
- Most readers like the overall organization of the piece, but are conflicted as to the ideal length (cut or expand by 50%).
- Every reader is in agreement that he or she has never read an essay like this one. (Which is not so surprising, since I have never written a creative nonfiction essay before, period. Simply said, I don't know what I am doing.)

At this point in the evolution of "The Fortunes," one thing becomes clear to me: I need to leave it alone for at least six weeks. Something is badly missing. Some simple stroke of the imagination, probably. But I am sick of this essay, am sick myself, and my essay is sick, too. So I leave it alone—not for six weeks, but for two entire months. I write about turnips instead. And then I start my home/family inventions, which grow into each other like vines. I start to get the feeling that I am really beginning to figure out how to write creative nonfiction essays—at least a little bit. "Passing 24 West: Semi-Charmed" comes out of the printer on November 2nd, and more pieces of my home/family essay appear.

This afternoon, November 13th, I am writing the diary of "The Fortunes," trying to apply to this one piece all the lessons learned. I feel guilty for having ignored this child, and am now in the uncomfortable position of having to analyze the process of creating an essay which is not finished yet. However, fate has intervened yet again. Early this morning, I have come upon Fortune #66 in a basket on the desk in my computer room. It is the very best fortune of them all, and will provide the glue for the entire essay. I see, in that one instant of reading the message, that the essay will be healed. I know what it will look like as a healthy essay. It is a fortune about music, and singing, and rejoicing. Hallelujah!

Today, December 4th, I realize that I'm learning a very good lesson about revising. At first, I think I have to take each person's comments seriously, so I dutifully record all of them on one copy of the essay. And then I realize that I am in control of the piece, and nobody else. So I do what I feel needs to be done with it, at the expense of overlooking some detail that might have improved the piece. I don't care if there is a shift in tone on page 7. I don't care if some people don't get why I believe in these things, or why they mean something to me. I'm driving to a point at the end, which is a serious one to me, and if people want me to be wry or funny about it, tough.

December 6th. I feel sorry for being bitchy back there. People gave me tons of feedback, and I was just overwhelmed by it, being new at this thing, and being in the first essay group. It's hard to please everybody, and now I know I don't have to. That's all. It's not so complicated anymore.

THE FORTUNES

I admit it: I save the fortunes from the cookies in Chinese restaurants. There are little collections of them all around the house—in drawers, baskets, organizer compartments, and even in my wallet. Never consciously have I tossed a fortune in the trash. They are my little fates, my mini horoscopes, and my conscience. They have voices.

Believing them to be special messages to me from a power who knows my every quirk and hidden potential, I take them to heart. Perhaps they are warnings, or as one strip says, "Many receive advice, only the wise profit by it." So I pay attention to them, thinking that there might be a reason for my having received this particular fortune in my cookie on this particular day. They are ponderable and karmic.

KINDNESS

Sometimes I have received the identical piece of wisdom twice. A cosmic insistence, a reinforcement of a truth that obviously I had not copped to before: "You have a kind and generous heart." Perhaps I was being admonished for my impatience, which apparently was the case in Manhattan (on pink paper) and in Tampa (on white). And sometimes a theme recurs, which I take as Zen spin, in case I still haven't internalized the original message: "You are kind-hearted and hospitable, cheerful and well-liked." (So I must really be, since I have received this cookie information several times.)

I have even had this revelation about my generosity rephrased: "You are never selfish with your advice or your help." Such fortunes come as elaborations on a simple idea, and result in one large amplification that takes place over time. This is comforting to me. I get the idea that I am basically a decent and kind person, and that I have not changed very much over the years. Or maybe it's just the idea that it is what's inside the cookie, or the person, that counts.

PATIENCE

I also admit, in addition to collecting fortunes, to being impatient. I have worked diligently on this facet of my personality, which I perceive as negative. Yet I am reminded more specifically: "You may have to be patient now—think, listen, and heed signs."

Sometimes there is a more specific message concerning my impatience, in case I hadn't considered the ramifications of this particular shortcoming before. I have been advised to "Curb a tendency to go off in all different directions." This fortune goes hard with me, because my mind behaves in just this way. I don't believe it's a fault, or an unadmirable quality in me, so I do feel somewhat inclined to argue, just a little, with this particular fortune, because I believe that mental forays are an intrinsic part of my life. I would not give them up for anything. "Going off in all different directions" is a sign of my mental agility, my drive to learn. I reserve the right do this, or to change my mind. I am not scatterbrained.

Yet there is another aspect to the "patience" fortunes, which I think is true. "It is much easier to begin a thing than to finish it." I know that I have always been pretty good out of the starting blocks, more sprinter than marathoner, and that I have difficulty completing projects. Still, it does help to be reminded of this shortcoming, even if a bit irritating. I do try to stick things out, if only because I know that I'm not predisposed that way. Overcompensation, I suppose. On the other hand, this fortune could simply be taken as encouragement to persevere.

BEAUTY

Another recurring theme from my cookies concerns beauty. This is not the vanity kind, not a call to brush up on my "Mirror, mirror on the wall" speech—although, as I have been counseled, "How you look depends on where you go." I take such these fortunes as reminders to stop and smell roses. Usually the message says, "You find beauty in ordinary things, do not lose this ability." So I slow down and look around for a few days, which is generally a thoughtful way to approach life. "Beauty in its various forms appeals to you." Certainly it does, since I have loved (and studied) music, art and poetry all my life. I have received this fortune twice, too. I suppose it never hurts to be reminded of something that was always in the forefront of my consciousness. At least I feel that these messages vindicate my personal aesthetics.

I do not like to think that thousands of people are getting the same messages as I am, even though I know they are. I realize that trite fortunes can apply to many people, but I have no trouble believing that the terse yet suggestive lines contained in the cookies are meant for me. That I sometimes receive them twice only reinforces this belief. Last Friday, in fact, the fortune cookie lottery bestowed upon each recipient a piece of wisdom that was absolutely appropriate to him or her. The aspiring teacher drew a fortune about education; the tapped-out doctoral student received financial advice; and I extracted words of encouragement about writing from the lopsided grin of the bent cookie.

I have read yet another fortune twice (pink and white paper, again): "You are contemplative and analytical by nature." This, of course, is true of my approach to musicology and writing. But it is even more true when combined with other cookie scraps which elaborate on the way art should be approached. I take all of them as further proof of my love of beauty, and smelling roses.

TRAVEL AND MONEY

The fourth cookie theme that has emerged over decades of egg rolls is travel, which seems also to have something to do with money. I have been told at various times that I "will travel far and wide for pleasure," or that I "will step on the soil of many countries." Perhaps I received one of these messages in Germany or France, or even Mississippi (which considers itself a sovereign state). Most ironically, I was informed, "You will be traveling and coming into a fortune." It is hardly surprising to uncover the intimate association of fortune and money, but to extract it from the inside of a cookie is like rediscovering the missing link. In any case, I was told, "You should be able to make money and hold on to it." That many fortunes have lotto numbers on the back is a fact which is not lost on me. However, since I hold onto whatever funds I have, according to the fortunes, I don't buy lottery tickets. On the other hand, I have obviously spent a great deal of money over the years on oriental food, in far-flung places—Hawaii, Los Angeles, Seattle, New York, Puerto Rico, Paris, Wiesbaden.

ADVICE

There have been messages in cookies which I should have heeded, but didn't. "Marriage is not a fast knot, but a slip knot." Definitely a slip knot: A divorce. Or, "You are soon going to change your present line of work." Corporate down-sizing was not far off. And some messages are wishful thinking on the part of the restaurant which served up a batch of tainted fried rice in Honolulu: "You have an iron constitution." A bottle of milk of magnesia later, I was not convinced.

There are fortunes which fall under the category of job advice. If only I had accepted career counseling from a cookie, which said, "You would make a good lawyer," I might be in a totally different place today. Or, it could simply be that this fortune originally belonged to my ex-husband, who is now defending white-collar crooks. (The same is probably true of the fortune which said, "You are a happy man.") Somehow the fortunes just ended up in my possession. Yet my father often told me that I would make a good lawyer, so a cookie verified his opinion at some point in my life, although he never said I would make a good man. Still, I suppose it's never too late to go to law school.

Then there is the motherly advice: "Keep your feet on the ground even though friends flatter you." I have always been the down-to-earth type, and probably less susceptible to flattery than most anyone I know. Yet this message is somewhat in conflict, at least in my mind, with another "parental advice" fortune that said, "Be sure to use your talents to attract others." There is the implication that while I should not fall for flattery, I should nevertheless make every attempt to charm other people. But if I consider that generosity and kindness are the talents referred to here, maybe I don't have a problem with this fortune after all, especially when I am told "You are talented in many ways."

There is a third category, which I call "life advice." It is somehow different from the other kinds of advice, because I can't imagine receiving it with regard to a job, nor can I hear my mother's voice in the fortune. It goes like this: "You're interested in higher education whether material or spiritual." This is undisputable truth. Like some of the other fortunes, it points out a direction which, over time, becomes obvious. I have no idea when I received this particular revelation of my personality, but it is one of the truest statements about me that I have ever bitten into.

Seldom have I drawn a fortune which I consider "standard" advice. In fact, this has happened only once, when I was informed, "You will enjoy good health." I should also mention at this point that my lone standard scrap is also the only time in my life that a cookie has lied to me. (I am diabetic.) If there's one thing I can't stand, it's lying. To hear dishonesty from the mouth of a cookie is outrageous, and somebody should be spoken to about this.

But since I'm a kind and generous person, I'm willing to admit that perhaps this cookie was not taking the broader view, like all the other cookies, and maybe—just maybe—I did enjoy good health that week, whenever it was. And putting the best construction on things, as I am prone to do, I'm willing to understand that sometimes oracles have bad days. So I should add "forgiveness" to the list of my traits, or view it as an extension of the generosity in me that the cookies have been telling me about all these years.

WORK

The fortunes about life's work are the most motivational, of course. I have many of these. Mostly they say things such as, "A good time to finish up old tasks." (Another cross-reference to some of the patience fortunes.) Or, "Many possibilities are open to you—work a little harder." These I tend to obey. "Work harder" is never bad advice. It's as though my parents really are in these cookies: "Work calmly and silently!" I can hear my mother saying, "All your hard work will soon pay off." This last one is stamped with two smiley faces, further proof that my mother had something to do with the baking of these bent almond triangles.

I work hard at writing, and I love words. Staring at a similar fortune, I am amused at first: "All your hard work will soon be paid off." Not all messages are grammatically correct, nor are their words spelled right. This one fortune seems fraught with irony, so I study it, puzzled. I begin to grow suspicious of the origin of this voice. Since I have always worked hard to discover the reasons for things, and what words mean, I subversively question advice from time to time, especially if phrased cryptically. This cookie has pseudo-authority, but I balk at arguing with it, because I also have the sense that hard work has big consequences, a different kind of pay-off: "Working hard will make you live a happy life." In this particular case, I would deduce that if I did not work hard, I would be miserable forever. So it is particularly nice to be told, "You have an ability to sense and know the higher truth." If I work hard to get to the bottom of a matter, really dig in, what I will find there will, in fact, turn out to be something higher.

HOME AND HAPPINESS

"The happiest circumstances are close to home." This strikes me as being another cryptic fortune. What, exactly, is home? Certainly it is not always where I am living, or where the government makes me say I live. For the nine years of my first marriage, my "home of record" was Memphis. I filed my taxes in Tennessee, voted by absentee ballot to an address in Shelby County. Yet I never lived there. I lived in Alabama, or New Jersey, or Germany. And surely the home I made then, wherever it happened to be, was rarely full of "happy circumstances."

But there is another way to look at this. "Happy events will take place shortly in your home." Could this mean I will be giving a party? Does it mean I will curl up with my books and my cats, with the windows open? Maybe it means that I will make more chicken soup? What I *think* it means, and what I will continue to believe, is that I will be generally content with my life, wherever I make my home. It means that I will make the best of things, no matter what nuisances occur. I am known for that. (I am kind and generous, after all.)

Home is difficult. Happiness is difficult. Yet I am told, "The current year will bring you much happiness." I really don't know what that means, either. Perhaps when I ate the cookie that foretold this, I had a relatively happy year.

When I think about the "home-and-happiness" fortunes, I am enough of a child to think of my parents, and Pennsylvania, where I was born. Or maybe happiness is my resilience (as my fortunes have explained); but maybe it is also hope, which I tend to think is not only a human tendency, but a character trait which is particularly evident in me. It's like listening to a piece of music. I know the tensions will resolve. Still, these fortunes are difficult.

The one fortune that makes my heart jump is, "Friends long absent are coming back to you." Nothing would make me feel more at home, or more happy, than to be in the company of friends who have been long away from me. I don't have many friends. At least not in the day-to-day sense. In fact, I have been known to love people whom I've never met or haven't seen in twenty years. This, for me, is normal. My attachments to people make me feel what most folks feel when they talk about "home" and "happiness." I could tell you who they are, but that would be silly. We are talking about fortune cookies here, and what the fortunes say about my friends seems as true as everything else. My friends, in the truest sense, *are* my home and my happiness.

POETRY

My friend Silvia is a gifted poet. And because she is, she understands me when I say that there is poetry in every cookie—and even that they contain poetic justice. Silvia told me, "I still have a yellowing fortune taped to my old electric typewriter about being honored by someone I respect. A week after I scarfed down that cookie, John Ashberry selected me as one of four writers to go to France on a fellowship. Coincidence? Never!" Two important ideas emerge here: first, that I am not alone in believing that fortunes can be predictions, or wish-fulfillments; and second, that I am not alone in saving them, hoarding them, treasuring them. They really mean something.

They function in my life as symbols in the truest and most poetic sense. In another way, I consider them symbols *of* my life. In rare instances, the fortunes themselves could be, are, poems. Such a discovery is like finding a little *Rubaiyat* cradled in the cookie:

When we take wine
with a dear friend,
a thousand cups
are still few.

It is possible to be creative with these strips of paper, to have fun with them. For example, they can be spliced into haiku:

You will have good luck
There is a true and sincere
someone you respect

Behind able men
overcome many hardships
for being honest

A pleasant surprise
You will soon be honored by
friendship between you

Good news will be brought
you have a reputation
one who goes all out

Words of empty tongue
you are one of the people
brought to you by mail

The irony of making Japanese poetry out of words from Chinese food is not lost on me. Nor is the notion that all poems are *found* poems which do not exist until we actually see them. Poems are everywhere, but we must make them ourselves.

MUSIC

This month, the guidance I've received in my food has concentrated on two ideas. The first is one I have borne in mind for a long time, and it still governs my way of living: "Let intuition rule this month and you will find success." I trust my intuition, and these days it is also telling me, "Speak only well of people and you need never whisper." This becomes an equation of intuition with conscience; an equation of kindness with speaking well of people; and of hunches with fortune.

The fortunes are often lyrical, and I suspect that songs could be made of them, that they could be made to rhyme, put together in such a way that together they would sing a kind of music that no individual fortune could.

Friends long absent
Are coming back to you;
You have an ability to sense
And know a higher truth:
When we take wine with friends,
A thousand cups are few.

Poetry and music are the biggest part of my life, my greatest inheritance. They are my family and my life-friends, what I listen to in bed and what I keep beside me all the time. I love them. In this respect, if I treat the fortunes as music or poetry, they are giving me enormously valuable advice about how to treat works of art. Above all, I will respect this wisdom.

I do think it is important, for example, to be kind and generous with art, and to work hard when dealing with it. I also believe that music represents a kind of travel which I have been lucky enough to experience all of my life. And I believe that not only is it beautiful and poetic, music is also full of advice—because compositions are models of experience, and I learn from them.

I always treat music with intuition, as my recent fortune advised. An earlier fortune also rings true, because I do sense a higher truth in music, and simply must write about it. Whether this comes as a result of intuition or hard work, it is still something I know I was meant to do, and that this is the kind of person I am. Here is where I am home, and happy.

Until today, I have never had a fortune taped in a special place to remind me of an important event. They are simply everywhere. But I still believe, in the aggregate collection of my fortunes, that I have been given important words about life. Over time, the messages have developed their own patterns and significance. Eventually, the thematic material has run together in a kind of impressionist music which sounds exactly like me. They are what I am composed of; they are my notes and my phrases. So I admit it: I save these fortunes, but more to the point, they save me. So this morning, I tape to my computer the one fortune which sums up everything I've been writing and thinking about: "Sing and rejoice, fortune is smiling on you."

W. BRIAN OVERCAST

Brambles

CONSIDER THIS:

"Brambles" was composed when Brian Overcast was enrolled in an essay-writing workshop while he was completing his MA degree in creative writing. Both Debbie and Brian include process narratives with their essays that tell the story of how they wrote their texts. After reading both essays and both process narratives, try to characterize each as "a writer." You can use the impressions and insights you gain from other readings in this chapter to help you respond to these authors' own reports of the writing life. Whereas Debbie analyzes types of fortune cookies, Brian analyzes his family. He defines them—as a classic nuclear unit—and then illustrates that unity. How does he complicate this apparently simple thesis? As you near the end of the essay, how do you react to the change in tone in this "nuclear" family's story?

WRITING PROCESS NARRATIVE FOR BRAMBLES

Although *Brambles* started as a side project that I worked on while revising the basement paper, it has developed into an important paper in its own right. Its importance lies in the fact that there were several landmark events that happened while writing this piece.

My primary goal at first was to simply keep writing. I wrote the freewrite off the top of my head, and was pleasantly surprised to find that the rudiments of a story had developed without the supreme effort that the Basement paper required. No outline this time. I don't think this paper was developed from an in-class prompt either, I just wrote the first line, "I grew up nuclear. Two parents, two kids, two car garage," and went from there. This is rare for me. Usually, the first paragraph is the hardest part of the story for me to write. (Landmark event #1.) At the end of the freewrite, I had developed the shell of a story, three pages, and was satisfied.

An interesting part about this first draft was that I wrote two endings to it. The first ending was:

The divorce of my mother and father still stings, but not like the sharpness of vodka. It stings like the summer I tried to help my father pick blackberries, when the menacing thorns pricked at my skin and tore at my clothes, the prickly vines drawing my blood and tears. As I was forced to flee, he went on without me, his back disappearing as he struggled deeper into the brambles.

This ending places more blame on my father for the divorce. This is the copy I sent home to my mother to read. I didn't want to hurt her feelings, which in turn caused me to write a lame ending. But I didn't like this compromise, so I wrote another ending:

The divorce of my mother and father still stings, but not like the sharpness of vodka. It stings like only the worst of ironies can. After all of those family meetings to guide my brother and me, after all those laws and mock contracts, my parents were the ones who broke the most sacred contract of all.

This ending I like much better, because it is closer to the truth. (Landmark event #2.) I chose to write the truth regardless of my parents feelings.

I chose to fat draft the *Brambles* paper next, since I was falling behind on it. (The Basement paper took a lot of my time.) The size doubled fairly easily, but would not go much further after that. I was satisfied with this draft, but I was a little afraid that the two halves (Florida and Cape Cod) did not fit well enough together. I also worked more on the second half of the paper when I was writing about the blackberry vodka. Anna had asked me to develop the second half further.

It was at this point that I experienced the Landmark event #3. I realized as I was revising the *Brambles* paper that a good portion of the Family Dinner section would fit nicely into my Basement paper. I wondered if it was okay to do this, to plagiarize myself. But, you (Wendy) always say to take risks, so I used that as my mental green light. And it fit nicely!

For the next draft, I went for a large scale revision. (This was after our conference.) The first thing I did was to cut $\frac{3}{4}$ of the first page, and the top $\frac{1}{4}$ of the second page. This was the portion about my reading habits, which we both liked, but it just didn't fit. I had to sit over it for about ten minutes first, though, searching for a way to fix it, to fit it in, but eventually I had to give in. *I just hate to cut.* But I got over it. I researched several '80's Family Sitcoms, at your suggestion, but the families weren't the strict nuclear that I was looking for, and I didn't feel like I could draw enough parallels between my family and the sitcom family, so I left it out. What I did add, was landmark event #4. I figured that not only could I fit paragraphs from *Brambles* into the Basement paper, but vice versa as well. So, I took back the original paragraphs, that had since been revised and reinserted them back into the Family Dinner section. I was swapping all over the place.

Other additions: Opened the paper describing the '80's mentality. (Still needs work), wrote about some good contracts, talked more about my parents in reference to the contracts, worked in more conflict about the divorce to set up the ending, etc.

When I was home over Thanksgiving break, I asked my mom if she had saved any of my contracts from childhood, but she hadn't. I was hoping to scan one into my paper. We talked a lot about the papers I have written for this class, and she told me that although she was upset when reading them, she was glad that I was expressing my feelings about the divorce. So, that was cool, and made me feel less restricted in what I can write.

In the final draft, I considered the suggestions of Terra, Carissa, Laura, and Debbie. Their primary suggestion was to further foreshadow the disintegration of my parent's marriage so that I could avoid the, "sucker-punch syndrome" at the end of my essay. I combated this by inserting a few sentences of foreshadowing, namely in the first paragraph, by lengthening the sitcom parallel, and on page four, when I inserted more about how our Family Dinners were no longer about family. I also transferred a few foreshadowing moments that I had developed in the basement paper. And not only did I add, but I also cut a portion on page six, ending a paragraph on the image of my father disappearing into the brambles. This was Laura's suggestion, and I feel it leaves the image open to more interpretation, leading to foreshadowing.

The other issue I had was the ending of my story, which I couldn't seem to get right. I reworked it by adding in more of the nuclear theme and the sitcom parallel. These two new paragraphs really strengthened the finish, I think, and also reduced the "sucker-punch syndrome." Also, the stylistic addition at the very end seems to stand out better now that it is isolated on its own page.

I feel satisfied with this piece now, and after *Brambles* and the basement paper, I am thoroughly worn out on the topic of my parents' divorce.

BRAMBLES

By the 1980's, everything was nuclear. Nuclear power plants ran our dishwasher and heated our home. There was nuclear waste. Two great nations pointed nuclear arms at each other. And TV sitcoms celebrated the nuclear family unit, from the *Cosby Show* to *Growing Pains.* In these shows, viewers could see how the American family was supposed to work: Parents and kids went through crises, argued out their problems, shed a few tears, then resolved it all with a laugh, a hug, and a moral message. In the sitcoms, the nuclear unit was tough, shared feelings, and never held a grudge for longer than thirty minutes. In the sitcoms, the nuclear unit stayed together.

I grew up nuclear. Two parents, two kids, a two car garage. My parents believed that a nuclear family was perfect—it insured success. Sometimes I wonder if my parents had a "how to" nuclear family book. We were certainly a textbook worthy example. Mother stayed at home, did the housework, helped my brother and me with our homework, and was a member of the Garden Club and PTA. My father earned the family income. I was a straight-A student at a private school. My brother, Stephen, was the best soccer player on his team. We were white bread, white collar, and fueled by uranium. We were real people trying to live a sitcom life.

Like the sitcoms, "The Family Dinner" was the most important part of our day. It was then that we discussed how school went, or soccer practice, or how my father's boss was a money-grubbing, penny-pinching son of a bitch. Reading the paper or even the nutritional information on a ketchup bottle was not allowed during dinner, only talk. In fact, my mother had a list of forbidden behaviors.

For example, putting an elbow on the table was okay, but two elbows was a crime. Kicking the leg of a sibling under the table or arguing about foot space was strongly discouraged. Also illegal: laughing until milk came out of my nose and playing with my food. Never, never did we bring the Gameboy to the table. Tetris and Super Mario would have to wait until later. All toys were checked at the kitchen door. But the most heinous crime of all, the top infraction of the list, was burping audibly. The higher the volume, the less ice cream I got after dinner. An intentional belch lasting over one second could send me to my room for the rest of the evening.

My father's only rule: Do not ever, under any circumstances, cry over a drink spilled on the dinner table. If my brother or I did spill our milk, he would yell and curse like a crusted sergeant. This, of course, made us cry more. At this point, my mother typically pushed back from the table, silently picked up her plate, and took her dinner back to her room. She dodged family arguments at any cost.

In an attempt to prevent these interfamily arguments, once a month after dinner we would hold a "Family Meeting." A family meeting was a chance for each member to air their respective concerns about how well the Overcasts were operating. We would discuss morals over meatloaf, and family laws between bites of lasagna. Naturally, my parents did most of the talking while my brother and I did most of the listening. These sessions covered various topics including: allowance raises, misplaced dirty laundry, unsanitary bathroom practices, homework quotas, and landscaping projects. After every meeting our family (my mother and father) would draw up a contract that we (my brother and I) would sign, stating new rules and objectives that we were to follow. These contracts were legal as far as our family law was concerned, and were to be adhered to at all times. Yet, when Stephen and I tried to write a contract to reduce the arguments between our parents, it went unsigned. Our nuclear unit was not always a fair one.

The most feared of all contracts was the landscaping contract. My parents used the word "landscaping" to dress up the words "yard work." My brother and I knew their trick, and we learned to hate that word. Landscaping usually involved one of two things—both undesirable. First, it meant weeding. I would estimate that thirty percent of our yard was made up of gardens my mother tended. These gardens were quite beautiful, but also a haven for weeds. A weeding contract meant bending over in the sun, pulling up weeds from the roots, and collecting them in a trash bag. A weeding contract meant cut fingers, dirt under our nails, and sore leg and back muscles. We never liked weeding, but we never liked the other landscaping contract either.

Mulching contracts meant a full day of work. First, my mom would run up to the local nursery and fill her station wagon with as much mulch as her trunk and back seat could hold. Then, I had to unload them and place the twenty pound bags into a cart, which my brother wheeled all over the yard to their final destinations. Finally, we mulched, and the smell of cypress filled the air. One of us poured, while the other distributed and smoothed. Mulching meant the same pain as weeding, but with an added twist—splinters. Too many to count. The cypress chips we handled all day took their toll on our hands, inserting a sliver of wood wherever they were soft.

The worst part was the reward for all this work: we were allowed to stay in the family. My father relished saying this each time we asked what we would get for a wasted Saturday. If we complained and asked for monetary rewards, he would either yell at our ungratefulness for all the work he did every day, or simply tell us that we had just earned our allowances for the week.

And so we hated yard work.

To be fair, not all contracts were bad. When I was eight, my mother set me up with a reading incentive contract. For every book I read I would earn a new GI Joe. This contract not only earned me a large collection of action figures, but also a foundation of literacy. Within this foundation, I realized that I actually enjoyed reading, and it has continued to give me pleasure ever since. But mostly, I found contracts to be undesirable.

My brother and I generally loved my mother's cooking, yet we soon became wary of eating at the dinner table, as family meetings and the ensuing contracts began to increase. Soon, our dinners were less about family time and more about rule making. My parents were trying so hard to be perfect—to have the smartest kids and the most successful family. But my brother and I weren't perfect, and neither were our parents. With their nuclear ideal falling apart, they increased their contract production, thinking that more structure would hold us all together.

Our refrigerator was nearly covered with these contracts. There was one that described yard work duties. Another detailed homework responsibilities. Contracts for grades, for work, for getting to soccer practice on time. Contracts for everything. Dinner soon became something of a mock congressional session. Platforms were discussed, laws were created, bills were vetoed. For this reason, my brother and I longed to eat in front of the TV, like the evil, non-nuclear families. We craved fast food and soda, and reading comic books while slurping a milk shake. Yet, all of these things were illegal, and they stayed that way for quite a while. Contracts were law, and our allowances counted on adhering to them.

Each year, however, we would get a break from family dinners. Every summer, we would vacation on Cape Cod where we stayed in an old, wood-shingled cottage. It was here where our parents showed signs that they were growing tired of the whole nuclear thing. In the Cape cottage, all laws were loosened and most contracts were null and void. There we could kick off our shoes and let them lay where they fell, if we even wore them. Food sometimes fell, and often rested. Our elbows rested, and no one cared. Burping was overlooked, my "C" in Geometry forgotten, and my brother's two month mulching contract postponed. Neither my father nor my mother wanted to have a family meeting. Our family congress simply went on vacation.

Another reason for our lack of family meals at the Cape was that my mother had deemed the small and antiquated kitchen insufficient for her cooking needs. The range heated unevenly, the gas stove was too dangerous, and she refused to cook with a microwave, claiming it "waved the taste goodbye." So, each summer she took a break from cooking, and my brother and I took a break from family dinners and everything that went along with them. We lived mostly on hot dogs, hamburgers, and other grilled food, for my dad was now the cook. The charcoal hibachi was his cooking appliance of choice, so he rarely set foot in the kitchen.

In fact, there were only two times a year that he used the kitchen. The first was when he cooked his annual lobster. He would spend a half day looking for the biggest lobster he could find, and cook him in a giant lobster pot until the crustacean was just the right color of pinkish orange. My parents would feast on the lobster with butter and lemon, tearing into its exoskeleton with rapture. They even ate the green contents of the digestive tract. *Ugh.* I hated lobster, and left my portion to my parents—all the more for them. I believe they really enjoyed grossing me out while I tried to quickly choke down my peanutbutter and jelly sandwich. I guess they owed me for all those dinner table burps back in Florida.

The only other time my father cooked in the kitchen was at the end of July, when he baked a pie. A blackberry pie. As the berries began to ripen, my father would visit his secret blackberry patches behind the cemetery. He would check once a week, taking a sampling to test, as he said, "for sweetness and acidity." When the day came for the picking, he would move off into the hat-high brambles, but not before fully covering his body from head to toe. The thorns of the blackberry were as numerous as they were merciless. My father would always leave at daybreak to avoid being seen, picking through the morning fog that shrouds most New England mornings.

My brother and I would typically have to wait until noon for him to return. The patch was over twenty yards deep and the work was slow because of the tangles. We would wait impatiently on the porch, anxious to hear his unofficial report on the berry crop for that year. Sometimes my brother and I spoke little, our hearts afraid of what could happen to our father in the brambles. We were afraid of the enormous and thorny bushes, and carried a mix of disappointment and pure gratitude when our father would not allow us to join him. As most sons, my brother and I wanted to be just like our father, but could not yet muster the courage to enter the blackberry patch. I tried to pick with him briefly once, but the menacing thorns tore my clothes and then my skin. They also sliced my pride. The prickly vines drew from my body both blood and embarrassed tears, forcing me to flee the tangled plants. Though I called my father to wait, he went on without me. He left me to cry in frustration as his back slowly disappeared deeper into the brambles.

We knew the success of his harvest would be determined by the coloring on his fingers—stained purple on an average year and nearly black on a good one. When he did return, he would be scratched-up and itchy, but smiling, holding a brown paper bag oozing purple juice at the seams. While my father took a shower, my brother, mother and I would separate the berries into three piles. One pile, the largest, would be for the pie filling. The second largest would be for us to eat as we pleased, which we often did as we separated the lot. It was common to hear, "I'll have to eat this one, it's a bit damaged," as we drew berries from the bag. The last pile, about the size of a handful, we would leave for my father. These berries had another purpose. In this pile only the best berries would do; the darkest in color, the most robust in size, the most symmetrical in shape. One dozen blackberries, as close to perfect as possible. These berries were reserved for the other tradition of my father's annual harvests—his blackberry vodka.

After scrubbing out scratches and picking out thorns, my father would emerge from the shower and make himself an honorary screwdriver to lower the level of the vodka. Then, he would take the bottle, the neck now empty, and fill it with the ripened berries until the liquid rose once again to a level of fullness. The bottle would then sit on the unused dining room table of the cottage for several weeks, waiting and maturing. Each day my brother and I would watch with fascination as the berries leached their juice into the vodka, infusing the alcohol with a cloud of purple flavor.

"Is it time yet?" we would ask.

"No," he would answer, "not until the last day."

On the morning of the last full day of vacation, my father would take his bottle and submerge it to the neck in a bucket of water. The bucket then went into the freezer, and by mid-afternoon, a block of ice had formed around the bottle, thereby insuring an icy sip for all 750 of the milliliters.

That night, my father would sit on our front porch with his friend, Johnny Button, and drink the vodka ceremoniously. They drank it neat, not needing any ice. At first, they would taste it gingerly, commenting on the nuances of the liquor and comparing it to the last year's batch. When the sun set and darkness began to intrude, they would continue to slowly sip the vodka, swapping stories late into the evening. I can still remember their intervals of laughter as *HA-HA's* echoed against the slatted walls of my room; drunk, happy laughter.

My father's friends often grew jealous of the fact he shared his prized beverage with only one person. They would conveniently drop-in unannounced on our final night, trying to get a taste of the nearly famous liquor. The thing is, my father would never share. He didn't believe anyone could appreciate the vodka as much as he and Johnny did. My mother would try it to be polite, but she didn't drink. So, it was their vodka, their tradition. The neighbors would hang outside of our porch like begging dogs, waiting to be let in, but my father would not budge. It's not that he was unkind, but the way my father saw it, he had suffered the brambles and was not going to share. Johnny and my father would send them off with their laughter.

The next morning our vacation was over and so was the fun. No, we weren't home yet, but the nuclear power that fueled our family had returned. Weeks of dirt was swept, cobwebs knocked down, and toilets scrubbed. I typically offered to clean the porch, interested to see if it had changed after the previous night of debauchery. But the porch always seemed to look the same, save two empty glasses and the vodka bottle, which was also empty—except for a stray blackberry or two. I would often smell the empty bottle, curious about the flavor it once contained.

I once touched my tongue to the concoction, cautiously, like testing hot tea. It repulsed me.

It's really a shame that I never shared in my father's tradition. He offered me a pull every year, yet even with the blackberries, the vodka was too sharp for my palette. I wish I had appreciated it then, for my father no longer visits the Cape. He doesn't share a bottle with Johnny. We don't have family dinners or meetings anymore either, for we are no longer a family. At least, not in the nuclear sense.

In 1992 my father and mother had a nuclear meltdown. After years of trying to live up to an ideal, their marriage had become strained. The uranium that fueled our family had reached its half-life. My father moved out. With the loss of a member our nuclear unit ceased exist.

I watched the sitcoms as they went into summer reruns, the TV families reliving the best episodes of their pseudo lives. But we didn't have reruns, only memories.

The divorce of my mother and father still stings, but not like the sharpness of vodka. It stings like only the worst of ironies can. After all of those family meetings to guide my brother and me, after all those laws and mock contracts, my parents were the ones who broke the most sacred contract of all.

It stings like the brambles.

CONNECTING TO READING

A. In a journal entry or in class freewrite, explore your own metaphors for composing as previously suggested, for example, "For me writing is like . . . ," and so on. Analyze these metaphors. What do they say about you as a writer? about your history with and attitudes toward writing? What media images of writers and/or writing do you think may have influenced your metaphors? What personal history? Tell stories.

B. In a group, use some of Winston Weathers's categories to share your own stories of composing. For instance, who or what is your muse? What is your preferred "scene of writing"? What do you think about drafting, outlining, grammar? In addition, share the ways family members have helped or hindered your development as a writer.

C. In a journal, using any of the readings in this chapter and an examination of your own history with writers or as a writer, compile a list of your own, indicating *10 ways to be a writer.* In class, with a group, draw on your journal entry to compile a list of the 10 ways that you can all agree upon.

D. For a class discussion, read Yolen and two other professional writers on their writing process (Paule Marshall, Winston Weathers, Terry Tempest Williams). What is similar about these pieces and what is distinct? (Look at both content and style.) Some of the members of your class may note that they become weary with reading these types of writings while others may find them useful and interesting: reflect together on that "fatigue" factor. How do those who find such narratives useful make sense of what they are reading for their writing? Make notes or write a journal entry and be prepared to share your insights.

E. On your own or with a partner, interview one or more artists on campus (writers, painters, musicians, actors) about their artistic process. Report back to your class on what you find. (To get a feeling for how detailed such information can be, look at the discussions in the writing process narratives for classroom authors Debbie Olander and Brian Overcast.) Or, interview one or more academic professionals to discover how lawyers, chemists, or anthropologists view their composing processes. Take notes and speak to the class from those notes.

CONNECTING TO WRITING

A. In a journal entry or during class, describe your writing process. (If you can't remember, keep notes on the next piece of writing you complete for any class.) Include all the specifics you can: time of day; place; atmosphere; technology (computer, by hand, etc.); decisions you made before, while, and after drafting; and so on. Then, draw your writing process. Share descriptions and drawings with group members in class and compile a group drawing: What elements of the writing process do you all have in common? You might now want to read the writing process narratives of this chapter's classroom authors, Debbie Olander and Brian Overcast. What more might both have told you about the process of writing the paper? What questions do you have for them?

B. In a journal entry, consider the disjunctions you find while reading in this chapter between your experiences as a writer and the experiences being described by other writers. For instance, Annie Dillard, quoted on page 5, suggests you have to like sentences to be a writer, and Lorrie Moore draws a distinct line between fact and fiction, while Terry Tempest Williams, in her lyric essay, claims, "I write to meet my ghosts. I write to begin a dialogue." Are any of those claims true or untrue for you? Why or why not? Explore three such disjunctions.

C. In class or on-line, conduct an interview with a writing partner. Share these with two other partners and write an explanation of what parts of the writing process are common to all four of you and what is distinctly different for each member. For a short sample (your group's should be longer), see the writing group report on page 5. To begin, in class or on-line, compile a list of 20 interview questions. Author Hilma Wolitzer wrote an essay called "Twenty Questions," in which she answered the most common queries put to her as an author, including: Do you use a word processor? Where do you get your ideas? What are you working on now? Who are your favorite writers? Are you married? Why do you write? Do you have a writing schedule and a special place to work? What advice do you have for young writers? Can writing be taught? What do you do when you're not writing? Do you revise? What is your response to reviews? Do you outline? and Do you think you would have continued to write if you hadn't been able to publish? Starting with your choice of these questions, compile your own list of 20 serious and humorous interview questions and then proceed.

D. To produce a short, two-page handout suitable for sharing with the class, take the results of your interviews with campus artists (see "Connecting to Reading," selection E, on page 48) and draw some connections between writing (especially your writing) and the process these artists use in creating their art. Make a list and then turn that list into an informal handout, or do the same exercise using interviews with scholars in professional fields.

E. In a journal entry, respond to the essays by classroom authors in this chapter—Debbie Olander and Brian Overcast. Although these writers' circumstances may be different than yours, the essays they write are similar to the ones you will be writing before long. Reflect on their work. What do you like or dislike? What is expected or unexpected? How is their writing like or unlike your own?

WRITING PROJECTS

1. Write your own "How I Write" essay. You can do this in several ways: answer some of the serious and humorous questions you previously compiled and shape a self-interview (or you and a classmate could interview each other and produce "how he/she" writes essays); create a personal narrative like Paule Marshall's; or use a mixture of all these forms, as undertaken by Winston/Weathers, who uses self-interview, narrative, and all sorts of stylistic options. Weathers's style would easily lend itself to writing a Web page or creating hypertext on your writing process. Or compose a "Why I Write" essay modeled on Terry Tempest Williams's article (or using the self-interview or informal essay formats).
2. Use the readings in this chapter (and advice found in Chapter 7) to help you write an informal research paper on how writers write. Cite the authors by name and essay title and note that all their works can be found in this book, which you will then cite, again, informally, in the body of your text. Imagine your essay appearing in a popular magazine such as *Vogue* or *Esquire.* After completing this essay, plan to give a 10-minute talk about your research to your classmates.
3. Find out more about Lorrie Moore, Paule Marshall, Richard Wilbur, and Terry Tempest Williams. Use the Web and library sources to prepare an introduction to this writer and her or his work for your classmates. Aim for a biographical essay of four to six pages. You might extend this introduction by finding another piece of this writer's published creative work. Continue your current paper or write a second short paper that introduces your classmates to a piece of creative writing by the author whom you have come to value.
4. After reading Debbie Olander's and Brian Overcast's process narratives, take an old essay that you have on hand and write a retrospective process narrative. Recall the way you wrote your essay in some detail. Then write a commentary on who you were then as a writer, with a writing process, and where you might go—given what you've learned in this chapter—to improve and enhance your writing process. You might want to cast this essay as advice to high school students. Or you might want to write an essay that grows from the working concept of "writing in high school versus writing in college," exploring how the methods used are the same and/or different.
5. Thinking of Paule Marshall's essay, examine who taught you to be a poet, a writer, a musician, an artist, or a lover of these or any other creative arts. Trace your investment to memories of your family, neighbors, or friends (focusing on one art and one influential group is likely to lead you into an essay of depth and insight rather than an essay that tries to cover too much, too fast).
6. There is a tension for me in compiling a chapter like this. It raises the issue of writing in school. Are Debbie Olander and Brian Overcast well served by labeling them "classroom authors"? How useful do you find the advice and

observations of practicing (often self-labeled "creative" writers) such as Lorrie Moore, Paule Marshall, and Richard Wilbur to the life you live as a writer in college? Write an extended open letter to your classmates about ways they can make school writing and real writing the same thing (Are they? Can they be?). If you don't like the open letter format, simply make this a position paper (for which you'll need to explore various theses to find the one you best believe in).

7. Look closely at Winston Weathers's essay construction. Where, if ever, have you read texts that are composed this way? Have you been allowed or encouraged to write a text that looks like this? If the form of his essay intrigues you, follow its form for an essay on any subject of your choice. Use your writing process narrative to discuss what you learned will happen when you use sidebars, Q and A, sentence fragments, interrupting subheadings, irony and parody, and so on. Of course, to imitate this style you'll need to analyze it in some depth and also choose an essay topic that you think would benefit from this type of textual thinking.
8. Study another writer. Writing research in the 1980s included researchers who watched writers actually compose their text. They trained these writers to speak aloud—verbalize—their decisions as they wrote. Find a willing partner in class, go to the computer lab, and each of you write a short piece—self- or class-assigned—using this method. Try to talk aloud to your interviewer the entire time you're making composing/drafting decisions (a tape recorder can be useful here). After a draft is finished, interview each other about the words on the page. Then, write an essay together that compares and contrasts your writing processes.
9. Like Lorrie Moore, write a parody of the writing process (or a writing process classroom) as you've experienced it. Her "How to Become a Writer" can lead you to ideas for "How to Have a Writing Process." It takes an intimate knowledge of a subject to poke good fun at it. By writing a parody you'll also be showing off all you know about examining the ways writers write.
10. Write an essay in which you ask 20 useful questions of yourself as a writer. And then answer them. Although you may answer humorously or narratively, your goal in this essay is also to inform. Have fun, but make a point (or points).

* * * *

I read once that some people start off by writing sentence by sentence or word by word and they never go back and revise. They just write headlong into it. Or some people always know the ending before they begin. It works in different ways for different people. When these stories started off they were really rough, but they changed and it wasn't just mindless or effortless. It was work.

—AMY TAN

Chapter 2

The Literacy Narrative

Thinking About the Literacy Narrative

> No one in my family read. I can't remember how I learned to read. It was all too long ago.
>
> —A 19-YEAR-OLD CLASSROOM AUTHOR

We have all had complicated experiences with language. It is crucial to our daily interactions with those we care about (as well as with those we don't care about). It enters our consciousness loud and long through ads, billboards, radio, TV. And it is subtle. When we take the time to tell stories of how we learned to use language and how we acquired the literate practices of reading and writing, these narratives let us see familiar selves in unfamiliar, but often productive new ways. The old self who didn't know how—or like—to read or write, over time may have become the new self. She's the woman who finds that her friends love to read her e-mails and ask her to help them with their essays and newsletters. The old high school cross-country runner who never read a book unless threatened with dismissal from the team may, by the end of law school, be the man who finds he can explain complicated court cases to his peers. For most of us, life just leads us to these new places. For the writer who considers his or her literacy autobiography, these sites of self-translation can provide insights into the journey, sometimes speeding it up, clarifying it, putting it into better, or at least new perspective. That happens because writing is a transformative act—it is the vehicle through which (in which?) we can make crossings into new intellectual and emotional territories.

Writing a literacy narrative—your story of coming into language, of learning how to read and write, of learning what reading and writing means to one's life—can do many things for you, the writer, and for your readers. Your literacy narrative can provide a place where you can look at and critique your schooling and challenge your education. You may choose to explore cultural and racial diversity. You may find yourself highlighting gender and cultural issues which affect you and writers like you. Writing a literacy narrative helps you understand the literature you read, allows you to study your own writing processes and growth as a writer and reader, and may help you create public voices and identities and explore professional goals.

I like this genre and the writing directions it suggests, because composing a literacy narrative seems a useful step in considering ways to become a better consumer of your intellectual opportunities. These narratives encourage you to think about who and what is helping you learn as well as who and what might be limiting your learning. Philosopher Ludwig Wittgenstein claimed, "The limits of my language mean the limits of my world." Examining literacy as a subject can call formerly held beliefs into question and/or affirm your fundamental understandings of how readers and writers influence and are influenced by the world.

For instance, many literacy specialists are exploring the ways home environments, local cultures, and gender construct us as literate individuals. Reading and writing takes place for different individuals under different circumstances. For me as a child. For you as a child. For each of us as adults. At home; in schools; and in our communities, regions, and countries. Who we are, where we grew up, and under what conditions all shape our literacy. And shape, too, the stories we tell to share those experiences. Examining your stories allows for self-learning, self-defining, and self-shaping as often as it produces entertaining and beguiling narratives. Through the literacy narrative, we make and remake, calibrate and recreate, we move from one understanding to a new, more enlightened understanding. When writing your own narrative, it may be useful to reflect on where you've come from as you enter college because this is, for many, also a time of career decisions and complicated lifestyle changes. You are on another literacy threshold.

Literacy specialists also propose that while we talk of and often experience ourselves as a single, unified consciousness, our personality is constructed, over time, from a variety of influences. Our family, schooling, and general life experiences, our cultural affiliations, and our racial and religious backgrounds co-contribute to who we are today as you'll clearly see in the readings that follow. Our lived experiences continue to add up in varied and interesting ways to . . . us.

The readings in this chapter include stories of struggle and accomplishment, leavened with ironic or humorous moments. They are generally serious because a great deal is at stake. Christy Brown and Domitila De Chungara discuss learning against the odds, detailing immense physical and economic handicaps. In his poem, Langston Hughes passionately examines the constraint of institutional settings. Barbara Mellix, Richard Rodriguez, and Amy Tan look at the way language and our home environments affect learning. In fact, most of these writers look at the ways race, class, and gender intersect in educational spaces. Eileen Simpson's struggle to understand how dyslexia complicated her learning usefully can be paired with an essay on the same subject by classroom author Chris Olson. These literacy narratives—including those of the classroom authors, undergraduate Andree Bacque and graduate student Stephen Armstrong that end this chapter—show how common themes display a powerful human face when explored in narratives that use effective and moving details. Bacque focuses on reading, and she explains how she consulted her mother to help prompt her memories. Armstrong didn't begin with the intention of constructing a literacy narrative, but his essay makes clear that his life as a student of literature has influenced him greatly and, because of that, his narrative still centers on literature and literacy.

Although themes occur and reoccur throughout the narratives gathered in this chapter, that doesn't suggest that the genre is worn out and overdone. Quite the reverse, it illustrates the generative nature of the form and assures you that there is always room for another literacy narrative—yours.

5

Chapter Readings

CHRISTY BROWN (1932–1981)

The Letter "A"

CONSIDER THIS:

Before you begin reading, you might find it useful to consider challenges you have faced in your life. For instance, how has being a member of a large or small; nuclear or blended; lower-, middle-, or high-income family influenced options you've had for learning? Equally, have you experienced a physical, emotional, and/or learning challenge that has changed the course of your life, particularly as it relates to your ability to read and write?

Christy Brown was born in Dublin, in the middle of a group of 22 children. His severe cerebral palsy made communication impossible; in fact, he was thought to be retarded until his dramatic discovery that he could control his left foot. He first used his foot to make letters, then learned to type and to write. In a *New York Times* interview, Christy Brown explained that he was spurred to create to come to terms with his affliction. Besides two autobiographies, Brown wrote fiction and poetry and his autobiography served as the basis for the acclaimed motion picture *My Left Foot* (1989) starring Daniel Day-Lewis. If you have seen this motion picture, tell your classmates about it. If not, consider renting it and viewing it before or after reading this passage to compare the two texts and to speculate on how you might identify a crucial scene in your literacy life.

Brown's work and his approach to writing despite his physical challenges has proved moving and inspirational to millions of people all over the world. After reading "The Letter 'A'" consider how writing has or could improve your life. Has anyone inspired you to write? Are you an inspiration for any of your family or friends? What, in particular, makes Brown's story so effective? What stylistic devices would you borrow from his text to help you write your own?

I was born in the Rotunda Hospital, on June 5th, 1932. There were nine children before me and twelve after me, so I myself belong to the middle group. Out of this total of twenty-two, seventeen lived, but four died in infancy, leaving thirteen still to hold the family fort.

Mine was a difficult birth, I am told. Both mother and son almost died. A whole army of relations queued up outside the hospital until the small hours of the morning, waiting for news and praying furiously that it would be good.

After my birth Mother was sent to recuperate for some weeks and I was kept in the hospital while she was away. I remained there for some time, without name, for I wasn't baptized until my mother was well enough to bring me to church.

It was Mother who first saw that there was something wrong with me. I was about four months old at the time. She noticed that my head had a habit of falling backward whenever she tried to feed me. She attempted to correct this by placing her hand on the back of my neck to keep it steady. But when she took it away, back it would drop again. That was the first warning sign. Then she became aware of other defects as I got older. She saw that my hands were clenched nearly all of the time and were inclined to twine behind my back; my mouth couldn't grasp the teat of the bottle because even at that early age my jaws would either lock together tightly, so that it was impossible for her to open them, or they would suddenly become limp and fall loose, dragging my whole mouth to one side. At six months I could not sit up without having a mountain of pillows around me. At twelve months it was the same.

Very worried by this, Mother told my father her fears, and they decided to seek medical advice without any further delay. I was a little over a year old when they began to take me to hospitals and clinics, convinced that there was something definitely wrong with me, some thing which they could not understand or name, but which was very real and disturbing.

Almost every doctor who saw and examined me labeled me a very interesting but also a hopeless case. Many told Mother very gently that I was mentally defective and would remain so. That was a hard blow to a young mother who had already reared five healthy children. The doctors were so very sure of themselves that Mother's faith in me seemed almost an impertinence. They assured her that nothing could be done for me.

She refused to accept this truth, the inevitable truth—as it then seemed—that I was beyond cure, beyond saving, even beyond hope. She could not and would not believe that I was an imbecile, as the doctors told her. She had nothing in the world to go by, not a scrap of evidence to support her conviction that, though my body was crippled, my mind was not. In spite of all the doctors and specialists told her, she would not agree. I don't believe she knew why—she just knew, without feeling the smallest shade of doubt.

Finding that the doctors could not help in any way beyond telling her not to place her trust in me, or, in other words, to forget I was a human creature, rather to regard me as just something to be fed and washed and then put away again, Mother decided there and then to take matters into her own hands. I was *her* child, and therefore part of the family. No matter how dull and incapable I might grow up to be, she was determined to treat me on the same plane as the others, and not as the "queer one" in the back room who was never spoken of when there were visitors present.

That was a momentous decision as far as my future life was concerned. It meant that I would always have my mother on my side to help me fight all the battles that were to come, and to inspire me with new strength when I was almost beaten. But it wasn't easy for her because now the relatives and friends had decided otherwise. They contended that I should be taken kindly, sympathetically, but not seriously. That would be a mistake. "For your own sake," they told her, "don't look to this boy as you would to the others; it would only break your heart in the end." Luckily for me, Mother and Father held out against the lot of them. But Mother wasn't content just to say that I was not an idiot: she set out to prove it, not because of any rigid sense of duty, but out of love. That is why she was so successful.

At this time she had the five other children to look after besides the "difficult one," though as yet it was not by any means a full house. They were my brothers, Jim, Tony, and Paddy, and my two sisters, Lily and Mona, all of them very young, just a year or so between each of them, so that they were almost exactly like steps of stairs.

Four years rolled by and I was now five, and still as helpless as a newly born baby. While my father was out at bricklaying, earning our bread and butter for us, Mother was slowly, patiently pulling down the wall, brick by brick, that seemed to thrust itself between me and the other children, slowly, patiently penetrating beyond the thick curtain that hung over my mind, separating it from theirs. It was hard, heartbreaking work, for often all she got from me in return was a vague smile and perhaps a faint gurgle. I could not speak or even mumble, nor could I sit up without support on my own, let alone take steps. But I wasn't inert or motionless. I seemed, indeed, to be convulsed with movement, wild, stiff, snakelike movement that never left me, except in sleep. My fingers twisted and twitched continually, my arms twined backwards and would often shoot out suddenly this way and that, and my head lolled and sagged sideways. I was a queer, crooked little fellow.

Mother tells me how one day she had been sitting with me for hours in an upstairs room, showing me pictures out of a great big storybook that I had got from Santa Claus last Christmas and telling me the names of the different animals and flowers that were in them, trying without success to get me to repeat them. This had gone on for hours while she talked and laughed with me. Then at the end of it she leaned over me.

"Did you like it, Chris? Did you like the bears and the monkeys and all the lovely flowers? Nod your head for yes, like a good boy."

But I could make no sign that I had understood her. Her face was bent over mine hopefully. Suddenly, involuntarily, my queer hand reached up and grasped one of the dark curls that fell in a thick cluster about her neck. Gently she loosened the clenched fingers, though some dark strands were still clutched between them.

Then she turned away from my curious stare and left the room, crying. The door closed behind her. It all seemed hopeless. It looked as though there was some justification for my relatives' contention that I was an idiot and beyond help.

They now spoke of an institution.

"Never!" said my mother almost fiercely, when this was suggested to her. "I know my boy is not an idiot; it is his body that is shattered, not his mind. I'm sure of that."

Sure? Yet inwardly, she prayed God would give her some proof of her faith. She knew it was one thing to believe but quite another thing to prove.

I was now five, and still I showed no real sign of intelligence. I showed no apparent interest in things except with my toes—more especially those of my left foot. Although my natural habits were clean, I could not aid myself, but in this respect my father took care of me. I used to lie on my back all the time in the kitchen or, on bright warm days, out in the garden, a little bundle of crooked muscles and twisted nerves, surrounded by a family that loved me and hoped for me and that made me part of their own warmth and humanity. I was lonely, imprisoned in a world of my own, unable to communicate with others, cut off, separated from them as though a glass wall stood between my existence and theirs, thrusting me beyond the sphere of their lives and activities. I longed to run about and play with the rest, but I was unable to break loose from my bondage.

Then, suddenly, it happened! In a moment everything was changed, my future life molded into a definite shape, my mother's faith in me rewarded, and her secret fear changed into open triumph.

It happened so quickly, so simply after all the years of waiting and uncertainty, that I can see and feel the whole scene as if it had happened last week. It was the afternoon of a cold, gray December day. The streets outside glistened with snow, the white sparkling flakes stuck and melted on the windowpanes and hung on the boughs of the trees like molten silver. The wind howled dismally, whipping up little whirling columns of snow that rose and fell at every fresh gust. And over all, the dull, murky sky stretched like a dark canopy, a vast infinity of grayness.

Inside, all the family were gathered round the big kitchen fire that lit up the little room with a warm glow and made giant shadows dance on the walls and ceiling.

In a corner Mona and Paddy were sitting, huddled together, a few torn school primers before them. They were writing down little sums onto an old chipped slate, using a bright piece of yellow chalk. I was close to them, propped up by a few pillows against the wall, watching.

It was the chalk that attracted me so much. It was a long, slender stick of vivid yellow. I had never seen anything like it before, and it showed up so well against the black surface of the slate that I was fascinated by it as much as if it had been a stick of gold.

Suddenly, I wanted desperately to do what my sister was doing. Then—without thinking or knowing exactly what I was doing, I reached out and took the stick of chalk out of my sister's hand—with my left foot.

I do not know why I used my left foot to do this. It is a puzzle to many people as well as to myself, for, although I had displayed a curious interest in my toes at an early age, I had never attempted before this to use either of my feet in any way. They could have been as useless to me as were my hands. That day, however, my left foot, apparently by its own volition, reached out and very impolitely took the chalk out of my sister's hand.

I held it tightly between my toes, and, acting on an impulse, made a wild sort of scribble with it on the slate. Next moment I stopped, a bit dazed, surprised, looking down at the stick of yellow chalk stuck between my toes, not knowing what to do with it next, hardly knowing how it got there. Then I looked up and became aware that everyone had stopped talking and was staring at me silently. Nobody stirred. Mona, her black curls framing her chubby little face, stared at me with great big eyes and open mouth. Across the open hearth, his face lit by flames, sat my father, leaning forward, hands outspread on his knees, his shoulders tense. I felt the sweat break out on my forehead.

My mother came in from the pantry with a steaming pot in her hand. She stopped midway between the table and the fire, feeling the tension flowing through the room. She followed their stare and saw me in the corner. Her eyes looked from my face down to my foot, with the chalk gripped between my toes. She put down the pot.

Then she crossed over to me and knelt down beside me, as she had done so many times before.

"I'll show you what to do with it, Chris," she said, very slowly and in a queer, choked way, her face flushed as if with some inner excitement.

Taking another piece of chalk from Mona, she hesitated, then very deliberately drew, on the floor in front of me, *the single letter "A."*

"Copy that," she said, looking steadily at me. "Copy it, Christy."

I couldn't.

I looked about me, looked around at the faces that were turned towards me, tense, excited faces that were at that moment frozen, immobile, eager, waiting for a miracle in their midst.

The stillness was profound. The room was full of flame and shadow that danced before my eyes and lulled my taut nerves into a sort of waking sleep. I could hear the sound of the water tap dripping in the pantry, the loud ticking of the clock on the mantel shelf, and the soft hiss and crackle of the logs on the open hearth.

I tried again. I put out my foot and made a wild jerking stab with the chalk which produced a very crooked line and nothing more. Mother held the slate steady for me.

"Try again, Chris," she whispered in my ear. "Again."

I did. I stiffened my body and put my left foot out again, for the third time. I drew one side of the letter. I drew half the other side. Then the stick of chalk broke and I was left with a stump. I wanted to fling it away and give up. Then I felt my mother's hand on my shoulder. I tried once more. Out went my foot. I shook, I sweated and strained every muscle. My hands were so tightly clenched that my fingernails bit into the flesh. I set my teeth so hard that I nearly pierced my lower lip. Everything in the room swam till the faces around me were mere patches of white. But—I drew it—*the letter "A."* There it was on the floor before me. Shaky, with awkward, wobbly sides and a very uneven center line. But it *was* the letter "A." I looked up. I saw my mother's face for a moment, tears on her cheeks. Then my father stooped and hoisted me onto his shoulder.

I had done it! It had started—the thing that was to give my mind its chance of expressing itself. True, I couldn't speak with my lips. But now I would speak through something more lasting than spoken words—written words.

That one letter, scrawled on the floor with a broken bit of yellow chalk gripped between my toes, was my road to a new world, my key to mental freedom. It was to provide a source of relaxation to the tense, taut thing that was I, which panted for expression behind a twisted mouth.

DOMITILA DE CHUNGARA (WITH MOEMA VIEZZER) (b. 1937)

Let Me Speak!

CONSIDER THIS:

Before you read this selection, make a brief list of your own experiences and interests in social and political activism (this can include issues you would like to address, steps you would like to take, as well as those you have addressed or taken). As you read, consider the differences and similarities of being an "activist" in the United States and in other countries.

Domitila Barrios de Chungara was born in Bolivia. After becoming a mining union leader and activist, she was twice jailed and tortured for her activities. She testified about these life experiences before the United Nations in 1975. The mines were closed in 1986, resulting in massive job loss. De Chungara has been an itinerant teacher since then, visiting rural areas and instructing people there about human and legal rights, among other things. *Let Me Speak!* is on one level her own oral history. But it's also described by collaborator and journalist Moema Viezzer as "the product of numerous interviews I had with her in Mexico and Bolivia, of her speeches . . . , as well as discussions, conversations, and dialogues she had with groups of workers, students, and university employees, people living in workers' neighborhoods, Latin American exiles living in Mexico, and representatives of the press, radio, and television." Viezzer carefully strove to retain Domitila's as well as her compatriots' vernacular. This work ranges from remembrances to personal conversations to more formal speeches and presentations. *Let Me Speak!* rises above one woman's experience to become a voice of her people and of workers everywhere.

To understand the challenges of collecting and compiling an oral history, work with a class partner after you read this narrative. Note three or four important events from your own literacy history. Share these with a partner and settle on the most interesting of each of your stories. *Tell* this story in detail to your writing partner, letting her transcribe it, and ask a few questions to clarify points (your partner does the same with you). Revise the story you heard and transcribed to share with other class writers who profiled each other. Try to identify one element in each story that might allow this single life to stand for experiences shared by a whole group of people.

Well, in 1954 it was hard for me to return to school after the vacation, because we had a house that was just a little room where we didn't even have a yard and we didn't have anyplace to leave the kids or anyone to leave them with. So we talked with the principal of the school and he gave me permission to take my little sisters with me. Classes were in the afternoon and in the morning. And I had to combine everything: house and school. So I'd carry the littlest one and the other one hung onto my hand, and Marina carried the bottles, and my sister, the other little one, carried the notebooks. And that's how all of us would go to school. In a corner we had a little crate where we'd leave the baby while we studied. When she cried, we'd give her her bottle. And my other little sisters wandered around from bench to bench. I'd get out of school, I had to carry the baby, we'd go home and I had to cook, wash, iron, take care of the kids. All that seemed very hard to me. I wanted so badly to play! And there were so many other things I wanted to do, like any other little girl.

Two years later, the teacher wouldn't let me take my sisters because they made too much noise. My father couldn't pay for a maid, since his wage wasn't even enough for the food and clothing we needed. For example, at home I always went barefoot; I only used my shoes to go to school. And there were so many things I had to do and it was so cold in Pulacayo that my hands would split open and a lot of blood would come out of my hands and feet. My mouth too, my lips would crack. And my face would also bleed. That's because we didn't have enough warm clothing.

Well, since the teacher had laid down the law, I began to go to school alone. I'd lock up the house and the kids had to stay in the street, because the house was dark, it didn't have a window, and they were terrified if I locked them in. It was like a jail, with just one door. And there wasn't any place to leave the kids, because at that time we lived in a neighborhood where there weren't any families. Only single men lived there.

Then my father told me to leave school, because I already knew how to read and I could learn other things by reading on my own. But I didn't obey him and I continued going to my classes.

Then one day the little one ate carbide ashes that were in the garbage pail, the carbide that's used to light the lamps. They'd thrown food on top of the ashes and my little sister, who I think was hungry, went to eat out of the can. She got a terrible intestinal infection and then she died. She was three years old.

I felt guilty about my little sister's death and I was very, very depressed. And even my father would say that it had happened because I hadn't wanted to stay home with the kids. I'd brought up that sister since she was born, so her death made me suffer a lot.

From then on I began to take much more care of my little sisters. Much more. When it was very cold and we didn't have anything to cover ourselves with, I'd grab my father's old rags and cover them with those, I'd wrap up their feet, their bellies. I'd carry them, try to entertain them. I devoted myself completely to the girls.

My father arranged it so that the mining company in Pulacayo gave us a house with a little yard, because it was very hard living where we were. And the manager, whose suits my father fixed, ordered them to give him a larger dwelling with a room, a kitchen, and a little corridor where we could leave the girls. And we went to live in a neighborhood in the mining camp, where the majority of the families were mine workers.

Sometimes we went hungry and there wasn't enough food, since my father could only afford a little. When you're small, it hard to live in poverty and with all kinds of problems. But that developed something strong in us: a great sensitivity, a great desire to help all the people. Our children's games always had something to do with our kind of life and with how we wanted to live. Also, during our childhood we'd seen that even though we didn't have much, my mother and father were always helping different families in Pulacayo. So when we saw poor people begging in the street, me and my sisters would start dreaming. We'd dream that one day we'd be big, that we'd have land, that we'd plant, and that we'd give those poor people food. And any time we had a little sugar or coffee or something else left over, and we heard a sound, we'd say: "A poor person's passing by. Look, here's a little rice, a little sugar." And we'd wrap it up in a rag and throw it out into the street for some poor person to pick up.

Once we threw out some coffee when my father was coming back from work. And when he came into the house he really scolded us and said: "How can you waste the little that we have? How can you throw out what costs me so much to earn for you?" And he really beat us. But those things were things that just occurred to us, we thought that that way we could help someone, see?

And so that's what our life was like. I was thirteen then. My father always insisted that I shouldn't go on with school, but I would beg him and I went on going. Of course, I never had enough school supplies. Some teachers understood, others didn't. And that's why they'd hit me, they'd beat me terribly because I wasn't a good student.

The problem was that my father and me had made a deal. He'd explained that he didn't have money, that he couldn't buy my supplies, that he couldn't give me anything for school. And so I had to arrange things as best I could. And that's why I had problems.

In the sixth grade I had a great teacher who knew how to understand me. He was a pretty strict teacher and on the first day that I didn't bring in all the supplies, he punished me very severely. One day he pulled me by the hair, slapped me, and, in the end, threw me out of school. I had to go home, crying. But the next day I went back, and through the window I watched what the kids were doing.

At one point the teacher called me:

"I suppose you haven't brought your supplies," he said.

I couldn't answer and started to cry.

"Come in. Go ahead, take your seat. And stay behind when school's over."

By that time one of the girls had told him that I didn't have a mother, that I cooked for my little sisters and all that.

At the end of school I stayed and then he said to me:

"Look, I want to be your friend, but you've got to tell me what's wrong. Is it true that you don't have a mother?"

"Yes, sir."

"When did she die?"

"When I was still in first grade."

"And your father, where does he work?"

"With the mine police, he's a tailor."

"Okay, what's the matter? Look, I want to help you, but you've got to be honest. What's the matter?"

I didn't want to talk, because I thought he was going to call my father in, like some teachers did when they were angry. And I didn't want him called in, because that's what the deal had been with him: I wasn't supposed to bother him or ask him for anything. But the teacher asked me more questions and then I told him everything. I also told him that I could do my homework, but that I didn't have notebooks, because we were very poor and my daddy couldn't buy them, and that years ago my father had wanted to take me out of school because he couldn't pay for it anymore. And that with a lot of sacrifice and effort I'd been able to get to sixth grade. But it wasn't because my father didn't want to, it was because he couldn't. Because, in spite of all the belief there was in Pulacayo that a woman shouldn't be taught to read, my father always wanted us to know at least how to do that.

It's true, my father was always concerned about our education. When my mother died, people would look at us and say: "Oh, the poor little things, five women, not one man . . . what good are they? They'd be better off dead." But my daddy would say proudly: "No, let my girls alone, they're going to live." And when people tried to make us feel bad because we were women and weren't much good for anything, he'd tell us that all women had the same rights as men. And we'd say that we could do the same things men do. He always raised us with those ideas. Yes, it was a very special discipline. And all that was very positive in terms of our future. So that's why we never considered ourselves useless women.

The teacher understood all that, because I told him about it. And we made a deal that I'd ask him for all the school supplies I needed. And from that day on we got on very well. And the teacher would give me and my little sisters all the supplies we needed. And that's how I was able to finish my last year in school, in 1952.

In school I learned to read, to write, and to get along. But I can't say that school really helped me to understand life. I think that education in Bolivia, despite the various reforms there've been, is still part of the capitalist system we live in. They always give an alienating education. For example, they make us see the motherland like a beautiful thing in the national anthem, in the colors of the flag, and all those things stop meaning anything when the motherland isn't well. The motherland, for me, is in every corner, it's also in the miners, in the peasants, in the people's poverty, their nakedness, their malnutrition, in their pains and their joys. That's the motherland, right? But in school they teach us to sing the national anthem, to parade, and they say that if we refuse to parade we aren't patriotic, and, nevertheless, they never explain our poverty, our misery, our parents' situation, their great sacrifices and their low wages, why a few children have everything and many others have nothing. They never explained *that* to me in school.

That's why I feel that we all have a responsibility to our children so that at home they learn to see the truth. Because if not, we're preparing future failures. And when they're a little bigger, they being to resist, and in the end, they turn out to be misfits, they don't even want to greet their parents anymore. But I think that we ourselves are to blame when we make our children live in a world of fantasy. There are times when parents don't even have a mouthful to eat, but they always get something for the children. And they don't show them how difficult the life we lead is and the children don't realize what reality is. And when they go to university, they don't want to say that they're miners' children, that they're peasants' children. And they don't know how to speak our language, I mean that they analyze everything and they explain everything in such a complicated way that we can't understand each other anymore. And that's a great mistake, because those who go to university learn so many things and we should all take advantage of that, shouldn't we? I do think that they should be able to speak and write in a scientific manner, but also one that we can understand and not always in a language which only they understand, with drawings and numbers, if you know what I mean. Because the military also understands numbers. And when they come to Siglo XX to talk over a problem with us, the first thing they do is bring a gigantic blackboard and gather us together and a guy comes out who starts to talk about money and stuff like that. The workers don't listen to them, they boo at them and tell them that they can take their numbers and go home. It's true, they boo at them.

So I think that the people who have had the chance to go to the university should talk our language, because we haven't been in the university and we don't understand much about numbers, but we *are* capable of understanding our national reality. That's why I say if they really want the people to be happy, those who study should maybe learn something about how to speak in our language with all the knowledge that they have, so that we too can understand everything that they learn. That would be very important and it would be a way to contribute, you might say, to the achievement of better living conditions for our country.

Thanks to all the consciousness of the Bolivian working class, the students really have changed a lot in the last few years. I see that in Bolivia the student movement is very strong, not only in the universities, but also in the colleges and schools. And a proof of that is that the government resorts to closing down the schools. Because that's the way to shut the students up, when they can't be shut up either with the tanks or planes which are used to attack the university. And each time the students rise up, the government begins to repress the movement leaders. Still, the students are always supporting us in our demands and are present with their solidarity when we go out on strike or have demonstrations or when our compañeros are put in jail.

But I also realize that many young people who supported us, and who seemed to be good revolutionaries, moved far away from us when they graduated as professionals. You no longer hear people talking about the student who'd say: "We'll bear the arms our fathers leave behind because we, their children, who have studied politics, economics, law, know how the people are deceived, we know what our fathers' lungs are like . . . ," and so forth. Out of the university comes the doctor, the lawyer, he or she gets a little job and the revolutionary disappears. We have to be careful that that doesn't happen, we have to be responsible to our class, we have to be consistent, do we not?

When I finished school, they gave me a job in the company grocery store in Pulacayo. That was in 1953. The next year my second sister also finished grade school and she also was able to get a job in a pastry shop. . . .

LANGSTON HUGHES (1902–1967)

Theme for English B

CONSIDER THIS:

Langston Hughes, once called the "Poet Laureate of Harlem," was a key figure of the Harlem Renaissance. He chronicled black urban life from the 1920s through the 1960s. Incredibly prolific, Hughes wrote poetry and prose, novels and plays and screenplays, short stories and children's books. He was also an editor and translator. Hughes, though, is best known for his poetry. What do you know about Harlem? The Harlem Renaissance? African-American poets and poetry? What, too, is a poet laureate? Before you read, as a class, pool your knowledge on these topics. If you come up with little detail, more research is in order.

Crucial to Hughes's approach to writing poetry is his concern with representing a distinctly black experience. Hughes sought to explain and highlight ordinary black life throughout his writing career. One central way Hughes did this was by incorporating "the meaning and rhythms of jazz" into his poems. When asked why he did this so often, he replied, "[J]azz to me is one of the inherent expressions of Negro life in America; the eternal tom-tom beating in the Negro soul—the tom-tom of revolt against weariness in a white world, a world of subway trains, and work, work, work; the tom-tom of joy and laughter, and pain swallowed in a smile." "Theme for English B" is a fascinating poem for the way it mixes voices, includes personal history *and* makes a political statement. Have each member of your writing group read the poem aloud, letting you hear it several times. Compose a one-page paraphrase of the poem and list the technical devices that makes Hughes's poem distinctive from other poems you've read. That is, explain what he does and how he does what he does.

The instructor said,

Go home and write
a page tonight.
And let that page come out of you—
Then, it will be true.

I wonder if it's that simple?
I am twenty-two, colored, born in Winston-Salem.
I went to school there, then Durham, then here
to this college on the hill above Harlem.
I am the only colored student in my class.
The steps from the hill lead down into Harlem,
through a park, then I cross St. Nicholas,
Eighth Avenue, Seventh, and I come to the Y,
the Harlem Branch Y, where I take the elevator
up to my room, sit down, and write this page:

It's not easy to know what is true for you or me
at twenty-two, my age. But I guess I'm what
I feel and see and hear, Harlem, I hear you:
hear you, hear me—we two—you, me, talk on this page.
(I hear New York, too.) Me—who?
Well, I like to eat, sleep, drink, and be in love.
I like to work, read, learn, and understand life.
I like a pipe for a Christmas present.
or records—Bessie, bop, or Bach.
I guess being colored doesn't make me *not* like
the same things other folks like who are other races.
So will my page be colored that I write?
Being me, it will not be white.
But it will be
a part of you, instructor.
You are white—
yet a part of me, as I am a part of you.
That's American.
Sometimes perhaps you don't want to be a part of me.
Nor do I often want to be a part of you.
But we are, that's true!
As I learn from you,
I guess you learn from me—

BARBARA MELLIX

From Outside, In

CONSIDER THIS:

We sometimes think of *authors* as those who wrote long enough ago to have been canonized in large literary anthologies. It's easy to forget that the writers we like are often working on campuses where we go to school (or shopping at the same mall where we shop). Barbara Mellix was born in South Carolina and educated at the University of Pittsburgh. She has taught writing at Pittsburgh and is currently an executive assistant dean in the College of Arts and Sciences there. Mellix makes the point that writing is creative in a very specific way; by writing one can bring "selves into being," with the attendant duties and joys that come with this kind of creation. This challenging, demanding, and ultimately hopeful approach is apparent throughout her essay "From Outside, In," as it explores the relationship of culture and language, in the particular case of the connections between standard English and black English.

Before or after reading Mellix's essay, consider the times you have had your language corrected, in large or small ways. How did you feel? Why did you accept or rebel against such correction? How did/do your parents' languages and/or beliefs about language affect you? Take into account how you'll feel about your own child's language (you can do this even if you don't have a child). What language do you expect your child to grow up speaking? One, more than one, a dialect? Will your child's speech appear accented or marked to another group of speakers? What family language roots do you want your child to remain in touch with? How do you think you'll react to your child using contemporary slang? Will you change your own language around your child? These questions require some inquiry into your own literacy history. What points in Mellix's essay could you use to support your own beliefs? What section best illustrates a point you're trying to make?

Two years ago, when I started writing this paper, trying to bring order out of chaos, my ten-year-old daughter was suffering from an acute attack of boredom. She drifted in and out of the room complaining that she had nothing to do, no one to "be with" because none of her friends were at home. Patiently I explained that I was working on something special and needed peace and quiet, and I suggested that she paint, read, or work with her computer. None of these interested her. Finally, she pulled up a chair to my desk and watched me, now and then heaving long, loud sighs. After two or three minutes (nine or ten sighs), I lost my patience. "Looka here, Allie," I said, "you too old for this kinda carryin' on. I done told you this is important. You wronger than dirt to be in here haggin' me like this and you know it. Now git on outta here and leave me off before I put my foot all the way down."

I was at home, alone with my family, and my daughter understood that this way of speaking was appropriate in that context. She knew, as a matter of fact, that it was almost inevitable; when I get angry at home, I speak some of my finest, most cherished black English. Had I been speaking to my daughter in this manner in certain other environments, she would have been shocked and probably worried that I had taken leave of my sense of propriety.

Like my children, I grew up speaking what I considered two distinctly different languages—black English and standard English (or as I thought of them then, the ordinary everyday speech of "country" coloreds and "proper" English)—and in the process of acquiring these languages, I developed an understanding of when, where, and how to use them. But unlike my children, I grew up in a world that was primarily black. My friends, neighbors, minister, teachers—almost everybody I associated with every day—were black. And we spoke to one another in our own special language: *That sho is a pretty dress you got on. If she don' soon leave me off I'm gon tell her head a mess. I was so mad I could'a pissed a blue nail. He all the time trying to low-rate somebody. Ain't that just about the nastiest thing you ever set ears on?*

Then there were the "others," the "proper" blacks, transplanted relatives and one-time friends who came home from the city for weddings, funerals, and vacations. And the whites. To these we spoke standard English. "Ain't?" my mother would yell at me when I used the term in the presence of "others." "You *know* better than that." And I would hang my head in shame and say the "proper" word.

I remember one summer sitting in my grandmother's house in Greeleyville, South Carolina, when it was full of the chatter of city relatives who were home on vacation. My parents sat quietly, only now and then volunteering a comment or answering a question. My mother's face took on a strained expression when she spoke. I could see that she was being careful to say just the right words in just the right way. Her voice sounded thick, muffled. And when she finished speaking, she would lapse into silence, her proper smile on her face. My father was more articulate, more aggressive. He spoke quickly, his words sharp and clear. But he held his proud head higher, a signal that he, too, was uncomfortable. My sisters and brothers and I stared at our aunts, uncles, and cousins, speaking only when prompted. Even then, we hesitated, formed our sentences in our minds, then spoke softly, shyly.

My parents looked small and anxious during those occasions, and I waited impatiently for our leave-taking when we would mock our relatives the moment we were out of their hearing. "Reeely," we would say to one another, flexing our wrists and rolling our eyes, "how dooo you stan' this heat? Chile, it just too hy*ooo*-mid for words." Our relatives had made us feel "country," and this was our way of regaining pride in ourselves while getting a little revenge in the bargain. The words bubbled in our throats and rolled across our tongues, a balming.

As a child I felt this same doubleness in uptown Greeleyville where the whites lived. "Ain't that a pretty dress you're wearing!" Toby, the town policeman, said to me one day when I was fifteen. "Thank you very much," I replied, my voice barely audible in my own ears. The words felt wrong in my mouth, rigid, foreign. It was not that I had never spoken that phrase before—it was common in black English, too—but I was extremely conscious that this was an occasion for proper English. I had taken out my English and put it on as I did my church clothes, and I felt as if I were wearing my Sunday best in the middle of the week. It did not matter that Toby had not spoken grammatically correct English. He was white and could speak as he wished. I had something to prove. Toby did not.

Speaking standard English to whites was our way of demonstrating that we knew their language and could use it. Speaking it to standard-English-speaking blacks was our way of showing them that we, as well as they, could "put on airs." But when we spoke standard English, we acknowledged (to ourselves and to others—but primarily to ourselves) that our customary way of speaking was inferior. We felt foolish, embarrassed, somehow diminished because we were ashamed to be our real selves. We were reserved, shy in the presence of those who owned and/or spoke *the* language.

My parents never set aside time to drill us in standard English. Their forms of instruction were less formal. When my father was feeling particularly expansive, he would regale us with tales of his exploits in the outside world. In almost flawless English, complete with dialogue and flavored with gestures and embellishment, he told us about his attempt to get a haircut at a white barbershop; his refusal to acknowledge one of the town merchants until the man addressed him as "Mister"; the time he refused to step off the sidewalk uptown to let some whites pass; his airplane trip to New York City (to visit a sick relative) during which the stewardesses and porters—recognizing that he was a "gentleman"—addressed him as "Sir." I did not realize then—nor, I think, did my father—that he was teaching us, among other things, standard English and the relationship between language and power.

My mother's approach was different. Often, when one of us said, "I'm gon wash off my feet," she would say, "And what will you walk on if you wash them off?" Everyone would laugh at the victim of my mother's "proper" mood. But it was different when one of us children was in a proper mood. "You think you are so superior," I said to my oldest sister one day when we were arguing and she was winning. "Superior!" my sister mocked. "You mean I'm acting 'biggidy'?" My sisters and brothers sniggered, then joined in teasing me. Finally, my mother said, "Leave your sister alone. There's nothing wrong with using proper English." There was a half-smile on her face. I had gotten "uppity," had "put on airs" for no good reason. I was at home, alone with the family, and I hadn't been prompted by one of my mother's proper moods. But there was also a proud light in my mother's eyes; her children were learning English very well.

Not until years later, as a college student, did I begin to understand our ambivalence toward English, our scorn of it, our need to master it, to own and be owned by it—an ambivalence that extended to the public-school classroom. In our school, where there were no whites, my teachers taught standard English but used black English to do it. When my grammar-school teachers wanted us to write, for example, they usually said something like, "I want y'all to write five sentences that make a statement. Anybody git done before the rest can color." It was probably almost those exact words that led me to write these sentences in 1953 when I was in the second grade:

> The white clouds are pretty.
> There are only 15 people in our room.
> We will go to gym.
> We have a new poster.
> We may go out doors.

Second grade came after "Little First" and "Big First," so by then I knew the implied rules that accompanied all writing assignments. Writing was an occasion for proper English. I was not to write in the way we spoke to one another: The white clouds pretty; There ain't but 15 people in our room; We going to gym; We got a new poster; We can go out in the yard. Rather I was to use the language of "other"; clouds *are,* there *are,* we *will,* we *have,* we *may.*

My sentences were short, rigid, perfunctory, like the letters my mother wrote to relatives:

> *Dear Papa,*
> How are you? How is Mattie? Fine I hope. We are fine. We will come to see you Sunday. Cousin Ned will give us a ride.
>
> Love,
> Daughter

The language was not ours. It was something from outside us, something we used for special occasions.

But my coloring on the other side of that second-grade paper is different. I drew three hearts and a sun. The sun has a smiling face that radiates and envelops everything it touches. And although the sun and its world are enclosed in a circle, the colors I used—red, blue, green, purple, orange, yellow, black—indicate that I was less restricted with drawing and coloring than I was with writing standard English. My valentines were not just red. My sun was not just a yellow ball in the sky.

By the time I reached the twelfth grade, speaking and writing standard English had taken on new importance. Each year, about half of the newly graduated seniors of our school moved to large cities—particularly in the North—to live with relatives and find work. Our English teacher constantly corrected our grammar: "Not 'ain't,' but 'isn't'." We seldom wrote papers, and even those few were usually plot summaries of short stories. When our teacher returned the papers, she usually lectured on the importance of using standard English: "I *am;* you *are;* he, she, or it *is,*" she would say, writing on the chalkboard as she spoke. "How you gon git a job talking about 'I is,' or 'I isn't' or 'I ain't'?"

In Pittsburgh, where I moved after graduation, I watched my aunt and uncle—who had always spoken standard English when in Greeleyville—switch from black English to standard English to a mixture of the two, according to where they were or who they were with. At home and with certain close relatives, friends, and neighbors, they spoke black English. With those less close, they spoke a mixture. In public and with strangers, they generally spoke standard English.

In time, I learned to speak standard English with ease and to switch smoothly from black to standard or a mixture, and back again. But no matter where I was, no matter what the situation or occasion, I continued to write as I had in school:

> *Dear Mommie,*
> How are you? How is everybody else? Fine I hope. I am fine. So are Aunt and Uncle. Tell everybody I said hello. I will write again soon.
>
> Love,
> Barbara

At work, at a health insurance company, I learned to write letters to customers. I studied form letters and letters written by co-workers, memorizing the phrases and the ways in which they were used. I dictated:

> Thank you for your letter of January 5. We have made the changes in your coverage you requested. Your new premium will be $150 every three months. We are pleased to have been of service to you.

In a sense, I was proud of the letters I wrote for the company: they were proof of my ability to survive in the city, the outside world—an indication of my growing mastery of English. But they also indicate that writing was still mechanical for me, something that didn't require much thought.

Reading also became a more significant part of my life during those early years in Pittsburgh. I had always liked reading, but now I devoted more and more of my spare time to it. I read romances, mysteries, popular novels. Looking back, I realize that the books I liked best were simple, unambiguous: good versus bad and right versus wrong with right rewarded and wrong punished, mysteries unraveled and all set right in the end. It was how I remembered life in Greeleyville.

Of course I was romanticizing. Life in Greeleyville had not been so very uncomplicated. Back there I had been—first as a child, then as a young woman with limited experience in the outside world—living in a relatively closed-in society. But there were implicit and explicit principles that guided our way of life and shaped our relationships with one another and the people outside—principles that a newcomer would find elusive and baffling. In Pittsburgh, I had matured, become more experienced: I had worked at three different jobs, associated with a wider range of people, married, had children. This new environment with different prescripts for living required that I speak standard English much of the time, and slowly, imperceptibly, I had ceased seeing a sharp distinction between myself and "others." Reading romances and mysteries, characterized by dichotomy, was a way of shying away from change, from the person I was becoming.

But that other part of me—that part which took great pride in my ability to hold a job writing business letters—was increasingly drawn to the new developments in my life and the attending possibilities, opportunities for even greater change. If I could write letters for a nationally known business, could I not also do something better, more challenging, more important? Could I not, perhaps, go to college and become a school teacher? For years, afraid and a little embarrassed, I did no more than imagine this different me, this possible me. But sixteen years after coming north, when my youngest daughter entered kindergarten, I found myself unable—or unwilling—to resist the lure of possibility. I enrolled its my first college course: Basic Writing, at the University of Pittsburgh.

For the first time in my life, I was required to write extensively about myself. Using the most formal English at my command, I wrote these sentences near the beginning of the term:

> One of my duties as a homemaker is simply picking up after others. A day seldom passes that I don't search for a mislaid toy, book, or gym shoe, etc. I change the Ty-D-Bol, fight "ring around the collar," and keep our laundry smelling "April fresh." Occasionally, I settle arguments between my children and suggest things to do when they're bored. Taking telephone messages for my oldest daughter is my newest (and sometimes most aggravating) chore. Hanging the toilet paper roll is my most insignificant.

My concern was to use "appropriate" language, to sound as if I belonged in a college classroom. But I felt separate from the language—as if it did not and could not belong to me. I couldn't think and feel genuinely in that language, couldn't make it express what I thought and felt about being a housewife. A part of me resented, among other things, being judged by such things as the appearance of my family's laundry and toilet bowl, but in that language I could only imagine and write about a conventional housewife.

For the most part, the remainder of the term was a period of adjustment, a time of trying to find my bearings as a student in a college composition class, to learn to shut out my black English whenever I composed, and to prevent it from creeping into my formulations; a time for trying to grasp the language of the classroom and reproduce it in my prose; for trying to talk about myself in that language, reach others through it. Each experience of writing was like standing naked and revealing my imperfection, my "otherness." And each new assignment was another chance to make myself over in language, reshape myself, make myself "better" in my rapidly changing image of a student in a college composition class.

But writing became increasingly unmanageable as the term progressed, and by the end of the semester, my sentences sounded like this:

> My excitement was soon dampened, however, by what seemed like a small voice in the back of my head saying that I should be careful with my long awaited opportunity. I felt frustrated and this seemed to make it difficult to concentrate.

There is a poverty of language in these sentences. By this point, I knew that the clichéd language of my Housewife essay was unacceptable, and I generally recognized trite expressions. At the same time, I hadn't yet mastered the language of the classroom, hadn't yet come to see it as belonging to me. Most notable is the lifelessness of the prose, the apparent absence of a person behind the words. I wanted those sentences—and the rest of the essay—to convey the anguish of yearning to, at once, become something more and yet remain the same. I had the sensation of being split in two, part of me going into a future the other part didn't believe possible. As that person, the student writer at that moment, I was essentially mute. I could not—in the process of composing—use the language of the old me, yet I couldn't imagine myself in the language of "others."

I found this particularly discouraging because at midsemester I had been writing in a much different way. Note the language of this introduction to an essay I had written then, near the middle of the term:

> Pain is a constant companion to the people in "Footwork." Their jobs are physically damaging. Employers are insensitive to their feelings and in many cases add to their problems. The general public wounds them further by treating them with disgrace because of what they do for a living. Although the workers are as diverse as they are similar, there is a definite link between them. They suffer a great deal of abuse.

The voice here is stronger, more confident, appropriating terms like "physically damaging," "wounds them further," "insensitive," "diverse"—terms I couldn't have imagined using when writing about my own experience—and shaping them into sentences like, "Although the workers are as diverse as they are similar, there is a definite link between them." And there is the sense of a personality behind the prose, someone who sympathizes with the workers: "The general public wounds them further by treating them with disgrace because of what they do for a living."

What caused these differences? I was, I believed, explaining other people's thoughts and feelings, and I was free to move about in the language of "others" so long as I was speaking *of* others. I was unaware that I was transforming into my best classroom language my own thoughts and feelings about people whose experiences and ways of speaking were in many ways similar to mine.

The following year, unable to turn back or to let go of what had become something of an obsession with language (and hoping to catch and hold the sense of control that had eluded me in Basic Writing), I enrolled in a research writing course. I spent most of the term learning how to prepare for and write a research paper. I chose sex education as my subject and spent hours in libraries, searching for information, reading, taking notes. Then (not without messiness and often-demoralizing frustration) I organized my information into categories, wrote a thesis statement, and composed my paper—a series of paraphrases and quotations spaced between carefully constructed transitions. The process and results felt artificial, but as I would later come to realize I was passing through a necessary stage. My sentences sounded like this:

> This reserve becomes understandable with examination of who the abusers are. In an overwhelming number of cases, they are people the victims know and trust. Family members, relatives, neighbors and close family friends commit seventy-five percent of all reported sex crimes against children, and parents, parent substitutes and relatives are the offenders in thirty to eighty percent of all reported cases. While assault by strangers does occur, it is less common, and is usually a single episode. But abuse by family members, relatives and acquaintances may continue for an extended period of time. In cases of incest, for example, children are abused repeatedly for an average of eight years. In such cases, "the use of physical force is rarely necessary because of the child's trusting, dependent relationship with the offender. The child's cooperation is often facilitated by the adult's position of dominance, an offer of material goods, a threat of physical violence, or a misrepresentation of moral standards."

The completed paper gave me a sense of profound satisfaction, and I read it often after my professor returned it. I know now that what I was pleased with was the language I used and the professional voice it helped me maintain. "Use better words," my teacher snapped at me one day after reading the notes I'd begun accumulating from my research, and slowly I began taking on the language of my sources. In my next set of notes, I used the word "vacillating"; my professor applauded. And by the time I composed the final draft, I felt at ease with terms like "overwhelming number of cases," "single episode," and "reserve," and I shaped them into sentences similar to those of my "expert" sources.

If I were writing the paper today, I would of course do some things differently. Rather than open with an anecdote—as my teacher suggested—I would begin simply with a quotation that caught my interest as I was researching my paper (and which I scribbled, without its source, in the margin of my notebook): "Truth does not do so much good in the world as the semblance of truth does evil." The quotation felt right because it captured what was for me the central idea of my essay—an idea that emerged gradually during the making of my paper—and expressed it in a way I would like to have said it. The anecdote, a hypothetical situation I invented to conform to the information in the paper, felt forced and insincere because it represented—to a great degree—my teacher's understanding of the essay, *her* idea of what in it was most significant. Improving upon my previous experiences with writing, I was beginning to think and feel in the language I used, to find my own voices in it, to sense that how one speaks influences how one means. But I was not yet secure enough, comfortable enough with the language to trust my intuition.

Now that I know that to seek knowledge, freedom, and autonomy means always to be in the concentrated process of becoming—always to be venturing into new territory, feeling one's way at first, then getting one's balance, negotiating, accommodating, discovering one's self in ways that previously defined "others"—I sometimes get tired. And I ask myself why I keep on participating in this highbrow form of violence, this slamming against perplexity. But there is no real futility in the question, no hint of that part of the old me who stood outside standard English, hugging to herself a disabling mistrust of a language she thought could not represent a person with her history and experience. Rather, the question represents a person who feels the consequence of her education, the weight of her possibilities as a teacher and writer and human being, a voice in society. And I would not change that person, would not give back the good burden that accompanies my growing expertise, my increasing power to shape myself in language and share that self with "others."

"To speak," says Frantz Fanon, "means to be in a position to use a certain syntax, to grasp the morphology of this or that language, but it means above all to assume a culture, to support the weight of a civilization." To write means to do the same, but in a more profound sense. However, Fanon also says that to achieve mastery means to "get" in a position of power, to "grasp," to "assume." This, I have learned—both as a student and subsequently as a teacher—can involve tremendous emotional and psychological conflict for those attempting to master academic discourse. Although as a beginning student writer I had a fairly good grasp of ordinary spoken English and was proficient at what Labov calls "code-switching" (and what John Baugh in *Black Street Speech* terms "style shifting"), when I came face to face with the demands of academic writing, I grew increasingly self-conscious, constantly aware of my status as a black and a speaker of one of the many black English vernaculars—a traditional outsider. For the first time, I experienced my sense of doubleness as something menacing, a built-in enemy. Whenever I turned inward for salvation, the balm so available during my childhood, I found instead this new fragmentation which spoke to me in many voices. It was the voice of my desire to prosper, but at the same time it spoke of what I had relinquished and could not regain: a safe way of being, a state of powerlessness which exempted me from responsibility for who I was and might be. And it accused me of betrayal, of turning away from blackness. To recover balance, I had to take on the language of the academy, the language of "others." And to do that, I had to learn to imagine myself a part of the culture of that language, and therefore someone free to manage that language, to take liberties with it. Writing and rewriting, practicing, experimenting, I came to comprehend more fully the generative power of language. I discovered—with the help of some especially sensitive teachers—that through writing one can continually bring new selves into being, each with new responsibilities and difficulties, but also with new possibilities. Remarkable power, indeed. I write and continually give birth to myself.

RICHARD RODRIGUEZ (b. 1944)

Going Home Again

CONSIDER THIS:

Consider a flashpoint issue: the English-only movement. Proponents of English-only believe standard written and spoken English should be the official (some believe the only) language of the United States. Proponents argue against bilingual education and offering tests in English as well as a learner's first language to nonnative speakers of English in U.S. schools. Take some time to consider your stance on the question. Also, as a class, list the pros and cons as you see them of both positions. Example: Pro—the United States is a melting pot of languages as well as of peoples, and although English is most often used, other languages should be offered and supported because a person's native language contributes to a great degree in composing that person, defining who he is. Con—the English-only position, outlined above. To amplify your thinking, gather the stories and beliefs of any students in your classroom for whom English is not a first language. Now consider the story of Richard Rodriguez who grew up in California speaking Spanish until he started attending Catholic grammar school. There, his teachers encouraged him to speak English and urged his parents to try to help him in this regard at home. After graduate school Rodriguez decided to become a writer and has since become one of the most prolific and reprinted essayists of his generation. His views against affirmative action and bilingual education have made him a controversial figure in many circles.

Rodriguez's writing often touches on the theme of what exactly American culture is and what one's place is within it, Mexican American or otherwise. He sums up his approach to the bilingual question this way: "[E]verybody has some part of their language that is in conflict with the public language." In a sense, you may find that "Going Home Again" could be read as an argument against Rodriguez's public position on this issue, and you can complicate his perspective by reading him in tandem with other authors in this chapter. After you finish reading Rodriguez, if your class opinion poll shows your class to be, in general, against bilingual education and support for other languages in the United States, research the other side—the side that argues for students' rights to their own language. (To begin, look at the English position statement of the National Council of Teachers, found on their Web page at: http://ncte.org) Conversely, if your class has already made a stronger case for students' rights to their own language, continue to research the English-only position further. What do you learn by giving each position thoughtful consideration? That is, instead of taking one position or the other, try to outline and examine the range and complexity of this literacy debate.

At each step, with every graduation from one level of education to the next, the refrain from bystanders was strangely the same: "Your parents must be so proud of you." I suppose that my parents were proud, although I suspect, too, that they felt more than pride alone as they watched me advance through my education. They seemed to know that my education was separating us from one another, making it difficult to resume familiar intimacies. Mixed with the instincts of parental pride, a certain hurt also communicated itself—too private ever to be adequately expressed in words, but real nonetheless.

The autobiographical facts pertinent to this essay are simply stated in two sentences, though they exist in somewhat awkward juxtaposition to each other. I am the son of Mexican-American parents, who speak a blend of Spanish and English, but who read neither language easily. I am about to receive a Ph.D. in English Renaissance literature. What sort of life—what tensions, feelings, conflicts—connects these two sentences? I look back and remember my life from the time I was seven or eight years old as one of constant movement away from a Spanish-speaking folk culture toward the world of the English-language classroom. As the years passed, I felt myself becoming less like my parents and less comfortable with the assumption of visiting relatives that I was still the Spanish-speaking child they remembered. By the time I began college, visits home became suffused with silent embarrassment: there seemed so little to share, however strong the ties of our affection. My parents would tell me what happened in their lives or in the lives of relatives; I would respond with news of my own. Polite questions would follow. Our conversations came to seem more like interviews.

A few months ago, my dissertation nearly complete, I came upon my father looking through my bookcase. He quietly fingered the volumes of Milton's tracts and Augustine's theology with that combination of reverence and distrust those who are not literate sometimes show for the written word. Silently, I watched him from the door of the room. However much he would have insisted that he was "proud" of his son for being able to master the texts, I knew, if pressed further, he would have admitted to complicated feelings about my success. When he looked across the room and suddenly saw me, his body tightened slightly with surprise, then we both smiled.

For many years I kept my uneasiness about becoming a success in education to myself. I did so in part because I wanted to avoid vague feelings that, if considered carefully, I would have no way of dealing with; and in part because I felt that no one else shared my reaction to the opportunity provided by education. When I began to rehearse my story of cultural dislocation publicly, however, I found many listeners willing to admit to similar feelings from their own pasts. Equally impressive was the fact that many among those I spoke with were *not* from nonwhite racial groups, which made me realize that one can grow up to enter the culture of the academy and find it a "foreign" culture for a variety of reasons, ranging from economic status to religious heritage. But why, I next wondered, was it that, though there were so many of us who came from childhood cultures alien to the academy's, we voiced our uneasiness to one another and to ourselves so infrequently? Why did it take *me* so long to acknowledge publicly the cultural costs I had paid to earn a Ph.D. in Renaissance

English literature? Why, more precisely, am I writing these words only now when my connection to my past barely survives except as nostalgic memory?

Looking back, a person risks losing hold of the present while being confounded by the past. For the child who moves to an academic culture from a culture that dramatically lacks academic traditions, looking back can jeopardize the certainty he has about the desirability of this new academic culture. Richard Hoggart's description, in *The Uses of Literacy,* of the cultural pressures on such a student, whom Hoggart calls the "scholarship boy," helps make the point. The scholarship boy must give nearly unquestioning allegiance to academic culture, Hoggart argues, if he is to succeed at all, so different is the milieu of the classroom from the culture he leaves behind. For a time, the scholarship boy may try to balance his loyalty between his concretely experienced family life and the more abstract mental life of the classroom. In the end, though, he must choose between the two worlds: if he intends to succeed as a student, he must, literally and figuratively, separate himself from his family, with its gregarious life, and find a quiet place to be alone with his thoughts.

After a while, the kind of allegiance the young student might once have given his parents is transferred to the teacher, the new parent. Now without the support of the old ties and certainties of the family, he almost mechanically acquires the assumptions, practices, and style of the classroom milieu. For the loss he might otherwise feel, the scholarship boy substitutes an enormous enthusiasm for nearly everything having to do with school.

How readily I read my own past into the portrait of Hoggart's scholarship boy. Coming from a home in which mostly Spanish was spoken, for example, I had to decide to forget Spanish when I began my education. To succeed in the classroom, I needed psychologically to sever my ties with Spanish. Spanish represented an alternate culture as well as another language—and the basis of my deepest sense of relationship to my family. Although I recently taught myself to read Spanish, the language that I see on the printed page is not quite the language I heard in my youth. That other Spanish, the spoken Spanish of my family, I remember with nostalgia and guilt: guilt because I cannot explain to aunts and uncles why I do not answer their questions any longer in their own idiomatic language. Nor was I able to explain to teachers in graduate school, who regularly expected me to read and speak Spanish with ease, why my very ability to reach graduate school as a student of English literature in the first place required me to loosen my attachments to a language I spoke years earlier. Yet, having lost the ability to speak Spanish, I never forgot it so totally that I could not understand it. Hearing Spanish spoken on the street reminded me of the community I once felt a part of, and still cared deeply about. I never forgot Spanish so thoroughly, in other words, as to move outside the range of its nostalgic pull.

Such moments of guilt and nostalgia were, however, just that—momentary. They punctuated the history of my otherwise successful progress from *barrio* to classroom. Perhaps they even encouraged it. Whenever I felt my determination to succeed wavering, I tightened my hold on the conventions of academic life.

Spanish was one aspect of the problem, my parents another. They could raise deeper, more persistent doubts. They offered encouragement to my brothers and me in our work, but they also spoke, only half jokingly, about the way education was putting "big ideas" into our heads. When we would come home, for example, and challenge assumptions we earlier believed, they would be forced to defend their beliefs (which, given our new verbal skills, they did increasingly less well) or, more frequently, to submit to our logic with the disclaimer, "It's what we were taught in our time to believe. . . ." More important, after we began to leave home for college, they voiced regret about how "changed" we had become, how much further away from one another we had grown. They partly yearned for a return to the time before education assumed their children's primary loyalty. This yearning was renewed each time they saw their nieces and nephews (none of whom continued their education beyond high school, all of whom continued to speak fluent Spanish) living according to the conventions and assumptions of their parents' culture. If I was already troubled by the time I graduated from high school by that refrain of congratulations ("Your parents must be so proud. . . . "), I realize now how much more difficult and complicated was my progress into academic life for my parents, as they saw the cultural foundation of their family erode, than it was for me.

Yet my parents were willing to pay the price of alienation and continued to encourage me to become a scholarship boy because they perceived, as others of the lower classes had before them, the relation between education and social mobility. Lacking the former themselves made them acutely aware of its necessity as prerequisite for the latter. They sent their children off to school in the hopes of their acquiring something "better" beyond education. Notice the assumption here that education is something of a tool or license—a means to an end, which has been the traditional way the lower or working classes have viewed the value of education in the past. That education might alter children in more basic ways than providing them with skills, certificates of proficiency, and even upward mobility, may come as a surprise for some, but the financial cost is usually tolerated.

Complicating my own status as a scholarship boy in the last ten years was the rise, in the mid-1960s, of what was then called "the Third World Student Movement." Racial minority groups, led chiefly by black intellectuals, began to press for greater access to higher education. The assumption behind their criticism, like the assumption of white working-class families, was that educational opportunity was useful for economic and social advancement. The racial minority leaders went one step further, however, and it was this step that was probably most revolutionary. Minority students came to the campus feeling that they were representative of larger groups of people—that, indeed, they were advancing the condition of entire societies by their matriculation. Actually, this assumption was not altogether new to me. Years before, educational success was something my parents urged me to strive for precisely because it would reflect favorably on *all* Mexican-Americans—specifically, my intellectual achievement would help deflate the stereotype of the "dumb Pancho." This early goal was only given greater currency by the rhetoric of the Third World spokesmen. But it was the fact that I felt myself suddenly much more a "public" Mexican-American, a representative of sorts, that was to prove so crucial for me during these years.

One college admissions officer assured me one day that he recognized my importance to his school precisely as deriving from the fact that, after graduation, I would surely be "going back to [my] community." More recently, teachers have urged me not to trouble over the fact that I am not "representative" of my culture, assuring me that I can serve as a "model" for those still in the *barrio* working toward academic careers. This is the line that I hear, too, when being interviewed for a faculty position. The interviewer almost invariably assumes that, because I am racially a Mexican-American, I can serve as a special counselor to minority students. The expectation is that I still retain the capacity for intimacy with "my people."

This new way of thinking about the possible uses of education is what has made the entrance of minority students into higher education so dramatic. When the minority group student was accepted into the academy, he came—in everyone's mind—as part of a "group." When I began college, I barely attracted attention except perhaps as a slightly exotic ("Are you from India?") brown-skinned student; by the time I graduated, my presence was annually noted by, among others, the college public relations office as "one of the fifty-two students with Spanish surnames enrolled this year." By having his presence announced to the campus in this way, the minority group student was unlike any other scholarship boy the campus had seen before. The minority group student now dramatized more publicly, if also in new ways, the issues of cultural dislocation that education forces, issues that are not solely racial in origin. When Richard Rodriguez *became* a Chicano, the dilemmas he earlier had as a scholarship boy were complicated but not decisively altered by the fact that he had assumed a group identity.

The assurance I heard that, somehow, I was being useful to my community by being a student was gratefully believed, because it gave me a way of dealing with the guilt and cynicism that each year came my way along with the scholarships, grants, and, lately, job offers from schools which a few years earlier would have refused me admission as a student. Each year, in fact, it became harder to believe that my success had anything to do with my intellectual performance, and harder to resist the conclusion that it was due to my minority group status. When I drove to the airport, on my way to London as a Fulbright Fellow last year, leaving behind cousins of my age who were already hopelessly burdened by financial insecurity and dead-end jobs, momentary guilt could be relieved by the thought that somehow my trip was beneficial to persons other than myself. But, of course, if the thought was a way of dealing with the guilt, it was also the reason for the guilt. Sitting in a university library, I would notice a janitor of my own race and grow uneasy; I was, I knew, in a rough way a beneficiary of his condition. Guilt was accompanied by cynicism. The most dazzlingly talented minority students I know today refuse to believe that their success is wholly based on their own talent, or even that when they speak in a classroom anyone hears them as anything but *the* voice of their minority group. It is scarcely surprising, then, though initially it probably seemed puzzling, that so many of the angriest voices on the campus against the injustices of racism came from those not visibly its primary victims.

It became necessary to believe the rhetoric about the value of one's presence on campus simply as a way of living with one's "success." Among ourselves, however, minority group students often admitted to a shattering sense of loss—the feeling that, somehow, something was happening to us. Especially from students who had not yet become accustomed, as by that time I had, to the campus, I remember hearing confessions of extreme discomfort and isolation. Our close associations, the separate dining-room tables, and the special dormitories helped to relieve some of the pain, but only some of it.

Significant here was the development of the ethnic studies concept—black studies, Chicano studies, et cetera—and the related assumption held by minority group students in a number of departments that they could keep in touch with their old cultures by making these cultures the subject of their study. Here again one notices how different the minority student was from other comparable students: other scholarship boys—poor Jews and the sons of various immigrant cultures—came to the academy singly, much more inclined to accept the courses and material they found. The ethnic studies concept was an indication that, for a multitude of reasons, the new racial minority group students were not willing to give up so easily their ties with their old cultures.

The importance of these new ethnic studies was that they introduced the academy to subject matter that generally deserved to be studied, and at the same time offered a staggering critique of the academy's tendency toward parochialism. Most minority group intellectuals never noted this tendency toward academic parochialism. They more often saw the reason for, say, the absence of a course on black literature in an English department as a case of simple racism. That it might instead be an instance of the fact that academic culture can lose track of human societies and whole areas of human experience was rarely raised. Never asking such a question, the minority group students never seemed to wonder either if as teachers their own courses might suffer the same cultural limitations other seminars and classes suffered. Consequently, in a peculiar way the new minority group critics of higher education came to justify the academy's assumptions. The possibility that academic culture could encourage one to grow out of touch with cultures beyond its conceptual horizon was never seriously considered.

Too often in the last ten years one heard minority group students repeat the joke, never very funny in the first place, about the racial minority academic who ended up sounding more "white" than white academics. Behind the scorn for such a figure was the belief that the new generation of minority group students would be able to avoid having to make similar kinds of cultural concessions. The pressures that might have led to such conformity went unexamined.

For the last few years my annoyance at hearing such jokes was doubtless related to the fact that I was increasingly beginning to sense that I was the "bleached" academic the minority group students found so laughable. I suppose I had always sensed that my cultural allegiance was undergoing subtle alterations as I was being educated. Only when I finished my course work in graduate school and went off to England for my dissertation year did I grasp how far I had traveled from my cultural origins. My year in England was actually my first opportunity to write and reflect upon the kind of material that I would spend my life producing. It was my first chance, too, to be free simultaneously of the distractions of course work and of the insecurities of trying to find my niche in academic life. Sitting in the reading room of the British Museum, I no longer doubted that I had joined academic society. Ironically, this feeling of having finally arrived allowed me to look back to the community whence I came. That I was geographically farther away from my home than I had ever been lent a metaphorical resonance to the cultural distance I suddenly felt.

But the feeling was not pleasing. The reward of feeling a part of the world of the British Museum was an odd one. Each morning I would arrive at the reading room and grow increasingly depressed by the silence and what the silence implied—that life as a scholar would require self-absorption. Who, I wondered, would find my work helpful enough to want to read it? Was not my dissertation—whose title alone would puzzle my relatives—only my grandest exercise thus far in self-enclosure? The sight of the heads around me bent over their texts and papers, many so thoroughly engrossed that they wouldn't look up at the silent clock overhead for hours at a stretch, made me recall the remarkable noises of life in my family home. The tedious prose I was writing, a prose constantly qualified by footnotes, reminded me of the capacity for passionate statement those of the culture I was born into commanded—and which, could it be, I had now lost.

As I remembered it during those gray English afternoons, the past rushed forward to define more precisely my present condition. Remembering my youth, a time when I was not restricted to a chair but ran barefoot under a summer sun that tightened my skin with its white heat, made the fact that it was only my mind that "moved" each hour in the library painfully obvious.

I did need to figure out where I had lost touch with my past. I started to become alien to my family culture the day I became a scholarship boy. In the British Museum the realization seemed obvious. But later, returning to America, I returned to minority group students who were still speaking of their cultural ties to their past. How was I to tell them what I had learned about myself in England?

A short while ago, a group of enthusiastic Chicano undergraduates came to my office to ask me to teach a course to high school students in the *barrio* on the Chicano novel. This new literature, they assured me, has an important role to play in helping to shape the consciousness of a people currently without adequate representation in literature. Listening to them I was struck immediately with the cultural problems raised by their assumption. I told them that the novel is not capable of dealing with Chicano experience adequately, simply because most Chicanos are not literate, or are at least not yet comfortably so. This is not something Chicanos need to apologize for (though, I suppose, remembering my own childhood ambition to combat stereotypes of the Chicano as mental menial, it is not something easily admitted). Rather the genius and value of those Chicanos who do not read seem to me to be largely that their reliance on voice, the spoken word, has given them the capacity for intimate conversation that I, as someone who now relies heavily on the written word, can only envy. The second problem, I went on, is more in the nature of a technical one: the novel, in my opinion, is not a form capable of being true to the basic sense of communal life that typifies Chicano culture. What the novel as a literary form is best capable of representing is solitary existence set against a large social background. Chicano novelists, not coincidentally, nearly always fail to capture the breathtakingly rich family life of most Chicanos, and instead often describe only the individual Chicano in transit between Mexican and American cultures.

I said all of this to the Chicano students in my office, and could see that little of it made an impression. They seemed only frustrated by what they probably took to be a slick, academic justification for evading social responsibility. After a time, they left me, sitting alone. . . .

There is a danger of being misunderstood here. I am not suggesting that an academic cannot reestablish ties of any kind with his old culture. Indeed, he can have an impact on the culture of his childhood. But as an academic, one exists by definition in a culture separate from one's nonacademic roots and, therefore, any future ties one has with those who remain "behind" are complicated by one's new cultural perspective.

Paradoxically, the distance separating the academic from his nonacademic past can make his past seem, if not closer, then clearer. It is possible for the academic to understand the culture from which he came "better" than those who still live within it. In my own experience, it has only been as I have come to appraise my past through categories and notions derived from the social sciences that I have been able to think of Chicano life in cultural terms at all. Characteristics I took for granted or noticed only in passing—the spontaneity, the passionate speech, the trust in concrete experience, the willingness to think communally rather than individually—these are all significant phenomena to me now as aspects of a total culture. (My parents have neither the time nor the inclination to think about their culture as a culture.) Able to conceptualize a sense of Chicano culture, I am now also more attracted to that culture than I was before. The temptation now is to try to preserve those traits of my old culture that have not yet, in effect, atrophied.

The racial self-consciousness of minority group students during the last few years, evident in the ethnic costumes, the stylized gestures, and the idiomatic though often evasive devices for insisting on one's continuing membership in the community of the past, is also an indication that the minority group student has gained a new appreciation of the culture of his origin precisely because of his earlier alienation from it. As a result, Chicano students sometimes become more Chicano than most Chicanos. I remember, for example, my father's surprise when, walking across my college campus one afternoon, we came upon two Chicano academics wearing serapes. He and my mother were also surprised—indeed offended—when they earlier heard student activists use the word "Chicano." For them the term was a private one, primarily descriptive of persons they knew. It suggested intimacy. Hearing the word shouted into a microphone by a stranger left them bewildered. What they could not understand was that the student activist finds it easier than they to use "Chicano" in a more public way, for his distance from their culture and his membership in academic culture permits a wider and more abstract view.

The Mexican-Americans who begin to call themselves Chicanos in this new way are actually forming a new version of what it means to be a Chicano. The culture that didn't see itself as a culture is suddenly prized and identified for being one. The price one pays for this new self-consciousness is the knowledge of just that— it is *new*—and this knowledge is not available to those who remain at home. So it is knowledge that separates as well as unites people. Wanting more desperately than ever to assert his ties with the newly visible culture, the minority group student is tempted to exploit those characteristics of that culture that might yet survive in him. But the self-consciousness never allows one to feel completely at ease with the old culture. Worse, the knowledge of the culture of the past often leaves one feeling strangely solitary. At home, I hear relatives speak and find myself analyzing too much of what they say. It is embarrassing being a cultural anthropologist in one's own family's kitchen. I keep feeling myself little more than a cultural voyeur. I often come away from family gatherings suspecting, in fact, that what conceptions of my culture I carry with me are no more than illusions. Because they were never there before, because no one back home shares them, I grow less and less to trust their reliability: too often they seem no more than mental bubbles floating before an academic's eye.

Many who have taught minority group students in the last decade testify to sensing characteristics of a childhood culture still very much alive in these students. Should the teacher make these students aware of these characteristics? Initially, most of us would probably answer negatively. Better to trust the unconscious survival of the past than the always problematical, sometimes even clownish, re-creations of it. But the cultural past cannot be assured of survival; perhaps many of its characteristics are lost simply because the student is never encouraged to look for them. Even those that do survive do so tenuously. As a teacher, one can only hope that the best qualities in his minority group students' cultural legacy aren't altogether snuffed out by academic education.

More easy to live with and distinguishable from self-conscious awareness of the past are the ways the past unconsciously survives—perhaps even yet survives in me. As it turns out, the issue becomes less acute with time. With each year, the chance that the student is unaware of his cultural legacy is diminished as the habit of academic reflectiveness grows stronger. Although the culture of the academy makes innocence about one's cultural past less likely, this same culture, and the conceptual tools it provides, increases the desire to want to write and speak about the past. The paradox persists.

Awaiting the scholarship boy who finally acknowledges the fact that his perceptions of reality have changed is the dilemma of action. The sentimental reaction to this knowledge entails merely a refusal to renew contact with one's nonacademic culture lest one contaminate it. The problem, however, with this sentimental solution is that it overlooks the way academic culture renders one capable of dealing with the transactions of mass society. Academic culture, with its habits of conceptualization and abstraction, allows those of us from other cultures to deal with each other in a mass society. In this sense academic culture does have a profound political impact. Although people intent upon social mobility think of education as a means to an end, education does become an end: its culture allows one to exist more easily in a society increasingly anonymous and impersonal. The truth is, the academic's distance from his own experience brings the capacity for communicating with bureaucracies and understanding one's position in society—a prerequisite for political action.

If the sentimental reaction to nonacademic culture is to fear changing it, the political response, typical especially of working-class and lately minority group leaders, is to see higher education solely in terms of its political and social possibilities. Its cultural consequences, in this view, are disregarded. At this time when we are so keenly aware of social and economic inequality, it might seem beside the point to warn those who are working to bring about equality that education alters culture as well as economic status. And yet, if there is one main criticism that I, as a minority group student, must make of minority group leaders in their past attacks on the "racism" of the academy, it is that they never distinguished between my right to higher education and the desirability of my actually entering the academy—which is another way of saying again that they never recognized that there were things I could lose by becoming a scholarship boy.

Certainly, the academy changes those from alien cultures more than it is changed by them. While minority groups had an impact on higher education, largely because of their advantage in coming as a group, within the last few years students such as myself, who finally ended up certified as academics, also ended up sounding very much like the academics we found when we came to the campus. I do not enjoy making such admissions. But perhaps now the time has come when questions about the cultural costs of education ought to be delayed no longer. Those of us who have been scholarship boys know in our bones that our education has exacted a large price in exchange for the large benefits it has conferred upon us. And what is sadder to consider, after we have paid that price, we go home and casually change the cultures that nurtured us. My parents today understand how they are "Chicanos" in a large and impersonal sense. The gains from such knowledge are clear. But so, too, are the reasons for regret.

EILEEN SIMPSON (b. 1919)

Dyslexia

CONSIDER THIS:

Growing up dyslexic (before the term was in common circulation), Eileen Simpson was called names like "stupid" and "lazy," although she was certainly neither of those things. While in graduate school, she met the poet (and her soon-to-be husband) John Berryman. He noticed some of her spelling mistakes and told her that her disorder had a name. This news alone was liberating, and this awakening helped her to start her fight against dyslexia.

Simpson describes what she learned during the writing of her graduate thesis: "It taught me that what I first put down on paper could only be brought up to an acceptable level if I was willing to stick with it through quadruple the number of drafts a student without my disability would have found necessary." Undeterred, she went on to finish her thesis and become a psychotherapist and an author. She's written three books of nonfiction and a novel.

Dyslexia (and other much discussed conditions like ADHD, attention deficit hyperactivity disorder) are loaded terms for most of us because popular media, policy statements and political groups, administrative systems and services, and our own life experiences complicate our understandings and beliefs about learning disabilities. At the same time, many of us haven't thoroughly researched these conditions. Before or after reading, and/or as you write about a similar issue, you might find it productive to follow the I-search process popularized by Kenneth Macrorie. 1) Detail what you already know/believe about the condition/issue; 2) research the condition/issue; and 3) tell the story of what you learned through this research. After writing down what you already know and believe, reading Eileen Simpson's and Chris Olson's essays in this chapter can start you on the path toward a more complete self-education.

Dyslexia (from the Greek, *dys,* faulty + *lexis,* speech, cognate with the Latin *legere,* to read), developmental or specific dyslexia as it's technically called, the disorder I suffered from, is the inability of otherwise normal children to read. Children whose intelligence is below average, whose vision or hearing is defective, who have not had proper schooling, or who are too emotionally disturbed or brain-damaged to profit from it belong in other diagnostic categories. They, too, may be unable to learn to read, but they cannot properly be called dyslexics.

For more than seventy years the essential nature of the affliction has been hotly disputed by psychologists, neurologists, and educators. It is generally agreed, however, that it is the result of a neurophysiological flaw in the brain's ability to process language. It is probably inherited, although some experts are reluctant to say this because they fear people will equate "inherited" with "untreatable." Treatable it certainly is: not a disease to be cured, but a malfunction that requires retraining.

Reading is the most complex skill a child entering school is asked to develop. What makes it complex, in part, is that letters are less constant than objects. A car seen from a distance, close to, from above, or below, or in a mirror still looks like a car even though the optical image changes. The letters of the alphabet are more whimsical. Take the letter *b*. Turned upside down it becomes a *p*. Looked at in a mirror, it becomes a *d*. Capitalized, it becomes something quite different, a *B*. The *M* upside down is a *W*. The *E* flipped over becomes Ǝ. This reversed *E* is familiar to mothers of normal children who have just begun to go to school. The earliest examples of art work they bring home often have I LOVƎ YOU written on them.

Dyslexics differ from other children in that they read, spell, and write letters upside down and turned around far more frequently and for a much longer time. In what seems like a capricious manner, they also add letters, syllables, and words, or, just as capriciously, delete them. With palindromic words (was-saw, on-no), it is the order of the letters rather than the orientation they change. The new word makes sense, but not the sense intended. Then there are other words where the changed order—"sorty" for story—does not make sense at all.

The inability to recognize that g, *g*, and *G* are the same letter, the inability to maintain the orientation of the letters, to retain the order in which they appear, and to follow a line of text without jumping above or below it—all the results of the flaw—can make of an orderly page of words a dish of alphabet soup.

Also essential for reading is the ability to store words in memory and to retrieve them. This very particular kind of memory dyslexics lack. So, too, do they lack the ability to hear what the eye sees, and to see what they hear. If the eye sees "off," the ear must hear "off" and not "of," or "for." If the ear hears "saw," the eye must see that it looks like "saw" on the page and not "was." Lacking these skills, a sentence or paragraph becomes a coded message to which the dyslexic can't find the key.

It is only a slight exaggeration to say that those who learned to read without difficulty can best understand the labor reading is for a dyslexic by turning a page of text upside down and trying to decipher it.

While the literature is replete with illustrations of the way these children write and spell, there are surprisingly few examples of how they read. One, used for propaganda purposes to alert the public to the vulnerability of dyslexics in a literate society, is a sign warning that behind it are guard dogs trained to kill. The dyslexic reads:

> Wurring
> Guard God
> Patoly

for

> Warning
> Guard Dog
> Patrol

and, of course, remains ignorant of the danger.

Looking for a more commonplace example, and hoping to recapture the way I must have read in fourth grade, I recently observed dyslexic children at the Educational Therapy Clinic in Princeton, through the courtesy of Elizabeth Travers, the director. The first child I saw, eight-year-old Anna (whose red hair and brown eyes reminded me of myself at that age), had just come to the Clinic and was learning the alphabet. Given the story of "Little Red Riding Hood," which is at the second grade level, she began confidently enough, repeating the title from memory, then came to a dead stop. With much coaxing throughout, she read as follows:

> Grandma you a top. Grandma [looks over at picture of Red Riding Hood]. Red Riding Hood [long pause, presses index finger into the paper. Looks at me for help. I urge: Go ahead] the a [puts head close to the page, nose almost touching] on Grandma

for

> Once upon a time there was a little girl who had a red coat with a red hood. Etc.

"Grandma" was obviously a memory from having heard the story read aloud. Had I needed a reminder of how maddening my silences must have been to Miss Henderson, and how much patience is required to teach these children, Anna, who took almost ten minutes to read these few lines, furnished it. The main difference between Anna and me at that age is that Anna clearly felt no need to invent. She was perplexed, but not anxious, and seemed to have infinite tolerance for her long silences.

Toby, a nine-year-old boy with superior intelligence, had a year of tutoring behind him and could have managed "Little Red Riding Hood" with ease. His text was taken from the *Reader's Digest's Reading Skill Builder,* Grade IV. He read:

> A kangaroo likes as if he had but truck together warm. His saw neck and head do not . . . [Here Toby sighed with fatigue] seem to feel happy back. They and tried and so every a tiger Moses and shoots from lonesome day and shouts and long shore animals. And each farm play with five friends . . .

He broke off with the complaint, "This is too hard. Do I have to read any more?"

His text was:

> A kangaroo looks as if he had been put together wrong. His small neck and head do not seem to fit with his heavy back legs and thick tail. Soft eyes, a twinkly little nose and short front legs seem strange on such a large strong animal. And each front paw has five fingers, like a man's hand.

An English expert gives the following bizarre example of an adult dyslexic's performance:

> An the bee-what in the tel mother of the biothodoodoo to the majoram or that emidrate eni eni Krastrei, mestriet to Ketra lotombreidi to ra from treido as that.

His text, taken from a college catalogue the examiner happened to have close at hand, was:

> It shall be in the power of the college to examine or not every licentiate, previous to his admission to the fellowship, as they shall think fit.

That evening when I read aloud to Auntie for the first time, I probably began as Toby did, my memory of the classroom lesson keeping me close to the text. When memory ran out, and Auntie did not correct my errors, I began to invent. When she still didn't stop me, I may well have begun to improvise in the manner of this patient—anything to keep going and keep up the myth that I was reading—until Auntie brought the "gibberish" to a halt.

RICHARD WRIGHT (1908–1960)

The Library Card

CONSIDER THIS:

The literacy narratives you're reading in this chapter range in levels of formality, and their authors differ in approaches to storytelling. Consider the effect of reading an autobiography written by a novelist such as Richard Wright compared to an oral history like that found in Domitila De Chungara's "Let Me Speak." As you read "The Library Card," ask yourself what makes this work distinct. Since you may have read it before, given that it is often included in anthologies, ask yourself, What about this text argues for continued inclusion in reading collections like this one?

Richard Wright was born to a sharecropper family in Mississippi and was largely self-educated. His novelistic autobiography set in that time, *Black Boy,* is widely considered to be his masterpiece. When asked why he wrote *Black Boy* he said he wanted to give a voice to "voiceless Negro boys." Wright recounts the hardship, the mindless racism and prejudice, and the occasional triumph of growing up black when and where he did. Some of the incidents recounted in the work seem so explosive as to be fictional, but for Wright this kind of heightened truth, "more real than the real," also seems to be exactly the point.

After you read, consider your own responses to the truth, or facticity, of literary nonfiction: does it help you or disappoint you as a reader to learn that some facts in a piece of nonfiction may have been changed to create a more interesting, readable, or emotionally accurate text? (This discussion continues in Chapter 8.)

One morning I arrived early at work and went into the bank lobby where the Negro porter was mopping. I stood at a counter and picked up the Memphis

Commercial Appeal and began my free reading of the press. I came finally to the editorial page and saw an article dealing with one H. L. Mencken. I knew by hearsay that he was the editor of the *American Mercury*, but aside from that I knew nothing about him. The article was a furious denunciation of Mencken, concluding with one, hot, short sentence: Mencken is a fool.

I wondered what on earth this Mencken had done to call down upon him the scorn of the South. The only people I had ever heard denounced in the South were Negroes, and this man was not a Negro. Then what ideas did Mencken hold that made a newspaper like the *Commercial Appeal* castigate him publicly? Undoubtedly he must be advocating ideas that the South did not like. Were there, then, people other than Negroes who criticized the South? I knew that during the Civil War the South had hated northern whites, but I had not encountered such hate during my life. Knowing no more of Mencken than I did at that moment, I felt a vague sympathy for him. Had not the South, which had assigned me the role of a non-man, cast at him its hardest words?

Now, how could I find out about this Mencken? There was a huge library near the riverfront, but I knew that Negroes were not allowed to patronize its shelves any more than they were the parks and playgrounds of the city. I had gone into the library several times to get books for the white men on the job. Which of them would now help me to get books? And how could I read them without causing concern to the white men with whom I worked? I had so far been successful in hiding my thoughts and feelings from them, but I knew that I would create hostility if I went about this business of reading in a clumsy way.

I weighed the personalities of the men on the job. There was Don, a Jew; but I distrusted him. His position was not much better than mine and I knew that he was uneasy and insecure; he had always treated me in an offhand, bantering way that barely concealed his contempt. I was afraid to ask him to help me to get books; his frantic desire to demonstrate a racial solidarity with the whites against Negroes might make him betray me.

Then how about the boss? No, he was a Baptist and I had the suspicion that he would not be quite able to comprehend why a black boy would want to read Mencken. There were other white men on the job whose attitudes showed clearly that they were Kluxers or sympathizers, and they were out of the question.

There remained only one man whose attitude did not fit into an anti-Negro category, for I had heard the white men refer to him as a "Pope lover." He was an Irish Catholic and was hated by the white Southerners. I knew that he read books, because I had got him volumes from the library several times. Since he, too, was an object of hatred, I felt that he might refuse me but would hardly betray me. I hesitated, weighing and balancing the imponderable realities.

One morning I paused before the Catholic fellow's desk.

"I want to ask you a favor," I whispered to him.

"What is it?"

"I want to read. I can't get books from the library. I wonder if you'd let me use your card?"

He looked at me suspiciously.

"My card is full most of the time," he said.

"I see," I said and waited, posing my question silently.

"You're not trying to get me into trouble, are you, boy?" he asked, staring at me.

"Oh, no, sir."

"What book do you want?"

"A book by H. L. Mencken."

"Which one?"

"I don't know. Has he written more than one?"

"He has written several."

"I didn't know that."

"What makes you want to read Mencken?"

"Oh, I just saw his name in the newspaper," I said.

"It's good of you to want to read," he said. "But you ought to read the right things."

I said nothing. Would he want to supervise my reading?

"Let me think," he said. "I'll figure out something."

I turned from him and he called me back. He stared at me quizzically.

"Richard, don't mention this to the other white men," he said.

"I understand," I said. "I won't say a word."

A few days later he called me to him.

"I've got a card in my wife's name," he said. "Here's mine."

"Thank you, sir."

"Do you think you can manage it?"

"I'll manage fine," I said.

"If they suspect you, you'll get in trouble," he said.

"I'll write the same kind of notes to the library that you wrote when you sent me for books," I told him. "I'll sign your name."

He laughed.

"Go ahead. Let me see what you get," he said.

That afternoon I addressed myself to forging a note. Now, what were the names of books written by H. L. Mencken? I did not know any of them. I finally wrote what I thought would be a foolproof note: *Dear Madam: Will you please let this nigger boy*—I used the word "nigger" to make the librarian feel that I could not possibly be the author of the note—*have some books by H. L. Mencken?* I forged the white man's name.

I entered the library as I had always done when on errands for whites, but I felt that I would somehow slip up and betray myself. I doffed my hat, stood a respectful distance from the desk, looked as unbookish as possible, and waited for the white patrons to be taken care of. When the desk was clear of people, I still waited. The white librarian looked at me.

"What do you want, boy?"

As though I did not possess the power of speech, I stepped forward and simply handed her the forged note, not parting my lips.

"What books by Mencken does he want?" she asked.

"I don't know, ma'am," I said, avoiding her eyes.

"Who gave you this card?"

"Mr. Falk," I said.

"Where is he?"

"He's at work, at the M——Optical Company," I said. "I've been in here for him before."

"I remember," the woman said. "But he never wrote notes like this."

Oh, God, she's suspicious. Perhaps she would not let me have the books? If she had turned her back at that moment, I would have ducked out the door and never gone back. Then I thought of a bold idea.

"You can call him up, ma'am," I said, my heart pounding.

"You're not using these books, are you?" she asked pointedly.

"Oh, no, ma'am. I can't read."

"I don't know what he wants by Mencken," she said under her breath.

I knew now that I had won; she was thinking of other things and the race question had gone out of her mind. She went to the shelves. Once or twice she looked over her shoulder at me, as though she was still doubtful. Finally she came forward with two books in her hand.

"I'm sending him two books," she said. "But tell Mr. Falk to come in next time, or send me the names of the books he wants. I don't know what he wants to read."

I said nothing. She stamped the card and handed me the books. Not daring to glance at them, I went out of the library, fearing that the woman would call me back for further questioning. A block away from the library I opened one of the books and read a title: *A Book of Prefaces.* I was nearing my nineteenth birthday and I did not know how to pronounce the word "preface." I thumbed the pages and saw strange words and strange names. I shook my head, disappointed. I looked at the other book; it was called *Prejudices.* I knew what that word meant; I had heard it all my life. And right off I was on guard against Mencken's books. Why would a man want to call a book *Prejudices*? The word was so stained with all my memories of racial hate that I could not conceive of anybody using it for a title. Perhaps I had made a mistake about Mencken? A man who had prejudices must be wrong.

When I showed the books to Mr. Falk, he looked at me and frowned.

"That librarian might telephone you," I warned him.

"That's all right," he said. "But when you're through reading those books, I want you to tell me what you get out of them."

That night in my rented room, while letting the hot water run over my can of pork and beans in the sink, I opened *A Book of Prefaces* and began to read. I was jarred and shocked by the style, the clear, clean, sweeping sentences. Why did he write like that? And how did one write like that? I pictured the man as a raging demon, slashing with his pen, consumed with hate, denouncing everything American, extolling everything European or German, laughing at the weaknesses of people, mocking God, authority. What was this? I stood up, trying to realize what reality lay behind the meaning of the words . . . . Yes, this man was fighting, fighting with words. He was using words as a weapon, using them as one would use a club. Could words be weapons? Well, yes, for here they were. Then, maybe, perhaps, I could use them as a weapon? No. It frightened me. I read on and what amazed me was not what he said, but how on earth anybody had the courage to say it.

Occasionally I glanced up to reassure myself that I was alone in the room. Who were these men about whom Mencken was talking so passionately? Who was Anatole France? Joseph Conrad? Sinclair Lewis, Sherwood Anderson, Dostoevski, George Moore, Gustave Flaubert, Maupassant, Tolstoy, Frank Harris, Mark Twain, Thomas Hardy, Arnold Bennett, Stephen Crane, Zola, Norris, Gorky, Bergson, Ibsen, Balzac, Bernard Shaw, Dumas, Poe, Thomas Mann, O. Henry, Dreiser, H. G. Wells, Gogol, T. S. Eliot, Gide, Baudelaire, Edgar Lee Masters, Stendhal, Turgenev, Huneker, Nietzsche, and scores of others? Were these men real? Did they exist or had they existed? And how did one pronounce their names?

I ran across many words whose meanings I did not know, and I either looked them up in the dictionary or, before I had a chance to do that, encountered the word in a context that made its meaning clear. But what strange world was this? I concluded the book with the conviction that I had somehow overlooked something terribly important in life. I had once tried to write, had once reveled in feeling, had let my crude imagination roam, but the impulse to dream had been slowly beaten out of me by experience. Now it surged up again and I hungered for books, new ways of looking and seeing. It was not a matter of believing or disbelieving what I read, but of feeling something new, of being affected by something that made the look of the world different.

As dawn broke I ate my pork and beans, feeling dopey, sleepy. I went to work, but the mood of the book would not die; it lingered, coloring everything I saw, heard, did. I now felt that I knew what the white men were feeling. Merely because I had read a book that had spoken of how they lived and thought, I identified myself with that book. I felt vaguely guilty. Would I, filled with bookish notions, act in a manner that would make the whites dislike me?

I forged more notes and my trips to the library became frequent. Reading grew into a passion. My first serious novel was Sinclair Lewis's *Main Street.* It made me see my boss, Mr. Gerald, and identify him as an American type. I would smile when I saw him lugging his golf bags into the office. I had always felt a vast distance separating me from the boss, and now I felt closer to him, though still distant. I felt now that I knew him, that I could feel the very limits of his narrow life. And this had happened because I had read a novel about a mythical man called George F. Babbitt.

The plots and stories in the novels did not interest me so much as the point of view revealed. I gave myself over to each novel without reserve, without trying to criticize it; it was enough for me to see and feel something different. And for me, everything was something different. Reading was like a drug, a dope. The novels created moods in which I lived for days. But I could not conquer my sense of guilt, my feeling that the white men around me knew that I was changing, that I had begun to regard them differently.

Whenever I brought a book to the job, I wrapped it in newspaper—a habit that was to persist for years in other cities and under other circumstances. But some of the white men pried into my packages when I was absent and they questioned me.

"Boy, what are you reading those books for?"

"Oh, I don't know, sir."

"That's deep stuff you're reading, boy."

"I'm just killing time, sir."

"You'll addle your brains if you don't watch out."

I read Dreiser's *Jennie Gerhardt* and *Sister Carrie* and they revived in me a vivid sense of my mother's suffering; I was overwhelmed. I grew silent, wondering about the life around me. It would have been impossible for me to have told anyone what I derived from these novels, for it was nothing less than a sense of life itself. All my life had shaped me for the realism, the naturalism of the modern novel, and I could not read enough of them.

Steeped in new moods and ideas, I bought a ream of paper and tried to write; but nothing would come, or what did come was flat beyond telling. I discovered that more than desire and feeling were necessary to write and I dropped the idea. Yet I still wondered how it was possible to know people sufficiently to write about them? Could I ever learn about life and people? To me, with my vast ignorance, my Jim Crow station in life, it seemed a task impossible of achievement. I now knew what being a Negro meant. I could endure the hunger. I had learned to live with hate. But to feel that there were feelings denied me, that the very breath of life itself was beyond my reach, that more than anything else hurt, wounded me. I had a new hunger.

In buoying me up, reading also cast me down, made me see what was possible, what I had missed. My tension returned, new, terrible, bitter, surging, almost too great to be contained. I no longer *felt* that the world about me was hostile, killing; I *knew* it. A million times I asked myself what I could do to save myself, and there were no answers. I seemed forever condemned, ringed by walls.

I did not discuss my reading with Mr. Falk, who had lent me his library card; it would have meant talking about myself and that would have been too painful. I smiled each day, fighting desperately to maintain my old behavior, to keep my disposition seemingly sunny. But some of the white men discerned that I had begun to brood.

"Wake up there boy!" Mr. Olin said one day.

"Sir!" I answered for the lack of a better word.

"You act like you've stolen something," he said.

I laughed in the way I knew he expected me to laugh, but I resolved to be more conscious of myself, to watch my every act, to guard and hide the new knowledge that was dawning within me.

If I went north, would it be possible for me to build a new life then? But how could a man build a life upon vague, unformed yearnings? I wanted to write and

I did not even know the English language. I bought English grammars and found them dull. I felt that I was getting a better sense of the language from novels than from grammars. I read hard, discarding a writer as soon as I felt that I had grasped his point of view. At night the printed page stood before my eyes in sleep.

Mrs. Moss, my landlady, asked me one Sunday morning:

"Son, what is this you keep on reading?"

"Oh, nothing. Just novels."

"What you get out of 'em?"

"I'm just killing time," I said.

"I hope you know your own mind," she said in a tone which implied that she doubted if I had a mind.

I knew of no Negroes who read the books I liked and I wondered if any Negroes ever thought of them. I knew that there were Negro doctors, lawyers, newspapermen, but I never saw any of them. When I read a Negro newspaper I never caught the faintest echo of my preoccupation in its pages. I felt trapped and occasionally, for a few days, I would stop reading. But a vague hunger would come over me for books, books that opened up new avenues of feeling and seeing, and again I would forge another note to the white librarian. Again I would read and wonder as only the naïve and unlettered can read and wonder, feeling that I carried a secret, criminal burden about with me each day.

That winter my mother and brother came and we set up housekeeping, buying furniture on the installment plan, being cheated and yet knowing no way to avoid it. I began to eat warm food and to my surprise found that regular meals enabled me to read faster. I may have lived through many illnesses and survived them, never suspecting that I was ill. My brother obtained a job and we began to save toward the trip north, plotting our time, setting tentative dates for departure. I told none of the white men on the job that I was planning to go north; I knew that the moment they felt I was thinking of the North they would change toward me. I would have made them feel that I did not like the life I was living, and because my life was completely conditioned by what they said or did, it would have been tantamount to challenging them.

I could calculate my chances for life in the South as a Negro fairly clearly now.

I could fight the southern whites by organizing with other Negroes, as my grandfather had done. But I knew that I could never win that way; there were many whites and there were but few blacks. They were strong and we were weak. Outright black rebellion could never win. If I fought openly I would die and I did not want to die. News of lynchings were frequent.

I could submit and live the life of a genial slave, but that was impossible. All of my life had shaped me to live by my own feelings and thoughts. I could make up to Bess and marry her and inherit the house. But that, too, would be the life of a slave; if I did that, I would crush to death something within me, and I would hate myself as much as I knew the whites already hated those who had submitted. Neither could I ever willingly present myself to be kicked, as Shorty had done. I would rather have died than do that.

I could drain off my restlessness by fighting with Shorty and Harrison. I had seen many Negroes solve the problem of being black by transferring their hatred of themselves to others with a black skin and fighting them. I would have to be cold to do that, and I was not cold and I could never be.

I could, of course, forget what I had read, thrust the whites out of my mind, forget them; and find release from anxiety and longing in sex and alcohol. But the memory of how my father had conducted himself made that course repugnant. If I did not want others to violate my life, how could I voluntarily violate it myself?

I had no hope whatever of being a professional man. Not only had I been so conditioned that I did not desire it, but the fulfillment of such an ambition was beyond my capabilities. Well-to-do Negroes lived in a world that was almost as alien to me as the world inhabited by whites.

What, then, was there? I held my life in my mind, in my consciousness each day, feeling at times that I would stumble and drop it, spill it forever. My reading had created a vast sense of distance between me and the world in which I lived and tried to make a living, and that sense of distance was increasing each day. My days and nights were one long, quiet, continuously contained dream of terror, erosion, and anxiety. I wondered how long I could bear it.

AMY TAN (b. 1952)

Mother Tongue

CONSIDER THIS:

You may find it useful to read Amy Tan's "Mother Tongue" along with Richard Rodriguez's "Going Home Again," for both works consider the effects of language on their lives and the lives of their parents. You've probably first encountered Tan by reading or hearing of her best-selling novel *The Joy Luck Club,* but you may not have known that Tan was born and raised in California, the daughter of Chinese immigrants, or that she was a published author before she was 10 years old, getting a piece she wrote about her neighborhood library into a local newspaper.

In a *Booklist* interview Tan mentioned that she didn't write a lot of fiction before she wrote *The Joy Luck Club.* "I did a lot of business writing, and as a business writer you do have to be very clear, maybe simple." Tan goes on to say that simple doesn't mean simplistic. She wrote her first novel for her mother and says she wanted the story and the emotion to come through cleanly, with a minimum of the writer's ego getting in the way. Her direct approach is perfectly suited to these goals.

Tan's frequent use of parable and legend is also a part of her Chinese-American heritage, but she resists pigeonholing herself in this way. When asked about being categorized, Tan told *Salon:* "I don't see myself, for example, writing about cultural dichotomies, but about human connections. All of us go through angst and identity crises. And even when you write in a specific context, you still tap into that subtext of emotions that we all feel about love and hope, and mothers and obligations and responsibilities." As you consider your own "Englishes" and the way you change your language to suit your context, consider also what other techniques you see Amy Tan using here or in her novels (in addition to parables, legends). What confuses you and what intrigues you; what techniques, as a writer, might you choose to emulate in your own literacy narrative?

I am not a scholar of English or literature. I cannot give you much more than personal opinions on the English language and its variations in this country or others.

I am a writer. And by that definition, I am someone who has always loved language. I am fascinated by language in daily life. I spend a great deal of my time thinking about the power of language—the way it can evoke an emotion, a visual image, a complex idea, or a simple truth. Language is the tool of my trade. And I use them all—all the Englishes I grew up with.

Recently, I was made keenly aware of the different Englishes I do use. I was giving a talk to a large group of people, the same talk I had already given to half a dozen other groups. The nature of the talk was about my writing, my life, and my book, *The Joy Luck Club.* The talk was going along well enough, until I remembered one major difference that made the whole talk sound wrong. My mother was in the room. And it was perhaps the first time she had heard me give a lengthy speech, using the kind of English I have never used with her. I was saying things like, "The intersection of memory upon imagination" and "There is an aspect of my fiction that relates to thus-and-thus"—a speech filled with carefully wrought grammatical phrases, burdened, it suddenly seemed to me, with nominalized forms, past perfect tenses, conditional phrases, all the forms of standard English that I had learned in school and through books, the forms of English I did not use at home with my mother.

Just last week, I was walking down the street with my mother, and I again found myself conscious of the English I was using, the English I do use with her. We were talking about the price of new and used furniture and I heard myself saying this: "Not waste money that way." My husband was with us as well, and he didn't notice any switch in my English. And then I realized why. It's because over the twenty years we've been together I've often used that same kind of English with him, and sometimes he even uses it with me. It has become our language of intimacy, a different sort of English that relates to family talk, the language I grew up with.

So you'll have some idea of what this family talk I heard sounds like, I'll quote what my mother said during a recent conversation which I videotaped and then transcribed. During this conversation, my mother was talking about a political gangster in Shanghai who had the same last name as her family's, Du, and how the gangster in his early years wanted to be adopted by her family, which was rich by comparison. Later, the gangster became more powerful, far richer than my mother's family, and one day showed up at my mother's wedding to pay his respects. Here's what she said in part:

"Du Yusong having business like fruit stand. Like off the street kind. He is Du like Du Zong—but not Tsung-ming Island people. The local people call putong, the river east side, he belong to that side local people. That man want to ask Du Zong father take him in like become own family. Du Zong father wasn't look down on him, but didn't take seriously, until that man big like become a mafia. Now important person, very hard to inviting him. Chinese way, came only to show respect, don't stay for dinner. Respect for making big celebration, he shows up. Mean gives lots of respect. Chinese custom. Chinese social life that way. If too important won't have to stay too long. He come to my wedding. I didn't see, I heard it. I gone to boy's side, they have YMCA dinner. Chinese age I was nineteen."

You should know that my mother's expressive command of English belies how much she actually understands. She reads the *Forbes* report, listens to *Wall Street Week,* converses daily with her stockbroker, reads all of Shirley MacLaine's books with ease—all kinds of things I can't begin to understand. Yet some of my friends tell me they understand 50 percent of what my mother says. Some say they understand 80 to 90 percent. Some say they understand none of it, as if she were speaking pure Chinese. But to me, my mother's English is perfectly clear, perfectly natural. It's my mother tongue. Her language, as I hear it, is vivid, direct, full of observation and imagery. That was the language that helped shape the way I saw things, expressed things, made sense of the world.

Lately, I've been giving more thought to the kind of English my mother speaks. Like others, I have described it to people as "broken" or "fractured" English. But I wince when I say that. It has always bothered me that I can think of no way to describe it other than "broken," as if it were damaged and needed to be fixed, as if it lacked a certain wholeness and soundness. I've heard other terms used, "limited English," for example. But they seem just as bad, as if everything is limited, including people's perceptions of the limited English speaker.

I know this for a fact, because when I was growing up, my mother's "limited" English limited *my* perception of her. I was ashamed of her English. I believed that her English reflected the quality of what she had to say. That is, because she expressed them imperfectly her thoughts were imperfect. And I had plenty of empirical evidence to support me: the fact that people in department stores, at banks, and at restaurants did not take her seriously, did not give her good service, pretended not to understand her, or even acted as if they did not hear her.

My mother had long realized the limitations of her English as well. When I was fifteen, she used to have me call people on the phone to pretend I was she. In this guise, I was forced to ask for information or even to complain and yell at people who had been rude to her. One time it was a call to her stockbroker in

New York. She had cashed out her small portfolio and it just so happened we were going to go to New York the next week, our very first trip outside California. I had to get on the phone and say in an adolescent voice that was not very convincing. "This is Mrs. Tan."

And my mother was standing in the back whispering loudly, "Why he don't send me check, already two weeks late. So mad he lie to me, losing me money."

And then I said in perfect English, "Yes, I'm getting rather concerned. You had agreed to send the check two weeks ago, but it hasn't arrived."

Then she began to talk more loudly. "What he want, I come to New York tell him front of his boss, you cheating me?" And I was trying to calm her down, make her be quiet, while telling the stockbroker, "I can't tolerate any more excuses. If I don't receive the check immediately, I am going to have to speak to your manager when I'm in New York next week." And sure enough, the following week there we were in front of this astonished stockbroker, and I was sitting there red-faced and quiet, and my mother, the real Mrs. Tan, was shouting at his boss in her impeccable broken English.

We used a similar routine just five days ago, for a situation that was far less humorous. My mother had gone to the hospital for an appointment, to find out about a benign brain tumor a CAT scan had revealed a month ago. She said she had spoken very good English, her best English, no mistakes. Still, she said, the hospital did not apologize when they said they had lost the CAT scan and she had come for nothing. She said they did not seem to have any sympathy when she told them she was anxious to know the exact diagnosis, since her husband and son had both died of brain tumors. She said they would not give her any more information until the next time and she would have to make another appointment for that. So she said she would not leave until the doctor called her daughter. She wouldn't budge. And when the doctor finally called her daughter, me, who spoke in perfect English—lo and behold—we had assurances the CAT scan would be found, promises that a conference call on Monday would be held, and apologies for any suffering my mother had gone through for a most regrettable mistake.

I think any mother's English almost had an effect on limiting my possibilities in life as well. Sociologists and linguists probably will tell you that a person's developing language skills are more influenced by peers. But I do think that the language spoken in the family, especially in immigrant families which are more insular, plays a large role in shaping the language of the child. And I believe that it affected my results on achievement tests, IQ tests, and the SAT. While my English skills were never judged as poor, compared to math, English could not be considered my strong suit. In grade school I did moderately well, getting perhaps B's, sometimes B-pluses, in English and scoring perhaps in the sixtieth or seventieth percentile on achievement tests. But those scores were not good enough to override the opinion that my true abilities lay in math and science, because in those areas I achieved A's and scored in the ninetieth percentile or higher.

This was understandable. Math is precise; there is only one correct answer. Whereas, for me at least, the answers on English tests were always a judgment call, a matter of opinion and personal experience. Those tests were constructed around items like fill-in-the-blank sentence completion, such as "Even though Tom was ________, Mary thought he was ________." And the correct answer always seemed to be the most bland combinations of thoughts, for example, "Even though Tom was shy, Mary thought he was charming," with the grammatical structure "even though" limiting the correct answer to some sort of semantic opposites, so you wouldn't get answers like, "Even though Tom was foolish, Mary thought he was ridiculous." Well, according to my mother, there were very few limitations as to what Tom could have been and what Mary might have thought of him. So I never did well on tests like that.

The same was true with word analogies, pairs of words in which you were supposed to find some sort of logical, semantic relationship—for example, "*Sunset* is to *nightfall* as ________ is to ________." And here you would be presented with a list of four possible pairs, one of which showed the same kind of relationship: *red* is to *stoplight, bus* is to *arrival, chills* is to *fever, yawn* is to *boring.* Well, I could never think that way. I knew what the tests were asking, but I could not block out of my mind the images already created by the first pair, "*sunset* is to *nightfall*"—and I would see a burst of colors against a darkening sky, the moon rising, the lowering of a curtain of stars. And all the other pairs of words—red, bus, stoplight, boring—just threw up a mass of confusing images, making it impossible for me to sort out something as logical as saying: "A sunset precedes nightfall" is the same as "a chill precedes a fever." The only way I would have gotten that answer right would have been to imagine an associative situation, for example, my being disobedient and staying out past sunset, catching a chill at night, which turns into feverish pneumonia as punishment, which indeed did happen to me.

I have been thinking about all this lately, about my mother's English, about achievement tests. Because lately I've been asked, as a writer, why there are not more Asian Americans represented in American literature. Why are there few Asian Americans enrolled in creative writing programs? Why do so many Chinese students go into engineering? Well, these are broad sociological questions I can't begin to answer. But I have noticed in surveys—in fact, just last week—that Asian students, as a whole, always do significantly better on math achievement tests than in English. And this makes me think that there are other Asian-American students whose English spoken in the home might also be described as "broken" or "limited." And perhaps they also have teachers who are steering them away from writing and into math and science, which is what happened to me.

Fortunately, I happen to be rebellious in nature and enjoy the challenge of disproving assumptions made about me. I became an English major my first year in college, after being enrolled as pre-med. I started writing nonfiction as a freelancer the week after I was told by my former boss that writing was my worst skill and I should hone my talents toward account management.

But it wasn't until 1985 that I finally began to write fiction. And at first I wrote using what I thought to be wittily crafted sentences, sentences that would finally prove I had mastery over the English language. Here's an example from the first draft of a story that later made its way into *The Joy Luck Club,* but without this line: "That was my mental quandary in its nascent state." A terrible line, which I can barely pronounce.

Fortunately, for reasons I won't get into today, I later decided I should envision a reader for the stories I would write. And the reader I decided upon was my mother, because these were stories about mothers. So with this reader in mind—and in fact she did read my early drafts—I began to write stories using all the Englishes I grew up with: the English I spoke to my mother, which for lack of a better term might be described as "simple"; the English she used with me, which for lack of a better term might be described as "broken"; my translation of her Chinese, which could certainly be described as "watered down"; and what I imagined to be her translation of her Chinese if she could speak in perfect English, her internal language, and for that I sought to preserve the essence, but neither an English nor a Chinese structure. I wanted to capture what language ability tests can never reveal: her intent, her passion, her imagery, the rhythms of her speech and the nature of her thoughts.

Apart from what any critic had to say about my writing, I knew I had succeeded where it counted when my mother finished reading my book and gave me her verdict: "So easy to read."

5

Classroom Authors

CHRIS OLSON

Learning to Read: For Me It's Been the Struggle of a Lifetime

CONSIDER THIS:

When he wrote this essay, Chris Olson was a university junior enrolled in an advanced article and essay writing class. Despite his long struggle with reading, he had become an English major by the time I met him and, after graduating, decided to study law. I haven't heard from him since writing a recommendation for his law school application, but I'm pretty sure that's because he is busy . . . reading . . . and completing his degree. I often talked to Chris about the strategies he had learned and might learn to improve his academic experience—these ranged from documenting his dyslexia and arranging for the extra time needed to take exams to learning to accept that while others could do their homework in a weekend morning and move on to social activities, he had to accept the fact that he'd be working on his projects all weekend. This was not because he wasn't as intelligent as his peers; Chris Olson's intelligence needed a longer time to work around the limitations placed on his expression by dyslexia.

A learning disability is not the only challenge that a student has to overcome to succeed in college. Before reading Olson's essay, you might think of all the challenges that you face. Imagine you were to write a letter to a younger brother or sister about how to apply for college, telling your sibling what impacted you most, and what obstacles stood in your way to becoming the literate citizen you hoped to become as you entered college. As a class, consider which of these were or are common problems for many of you. Which were or are unique to an individual or two?

Imagine having to double your study time because you just learned to read 3 years ago. Ever since I can remember, I have been a horrible student. I never understood much when I was little and was the troublemaker of the class, and always the one to be sent to the office. I made one trip to the office just about every day. On some days, when the teacher thought I had too much sugar in me, a second trip that would land me there the rest of the day. My parents did not have much to say about it at first, but when they had to leave work early and come pick me up because the school did not want me in their classrooms, things began to change.

I had made it up to the fifth grade, surprisingly only repeating third grade on the way. You can imagine the grades I was getting only being in class half the time. With the end of the fifth grade approaching, I received a letter in the mail explaining that I would have to repeat it. I was emotionally destroyed at that point. Twelve years old, a year older than most kids in the class, and I had to find out that I would be thirteen and still in the fifth grade. I began to think that teachers would not give me a break. They heard I was a bad kid, and the smallest little slip up and I was on my way. Sometimes I would be sent out not knowing what it was that I did. If I did not know what I did, how could I fix it, and then, did I want to? Their practices turned me against them, and I never won.

Upon receiving the letter, my folks had had enough. I was tested by the public school system a dozen times and they had no answers, which my parents desperately needed. I began to find myself not attending school very much. Instead I spent most of my remaining days of fifth grade undergoing tests. Still there were no answers.

Frustrated as hell at the no-answer scenario, my parents began to do some research of their own. They found Dr. Grosglen, who was world renowned for working and diagnosing learning disabilities. She worked out of the Mailmen Center for Child Development in Miami, and my parents squeezed me in to see her, which wasn't very easy. This was an intense time because it was just about my last hope. I underwent several days of testing—much of it I never understood, blocks with shapes and colors that had to match and pictures with odd shapes that didn't make sense. Just about the only thing that did make sense was the reading comprehension, and at this point I could hardly read. It was horrible not being able to read. I would sit in class and have stomach cramps from fear that the teacher would call on me to read a paragraph to the class, as they do in grade school.

When the testing ended there was a week wait before they brought me in to explain the results. I sat at a big oval office table that extended from one end of the room to the other, and had gentlemen in suits scattered about it as a Christmas tree would have ornaments. The angel at the top of the tree was Dr. Grosglen. It was from her that I would learn the fate of my struggle which was not over but just beginning. They explained to me that I suffered from what they called dyslexia, disturbance of the ability to read. She also explained that I had a slight attention deficit disorder. Despite all of this, she explained to me that my I.Q. was high, "above average" she said. "There is a lot of hope for you," she explained, "but you are going to have to work hard your entire life." I could not figure out what hard meant, but I knew I couldn't read. This scenario amazed me—the entire time I thought I was stupid, I wasn't. She went on to tell me that a lot of people suffered from this, and many are prominent. A few she named were Albert Einstein, Ben Franklin, Tom Cruise, and Cher.

Upon hearing the news, a few recommendations were made on where I should attend school. The chosen school was Vanguard, which specialized in cases such as mine. The school had no grades, so you worked at your own pace. My pace was 3 years, and much of those 3 years I learned to read and to function in the classroom. It all started with lousy reading comprehension books. Read the passage and answer the questions. It sucked and I quickly developed a distaste for it, but with persistence I finally came to the point where I could understand what I was reading. You see, at Vanguard it was a no-slacking environment, and they stressed control. Outside the small classrooms, I worked to be rewarded. Each night I would be given a certain amount of work that had to be done by the next day, and it had to be correct, absolutely correct. If it was incorrect, I would find myself doing the work at lunch instead of eating. And if it was not done correctly at lunch, I would find the work 3 hours later on my lap as my peers had fun in PE class. There was incentive for me to do the work then.

This is where I learned to read. For many days of the year, I sat lonely in the classroom learning and sounding out words. It was horrible. Sitting inside while my friends played outside in the warm south Florida sun drove me nuts, but I knew the only way out was to get the work done. It was a grueling process of learning to understand everything I read.

There seemed no doubt in my mind that after learning the concepts, I would conquer my disability and find a way. I just decided I was going to do it no matter what, so I dug in and improved. This is what gave me the confidence I have today—the struggle of learning to read. There was so much frustration and hardship, I had to get through it. It had to be over, and I was the only one who could end it.

I learned the basics, enough that I was admitted into a college prep school in Miami. I, for the first time in my life, amazed myself by breezing through a year there with a 2.9 grade point average, which I thought I would never do. It almost seemed too easy.

The real challenge came when I entered college. As a freshman, I quickly became overwhelmed with work. No matter how many hours I put into it, I got the same result. I began to notice students around me studying half the time I was and they ended up with better grades. What was going on? This seemed to be the case with every class. It was getting to the point that all I would do was study. It would extend from the time I woke up to late into the evening. I began to close the library. Still, I was not able to get above a "C" average. I began to pull my hair out. In high school I was an "A" student in algebra, and I was still not very good at reading, but as a college student, I was excellent in reading and failed math three times.

This has caused some very frustrating times in college. Most of the time I walked away from a test thinking that I definitely got an "A," only the next week to find it came back a "C." I often looked over a test after the fact and I would find the most basic mistakes. The markings of "B" and "D" on the answer sheet would often be backwards, among other fundamental mistakes. It wasn't that I did not know the material. This was caused by the dyslexia and it was the first time I began noticing what the doctor and I had spoke about. I would find, by going over the test with the teacher, that I knew all the material and even more. It was just the transition of it onto the test that became a problem—the same problem I had with comprehending what I was reading.

As a senior in college I seem to be more relaxed about my disability because I often can find my biggest mistakes. The small ones are what get away from me. Looking back on the days I had to learn to read, I realized that I learned a lot more than just reading. I learned to struggle and survive. It seems corny but reading has been the greatest struggle in life for me so far, and today I think I can read better than most people my age. My new goal is learning to spell and write. Things still come slowly to me, and I still find that I study twice as long as my peers. "But this too shall pass."

WRITING PROCESS NARRATIVE FOR "LEARNING TO READ"

Beginning with my first draft, I quickly became troubled with the way it was coming out of my brain onto the paper. I knew what I wanted to write about, but it just did not seem to want to come out. In my first draft I completed three pages, which were read in class by my peers. Surprisingly, they liked them, so it was possible that I was being too hard on myself. Although my classmates liked the first draft of the paper, I did not. In my opinion, I was not expressing the emotion and feeling that I felt so strongly about in the paper. It was not a clear reflection of what state I was in during the early years of learning to read.

I knew what I wanted to accomplish in the second draft. Reading has been so emotional for me, so I wanted to capture that in the paper. I find it harder sometimes to write about things I feel very emotional about because I see it in my head very clearly, which makes me leave out detail.

In planning the second draft of my paper, so I would not leave out detail as I did in the first draft; I took a piece of paper and made a list of all the topics I wanted to cover. Then next to each topic I wrote what was troubling or emotional about each one. This helped when I began to put the paper together. When I was lost in emotion I could look back on the reference sheet.

In revising the second copy, I looked at the reference you made on the copy. In two places I added more description or a scene to elaborate the setting. I also went through the paper and fixed the spelling and grammar errors.

E. ANDREE BACQUE

Drop Everything and Read

CONSIDER THIS:

When she wrote her literacy autobiography, Andree Bacque was a second-term, first-year writer. Her writing process cover sheet for "Drop Everything and Read," included here, tells you about her class drafting process, but it also tells you a little about Andree. She was willing to try a new topic, to ask for the help she needed from her mother (which turned out to be a pleasurable sort of research), to share her writing insecurities with a supportive writing group, and to take advice from her peers and her textbook when incorporating revision suggestions into a draft that she felt committed to. For most writers, it helps greatly to turn an outside assignment (from an editor, teacher, or supervisor) into a self-assignment, a piece of writing that pleases you, not only due to what you've managed to say but also due to what you've managed to learn by saying what you said. Like Andree, you might find the writing process cover sheet a useful device for giving yourself credit. The writer's job is to make the final product appear effortless, but the writer should also be recognized for taking risks, making wise decisions, and completing the extra thinking about process that shouldn't appear in the final draft but inevitably proves crucial for the success of that draft.

I must have always known reading was very important because the first memories I have as a child deal with books. There was not one morning that I don't remember mom smothered in her big blue chair reading the morning paper with nothing but the light of her lamp. And there is not one night when I don't remember mom sitting in bed reading her Bible, marking the psalms she liked with a bright yellow highlighter.

I always wanted to know what mom was reading. I was a curious five year old, and hearing my mom say, "I can't believe what's printed in the paper this morning," made me want to rip it out of her hands and read it myself. At night, mom would sometimes read me passages from her Bible, and I remember being extremely inspired by the elegant way the words sounded. I wanted to be like my mom and know all of the things she knew. So, I carried around my own Bible and each night, just to be like her, I would pretend like I was reading.

I remember our bookshelf reached the ceiling, and I remember fighting with my sister each night over which book mom would read. And I do mean each night. Although we could never agree on a book, we could agree that we wanted to be read to. (And our agreeing was extremely rare.) So, naturally reading became a nightly ritual. Mom must have read those books hundreds, maybe even thousands, of times because I still remember exact titles and can describe illustrations in them as if I was the artist. There were two that I particularly enjoyed. I don't remember the title to the first of these, but I remember popcorn being popped and popped and popped until it eventually filled the whole house and started flying out the doors and windows. My favorite, though, was entitled, *But No Elephants.*

The story took place in the middle of winter and was of an old caring woman. Each day a man would go to the old woman's home and beg her to take in an animal that he claimed was unable to survive in the cold. Each day she hesitantly brought another animal into her home always saying, "O.K., I'll take this one, But No Elephants!" Near the end of the story, the old woman had a cat watching television, a bird sitting at her table, a turtle in her bedroom, a cow in her kitchen, and many, many, more, but no elephants. Finally, the man went to her home with nothing to offer but the elephant. As you've probably guessed she took the elephant, and the story concluded with her and a multitude of animals looking through her window watching the man drive away. I love this story! More importantly, I think it was a vital step in my reading process because it made me want to read, rather hear books read, again and again. No matter how many times I heard the popcorn story or *But No Elephants,* I laughed each time. I still laugh. The enjoyment I experienced through these simple story books was the first time I realized that reading could be fun and entertaining.

My sister began school a year before I did, and when I was four I can remember Jeanne coming home with all sorts of neat books, workbooks, and on Fridays a special treat from her teacher. Of course, she never shared any of her neat things with me, and that year when she was in school and I wasn't seemed like it would last a century. Luckily, in less than a century it was my turn to bring home all of the exciting things that Jeanne once did.

"S e e S p o t r u n," I said struggling.

"Try it again, Andree," Mrs. Todd would say in the exact same voice she had used with her last twenty-six students. Mrs. Todd was a very tall woman with short brown hair. And although she sometimes seemed incredibly bored teaching us how to read, she always provided wonderful encouragement.

"See Spot run," I said again, but this time with great pride.

"Good job! Make sure you keep on practicing," Mrs. Todd would say, but this time with a slight bit more of enthusiasm. Then, I would eagerly run home and bore my parents to death reading over and over again, "See Spot run," and "The girl jumps."

I think this is how everyone learned to read. We would start off with the simplest sentences such as these, then grow into more complex sentences, then paragraphs, then stories, and then books. It seemed to be an unending journey, but even as a six year old I realized that knowing how to read could open many doors. When mom now said, "The C-A-N-D-Y is hidden on the top shelf," I knew where the candy was. My new reading ability enhanced my curiosity, and I wanted to know everything. I often found myself telling my mom to drive slower, so that I could read all of the signs we passed.

I loved to read, and in grammar school it was especially stressed. Everyday at a random time our principal, Mr. Stutes, would announce over the loud speaker, "It's time for 'DEAR.'" "DEAR" meant Drop Everything And Read, and that is exactly what we would do. It didn't matter if we were taking a test, we had to stop and read. Sometimes it would last for five minutes, sometimes twenty minutes, but we never missed a day. I read books from the library, school books, and magazines. If none of these were available, I even read the encyclopedias. I figured if our teacher would let us stop working math problems to read, it must be something extremely important . . . she was right.

Most of my reading through grammar, middle and high school was factual reading. I read for knowledge, and to make A's on my tests. Occasionally, I would read a novel that was assigned, but I didn't particularly enjoy this type of reading. I liked facts, things that were concrete. I thought anything abstract left too much room for argument. I don't think I ever once interpreted a piece of literary work the way my teacher wanted me to, so I stuck to the facts.

I suppose my preference of factual reading helped me become successful throughout my first thirteen years of school. Yet, now that I'm growing and the world I once knew as being so simple is becoming more and more complex, I find myself needing a way to escape. I found this escape in novels. First, I began with romance novels mostly written by Danielle Steel. She was a popular author with my friends, and most of the novels I read were recommended by them. I remember many, but one that sticks in my head most vividly is entitled *The Promise.* (This was also the first novel I remember reading and enjoying.) After becoming bored with romance novels, I went on to read the typical bestsellers. John Grisham is an author that I especially recall. I find it much easier to open a novel now rather than when I was in high school. I don't have to write down what I think happened or what technique I think the author was using when he or she wrote this. I just read to relax.

By opening a novel, I can leave behind my burdens and enter into a wonderful and mysterious place where I am now a new character. In these worlds I can become anyone. With each book lies a new setting, a new plot, and a new life to explore. The characteristics I experienced ranged drastically from places and people as beautiful as a young couple with a new found love deserted on a magical, tropical island to things as harsh as a father killing his young daughter's rapists in John Grisham's novel, *A Time to Kill.* I've realized that all books are not meant to be analyzed, and have very quickly found that the possibilities that lie within these books are limitless.

Simply being able to read has provided me with the knowledge and the craving to acquire more and more information. It saddens me to know that an illiterate person will never have my experiences or have the opportunities that I have in life. I never realized how important reading was until I imagined life without literacy. I think in many different aspects I took my ability to read for granted. I think many of us have. I read street signs, menus, billboards, labels, clothing, and the list goes on forever. I can't imagine life without the STOP; YIELD; Hamburger . . . $1.39; EXXON Gas Station Next Exit, and Levis signs that I encounter each day. I believe that everyone wants to learn and everyone wants to be able to understand what surrounds them. Otherwise, we wouldn't be here. I think we're taught to read because it's necessary for much of human understanding. It's funny, but the concept is that simple.

Reading is obviously a vital part of my life. It helps me to simply survive each day. I use reading to fulfill my passion to keep learning, and as a liberty to leave this confusing world and enter into a majestic place filled with beauty and imagination. It's amazing how "See Spot run," could trigger all this.

STEPHEN B. ARMSTRONG

A Trip to the Lake

CONSIDER THIS:

Stephen Blodgett Armstrong was born in 1970 in Hayward, California, and grew up in Annapolis, Maryland, the same town where James M. Cain, author of *The Postman Always Rings Twice,* grew up. After several years of traveling around the United States, finding employment as a chef, a teacher, and a reporter, he returned to school and composed this essay while enrolled in a graduate-level writing workshop. In 2000, Armstrong defended his master's thesis and is now pursuing his doctorate degree in creative writing. He lives in Tallahassee with his dog, a hyperactive dachshund named Madison.

Like Steve Armstrong, you may have just taken or be planning to take a trip abroad. This type of travel provides striking insights into American culture for many students. It is one thing to know your culture from the inside but quite another to reflect on it from several thousand miles or an ocean's distance. Equally dramatic is to see yourself from the viewpoint of other world citizens. When you travel, you find your literacy history travels with you, and you develop an interest in the cultures of other countries. While living in industrial Sheffield and reading English romantic poets, Armstrong decided to take a journey to Wordsworth country to better understand these poets and his reactions to their work. Before you read, consider intellectual journeys you have made or might make (and yes, these days, a trip to Graceland counts). Armstrong's essay is quite different from the thesis-driven essay you may be familiar with. What are the strengths of his approach? What would his essay look like if he were to follow a more traditional structure; that is, what would be lost and what gained?

WRITING PROCESS NOTE FOR "A TRIP TO THE LAKE"

I wrote this piece after an in-class invention on nature and ecology. Since my sophomore year of college, Wordsworth has appealed to me—significantly—because of his ability to evoke nature with his work. I mean by this, that, for me, Wordsworth has the ability to render the sublime observation with sublime execution. And when I went to England to study for a year, I felt that it was imperative to head to Wordsworth land to see the raw material he transformed into verse (much like going to Greenwich Village to better understand Lou Reed). At the University, however, the erudition and theories in the Romantic studies area alienated me. I felt that I was mis-spending my time reading Bloom, when I could/should head up to the Lakes. My friends, who, like T. S. Eliot, disdained Wordsworth and Coleridge, would not follow me. So, like the poet himself, I headed into the woods—alone. When I wrote this piece, in a burst about two months ago, I liked what I had. I brought it to you for your review and discussed the possibilities for revision in conference. Returning to the assignment, however, was a slow, resistant effort, and only recently did I muster the strength and understanding to resume the story, which is, I think, an ironic rite of passage.

A TRIP TO THE LAKE

In England, an undergraduate student begins to prepare—to revise—for finals months and months before they are given. And come the spring of that year, I'd been reading Wordsworth and Coleridge for three months rigorously, trying to understand the Romantic vision of God and nature. But I wasn't having much luck because I lived in a grotty industrial city named Sheffield, that had been bombed flat by the Nazis in the second war. And I read at a desk beside a glass window in my room, with a view of the dorm's dull blue car park and its pub, always wondering, *How did anybody ever find so much beauty in a place with so much metal and concrete like England?*

My view was narrowed, of course, by penury. I could not get out of the city to visit the nearby Peaks, a rolling range of high hills to the west. Nor could I find the time or fare to head up to Scotland or Wales, to view the rumoured beauty that clung to those lands like moss on a stone. My wilderness was in the pubs and the football fields and Victorian gardens scattered around the university. However, there was a window, at the top of a hospital downtown, near my friend JF's, that overlooked a rowboat lake cut from the remains of a quarry, where old men played bowls on a rectangular square of lime green lawn that made my heart ache. I don't know why the simple scene made my heart ache, but it did.

One afternoon I met with a professor to discuss the problems facing me, that I could only understand Wordsworth and Coleridge and the Sublime intellectually, I told him, and I lacked faith in the content of their works. I said to the professor, a blonde haired man with the face that was hooked and mean as Klaus Kinski's, "I believe in God, but I'm ambivalent about nature's role in perceiving Him."

"How can one feel ambivalently about nature?" he said. He had a photograph of his naked infant daughter standing in a bucket of water above his desk. A long thin finger worked at the space between the bridge of his nose and the corner of his jet black eye.

"Where I grew up I watched the workmen come in with bulldozers and tear down the woods to build a subdivision," I said. "And now, when I think of nature, if I do, I think of vulnerability—not the eternal."

"You haven't seen enough of the wild," the professor responded. And he turned from me, to finger the pages of a book about the life and work of Helen Frankenthaller.

"I've seen plenty," I said. And I left him there, in his tidy oak paneled office, under the window that I knew had a view of a prosthetics shop on the street below.

That night, at the pub, I found my friend JF and we chatted about my problem and the solution I was developing.

"Jan Frans," I said, "in order for me to understand Romantic poetry adequately, I think I have to head up to the Lake District to experience nature."

"Have fun," JF replied. He came from the Netherlands, where the developers turned the woods into canals and tulip fields thousands of years ago. I tried to appeal to him, to tell him that we might find nymphs in the English mountains and mermaids in the lakes, but my friend resisted. "I lack two things, Stevie," he said, "Money and interest."

"Well, I have plenty of interest," I said.

And the next day I went to the travel agent in the student union and purchased a ticket to the Lake District on credit. And that afternoon, with a ruck sack, my cowboy boots, and a copy of *The Prelude,* I boarded the train. It was dark when I arrived, and a storm ripped through the air, icy and ceaseless, soaking me on my hike from the one-light depot to the hostel that squatted on the edge of Lake Windermere.

When I woke up the next morning, my hair was still wet. I got up and struggled to the hostel's cafe where I ate eggs and toast and tomatoes and coffee. At a nearby shop, a card shop with a post office in it, I purchased a laminated folding map from an old man with a sty.

"Where's Dove Cottage?" I said.

"Here," he said, pointing to a black asterisk near a bending blue river.

"Cheers," I said.

And I headed out the door, under a ringing bell, into the cold and rainy morning. Lake Windermere lay like a lasso loop filled with grass green glass to my left. The shore, choked with spiky reeds and scattered with sheep droppings, squished beneath me. Forty minutes passed before I reached the lake's eastern rim, and there a meadow stretched as wide as Mama Cass's behind, stopping at the gray ankles of a rugged hill. The insides of my cowboy boots squeaked like piglets as I crossed the meadow and another forty five minutes passed before I reached the hill: obstacles like streams and cattle gates held me up. The ruck sack grew heavy quickly and its stretched arm straps slid down the sides of my shoulders continuously. Falling under an ever-increasing despondency, I wondered, *Why must I go through so many things alone?*

Nevertheless, when I reached the side of the gray hill,—so coarse, so unusual, so sensual—my heart leapt. I then proceeded up its side, hooking my fingers into crags and crevices where I could. The wind bit at my neck like a little dog. And at the top, which resembled a putting green since it was covered with grass and grass alone, a sheet of water swept along, like the first water that touches the street it will soon flood. My fingers held me to the grass: a tremendous wind jabbed and smacked at me, trying to knock me over the side of the green to my death thirty stories down. And as I stood there I became conscious, just slightly perhaps, of what Wordsworth may have meant when he wrote

> And I could hope my days to be
> Bound each to each by natural piety

In the valley below, a long wisp of cloud, as long as a train, pointed to an orange sun, smeared through the sky, like gold melting

Several hours later, I stood in a doorway of a stone house, watching the thick rain fall into the forest. The ancient house was pressed up against a one-lane road, like a gaunt prospector drinking at a stream. The road, slick and black, sank around a bend a quarter-mile away.

The rain wasn't going to give, I realized. It had been falling in sheets since noon, for two hours, but now a front had moved in, and, without a hat, the going was miserable. So I unbuckled my ruck sack and set it at my feet. Then I reached in for the pack of Old Virginia tobacco I'd brought and the cigarette papers. The rain, I discovered, had penetrated the ruck sack's nylon covering, had soaked through the sweat shirt that lay atop the bundle of clothes and goods I carried. The books—William's poems and Dorothy's journals—were wet, too. Fortunately, I'd wrapped the tobacco and papers inside a plastic Tesco bag.

With shivering fingers, I rolled a cigarette. I struck a weather proof match, lifted the burst of flame to the cigarette's tip, and inhaled. A terrible sense of boredom and isolation swept through me. Then a car flashed by, descended the hill, and disappeared.

Though the time, according to my watch, was half-three, my bones ached and my feet hurt so much, I thought it was later. And, by the map, I had another three hard miles to cover, over road and trail, before I reached Dove Cottage. The pain across my shoulders encouraged me to sit down on the stone steps where my wet feet rested, but I didn't give in. I knew that if I paused, if I indulged in comfort, I'd never make camp before nightfall. I might not find food, either. I was starving starving starving, needed a Cornish Pasty or a bag of crisps or whatever the tourist station I expected to find at Dove Cottage had to sell.

So, after the cigarette, I hoisted my pack over my shoulders. The soles of my boots started slapping the slippery road again. The forest rustled.

At half-four, I saw, but doubted my vision, a whitish building rising under the black blows of trees. A lorry, with emblems indicating some official capacity painted across its green doors, was parked beside the cottage's entrance. I saw a man, or a woman, with a dark hat and rain coat, standing beside the truck. A ranger, I suspected, guarding a national treasure.

As I ambled down the tiny road, letting its curved route lead me, my view was turned away from the white cottage to a wide, black river, that roared and quaked before the tourist station I had hoped I would find. *I'm here,* I told myself. *This is the place.*

The ranger person no longer stood at the cottage's door when I arrived. The truck, too, was gone, and now, a friendly, thin-faced man stood under the roof where it shaded folk from the falling rain. I said hello to him and asked him when the house and the museum closed.

"In fifteen minutes, sir," he told me. "Do hurry!"

I thanked the kind man with the thin face and entered the warm dark house with water dripping down my shoulders and my head. A young woman, dressed in clothes from an earlier century, received my ruck sack graciously.

"You've got but ten minutes, sir, so I won't charge you."

"Thank you so much," I replied.

Dove Cottage was lovely, really. Narrow hallways led to exhibits describing the life and contributions of the region's great poet. Upstairs, I saw the bed where he and his wife Mary slept for several years. A sign above a chair informed me that Coleridge had sat on it. A small, grainy window, overlooked the woods where Wordsworth so enjoyed walking.

The downstairs, strangely enough, reminded me of Graceland. Curators had left the house (they claimed) as Wordsworth kept it. Different rooms, serving different functions, had different looks. A glass showcase in the kitchen showed a tea bag that Wordsworth had used fifteen times during the rationing days of the war with France. In this showcase, as well, were the poet's spectacles which he wore to compensate for the blindness that began to beset him in middle-age. Pathetically, too, a blue stone sat beside the spectacles on a small cushion. A card explained that Wordsworth believed that if he pressed the blue stone to his eye, he might prevent further loss of his vision. My heart lurched for the poor man! Other signs spoke of Dorothy, who'd gone insane. A picture of Wordsworth's favorite daughter, who died young, hung in the kitchen as well. The longer I stood there, the more I felt like an intruder, a trespassing snoop. Strangely enough, the longer I stood there, the more I wished to be outside again, in the miserable rain, without a hat, walking.

The kind woman behind the counter returned my ruck sack to me.

"How long before the tourist station closes?" I said.

"Oh rush, sir. It closes in five minutes!"

A moment later, I stood outside Dove Cottage again. The sky was snot gray and black lines appeared where the clouds tumbled over one another. As I walked toward the river, however, a sign caught my eye. Arrow-shaped, someone had painted the words To Graves on it. I couldn't resist, you know. It seemed critical that I come as physically close as possible to the poet whose words brought me here.

A short black fence wrapped around his headstone. He slept the big sleep next to his wife, Mary. Above the three of us, the black trees rustled. "God bless you, William Wordsworth," I said.

Then, moving as quickly as I could in my soaking wet cowboy boots, I scrambled toward the tourist station, where I bought a tube of sausage spread, a block of cheese, and a weatherproof hat.

A shaky bridge lifted me over the boiling river to a meadow that eventually reached the bottoms of mountains lying miles away. I did not like the idea of pitching my pup tent in an open space such as this, and so I trudged along the river, in the direction of a copse of trees sprouting a mile or so ahead. As I walked, the weeds of the overgrown trail lashed at my legs. The river roared like an old Cadillac climbing a steep hill. Anxiety sank into me, blending with the cold night air, making my head hurt again.

But within a relatively short time, I entered the copse. The dark and the cold thickened under the heavy, dripping boughs. The river grew louder. Looking over to my left and right and behind me, I didn't see the ominous light from a farmer's house. Actually, I saw nothing but trees and the day's fading light dimming at the tops of them. Nevertheless, I found an adequate space to drop my gear and pitch my tent, a circular, flat, moss covered space, surround by great rocks.

I got to work. First, I unstrapped my pack and then the tent from the pack. Then I tested the ground with my fingers. I feared that the rock I could see might be the outward expressions of other, larger rocks, lying beneath the soil. My fingers, however, sank into ground as easily as a knife into a cut of beef. Relieved somewhat, I laid out the WW II-era tent, began to connect its numerous poles. The bloody contraption had brought me great misery before—but now, however, it frustrated me as it had never, never frustrated me before.

"Well goddam," I said, "goddam, goddam, goddam."

An hour in the black spitting rain passed before I had the thing set up. It sat there, small and fragile, A-shaped. I wouldn't even look at it. Instead, I sat on my heals and squeezed the tube of sausage into my mouth and gnawed on the block of cheese. The river's roar behind me taunted me, reminding me that I had forgotten to purchase bottled water from the now distant tourist station.

And then the feeling of isolation that had swept over me under the house an hour away from Dove Cottage swept over me again. I crawled into the tent and pressed my knees into the soft floor. I don't remember if I prayed. I should have prayed. I don't know what I was doing, but I did it until the hopeless feelings left me. And then I sat outside the tent again for the bloody contraption made me claustrophobic.

After dinner, my shaking fingers constructed another crummy cigarette. The smoke augmented my thirst and I quickly pushed it out on the soft ground and shoved the ruined butt in my pocket. Then I lay down. I looked up into the pitch black and listened as the rain smacked the tent. Moisture was seeping through and I know this because, as I laid there, I ran my fingers over the course, dripping canvas. An hour later, or two or three, I drifted into an empty, total sleep.

I don't know what time in the night the thumpings started. And I don't know how long the thumpings thumped before I woke up. But when I did, I felt the sides of the tent bulge toward me and felt the seeping rain water dribble on my face. Was a farmer on the other side, tapping the tent with his boots? Wet, aching, ravaged, a bizarre idea shot through my mind. What if it's God? I wondered. What if God is pressing my tent with his finger tips?

The thought horrified me.

When my eyes flickered open, the tent's canvas roof was the color of a lime. The river sounded milder than it had—like wet newspaper slowly being torn. I sat up and drew my sleeve across my cold, wet face.

Then I opened the tent's flap. It was quite bright outside, yet cold, like the inside of a refrigerator. I swept my eyes over what land I could see and saw only the mossy carpet, the wall of black trees, and the lichen-spotted boulders.

There was nothing else and no one. I fixed a cigarette and lit it and sat on my heels, a foot outside the tent. When I finished the cigarette, I found the tube of sausage. It still smelled okay, so I squeezed some on my finger. I washed it down with a bit of cheese. The salty flavors of the breakfast cut the acidic taste in my mouth better than toothpaste.

After I finished, I stood up and stretched my legs. I remembered my dream of God uncomfortably, standing there, looking at the unviolated land. My eyes dropped to the ground and they wandered to the sides of the tent.

The night before, in the setting light, I'd inventoried my little plot of land carefully, checking for rocks and snakes and other annoyances. I'd been satisfied that there was nothing to rip or penetrate or stain the WW II tent. But now, I saw, rising like miniature stacks of cannonballs, mounds of animal droppings were piled beside the tent.

A sheep abruptly baaa-ed from behind one of the boulders.

I remember very little of the rest of my trip to the Lake District. Eventually, I vaguely recall, I found Wordsworth's other house and saw the daffodils he planted in Dora's memory. I remember climbing another hill half-way and losing the heel of my boot. And I remember thinking, when the heel broke, "It's time to go now."

And then I hobbled through the rain and around Lake Windermere back to the train station. And on the train, I tried to read from *The Prelude.* But I was feeling terribly fatigued, and, as the train left the depot, I slipped into a deep and satisfying sleep.

CONNECTING TO READING

A. For a journal entry, choose two literacy narratives and read them together. Write a short introduction to these narratives (perhaps in the form of a letter from you to a friend whom you'd like to convince to read these texts) that answers these questions: Which do you find most effective and why? What does each author's story suggest to you about your own literacy? How much bearing does your own literacy past have on how you respond to each of these authors? After responding to and looking at the content of these narratives, spend some time analyzing them rhetorically. What effects did each writer achieve and by what methods? What might you borrow for your own narrative? Add notes on these elements in a second journal entry.

B. In class or on-line, each member of a reading group chooses two texts. Out of class, complete additional research on those two authors. Conduct a library and/or Web search for responses to some of each author's creative and scholarly publications. For the author about whom you can find the most information, compose an introduction to that writer's work that includes a biographical note, a list of his or her most well-known works, and sources for further reading that go beyond the information offered in this chapter. Several of the other authors are still writing and teaching. You may be able to find websites, university home pages, or current journal articles and writings by them. You could even e-mail them and interview them, briefly if they have time for such an interview.

For your group, compose an informal two-page handout, citing your sources. If two of you choose the same writer, which is likely, it will be interesting to compare the sources you found when you share your handouts in class.

C. In class, in a group, list the literacy narratives your group members chose to study. Note what you find in common among these writers. For example, what were their first reading or writing experiences? What were their parents' or family's attitudes toward reading? What effect did gender, race, and economic class have on their literacy? How did peers and/or writing groups influence them? Compare your chart with those of classmates in other groups and make a combined chart as part of your whole class discussion.

D. In class, with a partner, consider one classroom author along with one of your professional writers. Which do you relate to more and why? Are they more alike than different or more different than alike? Be ready to share your view with your classmates.

E. In a group, write 10 pieces of advice (a how-to sheet) for composing a literacy narrative based on your readings and analysis of the narratives in this chapter. What elements do literacy narratives have in common? What strategies do writers use when reporting and telling stories? Have a group member post this on the class website (if you have one) so other groups and other writers can consult your advice as they compose their own narratives.

CONNECTING TO WRITING

A. In a journal, as you read the narratives in this chapter, copy down quotes that you feel have relevance to your own literacy narrative and life. Try to collect at least 30 of these and then review them to see what, if anything, they have in common (you can use the double-entry journal technique described by Deborah Coxwell Teague in her essay "Making Meaning—Your Own Meaning—When You Read," found in Chapter 3. As a journal entry summary, write a paragraph reflecting on this collection of citations from the literacy narratives of others.

B. In a journal entry, describe how fitting in (or not fitting in) affected your literacy and helped you or forced you to make decisions about your schooling in kindergarten through high school.

C. On-line on a class discussion board, or in-class in a small group, share three informal writings about several themes/issues that arise in these narratives and have direct connections to your own literacy autobiography. For instance, for some of us, finding someone who appreciates our work can be a crucial point in our learning lives. Many of us can recount important interactions with teachers (whether that interaction was positive or negative). Overall, we can examine some of the following: our parents' literacy, a community attitude toward reading and writing that we encountered growing up, our sense of developing a (writer's) voice, and/or writing from or against our first language. Before undertaking this exploration, you might discuss the activity with a group or with your class to identify other recurring issues. Choose three to respond to and relate them to your own life, creating three short but separate exploratory writings. Ask classmates to tell you which of the three writings they find most promising and interesting and why.

D. In a journal entry or class discussion, analyze the writing style of these narratives. What do they have in common, and what is distinct about each writer's approach? (A chart might help here, too.) Which writers use devices that you would be comfortable using yourself? (Why are you comfortable with them?) Which writers use devices that you didn't expect or that you haven't tried? Will you now? Why or why not?

E. In a group discussion, consider other times in your schooling when you've been asked to write a literacy narrative, even if you didn't know at the time that that's what it might have been called. A prime instance is the college entrance essay. With your group, note other occasions on which you've been asked to write such a narrative or read one written by another author. Share your list with the class.

WRITING PROJECTS

1. What do you remember about learning to read and write? In what way are you the same or a different reader than you were back then? You might find it useful to prewrite on this topic by choosing important dates/memories, such as being read to, visiting the library as a child, starting kindergarten, writing your first paper, memorable teachers, out-of-school writing and reading memories, and so on. Jot down 10 or 12 of these moments/memories and explore each informally. Freewrite. Free associate. In doing this, you will no doubt find a lead for a narrative. Write that narrative. Andree Bacque's process cover sheet explains how she undertook a similar exercise and turned similar writings into a literacy narrative.
2. Make a list of all the members of your immediate family—those you lived with when you were between ages 2 and 10. After their names, write the occupations they had then and describe the locations and the scenes in which you remember seeing them most often. Now, describe each as a reader. What did he or she read? When? How often? What feelings and beliefs about reading did he or she express? Paint a word picture of this person reading something—anything—to the best of your descriptive abilities. If you can't remember exactly, make up a reasonable description and/or work from old photos or join your memories to that of another family member, one you call up or e-mail and interview.) Join these pictures or snapshots into a narrative.
3. Visit the children's book section in your public library (or visit a local elementary school library). I'm willing to predict that you'll find forgotten and

favorite books call out to you from the shelves and reignite memories. Reread several books and write a journal entry. What do you find different reading the book today? What memories of reading or being read to does the book prompt? If you have children, have you read this book to/with your own child? Why or why not? If you plan to have children, will you read this book—and what other books—to/with them? At home, use your journal entry to compose an open letter to that child, describing to him or her your feelings about literacy, yours and that child's.

4. In class or at home, draw the floor plan of the house, apartment, trailer, or living space where you lived when you were first learning to read. On the diagram, label each room: kitchen, bedroom, bathroom, and so on. Then number each room. At the bottom of the page, for each number, write notes toward a story you might tell concerning you and reading/writing that took place in that room. Continue until you've completed notes for each room in the house. For some, numbering outdoor locations/making story notes, can be productive, too. Share some stories with classmates to find which interest them as listeners/readers. Later, choose one story and expand it into a draft for your literacy narrative.
5. Take five of the most memorable quotes from literacy narratives that you collected (Connecting to Writing, activity A) and place each on a separate page in a new file on your computer. Use each as a prompt for writing a literacy vignette of your own. Link these vignettes together with short subtitles as you might lay out a sequence of photos in a photo album.
6. Reread the literacy narratives in this chapter and collect five statements you find provocative, promising, problematic. Type each into a new file and then start talking to it, about it, against it, for it, beside it, beyond it. Eventually, you should develop enough starts (if you're not already plunging into a draft) to respond to your responses. Set up a second column and write about your writings. Be a teacher. Be a skeptic. Be a classmate. Be a parent. Be a second-self. Be your younger self writing to your older self, and vice-versa. Extend and explore your earlier exploration. Look for key phrases, repetitions, new insights. Take one of these, or a collage of all of this—and tell a story; create a literacy narrative.
7. Several of the literacy narratives, Christy Brown's and Domitila de Chungara's in particular, describe a learner having to overcome physical or economic obstacles. The works by de Chungara, Amy Tan and Barbara Mellix, for instance, describe literacy from a woman's perspective. Most of the writers, but particularly Richard Rodriguez and Amy Tan, explore the influence of family. Choose one of these lenses to emphasize while writing or revise your own literacy narrative and/or write yours in a way that considers *all* these lenses, using them as an organizing principle.
8. After examining all the narratives in this chapter for statements about/attitudes toward public schooling, write an essay where you use these writers as research background for exploring your own attitudes and beliefs about schooling.

9. Consider the effects of economic class on literacy. If you did not face economic adversity and/or cultural difficulties coming into the U.S. school system, write an essay that considers your particular circumstances, as in Andree Bacque's essay. To add texture and to complicate your own narrative, reflect on what your learning life might have been like had you encountered the very different conditions described in some of the narratives in this chapter. A place to begin your drafting could be with a freewrite where you compare and contrast your own learning story to each of those here: Like [name], I. . . . Unlike [name], I. . . .

10. Write a poem as a literacy narrative as Langston Hughes does; as a parody; as a series of vignettes (influential individuals in your life); or as an anti-narrative, written to explain how someone might *not* value literacy. Then, use this short writing as part of the framework of your more essay-like literacy narrative. Reflect on what you learned by writing *creatively* and how that writing illuminates (if it does) the points you want to make about your coming into (or not coming into) reading, writing, or more proficient language use.

* * * *

To value self-investment, to avoid premature closure, to see revision as discovery, to go beyond the predictable, to risk experimentation, and, above all, to trust your own creative powers are necessary for all good writing, whether it is a freshman theme, a poem, a term paper. . . . Few of us reward risk taking that fails with a better grade than polished but pedestrian texts. We are more product-oriented, judging assignments as independent of one another rather than as part of a collective and ongoing body of work. No wonder that students interpret our message as "Be careful, not creative!"

—MIMI SCHWARTZ

Considering Community and Audience

Thinking About Your Interactions with Other Writers and Readers

> This is the first time I've had an English class where groups were formed. I found that I had an easier time talking in the groups than in class discussion. So I must say that it has value in letting me get my ideas across to other people in class, with much less apprehension.
>
> —ANONYMOUS CLASSROOM AUTHOR

You may never have thought of yourself as a rhetorician. But you are. Every day, in a number of different ways, you attempt to persuade someone to think the way you think. You have real and imagined audiences for your ideas. You may be trying to get your student loan processed more quickly or to convince a good friend to visit you this weekend. Because your partner (child, parent, friend) didn't understand what you meant last night at dinner, you're explaining to him today how he misinterpreted what you said and encouraging him to consider your words in a different light. You have personal and public audiences with whom you need to communicate. You may be running for elected office and want someone's vote, or you may be serving a customer at work, hoping to convince her to purchase a brand of computer that you particularly believe in. The last two uses of rhetoric—political and consumer rhetoric—are the sorts that most of us associate with the term. However, as a member of a number of communities, you are constantly acting on and being acted upon by different persuasive individuals, images, texts, and events. Teachers, classmates, friends, parents, neighbors, community members, and public figures influence and are influenced by you.

Equally often, you move from oral to written persuasive discourse: "I am returning this sweater because . . ."; "I am an excellent candidate for your law school since . . ."; "If you care about this issue, you will join me by contributing. . . ." At any moment of the day then, you are adjusting your communication, making it more clear, persuasive, and appropriate to the given subject and the given audience. You "read" a situation and you respond to it based on your analysis of what would be most effective and most appropriate to the occasion. It makes sense, then, to study the art of written persuasion, to study how writers affect the world through language, and to do that, we study how language works within communities.

The minute you enter a writing classroom, you become part of a community with common goals: to learn about writing processes, to improve each community member's writing, to develop lifelong writing abilities. With others in this group, you develop your drafts and examine them, sharing insights and arguments with peer readers and your teacher. It's rare that writers actually get to see their texts being read in this manner; to talk to their readers; or to have an immediate, actual, interested, and knowledgeable audience. By paying attention to peer response, you develop the useful skill of predicting the way more distant audiences will understand and respond to your texts. That's not to say, though, that you should always write to an audience since there are times when you have to explore ideas on your own. Nor is it a simple thing to write to or for your peers. But writing and sharing in a workshop situation generally proves valuable to writers. In his selection in this chapter, Toby Fulwiler offers advice for making the most of these audiences.

In Chapter 1, we looked at assumptions that writers write alone and newer understandings that they both do and don't. They write within a network of communicative relationships. In the following interview, playwright John Edgar Wideman explains to Renee Olander how writers navigate between the demands of public readers (audiences) and the necessity of developing a voice, a way of saying what needs to be said:

[RENEE] OLANDER: Do you have a reader in mind as you write, an image of an audience you hope to reach?

[JOHN EDGAR] WIDEMAN: At times in my life I have. When I was younger I always had very specific voices, and that is a sign of a younger writer. It means that writing for you, or for me, is an imitation of something that's already out there, something that pleases you, something that turns you on, and you're trying to reproduce it in some way with a little twist of your own voice. But I think that over time, something else happens and you begin to talk to yourself, to talk to the other books you've written, and the voice becomes much more internalized. Maybe you lose some of that grand ambition which is part of being a beginning writer—you begin to settle for what you have, and to listen more closely and pay more attention to your own voice and its energy and whatever its limits might be.

Luckily, you don't have to hold an "image of an audience" in your mind, and just hope for the best, at least not right now. Instead, you can share your rhetorical efforts, your drafts, with your classmates. As you do, you'll want to consider issues like the following: What constitutes a "safe" audience for a writer? How does a writer know how to shape a text for a particular audience? Are there times when it's important to ignore an imagined audience? To adapt to it? What happens—and can be learned—by shaping the same text for two different audiences? How do you write for a community you don't feel comfortable in or know very well? How do you imagine yourself in the company of such an audience? And so on.

So far I've perhaps made community membership seem easy, simple, something to be outlined, understood, and attended to. But membership, of course, is part of a negotiation between individuals. And although we enter our communities by birth, accident, or intention, rarely is passage through or participation within a community without complications. We can be invited to join a community. That's why a small peer response group can be a pleasant surprise to writers who don't like to share their drafts or discussion with a larger, less well-known community of the entire class. We can be forced to join a community: being enrolled in a certain classroom by the registrar because no other sections are available. We can be kept out of a community because we don't have the prerequisite, we had a time conflict, or our writing sample wasn't judged appropriate. And once arrived, we can find consensus stifling or supportive (and sometimes both). We can choose to disregard some of our communities (global concerns about armaments or ecology) but find we do so at our own peril. Negotiating community memberships is complicated, and we have to remember that we can be kept from joining in discussions for reasons we want to challenge or resist.

Nonetheless, community and audience concerns undergird our lives as writers. The readings in this chapter should help you investigate the concepts just outlined. To do that, this chapter features authors who focus on the communities you are entering and participating in at the college level. The university, with its colleges, divisions, fields, and subfields offers a stimulating microcosm of community issues. To understand discourse negotiations that take place there, we need to consider the art of rhetoric, classical and contemporary. In the readings in this chapter, Edward Corbett and Robert Connors offer an encyclopedic overview of classical rhetoric and outline its continuing importance to students of writing. Since you are probably using this book in a college writing classroom, it's appropriate to investigate the discourse of college academics. Mike Rose defines such an audience and Stanley Witkin illustrates how one such community—that of social work—formed, and how its members create meaning together by observing and negotiating evolving sets of textual conventions.

As part of his own literacy narrative, Gerald Graff explores the problems he had accessing academic discourse: the language of scholars in university and college settings. Interestingly, he's now considered an insider within the very community he once considered alien. John Agard's poem voices resistance to the same academic discourse community that Graff now thoroughly represents, setting the scene for letting you examine how communities both include and exclude members. In a slightly different vein, Rita Dove looks at the tensions between artistic and professional life. To underline the point that community is as much about difference as it is about similarity, Fan Shen explores his "English" and "Chinese" identities. Toby Fulwiler offers some nuts-and-bolts advice for considering two key audiences for college writers: classmates and teachers. Deborah Coxwell Teague explains how communities of readers make meaning when they read, explaining that meaning is a negotiation between reader and text that requires active attention, and, often, rereading. In the final essays of this chapter, classroom author Benjamin Lauren uses an unsympathetic "audience," a banker met on a plane, as a foil for his narrative; and Kenneth Reeves studies a particular community, that of B movie fans, and shares his interview-based research with interested readers.

5

Chapter Readings

EDWARD P. J. CORBETT (1919–1998) AND
ROBERT J. CONNORS (1952–2000)

A Brief Explanation of Classical Rhetoric

CONSIDER THIS:

A pioneer of composition studies who taught at Creighton University, Loyola of Chicago, and Ohio State University, Edward P. J. Corbett was an expert in both classic and modern rhetoric, and strove especially to make the discipline of classic rhetoric relevant to the modern student's life. In his *Little English Handbook* he promoted the teaching of "public prose. . . . That dialect of written English most commonly used in the newspapers, magazines, and books" that educated people read. Corbett had nothing against other, less formal, dialects. Rather, he chose to clarify the situations in which writers "must use the written language in order to record or communicate their thoughts, needs, and feelings." One of Corbett's students, invited to help revise the fourth edition of *Classical Rhetoric for the Modern Student* 33 years after the original edition, Robert J. Connors, was a well-regarded historian of rhetoric in his own right and professor of English and director of the Writing Center at the University of New Hampshire.

Before you begin to read about classical rhetoric, list the attributes of "public prose," as you understand it. What makes public prose sound different, say, than your personal journal writing, or the way you and your friends talk? Now, make a list of all the areas in your life where you use persuasion. That is, in the course of a day, week, month, or year, who do you try to persuade to do what? Consider whether you tend to use logical, emotional, or ethical appeals (for instance, when challenging a referee's call or asking your boss for a raise) and how your understanding of your audience helps you make such a decision (if you make such decisions beforehand). When you read this selection on classical rhetoric, you'll encounter a great number of classifications; it may help to work with a group to outline the information you're presented with.

Although modern students may often have heard the term *rhetoric* used, they probably do not have a clear idea of what it means. Their uncertainty is understandable, because the word has acquired many meanings. Rhetoric may be associated in their minds with the writing of compositions and themes or with style—figures of speech, flowery diction, variety of sentence patterns and rhythms—or with the notion of empty, bombastic language, as implied in the familiar phrase "mere rhetoric." Maybe tucked away somewhere in their consciousness is the notion of rhetoric as the use of language for persuasive purposes.

What all these notions have in common is that rhetoric implies the use or manipulation of words. And, indeed, a look at the etymology of the word *rhetoric* shows that the term is solidly rooted in the notion of "words" or "speech." The Greek words *rhēma* ("a word") and *rhētor* ("a teacher of oratory"), which are akin, stem ultimately from the Greek verb *eirō* ("I say"). Our English noun *rhetoric* derives from the Greek feminine adjective *rhetorikē*, which is elliptical for *rhetorikē technē* ("the art of the rhetor or orator"). English got its word immediately from the French *rhétorigue.*

This investigation of the etymology of the term brings us somewhat closer to the original meaning of rhetoric: something connected with speaking, orating. From its origin in 5th century B.C. Greece through its flourishing period in Rome and its reign in the medieval *trivium,* rhetoric was associated primarily with the art of oratory. During the Middle Ages, the precepts of classical rhetoric began to be applied to letter-writing, but it was not until the Renaissance, after the invention of printing in the fifteenth century, that the precepts governing the spoken art began to be applied, on any large scale, to written discourse.

Classical rhetoric was associated primarily with persuasive discourse. Its end was to convince or persuade an audience to think in a certain way or to act in a certain way. Later, the principles of rhetoric were extended to apply to informative or expository modes of discourse, but in the beginning, they were applied almost exclusively to the persuasive modes of discourse.

Rhetoric as persuasive discourse is still very much exercised among us, but modern students are not likely to have received much formal training in the art of persuasion. Frequently, the only remnant of this training in the schools is the attention paid to argumentation in a study of the four forms of discourse: Argumentation, Exposition, Description, and Narration. But this study of argumentation usually turns out to be an accelerated course in logic. For the classical rhetorician, logic was an ancillary but distinct discipline. Aristotle, for instance, spoke of rhetoric as being "an offshoot" or "a counterpart" of logic or, as he called it, dialectics. The speaker might employ logic to persuade the audience, but logic was only one among many "available means of persuasion." So those who study argumentation in classrooms today are not really exposed to the rich, highly systematized discipline that earlier students submitted to when they were learning the persuasive art.

Although classical rhetoric has largely disappeared from our schools, there was a time when it was very much alive. For extended periods during its two-thousand-year history, the study of rhetoric was the central discipline in the curriculum. Rhetoric enjoyed this eminence because, during those periods, skill in oratory or in written discourse was the key to preferment in the courts, the forum, and the church. One of the reasons why the study—if not the practice—of rhetoric has declined in our own times is that in an industrial, technological society like our own, there are avenues to success other than communication skills. Part of the folklore of America is that in the years from about 1870 to 1910, some barely literate men became millionaires—some of whom, ironically, later founded libraries and endowed universities.

One fact that emerges from a study of the history of rhetoric is that there is usually a resurgence of rhetoric during periods of social and political upheaval. Whenever the old order is passing away and the new order is marching—or stumbling—in, a loud, clear call goes up for the services of the person skilled in the use of spoken or written words. One needs only to hearken back to such historical events as the Renaissance in Italy, the Reformation in England, and the Revolution in America to find evidence of this desperate reliance, in times of change or crisis, on the talents of those skilled in the persuasive arts. As Jacob Burckhardt has pointed out in *The Civilization of the Renaissance in Italy*, the orator and the teacher of rhetoric played a prominent role in the fifteenth-century humanistic movement that was casting off the yoke of the medieval church. After Henry VIII broke with Rome, the Tudor courts of England resounded with the arguments of hundreds of lawyers engaged to fight litigations over confiscated monastic properties. Students of the American Revolution need recall only Tom Paine's incendiary pamphlets, Patrick Henry's rousing speeches, Thomas Jefferson's daring Declaration of Independence, and Hamilton's and Madison's efforts to sell constitutional democracy in the *Federalist Papers* to be convinced that in time of change or upheaval, we rely heavily on the services of those equipped with persuasively eloquent tongues or pens. Something of the same kind of rhetorical activity is raging today among the nationalists fighting for independence in African and Asian countries. More recently in our own country, we witnessed the furious rhetorical activity, expressed in both words and physical demonstrations in the pro-choice/right-to-life debates.

THE FIVE CANONS OF RHETORIC

Inventio is the Latin term (*heuresis* was the equivalent Greek term) for "invention" or "discovery." Theoretically, orators could talk on any subject, because rhetoric, as such, had no proper subject matter. In practice, however, each speech that orators undertook presented a unique challenge. They had to find arguments that would support whatever case or point of view they were espousing. According to Cicero, the speaker relied on native genius, on method or art, or on diligence to help find appropriate arguments. Obviously, that individual was at a great advantage who had a native, intuitive sense for proper arguments. But lacking such an endowment, a person could have recourse either to dogged industry or to some system for finding arguments. *Inventio* was concerned with a system or method for finding arguments.

Aristotle pointed out that there were two kinds of arguments or means of persuasion available to the speaker. First of all, there were the non-artistic or non-technical means of persuasion (the Greek term was *atechnoi pisteis*). These modes of persuasion were really not part of the art of rhetoric; they came from outside the art. Orators did not have to *invent* these; they had merely to use them. Aristotle named five kinds of non-artistic proofs: laws, witnesses, contracts, tortures, oaths. Apparently, the lawyer pleading a case in court made most use of this kind of proof, but the politician or the panegyrist could use them too. The representatives today, for instance, who are trying to persuade the citizens to adopt a sales tax quote statistics, legal contracts, existing laws, historical documents, and the testimony of experts to bolster their case. They do not have to invent these supporting arguments; they already exist. True, there is a sense in which they have to find such supporting arguments. They have to be aware that they exist, and they have to know what departments or records to go to in order to discover them. (One of the sections in the next chapter will provide expositions of some of the standard reference books that can supply the facts, figures, testimonies to support arguments.) But the representatives do not have to imagine these arguments, to think them up—to invent them, in the classical sense of that term.

The second general mode of persuasion that Aristotle spoke of included artistic proof—"artistic" in the sense that they fell within the province of the art of rhetoric: *rational* appeal (*logos*), *emotional* appeal (*pathos*), and *ethical* appeal (*ethos*). In exercising the rational appeal, the speaker was appealing to the audience's reason or understanding. The speaker is "arguing," in other words. When we argue, we reason either *deductively* or *inductively*—that is, we either draw conclusions from affirmative or negative statements (e.g., No man can attain perfect happiness in this life; John is a man; therefore John cannot attain perfect happiness in this life) or make generalizations after observing a number of analogous facts (e.g., Every green apple that I bit into had a sour taste. All green apples must be sour.) In logic, the deductive mode of arguing is commonly referred to by the term that Aristotle used, the *syllogism*. In rhetoric, the equivalent of the syllogism was the *enthymeme*. The rhetorical equivalent of *full induction* in logic is the *example*. Since the next chapter will provide an elaborate explanation of syllogism, enthymeme, induction, and example, we will not dwell on them here.

A second mode of persuasion is the emotional appeal. Since people are by nature rational animals, they should be able to make decisions about their private and public lives solely by the light of reason. But they are also endowed with the faculty of free will, and often enough their will is swayed more by their passions or emotions than by their reason. Aristotle expressed the wish that rhetoric could deal exclusively with rational appeals, but he was enough of a realist to recognize that a person is often prompted to do something or accept something by his or her emotions. And if rhetoric was, as he defined it, the art of discovering "all the available means of persuasion," then he would have to give a place in his *Rhetoric* to an investigation of the means of touching the emotions. Accordingly, he devoted the major portion of Book II of his *Rhetoric* to an analysis of the more common human emotions. This was the beginning of the science of human psychology. If the orator was to play upon people's emotions, he must know what those emotions were and how they could be triggered off or subdued.

A third mode of persuasion was the ethical appeal. This appeal stemmed from the character of the speaker, especially as that character was evinced in the speech itself. A person ingratiated himself or herself with an audience—and thereby gained their trust and admiration—if he or she managed to create the impression that he or she was a person of intelligence, benevolence, and probity. Aristotle recognized that the ethical appeal could be the most potent of the three modes of persuasion. All of an orator's skill in convincing the intellect and moving the will of an audience could prove futile if the audience did not esteem, could not trust, the speaker. For this reason politicians seeking election to public office take such great care to create the proper image of themselves in the eyes of the voters. It was for this reason also that Cicero and Quintilian stressed the need for high moral character in the speaker. Quintilian defined the ideal orator as "a good man skilled in speaking." In his *Nicomachean Ethics,* Aristotle explored the *ēthos* proper for the individual; in his *Politics,* the *ēthos* proper for individuals living together in a society.

The method that the classical rhetoricians devised to aid the speaker in discovering matter for the three modes of appeal was the *topics. Topics* is the English translation of the Greek word *topoi* and the Latin word *loci.* Literally, *topos* or *locus* meant "place" or "region" (note our words *topography* and *locale*). In rhetoric, a topic was a place or store or thesaurus to which one resorted to find something to say on a given subject. More specifically, a topic was a general head or line of argument which suggested material from which proofs could be made. To put it another way, the topics constituted a method of probing one's subject to discover possible ways of developing that subject. Aristotle distinguished two kinds of topics: (1) the special topics (he called them *idioi topoi* or *eidē*); (2) the common topics (*koinoi topoi*). The special topics were those classes of argument appropriate to particular kinds of discourse. In other words, there were some kinds of arguments that were used exclusively in the law courts; some that were confined to the public forum; others that appeared only in ceremonial addresses. The common topics, on the other hand, were a fairly limited stock of arguments that could be used for any occasion or type of speech. Aristotle named four common topics: (1) more and less (the topic of degree); (2) the possible and the impossible; (3) past fact and future fact; (4) greatness and smallness (the topic of size as distinguished from the topic of degree). In the text itself we will see how the topics are put to work.

All of the considerations reviewed in the last two or three pages fell within the province of *inventio.* Chapter II, entitled "Discovery of Arguments," will be concerned with this aspect of rhetoric—how to "discover"' something to say on some given subject, which is the crucial problem for most writers. The chief reason for writers' inarticulateness on certain subjects is the lack of experience or reading background that can stock their reservoir of ideas. At other times, their inarticulateness stems from their inability to look into a subject to discover what they already know about the subject. Since *inventio* is a systematized way of turning up or generating ideas on some subject, writers may find this rhetorical approach helpful.

The second part of rhetoric was *dispositio* (Greek, *taxis*), which may be translated as "disposition," "arrangement," "organization." This was the division of rhetoric concerned with the effective and orderly arrangement of the parts of a written or spoken discourse. Once the ideas or arguments are discovered there remains the problem of selecting, marshalling, and organizing them with a view to effecting the end of the discourse.

In the simplest terms, one might say that any discourse needs a beginning, a middle, and an end; but this division is self-evident and not much help. Rhetoricians spelled out the divisions of a discourse more specifically and functionally. Aristotle held that there were really only two essential parts of a speech: the statement of the case and the proof; but he was ready to concede that in practice orators added two more parts: an introduction and a conclusion. Latin rhetoricians, like the author of the *Ad Herennium*, further refined these divisions, recognizing six parts: (1) the introduction (*exordium*); (2) the statement or exposition of the case under discussion (*narratio*); (3) the outline of the points or steps in the argument (*divisio*); (4) the proof of the case (*confirmatio*); (5) the refutation of the opposing arguments (*confutatio*); (6) the conclusion (*peroratio*).

Such a division may strike writers as being arbitrary, mechanical, and rigid. Two things may be said in defense of this conventional pattern. It did set forth clear principles of organization, and inexperienced writers need nothing so much as simple, definite principles to guide them in arrangement of material. Then too the rhetoricians allowed for some adjustments in this scheme. Accepting the Aristotelian notion of the "available means of persuasion," they acknowledge that on some occasions it was expedient to omit certain parts altogether (for instance, if one found it difficult to break down the opposing arguments, it might be advisable to omit the stage of *confutatio*) or to re-arrange some of the parts (for instance, it might be more effective to refute the opposing arguments *before* advancing one's own arguments).

Unquestionably, there is a close interrelation between *inventio* and *dispositio*, and in many rhetoric books these two divisions were treated under one head. Disposition was looked upon as just another aspect of invention; *inventio* was the originative aspect, and *dispositio* was the organizing aspect. As one may learn from the history of rhetoric in the Appendix, Peter Ramus and his followers, like Francis Bacon, wanted to relegate invention and disposition to the province of logic and to limit rhetoric to considerations of style, memory, and delivery. Chapter III of this text, entitled "Arrangement," will deal with this aspect of rhetoric.

The third part of rhetoric was *elocutio* (Greek, *lexis* or *hermēneia* or *phrasis*). The word *elocution* means something quite different to us from what it meant to the classical rhetorician. We associate the word with the act of speaking (hence, the elocution contest). This notion of speaking is, of course, implicit in the Latin verb from which this word stems, *loqui*, "to speak" (cf. Greek, *legein*, "to speak"). We have a number of English words based on this Latin verb: *loquacious*, *colloquial*, *eloquence, interlocutor.* It was after the revival of interest in delivery in the second half of the eighteenth century that the word *elocution* began to take on its present meaning. But for the classical rhetorician, *elocutio* meant "style."

Style is a difficult concept to define, although most of us feel we know what it is. Famous definitions of style, like Buffon's "style is the man," Swift's "proper words in proper places," Newman's "style is a thinking out into language," and Blair's "the peculiar manner in which a man expresses his conceptions," are apt, but they are just vague enough to tease us out of thought and just general enough to give us a sense for style without giving us a clear definition of it. None of the major rhetoricians attempted to give a definition of style, but most of them had a great deal to say about it; in fact, some of the Renaissance rhetorics were devoted exclusively to a consideration of style.

One of the points that elicited a great deal of discussion was the classification of styles. Various terms were used to name the kinds of style, but there was fundamental agreement about three levels of style. There was the *low* or *plain* style (*attenuata, subtile*); the *middle* or *forcible* style (*mediocris, robusta*); and the *high* or *florid* style (*gravis, florida*). Quintilian proposed that each of these styles was suited to one of the three functions that he assigned to rhetoric. The plain style was most appropriate for *instructing* (*docendi*); the middle for *moving* (*movendi*); and the high for *charming* (*delectandi*).

All rhetorical considerations of style involved some discussion of *choice of words,* usually under such heads as correctness, purity (for instance, the choice of native words rather than foreign words), simplicity, clearness, appropriateness, ornateness.

Another subject of consideration was the *composition or arrangement of words* in phrases or clauses (or, to use the rhetorical term, *periods*). Involved here were discussions of correct syntax or collocation of words; patterns of sentences (e.g., parallelism, antithesis); proper use of conjunctions and other correlating devices both within the sentence and between sentences; the euphony of sentences secured through the artful juxtaposition of pleasing vowel and consonant combinations and through the use of appropriate rhythmical patterns.

A great deal of attention was paid, of course, to *tropes* and *figures* (Greek, *schēmata,* hence the English term *schemes,* which was often used in place of *figures*). Since the concept of tropes and schemes is very complex, it is better that we defer any definition and illustration of these terms to the appropriate section of the text.

Also involved in considerations of style were arguments about (1) the functional vs. the embellishing character of style; (2) Asianism vs. Atticism; (3) the written style vs. the spoken style; (4) economy of words vs. copia of words. These points of discussion are rather peripheral matters, but it is remarkable how much time and energy the rhetoricians devoted to such controversies. The fourth chapter of this book will be devoted to consideration of style.

The fourth part of rhetoric was *memoria* (Greek, *mnēmē*), concerned with memorizing speeches. Of all the five parts of rhetoric, *memoria* was the one that received the least attention in the rhetoric books. The reason for the neglect of this aspect of rhetoric is probably that not much can be said, in a theoretical way, about the process of memorizing; and after rhetoric came to be concerned mainly with written discourse, there was no further need to deal with memorizing. This process did receive, however, some attention in the schools of rhetoric set up by the sophists. The orator's memory was trained largely through constant practice (just as professional actors today acquire an amazing facility in memorizing a script), but the rhetors did suggest various mnemonic devices that facilitated the memorizing of speeches. The courses that one sometimes sees advertised in newspapers or magazines—"I Can Give You a Retentive Memory in Thirty Days"—are modern manifestations of this division of rhetoric. There will be no consideration in this book of this aspect of rhetoric.

The fifth division of rhetoric was *pronuntiatio* (Greek, *hypokrisis*) or delivery. As in the case of *memoria,* the theory of delivery was conspicuously neglected in the rhetoric texts until the elocutionary movement began about the middle of the eighteenth century. But most rhetoricians would acknowledge the importance of effective delivery in the persuasive process. When Demosthenes, the greatest of the Greek orators, was asked what he considered to be the most important part of rhetoric, he replied, "Delivery, delivery, delivery." Despite the neglect of delivery in the rhetoric books, a great deal of attention was devoted to this aspect in the Greek and Roman schools of rhetoric. Skill in delivery can best be acquired, of course, not by listening to theoretical discussions of this art but by actual practice and by analyzing the delivery of others. Understandably enough, discussions of delivery, as well as of memory, tended to be even more neglected in rhetoric texts after the invention of printing, when most rhetorical training was directed primarily to written discourse.

Involved in the treatment of delivery was concern for the management of the voice and for gestures (*actio*). Precepts were laid down about the modulation of the voice for the proper pitch, volume, and emphasis and about pausing and phrasing. In regard to action, orators were trained in gesturing, in the proper stance and posture of the body, and in the management of the eyes and of facial expressions. What this all amounted to really was training in the art of acting, and it is significant that all the great orators in history have been great "hams."

There is no denying the importance of delivery in effecting the end that one sets for oneself. Many speeches and sermons, however well prepared and elegantly written, have fallen on deaf ears because of inept delivery. Writers lack the advantage a speaker enjoys because of their face-to-face contact with an audience and because of their vocal delivery; the only way in which writers can make up for this disadvantage is by the brilliance of their style.

THE THREE KINDS OF PERSUASIVE DISCOURSE

All rhetoricians distinguished three kinds of orations, and this tripartite classification is well-nigh exhaustive. First, there was *deliberative* oratory, also known as *political, hortative,* and *advisory,* in which one deliberated about public affairs, about anything that had to do with politics, in the Greek sense of that term—whether to go to war, whether to levy a tax, whether to enter into an alliance with a foreign power, whether to build a bridge or a reservoir or a temple. More generally, however, deliberative discourse is that in which we seek to persuade someone to do something or to accept our point of view, as in the two pieces we considered at the beginning of this chapter. According to Aristotle, political oratory was always concerned about *future* (the point at issue is something that we will or will not do); its special topics were the *expedient* and the *inexpedient;* and its means were *exhortation* and *dehortation.*

Second, there was *forensic* oratory, sometimes referred to as *legal* or *judicial* oratory. This was the oratory of lawyers in the courtroom, but it can be extended to cover any kind of discourse in which a person seeks to defend or condemn someone's actions. (Richard Nixon's famous "Checkers" speech before a nationwide television audience can be considered as an example of forensic rhetoric; and Newman's *Apologia Pro Vita Sua* is another example of forensic discourse.) Forensic oratory, according to Aristotle, was concerned with *past* time (court trials are always concerned with actions or crimes that took place in the past); its special topics were *justice* and *injustice;* and its means were *accusation* and *defense.*

Third, there was *epideictic* oratory. This species has had a variety of other titles: *demonstrative, declamatory, panegyrical, ceremonial.* It is the oratory of display, the kind of oratory exemplified in the *Gettysburg Address* and in the old-fashioned Fourth of July speeches. In this kind of discourse, one is not so much concerned with persuading an audience as with pleasing it or inspiring it. *Ceremonial* discourse—the term we use in this text—is the most "literary" and usually the most ornate of the three kinds of discourse. Aristotle had to strain to fit a proper time-province to this form of oratory, but in the interests of neatness he laid it down that ceremonial oratory was concerned primarily with the *present.* Its special topics were *honor* and *dishonor,* and its means were *praise* and *blame.* The ancients made no provision in their rhetorics for sermons or homiletics. But later, when rhetoric was studied in a Christian culture, the art of preaching was usually considered under the head of epideictic oratory—even though preachers are also concerned with people's past and future actions.

THE RELEVANCE AND IMPORTANCE OF RHETORIC FOR OUR TIMES

The kind of complicated, formalized system of rhetoric described in the previous sections may seem to be remote from the concerns and needs of contemporary society. Indeed, some exercises that students in Greek and Roman schools were subjected to are totally dispensable. Practices and principles should not be retained simply because they are venerable with age. They should be retained only if they prove relevant and useful.

Let it be said, first of all, that rhetoric is an inescapable activity in our lives. Every day, we either use rhetoric or are exposed to it. Everyone living in community with other people is inevitably a rhetorician. A parent constantly uses rhetoric on a child; a teacher, on his or her students; a salesperson, on customers; a supervisor, on workers. During every half hour that we spend in front of a television set, we are subjected three or four times to somebody's efforts to get us to buy something. During election time, we are bombarded by candidates' appeals for our vote. Even when we are driving on the streets and highways, our eyes are constantly assaulted by sales pitches on huge billboards.

Advertising may be the most ubiquitous example of an activity that practices what Aristotle preached. But many other fields of endeavor in modern life rely on rhetoric too. The diplomat is a traveling rhetorician with portfolio. The public-relations agent is a practitioner of ceremonial rhetoric, that variety of rhetoric that seeks to reflect credit on a person or an institution. Law is such a many-faceted profession today that many lawyers never get a chance to practice the forensic brand of rhetoric in the courtroom; but even those lawyers whose principal function is to prepare briefs for the Clarence Darrows of the courtroom can be said to be engaged in the *inventio* and *dispositio* aspects of rhetoric. Insurance agents and sales personnel of various kinds practice deliberative rhetoric, often very effectively, every day. Preachers, press-agents, senators and representatives, counsellors, union leaders, business executives, lobbyists are as actively exercising their rhetorical skills today as they ever were.

There are some forms of rhetoric practiced today that we regard with suspicion, even disdain. One of these is propaganda. The term *propaganda* was once a neutral sort, signifying the dissemination of truth. But because some people have used propaganda for unscrupulous purposes, *propaganda* has taken on decidedly unfavorable connotations. Closely allied to this disreputable form of rhetoric is demagoguery. The names of the most successful of the twentieth-century demagogues are etched so deeply into our memories that they need not be specified here. These were the exploiters of specious arguments, half-truths, and rank emotional appeals to gain personal advantage rather than to promote the public welfare. Another variety of dangerous rhetoric is brainwashing. A definitive analysis of this diabolical technique has yet to be written, but a beginning has been made in the terrifying final chapters of George Orwell's novel *1984.* Another term has been taken from Orwell's novel to designate another dangerous form of rhetoric, *doublespeak*—a deliberate attempt to use language in such a way as to deceive or confuse listeners or readers. A good argument for an intensive study of rhetoric is that citizens might thereby be put on their guard against the onslaughts of these vicious forms of persuasion.

If "rhetoric" is such a pervasive activity in contemporary society, it behooves us to be aware of the basic strategies and principles of this ancient art. If nothing else, a knowledge of this art will equip us to respond critically to the rhetorical efforts of others in both the oral and written forms. As originally conceived, rhetoric was primarily a synthetic art—an art for "building up," for "composing," something. But rhetoric can also be used as an analytical art—an art for "breaking down" what has been composed. As such, it can make us better readers. As Malcolm Cowley once pointed out, the New Criticism of writers like Cleanth Brooks and Robert Penn Warren represented an application of rhetorical principles to the close reading of poetic texts. Mortimer Adler's *How to Read a Book* presented a rhetorical technique for the reading of expository and argumentative prose. Wayne C. Booth, in his book *The Rhetoric of Fiction,* has shown us the subtle operations of rhetoric in such narrative forms as the short story and the novel. And a knowledge of rhetoric can help us to respond critically and appreciatively to advertisements, commercials, political messages, satires, irony, and doublespeak of all varieties.

Rhetoric can also assist us in becoming more effective writers. One of the chief values of rhetoric, conceived of as a system for gathering, selecting, arranging, and expressing our material, is that it represents a *positive* approach to the problems of writing. Students have too often been inhibited in their writing by the negative approach to composition—don't do this, beware of that. Classical rhetoric too had its negative prescriptions, but, in the main, it offered positive advice to help writers in the composition of a specific kind of discourse directed to a definite audience for a particular purpose. Rhetoric cannot, of course, tell us what we must do in any and every situation. No art can provide that kind of advice. But rhetoric can lay down the general principles that writers can adapt to fit a particular situation. At least, it can provide writers with a set of procedures and criteria that can guide them in making strategic decisions in the composition process.

Students may fear that an elaborately systemitized approach to composition will inhibit rather than facilitate writing. There is no denying that formula can retard and has retarded inventiveness and creativity. But to admit that formula *can* inhibit writers is not to admit that it invariably does. Almost every one of the major English writers, from the Renaissance through at least the eighteenth century—Chaucer, Jonson, Shakespeare, Milton, Dryden, Pope, Swift, Burke—had been subjected to an intensive rhetoric course in their grammar school or university. If one cannot claim that the study of rhetoric made them great writers, one might yet venture to say that the study of rhetoric did not prevent them from becoming great writers and might even have made them better writers than they would have been on genius alone.

Lest any false hopes be raised, however, let it be affirmed that this adaptation of classical rhetoric offers no magic formula for success in writing. Students will have to work hard to profit from the instruction offered in this book, for it is not all easy to understand, and what is learned must be applied.

The road to eloquence is a hard road and a lonely road, and the journey is not for the faint-hearted. But if, as we are told, the ability to use words to communicate thoughts and feelings is our most distinctively human accomplishment, there can be few satisfactions in life that can match the pride a person feels when he or she has attained mastery over words. As Quintilian said, "Therefore let us seek wholeheartedly that true majesty of expression, the fairest gift of God to man, without which all things are struck dumb and robbed both of present glory and the immortal acclaim of posterity; and let us press on to whatever is best, because, if we do this, we shall either reach the summit or at least see many others far beneath us."

MIKE ROSE (b. 1944)

The Discourse of Academics

CONSIDER THIS:

Born to immigrant parents and raised in South Central Los Angeles, Mike Rose is author of *Lives on the Boundary,* a book-length literacy narrative and study of schooling. A professor at UCLA, he has also taught at the grade school and high school levels. Rose believes that "America is being created" in classrooms around the country. He came to that conclusion, for him mainly a positive one, by observing teacher and student interactions in a number of different settings in public schools across the United States. He describes his research methodology this way: "I am generally interested in thinking and learning and the various methods we use to study, foster, and write about them." Further, he says, "I'm interested in ways to bridge or combine modes of inquiry. How can we in principled ways rethink the barriers that often exist among disciplines, among methodologies, and among scholarly and non-scholarly languages?"

As you begin to read this excerpt, think about your own definition of "school talk" or, more elegantly, the language used by scholars in the academy. That is, do you speak in a classroom the way you speak outside of the classroom? If not, what prompts any language shifts you make? Did you ever, as Rose suggests, enter a classroom and feel puzzled by what was going on? Similarly, have you ever entered a new course and listened to the professor on the first day and felt sure, simply by the way she discussed her topic, that you were about to be left at the station? What was confusing, confounding, or unexpected about the professor's discussion in such an instance? Even if you feel comfortable entering new communities where specialists speak in field-specific language, what techniques do you employ to increase your chances of getting along, understanding, and finding a way to talk?

The discourse of academics is marked by terms and expressions that represent an elaborate set of shared concepts and orientations: alienation, authoritarian personality, the social construction of the self, determinism, hegemony, equilibrium, intentionality, recursion, reinforcement, and so on. This language weaves through so many lectures and textbooks, is integral to so many learned discussions, that it's easy to forget what a foreign language it can be. Freshmen are often puzzled by the talk they hear in their classrooms, but what's important to note here is that their problem is not simply one of limited vocabulary. If we see the problem as knowing or not knowing a list of words, as some quick-fix remedies suggest, then we'll force glossaries on students and miss the complexity of the issue. Take, for example, *authoritarian personality.* The average university freshman will know what *personality* means and can figure out *authoritarian;*. the difficulty will come from a lack of familiarity with the conceptual resonances that *authoritarian personality* has acquired in the discussions of sociologists and psychologists and political scientists. Discussion . . . you could almost define a university education as an initiation into a variety of powerful ongoing discussions, an initiation that can occur only through the repeated use of a new language in the company of others. More than anything, this was the opportunity people like Father Albertson, my Shakespeare teacher at Loyola, provided to me. The more comfortable and skillful students become with this kind of influential talk, the more they will be included in further conversations and given access to further conceptual tools and resources—the acquisition of which virtually defines them as members of an intellectual community.

All students require such an opportunity. But those coming to the university with less-than-privileged educations, especially those from the lower classes, are particularly in need. They are less likely to have participated, in any extended way, in such discussions in the past. They won't have the confidence or the moves to enter it, and can begin to feel excluded, out of place, put off by a language they can't command. Their social marginality, then, is reinforced by discourse and, as happened to me during my first year at Loyola, they might well withdraw, retreat to silence.

This sense of linguistic exclusion can be complicated by various cultural differences. When I was growing up, I absorbed an entire belief system—with its own characteristic terms and expressions—from the worried conversations of my parents, from the things I heard and saw on South Vermont, from the priest's fiery tales. I thought that what happened to people was preordained, that ability was a fixed thing, that there was one true religion. I had rigid notions about social roles, about the structure of society, about gender, about politics. There used to be a rickety vending machine at Manchester and Vermont that held a Socialist Workers newspaper. I'd walk by it and feel something alive and injurious: The paper was malevolent and should be destroyed. Imagine, then, the difficulty I had when, at the beginning of my senior year at Mercy High, Jack MacFarland tried to explain Marxism to us. How could I absorb the language of atheistic materialism and class struggle when it seemed so strange and pernicious? It wasn't just that Marxist terms-of-art were unfamiliar; they felt assaultive. What I did was revert to definitions of the social order more familiar to me, and Mr. MacFarland had to draw them out of me and have me talk about them and consider them alongside Marx's vision and terminology, examining points of conflict and points of possible convergence. It was only then that I could appropriate Marx's strange idiom.

Once you start to think about underprepared students in terms of these overlapping problem areas, all sorts of solutions present themselves. Students need more opportunities to write about what they're learning and guidance in the techniques and conventions of that writing—what I got from my mentors at Loyola. They need more opportunities to develop the writing strategies that are an intimate part of academic inquiry and what has come to be called critical literacy—comparing, synthesizing, analyzing—the sort of thing I gave the veterans. They need opportunities to talk about what they're learning: to test their ideas, reveal their assumptions, talk through the places where new knowledge clashes with ingrained belief. They need a chance, too, to talk about the ways they may have felt excluded from all this in the past and may feel threatened by it in the present. They need the occasion to rise above the fragmented learning the lower-division curriculum encourages, a place within a course or outside it to hear about and reflect on the way a particular discipline conducts its inquiry: Why, for example, *do* so many psychologists who study thinking rely on computer modeling? Why is mathematics so much a part of economics? And they need to be let in on the secret talk, on the shared concepts and catchphrases of Western liberal learning.

There is nothing magical about this list of solutions. In fact, in many ways, it reflects the kind of education a privileged small number of American students have received for some time. The basic question our society must ask, then, is: How many or how few do we want to have this education? If students didn't get it before coming to college—and most have not—then what are we willing to do to give it to them now? Chip and I used to talk about our special programs as attempts to create an Honors College for the underprepared. People would smile as we spoke, but, as our students would have said, we were serious as a heart attack. The remedial programs we knew about did a disservice to their students by thinking of them as *remedial.* We wanted to try out another perspective and see what kind of program it would yield. What would happen if we thought of our students' needs and goals in light of the comprehensive and ambitious program structures more often reserved for the elite?

GERALD GRAFF (b. 1937)

Disliking Books at an Early Age

CONSIDER THIS:

Gerald Graff was born in Chicago and has taught at Northwestern University and the University of Chicago. Graff won the American Book Award in 1993 for *Beyond the Culture Wars.* Graff ponders the differences between academic writing and writing for the general public. In an interview for the *Chicago Humanities Journal,* he said, "When I write, it often feels as if I am trying to rediscover the 'lay' person I was before I became a professional academic, as if I am trying to write that lay person's perspective into my text. I figure that if I can recover and incorporate that self into my text, I'll appeal to a wider audience as well as to an academic audience and will avoid the oppressive 'in-group' tone of so much academic writing."

Graff also considers similar issues when starting out to write for the larger audience. In his preface to *Beyond the Culture Wars,* he states: "Writing for a general audience is not an easy thing for the average academic. As writers we academics are spoiled. We are used to writing for other academics, usually those in our particular fields, and this protection from outside perspectives lets us fall into cozy ways of thinking and expressing ourselves." Do these comments shed some light on Graff's statements about his early dislike of books and its effect on his teaching literature? Does Mike Rose's discussion of academic discourse shed some light on Graff's assertions? What parts, if any, of Graff's narrative do you respond to most?

I like to think I have a certain advantage as a teacher of literature because when I was growing up I disliked and feared books. My youthful aversion to books showed a fine impartiality, extending across the whole spectrum of literature, history, philosophy, science, and what was known by then (the late 1940s) as social studies. But had I been forced to choose, I would have singled out literature and history as the reading I disliked most. Science at least had some discernible practical use, and you could have fun solving the problems in the textbooks with their clear-cut answers. Literature and history had no apparent application to my experience, and any boy in my school who had cultivated them—I can't recall one who did—would have marked himself as a sissy.

As a middle-class Jew growing up in an ethnically mixed Chicago neighborhood, I was already in danger of being beaten up daily by rougher working-class boys. Becoming a bookworm would only have given them a decisive reason for beating me up. Reading and studying were more permissible for girls, but they, too, had to be careful not to get too intellectual, lest they acquire the stigma of being "stuck up."

In *Lives on the Boundary*, a remarkable autobiography of the making of an English teacher, Mike Rose describes how the "pain and confusion" of his working-class youth made "school and knowledge" seem a saving alternative. Rose writes of feeling "freed, as if I were untying fetters," by his encounter with certain college teachers, who helped him recognize that "an engagement with ideas could foster competence and lead me out into the world." Coming at things from my middle-class perspective, however, I took for granted a freedom that school, knowledge, and engagement with ideas seemed only to threaten.

My father, a literate man, was frustrated by my refusal to read anything besides comic books, sports magazines, and the John R. Tunis and Clair Bee sports novels. I recall his once confining me to my room until I finished a book on the voyages of Magellan, but try as I might, I could do no better than stare bleakly at the pages. I could not, as we would later say, "relate to" Magellan or to any of the other books my father brought home—detective stories, tales of war and heroism, adventure stories with adolescent heroes (the Hardy Boys, *Hans Brinker, or The Silver Skates*), stories of scientific discovery (Paul de Kruif's *The Microbe Hunters*), books on current events. Nothing worked.

It was understood, however, that boys of my background would go to college and that once there we would get serious and buckle down. For some, "getting serious" meant prelaw, premed, or a major in business to prepare for taking over the family business. My family did not own a business, and law and medicine did not interest me, so I drifted by default into the nebulous but conveniently noncommittal territory of the liberal arts. I majored in English.

At this point the fear of being beaten up if I were caught having anything to do with books was replaced by the fear of flunking out of college if I did not learn to deal with them. But though I dutifully did my homework and made good grades (first at the University of Illinois, Chicago branch, then at the University of Chicago, from which I graduated in 1959), I continued to find "serious" reading painfully difficult and alien. My most vivid recollections of college reading are of assigned classics I failed to finish: *The Iliad* (in the Richmond Baltimore translation); *The Autobiography of Benvenuto Cellini,* a major disappointment after the paperback jacket's promise of "a lusty classic of Renaissance ribaldry"; E. M. Forster's *A Passage to India,* sixty agonizing pages of which I managed to slog through before giving up. Even Hemingway, Steinbeck, Fitzgerald, whose contemporary world was said to be "close to my own experience," left me cold. I saw little there that did resemble my experience.

Even when I had done the assigned reading, I was often tongue-tied and embarrassed when called on. What was unclear to me was what I was supposed to *say* about literary works, and why. Had I been born a decade or two earlier, I might have come to college with the rudiments of a literate vocabulary for talking about culture that some people older than I acquired through family, high school, or church. As it was, "cultured" phrases seemed effete and sterile to me. When I was able to produce the kind of talk that was required in class, the intellectualism of it came out sounding stilted and hollow in my mouth. If *Cliffs Notes* and other such crib sheets for the distressed had yet come into existence, with their ready-to-copy summaries of widely taught literary works, I would have been an excellent customer. (As it was, I did avail myself of the primitive version then in existence called *Masterplots.*)

What first made literature, history, and other intellectual pursuits seem attractive to me was exposure to critical debates. There was no single conversion experience, but a gradual transformation over several years, extending into my first teaching positions, at the University of New Mexico and then Northwestern University. But one of the first sparks I remember was a controversy over *The Adventures of Huckleberry Finn* that arose in a course during my junior year in college. On first attempt, Twain's novel was just another assigned classic that I was too bored to finish. I could see little connection between my Chicago upbringing and Huck's pre–Civil War adventures with a runaway slave on a raft up the Mississippi.

My interest was aroused, however, when our instructor mentioned that the critics had disagreed over the merits of the last part of the novel. He quoted Ernest Hemingway's remark that "if you read [the novel] you must stop where the nigger Jim is stolen by the boys. This is the real end. The rest is cheating." According to this school of thought, the remainder of the book trivializes the quest for Jim's freedom that has motivated the story up to that point. This happens first when Jim becomes an object of Tom Sawyer's slapstick humor, then when it is revealed that unbeknownst to Huck, the reader, and himself, Jim has already been freed by his benevolent owner, so that the risk we have assumed Jim and Huck to be under all along has really been no risk at all.

Like the critics, our class divided over the question: Did Twain's ending vitiate the book's profound critique of racism, as Hemingway's charge of cheating implied? Cheating in my experience up to then was something students did, an unthinkable act for a famous author. It was a revelation to me that famous authors were capable not only of mistakes but of ones that even lowly undergraduates might be able to point out. When I chose to write my term paper on the dispute over the ending, my instructor suggested I look at several critics on the opposing sides—T. S. Eliot and Lionel Trilling, who defended the ending, and Leo Marx, who sided with Hemingway.

Reading the critics was like picking up where the class discussion had left off, and I gained confidence from recognizing that my classmates and I had had thoughts that, however stumbling our expression of them, were not too far from the thoughts of famous published critics. I went back to the novel again and to my surprise found myself rereading it with an excitement I had never felt before with a serious book. Having the controversy over the ending in mind, I now had some issues *to watch out for* as I read, issues that reshaped the way I read the earlier chapters as well as the later ones and focused my attention. And having issues to watch out for made it possible not only to concentrate, as I had not been able to do earlier, but to put myself into the text—to read with a sense of personal engagement that I had not felt before. Reading the novel with the voices of the critics running through my mind, I found myself thinking things that I might say about what I was reading, things that may have belonged partly to the critics but also now belonged to me. It was as if having a stock of things to look for and to say about a literary work had somehow made it possible for me to read one.

One of the critics had argued that what was at issue in the debate over *Huckleberry Finn* was not just the novel's value but its cultural significance: If *Huckleberry Finn* was contradictory or confused in its attitude toward race, then what did that say about the culture that had received the novel as one of its representative cultural documents and had made Twain a folk hero? This critic had also made the intriguing observation—I found out only later that it was a critical commonplace at the time—that judgments about the novel's aesthetic value could not be separated from judgments about its moral substance. I recall taking in both this critic's arguments and the cadence of the phrases in which they were couched; perhaps it would not be so bad after all to become the sort of person who talked about "cultural contradictions" and the "inseparability of form and content." Perhaps even mere literary-critical talk could give you a certain power in the real world. As the possibility dawned on me that reading and intellectual discussion might actually have something to do with my real life, I became less embarrassed about using intellectual formulas.

It was through exposure to such critical reading and discussion over a period of time that I came to catch the literary bug, eventually choosing the vocation of teaching. This was not the way it is supposed to happen. In the standard story of academic vocation that we like to tell ourselves, the germ is first planted by an early experience of literature itself. The future teacher is initially inspired by some primary experience of a great book and only subsequently acquires the secondary, derivative skills of critical discussion. A teacher may be involved in instilling this inspiration, but only a teacher who seemingly effaces himself or herself before the text. Any premature or excessive acquaintance with secondary critical discourse, and certainly with its sectarian debates, is thought to be a corrupting danger, causing one to lose touch with the primary passion for literature.

This is the charge leveled against the current generation of literature teachers, who are said to have become so obsessed with sophisticated critical theories that they have lost the passion they once had for literature itself. They have been seduced by professionalism, drawn away from a healthy absorption in literature to the sickly fascination with analysis and theory and to the selfish advancement of their careers.

This hostility to recent theory would not have been so powerful, however, if it were not overlaid on an older set of resentments that long predate the rise of deconstruction and poststructuralism, resentments at literature's having become an academic "field" to begin with. Today's attacks on literary theory are often really attacks on literary criticism, or at least on criticism of the intensely analytic kind that academics practice, which has always been suspected of coming between readers (and students) and the primary experience of literature itself. This resentment is rooted in anxieties about the increasing self-consciousness of modern life, which often leaves us feeling that we are never quite living but only endlessly talking about it, too often in some abstract professional vocabulary. The anxieties are expressed in our romantic literary tradition, which protests against the urban forms of sophistication that, it is believed, cause us to lose touch with the innocence of childhood and our creative impulses.

To those who have never reconciled themselves to the academicization of literature, the seeming overdevelopment of academic criticism with its obtrusive methodology and its endless disputes among interpretations and theories seems a betrayal not just of literature and the common reader but of the professor's own original passion for literature. In a recent letter to an intellectual journal one writer suggests that we should be concerned less about the oft-lamented common reader whom academic critics have deserted than about "the souls of the academics and literati themselves, who, as a result of social and professional pressures, have lost touch with the inner impulses that drew them to the world of books in the first place." What the writer of this letter cannot imagine is that someone might enter academic literary study because he actually *likes* thinking and talking in an analytical or theoretical way about books and that such a person might see his acceptance of "professional pressures" not as a betrayal of the "inner impulses" that drew him "to the world of books in the first place" but as a way to fulfill those impulses.

The standard story ascribes innocence to the primary experience of literature and sees the secondary experience of professional criticism as corrupting. In my case, however, things had evidently worked the other way around: I had to be corrupted first in order to experience innocence. It was only when I was introduced to a critical debate about *Huckleberry Finn* that my helplessness in the face of the novel abated and I could experience a personal reaction to it. Getting into immediate contact with the text was for me a curiously triangular business; I could not do it directly but needed a conversation of other readers to give me the issues and terms that made it possible to respond.

As I think back on it now, it was as if the critical conversation I needed had up to then been withheld from me, on the ground that it could only interfere with my direct access to literature itself. The assumption was that leaving me alone with literary texts themselves, uncontaminated by the interpretations and theories of professional critics, would enable me to get on the closest possible terms with those texts. But being alone with the texts only left me feeling bored and helpless, since I had no language with which to make them mine. On the one hand, I was being asked to speak a foreign language—literary criticism—while on the other hand, I was being protected from that language, presumably for my own safety.

The moral I draw from this experience is that our ability to read well depends more than we think on our ability to *talk well* about what we read. Our assumptions about what is "primary" and "secondary" in the reading process blind us to what actually goes on. Many literate people learned certain ways of talking about books so long ago that they have forgotten they ever had to learn them. These people therefore fail to understand the reading problems of the struggling students who have still not acquired a critical vocabulary.

The standard story of how we learn to read provides little help in dealing with such problems. Seeing criticism (and critical debate) as a distraction from the "primary" experience of literature itself, the standard story implies that the business of teaching is basically simple: Just put the student in front of a good book, provide teachers who are encouraging and helpful, and the rest presumably will take care of itself. The traditional maxim that sums up this view is that a good book "essentially teaches itself." The great teacher is one who knows how to let the book teach itself. And it is true that in the spell cast by such a teacher, it often *seems* as if the work is itself speaking directly to the student without intervention from the teacher's interpretations and theories. But this spell is an illusion. If books really taught themselves, there would be no reason to attend classes; students could simply stay home and read them on their own.

Nevertheless, the standard story remains seductive. Much of the appeal of Allan Bloom's *The Closing of the American Mind* lies in its eloquent restatement of the standard story, with its reassuringly simple view of reading and teaching: "a liberal education means reading certain generally recognized classic texts, just reading them, letting them dictate what the questions are and the method of approaching them—not forcing them into categories we make up, not treating them as historical products, but trying to read them as their authors wished them to be read." What has gone wrong, Bloom suggests, is that instead of letting the texts themselves dictate the questions we ask about them, a generation of overly professionalized teachers has elevated its own narcissistic interests over those of the author and the students. These teachers, as Bloom puts it, engage in "endless debates about methods—among them Freudian criticism, Marxist criticism, New Criticism, Structuralism and Deconstructionism, and many others, all of which have in common the premise that what Plato or Dante had to say about reality is unimportant."

It sounds so commonsensical that only a desiccated academic could disagree. What could be more obvious than the difference between "just" reading books, as ordinary readers have always done, and imposing theories and isms on books, as methodology-crazed academics do? The question, however, is whether anyone ever "just" reads a book the way Bloom describes. We need go no further than Bloom's own quoted statements to see that he himself does not practice the doctrine he preaches. When Bloom invokes the names of Plato and Dante, he does *not* let these authors dictate the questions that govern his discussion but "forces" them into categories he, Allan Bloom, with his twentieth-century preoccupations, has "made up." After all, what did Plato and Dante know about Freudians, Marxists, cultural relativists, and the other contemporary targets of Bloom's polemic? In using Plato and Dante to attack the intellectual and educational trends of his own time, Bloom is not reading these writers as they wished to be read but is *applying* them to a set of contexts they did not and could not have anticipated. This is not to say that Bloom is unfaithful to Plato's text, only that he does not passively take dictation from Plato's text but actively selects from it for his own purposes—just as he accuses theorists of doing.

The philosopher Richard Rorty has succinctly pointed out the trouble with Bloom's "just read the books" theory. Rorty acknowledges that interpreters are obliged "to give authors a run for their money," respecting "an author's way of talking and thinking, trying to put ourselves in her shoes." He argues, however, that "it is not clear how we can avoid forcing books into 'categories we make up. . . .'" We cannot help reading books, Rorty says, "with questions in mind—not questions dictated by the books—but questions we have previously, if vaguely, formulated." Rorty's point is not that reading is merely subjective but that it is inevitably *selective.* It is not that any reading of Plato is as good as any other but that even the most reliable reading has to select certain aspects of the text to emphasize, and the selection will be conditioned by the contingent situations in which the text is read. I would restate Rorty's point this way: As readers we are necessarily concerned with *both* the questions posed by the text and the questions we bring to it from our own differing interests and cultural backgrounds. Bloom thinks he can chose between "just reading" Plato and Dante and applying a "method" to them as do academic Freudians and Marxists. But Bloom's way of reading, which is influenced by his mentor the philosopher Leo Strauss, is as much a "method" as any other, bringing its special set of interests and principles of selection that are not dictated by Plato or Dante.

In teaching any text, one necessarily teaches an interpretation of it. This seems so obvious as to be hardly worth restating, but what follows from it is not obvious and is resisted violently by many who oppose the spread of theory. It follows that what literature teachers teach is not literature but criticism, or literature as it is filtered through a grid of analysis, interpretation, and theory. "Remarks are not literature," said Gertrude Stein in a now-celebrated observation, and Stein was right: Teachers cannot avoid interposing "remarks" between literature and their students—remarks, we hope, that illuminate the works and help our students take personal possession of them, but remarks nevertheless.

If teachers cannot avoid translating the literature they teach into some critical language or other, neither can students, for criticism is the language students are expected to speak and are punished for not speaking well. Inevitably the students who do well in school and college are those who learn to talk more or less like their teachers, who learn to produce something resembling intellectualspeak.

By what process do we imagine students will learn this language? The assumption seems to be that it will happen by a kind of osmosis, as students internalize the talk that goes on in class until they are able to produce a reasonable facsimile of it. However, as a recent textbook writer, Gordon Harvey, points out, not all students "can make this translation, since it requires that they intuit a whole set of intellectual moves and skills . . . too basic for experienced writers to notice themselves carrying out." The polite fiction that students will learn to make the "intellectual moves" by being in the presence of them for several hours a week is usually just that, a polite fiction.

Again, the problem is that what students are able to say about a text depends not just on the text but on their relation to a critical community of readers, which over time has developed an agenda of problems, issues, and questions with respect to both specific authors and texts and to culture generally. When students are screened from this critical community and its debates, or when they experience only the fragmentary and disconnected versions of it represented by a series of courses, they are likely to either be tongue-tied in the face of the text itself or to respond in a limited personal idiom, like the student who "relates to" Hamlet because he, too, had a mean stepfather.

In short, reading books with comprehension, making arguments, writing papers, and making comments in a class discussion are *social* activities. They involve entering into a cultural or disciplinary conversation, a process not unlike initiation into a social club. We obscure this social dimension when we conceive of education as if it were a process of contemplating important truths, values, and "cultural literacy" information in a vacuum and consequently treat such student tasks as reading assignments, making arguments, writing papers, and entering class discussions as if they were a matter of performing abstract procedures in a social void. Choose a topic that interests you, freshman writers are told; organize your paper logically around a central idea, and remember to support your thesis with specific illustration and evidence. Such advice is usually more paralyzing than helpful because it factors out the social conversation that reading, writing, and arguing must be part of in order to become personally meaningful.

Choosing a topic that interests you or making an effective argument depends on having a sense of what *other people* are saying, of what the state of the discussion is. Before my exposure to the critical debate on *Huckleberry Finn,* I had been trying to generate that discussion out of myself, something I did not know how to do. Exposure to the debate made me less of an outsider, provided me with a social community that gave my reading stimulus and direction. I could now discover what my teachers meant by "enjoying literature" because this had ceased to be a matter of vainly struggling to achieve some mysterious and rarefied experience. Relation to a community made the intimacy of literary experience possible.

JOHN AGARD (b. 1949)

Listen Mr. Oxford Don

CONSIDER THIS:

John Agard was born in Guyana, and as a young man taught French, English, and Latin. He also worked as a librarian, editor, and newspaper writer. He moved to England in 1977 and concentrated on writing poetry. He won the Cuban Casa de las Americas prize for poetry in 1982 and a Paul Hamlyn Award in 1997. He writes poetry and stories for people of all ages. Part of him, however, never left the Caribbean: "[M]y childhood in Guyana formed my consciousness. It is part of my mental landscape." Caribbean influences in syntax, meter, and subject matter permeate his work. Much of Agard's work also has an irresistible sense of whimsy and playfulness about it. When asked about his poetry's beginnings in a BBC interview, Agard gives a hint of this when he says, "I can't recall my first poem, but an early one was about a schoolboy in the classroom thinking about how he had to take his exams. I really hadn't studied for the exams so I was playing around, and I began writing a poem. I was about 16."

Think about your own connections to classrooms and the language of classrooms. Supportive teachers like to remind you that "There are no dumb questions," but most learners still feel that there are questions we shouldn't ask. Can you think of one time you wanted to but didn't ask for clarification in a classroom? Share these moments in a group. After reading Agard's poem, think of what sort of a poem you could make to address one of those moments; what would be your own, "Listen . . ." poem? Or, you could draw a poem topic from any of the readings in this chapter. What poem might Gerald Graff or Rita Dove or Fan Shen write to embody one of the points made in their essays?

Me not no Oxford don
me a simple immigrant
from Clapham Common
I didn't graduate
I immigrate

But listen Mr Oxford don
I'm a man on de run
and a man on de run
is a dangerous one

I ent have no gun
I ent have no knife
but mugging de Queen's English
is the story of my life

I don't need no axe
to split/ up yu syntax
I don't need no hammer
to mash/ up yu grammar

I warning you Mr Oxford don
I'm a wanted man
and a wanted man
is a dangerous one

Dem accuse me of assault
on de Oxford dictionary/
imagine a concise peaceful man like me/
dem want me serve time
for inciting rhyme to riot
but I tekking it quiet
down here in Clapham Common

I'm not a violent man Mr Oxford don
I only armed wit mih human breath
but human breath is a dangerous weapon
So mek dem send one big word after me
I ent serving no jail sentence
I slashing suffix in self-defence
I bashing future wit present tense
and if necessary

I making de Queen's English accessary/to my offence

RITA DOVE (b. 1952)

To Make a Prairie

CONSIDER THIS:

Rita Dove was born in Akron, Ohio, and earned an M.F.A from the University of Iowa. She has been the Poet Laureate of the United States and has won the

Pulitzer Prize for her poetry, among numerous other honors and awards. Currently, she is Commonwealth Professor of English at the University of Virginia. Dove does not necessarily consider herself a "black poet" or a "woman poet." Upon winning the Charles Frankel Prize, she said, "There are times when I am a black woman who happens to be a poet and times when I am a poet who happens to be black. There are also times when I am more conscious of being a mother or a member of my generation. It's so hopelessly confused that I don't make a big deal out of it." Dove is concerned about the arts' place in the everyday world and suggests that art can take a more prominent role than she previously thought. In an interview for Bookreporter.com she said, "For many years, I thought a poem was a whisper overheard, not an aria heard. I have come to realize there is also a poem I can write that has a larger presence."

How important are the arts to you? What activity do you define as an "art," and how vital is it to your sense of community? Are you an artist? Why or why not? If so, how do you define yourself as such? If not, what "art" would you like to become involved in (wishful thinking is fine here, even encouraged)? Why? What community would that place you in, and what would your audience expect from you?

When I was inducted into Phi Beta Kappa at Miami University (Ohio) two decades ago this year, many of the presiding faculty were aghast when I answered their query concerning my career plans with "I want to be a poet." The implied sentiment was "How can you throw away your education?"—as if declaring one's intention to be a poet was analogous to putting on a dunce cap.

Phi Beta Kappa's motto, "philosophy or the love of knowledge is the guide of life," puts it well. Wisdom is the *guide* of life—not the goal. Intelligence is a desirable commodity, but, as one character in Madeleine L'Engle's book *A Wind in the Door* says, "The naked intellect is an extraordinarily inaccurate instrument." Intellectual achievement requires imagination.

I want to discuss here an activity which, although often smiled at or benevolently dismissed in children, is barely tolerated in adolescents, rarely commended in the boardroom, and, to the best of my knowledge, never encouraged in schools—but without which no bridges would soar, no light bulbs burn, and no Greek warships set out upon Homer's "wine-dark sea." That activity is daydreaming—an activity so prevalent that we had to jerryrig a word, an oxymoron of sorts, because, so to speak, the default for dreaming is night. *Daydreaming.* There's a loftier expression for it, of course—reverie. But "daydreaming" is the word that truly sets us adrift. It melts on the tongue. The French phenomenologist Gaston Bachelard speaks of a "dreaming consciousness" and calls poetic reverie a "phenomenology of the soul," a condition in which "the mind is able to relax, but . . . the soul keeps watch, with no tension, calmed and active."

Many of you have heard the story of Thomas Edison's method for courting inspiration: whenever he became stymied, he would take a nap, and often the solution to his problem would come to him in his sleep. Herbert Marcuse calls this kind of daydreaming the drive toward *Eros,* as opposed to—what else?—

Thanatos, or death. And what is the ultimate expression of this drive toward Eros? Child's play, which Marcuse defines by saying that playing as a child plays is its own goal, its own contentment, whereas work serves a purpose that lies outside the self.

When I was a child, I loved math—the neatness of fractions, all those pies sliced into ever-diminishing wedges. I adored unraveling the messy narratives of story problems, reducing them to symbols. I did this with the singlemindedness of a census taker. However, there were two stumbling blocks in my mathematical education. The first occurred when I was forced to drill with flash cards; although there are absolute answers with flash cards, there is no end of the series: one correct solution merely prompts the next problem. Something about this procedure frightened me; I believe I recognized in it some metaphor for the numbing repetitions of daily existence—taking out the garbage, doing the dishes, washing laundry, driving to the office, working from 9 to 5. . . . Here's a poem I wrote on the subject:

FLASH CARDS

In math I was the whiz kid, keeper of oranges and apples.
What you don't understand, master, my father said; the faster
I answered, the faster they came.

I could see one bud on the teacher's geranium,
one clear bee sputtering at the wet pane.
The tulip trees always dragged after heavy rain
so I tucked my head as my boots slapped home.

My father put up his feet after work
and relaxed with a highball and *The Life of Lincoln.*
After supper we drilled and I climbed the dark
before sleep, before a thin voice hissed
numbers as I spun on a wheel. I had to guess.
Ten, I kept saying, *I'm only ten.*

I hit the second snag in tenth grade, a few weeks into geometry. My homework assignment was to prove a theorem. But how could I even begin if I had to use points and lines and planes in order to prove it—points with no dimension, lines without thickness, and planes that had no length or width or area or perimeters, but stretched into infinity?

I asked my brother, who was two years older and had weathered geometry without a whimper, but his only advice was "You have to sit down and think about it until you get it." He let me use his desk to do this thinking. And so I sat for 20 minutes, for half an hour, trying to imagine what didn't exist. I began to daydream, and my eyes drifted to the ceiling . . . a plane. No, a representation of a plane; and, though I couldn't see it, the ceiling continued beyond the walls of my brother's room, into the hall and above my bedroom and my parents' bedroom—and if I could imagine the ceiling beyond that closed door, why not a ceiling that went on past the house and the neighborhood, all the way to Forever? Walls met ceiling, forming lines that did the same trick. Where ceiling and two walls met, a point . . .

GEOMETRY

I prove a theorem and the house expands:
the windows jerk free to hover near the ceiling,
the ceiling floats away with a sigh.

As the walls clear themselves of everything
but transparency, the scent of carnations
leaves with them. I am out in the open
and above the windows have hinged into butterflies,
sunlight glinting where they've intersected.
They are going to some point true and unproven.

Some Stereotypes

There are a thousand and one myths about artists in general, writers in particular, and specifically poets: Poets, the legend goes, are eccentric, not quite of this world; poets are blessed with imagination that the rest of us can never hope to approach. Poets lead wild—or at the very least, wildly disorganized—lives and say outrageous things in polite company. And lo, poets may even be the prophets of our time. The prevailing notions our society harbors about the creative arts make it difficult for artists, and especially that lofty breed of poets, to be taken seriously.

Oddly enough, there is the converse myth that poetry is difficult—hermetic, cerebral stuff, impossible for the mere mortal to comprehend. I cannot tell you on how many occasions I have read poetry in a church basement or high school classroom, only to have someone come up afterwards and exclaim: "I never knew poetry could be like that—why, that was fun!"

What this tells us about our society is that we regard the creative arts with a degree of apprehension, perhaps even suspicion. We do not expect the arts to be accessible, nor do we see any reason to incorporate the arts into our everyday or professional lives. And so, unfortunately, for many students, the years at the university and the few years beyond, in graduate study, may be the last opportunity to live in an environment where intellectual discourse and artistic expression are acknowledged and considered essential.

Of course, stereotypes cut both ways. The flip side of the coin is the assumption that intellect and imagination do not mix. This might be, partly at least, a result of one of our century's most dangerous signs of progress—the concept of specialization.

Let me illustrate this point. In the winter of 1984, when I was giving a series of lectures on the East Coast, a severe storm closed many airports along the seaboard, forcing plane passengers to scramble for the trains. I was on my way to New York City from Providence, Rhode Island, with my husband and infant daughter. The train was so crowded that people were standing—even sitting—in the aisles and in the passageways between cars. In that situation there was no question of chivalry: no one stood up to give me a seat. After about an hour, a seat became free and the young man standing nearest to it—and therefore, according to the laws of survival of the fittest, entitled to it—sat down, then turned and motioned for me to take his place. After another half-hour of travel, the seat next to me became vacant, so I was able to scoot over and give my cavalier a chance to rest his feet.

We began a careful conversation: first about the weather, then my daughter's vital statistics (she was blissfully asleep), and finally, we turned to occupation. "What do you do?" I asked, and was puzzled by his obvious hesitation before the reply came: "I'm . . . I'm a microbiologist." Pause. Then he added, "I usually don't tell people that. It tends to stop conversation."

"So what do you usually tell people?" I asked.

"Oh, that I work in a lab. Or that I study diseases. And what about you?" He turned the tables: "What do you do?" Now it was my turn to hesitate before I answered:

"I'm a poet."

"Oh!" he exclaimed. "That's wonderful!"

"And isn't microbiology wonderful, too?" I asked.

"Sure," he conceded, "but when I tell people I'm a microbiologist, they're so afraid they won't understand anything I say, they never ask any further. It gets to be a bummer."

"Yeah," I said, "I know what you mean." And I did; many a time I had experienced that awkward silence toward me as a poet. I never knew, however, that there were scientists who suffered the same blues.

"So tell me," I went on, "what exactly *do* you do as a microbiologist?" What followed was a fascinating account of this man's work with the molecular structure of DNA. He described how, aided by an electron microscope, he "walked" the length of a healthy DNA strand, taking notes along the way on the distinguishing traits of every cell. He then compared these observations with the reports from similar "walks" along DNA strands from people who had multiple sclerosis. By comparing these scientific diaries, he hoped to pinpoint the determining traits for one of the world's most devastating and mysterious diseases.

What impressed me especially about his account was the language he used to describe his work. In order to make this complicated process accessible to a lay person, he resorted to a vivid pictorial—even poetic—vocabulary. When I asked him whether he and his colleagues used the same metaphors in the lab, he seemed surprised. "Well," he replied, "we have specific technical terms of course, but we use some of these words, too. What else can you call it but taking a walk?"

Yes, what else could you call it? Here I was talking with a top-level scientist whose work was so specialized that it had to invent its own language in order to be able to imagine its own investigations. And at this point, when imagination enters, we also enter the domain of poetry.

MAKING A PRAIRIE

To make a prairie,

Emily Dickinson wrote,

it takes a clover and one bee,
One clover, and a bee,
And revery.
The revery alone will do,
If bees are few.

To make a prairie—or a light bulb, or the quantum theory of mechanics—you need revery. Daydreaming. The watchful soul in the relaxed mind.

A liberal education is intended to make people flexible, able to cope with the boundless changes that accelerating civilization will confront them with. So much of modern university education has become a closed society with privileged access to certain mysteries, a microcosm where palpable interaction with the physical world has been suspended in the interests of specialized knowledge. The Industrial Revolution, whose most poignant symbol is the assembly line, made specialization practical; now the Technological Revolution, whose symbol might be the silicon chip, makes specialization imperative.

But technological advances also de-emphasize the individual, reducing the grand gestures of the soul to so many impressions on a grain of sand. The humanities, with their insistence on communication and their willingness to admit paradox into the contemplation of truth, are too often silenced by the bully's club of empirical data. There's a Mother Goose rhyme that goes:

If all the world were paper,
And all the sea were ink;
If all the trees were bread and cheese,
What should we have to drink?

Yes, indeed—for if we assign a category to every wish and leave the fulfillment of these wishes to one discipline, we may be fed but not nourished; someone is sure to forget the lemonade. The groundwork laid in college stresses the connectedness of all learning. The task upon leaving college and entering into the intricacies of a chosen discipline is to avoid being narrowed into a mere functionary of a professional specialization.

How restless and curious the human mind is, how quick the imagination latches onto a picture, a scene, something volatile and querulous and filled with living, mutable tissue! The mind is informed by the spirit of play. The most fantastical doodles emerge from wandering ballpoint pens in both the classroom and the board meeting. Every discipline is studded with vivid terminology: In geometry various shapes are defined as "random slices of Swiss cheese," chains, or self-squared dragons. There are lady's slippers in botany and wingbacks in football games. There are onomatopoetic bushwhackers in the jungles of Nicaragua; there are doglegs on golf courses and butterfly valves in automobiles. The theory of quark confinement could be a quantum physicist's definition of the human soul. Astronomy has black holes with "event horizons"—the orbital path around a black hole where time stands still, the point beyond which one is drawn inextricably into the core of the imploding star. Every discipline craves imagination, and you owe it to yourself to keep yours alive.

In ancient Rome, every citizen possessed a genius. The genius was a personal spirit that came to every person at birth; it represented the fullness of one's potential powers. This genius was considered a birthright, but it needed to be nourished in order to survive. Now, in our narcissistic age children celebrating a birthday expect gifts to shower upon them from the outside, but the ancient Roman was expected to make a birthday sacrifice to his or her genius. If one served one's genius well during life, the genius became a *lars*, or household god, after one's death. If one neglected one's potential, the genius became a spook, a troublesome spirit who plagued the living.

Poets do not have a monopoly on imagination: the world will be ever unfolding, as long as one can imagine its possibilities, as long as one honors one's spirit—or, as the Romans would have said, one's "genius"—and lets the fresh air blow in, fragrant, from the flowering prairie.

FAN SHEN

The Classroom and the Wider Culture: Identity as a Key to Learning English Composition

CONSIDER THIS:

Fan Shen was born in China and studied at Lanzhou University and Marquette University. He has taught at Rockland Community College and is currently a member of the English faculty at Rochester Community and Technical College. Shen has examined the interplay between Chinese and American cultures that he first noticed while studying composition in America.

Before reading this essay, conduct some class surveys and take a self-inventory. First, find out how many of your classmates are proficient in more than one language. How many feel bicultural? How many have spent significant periods of time in more than one culture? What cultural identities do you hold? How do you experience those identities? Do you inhabit them simultaneously, or shift and switch identities? Do you try to ignore portions of your cultural identity? Does American academic culture make you feel like you need to suppress or assert particular portions of your cultural identity? After reading Shen's essay, you may want to return to these inventories and explore them further, asking if you have more than one "I" and different senses of "self."

One day in June 1975, when I walked into the aircraft factory where I was working as an electrician, I saw many large-letter posters on the walls and many people parading around the workshops shouting slogans like "Down with the word 'I'!" and "Trust in masses and the Party!" I then remembered that a new political campaign called "Against Individualism" was scheduled to begin that day. Ten years later, I got back my first English composition paper at the University of Nebraska-Lincoln. The professor's first comments were: "Why did you always use 'we' instead of 'I'?" and "Your paper would be stronger if you eliminated some sentences in the passive voice." The clashes between my Chinese background and the requirements of English composition had begun. At the center of this mental struggle, which has lasted several years and is still not completely over, is the prolonged, uphill battle to recapture "myself."

In this [paper] I will try to describe and explore this experience of reconciling my Chinese identity with an English identity dictated by the rules of English composition. I want to show how my cultural background shaped—and shapes—my approaches to my writing in English and how writing in English redefined—and redefines—my *ideological* and *logical* identities. By "ideological identity" I mean the system of values that I acquired (consciously and unconsciously) from my social and cultural background. And by "logical identity" I mean the natural (or Oriental) way I organize and express my thoughts in writing. Both had to be modified or redefined in learning English composition. Becoming aware of the process of redefinition of these different identities is a mode of learning that has helped me in my efforts to write in English, and, I hope, will be of help to teachers of English composition in this country. In presenting my case for this view, I will use examples from both my composition courses and literature courses, for I believe that writing papers for both kinds of courses contributed to the development of my "English identity." Although what I will describe is based on personal experience, many Chinese students whom I talked to said that they had had the same or similar experiences in their initial stages of learning to write in English.

IDENTITY OF THE SELF: IDEOLOGICAL AND CULTURAL

Starting with the first English paper I wrote, I found that learning to compose in English is not an isolated classroom activity, but a social and cultural experience. The rules of English composition encapsulate values that are absent in, or sometimes contradictory to, the values of other societies (in my case, China). Therefore, learning the rules of English composition is, to a certain extent, learning the values of Anglo-American society. In writing classes in the United States I found that I had to reprogram my mind, to redefine some of the basic concepts and values that I had about myself, about society, and about the universe, values that had been imprinted and reinforced in my mind by my cultural background, and that had been part of me all my life.

Rule number one in English composition is: Be yourself. (More than one composition instructor has told me, "Just write what *you* think.") The values behind this rule, it seems to me, are based on the principle of protecting and promoting individuality (and private property) in this country. The instruction was probably crystal clear to students raised on these values, but, as a guideline of composition, it was not very clear or useful to me when I first heard it. First of all, the image or meaning that I attached to the word "I" or "myself" was, as I found out, different from that of my English teacher. In China, "I" is always subordinated to "We"—be it the working class, the Party, the country, or some other collective body. Both political pressure and literary tradition require that "I" be somewhat hidden or buried in writings and speeches; presenting the "self" too obviously would give people the impression of being disrespectful of the Communist Party in political writings and boastful in scholarly writings. The word "I" has often been identified with another "bad" word, "individualism," which has become a synonym for selfishness in China. For a long time the words "self" and "individualism" have had negative connotations in my mind, and the negative force of the words naturally extended to the field of literary studies. As a result, even if I had brilliant ideas, the "I" in my papers always had to show some modesty by not competing with or trying to stand above the names of ancient and modern authoritative figures. Appealing to Mao or other Marxist authorities became the required way (as well as the most "forceful" or "persuasive" way) to prove one's point in written discourse. I remember that in China I had even committed what I can call "reverse plagiarism"—here, I suppose it would be called "forgery"—when I was in middle school: willfully attributing some of my thoughts to "experts" when I needed some arguments but could not find a suitable quotation from a literary or political "giant."

Now, in America, I had to learn to accept the words "I" and "Self" as something glorious (as Whitman did), or at least something not to be ashamed of or embarrassed about. It was the first and probably biggest step I took into English composition and critical writing. Acting upon my professor's suggestions, I intentionally tried to show my "individuality" and to "glorify" "I" in my papers by using as many "I's" as possible—"I think," "I believe," "I see"—and deliberately cut out quotations from authorities. It was rather painful to hand in such "pompous" (I mean immodest) papers to my instructors. But to an extent it worked. After a while I became more comfortable with only "the shadow of myself." I felt more at ease to put down *my* thoughts without looking over my shoulder to worry about the attitudes of my teachers or the reactions of the Party secretaries, and to speak out as "bluntly" and "immodestly" as my American instructors demanded.

But writing many "I's" was only the beginning of the process of redefining myself. Speaking of redefining myself is, in an important sense, speaking of redefining the word "I." By such a redefinition I mean not only the change in how I envisioned myself, but also the change in how *I* perceived the world. The old "I" used to embody only one set of values, but now it had to embody multiple sets of values. To be truly "myself," which I knew was a key to my success in learning English composition, meant *not to be my Chinese self* at all. That is to say, when I write in English I have to wrestle with and abandon (at least temporarily) the whole system of ideology which previously defined me in myself. I had to forget Marxist doctrines (even though I do not see myself as a Marxist by choice) and the Party lines imprinted in my mind and familiarize myself with a system of capitalist/bourgeois values. I had to put aside an ideology of collectivism and adopt the values of individualism. In composition as well as in literature classes, I had to make a fundamental adjustment: if I used to examine society and literary materials through the microscopes of Marxist dialectical materialism and historical materialism, I now had to learn to look through the microscopes the other way around, i.e., to learn to look at and understand the world from the point of view of "idealism." (I must add here that there are American professors who use a Marxist approach in their teaching.)

The word "idealism," which affects my view of both myself and the universe, is loaded with social connotations, and can serve as a good example of how redefining a key word can be a pivotal part of redefining my ideological identity as a whole.

To me, idealism is the philosophical foundation of the dictum of English composition: "Be yourself." In order to write good English, I knew that I had to be myself, which actually meant not to be my Chinese self. It meant that I had to create an English self and be *that* self. And to be that English self, I felt, I had to understand and accept idealism the way a Westerner does. That is to say, I had to accept the way a Westerner sees himself in relation to the universe and society. On the one hand, I knew a lot about idealism. But on the other hand, I knew nothing about it. I mean I knew a lot about idealism through the propaganda and objections of its opponent, Marxism, but I knew little about it from its own point of view. When I thought of the word "materialism"—which is a major part of Marxism and in China has repeatedly been "shown" to be the absolute truth—there were always positive connotations, and words like "right," "true," etc., flashed in my mind. On the other hand, the word "idealism" always came to me with the dark connotations that surround words like "absurd," "illogical," "wrong," etc. In China "idealism" is depicted as a ferocious and ridiculous enemy of Marxist philosophy. Idealism, as the simplified definition imprinted in my mind had it, is the view that the material world does not exist; that all that exists is the mind and its ideas. It is just the opposite of Marxist dialectical materialism which sees the mind as a product of the material world. It is not too difficult to see that idealism, with its idea that mind is of primary importance, provides a philosophical foundation for the Western emphasis on the value of individual human minds, and hence individual human beings. Therefore, my final acceptance of myself as of primary importance—an importance that overshadowed that of authority figures in English composition—was, I decided, dependent on an acceptance of idealism.

My struggle with idealism came mainly from my efforts to understand and to write about works such as Coleridge's *Biographia Literaria* and Emerson's "Over-Soul." For a long time I was frustrated and puzzled by the idealism expressed by

Coleridge and Emerson—given their ideas, such as "I think, therefore I am" (Coleridge obviously borrowed from Descartes) and "the transparent eyeball" (Emerson's view of himself)—because in my mind, drenched as it was in dialectical materialism, there was always a little voice whispering in my ear "You are, therefore you think." I could not see how human consciousness, which is not material, could create apples and trees. My intellectual conscience refused to let me believe that the human mind is the primary world and the material world secondary. Finally, I had to imagine that I was looking at a world with my head upside down. When I imagined that I was in a new body (born with the head upside down) it was easier to forget biases imprinted in my subconsciousness about idealism, the mind, and my former self. Starting from scratch, the new inverted self—which I called my "English Self" and into which I have transformed myself—could understand and *accept*, with ease, idealism as "the truth" and "himself" (i.e., my English Self) as the "creator" of the world.

Here is how I created my new "English Self." I played a "game" similar to ones played by mental therapists. First I made a list of (simplified) features about writing associated with my old identity (the Chinese Self), both ideological and logical, and then beside the first list I added a column of features about writing associated with my new identity (the English Self). After that I pictured myself getting out of my old identity, the timid, humble, modest Chinese "I," and creeping into my new identity (often in the form of a new skin or a mask), the confident, assertive, and aggressive English "I." The new "Self" helped me to remember and accept the different rules of Chinese and English composition and the values that underpin these rules. In a sense, creating an English Self is a way of reconciling my old cultural values with the new values required by English writing, without losing the former.

An interesting structural but not material parallel to my experiences in this regard has been well described by Min-zhan Lu in her important article, "From Silence to Words: Writing as Struggle" (*College English* 49 [April 1987]: 437–48.) Min-zhan Lu talks about struggles between two selves, an open self and a secret self, and between two discourses, a mainstream Marxist discourse and a bourgeois discourse her parents wanted her to learn. But her struggle was different from mine. Her Chinese self was severely constrained and suppressed by mainstream cultural discourse, but never interfused with it. Her experiences, then, were not representative of those of the majority of the younger generation who, like me, were brought up on only one discourse. I came to English composition as a Chinese person, in the fullest sense of the term, with a Chinese identity already fully formed.

IDENTITY OF THE MIND: ILLOGICAL AND ALOGICAL

In learning to write in English, besides wrestling with a different ideological system, I found that I had to wrestle with a logical system very different from the blueprint of logic at the back of my mind. By "logical system" I mean two things: the Chinese way of thinking I used to approach my theme or topic in written discourse, and the Chinese critical/logical way to develop a theme or topic. By English rules, the first is illogical, for it is the opposite of the English way of approaching a topic; the second is alogical (non-logical), for it mainly uses mental pictures instead of words as a critical vehicle.

The Illogical Pattern. In English composition, an essential rule for the logical organization of a piece of writing is the use of a "topic sentence." In Chinese composition, "from surface to core" is an essential rule, a rule which means that one ought to reach a topic gradually and "systematically" instead of "abruptly."

The concept of a topic sentence, it seems to me, is symbolic of the values of a busy people in an industrialized society, rushing to get things done, hoping to attract and satisfy the busy reader very quickly. Thinking back, I realized that I did not fully understand the virtue of the concept until my life began to rush at the speed of everyone else's in this country. Chinese composition, on the other hand, seems to embody the values of a leisurely paced rural society whose inhabitants have the time to chew and taste a topic slowly. In Chinese composition, an introduction explaining how and why one chooses this topic is not only acceptable, but often regarded as necessary. It arouses the reader's interest in the topic little by little (and this is seen as a virtue of composition) and gives him/her a sense of refinement. The famous Robert B. Kaplan "noodles" contrasting a spiral Oriental thought process with a straight-line Western approach may be too simplistic to capture the preferred pattern of writing in English, but I think they still express some truth about Oriental writing. A Chinese writer often clears the surrounding bushes before attacking the real target. This bush-clearing pattern in Chinese writing goes back two thousand years to Kong Fuzi (Confucius). Before doing anything, Kong says in his *Luen Yu (Analects),* one first needs to call things by their proper names (expressed by his phrase "Zheng Ming"正名). In other words, before touching one's main thesis, one should first state the "conditions" of composition: how, why, and when the piece is being composed. All of this will serve as a proper foundation on which to build the "house" of the piece. In the two thousand years after Kong, this principle of composition was gradually formalized (especially through the formal essays required by imperial examinations) and became known as "Ba Gu," or the eight-legged essay. The logic of Chinese composition, exemplified by the eight-legged essay, is like the peeling of an onion: layer after layer is removed until the reader finally arrives at the central point, the core.

Ba Gu still influences modern Chinese writing. Carolyn Matalene has an excellent discussion of this logical (or illogical) structure and its influence on her Chinese students' efforts to write in English. A Chinese textbook for composition lists six essential steps (factors) for writing a narrative essay, steps to be taken in this order: time, place, character, event, cause, and consequence. Most Chinese students (including me) are taught to follow this sequence in composition.

The straightforward approach to composition in English seemed to me, at first, illogical. One could not jump to the topic. One had to walk step by step to reach the topic. In several of my early papers I found that the Chinese approach—the bush-clearing approach—persisted, and I had considerable difficulty writing (and in fact understanding) topic sentences. In what I deemed to be topic sentences, I grudgingly gave out themes. Today, those papers look to me like Chinese papers with forced or false English openings. For example, in a narrative paper on a trip to New York, I wrote the forced/false topic sentence, "A trip to New York in winter is boring." In the next few paragraphs, I talked about the weather, the people who went with me, and so on, before I talked about what I learned from the trip. My real thesis was that one could always learn something even on a boring trip.

The Alogical Pattern. In learning English composition, I found that there was yet another cultural blueprint affecting my logical thinking. I found from my early papers that very often I was unconsciously under the influence of a Chinese critical approach called the creation of "yijing," which is totally nonWestern. The direct translation of the word "yijing" is: yi, "mind or consciousness," and jing, "environment." An ancient approach which has existed in China for many centuries and is still the subject of much discussion, yijing is a complicated concept that defies a universal definition. But most critics in China nowadays seem to agree on one point, that yijing is the critical approach that separates Chinese literature and criticism from Western literature and criticism. Roughly speaking, yijing is the process of creating a pictorial environment while reading a piece of literature. Many critics in China believe that yijing is a creative process of inducing oneself, while reading a piece of literature or looking at a piece of art, to create mental pictures, in order to reach a unity of nature, the author, and the reader. Therefore, it is by its very nature both creative and critical. According to the theory, this nonverbal, pictorial process leads directly to a higher ground of beauty and morality. Almost all critics in China agree that yijing is not a process of logical thinking—it is not a process of moving from the premises of an argument to its conclusion, which is the foundation of Western criticism. According to yijing, the process of criticizing a piece of art or literary work has to involve the process of creation on the reader's part. In yijing, verbal thoughts and pictorial thoughts are one. Thinking is conducted largely in pictures and then "transcribed" into words (Ezra Pound once tried to capture the creative aspect of yijing in poems such as "In a Station of the Metro." He also tried to capture the critical aspect of it in his theory of imagism and vorticism, even though he did not know the term "yijing.") One characteristic of the yijing approach to criticism, therefore, is that it often includes a description of the created mental pictures on the part of the reader/critic and his/her mental attempt to bridge (unite) the literary work, the pictures, with ultimate beauty and peace.

In looking back at my critical papers for various classes, I discovered that I unconsciously used the approach of yijing, especially in some of my earlier papers when I seemed not yet to have been in the grip of Western logical critical approaches. I wrote, for instance, an essay entitled "Wordsworth's Sound and Imagination: The Snowdon Episode." In the major part of the essay I described the pictures that flashed in my mind while I was reading passages in Wordsworth's long poem, *The Prelude.*

> I saw three climbers (myself among them) winding up the mountain in silence "at the dead of night," absorbed in their "private thoughts." The sky was full of

> blocks of clouds of different colors, freely changing their shapes, like oily pigments disturbed in a bucket of water. All of a sudden, the moonlight broke the darkness "like a flash," lighting up the mountain tops. Under the "naked moon," the band saw a vast sea of mist and vapor, a silent ocean. Then the silence was abruptly broken, and we heard the "roaring of waters, torrents, streams/innumerable, roaring with one voice" from a "blue chasm," a fracture in the vapor of the sea. It was a joyful revelation of divine truth to the human mind: the bright, "naked" moon sheds the light of "higher reasons" and "spiritual love" upon us; the vast ocean of mist looked like a thin curtain through which we vaguely saw the infinity of nature beyond; and the sounds of roaring waters coming out of the chasm of vapor cast us into the boundless spring of imagination from the depth of the human heart. Evoked by the divine light from above, the human spring of imagination is joined by the natural spring and becomes a sustaining source of energy, feeding "upon infinity" while transcending infinity at the same time. . . .

Here I was describing my own experience more than Wordsworth's. The picture described by the poet is taken over and developed by the reader. The imagination of the author and the imagination of the reader are thus joined together. There was no "because" or "therefore" in the paper. There was little *logic.* And I thought it was (and it is) criticism. This seems to me a typical (but simplified) example of the yijing approach. (Incidentally, the instructor, a kind professor, found the paper interesting, though a bit "strange.")

In another paper of mine, "The Note of Life: Williams's 'The Orchestra,'" I found myself describing my experiences of pictures of nature while reading William Carlos Williams's poem "The Orchestra." I "painted" these fleeting pictures and described the feelings that seemed to lead me to an understanding of a harmony, a "common tone," between man and nature. A paragraph from that paper reads:

> The poem first struck me as a musical fairy tale. With rich musical sounds in my ear, I seemed to be walking in a solitary, dense forest on a spring morning. No sound from human society could be heard. I was now sitting under a giant pine tree, ready to hear the grand concert of Nature. With the sun slowly rising from the east, the cello (the creeping creek) and the clarinet (the rustling pine trees) started with a slow overture. Enthusiastically the violinists (the twittering birds) and the French horn (the mumbling cow) "interpose[d] their voices," and the bass (bears) got in at the wrong time. The orchestra did not stop, they continued to play. The musicians of Nature do not always play in harmony. "Together, unattuned," they have to seek "a common tone" as they play along. The symphony of Nature is like the symphony of human life: both consist of random notes seeking a "common tone."

For the symphony of life
Love is that common tone
  shall raise his fiery head
    and sound his note.

Again, the logical pattern of this paper, the "pictorial criticism," is illogical to Western minds but "logical" to those acquainted with yijing. (Perhaps I should not even use the words "logical" and "think" because they are so conceptually tied up with "words" and with culturally based conceptions, and therefore very misleading if not useless in a discussion of yijing. Maybe I should simply say that yijing is neither illogical nor logical, but alogical.)

I am not saying that such a pattern of "alogical" thinking is wrong—in fact some English instructors find it interesting and acceptable—but it is very non-Western. Since I was in this country to learn the English language and English literature, I had to abandon Chinese "pictorial logic," and to learn Western "verbal logic."

IF I HAD TO START AGAIN

The change is profound: through my understanding of new meanings of words like "individualism," "idealism," and "I," I began to accept the underlying concepts and values of American writing, and by learning to use "topic sentences" I began to accept a new logic. Thus, when I write papers in English, I am able to obey all the general rules of English composition. In doing this I feel that I am writing through, with, and because of a new identity. I welcome the change, for it has added a new dimension to me and to my view of the world. I am not saying that I have entirely lost my Chinese identity. In fact I feel that I will never lose it. Any time I write in Chinese, I resume my old identity, and obey the rules of Chinese composition such as "Make the 'I' modest," and "Beat around the bush before attacking the central topic." It is necessary for me to have such a Chinese identity in order to write authentic Chinese. (I have seen people who, after learning to write in English, use English logic and sentence patterning to write Chinese. They produce very awkward Chinese texts.) But when I write in English, I imagine myself slipping into a new "skin," and I let the "I" behave much more aggressively and knock the topic right on the head. Being conscious of these different identities has helped me to reconcile different systems of values and logic, and has played a pivotal role in my learning to compose in English.

Looking back, I realize that the process of learning to write in English is in fact a process of creating and defining a new identity and balancing it with the old identity. The process of learning English composition would have been easier if I had realized this earlier and consciously sought to compare the two different identities required by the two writing systems from two different cultures. It is fine and perhaps even necessary for American composition teachers to teach about topic sentences, paragraphs, the use of punctuation, documentation, and so on, but can anyone design exercises sensitive to the ideological and logical differences that students like me experience—and design them so they can be introduced at an early stage of an English composition class? As I pointed out earlier, the traditional advice "Just be yourself" is not clear and helpful to students from Korea, China, Vietnam, or India. From "Be yourself" we are likely to hear either "Forget your cultural habit of writing" or "Write as you would write in your own language." But neither of the two is what the instructor meant or what we want to do. It would be helpful if he or she pointed out the different cultural/ideological connotations of the word "I," the connotations that exist in a group-centered culture and an individual-centered culture. To sharpen the contrast, it might be useful to design papers on topics like "The Individual vs. The Group: China vs. America" or "Different 'I's' in Different Cultures."

Carolyn Matalene mentioned in her article (789) an incident concerning American businessmen who presented their Chinese hosts with gifts of cheddar cheese, not knowing that the Chinese generally do not like cheese. Liking cheddar cheese may not be essential to writing English prose, but being truly accustomed to the social norms that stand behind ideas such as the English "I" and the logical pattern of English composition—call it "compositional cheddar cheese"—is essential to writing in English. Matalene does not provide an "elixir" to help her Chinese students like English "compositional cheese," but rather recommends, as do I, that composition teachers not be afraid to give foreign students English "cheese," but to make sure to hand it out slowly, sympathetically, and fully realizing that it tastes very peculiar in the mouths of those used to a very different cuisine.

STANLEY L. WITKIN (b. 1947)

Writing Social Work

CONSIDER THIS:

Stanley L. Witkin earned advanced degrees from the University of Wisconsin and is currently a professor at the University of Vermont's School of Social Work. As editor-in-chief of the journal *Social Work,* Witkin is highly aware of audience expectations and the interaction of reading and writing processes. He points out that "Writing is considered a skill, even a craft, that requires continuous practice and feedback. Reading, in contrast, is considered a kind of language proficiency that students already possess by the time we meet them. Writing is viewed as active, reading as passive. Writers produce something, readers consume. The characteristics of good writing, such as clarity and proper use of grammar, are generally known. Good reading is harder to pin down, or when it is, it gets defined narrowly as 'comprehension.'" As a journal editor, Witkin has a responsibility for "reading" his field. In this editorial about the writing of social scientists, he describes the traditional writing style of the field and four alternative essay formats. In reading this editorial, what do you learn about writing in social work? How is it like or unlike writing, as you know it, in other disciplines?

I am sitting on a hard wooden chair with a small round seat. My laptop computer sits stoically in front of me on a smooth wooden table scattered with papers and diskettes. Although it is June the temperature gauge just outside my large window reads 8 degrees centigrade (about 45 degrees Fahrenheit). I watch a large black and white magpie hop around in front of a red wooden building with a metal roof that faces the window. The building is the "sauna house" of the University of Lapland. I have returned to Finland to participate in another international summer school.

I am feeling restless, fighting with myself to stay at the computer and continue working on this editorial. It is due soon after I return to the United States, and I would like to have it mostly completed while I am here. I remind myself that I love to write, at least some of the time. Like when I have just finished a writing project and the exquisite pain of searching for the "right" words and the talking-to-myself struggle to stay focused are memories. I am also thinking about whether what I am writing now—these words—can be part of the editorial. After all, I say to myself, part of this issue of *Social Work* is about writing, and I am writing about writing.

Maybe I am just trying to write my way into this editorial. It is not that I lack ideas; in fact, the opposite is true. My struggle is how to express and organize them, to make them coherent and interesting—within a small number of pages. There are infinite ways to write about writing. Yet each beginning, each formulation, points me in a different direction—toward certain conceptions and understandings and away from others. Which ones will be enacted through my writing? Which will be given form, and which will remain in the ethereal world of thought? Can I even know what these ideas are until I write them down? (I am reminded of Lamott's [1994] comment that "Very few writers know what they are doing until they've done it"). These are big questions for a little essay.

At the same time, I am excited about introducing alternative writing formats into *Social Work.* For a profession that depends so heavily on writing, this topic gets little attention. The stylistic and structural requirements of our journals are rarely questioned or examined in relation to our professional goals. But the way we write is important, very important to how we learn and what we know. What follows are some of my thoughts on this subject.

WRITING SCIENCE

By the 17th century there came to be a distinction between literary and scientific forms of writing. The former, associated with the arts, culture, and humanities, was concerned with language itself, how it might be used to express, explore, analyze, and create. For science, however, language simply was a vehicle for recording the regularities of nature and the methods for producing those regularities. By and large, academic and professional journals, including *Social Work,* have adopted the writing format developed for scientific writing.

Writing science (or research) requires adherence to a prescribed structure that looks something like the following: statement of the problem, literature review, method, results, and discussion. This structure both reflects various assumptions about knowledge and serves the needs of certain segments of the scientific community. For example, following this structure gives texts an aura of authority, equating particular accounts of the world as "reality." It also keeps contributors in line. "One gets published by conforming to the literary style of a discipline-presenting argument in a way that adheres to literary canons (e.g., paying obeisance to those given high status, using its referencing style, and methodologies, presenting findings, beginnings."

Science writing assumes that language reflects the world as observed by the researcher. Writing is largely passive, an objective recording of activities and events. As Bazerman put it, "To write science is commonly thought not to write at all, just simply to record the natural facts." Literary merit is not considered important. In fact, concern with issues of style is considered tangential or even worse, as contributing to subjectivity or bias. Science is a literary genre that denies its own "literariness."

The writing format developed for describing experiments is the paragon of scientific writing. This powerful literary genre evolved over the past three and a half centuries following the publication of the first scientific journals. A current expression of this genre—and the most common in social work journals—is the style developed by the American Psychological Association (aka "APA style"). To my knowledge, this style of writing is taught in most social work programs in the United States as the proper way to write about the weighty subjects we address. Why would social work adopt a writing style developed for the reporting of psychological research? I suspect it had something to do with the profession's perennial quest to be accorded the recognition and status of science-based professions like psychology and psychiatry. Nevertheless, as a variant of scientific writing, some characteristics of APA style should concern social workers.

APA STYLE

APA style tends to create what Billig calls "depopulated texts"—that is, texts devoid both of authors or "subjects." Little is known about authors other than their name, degrees, and professional affiliations. Similarly, research subjects are presented in scant detail. We know little about them as people. And when they are described, it is not in their own words, but in the language of theory or methodology.

A presumed hallmark of scientific writing is its objectivity. Its offshoot, neutrality, is a value to which authors are expected to adhere. But as a cultural activity, writing always expresses values. There simply are no "pure" ways of representing the world. Our choice of words, emphases, or literary tropes tends to generate one picture, whereas other, but equally legitimate, choices might generate a different picture. This false sense of neutrality is compounded by the identification of some areas of ethical concern such as gender bias, but silence on others, for example, treating people as objects.

For those interested in alternative forms of writing or nonpositivist forms of knowledge, APA style acts as a gatekeeper, discouraging their participation or "marginalizing" their contributions. I suspect that for many practitioners, the challenge of fitting their ideas into the procrustean bed of APA style keeps them from ever putting pen to paper (or fingers to keyboard). Given the range and complexity of issues addressed by our profession, as well as our value framework, such a position seems ill-advised.

POSTMODERN CHALLENGES

Interest in alternative forms of writing coincides with the emergence of the postmodern critique of Western enlightenment thinking. Previously unassailable notions such as progress, objectivity, and rationality have all been subject to critique—"unpacked" and reassembled as historical and cultural expressions. As applied to writing, particularly professional and scientific writing, language as a true representation of objective reality now competes with an understanding of language as constitutive of reality. According to this latter position, how we write directs attention to certain things and not others and favors certain conceptions, viewpoints, and interpretations over others. As Billig noted, "Writing practices are not merely means to persuade readers of "facts," but those "facts," of which the readers are to be persuaded, are themselves constituted through writing."

How we write not only influences what we know but how we know. Writers, whether scientific or not, use various rhetorical and literary devices, such as forms of argument, metaphors, and the like to support their positions. In this sense writing is a form of practice and inquiry. Practitioners are beginning to recognize these aspects of writing and are using them as useful adjuncts to their work.

If writing is a form of inquiry, then alternate forms of writing are like different methodologies in their ability to generate different social realities. The various uses of language, as Laurel Richardson notes, are "competing ways of giving meaning and of organizing the world [making] language a site of exploration, struggle." Thus, through our writing practices social workers participate in this generation, exploration, and struggle. Do these practices express the profession's values and aims? If they did, then the people who populated our texts would be fully human, social beings. Individuals, groups, organizations, and communities would be sites of possibilities—for change, growth, and transformation. As much as possible, our language would be widely accessible and our writing formats sufficiently varied so that a broad range of people could participate in our discourses. Our writing would be a vehicle for the pursuit of cherished values such as human rights and social justice. It would be critical and reflexive, questioning domination including the authority of authors. Some of these qualities are illustrated in the articles, practice update, commentaries, and letters included in this issue.

A GLIMPSE AT SOME ALTERNATIVES

Four articles solicited for this issue—by Rose, Weick, Sternbach, and Donahue—represent, more or less, literary styles typically not seen in professional, academic journals: personal essay (Rose and Weick), memoir (Sternbach), and autoethnography (Donahue). In addition, an atypical article by Kanuha, although more representative of a standard academic format, displays features of these styles.

Essay

According to my Random House Webster's Unabridged Dictionary, an essay is a literary composition on a particular theme or subject. It tends to be written in ordinary language and is "generally analytic, speculative, or interpretative." From this perspective, the three styles noted above can be viewed as variants on the essay.

Essays, as Goldstein (1993) reminds us, have a long history in social work, including works by such notables as Mary Richmond and Grace Coyle. Writing essays stimulates thinking and expands conceptual and literary boundaries. "This literary form awakens our critical and reflective thinking about essentially ambiguous, personal, or social issues. It encourages the use of imagery, metaphor, and other elements of style that may capture qualities of human circumstances in play outside the margins of scientific discourse."

Personal Essay. Compared with the essay, the personal essay is more intimate. "The essayist gives you his thoughts, and lets you know, in addition, how he came by them." Personal disclosures form the basis of a relationship between authors and readers. This is not dispassionate reporting from invisible authors, but a narrative in which the authorial presence is integral to the story being told. Rose tells us about how his encounter with a young, defiant client generated an epiphany that led him to question the relevance of his professional education. We learn from Kanuha about the relationship between "a life experience of being multiply stigmatized" and her choice of a dissertation topic. Weick discusses the parallels between women as caretakers and the development of the social work profession in a way that is intertwined with her own socialization as a woman. She is not outside of the text, but an intimate part of it. Indeed, when she talks about the struggles of the profession to be heard, you sense that she also is talking about herself.

Memoir. The memoir is a record of events written by a person having intimate knowledge of them and based on personal observation (Random House Webster's Unabridged Dictionary, 1996). Although autobiographical, the memoir tends to be more limited in scope than an autobiography, usually focusing on particular events or themes. "The memoirist both tells the story and muses upon it, trying to unravel what it means in light of her current knowledge." Thus, Sternbach shares with us his experience of working in a men's maximum-security prison while reflecting on his experience and its effect on his present-day professional practice.

Kanuha reflects on her experience of conducting her dissertation research as both an insider (lesbian woman of color) and outsider (researcher). This process of reflection and meaning making benefits not only the author, but also the readers. Commenting about how his students profited from reading memoirs, noted author Jay Parini (1998) wrote, "They are learning quite explicitly how to construct a self, how to navigate the world, and—perhaps most usefully—how to gain some purchase on the world through the medium of language." Such lessons are no less important for social workers than English majors.

Autoethnography. An autoethnography is "a form of self-narrative that places the self within a social context." While focusing on the personal experience of the writer, it communicates about social and cultural contexts. One use of autoethnography, as illustrated in the essay by Donahue, is to compare lived experience against established knowledge. By doing so, autoethnographers reveal the limitations of such knowledge while providing an alternative representation. For example, Tillmann-Healy (1996) in her moving autoethnography about her ongoing struggle with bulimia, noted that the focus (of the literature) on "curing the disease" although admirable, "obscures the emotional intensity of bulimia and fails to help us understand what bulimia *means* to those who live with it every day and what it *says* about our culture." Similarly, Donahue helps us understand what struggling with debilitating depression means and how that struggle can be exacerbated by the conflicting messages of those espousing different causal theories and intervention approaches.

COMMONALITIES

Despite the differing emphases of these literary styles, the essays share certain features, which I call author visibility, striving for authenticity, and connection and mutuality. Although the latter two features are not integral to these literary styles, I wonder if an authorial presence, use of the personal voice, and flexibility of expression invite the articulation of such fundamental values and beliefs.

The Visible Author

Relative to the standard academic article, where our only knowledge of authors is their academic or agency affiliation, the authors of these essays are highly visible and "exposed." They are real, "flesh and blood" people writing openly from their histories, social contexts, and experience. Ideas and lives are intertwined. Such disclosure is risky, yet this risk taking generates the rich, human context that gives these ideas their verisimilitude. Thus, we read about the 24-year-old Stephen Rose "white, recently married, middle-class, and the proud possessor of a quite new MSW" as he becomes painfully aware of his unwitting participation in a system of professional domination through the "ownership of meaning of another's person's experience through the delegated power to interpret it." We learn of the family and personal influences on Ann Weick's decision to become a social worker, her brave disclosure that this "inclination toward social work was entirely conventional" and of her journey toward the realization that her "first voice"—the voice of women—has been suppressed despite its being "the essential voice of social work." We "hear" Valli Kanuha's struggle to maintain an analytical stance when interviewing people whose "deeply personal and oftentimes painful life histories . . . mirrored many of my own experiences as a young lesbian coming of age in the 1950s." We enter with Jack Sternbach, the maximum security Foothills Correctional Institution where the hippie-looking professor's "arrogance was matched only by my ignorance, and both were balanced by my innocence." We follow him through his sometimes scary and ultimately enlightening encounters with inmates that taught him "about manhood that shook and shaped me then and provided the ground for much of my subsequent life work and personal development." We accompany Anne Donahue as she moves painfully toward an all-encompassing and immobilizing depression. "What is the whirlpool sucking at me? Fear of losing all control of my mind, instantly. I'm drowning." And we get a sense of the consequences of our theoretical debates when they leave out the people whose conditions they are attempting to explain.

Striving for Authenticity

All five authors address and endeavor to live what I would call an authentic life: integrating deeply held personal beliefs with professional ones, or, in the case of Donahue, having those beliefs respected by professionals. ("I may have been suffering from severe, recurrent depression, but I had life values and goals that were my right to have." In each case this striving has led to important life changes. For Donahue it has meant going public with her story and advocating for laws that treat people burdened with psychiatric labels first and foremost as human beings. For Kanuha, too, it has meant writing about her personal-professional struggles and proposing "more reflexive, multimethod approaches for the study of social problems." For Rose it has meant exposing oppressive social arrangements and generating situations in which others could define their own lives. For Weick it meant understanding that we will never be able to assert our identity if we continue to do so with a borrowed voice. Rather, we must learn to speak openly in our own voice—the caretaking voice of passion, commitment, dedication, and vision. For Sternbach it meant integrating the lessons he learned at Foothills into his life and psychotherapy practice with men.

Connection and Mutuality

The necessity of relational connection and mutuality resonates throughout the essays. Sternbach states it most directly, "What I have to offer others has little value unless it is embedded in mutuality." Weick relates these qualities to women's use of their first voice: "In these times, conversation invariably is connected in some obvious and deep way with human relationships." For Rose, it is part of his epiphany, "Somehow, in this crucible, I began to identify and experience *validity* and its corollary, authentic recognition in mutually produced relationships." Kanuha's identification as an "insider" who has intimate familiarity with the experiences of her research participants is integral to the information her inquiry generates. "The degree and kinds of shared laughter, unfinished phrases, or specific terminology represented the 'knowing' and familiar references that characterize interactions between those who share cultural ways that are profoundly ingrained." Finally, for Donahue it is an indispensable part of the helping process: "Whether medication or talk therapy or both; whether peer intervention and recovery or self-empowerment—all become pointless if not within a context of understanding of the continuum of the mediating intellect and the deeply personal differences of choices and values, and of the lived experience of immobilizing anguish."

As you can tell, I have learned much from these essays. I hope you do as well. Writing essays will not solve our problems nor will it replace other forms of inquiry. But I do believe that expanding our writing practices to include essays and other literary styles can help the social work community "to understand itself, converse well, and make choices." Let us not so privilege one literary format that the profession, as Ann Weick eloquently writes, "let slip through its fingers the language that fills its veins with the fullest expression of human experiences and that most essentially gives social work its distinctive character as a profession."

Endnotes

1. Readers will note that I do not use the typical referencing style of the journal in this section of the editorial. I do this to make a point about the influence of stylistic conventions (see note 7).
2. See L. Richardson, *Writing Strategies: Reaching Diverse Audiences* (Newbury Park, CA: Sage Publications, 1990).
3. There are some notable exceptions in social work. For example, the journal *Narratives,* whose founding editor was Sonia Abels, has been a leader in publishing alternative forms of writing. Also, in the past few years, the journal *Families in Society,* under the editorship of Howard Goldstein, has published several essays.
4. See B. Agger, *Reading Science: A Literary, Political, and Sociological Analysis* (Dix Hills, NY: General Hall, 1989).
5. See C. Bazerman, *Shaping Written Knowledge* (Madison: University of Wisconsin Press, 1988, p. 14).
6. See Bazerman, *supra,* for a history of the experimental article.
7. APA style discourages the use of endnotes as seen here. Footnotes or endnotes facilitate authors' reflections on their ideas and "offer the possibility of creating parallel text" (D. Vipond, "Problems with a Monolithic APA Style" [Comment], *American Psychologist, 51* [1996]: 653).
8. See M. Billig, "Repopulating Social Psychology: A Revised Version of Events," in *Reconstructing the Psychological Subject* (1998, pp. 126–152), eds. B. Bayer & J. Shotter (Thousand Oaks, CA: Sage Publications).
9. I am not advocating that we compromise confidentiality, and I doubt whether this concern has much to do with the lack of translation of

information about clients or research participants. There are ways we can describe people without revealing their identities. Ironically, the hiding of information may inadvertently foster the notion of subject or client as a stigmatized identity.

10. See G. S. Budge & B. Katz, "Constructing Psychological Knowledge: Reflections on Science, Scientists, and Epistemology in the APA Publications Manual," *Theory & Psychology*, 5[1995]: 217–231.
11. I am not referring only to quantitative approaches, as "nonquantitative approaches often proceed in much the same way without relying explicitly on techniques of statistical inference. At issue is not quantification per se but the way that text . . . establishes its epistemological authority (see Agger, *supra* at note 4, p. 4).
12. See Billig, *supra* at note 8, p. 128.
13. I have found the writings of Laurel Richardson on this topic to be particularly illuminating. See, for example, note 2, and "Writing: A Method of Inquiry," in *Handbook of Qualitative Research* (1994, pp. 516–529; 2nd ed., 2000, pp. 923–948), eds. N. K. Denzin & Y. S. Lincoln (Thousand Oaks, CA: Sage Publications).
14. For example, see B. A. Esterling, L. L'Abate, E. J. Murray, & J. W. Pennebaker, "Empirical Foundations for Writing in Prevention and Psychotherapy: Mental and Physical Health Outcomes," *Clinical Psychology Review, 19*[1999]: 79–96.
15. Richardson, 1994, *supra* at note 12, p. 518.

References

Barrington, J. (1997). *Writing the memoir.* Portland, OR: Eighth Mountain Press.

Denzin, N. K. (1997). *Interpretive ethnography.* Thousand Oaks, CA: Sage Publications.

Goldstein, H. (1993). Writing to be read: The place of the essay in social work literature. *Families in Society, 74*, 441–446.

Lamott, A. (1994). *Bird by bird.* New York: Doubleday.

Lopate, P. (1994). Introduction. In P. Lopate (Ed.), *The art of the personal essay.* New York: Doubleday.

Parini, J. (1998, July 10). The memoir versus the novel in a time of transition. *Chronicle of Higher Education*, p. A40.

Reed-Danahay, D. E. (1997). *Auto/ethnography: Rewriting the self and the social.* Oxford: Berg.

Tillmann-Healy, L. M. (1996). A secret life in a culture of thinness: Reflections on body, food, and bulimia. In C. Ellis & A. P. Bochner (Eds.), *Composing ethnography: Alternative forms of qualitative writing* (pp. 76–108). Walnut Creek, CA: Altamira Press.

Witkin, S. L. (1999). Letter from Lapland. *Social Work, 44*, 413–415.

TOBY FULWILER (b. 1942)

The Role of Audiences

CONSIDER THIS:

Toby Fulwiler is a foundational figure in the writing-across-the-disciplines movement in U.S. universities. He received his Ph.D. from the University of Wisconsin, taught at Wisconsin and at Michigan Technological University, and retired from the English Department at the University of Vermont. Fulwiler is concerned with "the role of writing in learning." In *Angles of Vision,* he puts the relationship quite succinctly: "When we write about anything, we learn it better." Fulwiler also makes a bridge between getting started and considering other, future audiences by declaring that a writer's first audience is always him- or herself: "I think the most important reason to write in the first place is for ourselves, for what happens in our own minds when we make concrete or otherwise scattered and fragmentary thought. Finding words, generating sentences, constructing paragraphs is also our way of finding, generating, and constructing the meaning of our world." Only then, he feels, will writers be likely to have things to say that others might enjoy reading later: "When we write to ourselves, as we do in journals, diaries, and notebooks, we concentrate on what we are thinking about, rather than the shape of our words or how some distant audience will react to them." Fulwiler suggests that if we have something to say to ourselves, we take the first step toward having something meaningful to say to another audience.

Before reading Fulwiler's advice take a poll of classmates and see what they think about audience. Is audience a large or small consideration as they begin, continue, and complete a draft? How do they envision an audience for their writing, if they do?

> For me, in most cases, I'm writing because I have to, not because I want to. . . . I'm usually writing for a grade, it puts on more pressure. Most of the time people communicate through talking. Talking is more natural, you can read other people's expressions—it's easier to sense if you're right or wrong.
>
> —First-Year College Student, Anonymous

Many jobs in business, government, and education involve writing for different audiences. In the course of daily business, you may write memos to co-workers, letters to complete strangers, reports to your boss, and notes to yourself. Even if you've never been required to write at work, you probably learned about audience expectations simply by having written for various teachers in passing from one grade to the next in school, and by writing letters to friends and parents, and thank-you notes to aunts, uncles, and grandparents. In fact, most of us had already learned to distinguish one audience from another before we learned to read or write, as we used oral language to communicate with different people.

WRITING AND TALKING

Most of us would agree with the writer above who believes that talking is easier than writing. For one thing, most of us talk more often than we write—usually many times in the course of a single day—and so get more practice. For another, we get more help from people to whom we speak face to face than from those to whom we write. We see by their facial expressions whether or not listeners understand us, need more or less information, or are pleased with our words. Our own facial and body expressions help us communicate as well. Finally, our listening audiences tend to be more tolerant of the way we talk than our reading audiences are of the way we write: nobody sees my spelling or punctuation when I talk, and nobody calls me on the carpet when, in casual conversation, I blow an occasional noun–verb agreement or mis-use the subjunctive (whatever that is).

However, writing does certain things better than speaking. If you miswrite, you can always rewrite and catch your mistake before someone else notices it. If you need to develop a complex argument, writing affords you the time and space to do so. If you want your words to have the force of law, you can make a permanent (written) record to be reread and studied in your absence. And if you want to maintain a certain tone or coolness of demeanor, this can be accomplished more easily in writing than in face-to-face confrontations.

Because most readers of this book are likely to be students, we will look at some of the audiences for whom students most commonly write and see what help is to be had.

WRITING FOR TEACHERS

When you are a student in high school, college, or graduate school, your most common audiences are teachers who have requested a written assignment and who will read and grade what you produce. But teachers are an especially tough audience for most of us.

First, teachers often make writing assignments with the specific intention to measure and grade you on the basis of what you write. Second, teachers often think it their civic duty to correct every language miscue you make, no matter how small. Third, teachers often ask you to write about subjects you have no particular interest in—or worse, to write about *their* favorite topics! Finally, your teachers usually know more about the subject of your paper than you do because they are the experts in the field, which puts you in a difficult spot: you end up writing to *prove* how much you know more than to share something new with them.

You can't do much about the fact that teachers will use your writing to evaluate you in one way or another—they view it as part of their job, just as they do when making assignments "for your own good" (but not necessarily interest). However, as an individual writer, you can make choices that will influence this difficult audience positively—especially if you understand that most of your instructors are fundamentally caring people.

In the best circumstances, instructors will make writing assignments that give you a good start. They do this when they make clear their expectations for each assignment, when they provide sufficient time for you to accomplish the assignment, when they give you positive and pointed feedback while you are writing, when they create a climate in which it's clear that the subject belongs to *you,* not to them or the text or the school, and when they evaluate your papers according to criteria you both understand and agree with.

But regardless of how helpful you find your teacher, at some point you have to plan and write the paper using the best resources *you* can muster. Even before you begin to write—or as you think about the assignment through writing about it—you can make some important mental decisions that will make your actual drafting of most assignments easier:

1. Read the assignment directions carefully before you begin to write. Pay particular attention to instruction words such as "explain," "define," or "evaluate"—terms that mean something quite different from one another. Most of the time when teachers develop their assignments, they are looking to see not only that you can demonstrate what you know, think logically, and write clearly—they also want to see if you can follow directions.
2. Convince yourself that you are interested in writing this assignment. It's better, of course, if you really *are* interested in writing about *Moby Dick* or the War of 1812 or photosynthesis, but sometimes this isn't the case. If not, you've got to practice some psychology on yourself because it's difficult to write well when you are bored. Use whatever strategies usually work for you, but if those fail, try this: locate the most popular treatment of the subject you can find, perhaps in a current newsstand or by using the *Reader's Guide to Periodical Literature.* Find out what has made this subject newsworthy, tell a friend about it (Did you know that . . . ?), write in your journal about it, and see what kind of questions you can generate. There is a good chance that this forced engagement will lead to the real thing.
3. Make the assignment your own. This can be done by any of the following methods: (a) recasting the paper topic in your own words, (b) reducing the size/scope of the topic to something manageable, or (c) relating it to an issue with which you are already familiar. Modifying a writing task into something both interesting and manageable dramatically increases your chances of making the writing less superficial because you're not biting off more than you can chew and because the reader will read caring and commitment between the lines.
4. Try to teach your readers something. At the least, try actually to communicate with them. Seeing your task as instructional puts you in the driver's seat and gets you out of the passive mode of writing to fulfill somebody else's expectations. In truth, teachers are delighted when a student paper teaches them something they didn't already know; it breaks the boredom of reading papers that are simple regurgitations of course information.
5. Look for a different slant. Teachers get awfully tired of the same approach to every assignment, so, if you are able, approach your topic from an

unpredictable angle. Be sure you cover all the necessary territory that you would if you wrote a more predictable paper, but hold your reader's attention by viewing the terrain somehow differently: locating the thesis in *Moby Dick* from the whale's point of view; explaining the War of 1812 through a series of dispatches to the London *Times* from a British war correspondent; describing photosynthesis through a series of simulated field notebooks. (I provide these examples only to allude to what may be possible; teacher, subject, and context will give you safer guidelines.)

6. Consider your paper as a problem in need of solution or a question in need of an answer. The best way to start may be to try to write out in one sentence what the problem or question actually is, and to continue with this method as more information begins to reshape your initial formulation. For example, the question behind this chapter is: What is the role of audience in writing? The chapter itself is an attempt at answering. (The advice of my high school math teacher to help solve equations may be helpful here: What am I given? What do I need to know?) Approaching it this way may help you limit the topic, keep your focus as you both research and write, and find both a thesis and a conclusion.
7. View the paper topic from your teacher's perspective. Ask yourself how completing this paper helps further course goals. Is it strictly an extra-credit project in which anything goes? Or does the paper's completion also complete your understanding of the course?

Each of these ideas suggests that you can do certain things psychologically to set up and gain control of your writing from the outset. Sometimes none of these suggestions will work, and the whole process will simply be a struggle; it happens to me in my writing work more often than I care to recount. But often one or two of these ideas will help you get started in the right direction. In addition, of course, it helps to consult the teacher with some of your emerging ideas. Because the teacher made the assignment, he or she can best comment on the appropriateness of your choices.

WRITING TO CLASSMATES

Next to the teacher, your most probable school audience is your peers. More and more teachers are finding value in asking students to read each other's writing, both in draft stages and in final form. You will probably be asked to share your writing with other students in a writing class, where both composing and critiquing papers are everybody's business. Don't be surprised if your history or biology teacher asks you to do the same thing. But equally important to remember is that you could initiate such sharing yourself, regardless of whether your teacher suggests it; the benefits will be worth it.

Writing to other students and reading their work is distinctly different from simply talking to each other; written communication demands a precision and clarity that oral communication does not. When you share your writing with a peer, you will be most aware of where your language is pretentious or your argument stretched too thin. If you ask for feedback, an honest classmate will give it to you—before your teacher has to. I think that students see pomp and padding as readily as teachers do and are equally put off by it. What's the point in writing pretentiously to a classmate?

The following are some of the possible ways to make sharing drafts profitable:

1. Choose people you trust and respect to read your draft. Offer to read theirs in return. Set aside enough time (over coffee in the snack bar?) to return drafts and explain your responses thoroughly to each other.
2. When possible, *you* decide when your draft is ready to share. I don't want someone to see a draft too early because I already know how I am going to continue to fix it; other times, when I am far along in the process, I don't want a response that suggests that I start all over. There's a balance here: it's better that I seek help on the draft before I become too fond of it, when I tend to get defensive and to resist good ideas that might otherwise help me.
3. Ask for specific responses on early drafts. Do you want an overall reaction? Do you have a question about a specific section of your paper? Do you want help with a particularly intricate argument? Do you want simple editing or proofreading help? When you share a draft and specify the help you want, you stay in control of the process and lessen the risk of your reader's saying something about your text that could make you defensive. (I'm very thin-skinned about my writing—I could lose confidence fast if I shared my writing with nonsupportive people who said anything they felt like about my work.)
4. When you comment on someone else's paper, use a pencil and be gentle. Remember how you feel about red ink (bad associations offset the advantages of the contrasting color), and remember that ink is permanent. Most writers can't help but see their writing as an extension of themselves. Writing in erasable pencil *suggests* rather than *commands* that changes *might* rather than *must* be made. The choice to do so remains where it should, with the writer rather than the reader.
5. Ask a friend with good language skills to proofread your paper before submission. Most readers can identify problems in correctness, clarity, and meaning more easily in another person's work than in their own. When students read and respond to (or critique) each other's writing, they learn to identify problems in style, punctuation, and evidence that may occur in their own writing.

PUBLICATION

Writing for publication is something you may not have to do while you're still in school. Conversely, you may have already done so in letters to the newspaper editor or articles for a school paper. However, you may have a teacher who wants you to experience writing for an audience that doesn't know who you are. When you write for an absent audience, there are a few things to keep in mind:

1. Assume ignorance unless you know otherwise. If you assume your audience knows little or nothing about what you are writing, you will be more likely to give full explanations of terms, concepts, and acronyms. Because you will never know exactly into whose hands your published piece will fall, it's always better to over- than to underexplain. (This suggestion, of course, is also a good one to use for known academic audiences. The cost of elaborating is your time; the cost of assuming too much will be a lower grade.)
2. Provide a full context that makes it clear why you are writing. This is true in books, articles, reviews, and letters to the editor. You can often do this in a few sentences early in your piece, or you can provide a footnote or endnote. Again, no harm is done if you provide a little extra information, but there is a real loss to your reader if you do not.
3. Examine the tone, style, and format of the publisher before you send your manuscript. You can learn a lot about the voice to assume—or avoid—by looking at the nature of other pieces published in this medium.
4. Use the clearest and simplest language you can. I want to be careful here not to be prescriptive, because the level of language you choose is dependent on your analysis of the situation in which you're writing. However, I would not try overly hard to sound erudite, urbane, or worldly; too often the result is pretension, pomposity, or confusion. Instead, let your most comfortable voice work for you, and you'll increase your chances of genuinely communicating with your reader.
5. If you are worried about having your manuscript accepted, send a letter of inquiry to see what kind of encouragement the editor gives you. This gives you a better indication of what the editor wants; it also familiarizes him or her with your name, increasing your chances of a good reading.

YOURSELF

One more audience is especially worth commenting on: yourself: Regardless of your intended audience, you, too, must be pleased with your writing. You want it to represent you well. You want just the right combination of thought and expression to create just the right impression. Our first audience is always ourselves. We must think our own writing "good."

In exploratory writing, your focus is primarily on your ideas. But when you write for a teacher, classmate, or editor, you are most likely to please them when you please yourself first. The following suggestions may help you do that:

1. Read aloud to yourself from your own writing. Listen to the rhythms of your words and sentences: Do you like them? Do they sound natural or forced? (If you are a native speaker of English, your ear should tell

you these things. If you are not, read them to a native speaker for a reaction.)

2. Edit. Allow time to reread your finished paper, looking for repetitions, inexact explanations, imprecise words, useless words, and clear-cut mistakes.
3. Proofread. The last act of editing is proofreading to catch typos and simple errors. Because I write on a computer that has a program to check my spelling, I use that first. But that won't catch mistaken correct spellings ("their" for "there"), typos that accidentally create correct words ("do" for "so"), usage or punctuation mistakes, or omitted words. In the end, I must proofread the old-fashioned way, reading slowly, moving a ruler down line by line, forcing myself to read every word.

Writing to different audiences will be a fact of your working life, whether you are in business, engineering, law, medicine, politics, teaching, foreign service, etc. Those of you who excel at it may well get the early promotions. You will learn to do it, one way or another, when you have to. Why not start now?

DEBORAH COXWELL TEAGUE (b. 1953)

Making Meaning—Your Own Meaning—When You Read

CONSIDER THIS:

Deborah Coxwell Teague is director of First-Year Writing at Florida State University. She holds advanced degrees in reading and language arts and in rhetoric and composition, has taught both middle and high school, and has directed the university's Reading/Writing Center. Teague studies and writes about reading, writing assessment, and teacher education and says that reading and writing shaped the person she is today. She recalls, "I grew up in a small southern town, the daughter of conservative, extremely protective parents, and without books to read, I think I would have lost my mind." She says that reading about others' experiences and their ideas and writing about her own world and the world beyond helped her make sense of who she was and who she might become. "Sure, reading and writing are essential skills for succeeding in school and in business, but that's just the beginning, and that's why I love being a teacher," says Teague. "Teaching gives me the opportunity to help individuals discover how reading and writing can influence and expand their worlds." Teague's essay can help you reflect on the changes you experience as you move from high school to college culture (if that's the case) or from one learning community to another. She also shows us that reading and writing are interactive processes. Writers need audiences, and actual and imagined readers influence the choices we make as we compose.

Some of us consider ourselves to be more of a reader than a writer (or the reverse). Which is true for you? In Chapter 2 you investigated how you became a reader and a writer, and when reading this selection, consider how you improve as a writer (and how much that improvement depends on understanding reader–writer interactions). Teague's essay offers a useful parallel to the discussion about reading for college writing that you find in the introduction to *On Writing: A Process Reader.*

When I first began teaching high school English, I wondered if I had somehow completely missed out on an extremely important part of teacher training. I wondered if I had been absent—or perhaps I'd been doing some serious day dreaming—the day my college professor passed out the guide that revealed the secret to discovering the one true, correct meaning of a piece of literature. You see, when I was a high school student, my English teachers always had the answers, or at least I thought they did. Anytime we high school students were told to read a short story, a poem, or an essay for class, my teachers knew exactly what the selection meant. They knew precisely what the author was trying to communicate to the reader in the short story, poem, or essay. They had all the right answers. They had the knowledge and they gave it to us, their students. But when I became a teacher and assigned a short story, a poem, or an essay for my students to read, I was never sure I knew exactly what the author was trying to say to the reader. I knew what *I thought* the selection meant; I knew how *I interpreted* the text—but I didn't know if my interpretation was the correct one.

I clearly remember the dazed and confused looks on my high school students' faces when I first asked them what they thought about a selection I had asked them to read for class. "What do you think the author is saying in this poem?" I asked, and most of them looked at me as if I had lost my mind. I was the teacher. I was supposed to tell them what the author meant, not ask their opinions. I was supposed to know beyond the shadow of a doubt what the author had intended when she wrote the poem—but I didn't. I thought about discussing my problem—my shortcoming—with my colleagues, but I didn't want to let them know I wasn't the wonderful young teacher I fancied they thought I was. So I kept my thoughts to myself and continued to ask my students to read closely and share their interpretations with me and with the rest of the class. Together, we attempted to construct meanings for the texts we read.

That was more than just a few years ago, and since then I've made a discovery: My teachers were faking it—at least in some respects. They probably did not even realize they were faking it, but they were—at least some of the time. They had never sat down with William Shakespeare, Emily Dickinson, or Langston Hughes to discuss the one "true" meaning of *Romeo and Juliet, I'm Nobody! Who Are You?* or *Dream Deferred.* But when we discussed those literary selections in class, they *acted* as if they had all the answers. Looking back, I realize now that they did have many of the answers, and even when they didn't, their intentions were probably good: They were older and wiser than their students;

they were more experienced readers and knew how to read a text closely; they had background information about the author that we, their students, did not have; they had knowledge of the historical and cultural contexts in which the selection had been written; and they were the literature teachers—the ones who were *supposed* to have the answers. Yes, they faked it when they led me to believe that they possessed the one, the true, the only correct way to interpret the text, but they weren't faking it when they shared information regarding plot, characters, point of view, or facts about the author's life and the historical and social contexts surrounding the literature.

In some of the writing classes you take at the college level, you will probably be assigned works of literature to read—short stories, poems, essays, perhaps plays and novels—but don't be surprised if your writing teacher doesn't ask you to focus on plot, character, and point of view. Don't be surprised if your writing teacher never asks you to write a formal literary analysis. And don' t be surprised if your writing teacher refuses to fake it. In fact, she will probably tell you that there is no one correct way to interpret a text—that the interpretation depends on a number of factors such as the reader's experiences, knowledge, and feelings—and that her primary interest is in *your* interpretation and in how you reached it.

Okay, sounds easy, you might be thinking at this point. *After all, if there's one right answer, how hard can it be?*

Sorry if I misled you. The reading you do for a writing class isn't as easy as it might sound. The easy classes, for me anyway, the ones that did not require much effort on my part, were the ones in which my teacher had all the answers and all I had to do was memorize the facts. That's not likely to be the scenario in a writing class. The reading you do for writing classes requires next to no memorization. The reading does, however, require lots of thinking about and writing about what you read, and lots of rereading, rethinking, and rewriting as you go about making meaning—your meaning—of the text.

We teachers sometimes forget that not all of our students know how to read.

What is she talking about? you might be thinking. *She's talking about college students, right? Come on, if you re in college, you know how to read.*

Not necessarily—not the way I'm talking about anyway,

A few years ago, toward the beginning of the semester, I asked the students in my second-semester first-year writing class to read Alfred, Lord Tennyson's *Ulysses* for class. I love that poem; it's been one of my favorites for years, and I fully expected my students to be as excited about it as I was. I could hardly wait to hear their responses. We had read and discussed two or three pieces of literature at this point in the semester, and they had never failed to come to class full of ideas and ready for discussion. However, on the day we were to discuss *Ulysses,* my request for their responses, for their ideas, was met with silence and bowed heads as they stared at the texts before them on their desks.

"Well, what did you think of the poem?" I asked a second time. More silence. My first thought was that no one had read it, but then I realized that surely they had made time to read a two-page poem. They knew better than to think I would stand before them and deliver a lecture on the assigned reading. They knew I would ask for their ideas and opinions. More silence.

Finally one student spoke up. "I read it, but I couldn't figure it out. It was dumb."

Whoa—hold on there, young man. This is one of my favorite poems of all time and you are calling it dumb? Just who do you think you are? I somehow managed to keep my thoughts from coming out of my mouth, but doing so took a monumental effort.

"Yeah, I couldn't make any sense of it either," another student voiced.

"How many times did you read it," I asked, fully expecting my students to tell me that they had read it two, perhaps three times.

My students looked at each other and then looked at me as if I had asked the most stupid question they had ever heard. "Once, of course," came the reply.

At that point I realized that I had made several mistakes. To begin with, I had never talked with them about *how* to read. I had planned to—it was in my lesson plans—but I had gotten caught up in the maddening pace of the semester and hadn't made time for any talk of *how* to read. The other selections I had asked my students to read were easy to comprehend—one reading and they were able to share their thoughts and ideas with the rest of the class. The other texts we had read required no background knowledge of heroes from Greek mythology and contained no references to "the rainy Hyades" (10) or "the ringing plains of windy Troy" (17). The other texts were written in twentieth-century English and contained no sentences such as "Yet all experience is an arch wherethrough/Gleams that untraveled world, whose margin fades/For ever and for ever when I move" (19–21). I realized that I had not thought of *Ulysses* as a difficult text because I had read it so many times over the years that I could repeat most of it from memory. I had read Homer's *Odyssey* and Dante's *Inferno,* and I understood the many references made in *Ulysses;* my first-year students, however, did not. At the least, I should have provided them with background information before assigning the poem, and I most certainly should have explained that this poem—like many of the selections assigned in a writing class—would require multiple readings.

Reading a selection more than once might at first sound like an unnecessary, unpleasant, redundant chore, but if you think about it, you've probably read many texts repeatedly. As children, most of us love to be read our favorite books over and over, until we know the words by heart. My little ones, now 3 and 4 years old, have had me read *Where the Wild Things Are* (Sendack 1963), *Runaway Bunny* (Brown 1942), and *Madeline* (Bemelmans 1939) so many times that they now "read" the books to me. And many of us can think of a favorite movie we've "read" over and over until we know every line, every look, every move before we see it on the screen.

To read *Where the Wild Things Are, Titanic,* or *Star Wars* over and over is one thing—to read an assigned text more than once is something else altogether—right? Not completely. Although our motives might be different, the result of the rereading is much the same. When we reread, at least the first several times, we almost always learn something new with each reading—we make connections and pick up on details we didn't notice the first or perhaps even the second time we read the text. Am I saying that we should read every assigned text over and over? No. I am saying that many texts, especially those assigned for reading in a writing class, need to be read closely—more closely than one reading allows.

Rereading is only one of many activities that can help us read a text closely. Several other strategies that can help include selective underlining, making marginal comments, keeping a reading response journal, and keeping a double-entry notebook.

SELECTIVE UNDERLINING

Making marks in a text is often a difficult habit for college students to learn. In high school, most of the books you used probably belonged to the school system and were passed down from one student to another, and you were more than likely told to make no marks whatsoever in them. Now that you're in college and your books belong to you, you might be tempted to keep your books "clean" so that you can get a better price for them when you sell them back to the bookstore at the end of the semester. Don't give in to this temptation. Write in your books. Think of it as an investment in your education. Besides, the minuscule amount the bookstore will give you for your books is hardly worth what you'll lose if you refrain from making your books—and the information in them—your own.

As you read a text, underline or highlight words, phrases, and sentences that stand out to you. The words you decide to underline will depend to a large extent on your reasons for reading. For the reading you do in a writing class, you'll probably want to underline words, phrases, and sentences that are especially striking to you—for whatever reason. If you're reading an essay on a controversial topic, you might underline the main points the author makes in the argument. If you're reading a poem, you might underline phrases that, in your opinion, are beautifully written and/or especially meaningful to you. If you're reading a short story, you might underline parts of the story that remind you of similar experiences you've had. The parts of a text that you decide to underline are likely to be quite different from what someone else underlines—and that's fine. Underlining can help you pay closer attention as you read than you would without a marker in hand, and underlining also can help you later when you review the text.

MAKING MARGINAL COMMENTS

In addition to underlining as you read, get in the habit of making notes to yourself in the margins. When I am reading a challenging text, one that is difficult for me to understand, or perhaps one that is not especially interesting to me, I've found that I'm less likely to let my mind wander as I read—less likely to be thinking about what I might eat for dinner that night or what I'm going to do over the weekend—if I make notes in the margin as I go along. I might write a phrase or a sentence in the margin beside each paragraph summing up the main point of the paragraph. If I finish reading a paragraph and have no idea what point the author was trying to make, I read it again. This strategy forces me to read more closely and keep my mind on what I'm reading.

Marginal comments serve lots of other useful purposes. When you're reading an essay on a controversial topic, you might respond to the author's argument in the margins of the text. If you disagree with the author's point, respond in the margin. If you don't think the author is providing sufficient evidence to prove her point, make a note of your reaction in the margin. When you're reading a short story and you make a connection between something that happens in the story and a personal experience, jot down a note in the margin. Marginal comments allow you to carry on a conversation with the text as you read.

KEEPING A READING RESPONSE JOURNAL

This is a useful tool that provides a place for you to respond more fully than you might respond in marginal comments as you read a text. If you decide to keep a reading response journal, use it as a place to do more than simply summarize what you've read. Think of the journal as a place to carry on a more extended dialogue with the text. You might explore why you particularly disliked or liked a selection. If you disliked the selection, what caused your reaction? Did you disagree with the author's opinion? If so, how does your opinion differ from the author's? Did the author fail to make a strong argument? How could the argument have been made stronger? Do you feel the author was biased? If so, in what particular ways did the bias come across in the text? If you were not interested in the subject matter being discussed, what do you think caused your lack of interest? How is your opinion of the selection related to what's going on in your own life? Explore places in the text where you felt confused. What do you think caused the confusion? Explore places in the text where you had questions. If you especially enjoyed a particular selection, what was there about it that made you like it? Explore parts of the selection to which you could especially relate. Explore experiences in your own life that came to your mind as you read the selection.

KEEPING A DOUBLE-ENTRY NOTEBOOK

The first time I was told to keep a double-entry notebook, I was less than excited about the assignment. We were told to draw a line down the middle of the page. On one side of the line we were to record phrases, lines, and/or passages from the text, and on the other side of the line we were to respond to what we had recorded. The whole assignment sounded to me like a lot of unnecessary busy work. I was wrong; it wasn't busy work. And today, years later, I still have that first double-entry notebook. There's something about recording others' ideas, and then responding to them that makes a text more meaningful for the reader. Keeping a double-entry notebook forces the reader to enter a dialectic—a discussion—with the author. No longer is the reader an outsider—a voyeur—looking on yet remaining invisible. Responding to the text requires involvement and helps the reader make his or her own meaning from the words on the page.

The reading you do for a writing class requires much more than reading for the main idea or reading so that you can write a plot summary or a character sketch. It requires more than reading to remember the characters' names and who did what to whom at what time and in what place. Reading for a writing class requires that you do much more than memorize what someone else tells you is the author's main intent or purpose.

Instead, the reading you do for a writing class requires involvement. It requires that you see reading as much more than simply mentally processing words on a page. It requires that you see reading as a process of investigation and reflection. It requires that you do some serious thinking about the way you read—about the way you go about making meaning of a text. It requires that you enter a dialectic—a conversation, your conversation—with the text. The reading you do for a writing class requires you to respond to the text, to make your own interpretation of the author's purpose for writing, and to make connections between the author's experiences, thoughts, and ideas, and your own. The reading you do for a writing class requires you to make your own meaning of the words on the page and to be ready to share that meaning with others. You may discover that your interpretation of a particular text is quite different from your classmates' or your teacher's—and that's okay. In a writing class, there's no need for anyone to fake it. Just read closely and make your own meaning.

Works Cited

Bemelmans, Ludwig. 1939. *Madeline.* New York: Viking.

Brown, Margaret Wise. 1942. *Runaway Benny.* New York: HarperCollins.

Sendak, Maurice. 1963. *Where the Wild Things Are.* New York: Harper & Row.

Tennyson, Alfred. 1993. "Ulysses." *Windows.* Eds. Jeff Rackham and Olivia Bertagnolli. 483–84. New York: HarperCollins.

5

Classroom Authors

BENJAMIN LAUREN

What Are We Doing with Our Pennies?

CONSIDER THIS:

Benjamin Lauren was a graduate student in creative writing when he wrote this essay. The class assignment was to write in the manner of the short "Talk of the Town" essays found at the beginning of each week's *New Yorker* magazine. These writings focus on place, person, or event. Ben's does all three and his essay also illustrates the ways individuals from two different cultures, in this case student and banker, can be talking at amusing cross purposes. Ben uses the banker as a foil for his own reverie on a candy store in his past, but he also ends with a quiet observation about memory. "I had a problem finishing the essay," he notes in his process narrative, "until I remembered the ending of a poem I had written last year that never seemed to go anywhere. The lines were, 'I forgot about Jesse and ate lunch. Then I forgot about lunch.' I realized that this was exactly what I did with my memory of John's Root Beer stand while I was half listening to the banker speak about pennies. So I actually generated the ending for this a year ago." If you're a student of people and culture like Ben, you've likely noticed that travel offers many moments for meditation.

Recently, I was flying to Milwaukee when the banker next to me began explaining that banks are having a hard time stocking pennies. He was a chubby man with chipmunk cheeks and smelled of Brut aftershave. Just when I began imagining where he was storing all of those pennies, he said, "consumers are literally piggybanking their pennies and cashing them in all at once." I knew what he was describing because I had done this in the past, a habit I'd started as a child—emptying my parents' Folgers cans and cutting a coin-sized slit into the cover to store all of my pennies. The difference now is when I was young, my friends and I didn't deposit our pennies into our savings accounts or cash them in when we'd take our yearly vacations. We'd take our pennies up the street to John's Root Beer stand and spend them on candy. John's was my neighborhood's secret. It wasn't popular for its Root Beer—it was popular because it was up the street.

The stout banker adjusted restlessly in his small seat and knocked me in the chest with his elbow, which brought me back into our conversation that he was having with himself. He didn't notice that he had hit me, and went on, "I mean, take my bank for example. We asked the reserve for so many pennies, and they only gave us half of our order. There are 200 billion of these suckers in circulation all around the world!" But I drifted off again—I had already been imagining the candy I had bought when I was younger with all of my pennies. There was the rope licorice, the Bazooka bubble-gum, Tootsie Rolls, and jawbreakers. I actually tried to break my jaw several times, but it never worked. The owner of John's thought it was a good idea to paint the stand orange so that it stuck out to the passerby. It was the shiniest and brightest orange paint that I had ever seen.

I grunted a "wow" at the man so I could daydream more about John's in the fall before winter closed them down until spring, and my friends and I would jump in the huge pile of leaves in the back of the stand. The man took my grunt as a signal that I was interested in what he was ranting about. I remembered how my friends and I would wait until customers would leave and we'd check to see if they had left any pennies on their orange John's trays on the orange picnic tables that surrounded the stand. For some unknown reason, a lot of people would leave a few pennies behind. Maybe they knew about our candy habits.

The banker ate some peanuts and went on, now sweating. "Can you believe that merchants have to ask people for exact change because they have no pennies in their drawers? And banks can't do anything about it!" I shrugged and said, "Why don't they just press more?" That was a mistake. He filled his cheeks with air and said, "Because they are a bunch of idiots anyway." And by looking at him, I encouraged him to go on as I thought about John's, jingling the change in my pocket. "With this change I could get at least some rope licorice," I thought. The taste came back into my mouth. It reminded me of how a burning cherry candle smells. I thought of the antique milk jar on my dresser and smiled to myself. If this sweaty man only knew about the pennies I horded in that jar. My mother used to joke with me when I was eight that I had all of the pennies in the world stored away in coffee cans. The more the banker went on, the more I thought my mother may have been right. "That's just it," he said on the downside of a particularly long breath, "I'd like to know—what are we doing with our pennies?"

I looked up from my folded hands resting on my tray table next to my ginger ale and pretzels. "Saving them for postage," I said. "And for candy." I don't think he understood my sarcasm. But that is what I do with my pennies. Except now I buy candy a lot less, only sometimes dabbling a bit in my saccharin childhood. He went on, "No, I'll tell you what they're doing . . . ." But I didn't listen to where his explanation went. I thought of John's some more and then I forgot about it, just like I did when I was child.

KENNETH REEVES

"Freaks" and Geeks

CONSIDER THIS:

Writing for the same assignment, to create a work suitable for the "Talk of the Town," Kenneth Reeves, a graduate student in English education when he composed this essay, focused on a distinct culture, movie aficionados, particularly

B movie fans, embodied in the person of his interview subject, Mark Asaf. As he ushers us into this world (along the way sharing his own love of this movie genre), Reeves educates us concerning community members' habits and values. At the same time, Reeves's essay is also, in its way, a preview/review of a recently released B movie.

Before you read, you might think of other hobbyists and fanatics you know. What are the attributes of someone obsessed with a topic, a collection, a sport, a particular lifestyle? How do you know they're far gone in their passion for this subject or activity? What are your own obsessions and passions and how have these directed you toward particular communities of like-minded individuals? In particular, how did you access the language and rhetoric of that culture?

Mark Asaf has a passion for B movies that started when he was nine years old. "The first monster movie I ever saw was *Frankenstein* (James Whale, 1931)," he says with a gleam, "and I've loved them ever since." Ace is, among other things, a collector of B-movie memorabilia. It started out small, a few yellowing marquee posters in tasteful frames with favorite titles like *The Giant Claw* (Fred F. Sears, 1957) and *The Monolith Monsters* (John Sherwood, 1957) hanging in the dining room. Gort surveys the piano with steely disinterest from a poster for *The Day the Earth Stood Still* (Robert Wise, 1951) over by the kitchen.

Sitting among these talismans of second-string classics, I start thinking about the upcoming release of the first authentic B movie of the 2002 summer season and feel my eternal internal debate recommence. On the one hand, lurid scenes of riding-mower-sized spiders leaping at motorcross-jumping dirt bikes in the noonday Mojave sun promises the tawdry sort of gratification every true B-movie aficionado craves in the secret depths of his soul. On the other hand, it's going to be a lousy movie.

But then, isn't that the point? These days, B movies are bad by definition, and those of us who enjoy them can see within a doomed irony that rivals Aeschylus' Orestian efforts, while admittedly lacking his Promethian talent. Watching a movie whose plot, premise, and script can yield at best a slightly-less-than-mediocre film get treated by its auteurs as the height of entertainment and humor is, in itself, both humorous and entertaining. On the other hand, it's going to be a lousy movie.

As Ace and I start dropping obscure titles at each other, I realize that it takes a special breed to appreciate the underlying pathos of such blatantly awful films, a breed with unhealthy levels of morbid curiosity and a surprisingly absurdist sense of humor. A breed with a craving for popcorn and unintentional satire. Why, I used to wonder as I'd watch yet another slime-covered creature stalk predictably out of the shadows, do they keep on making this crap? And I would inevitably lead me to ponder the most logical rebuttal: why do we keep on watching this crap?

Because there's something mesmerizing about B movies, a sort of car-wreck hypnosis that keeps them from hurting too much. They are almost primal in their black-and-white moral simplicity, clearly defining the boundaries between cleft-chinned good and the sort of implacable evil that just has to die. We know from the opening scenes who's going to live and which vial of green serum will transform some of the local fauna into those rampaging hellbeasts we saw in the previews. Every B movie has an inherent conservatism that is oddly comforting, a definitive sense of order that goes beyond the rational, and it is that very unjustifiable comfort that makes their allure so compelling. No one truly believes (no one can believe truly) that such films have any redeeming qualities, but we like them anyway.

Opening the door of a bulky cottage in his backyard, Ace tells me that five years ago he bought some rows of chairs from an old movie theater that was giving up the ghost. Over the next few months, he remade this detached apartment behind his house into a private theater for the newest additions to his collection: 16mm film reels. "The first film we watched in here was *Vertigo* (Alfred Hitchcock, 1958), but that's not exactly a B movie," he says, touching the textured black casing of his projector. A screen covers the back wall, pulled down from the fixture screwed into the ceiling, and a cabinet beside the projector holds most of Ace's reels. "Have you seen *The Giant Gila Monster* (Ray Kellogg, 1959)?" He crouches down in front of the cabinet and opens a door. "I've got it right here."

According to Ace, 16mm collectors are a dedicated bunch who swap and sell thousands of titles from all different genres. Especially rare films can go for hundreds of dollars, but most cost less than fifty bucks. B-movie reels are fairly common, but Ace grudgingly admits that it's a niche market among collectors so availability can be a little spotty. The real cost of collecting film, he claims, lies in the equipment. A good projector can run half a grand or more, and a decent screen is a few hundred on top of that. I found an authentic popcorn machine on eBay for only $236 (butter flavoring not included), but the auction still had eight hours left. In addition to equipment, however, the 16mm collector also needs space. "Ten feet is about the minimum distance," Ace says, "the screen should be at least that far back."

Originally, studios made B movies as fodder for the double-feature market, a sort of cinematic hors d'oeuvre to their A-list films featuring actors with talent. The fact that some were so bad they couldn't help but become popular was the same sort of fortuitous accident that brought us penicillin. When vast improvements in the quality of special effects put the final bits of plastic moss on the cheesily-tilted styrofoam tombstone of Fifties' rubber-suit monster flicks some time in the late Sixties, the traditional B-movie spirit of hopelessly earnest myopia changed into a sort of smirky self-satire. The new brand of B relies heavily on campy humor, allusions to pop culture, and an unrepentant pandering to our love of two-dimensional characters. Films like *Deep Rising* (Stephen Sommers, 1998) and *Tremors* (Ron Underwood, 1989)—one of the genre's all-time best—succeed in fusing such traits into a gestalt whose very silliness makes them deeply witty. Unfortunately, such successes are increasingly rare, and this is the source of my internal debate. Because I know it's going to be a lousy movie.

Back on Ace's couch, I have a perfect view of the poster for *The Wasp Woman* (Roger Corman, 1959) that hangs over his TV. "Monster movies stretch the bounds of fiction," he replies, "they make more things possible. I think that's why I like them." We've been discussing the merits of B movies as a genre, and neither of us has been able to satisfactorily explain their appeal. "You should check out bmonster.com," he says, giving up. "They're a really good source of information about monster movies." When I bring up this summer's arachno-schlock thriller, Ace smiles again. "I'm not going opening night," he nods, "but I'm definitely seeing it on a big screen."

I admire his dedication, but I'm not sure I'll even go. I've seen enough in the commercials to have a pretty good idea how bad the acting's going to be, and those "funny" soundbites are even worse. On the other hand, they did name it *Eight Legged Freaks* (Ellory Elkayem, 2002). . . .

CONNECTING TO READING

A. Make a journal entry in which you consider yourself a member of communities (as Benjamin Lauren was a student and not a banker, as Mark Asaf and, likely, Kenneth Reeves, belong to the B-movie fan base). To do this, list all the forums, locations, or groups where you meet with two or more other individuals to whom you are united by some common bond or effort. My list might include: writing group, English department, family dinner, teachers' associations, and friends who meet bimonthly for dinner at San Miguel Mexican restaurant. These are the people I meet with and talk to regularly. I write to some but not all of them. I also have a number of other written discourse communities: the English department e-mail listserv; my three sisters (we share group e-mails); the local newspaper (should I care to write a letter to the editor); and so on. Consider your list and freewrite about the attributes of membership required for each of your communities. Do you have to participate in not just label yourself as a member, to be part of a community? In a second freewrite, discuss the ways in which one becomes a good member and/or loses membership rights for one of your communities. What are the responsibilities of membership? The actions of a member in good standing? How do you know what you know about this community (its rules, responsibilities, and so on)? In class, compare your final freewrite with those of members of a small discussion group. A number of the authors in this chapter reflected on public and school communities, did you?

B. In your next journal entry—having defined communities and the process of being a community member—investigate communication as an aspect of community membership. Consider how you change as a communicator as you address each of your varied audiences (how would the banker in Benjamin Lauren's essay speak when he is not on the plane but in the bank's monthly board meeting instead, for instance?). Do you use the same written language in a personal e-mail as you do in a letter to the editor or to your supervisor suggesting changes in job conditions? If not, how does your language change and why? How do you know what shifts to make? What are the costs of making or not making such accommodations? Tell some stories as you consider whether or not you are a rhetorician as defined by Edward Corbett and Robert Connors.

C. On a course discussion board (if you have one) or in a journal entry, make the case for academic discourse, using any of these authors to help you, particularly Mike Rose, Gerald Graff, Stanley Witkin, and Kenneth Reeves. Why is it necessary for professionals to use specialized language? What is that language in service of? Do your peers agree or disagree with you? (After this you might want to make the countercase against such discourse, starting from your reading of John Agard's poem.)

D. In class, with a partner, share your observations about two chapter authors who express hesitations about, confusions with, or challenges to the way communities ask their members to act, speak, or think as a condition of membership and/or advancement (consider, for instance, Dove, Agard, Shen). What objections or concerns might be offered to the idea that to be a social scientist, for instance, you need to talk the way social scientists talk or that to be an English speaker in good standing you must be fluent in "public" prose? After your discussion, summarize your observations in a follow-up journal entry.

E. In a class discussion, explore the ways culture (or cultures) influence and shape you as a writer. Share some stories of this sort of influence. What is lost when you subsume your cultural individuality into a larger community? Why (and when) might you want to or not want to do this? You might want to follow Deborah Coxwell Teague's advice for keeping a double-entry notebook by reading Fan Shen's essay, making a journal entry, and then rereading that essay with these questions in mind to reflect on your original reading response. Doing so will prepare you to be an active and informed discussion participant.

CONNECTING TO WRITING

A. To compose an informal handout to be shared with your classmates, investigate the writing conventions in particular and the discourse conventions in general for your declared major or an area of possible career interest to you. Begin by consulting several of your textbooks, professors, and their professional journals. What sorts of talk count? What type of prose is common? What field-specific jargon or language is used? What type of research counts for making knowledge in the field? How can you tell an insider from an outsider? What subspecialties of the field can you identify? What factions exist? What are the big arguments going on in the field? Report on what you've learned in a one- to two-page report on becoming a . . . (physicist, Shakespearean scholar, marine biologist, nurse practitioner, criminologist, etc.).

B. Informally explore audience considerations by revising a paper that you wrote for one course. Rewrite a section of this paper for a "lay" audience. In your journal or on a Web posting that consists of the original passage and a revision, reflect on the changes you made for your new target audience and why.

C. As a group, choose a controversial issue. Have each group member consult a handbook of rhetoric (perhaps Corbett and Connors) or the persuasion section of a writing handbook to find out more about the *topics* you can use in arguing any case. Use these to *discover* the possible arguments you could deploy about a controversial subject such as whether or not we should allow stem cell research. In your group, brainstorm and apply as many of the topics as you can to see how they might help you generate your best, most persuasive, argument. Keep notes and compose a handout for the class, illustrating the process for using topics to discover effective arguments. If you have a class listserv, post these notes as a class guide to argumentation and resource for future papers.

D. Freewrite for 20 minutes in your journal on a provocative sentence from any of the essays in this chapter and use it as a prompt for exploring your thoughts about audience and/or community. Revise this into a one-page, informal, exploratory, reflective position statement that you can post on-line or share with class members.

E. In a journal entry, describe your own experiences with teacher and peer audiences and classroom writing communities. Tell stories. Have these experiences been positive or negative or mixed? Why? What are your strengths and weaknesses as a writing workshop member? How do you feel when peers and/or teachers respond to your writing? What do you wish you could change about such responses? Why? Use this entry to help you contribute to a class discussion on the same topic. Be prepared to read one of your stories, illustrations, or vignettes.

WRITING PROJECTS

1. Compose and design an introduction to your major for entering first-year students (you may choose to coauthor with another class member in the same major). Think of this as a brochure or short handout that potential majors might pick up on their campus tour or refer to on the Web. Why should they consider this major? What is required to join the community? What are the benefits and responsibilities of this course of study? Where can they go to learn more? You might want to include an "insider's guide" to special language and terms used in courses, ways to accelerate or improve one's chances to become a welcomed insider to that program and/or department, and so on. Formulate this as a Web page or illustrate the brochure if you have computer access and digital capabilities.
2. To compose an open letter to an audience of non-U.S. students who have recently arrived on your campus, investigate the campus resources available to students from other cultures and countries. What are the goals of those who run these sites and/or provide these services? What can an interested monocultural campus resident do to become more cross-culturally involved (or, vice-versa, what can a student from abroad do to become more involved in general campus activities)? This project lends itself to interviewing, illustrating, coauthoring, and Web posting as well.

3. Write a persuasive letter to the editor of your school or city newspaper on a topic about which you feel strongly. Use classical topics as outlined by Edward Corbett and Robert Connors to help you discover your best arguments. After you've completed your draft, decide if you noticed yourself writing any differently when you shifted from a classroom to a civic audience. How? Revise the letter and send it to the editor.
4. Write a personal essay modeled on that of Gerald Graff, Fan Shen (for a more scholarly model), Benjamin Lauren, or Kenneth Reeves (for a more literary model). Borrow either the essayist's general topic or style (or both).
5. Write an autoethnography. Write about a personal issue but place it in a social context; compare your lived experience to established knowledge. As Stanley Witkin points out, you might write about your eating disorder, but you would also research such disorders and share that research. You might write about your struggle with an absent parent, but you'd also research divorce in the United States. You might explore your excitement about learning to scuba dive and contextualize your experiences with information about trends and developments in the sport.
6. Write a poem (or song) of protest, as Aagard did, and examine the work of such a poem in an accompanying essay that explores what the poem accomplishes for you that an essay might not. Or integrate a poem of protest into an essay of protest or social analysis.
7. Write an essay that explores your connection to the academic community you are now inhabiting. How did you decide to come to college? What in your past helped or hindered you? Now that you're here, how do you feel about entering this community? What are your struggles? Hopes? What are your predictions about where you'll be 5, 10, or 20 years from now? Both Gerald Graff's and Rita Dove's essays may offer ideas or prompts for such an essay.
8. I know a number of writers who claim they write for themselves. Is that true for you? Can it be true for any writer? How do audiences help and hinder a writer? What is your sense of who you write for and why? Use any of the authors in this chapter to help you explore the topics of the writer's audience or reading like a writer.
9. Write an essay on culture. Discuss the issue of what you like or dislike about your culture (of course, you need to define culture). Think, for instance, of stories or movies where individuals are cut off from their culture: shipwrecks (*The Tempest, Robinson Crusoe*) and castaways (Tom Hanks in *Castaway; Survivor*). You could shape this as a shipwreck narrative: What would you take with you? What are the essentials of your culture/communities?
10. Consider the future. How has technology changed our definition of community? of world cultures? How do you think these changes will play out in the future? In regard to these issues, project yourself in 25, 50, or 100 years into the future. Equally, you might want to consider the future of writers and writing, the book, any printed text.

* * * *

That's why I write a lot with other people. That and it's never quite as lonely. That and it's just plain more fun. You get to talk a lot. You get to hear yourself think. The best collaborations I've had were those where there was a lot of talk, where we would talk out the ideas and write as we talked, dictate the piece. The first draft would be a conglomerate of stuff—talked-out ideas, sixteen examples, a ramble or two here and there. A draft much like my [own] first drafts—way too long, a few gems hidden within a jungle. Then, each of us would try our hand at making it right—working on this part here, that part there, adding and deleting, whatever it needed. Then we would meet and see what we had and cut and write and add and subtract together. . . . The writing never seemed hard either—time consuming but not hard.

—LIL BRANNON

Chapter 4

Writing to Find Your Topic: Inventing, Exploring, Discovering

Thinking About Getting Started

> When I first started to write, I would sit for hours trying to think of something worthwhile to write about. So many things passed through my mind but not one seemed important enough to write about; nature, animals, helping others, and love were only a few topics. All of these topics are so broad, but I, as a young writer, thought I could tackle them. I didn't know then that I could never give these subjects justice unless I broke them down and wrote about the specifics in each.
>
> You will see that as you do mature in your thinking as well as your writing, how much easier it is to find subjects for your works. Actually, they seem to find you. As I think back on all the times I sat clueless about what to write, I realize I actually had thought of a million things to write about. Now I wonder if I'll ever have enough years in my life to write about each one in my own way.
>
> —MISSY, CLASSROOM AUTHOR

Invention activities provide insights into the ways writers actually write. In essence, all writers apprentice themselves to other (often more adept) writers by reading and imitating the more successful writer's work and then by giving themselves assignments that challenge their own skills and abilities. Invention, as you discovered in the last chapter, was one of the five canons of classical rhetoric. According to Edward P. J. Corbett in his *Classical Rhetoric for the Modern Student*, "*Inventio* is the Latin term . . . for "invention" or discovery." . . . *Inventio* was concerned with a system or method for finding arguments. In this chapter, we're focusing on invention as discovery.

Although other writers and writing teachers can develop these activities for you, you can create them yourself. They require rhetorical reading, the analysis of writer, subject and reader relationships, and the analysis of genre characteristics. *Genre* is a word we use to talk about types of writing (nonfiction, poetry, drama, and fiction, as well as variations within types; for instance, fiction includes westerns, romances, science fiction, and so on). Overall, in this sort of rhetorical analysis you're looking carefully at a text to copy its most admirable characteristics. To create an essay invention exercise, I read like a writer, looking at a series of essays with common themes or with interesting content and style. I consider how they are titled. I consider how they are organized. I read for techniques that I can fashion into self-assignments.

These exercises and self-assignments come from being a student of essay writing and working with classroom authors. They also come from reading the essays and working backwards; You might say, "This essayist achieved this effect: I bet if I did this and this and this, I could achieve the same or a similar effect in my own work." Careful analysis results in useful imitation. And analysis and imitation are skills I encourage you to cultivate because, lifelong, as a writer, you'll be inventing your own approaches to "assignments" and even the assignments themselves. Invention exercises work, so well, in fact, that several general techniques are now promoted in most writing classes. Here is an overview of those techniques that writers use most often.

- *Freewriting:* Write about anything for a set amount of time (5 or 10 minutes). Don't stop writing or reread. If you get stuck, repeat the last word you wrote until the boredom of doing so unsticks you. When freewriting at the computer, turn off your monitor and type rapidly to speed your thoughts. Stop your freewriting, reread it, and circle the most interesting discovery.
- *Guided Freewriting:* Same as above; however, you start writing in response to a particular (invention) prompt.
- *Listing and Brainstorming:* When you get ready to go to the store, you often make a list of all the things you think you need. Do the same with your writing. Quickly write down short notes related to your topic, or brainstorm a topic by listing everything you're interested in/concerned with at that moment.
- *Group Brainstorming:* Several individuals dictate ideas to a group recorder, or group members write on an agreed-upon topic and compile a master list. Another variation is to read something you've written to a group and ask them to help you add ideas and details.
- *The Reporter's Formula:* Alone or with a group, ask *who, what, where, when, why,* and *how* about your topic or subject. Freewrite your answers to each question and then use your discoveries to start a draft.
- *Clustering:* Alone or with a group, list a core word or term in the center of your paper or on a chalkboard. Brainstorm related networks of concepts, events, and details. Use connecting lines to indicate relationships.
- *Cubing:* Alone or with a group, take six perspectives on a topic or subject: *describe it, compare it, associate it, analyze it, apply it, argue for or against it.* Freewrite your answers to each perspective and then use your discoveries to start a draft.

- *Looping and Center-of-Gravity Sentences:* Freewrite for 10 minutes, then stop, reread, and circle the most important sentence. Next, begin again, starting with the circled sentence. Write 10 minutes more. Stop, reread, and again circle the most important sentence. Start again, using the second circled sentence. Complete three or more loops, finding several center-of-gravity sentences along the way.
- *Making an Authority List:* List 30 things you know a lot about or could be considered an authority on (especially if you list a specific audience; for instance, we're all "authorities" on going to high school when talking to anyone under the age of 14). Then circle the three items on your list that you've never written about. Rank them in the order of interest to you or share your list with class members and have them circle those items they know little about. Ask them to rank in order the five items they'd be most interested in reading about. Use their help to decide which two topics to explore. Write a five-minute freewrite on each item and decide which seems to have the most essay potential.

Invention techniques can be used to help you discover more about a topic or thesis you already have and/or to *expand* a draft in progress. At the same time, by reading generally in areas of interest to you and then applying some of these techniques to what you discover (possibly by starting with a provocative quote from your reading), you'll soon find a topic developing. My goal when assigning these inventions or when writing on some of them with classroom authors is to be sure that everyone goes home with ideas and possibilities. Sometimes it's extremely useful to explore several ideas before fixing on one. Inventions and journal writing help you conduct and organize your explorations.

Many professional writers keep writing journals which exist under a variety of aliases: notebooks, daybooks, diaries, almanacs, calendars, monthlies, logs, dialog journals, field accounts, ledgers, sketchbooks, or taped logs. Anne Lamott uses index cards like others use journals. Others of us keep journals on our computer or by saving our e-mails. Your journal can help you conduct self-explorations and/or clarify your values. It can provide a secure place for drafting, sketching, and collecting (I often print my poems and drafts and then paste them into my spiral-bound journal and add cartoons, ads, photographs, short notes, and lists). They can be used for dialogue with yourself (in the form of a double-entry journal) or with others (by sharing responses in groups and responding to each other's entries).

To introduce the essays in his edited collection *The Journal Book,* Toby Fulwiler lists the attributes of productive journals. The more a journal exhibits these attributes, the more successful it probably has been for the writer. A productive journal, he finds, will have several important characteristics. It will be written in an informal style and use *I,* the first person pronoun. It will use informal punctuation and punctuation for effect—dashes, underlining, block caps, or exclamation points. It will follow the rhythms and patterns of everyday speech. In addition, a successful class journal usually exhibits experimentation.

It consists of frequent and long entries; includes entries you initiate; is usually arranged in chronological order; and, overall, both explores and informs.

In analyzing his own daybook entries in *A Writing Teacher Teaches Writing,* Donald Murray finds that these include the following: observations, questions, lines, notes, plans, titles, leads (beginnings), quotations from other writers, outlines, diagrams, drafts, ideas for pieces, discussions with himself, postcards or pictures, paragraphs from newspapers, chunks of drafts that haven't worked, titles of books to read, prewriting, and notes on lectures. You can see that the writer's journal is very flexible and can be stored on a computer, collaged into a bound book or scrapbook, or even be kept in a large box.

In the readings that follow, Spike Lee's journal entries on the making of his film *Do the Right Thing* show how versatile the journal can be and provide a sample of journal writing for considering Fulwiler's observations as do the journal entries you've been keeping as a result of prompts in this textbook. Next, Anne Lamott explains how index cards help her keep lists and memories, much as a journal would. She argues that they allow her to capture more of what she observes and feels as a writer; in effect, index cards work for her as they might work for you, as memory aides and potential future writing prompts.

As we move on to focused invention exercises, Katharine Haake provides a writing exercise based on Richard Hugo's suggestion that all writers have a triggering subject. Haake's exercise is followed by a series of classroom handouts that offer you a number of encouragements for discovering a topic by writing. Invention exercises like these are derived by reading rhetorically, by looking at finished texts and saying, To write a text like this, what might the writer have been thinking? What might the writer have chosen to do? I enjoy reading classroom authors' process narratives, in part, because they teach me how better to make such readings of professional writers. When you see an author you admire investigate an unusual subject or use an effective technique, it's only natural to want to do the same yourself. The classroom handouts "Invention Exercises—Writing to Find Your Topic" direct you to subjects and approaches that have proven useful for any number of writers in the past.

Writers are pragmatic: They read for ideas. They're also careful observers of the world around them. Raymond Carver's poem "Sunday Night" suggests that a writer's consciousness is, in fact, the greatest invention instrument of all. His words remind us to "make use" of the world we experience and observe as well as of the writing prompts and self-assignments that allow us to gather and grow those observations into effective prose. Classroom authors Leah Marcum and Scott Arkin explore the brave new territories of the Internet, a medium that can be very exciting for personal journals and/or for dialoging with another writer. Although not talking exclusively about journaling, these writers' experiences can inform your thinking (and you probably have your own stories to share about life on the Internet or using classroom discussion boards).

5

Chapter Readings

SPIKE LEE (b. 1957)

Journal Entries: *Do the Right Thing*

CONSIDER THIS:

You may have viewed several of Spike Lee's films. In a group, discuss what characterizes his work. If you've viewed *Do the Right Thing* (or have the chance to do so before or after reading this entry), share your initial response to this film. Spike Lee, a native of Atlanta, went to Morehouse College and New York University's film school. Lee won the Student's Academy Award for his 1982 film *Joe's Bed-Stuy Barber Shop: We Cut Heads,* and received an Academy Award nomination for the documentary *Four Little Girls* (1999).

Lee credits his parents for his interest in the arts and has a complex view of himself as a "black filmmaker." In an interview with *IndieWire,* he said, "I have no problems with white America looking at me as a black man because I understand the mind-set and where we are in this country. I think the majority of white Americans are unable to look at somebody black and not the color of their skin first. That's just the reality." But Lee resists the idea of being a spokesperson. He told *American Visions,* "All my views have been solely my views, and I think that there are African American people who agree with me, but we also have African Americans who don't agree." As you read Lee's journal, you may want to reflect on his statements about being (or not being) a spokesperson for other African Americans. Even more, you may wish to consider the ways he makes use of a journal to explore and develop his art. How do you sense this journal functioned for him as a filmmaker? What types of reflection can you identify? Do you predict that he will continue to keep a journal?

DECEMBER 25, 1987

It's nine in the morning and I'm sitting down to get started on my next project, *Do the Right Thing.* I hope to start shooting next August. I want the film to take place over the course of one day, the hottest day of the year, in Brooklyn, New York. The film has to look hot, too. The audience should feel like it's suffocating, like *In the Heat of the Night.*

I'll have to kick butt to pull things together by August. If I'm not happy with the script, I'll hold off until the following summer. It's better to go at it right away, though, like Oliver Stone did by following *Platoon* with *Wall Street.*

I want most of the film to take place on one block. So, I need to scout a block in Brooklyn with vicious brownstones. We can build sets for the interiors, but most scenes will take place in the street and on stoops and fire escapes.

Its been my observation that when the temperature rises beyond a certain point, people lose it. Little incidents can spark major conflicts. Bump into someone on the street and you're liable to get shot. A petty argument between husband and wife can launch a divorce proceeding. The heat makes everything explosive, including the racial climate of the city. Racial tensions in the city are high as it is, but when the weather is hot, forget about it. This might be the core of a vicious climax for the film.

This block is in a Black neighborhood in Brooklyn. On one corner is a pizza parlor run by an Italian family who have refused to leave the neighborhood. One of the young Black characters will have a job at the pizzeria.

Although the Black and Puerto Rican block residents seem to get along with the Italian family, there is still an undercurrent of hostility. Of course this tension explodes in the finale. There should be a full-scale riot—all hell should break loose. Something provocative must set it off, like a cop shoots a kid and brothers go off. Then the rains come. I know, I know, sounds corny. But goddamn, this is only the first page.

The look of the film should be bright. The light in daytime should be an intense white light, almost blinding, and the colors, bright. I mean Puerto Rican bright. AFROCENTRIC bright. Everybody will be wearing shorts and cutoff jeans. Men will be shirtless, women in tube tops.

The image of this pizzeria keeps coming into my mind. It's gonna be important in the end. It's gonna be important. I see my character working there. He hates it there, but he's gotta have a job.

Sometime soon the characters will start talking to me very specifically. I will hear their individual voices and put their words down on paper.

For the entire mouth of January I'm gonna put my ideas down on legal pads. I think I'll have enough material to start writing the actual script on or around the first of February. Now mind you, February is also the month *School Daze* opens. But I'll try to be disciplined and not miss a day.

God willing, I'll finish my first draft around the beginning of March. That would give me five months before the first of August, when I want to start shooting. I can shoot all my exterior scenes in August and save my interiors for cover sets. That would be ideal. I would like the luxury of a ten-week shoot—at least.

DECEMBER 27, 1987

I would like this script to be circular. Every character should have a function. If a character is introduced, he or she should appear again and advance the script in some way.

I may use an image that reappears throughout the film. In *The Last Emperor* it was the cricket. Seeing the cricket at the end of the film made it magical for me.

After the climax of the film, I would like to have a coda. This scene could take place the morning after the riot. We see the aftermath from the night before. It's not so hot on this day, and folks seem to have regained their senses. I'll have to think of a way to convey this.

It's early, but I don't want anyone to die in the riot. Some people will get hurt. Some will definitely get fucked up, but as of now, no one will be killed.

While I was in the grocery today I heard a radio newscast that two Black youths had been beaten up by a gang of white youths in Bensonhurst. The two Black kids were hospitalized. They were collecting bottles and cans when they got jumped. This happened on Christmas night. Just the other day some Black kids fired up a white cab driver in Harlem. New York City is tense with racial hatred. Can you imagine if these incidents had taken place in the summer, on the hottest day of the year? I'd be a fool not to work the subject of racism into *Do the Right Thing.*

The way I see it, we'll introduce the subject very lightly. People will expect another humorous film from Spike Lee, but I'll catch them off guard. Then I'll drop the bomb on them, they won't be prepared for it.

If a riot is the climax of the film, what will cause the riot? Take your pick: an unarmed Black child shot, the cops say he was reaching for a gun; a grandmother shot to death by cops with a shotgun; a young woman, charged with nothing but a parking violation, dies in police custody; a male chased by a white mob onto a freeway is hit by a car.

It's funny how the script is evolving into a film about race relations. This is America's biggest problem, always has been (since we got off the boat), always will be. I've touched upon it in my earlier works, but I haven't yet dealt with it head on as a primary subject.

I need to use my juice to get the testimony of Cedric Sandiford and other key witnesses in the Howard Beach case. We're not only talking Howard Beach: It's Eleanor Bumpers, Michael Stewart, Yvonne Smallwood, etc.

If I go ahead in this vein, it might be in conflict with the way I want to tell the story. It can't be just a diatribe, WHITE MAN THIS, WHITE MAN THAT. The treatment of racism will have to be carried in the subtext until the end of the film. Then again, being too avant-garde, too indirect, might trivialize the subject matter. Any approach I take must be done carefully and realistically. I won't be making any apologies. Truth and righteousness is on our side. Black folks are tired of being killed.

This is a hot one. The studios might not want to touch this film. I know I'll come up against some static from the white press. They'll say I'm trying to incite a race riot.

The entire story is starting to happen in my mind. "The hottest day of the summer" is a good starting point, but I need more. I'll be examining racial tensions and how the hot weather only makes them worse. These tensions mount, then something happens outside or inside of the pizza parlor that triggers a major incident.

Now I'm grounded. I know what I'm doing. It will be told from a Black point of view. I've been blessed with the opportunity to express the views of Black people who otherwise don't have access to power and the media. I have to take advantage of this while I'm still bankable.

The character I play in *Do the Right Thing* is from the Malcolm X school of thought: "An eye for an eye." Fuck the turn-the-other-cheek shit. If we keep up that madness we'll be dead. YO, IT'S AN EYE FOR AN EYE.

It's my character who sees a great injustice take place and starts the riot. He turns a garbage can upside down, emptying the trash in the street. Then he goes up to the pizza parlor screaming, "An eye for an eye, Howard Beach," and hurls the garbage can. It flies through the air in slow motion, shattering the pizza parlor's glass windows. All hell breaks loose. Everyone takes part in the riot, even the old woman who sits in her window watching the block. This is random violence. But before this, the cops do something that escalates the conflict to violence. They might even kill someone. The riot takes off, and it's the Italians in the pizza parlor who have to pay.

In the riot scene, it might be vicious if no words were spoken until my character throws the garbage can in the window and screams "Howard Beach."

The subject matter is so volatile, it must be on the QT. No way are people gonna read the script, especially agents. I'm not giving out information on the film until it's about to be released. Mum's da word.

[JANUARY 1, 1987]

It has to be a small incident that leads to the film's final confrontation. This incident will appear to be nothing at first, then it turns into something bigger, then it turns into something bigger again. Add the combustible atmosphere of the hottest day of the year and you have a big disturbance, a race riot.

I know my character will throw the garbage can through the pizzeria window. This is prompted by a beating by the cops. But what prompted the cops? An idea came to me this morning. At Brooklyn College a couple of years ago there was a major disturbance between Black and white students that involved a jukebox. The Jewish kids wanted to listen to their music, the Blacks wanted to hear theirs. Somehow a fight started. That's the little incident I need.

What would happen if a Black youth came into the pizzeria with a giant box blasting rap? A box so loud people can't hear themselves think. This guy could be Joe Radio! The music has to be some vicious rap record. How 'bout a dope beat with a rap using the names of Black people along with a chorus of "Uplift the Race, By Any Means Necessary"?

Joe Radio comes into the pizzeria with his box booming. The owner tells him to turn it off. Joe Radio, or even better, Radio Raheem, just turns it up louder and orders his slice. The owner refuses to wait on anybody till Raheem takes the noise outta his store.

The owner's sons play Rocky Balboa and use force to remove Raheem. The climax is set in motion. A scuffle breaks out, the cops are called. Any time cops see a white person struggling with a Black person, you know who they're gonna go after. They put a choke hold on Raheem. He falls to the ground like a sack of potatoes. The cops try to revive him; they play it like he's faking. Get up, get up, they're yelling at him.

Finally the cups see what they've done to Raheem. They try to get him outta there without people knowing the deal, but it's too late. Word goes through the already volatile crowd: Radio Raheem is dead, they killed him. I hear this and pick up the garbage can, dump the garbage in the street, and scream "Howard Beach." The missile flies through the air in slo-mo, breaking the plate glass storefront, and the riot begins.

So that's what I'm talking about. How a little incident compounds tensions between Blacks and Italians and becomes a full-scale race riot. And how the hot weather adds fuel to the fire.

[JANUARY 2, 1988]

. . . There must be a resolution of some sort after the riot. For the most part, the Black uprisings in the sixties took place in poor, inner-city, neighborhoods. The buildings hit are still burnt-out shells, they were never replaced. The only people hurt in the long run were the Black people who lived in those communities. That's why this film must have a coda on the end. I'd get myself hung by showing violence for violence's sake.

In the first light of day, we can see the damage that was done the previous night. The pizzeria is totalled. Fire is still smouldering from the wreckage. My character is walking toward the pizzeria. He's not gloating or anything. He hears someone rummaging through the remains—it's the owner. Henceforth the owner's name is SAL and the pizzeria is SAL'S FAMOUS PIZZERIA.

Sal looks like he's on a mission. He finally stops when he notices my character standing there looking at him. This is where the most poignant scene should take place. It has to be subtle. It can't be any of this We-Are-the-World, We-Are-All-God's-Children, We-Can-Work-It-Out shit, either. But it has to be honest.

[FEBRUARY 14, 1988]

Remember how in *Raging Bull,* jealousy was Jake La Motta's Achilles' heel? Well, for Mookie it's money, money, and mo' money. He is constantly counting his money, arranging the dollar bills so they face the same way. It's about being paid.

I was searching for a reason why Mookie should go back to Sal's Pizzeria the morning following the riot. Now I've got it. Mookie goes back there to find Sal because he wants to get paid. Mookie never got paid by check, always in cash, he's off da books.

Sal can't believe Mookie has the gall to ask for his money. Sal doesn't want to hear it. His business has been burnt down to the ground and this guy Mookie wants to get paid. The dialogue isn't there yet, but that's definitely the final scene.

About the riot. As the crowd torches the pizzeria, the Fire Department arrives on the scene. Before firemen turn their hoses on the fire, they direct the water toward the people to disperse them. So we're back to Montgomery and Birmingham, Alabama; the only thing missing is Bull Connor and the German shepherds.

I had written earlier about a torrential downpour that comes at the height of the uprising. Now I have this idea about the crowd getting hosed. When I don't read my notes, I miss making these connections. Alright, alright, I'm gonna read all my notes tonight.

FEBRUARY 28, 1988

Yesterday I began work on the script. Well, actually, I began the last work before the actual writing of the script. I put down all the ideas or scenes and dialogue on three-by-five index cards. TOMORROW, I'll begin to write this motherfucker.

This morning I got up early to go to my corner store, T and T, to buy the paper. The young guys who work there had a Run-D.M.C. tape on. The owner, an old Italian guy, says, "What da fuck is dat? Turn that jungle music off. We're not in Africa. It's giving me a stomach ache." Sooner or later it comes out. Okay, so you don't like rap music. But why does it have to be about jungle music and Africa? I should have Sal say the same words to Radio Raheem in the movie.

FEBRUARY 29, 1988

It's the last day of February and I'm exactly where I want to be. I'm in a creative mood. I've finished making my three-by-five cards outlining every scene. March, the month I was born in, begins tomorrow. I'm ready and fired up.

MARCH 5, 1988

Last night I went to see Michael Jackson perform at Madison Square Garden. *School Daze* opened in ten more markets today. I had two hours of phone interviews this morning. It's 3:00 P.M. now and I haven't done any actual writing on the script. Instead, I read over what I wrote yesterday.

MARCH 6, 1988

When I stopped writing today I was up to page 48; that's roughly twenty-four typed pages. That's almost a third of the script down and this is only the fifth day of writing. I'm pleased with myself. I'm not trying to rush through this stuff either.

I have the next forty or so scenes on index cards lined up in order. I need to keep Mookie in the forefront. But, I can't forget about his sister Jade, and, I have to include Mookie's woman, the one he does the ice cube number with.

This weekend has been great. I've been writing my butt off. I'm not gonna take any more days off, just write straight through to the end.

MARCH 8, 1988

I'm into my second week of writing and I'm halfway through the first draft. I feel good about it. I have at least two or three more drafts coming, but the first one I can go to Paramount Pictures with. It's also the draft I can show to Bob De Niro [Lee's first choice to play Sal] and my key production staff. I hope to go to Cannes and I can work on a second draft there.

Now that I'm halfway through, I can focus on Mookie's thing about getting paid. I have to keep in mind how the change from day to dusk then night affects what's happening in the story. In the summer, though, it really doesn't get dark till eight o'clock or so.

MARCH 10, 1988

I wrote like a madman yesterday from 7:00 A.M. to noon. In the evening I went to see the Knicks lose to the Lakers.

When I stopped writing I was on page 111, which is something like fifty-five typewritten pages. That's great considering I haven't been at it for a full two weeks yet. There's no doubt in my mind now that a crisp, lean, and mean ninety-page script will be ready in time for us to shoot in August. Monty and I should sit down now and start assembling a production staff.

MARCH 13, 1988

It's early Sunday morning, a week before my birthday. Today begins my third week on the first draft of *Do the Right Thing*. I should finish by the end of this week.

MARCH 14, 1988

Yesterday I let Lisa Jones read what I have written so far. She was laughing a lot, so that's a good sign. When I stopped writing I was on page 144; roughly seventy-two typewritten pages. I'm up to the point where the uprising begins. I'll finish before I go to Los Angeles this Friday.

I gotta watch it, the ending I'm talking about. I can't let the last scene between Mookie and Sal be too chummy. Remember, Sal has had his business burnt to the ground. Also, what are Sal, Vito, and Pino gonna do when the pizzeria goes up in flames? Do they stand there and watch or what? Think about it, Spike, think about it.

MARCH 15, 1988

I didn't write yesterday. I was too sleepy, but I did wake up at six this morning and I'm about to bust it out. Y'know the deal.

MARCH 17, 1988

Tuesday morning I finished the first draft of *Do the Right Thing*. It came in at roughly eighty-seven typed pages. It's the fastest script I have ever written. In all, the actual writing of the first draft took fifteen days, but I have been taking notes since December.

The first draft may be finished, but that doesn't mean my work is done. More work is still to come on script. I have three or four more drafts. Typewritten, it might be four or five pages less than ninety. We hope to start shooting on the first of August, a little over four months from now. Time is not to be wasted.

I'm on a five-hour flight to Los Angeles. Before we took off, I read Jim Jarmusch's new script *One Night in Memphis.* There are similarities between our scripts. I like the form he uses. It's three interwoven stories that take place in a rundown hotel in Memphis, Tennessee. Jim is giving a role to my brother Cinque, which is good. It means Cinque can't work on my film, but it's better that he get a chance to act for Jim.

Yes yes, y'all, it's time to write the second draft of *Do the Right Thing.* There are a few critical points I have to expand:

1. The relationship between Mookie and Tina.
2. The relationship between Mookie and Radio Raheem.
3. How ML and Sweet Dick Willie rank on Coconut Sid about being West Indian.
4. Tina has to be introduced earlier. I'd like to do it by showing Tina, her child, and her mother; but not let it be known right away that Tina is Mookie's girlfriend.
5. I want to pay homage to *Night of the Hunter.* You know those brass-knuckle name rings that kids are wearing now? They're gold-plated and spread across four fingers. Radio Raheem will wear two of these. The one on his left hand will read "L-O-V-E," on his right, "H-A-T-E," just like Robert Mitchum's tattoos in *Night of the Hunter.* Radio Raheem tells Mookie a story about the rings that will be a variation on Robert Mitchum's tale of his tattoos. Vicious.

One of the problems of the ending of the film as it stands is that Mookie is too impartial when the riot breaks out. He has to be on Radio Raheem's side from the beginning, even if he doesn't get physically involved.

I want to stay away from still photographs for the opening credits. I used stills in *She's Gotta Have It* and *School Daze.* I have been thinking about credits written in white chalk on a city street. Black asphalt. We could shoot them with a Louma crane.

JUNE 7, 1988

I'm writing like a madman to finish the second draft of *Do the Right Thing.* I have to go out to L.A. next Thursday to meet with the head honchos at Universal. I'll implore them to promote the film properly and spend the money that needs to be spent.

JUNE 10, 1988

The second draft of *Do the Right Thing* came in at ninety-two and one-eighth pages. Lean and mean. If we have a 39-day shooting schedule, we can average

2.3 pages a day, which is nothing. If the weather cooperates, the shoot should be fast and smooth.

JUNE 13, 1988

Now that the second draft is done and most of the principal casting is complete, I can start planning the shots for the film. Time is slipping by. When I get back from London, there will be exactly one week left before we shoot. That's no time at all. Tomorrow Ernest and I are gonna spend some time together talking over the script, thinking about shots, lighting, and camera moves.

The final shot of the film should be similar to that stylized shot in *Hair* where everyone comes out at once onto an empty street. As Mookie walks away from Sal's, the empty street comes to life.

AUGUST 7, 1988 [LAST JOURNAL ENTRY]

We've been shooting for three weeks; we're almost at the halfway point.

I'm learning so much more with each film. It's been said that directing films is like being a psychologist. It's so true. Actors are quirky people. I'm learning to deal with them. Larry Fishburne's big complaint on *School Daze* was I didn't communicate enough. I've taken this to heart on *Do the Right Thing.*

I've come to see that my style of directing is about a controlled freedom, if there is such a thing. I give actors an enormous amount of freedom to shape their characters. I try to give them the framework or boundaries to work in. For some actors, this presents a problem. In the past they've been restricted and held back. When they are given the ball and told to run with it, they don't know what to do.

When this film is released people are gonna make a big deal out of the fact that this is my first film to use white actors. I know I'm gonna hear the question again and again, "Spike, is there a difference between directing Black actors and white actors?" and I'll answer, "Sir, I think that's a stupid-ass question."

It's a great pleasure to make this film in Brooklyn, in Bedford-Stuyvesant. Y'know Spike, you're lucky. I'm young, Black, and doing what I want to do. That's why I say my prayers every night. I'm doing what makes me the happiest; that's making films.

I've said this so often before, but why not again? Ninety-five percent of the people on this planet work all their lives, get up every morning, and drag themselves in a job they hate, a job they really despise. They end up going to the grave that way. It's sad, but true. I'm one of the lucky ones, but that doesn't mean I go around singing "Don't Worry Be Happy." Sometimes on the set, while we're setting up for a shot, I look around and watch everyone working. I see all these young, talented Black artists and technicians and I feel just fine. It's a good feeling to be in a position to hire people who need jobs, people who deserve jobs. Of course we can't hire everyone, but we're doing what we can.

ANNE LAMOTT (b. 1954)

Index Cards

CONSIDER THIS:

Do you think writers think in special ways? What about artists or specialists in any field? What characterizes the thinking habits in an area in which you're an expert (cooking, playing soccer, shopping)? What, to you, illustrates the ways writers think that are distinct and important for their work?

Anne Lamott was born in San Francisco and educated at Goucher College. She received a Guggenheim fellowship in 1985. Her fiction is noted for its close observation about domestic affairs and its sharp sense of humor. Her book *Bird by Bird* offers some wonderfully straightforward advice about the writing process: "The very first thing I tell my new students on the first day of a workshop is that good writing is about telling the truth." But where does one start? "Start with your childhood, I tell them. Plug your nose and jump in, and write down all your memories as truthfully as you can." And how does one really become a writer? "You sit down. . . . You try to sit down at approximately the same time every day." Do you have habits that at all resemble Lamott's? Do you keep lists? On what? In what form? What happens to them when you're done with them?

I like to think that Henry James said his classic line, "A writer is someone on whom nothing is lost," while looking for his glasses, and that they were on top of his head. We have so much to remember these days. So we make all these lists, filled with hope that they will remind us of all the important things to do and buy and mail, all the important calls we need to make, all the ideas we have for short stories or articles. And yet by the time you get around to everything on any one list, you're already behind on another. Still, I believe in lists and I believe in taking notes, and I believe in index cards for doing both.

I have index cards and pens all over the house—by the bed, in the bathroom, in the kitchen, by the phones, and I have them in the glove compartment of my car. I carry one with me in my back pocket when I take my dog for a walk. In fact, I carry it folded lengthwise, if you need to know, so that, God forbid, I won't look bulky. You may want to consider doing the same. I don't even know you, but I bet you have enough on your mind without having to worry about whether or not you look bulky. So whenever I am leaving the house without my purse—in which there are actual notepads, let alone index cards—I fold an index card lengthwise in half, stick it in my back pocket along with a pen, and head out, knowing that if I have an idea, or see something lovely or strange or for any reason worth remembering, I will be able to jot down a couple of words to remind me of it. Sometimes, if I overhear or think of an exact line of dialogue or a transition, I write it down verbatim. I stick the card back in my pocket. I might be walking along the salt marsh, or out at Phoenix Lake, or in the express line at Safeway, and suddenly I hear something wonderful that makes me want to smile or snap my fingers—as if it has just come back to me—and I take out my index card and scribble it down.

I have an index card beside me right now on which I scribbled, "Pammy, Demi Moore." Those words capture an entire movie for me, of one particular day last year, six months before Pammy died.

We were outside in her garden. The sky was blue and cloudless, everything was in bloom, and she wore a little lavender cotton cap. She was doing very well that day, except that she was dying. (My father's oncologist once assured him, "You're a very, very healthy fifty-five-year-old man, except, of course, for the brain cancer.") We were lying on chaise lounges, in T-shirts and shorts, eating miniature Halloween chocolate bars. Sam was pulling Pammy's two-year-old daughter Rebecca around the garden in a little red wagon.

"I'm a little depressed," Pammy said. One day not long before, she had said that all she had to do to get really, really depressed was to think of Rebecca, and all she had to do to get really, really *joyful* was to think of Rebecca. "I'm actually quite depressed," she said.

"I don't see why."

"What's the silver lining here? I can't seem to remember today."

"The silver lining is that you're not going to have to see any more naked pregnant pictures of Demi Moore."

She looked at me for a moment with real wonder. "God," she said, "that's a lot—I hadn't even thought of that." And she was very funny again for the rest of the day, happy to be with the children and me.

It was such a rare scene that you would think I would remember it forever. I used to think that if something was important enough, I'd remember it until I got home, where I could simply write it down in my notebook like some normal functioning member of society.

But then I wouldn't.

I'd get home, remembering that I had thought of or heard the perfect image or lines to get my characters from the party in the old house on the hill to their first day on the new job, or to their childhood playhouse, or wherever it was that they seemed to think they were supposed to be next. And I'd stand there trying to see it, the way you try to remember a dream, where you squint and it's right there on the tip of your psychic tongue but you can't get it back. The image is gone. That is one of the worst feelings I can think of, to have had a wonderful moment or insight or vision or phrase, to know you had it, and then to lose it. So now I use index cards.

One of the things that happens when you give yourself permission to start writing is that you start thinking like a writer. You start seeing everything as material. Sometimes you'll sit down or go walking and your thoughts will be on one aspect of your work, or one idea you have for a small scene, or a general portrait of one of the characters you are working with, or you'll just be completely blocked and hopeless and wondering why you shouldn't just go into the kitchen and have a nice glass of warm gin straight out of the cat dish. And then, unbidden, seemingly out of nowhere, a thought or image arrives. Some will float into your head like goldfish, lovely, bright orange, and weightless, and you follow them like a child looking at an aquarium that was thought to be without fish. Others will step out of the shadows like Boo Radley and make you catch your breath or take a step backward. They're often so rich, these unbidden thoughts, and so clear that they feel indelible. But I say write them all down anyway.

Now, I have a number of writer friends who do not take notes out there in the world, who say it's like not taking notes in class but *listening* instead. I think that if you have the kind of mind that retains important and creative thoughts—that is, if your mind still works—you're very lucky and you should not be surprised if the rest of us do not want to be around you. I actually have one writer friend—whom I think I will probably be getting rid of soon—who said to me recently that if you don't remember it when you get home, it probably wasn't that important. And I felt eight years old again, with something important to say that had suddenly hopped down one of the rabbit holes in my mind, while an adult nearby was saying priggishly, "Well! It must not have been very important then."

So you have to decide how you feel about this. You may have a perfectly good memory and be able to remember three hours later what you came up with while walking on the mountain or waiting at the dentist's. And then again, you may not. If it feels natural, if it helps you to remember, take notes. It's not cheating. It doesn't say anything about your character. If your mind is perhaps the merest bit disorganized, it probably just means that you've lost a little ground. It may be all those drugs you took when you were younger, all that nonhabit-forming marijuana that you smoked on a daily basis for twenty years. It may be that you've had children. When a child comes out of your body, it arrives with about a fifth of your brain clutched in its little hand, like those babies born clutching IUDs. So for any number of reasons, it's only fair to let yourself take notes.

My index-card life is not efficient or well organized. Hostile, aggressive students insist on asking what I *do* with all my index cards. And all I can say is that I have them, I took notes on them, and the act of having written something down gives me a fifty-fifty shot at having it filed away now in my memory. If I'm working on a book or an article, and I've taken some notes on index cards, I keep them with that material, paper clip them to a page of rough draft where that idea or image might bring things to life. Or I stack them on my desk along with the pages for the particular chapter or article I'm working on, so I can look at them. When I get stuck or lost or the jungle drums start beating in my head, proclaiming that the jig is about to be up and I don't know what I'm doing and the well has run dry, I'll look through my index cards. I try to see if there's a short assignment on any of them that will get me writing again, give me a small sense of confidence, help me put down one damn word after another, which is, let's face it, what writing finally boils down to.

There are index cards on my desk that record things I thought of or saw or remembered or overheard in the last week or so. There are index cards from a couple of years ago. There is even one index card from six or seven years ago, when I was walking along the salt marsh between Sausalito and Mill Valley. Bicyclists were passing me on both sides, and I wasn't paying much attention until suddenly a woman rode past wearing some sort of lemon perfume. And in a split second I was in one of those Proustian olfactory flashbacks, twenty-five or so years before, in the kitchen of one of my aunts, with her many children, my cousins, on a hot summer's day. I was the eldest, at eight or so, and my aunt and uncle had just gotten divorced. She was sad and worried, and I think to soothe herself and help her wounded ego, she had done a little retail therapy: she'd gone to the store and spent several dollars on a lemonade-making contraption.

Of course, it goes without saying that to make lemonade, all you need is a pitcher, a lemon-juice squeezer, ice cubes, water, lemons, and sugar. That's all. Oh, and a long spoon. But my aunt was a little depressed, and this lemonade-making thing must have seemed like something that would be fun and would maybe hydrate her life a little, filling her desiccated spirit with nice, cool, sweet lemonade. The contraption consisted of a glass pitcher, with a lemon squeezer that fit on top and that had a holding tank for the lemon juice. What you did was to fill the pitcher with water and ice cubes and sugar, then put the squeezer—with its holding tank—on top, squeeze a bunch of lemons, then pour the lemon juice from the holding tank into the pitcher. Finally, you got your long spoon and stirred. The lemon googe and seeds stayed on top in the juice squeezer. The whole thing was very efficient, but if you thought about it too long, totally stupid, too.

So there we were in the kitchen, the five cousins and me, crowded around her at the sink as she proudly made us lemonade. She put the cold water in the pitcher, added ice cubes, lots of sugar, put the juicer lid on top, squeezed a dozen lemons, and then began to take glasses down from the cupboards. Wait! we older ones wanted to cry out, you haven't poured in the lemon juice. Stop! Mistakes are being made! But she got out jelly glasses, plastic glasses, a couple of brilliant aluminum glasses, and poured seven servings. There we were, six anxious black-belt codependents, unable to breathe, with a longing for everything to be Okay and for her not to feel sad anymore. She raised her glass to us as a toast, and we all took sips of our sugary ice water, and my aunt's hands were so lemony from cutting and squeezing all those lemons that she must have tasted lemon. We all stared at her helplessly as we drank our sugar water, then smiled and raised our glasses like we were doing a soft-drink commercial, and held them out for more.

I perfectly remembered, there on the salt marsh, the crummy linoleum on my aunt's kitchen floor, graying beige speckled with black, and how it wore away to all black near the sink, and how at its most worn place, rotten wood showed through. And how all those cousins, some so young they must have thought ice-cold sugar water was about as good as the getting got, stood at the sink with us older kids, in a ring around my aunt. And how close I felt to them all, how much a part of the wheel.

It touches me so deeply, the poignancy of the crummy linoleum, of my aunt's pain and her pride in her lemonade-making machine, of all the ways in which we try to comfort ourselves, of her wanting to make us better lemonade, of us wanting to make her better, the enthusiasm with which we drank and held out our glasses, as if we were hoisting steins at Oktoberfest. And I hadn't remembered any of this in twenty-five years.

Now, maybe I'm not going to use it anywhere. All the index card says is "The lemonade-making thing." But it's like a snippet from a movie, a vignette of a family in pain, managing to survive, one of those rare moments when people's hearts are opened by disappointment and love, and for just a few minutes, against all odds, everything is more or less Okay.

Sometimes I'll be driving along, and all of a sudden words form in my mind that solve some technical problem for me. I may have been trying all morning long to show that time has been passing for my characters, without resorting to old-movie techniques where leaves of a calendar blow out the window or the hands of a clock spin. These techniques do not translate well to the written word. It's a wonderful feeling when you're reading something by someone else, and the writer has aged exactly the right detail so that you know the story is picking up again sometime later. Sometimes the seasons change, or children start school, or beards grow long, or pets go gray. But sometimes in your own writing you can't find the way to make time pass invisibly, and you will not be aided in this by sitting at your desk staring bitterly at your words, trying to will it to happen. Instead, all of a sudden when you're wrestling with the dog or paying the electric bill, you might look up and know that something is coming to you that might really matter, only you can't quite reel it in. It's like watching someone on a ventilator rise again and again to the surface, like a trapped fish, and you stay with the person, and sometimes he or she blinks awake. And so, if you hold some space open, an image may come to you. Then, for goodness sakes, jot it down.

I have an index card here on which is written, "Six years later, the memory of the raw fish cubes continued to haunt her," which I thought might make a great transitional line. But I have so far not found a place for it. You are welcome to use it if you can.

I eventually throw away a lot of my index cards, either because I use what's on them in a paragraph somewhere or because it turns out that the thought wasn't all that interesting. Many index cards on which I write in the middle of the night tend to be incoherent, like some incredibly bright math major thinking about oranges or truth while on LSD. Some contain great quotes that I share with my students, although I unfortunately often forget to write down whose quote it is. Like this one, for instance: "What lies behind us and what lies before us are tiny matters, compared to what lies within us." Now, I'm almost positive Ralph Waldo Emerson said this, but with my luck some critic will point out that it was really Georgette Mosbacher. (Who was it that said, "A critic is someone who comes onto the battlefield after the battle is over and shoots the wounded"? I have it written on an index card somewhere. . . .) Other cards just sort of live with me, in little piles and drifts. My son will probably have to deal with them someday, after my death. They are my equivalent of all the cats that those nutty Bouvier aunts own. But my cards do not smell or shed or go wee-wee on the floors, and I think Sam should be aware that he is getting off easy. Most of them will not make much sense to him. There are many with just one or two words on them that would have reminded me of entire scenes and empires, but he will have to stand there scratching his head.

But he will also find some dated in the early nineties, and they will contain complete stories about how he blew me away, how he made me shake my head with wonder and a kind of relief. Like this one, dated 9-17-93:

> Sam and I walked Bill and Adair up to their car after dinner. Crisp cold starry night. Bill, holding Sam, inhaled deeply. "Doesn't it smell wonderful, Sam?" he said. Sam inhaled deeply, too, like he was smelling a delicious meal, looked off into space, and said, "It smells like moon."

Now that memory won't be lost. I'm not sure if I will use it in my writing—actually, I guess I just did—but I know it won't be lost.

Nor will the details of an early morning the two of us spent recently in an emergency room, where Sam was having his first asthma attack. We were both afraid and sad and did not quite know what was going on, but Sam was hooked up to a nebulizer, with a mask over his mouth and nose, and I was sitting beside him on his bed, wishing I had thought to grab a toy as we left the house. So I looked inside my purse and managed to come up with a tiny box of crayons from a restaurant and two used index cards. One contained a shopping list, the other a brief description of the sky.

I drew a terrible giant on the blank side of each card. Sam, sucking away at his mask, watched me with fear. Next I poked holes in each of the giants' right hands, and stuck tongue depressors through the holes. Then I staged a vigorous, clicking sword fight. Sam's eyes grew wide, and he smiled. After a long while he could breathe again freely, and we were told we could go home. But before we did, I dismantled the giants, stuck the card with the shopping list in my back pocket and, on the back of the other, scribbled down this story.

KATHARINE HAAKE (b. 1952)

Exercise 1: Beyond the End of Writing

CONSIDER THIS:

A third-generation Californian, Katharine Haake is a professor of English at California State University, Northridge, where she specializes in critical and narrative writing and theory. She is the coauthor of *Metro: Journeys in Writing Creatively* and explores feminist and creative writing theory in *What Our Speech Disrupts.* Her recent fiction includes *The Height and Depth of Everything: Stories* and *That Water, Those Rocks: Narrative Reflections* (University of Nevada Press). In her introduction to this exercise, Haake shares Richard Hugo's idea of writers' "triggering subjects" and also his discussion of writers' assumptions. Before reading this discussion and trying the exercises, share with group members some of your own assumptions about writing and your advice to other writers.

Compile a list of subjects that seem to you to "trigger" writers in general and each of you as writers in particular. Think of this discussion as a warm-up for Haake's exercise. At some point, you may want to consider how it will affect this "assumption experiment" if you begin with the intention of writing fiction or nonfiction.

> It is the childish delight at combinatorial play that induces the painter to try out patterns of lines and colors and the poet to attempt combinations of words. At a certain stage something clicks, and one of the combinations obtained by its own mechanisms, independently of any search for meaning or effect on some other level, takes on an unexpected sense or produces an unforeseen effect that consciousness could not have achieved intentionally.
>
> —ITALO CALVINO, "CYBERNETICS AND GHOSTS"

In his book *The Triggering Town,* Richard Hugo argues that those of us who write have somewhere deep inside a subject that "triggers" writing. We know this is true because, to varying extents, we feel impassioned and driven in our writing, which frequently seems to grow, like gods out of the weather, from the same material, or problem, or idea, or passion. Hugo's own triggering subject had always been, he said, a small town in the American West that had seen better days and was now in decline.

Perhaps you know the kind of town he means. You're driving for hours across the vast emptiness we know as the American West. Maybe you see mountains in the distance; maybe you are moving away, toward the flat reaches of plains. You're going fast, and inside you have that feeling between awe and despair, something in this endless stretch of land you recognize but cannot name, something very close to longing. Then, out of nowhere, a town rears up, replete with its own mute history and loss. You want to stop. You want to have a hamburger and cherry coke at the cafe. You want, for an instant, to disappear into whatever has held this place together through its long and complex history, but you know, too, you're an outsider, and should pass.

Whenever he saw such a town, Hugo said, it triggered whatever it was inside him that wanted to write a poem. But, he continued, for each piece of writing there are always two subjects: the triggering subject, the one that "sparked" the writing; and the subject that is discovered in the act of writing the piece. And this, he says, occurs during a process in which the writer transfers allegiance from the first, the triggering subject, to the words, the language it triggers. For in addition to our triggering subject, Hugo says we all have inside us a unique and private language. This is not to be confused with any of the models of high literary writing we may aspire to. This language is our own and must be distinguished from all the different kinds of language we think we're supposed to sound like. Learning to write, Hugo says, is a process of learning to sound like ourselves, in which we must commit our most passionate attention to the language itself inside us, and not to the subject that sparks it. This is what he calls "writing off the subject."

And here's the most curious thing, a certain alchemy of writing: the more you pay attention to working the actual words in your head instead of what you think you want them to mean, the closer they will come to your intention.

The title essay of Hugo's book includes the following:

> Assumptions lie behind the work of all writers. The writer is unaware of most of them, and many of them are weird. Often the weirder the better. Words love the ridiculous areas of our mind. But silly or solid, assumptions are necessary elements in a successful base of writing operations. It is important that a [writer] not question his or her assumptions, at least not in the middle of composition. Finish the [writing] first, then worry, if you have to, about being right or sane.
>
> Whenever I see a town that triggers whatever it is inside me that wants to write a poem, I assume at least one of the following:
>
> The name of the town is significant and must appear in the title.
>
> The inhabitants are natives and have lived there forever. I am the only stranger.
>
> I have lived there all my life and should have left long ago but couldn't. . . .
>
> The churches are always empty.
>
> A few people attend church but the sermons are boring.
>
> Everybody goes to church and the sermons are inspiring. . . .
>
> I am an eleven-year-old orphan. . . .
>
> The grain elevator is silver. . . .
>
> Dogs roam the streets. . . .
>
> Wind blows hard through the town except on Sunday afternoons a little before noon when the air becomes still.
>
> The air is still all week except on Sunday afternoons when the wind blows.
>
> Once in awhile an unlikely animal wanders into town, a bear or cougar or wolverine. . . .
>
> There is always a body of water, a sea just out of sight beyond the hill or a river running through the town. Outside of town a few miles is a lake that has been the scene of both romance and violence. . . .

The list continues, by turns whimsical, sad, fantastic, realistic, twisted. As in many useful models for writing, it requires that we hold contradictory tenets to be simultaneously true and embrace a both/and vision, the uncommon logic on which writing depends.

Elsewhere, Hugo offers additional good advice (4–8). For example:

1. [Don't] push language around to make it accommodate what [you have] already conceived to be the truth. ["How can I know what I mean until I see what I've said?"—E. M. Forster]
2. Talk about something else before you run out of things to say about [your triggering subject]. Don't be afraid to jump ahead.
3. Depend on rhythm, tonality, and the music of language to hold things together. [Use words for the sake of sound.]

4. The initiating subject should trigger the imagination as well as the [writing].
5. The [writer's] relation to the triggering subject should never be as strong as (must be weaker than) [her/]his relation to [her/]his words. The words should not serve the subject. The subject should serve the words.
6. The [writing] grows from an experience, either real or imagined.
7. Seldom [find] room for explanations, motivations, or reason. [Or, as François Camoin says, "Never apologize, never explain."]
8. Think small.

And here's one from François and me: *Don't think.*

This exercise asks you to play with the concept of language and subject in a process that Hugo calls writing "off the subject."

Begin by naming your triggering subject. This does not have to be one single thing that always drives your writing, because such a thing changes over time to reflect your changing interests and self, and also may take years to discover. But whatever you choose as your subject, it must be important to you in some fundamental way. You have to care about it deeply. It has to *count.*

Your first question here is: *What is it?*

Boys at play on a field, the river that ran by your childhood house, your eccentric Aunt Trudy, volcanoes. Soccer. Botany. What you know how to build. A master family myth.

Once you have named your "triggering subject" write a list of ten "assumptions" you might make about this subject. Your assumptions may be a sentence, several sentences, a small paragraph, but they should be characterized by what Cynthia Ozick calls "the recognition of the particular"—detail, minute observation, whatever distinguishes your observation ("assumption") from what anyone else might say about the same thing.

Number your first ten assumptions.

Read them out loud.

Think about them.

Now, use each of your first ten assumptions as a new "triggering subject"—one more particularized than the one you began with, but still related—and start over again, ten new assumptions, each containing something specific—a color, a named scent, material objects.

That makes one hundred and ten assumptions. If you have time, write one assumption off each of those, doubling your total, and if that doesn't get you "writing off the subject," go back and start over again.

Variations

1. Go back over the list of assumptions you made, and without changing any of them, write a story by linking selected assumptions together in a different order.

2. Choose ten of your favorite assumptions and write a story in ten parts, each beginning with one of the assumptions.
3. Write a poem with words or phrases from your assumptions.
4. Choose your favorite assumptions, as many as you like, and expand them each into a paragraph, a page, a story.
5. Begin again with an entirely new subject—or the same one.

Note: This exercise will seem, at times, extreme. You will want to stop. You may begin to doubt, or curse, or sweat the proverbial writerly blood. But keep going, because if you persevere beyond the end of writing, you will reach a second wind where writing may begin again, and then again again.

Do it all.

PARTIAL STUDENT SAMPLE

The Assumptions of Rebbecca Brown

1. He wears a long black jacket that is shiny with raindrops or sweat.
2. He is not a he.
3. Underneath her fingernails colors flow over each other in waves and make the sound of wind rustling leaves.
4. The man who lies in the box is sleeping and bloated. There is something still under his eyes. He is my uncle with the broken ear and small squeaky dog named Trix.
5. Air has no weight or blood to fix it firmly.
6. The captain did not lose his ring over the rim of the rocking sea. It was given to the water so a piece of his fixed place would sink and carry his breath to the bottom of loving sand.
7. There are small crooked whispers that tickle and find a nice spot under eyelids to flutter and feel soft.
8. She can not sleep because her eyes are filled with too much light.
9. People go there in glimmering golden autos with gold bracelets gold smiles gold everywhere. Even their hair smells golden.
10. To leave is to become lost.

He wears a long black jacket that is shiny with raindrops or sweat.

1. The train was too much trouble so he walked with his black weight to a new town too tiny to notice.
2. It rains every other hour under the trees. The heat sweats them out of pressure and their water falls on the sleeping man.
3. The jacket was bought from a sad long lady with weeds and licorice leaning out of her pockets. Her teeth were gray and sticky.

4. He had an uncanny ability to sweat, even while he was still.
5. The sun in Mexico swelters.
6. The rain in Seattle soaks.
7. His galoshes squeak like the mouse he found in his cabinet.
8. He whistles while walking on the dark melting snow.
9. The lining is red with white dots and is ripped near his fragile thin wrists.

He is not a he.

1. He only looks like a he who is tired of working under the cooked sun.
2. He was a she so he can't really be a she as she had the he installed permanently and discreetly.
3. He is a cat and it is wrong to call him "he" when he meows instead of saying "me."
4. He is not and she is not.
5. He is my mother who makes malt-o-meal and sews my fraying mittens.
6. He lies all the time and changes his sex like his socks.
7. He is a floating particle above my head now, and has no eyes or hair.
8. He is music when he sings. He loses himself, his he, and becomes something beautiful, like clean air or clear water.
9. He talks to his many selves who are they, all one. He she we they one two three he four she three we.
10. He is a sad sorry frightened thing with pointy ears that hear everything dissolve into hums.

Underneath her fingernails colors flow over each other in waves and make the sound of wind rustling leaves.

1. When she is typing, her nails click and spark over keys. She likes to type in the dark when it is quiet so that the sound shines.
2. The leaves that fell from the tree outside of her window were brown and orange. Like all trees. Like all girls she was not impressed by brown and orange. She liked red and green and yellow, the colors of growing things.
3. She painted. She liked the sound of brushes against the canvas. She liked the look of color when it accidentally got stuck underneath her nails. She waited. She painted. She waited.
4. When it was quiet, she could hear the colors shifting under her long, delicate nails. She had been painting the underside of her nails since she was thirteen and her mother bought her her first jar of polish. It was "candy cane red." When she first painted her nails, it was on the outside, and a bad thing had happened. She never wanted to be attractive again. Candy canes are too bright. She must paint the underside so that the beauty and brightness are dulled and opaque.

5. When she sees her nails underneath the microscope she can imagine the sound of the leaves that rustled when she was a little girl looking for bugs to dissect.
6. Shhhhhhhhhhhhhh. Shhhhhhhhhhhhh Shhhhhhhhhhhh.

5

Classroom Handouts

Invention Exercises: Writing to Find Your Topic

CONSIDER THIS:

These exercises touch on several of the big topics: home, the natural world, food, and family and will provide triggering subjects for most writers. Were some of these subjects on the list you compiled before reading Katharine Haake's exercise? After trying some of these inventions, you might create your own invention exercise by substituting your own triggering subjects for any of the sequences of individual prompts found here.

EXPLORING: FINDING SIGNIFICANCE BY INVENTING YOUR OWN HURRICANE

All writers draw from common topics: love, death, family. It is the way you invest those topics with personal connections and share your particular angle of vision that makes a big topic particular, resonant, and important to your readers. Part of the writer's work, then, is to discover which topics have power for them. When we read about natural disasters, we often marvel at the resilience of those who were involved in earthquakes, fires, flash floods, tornados, and hurricanes. Imagining yourself in such a situation allows you to consider what matters to you.

1. When the big one arrives and you have 24 hours notice, what do you save from your
   - **a.** family home when you were age ________ (choose an age)
   - **b.** home today

   For option (a) and then option (b), write a paragraph, considering what you'd choose with just four hours' notice. In a separate response, consider what you'd choose with just 30 minutes' notice for each option.
2. From each of the above four options, choose one item and expand on it in another informal paragraph.
3. Do any items appear in both your (a) and (b) scenarios? What does it mean that you have kept (and would save) these items over time? Write another paragraph exploring this.

Consider these items/writings as talismanic lodestones and explore their significance in a piece of nonfiction or fiction.

REDISCOVERING: YOUR FAMILY, YOUR HOME

Our families shaped who we are today, but it's sometimes hard to remember more than stylized snapshots of the past. That is, to get past your own self-censor, you need to close your eyes, remember, recall. When I take myself on a tour of my family home from when I was seven, I begin to recall where the bathroom light switch was, how many steps led up to the front porch, the color of the kitchen curtains, the smell of the piano keys. Memory exercises can help writers recall specific details and also free them to invent those they need to better create the "feel" of past events. For instance, draw the floor plan of an early family home. Label each room with a number and, on a separate sheet of paper, tell a family story having to do with each room.

Moving Belongings from One Room to Another

Return to your writings on your memories of an early family home. Now choose the most important room of that dwelling, and move items that you care about from other rooms into that crucial room. Next furnish the room with all the people who were important to you at that time of life (family members, friends, relatives, schoolmates). In some writings, explore this now crowded room: what is significant about it under these conditions?

INVENTING: A ROOM OF YOUR OWN

What is your ideal room? Describe it. Furnish it. What is its significance to you? If you are imagining one, what is keeping you from getting to that room? If you are remembering a room from your past, what would you give to get back there or to recreate it today (maybe in some ways you have)?

Use these memory-as-it-was and memory-as-it-could-be exercises to explore an important event, object, or person from the past.

Share some of your freewrites with a small group. As a group, come up with some other prompts for remembering *home* that you can share with others at the end of class today.

EXPLORING, DISCOVERING, AND INVENTING: WRITING ABOUT THE ENVIRONMENT AND FOOD AND FAMILY

Finding Your Nature—Writing Prompts

- Before reading the definitions below, define "nature" for yourself.
- How do humans fit into your definition/understanding of nature?
- Now, which of the following definitions "fit" your sense of nature? How encompassing and/or exclusive is your definition/expectation for the word? Do the definitions of naturalist, natural science, and/or natural history modify your definition of nature? (Definitions are taken from *Webster's New World Dictionary*, second college ed.)

Nature: (1) the essential characteristic of a thing: essence; (7) the sum total of all things in time and space; (10) the entire physical universe; a simple way of life close to or in the outdoors; (11) natural scenery, including the plants and animals that are part of it.

Naturalist: a person who studies nature, especially by direct observation of animals and plants.

Natural science: the systematized knowledge of nature and the physical world, including zoology, botany, chemistry, physics, geology, and so on.

Natural history: the study of zoology, botany, mineralogy, geology, and other subjects dealing with the physical world, especially in a popular, nontechnical manner.

- What place would you claim as a place where you feel most at home, can best name (or are interested in learning how to name)? Why?
- Choose one sentence frame to explore:

  I've always had a ________ relationship with the natural world (and continue).

  Until recently, I had a ________ relationship with the natural world. Recently though . . . (and continue).
- Are you a naturalist, nature writer, nature lover (or hater)?
- What animal most fascinates you? What animal would you choose to study further? What animal do you most associate with, i.e., as a spirit guide or representative of some aspect of you or your inner and/or spiritual nature? Why? How did you come to an understanding of this relationship?
- What landscape makes you feel most at home? Most wild? Most at risk? Most natural?
- What animal, plant, or geology speaks most to you and why?
- Are you a cultivator? Do you have a black or a green thumb? Do you admire/disdain/prefer wild or cultivated plant life?
- What education should a nature writer undertake? What skills should a nature writer possess?
- What do you think about/relate to the following terms: urban, suburban, rural, country, wild(erness)? Where would a naturalist situate him/herself in each location? Can you be a nature writer in each setting?
- Research—primary, secondary. Do you have to experience a natural phenomena to write about it?
- I'd rather experience nature than read about it. I'd rather read about nature than experience it. Situate yourself in this discussion.
- Given a grant, what animal, ecosystem, plant, landscape, or weather phenomena would you investigate? (This can range from your backyard to Tibet.)

Complete five to seven of these freewrites at home at your computer. Make four copies of one or two single-spaced pages to share in class.

Writing About Food and Family

Chocolate

Nothing new can be said about chocolate, and where it is concerned, clichés ring true. Chocolate cures heartache—or at least postpones it for awhile. You are never too young or too old for chocolate. Life is like a box of chocolates (Forrest Gump, among others). A chocolate in the mouth is worth two on the plate. Chocolate is healthy; it comes from a bean. I never met a chocolate I didn't like (Deanna Troi on *Star Trek: The Next Generation*). Some people eat to live; others live to eat; I live to eat chocolate. Chocolate sweetens life, and without it stress wouldn't make so many people overweight.

Chicken Alfredo

When my parents drove me to college, dragging my heels along the highway in an attempt to delay the inevitable, I met a boy who likes to cook. He sautéed chicken and slices of onion in olive oil spiced with garlic, basil, black pepper, and a dash of red pepper. The warm, spicy smell of the kitchen reminded me of home; it permeated my clothing and reminded me that there was nothing to fear. He mixed in Alfredo sauce.

Standing in the hot kitchen, drops of sweat beaded on the back of my neck, and I swept my hair up into a sloppy chignon. Pieces of hair too short to reach it fell in front of my face, and even in this environment, he made me feel beautiful, unafraid.

The creamy white chicken arrived on my plate atop a bed of angel hair pasta. Each ingredient had changed, combining with the others to form a feast. He showed me that change should be zesty and exciting, not bland and suspicious. Before him, I thought it something ugly to be feared and dreaded. In fact, if I had had any choice in the matter, I wouldn't have left my parents' home to meet my future. The feast became more evident with each bite of what would soon become my favorite meal.

One year later, the two of us stood in the kitchen again, as had become routine by that time. He decided to cook again the meal that I loved so much, this time adding more than just spices to the chicken. He poured himself into the dish, and I felt his hurts and regrets as I twirled the strands of angel hair onto the fork. Another year passed, and we grew closer together. I cooked the chicken this time, and he sat behind the counter, watching me make a meal to share with him. He ate a bite of chicken and said, "This is love."

—Colleen Leary

You're standing in the line at the market, cart full of food, surrounded by popular magazines that display dishes and recipes; you leaf through one after another, wondering who ever cooks these dishes, wondering if the checker ever marvels at the odd food combinations customers like you place on the conveyor belt: one item because it's healthy, one item because your grandmother always bought that brand, one item because you can now buy something no one in your family could stand to share, one item to make a special meal for a special person. Or, you wake up late at night and find yourself watching the cooking show. Or, you walk into a café, cafeteria, fair, movie theater, hamburger joint, bakery, house and you smell an aroma that reminds you of . . . and takes you back to . . . . You bite into, or sip, or taste, or nibble a . . . and you're transported here and there.

Food triggers memory. Family food customs help define us. Food and family are inextricably entwined (and so, in their ways, are food and sex: think of indulgent movie scenes). Food is comfort and food is a sensual trigger that opens up the pathways to story (and essay). Food is also business: family business, cultural icon (brand names), and art (the menu, the review, the critic).

To begin to (re)discover your own connections to food (and family), choose from the following invention prompts:

1. Write about any six of the following words (in any order): appetite, hunger, food, milk, fat, sugar, spice, meat, mother, father, sister, brother, grandmother, grandfather, lover, feast, famine, bread, chocolate, simmer, friend.
2. List the foods different family members like. Choose one and describe that person eating the food, note sensations, emotions, and then end with the relative saying something aloud.
3. Write about a "scene" of eating in the third person. Watch a friend or family member eat; describe and interpret his/her actions.
4. Share a recipe and a story that goes with that recipe.
5. Write about eating and times of day and/or eating in different locations.
6. Tell someone something about food that you've never been willing or able to express before. Explain something about you, food, and your memories of food.
7. Write about a joyous moment with food, celebration, and satiety.
8. Write about loss or absence and eating.
9. Write about the humor of foods. Write about their colors, tastes, smells, and textures.
10. Note some clichés—like, *You are what you eat*—and use the truism as a springboard for more insightful thinking.
11. List five foods you used to eat often in your childhood but don't any longer. Write the words on blank paper and explore why you did then but don't now. Do the reverse: list five foods you still eat, will probably always eat, and explore why.
12. Free associate a list of 20 foods (perhaps in a group). Choose five and invent a story in paragraph form about each food (as Colleen Leary did, previously). The stories are linked only in that you're the person stringing them together. They don't have to be (but may be) in order or in the same style or voice.

    Grandma Lib would call me for lunch. She would extract brilliantly colored fiesta wear from her almond toned fridge and carefully place each item in its place on the banged up oak table. One turquoise plate presenting layered thin cold cuts, turkey and roast beef. One deep red plate holding sliced cheeses, the varieties changing but always including Grandma Lib's favorite of Swiss. One buttered colored dish with slices of pears or melon balls, sometimes other fruits depending on what was on special at Dave's Grocery, a narrow market with four aisles we frequented often to blow our dollar allowance on candy and trading cards. A large container of cottage cheese, striped with red labeling. One green dish with tomatoes, sliced and salted. One large flowered plate of lettuce separated with dampened paper towels. The mayo and mustard set the center of the table next to the Pepperidge Farm white bread, sliced so thin that the tomato juice always seeped through creating a salmon pink sponge. In five minutes flat, her kitchen table became a patchwork quilt of loud summer colors and simple food tasting of freshness and comfort.

—Rachel Harrington

Complete five to seven of these freewrites at home at your computer. Make four copies of one or two single-spaced pages to share in class.

RAYMOND CARVER (1938–1988)

Sunday Night

CONSIDER THIS:

Raymond Carver was born in Clatskanie, Oregon, and died of lung cancer in Port Angeles, Washington. He earned an M.F.A. from the University of Iowa and taught at Berkeley, Syracuse University, and the University of Iowa. Carver's stories formed the basis for Robert Altman's acclaimed film *Short Cuts.* His numerous awards and honors include the National Endowment for the Arts award, a Guggenheim fellowship, and the Mildred and Harold Strauss Living Award. Carver is known for incorporating incidents drawn from his life in the Pacific Northwest into his work, but he approached such raw material in a very specific way. In an interview he said, "I use certain autobiographical elements, something—an image, a sentence I heard, something I saw, that I did, and then I try to transform that into something else. Yes, there's a little autobiography and, I hope, a lot of imagination."

Carver wrote mostly short stories and poetry. He saw similarities between the two forms: "I believe a plotline is very important. Whether I am writing a poem or writing prose I am still trying to tell a story." He also saw some advantages in poetry: "The nice thing about a poem is that there is instant gratification. And if something goes wrong, it's right there. It would be a hard thing for me to work for months on a novel and then have it be bad. It would be a tremendous investment for me, and I don't have a very long attention span." When you read Carver's poem, do you detect what you think of as "autobiographical" sparks? What elements from your own life would you substitute for those in the poem? what weather, evening occupation, type of music, type of car, individual, doing what? What do you make use of in your writing? What small, overlooked elements might actually loom large in your compositions? To what might you add your imagination?

Make use of the things around you.
This light rain
Outside the window, for one.
This cigarette between my fingers,
These feet on the couch.
The faint sound of rock-and-roll,
The red Ferrari in my head.
The woman bumping
Drunkenly around in the kitchen . . .
Put it all in,
Make use.

Classroom Authors

SCOTT ARKIN

IChat

CONSIDER THIS:

Scott Arkin was an undergraduate English writing major when he wrote this essay. Before you read it, share your "history of using the Internet" with members of your group. The Internet world is changing so quickly, it's difficult to narrate our experiences there. What in Scott's essay—if anything—do you already find out of date? What in this essay would you expect he would have to revise, rethink five years from now?

WRITING PROCESS NOTE FOR "ICHAT"

This paper has come a long way since its birth. (And at least there was no screaming and blood with this baby.) As I mentioned in my Executive Summary (which is attached to Draft 2), the class workshop really helped me concentrate on my ideas. It made me realize that I was trying to cover too much in a single paper. So after much work, I chopped up Draft 2 and shot out my Final Paper. There are three main changes: 1. Added more secondary research. 2. Cut out the entire section on swearing/lying online. 3. Included a section on new words/terms from the Internet/online. By doing those three things I was able to develop more about the Language of the paper, which was the main idea. I wanted to get across all the new language developments that are happening online, and I think I accomplished that very well. Of course, I also made some minor revisions, but I definitely think now my main idea is coming across much better.

I do admit I didn't stick to my Executive Summary Revision Timeline. I was planning to spend more time earlier, rather than later on Paper 2. However, I got quite caught up in Paper 3 and therefore my timeline got switched around. But even so, I had plenty of opportunities to revise it just how I wanted. Unlike Paper 1 and Paper 2, I mainly wrote Paper 2 in the school's computer lab. I think that also helped me develop the whole online language theme since I was able to easily and quickly find research off the Internet. And I think it came out excellent.

ICHAT

My first online experience was when I was in 9th grade. My dad brought home his laptop (which back then was the size of a suitcase) and it had a software program on it called America Online. So I "logged on," entered in my dad's credit card number and had to pick a screen-name: so I tried "Scott" then "ScottA" but no luck. Next I tried a few cartoon character names, but they were also taken. So I got mad that I couldn't get a stupid name to work. So I typed in "StupidCow" thinking I could go back and change it later. Well little did I know, the computer took it and then wisked me away to their service. I attempted to go back and change it, but it wouldn't let me. So after a minute or two of discouragement, I entered my first chat room. And I thought it was the coolest thing in the world. I was immediately taken aback by how many people were in there chatting. One was from Oklahoma, another from New York, and another from Washington. I was just in awe at how all these different people, from different parts of the continent were in this same virtual room as I was. And they were talking to me, "Hey StupidCow, how are you?", "Welcome StupidCow!", "Can I milk you StupidCow?" It then dawned on me—I could meet women on this thing! Yeah Baby!! Of course I quickly realized who the hell is going to talk to someone named StupidCow. That ended my cyber-sex life.

The Internet started in the 1960s as a project for the United States Department of Defense's Advanced Research Projects Agency (ARPA). Using government funds, they began development of a computer network to exchange information (originally, designed in case there was a war). Over the next few years, and as new technologies were created, through ARPA, corporations, and universities the computer architecture developed to begin routing data over the ARPA network that spanned the United States. Eventually, with the full network in place in the 1970s, services emerged such as sending and receiving files (FTP), mail (e-mail), and eventually the World Wide Web was born in 1989. From there, Internet Service Providers, such as America Online, used the backbone of the network for their own services.

The more I used America Online, the more I became addicted to chat rooms, e-mail and Instant Messages. Being able to communicate with so many different people so quickly was the neatest thing in the world to me. However, back then AOL charged by the hour—so I had to mow a lot of lawns to pay my dad back. Even so, after experiencing the online world it made me realize how open everybody was—when you talked to someone, you didn't know whether they were pretty or ugly, fat or skinny, smelly or sweet, black or white, frizzy haired or bald—it didn't matter. You only based people on what they said, not what they looked like. Barriers were broken. You didn't know if somebody had an accent unless they told you, nor could you tell if they were from a foreign country (especially since everybody's typing skills were so poor). And everybody was using a new language online—one filled with acronyms, smileys and new dot com words.

StupidCow: What's LOL?
MikeR324: Laughing Out Loud
StupidCow: Thanks.
CareBear: Where ya from Stupid? :-)
StupidCow: Florida. What's :-)?
CareBear: Turn your head sideways. BRB
D0me4Evr: asdlkjasdljkahafglk. The wOrLd is CoMing To aN End!
KoolGuy7: Hey there sexy CareBear, wanna get a private room???

Dave Barry's Smiley List:

:-) Happy person with a nose.

:-(Sad person with a nose.

:—-(Person who is sad because he or she has a large nose.

:-D Person laughing.

:-D* Person laughing so hard that he or she does not notice that a 5-legged spider is hanging from his or her lip.

:-l Person unsure of which long-distance company to choose.

>8-O-(§) Person just realizing that he or she has a tapeworm.

;-) Person winking.

.-) Person who can still smile despite losing an eyeball.

:-OWW Person vomiting a series of Slim Jims.

:-Q Person who just had cybersex and is now enjoying a post-coital cybercigarette.

Smileys (also called Emoticons) are just one new form of language being created on the Internet universe. It was created as a means to express a person's emotions. Whether they're happy :-) or sad :-(, they're laughing :-D or they're sticking their tongue out :-P at you. They can wink ;-) at you or give you a smooch :-* on the cheek. Hundreds were created so one person would know how the other is feeling. And over the past few years they became a common new language online. If you enter any chatroom, it will be filled with familiar and not-so-familiar smileys being sent back and forth. As well as in e-mails, smileys are a natural addition to any sentence so the reader knows how it was meant.:) While in person you can read their body language, on the phone you can hear their tone of voice, but online there had to be a way to express one's emotions, and smileys were created. They're a natural key stroke to anybody who's a regular in the online chatting world. Some people can be very sarcastic or silly online, and by using a ;-) after their sentence, you immediately know they were just kidding (like if they say they have to go because the people from the Publisher's Clearinghouse are at their door).

Another form of communication is online acronyms: LOL, BRB, AFK, ROTFLMAO (*Laughing Out Loud, Be Right Back, Away From Keyboard, Rolling On The Floor Laughing My Ass Off*) and many, many more. Acronyms are a part of online language just as much as smileys are. You can easily come up with your own and confuse the people you're talking to—which can be quite fun as well. IMHOYNTTAS (*In My Humble Opinion You Need To Take A Shower*). Or you can create a new language between you and your friends. Just as teenagers came up with number codes for their beepers to tell their friends that "I'm Bored", "Call me later" or even "Billy Bob just kissed me behind the basketball court." Acronyms are the shorthand of the online community, where people are ever ready to express their ideas and thoughts as quickly as possible. Every group of people have their own personal codes and shorthands. Whether it's a math club, technical job, Save the Trees organization or even religion, each one has its terms and lingo that help define it. And if you were transplanted into a new different group of people, it would take you awhile to learn their lingo. Just as if you're starting a new job, you usually go through a period of "training" that gets you up to speed with that company's terms.

In the Age of Information, new words are being created faster than Webster can add them to his dictionary. It started with the beginnings of the Internet when the word "cyberspace" was coined—which began an influx of cyber words like "cybersex" and "cyberworship." Then came along "e" with "e-mail," "e-commerce," "eTrade," and "eBay." Sooner after, "i" became the popular letter of choice to create new words like "iMac." Technology has always influenced vocabulary—as new devices are invented, people come up with terms to use and explore them. According to Michael Agnes, Editor in Chief of *Webster's New World Dictionary,* "The percentage of technical language that impinges on the average person is rather small. We like to see a word have a solid track record over at least three years before including it." But even if not every new word is included, the "speed and informality of the Internet is credited with changing the way that Americans are writing and thinking of both print and text" explains Dana Hull's "e-Prefix" article. And e-mail is the perfect tool for the Information Age—it provides short, quick exchanges between people, allowing them to get their ideas across as efficiently as possible.

:-{8 Person who is unhappy with the results of her breast-enlargement surgery.

:V:-| Person who cannot figure out why nobody wants to talk to him or her, little suspecting that there is an alligator on his or her head.

~oE]:-| Fisherperson heading for market with a basket on his or her head containing a three-legged octopus that is giving off smell rays.

>:-[-{9 Person who is none too pleased to be giving birth to a squirrel.

As the Internet world grows, new communities are formed—whether they be interest- or hobby-based, religion, gender, work-related, etc. And these communities use different languages and means to express their ideas. One community may discuss their needlecraft tips in a message board, while another group shares their favorite Leonardo DiCaprio movies in a chat room, while another group posts information about the Presidential Election on a web page. And as these communities grow, so do their people and languages. My girlfriend often shares & receives cooking tips from a listserve of hundreds of people around the world—and they usually send native cuisines that are quite disgusting (because of the needed animal body parts) to a typical American. And while they might not speak each other's language perfectly, they can communicate effectively enough to get their ideas (and cooking tips) across.

BOB1978: Did you hear they're coming out with another Blair Witch movie?
YOYO69: Yeah this time she blows her nose before going on camera.
BesoMi: Yo conoce que Leonardo DiCaprio es en la movica.
SuzyBGood: Oh Leo! He's my hero! I want to take off all his clothes and . . .

I think some people are afraid that their identities will be lost in this new medium. That everybody will speak the same language (Klingon), and lose their past culture. I believe it's the opposite though, that their own customs and traditions will flourish as new people are able to learn about them. Language changes over time—it develops as new words combine with the old. Just as Old English looks nothing like Modem English (for example, "thank you" in Old English would be "Ic flancie fle"), what we write today may look like a foreign language to students more than a hundred years from now. But it's all built upon the past. It's as if we're all immigrants to a new land, and our languages will get thrown into a melting pot and out will come some yummy fondue.

With 6 billion people in the world and only a few hundred million online as of now, there's lots of room for expansion and diversification. People are coming up with new words and terms that express their thoughts. The advent of the Internet has brought a new creation of our ever-changing language into the open. We're more likely to express new ideas, and our ideas can be seen by potentially millions and millions of people spanning the globe. And as new peoples and cultures get on the Internet, their own learnings and languages will be intertwined with what's out there now. As universal as the words "adios" and "okay" are throughout the world today, things like a :-) will be common throughout the world in the future.

LEAH V. MARCUM

You've Got Mail (Whether You Want It or Not)

CONSIDER THIS:

Leah Marcum was an undergraduate English writing major when she wrote this essay. As you'll discover when you read her process cover sheet, her essay discusses what she considers to be e-mail abuse. Before you read, what have you found, personally, to be problematic about writing on or with the Internet? What issues about Internet use concern you as a student, an employee, a parent (if you have children or plan to have children)? If you've experienced a problem with Internet use, how have you addressed it? After reading Leah's essay, decide if you'd respond in a similar or different way and why.

WRITING PROCESS NARRATIVE FOR "YOU'VE GOT MAIL"

Even though I thought I'd write about something else, Wendy told us to write about something that we feel passionate about. Well, that could be a lot of things, but I remembered that an incident happened over a year ago that affected me and my husband quite a lot, and I always thought that I should write about it. It was hard, though, because I still have a lot of uncomfortable feelings about the incident. A male friend of my husband's e-mailed an X-rated photo of a woman who looked a lot like me. It was such a shock because the personality of this man just didn't lend itself to that kind of action, and because there had never been the slightest hint that he *would* think of me in any way other than a platonic friend. I felt abused in the way that women feel abused when men cat-call to them on the street—you just can't respond without having an icky confrontation. Anyhow, that's what I decided to write about, even though I knew I'd have some trouble with it.

After sharing the first rough draft, my 3-person group gave me encouragement to go ahead with this topic. They suggested that I begin with the actual e-mail sent, and put it in a typical e-mail format. I agreed. They thought the name "E-mail Abuse" was okay, and they agreed with my ideas to add other categories of e-mail abusers. I still don't know how I'll conclude.

The full draft is looking pretty good. I like the beginning with the e-mail format because it's eye-catching. I've added other categories of e-mail abusers, and have concluded with a plea for people to just be considerate before sending stuff that isn't appropriate for the recipient.

The workshop response was interesting. Two or three people (one woman) felt sorry for the friend who sent the X-rated photo, because he was no longer our friend. Others in the group sympathized with my viewpoint. I realized, though, that I needed to make it clear that, while Ed was an old friend, he wasn't a *close* friend. One person seemed to resent that I didn't like getting the barrage of e-mail that I do. He said he just sends out whatever he wants regardless of the recipient, and that I shouldn't be asking people to think twice before sending. I always like his comments, but I don't want to change the tone of my paper or the gist of my complaint. Besides, he was the only one who felt that way. The group didn't like the name because "abuse" didn't really fit. Most of the examples I gave were just annoyances instead. They also reminded me that other unwelcome e-mail includes "urban legends" and chain letters.

I've changed the title, clarified and minimized the relationship with Ed, got rid of the "abuse" theme (opting for annoying instead), included urban legends, and added Town Criers as another category. I rewrote a lot of text because some of it seemed disjointed. I'm a little concerned that I started out with a pretty serious topic, then applied a cynical/humorous tone to the body of it, then concluded on a serious note. Maybe that's okay—I'll put it aside and read it again after awhile to see how it sounds.

Okay, this is it, Final Portfolio copy. I decided that the first part of the paper was okay. It's serious, but not in an extremely solemn way. For the ending, I finally thought of something tart to say about the annoying e-mailers so it could end on a funny note. To bed.

YOU'VE GOT MAIL (WHETHER YOU WANT IT OR NOT)
THE ANNOYING PRACTICE OF E-MAILING ANYTHING AND EVERYTHING TO ANYBODY AND EVERYBODY

To: Dave & Leah
From: Ed C.
Subject: 3 attachments

I've included three separate attachments with this e-mail:

1) Information about the software I told you about;
2) A picture of the vacation house I bought in North Carolina (you'll have to join me there sometime!); and
3) A picture of a young lady who looks remarkably like Leah. Warning! This is an X-rated photo, so if you 're offended by nudity, don 't open it!

Love, Ed

It never occurred to me that the "X-rated" photo might be real. Ed always sent the best e-mail jokes of anyone we knew, and I figured that the photo would be a funny cartoon. Ed was a very conservative, fifty-five year old man who never told dirty jokes or behaved in any questionable way. He was a former business associate of my husband's and we socialized with him quite a bit. I couldn't say that we were the closest of friends, but we had spent so much time together that a very pleasant, casual friendship had developed over the years.

We especially liked getting e-mail from Ed because the quality of his jokes, games, and references to interesting web sites generally surpassed those that other people sent. You know, the ones that have been thoughtlessly forwarded to fifty other people and still have everyone else's address on them, so that you have to keep opening them, and opening them, and opening them until you finally get to the joke or the site, which is never worth the effort that you've expended to get there. Unlike *those* e-mail messages, I always opened Ed's e-mail with pleasure.

It took a while for the "X-rated" picture to assemble, and as each section from top to bottom actually formed an identifiable naked body part, my face turned red and I felt like I'd been slapped. The young woman in the photo was bending over a little so that her breasts hung forward. Her eyes were half closed, and she was licking the corner of her upper lip. As Ed had said, she *did* look remarkably like me when I was young and slender: shoulder-length red hair, blue eyes, freckles, long arms and legs, and our faces shared the same shape. But this was a soft-porn photo, from a web site called "Naked Redheads."

Frozen in disbelief that this middle-aged man, who had always been courteous toward me, and who never even told off-color jokes, could have sent such a photo to us, just blew me away. Surely, I thought, he would never have shown up in person at our house and whipped out a *Hustler* magazine to show us a redhead who looked similar to me! What is it about e-mail that would foster this thoughtless behavior?

Ed isn't the only one who has sent unwelcome e-mail to us, of course. Just like everyone else, we've received unsolicited advertisements for X-rated websites, as well as promotions for every other imaginable business in the world. I never figured there was much I could do about the advertising onslaught, so I've always deleted it without a second thought. However, annoying e-mail from people we actually know is another matter. Even though most unwelcome e-mail comes from people we have only a casual relationship with—they're not our closest companions—I still think of them as friends and, as such, I have always felt obligated to look at what they're sending. So I look, and I am always amazed at the things they say and the stuff they send, without the slightest consideration that it might not be meaningful or appropriate for us. I just know that they would never have the temerity to say to our faces the same things they say on e-mail.

Some of the most annoying messages that we routinely get are from our Christian friends. My husband and I are not involved in an organized religion (which is not to say that we don't have a healthy sense of spirituality). Generally speaking, most people who know us are aware that we're not church-goers and no one has ever made an issue of it. However, three of those friends evidently feel the need to bombard us on nearly a daily basis with e-mail "forwards" of proselytizing stories or tales of modem day miracles or lists of ways people should behave if they want to get into heaven. We recently got a list of "Emergency Phone Numbers" from a Christian acquaintance. There were thirty entries for emergencies like, "When you have sinned . . . Call John 14. When your prayers grow narrow and selfish . . . Call Psalm 67." There is always a heavy undercurrent of "do it the Christian way, or else." Do they think that we will suddenly "see the light" through receipt of these rote messages? Do they think that we *like* getting these little unsolicited lessons? I can only imagine that they think we are bad people (although they wouldn't hesitate to be our guests for dinner), and that they are trying to save us from hellfire and damnation—but why don't they do it in person instead of hiding out in cyberspace?

Second only to the religion pushers on my e-mail black list are the Republican friends who know that my husband and I are Democrats. In person, we can all discuss the issues and voice our differing opinions without a fistfight breaking out. In fact, the relationship with these people is so amicable that sometimes we are all able to reach a consensus (no easy feat these days). Yet, several times a week, our Republican friends send the most mean-spirited, anti-Democrat jokes and cartoons one could imagine. Just like our Christian friends, I wonder what in the world gets into them?

Another category of annoying e-mailers are the ones that take on the role of moralizers. Similar to the Christians (and often overlapping), the Moralizers send touching, poignant little stories in which people sacrifice themselves for the greater good. They also share pieces with titles like, "Today I Can Be Thankful For:" followed by a three-page list of responses like, "The alarm that goes off in the early morning because it means that I'm alive," and "The piles of laundry because it means I have clothes to wear," and "The space I find at the far end of the parking lot because it means I am capable of walking." The Moralizers are generally older friends who have retired and evidently spend every day at their computer forwarding these stories one after another around the globe (to judge from the scores of addresses on their missives). I guess they think we enjoy reading these little parables, day after day, ad nauseam.

Other offenders are those who send lawyer-bashing jokes (my husband is an attorney) in which lawyers are always the scum of the earth, dishonest, better off dead, etc. Oh, ha ha. Then there are those well-meaning people who think of themselves as the town crier. Town Criers are the ones who warn everyone on their e-mail address list to beware of the latest killer computer viruses ("It will MELT your hard drive!!!). Or they warn everyone they know that they should boycott Proctor and Gamble products because the CEO of the company gives all of the company's profits to the Church of Satan. They are also the ones who spread urban legends and beg us to *please* not flash our headlights at night because it's a signal to vicious gang initiates to kill you. The Town Criers usually follow up a few days later with sheepish apologies for sending stuff that has no basis in fact, but that doesn't stop them from sending future alarming notices.

I do get annoyed with the preponderance of e-mail messages by people who don't seem to care whether the message has anything to do with us or not, but there is one aspect of getting these messages that keeps me fascinated: the senders exhibit a secret side of their personality that I don't think I'd otherwise see.

For instance, we know one couple who recently married despite dire predictions of marital doom from all of their friends. All of her e-mails are male-bashing jokes; all of his put down women. We have watched over time as their e-mails have gotten more and more vicious about the opposite sex, and we expect a divorce announcement any day now.

Another friend reveals his fascination with aberrant sexual practices by sending off-color jokes and stories that involve sex with animals, sex with groups, sex on the Thanksgiving dinner table in front of all the relatives, sex in bathrooms, on trampolines, underwater and the like. None of his jokes are terribly graphic or gross, but they do say something about his own sexual predilections. I find myself wondering if he realizes how obvious his penchant for unusual sex is?

Again, we have spent a lot of social time with these e-mail abusers, annoyers and/or personality revealing friends and acquaintances, and they have never behaved in any way that I would have thought of as questionable as long as we're face-to-face. The discrepancy between their in-person personality and their e-mail personality is a puzzler, so I started talking (over the phone) to some of the offenders about it. I approached them in such a way that they didn't need to get defensive, by telling them I was doing an article for a writing class, and had noticed that their e-mails fell into one of several categories. Why did they focus on sending the things they did, I asked, instead of a personal note?

Some people (the Christians and the Moralizers) acted surprised and said that they hadn't even realized what they were doing. They were just sending along stuff that they had received and enjoyed and thought that we would enjoy, too. I'm not at all sure I buy that, since they all know where we stand on the issue of organized religion and because we have never given any indication that we are moralists. But I let them off without a struggle, and since then I have (gratefully) begun to get personal notes instead of the religious tracts and morality stories that plagued my computer screen before.

There was no need to fan the flames of the warring couple, I decided, but I did ask our (possibly) sexually aberrant friend about the nature of his jokes. He quite frankly said that those jokes were the only kind he liked, and he didn't care who knew it. Okay!

One Town Crier reported that sending along urgent messages made him feel important. He didn't give any acknowledgment that the messages were usually wrong, and I didn't have the heart to burst his bubble. There's a reason computers have a "delete" button, and I'll definitely be using it for those "urgent" messages.

The Lawyer Basher was unable to explain why he thought my husband would laugh at being called dishonest and better-off-dead and a bottom feeder. Then he told me a lawyer joke. "Delete."

I didn't bother surveying the Republicans. They seem to be on a national mission to beat the Democratic Party to death through nasty name-calling, and I rather like taking a pacifist stance just to underscore the difference between the two groups.

Ed was also not part of my survey. My husband called Ed shortly after he sent the fateful X-rated e-mail, and discussed the whys and wherefores of his ill-chosen action. All he could offer was that he'd always had a thing for redheads, which had led him to the Naked Redheads site. When he saw the young woman who looked like me, he just sent it to us, he said, without thinking. Upon further digging, though, he admitted that he'd had a little crush on me when David and I first got married—and that was when his "thing" for redheads began. He was apologetic, but he also sounded a little put out that he was being questioned. He and my husband have remained cordial business associates, but I'm relieved that he never asked to visit with us again in our home. I don't believe I could ever think of Ed with the same ease that I had before.

Unlike Ed, most senders of unwanted e-mail messages don't end up having to pay any consequences for their lack of judgment. As near as I can tell from my own observations and from the informal survey I did, people tend to think of e-mail as something less than tangible: they see something *they* like (or want to poke at you with), push a couple of buttons, and *poof!* it's gone. And because it's gone so quickly (no face-to-face accountability, and no piece of paper with the incriminating evidence), I think, too, that there's a sense of anonymity. It's like covertly shooting a spit ball at someone, and then acting nonchalant.

Doing the survey has relieved the bulk of unwanted e-mails from my in-box, but I would put out a plea to anyone who reads this: When you're going to send an e-mail to someone, ask yourself, "Would I say this to them in person?" Or, "Would I hand them a piece of paper with this message on it? Would I share this picture in a magazine if they were sitting next to me?" If you can't answer, "Yes," please think of someone else who you know will enjoy it. Or, at the very least, instead of sending it to me, forward it to a Christian, a Moralizer, a Republican or a Town Crier. I know they'll receive it in the spirit it's given.

CONNECTING TO READING

A. With your group, share your past history as "someone who writes journals." To do this, consult the discussion about journal keeping in this chapter as well as the selection by Spike Lee. Many writers and teachers believe journaling is a sound method for learning in any subject area and a crucial technique for improving as a writer. What would you each need to do to make journaling a better learning and writing technique in your writer's tool kit?

B. Write a journal entry that you can share with your class writing group based on further research into journal keeping. At your local bookstore, public or university library, or on the Internet, you'll quickly find authors who discuss journal keeping and the history of journal writing. Browse several of these sources. You might begin with Sharyn Lowenstein's essay "A Brief History of Journal Keeping" found in *The Journal Book,* edited by Toby Fulwiler (Portsmouth, NH: Boynton/Cook Heinemann 1987).

C. Keep a double-entry notebook as you read any essay in this book. Post a section from this entry on your class discussion board (or bring copies to class) so that your class can compare how this technique works when undertaken by different writers.

D. With your group, in class, try exploring the same topic (you should agree on a topic beforehand, using one of the prompts or sequences covered in the invention handouts—home, nature, food, and family). Each member of the group will use a different invention response method—clustering, reporter's formula, cubing, and so on—to explore the topic. Share your results. Try to examine how each technique works and why a writer might or might not choose it to investigate a particular topic. If there is time, repeat with a different topic and ask each member to choose a different technique. Or, if you prefer, repeat with the same topic but have each member respond using a different invention lens. Again, compare your results and investigate the uses of these techniques.

E. As a group, consider Katharine Haake's "Beyond the End of Writing" and, together, explain to each other how you would follow her writing directions. Then consider your favorite of the classroom invention handouts. First, read all the writing samples aloud in your group. Then, each member should circle the five writing prompts that interest him or her most. Again, see if you're similar in your choices or very different.

CONNECTING TO WRITING

A. At home, choose your favorite general freewriting technique and one you've rarely used from those outlined in the introduction to this chapter. Apply these techniques to any current writing assignment for any class you are enrolled in. Share copies of your results with your group.

B. At home, continue with Connecting to Reading, activities D or E from this chapter. Complete Katharine Haake's exercise and/or your favorite prompts from the classroom handouts. Share the results in class groups or on the class discussion list.

C. To write a journal entry on your own journal-keeping practices, find an old set of personal or class journals. Use Toby Fulwiler's analysis of effective journal practices, Donald Murray's self-analysis of his daybooks, and your reading of Spike Lee's journals to help you analyze your own practices. Share your observations in a class discussion.

D. E-mail a classmate about e-mail. After reading Scott Arkin's and Leah Marcum's essays, compose a short e-mail–related narrative (or two) based on your own experiences. Comment on your partner's narrative in a return e-mail. Copy this dialogue into your course journal if you're keeping one.

E. Compose an open letter to an actual friend (that you will share with a small group or the whole class), expanding on Raymond Carver's seemingly simple advice. Is it? Why or why not? Relate it to what you've learned about writers and their processes and life histories in Chapters 1 and 2. Cite the observations of other writers found in this textbook to support your claims. Feel free to send the friend the letter also.

WRITING PROJECTS

1. Examine your own history of journal writing. Make yourself into a case study, using the research you did into your history of journal keeping and documenting your claims and observations with quotes from your own journal(s). If you've kept a journal for some time, you might use the title "Changing as a Writer" (or "Journal Keeper"), or you may focus your narrative on journaling, something along the lines of "Me and My Journal." Let this meditation on journals and journal keeping reveal aspects of your writing process or writing life in any way, with any title, that you choose. If you've never kept a journal, explore why not and consider what benefits journal writing may have for you. Make the case against your own current practices.

2. Write an essay about e-mail. Expand your vignettes about your experiences with e-mail or quote them as part of your essay. For this paper, consider doing some research on the Internet and/or e-mail; movies like *You've Got Mail* count, but look also at books, articles, Scott Arkin's and Leah Marcum's essays in this chapter, and the far reaches of the Internet itself.
3. For your essay, discover a topic by using the "authority list," described in the introduction to this chapter. Compose an essay on your "authority" subject, directed to a particular audience or community of readers.
4. Develop an essay based on your responses to "Beyond the End of Writing" or one or more of the prompts in the invention handouts for this chapter. As you complete this essay, keep a process journal—a double-entry technique in itself, only this time you're reflecting on composing instead of on reading—and use that journal to compose your process narrative to accompany the essay.
5. Develop an essay from any of the writing projects in any of the chapters of this book using a number of the general invention techniques listed in the chapter introduction as a method for enlarging (sections of) each draft that you produce. Again, keep a drafting journal so you can compose a solid writing process narrative.
6. Begin your essay with a quote from a writer in the manner of Anne Lamott. Write a personal narrative about one aspect of your writing process. Study your practices. What is the result of this practice for you? How might another writer benefit from doing what you do (or why should other writers avoid your practices)? If possible, include a family anecdote or an illustrative story, meditate on the importance of this practice to your life in general, illustrate the practice using your own texts, and work to achieve a strong sense of closure. (You may have noticed I just read Lamott's text rhetorically to create the prompts for an exercise that might allow you to write a successful version of your own essay that grows from hers.)
7. In your essay, respectfully disagree with one or more of the authors in this chapters or offer a discussion of their advice that also suggests warnings, alternatives, options. Using well-described personal examples, explain the possible negative aspects of being asked to keep a journal or do in-school writing exercises. If possible, document your claims using samples from your own journals and in-class writings. Finally, suggest viable alternatives for allowing novice writers and/or blocked writers and/or disengaged writers to get going on a writing project.
8. Compose an introduction to and review of Richard Hugo's influential book *The Triggering Town,* mentioned in Katharine Haake's exercise. His collection offers advice to interested creative writers and teachers of writing. Connect his work to your life as a writer. Which of his essays in this collection would you recommend to classmates and why? Which don't seem to

apply and why? Pull out some quotes and freewrite on them; then look for an organization pattern for your paper. Introduce us to Hugo's work and explore what is still relevant for today's writers and what might be old-fashioned or of less use. Consider, for instance, his images of writers, any gendered language, any acknowledgement or lack of the same of multicultural writers, of those who work in cyberspace, and so on.

9. Compose a response to or review of Peter Elbow's highly influential book *Writing Without Teachers* for other class readers. To do this, you'll need to read in the *genre* of reviews to find a format you like. Do you think *Writing Without Teachers* is justly or unjustly considered a key text for contemporary writers, and why?
10. Return to a paper topic you've always wanted to write about and compose that paper now. Freewrite about why you haven't done so before. Now, use any of the techniques presented in this chapter to help you write a draft of this paper. As in the previous exercise, use the initial freewrite as the first entry in your writing process narrative journal for this essay. Try to spend at least one-third or one-half of your total available writing time on the journal, analyzing the development of this paper as you complete your draft.

* * * *

The hardest part of writing is pushing through to the end of the first draft. I don't read each day's work before I start the next day's work. If I stop, and reread and work over each day's work, it's a temptation to make each chapter a perfect jewel as I go, and by the time I get to the end of the book I might find that what I wrote at the beginning was all wrong. I lose my perspective if I work on the writing too intensively page by page. It's better to push on and complete a first draft, and then to the revising.

—Beverly Cleary

Chapter 5

Form to Develop Your Thoughts: Modes, Topics, Genres

Thinking About How Form and Structure Help Develop a Topic You Already Have

> Since freshman year, I have learned a lot. I've learned to shop for a week on twenty dollars. I've learned to pack up and move efficiently. I've learned that writing is an art applied to communication and that I have a tendency to stray from the communication aspect. I've learned to be honest with myself first, then people are honest with me. I've learned that I only need to water my plants once a week. I've learned to write papers like molding clay. Write like crazy, stop and turn it to the light, examine it. And never, never put it in the kiln until it can speak without you.
>
> –ANONYMOUS CLASSROOM AUTHOR

Once upon a time, you were regularly told exactly what to do with your writing. It felt like a juggling act: first you had to respond to a set topic, and about that topic you felt obliged to write for a specified number of pages, and within those pages you had to accomplish several things. You may have been told that paragraphs needed to begin with a topic sentence; have unity, coherence, and clarity; and be five to eight sentences long. You were told to write a series of papers across a term but to do so in a certain order: in the first describe a memorable landscape, in the second narrate a life-changing experience, in the third explain why democracy is essential to the stability of the free world, and in the fourth persuade your congressperson to vote for or against gun control legislation. While writing each paper, you were encouraged to develop your life-changing narrative using examples and illustrations as well as vivid, particular detail. To discuss democracy you were required to define terms and explore cause and effect. To persuade your elected representative, you made legal, ethical, and emotional appeals (but were cautioned to focus on the former more than the latter).

It's no surprise that writing according to these directions often failed to engage either the reader (too often only your teacher) or the writer (you). There was little room to discover what you wanted to say and why. And while obeying multiple composing constraints, you were endeavoring to do so with perfect form.

That's just the trouble. Under so many prescriptions, writers feel like they are *merely* performing or writing to show knowledge. Certainly it is more efficient for a teacher to supply students with topics, forms, and genres like the personal essay or the persuasion paper. The teacher can specify skills for mastery, the student can attempt to master, and be faulted or rewarded for achieving a certain sort of technical excellence. In fact, some students seem to prefer this sort of firm guidance because it doesn't push them to explore on their own, to take risks. However, expert writers remind us that without exploration, experimentation, and risk-taking there is little growth. Certainly there are situations still when all of us have to perform under pressure and where clear, competent work is valuable and to be valued, as when we write an exam, are asked to complete a paper with very short notice, or need to finish a project in a single sitting. Having some of these skills is certainly a relief and quite necessary at times, but the writer who wants to mature needs to engage forms and not be intimidated by them.

For many reasons, writing instruction in certain required college classes in the later part of the twentieth century looked, sounded, and developed in the manner I've just outlined. Contemporary writing classrooms are often much different. Writers in them are considered to be intelligent adult learners who have something to say but who also need support in learning the best way to accomplish their writing aims. In such courses, writing purposes are assumed to be part of a mutual negotiation between writer and the writer's goals; between a student's aims and the teacher's aims for the course; between author and assignment. When used to support you in your writing, many of the techniques we survey in this chapter can be very useful in both sorts of classrooms.

The rule-oriented writing classes of the past insisted that form was more important than content. This directive came from the assumption that form could generate solid content with machine-line regularity. But humans, writers at work, aren't assembly line technicians. And form and content, of course, are partners. Sometimes you want to explore the challenge of a genre (poetry, the sonnet in particular; fiction, flash-fiction in particular; the scientific report, the lab report in particular; the literary essay, a response to a recent novel or current film in particular). Sometimes you decide it would be useful to master a technique like comparison/contrast organization options; the essay-test response, which relies on a thesis and tight organization; logical argumentation structures that are essential, for instance, in the practice of law because once you do, you'll be able to internalize that strategy and feel able to use it when necessary.

Contemporary writing reference books call modes and topics "patterns of organization" and usually list these as narration, description, cause and effect, analogy, example and illustration, classification and division, process analysis, comparison and contrast, and definition. When working to persuade, you consider logical, emotional, and ethical appeals. In classical rhetoric, common topics were used to help orators find the best available means to make their case. Orators were encouraged to try these topics, to discover their limits and strengths, to practice. For this, they used definition and comparison, explored relationships and circumstances, and used expert testimony (from authorities, testimonials, statistics, maxims, laws, and previous examples or precedents). So, too, you could argue for or against gun control by defining what you mean by "control": by comparing laws of the past to a newly proposed law; by exploring the relationship of gun availability to violence; by considering circumstances under which the law you support would be desirable or undesirable; and by sharing statistics, relevant laws, legal precedents, and previous legal testimony. You could use logical appeals (legal precedents) but mix them with emotional appeals (testimony from a parent whose child has been killed by another child who had access to an unsecured family handgun) and ethical appeals (maxims). Conceivably, your entire paper could be organized by cause and effect or by example and illustration or by comparison and contrast.

Quickly, you realize why it's unlikely that any writer would choose to deploy all these strategies in a single text. In fact, the writer might choose only one or two methods for any given situation. Or the writer might use modes, topics, and appeals to explore a subject during initial drafts (because they are generative techniques) but then decide to focus on particular aspects (leaving out the emotional appeal, perhaps, or focusing on statistics more than on testimonials).

Instead of arguing for or against modes and topics, in this chapter I encourage you to investigate them. The writers included here use form seriously and playfully. With Edward P. J. Corbett and Robert J. Connors, you'll share a rhetorical discussion of why and how to formulate a thesis. Next, you'll read a series of texts where the writer has relied on some, but, of course, not all, of these techniques. For these authors, formal structures provide artistic and communicative scaffolding not straight jackets. For instance, Evans Hopkins and Brent Staples include description and narration in their explorations of authority, race, and class; in their essays, persuasions about the problems of racism are both tacit and explicit. Donna Steiner examines two powerful subjects—love and alcoholism—and mixes modes to do so; you'll find her telling stories, describing, defining, using rhetorical questions, and several other identifiable techniques. Haunani-Kay Trask and Sherman Alexie make strong arguments about culture; both compare and contrast their minority culture with dominate ones, using logical, ethical, and pathetic appeals. Diane Ackerman and Jamaica Kincaid define and describe (hummingbirds, tourists). Barry Lopez transcends our expectations for the comparison and contrast form when he compares a truck and a horse, and my essay tests the limits of both the comparison and contrast form (life in Alaska and life in Florida) within the demands of the five-paragraph essay that Leonora Smith critiques in her poem of the same name.

Classroom authors, too, use varied and effective patterns. Maggie Gerrity mixes memoir with critique to produce her argument while Sandra Giles provides a descriptive report in the final draft of her essay (shared in an early and final draft). Amanda Fleming's essay illustrates how the same topic, cast in two very different molds, produces dramatically different—yet clearly related—effects.

While I encourage you to identify each writer's choices as you notice them played out in a text, as I've begun to do here, you'll also want to imagine how each author could have taken other paths, chosen other equally effective ways to explore their subjects and develop their writing. You can perform the same sorts of analysis using essays in other chapters as well. Even as you say, "This essay relies on descriptive details," you will want to ask, also, "What would have happened if the author had included some statistics or provided a better definition of her terms?"

When investigating any form, I encourage you to play by the rules as long as they feel profitable but be willing to break free from constraints to support your developing text. In this I echo George Orwell's famous writing advice in his essay "Politics and the English Language": "Break any of these rules sooner than say anything outright barbarous." In much the same way, thesis statements should aid not hinder your writing aims. Methods of organization may be useful to a point, but something in your vision, your subject, or your paper may require you to consider alternate ideas; move your thesis to a new and unexpected spot in your essay; sandwich a short, sharp, single-sentence paragraph between two much longer ones; or appeal strongly to the emotions of your readers. When you do this, you have turned your paper to the light, examined it, and made sure you've done what's best for the composing situation. That is, you have learned from your careful engagements with generative conventions, but you haven't let them overawe you or overdetermine what you are trying to say.

Chapter Readings

EDWARD P. J. CORBETT (1919–1998) AND
ROBERT J. CONNORS (1952–2000)

Formulating a Thesis

CONSIDER THIS (See Authors' Introductions in Chapter 3):

In a group, relate your past experiences with writing thesis statements. How have you been trained? How effective have you been in drafting them? Edward Corbett and Robert Connors argue strongly for the use of the thesis statement. Their cardinal principle is that a thesis statement should take the form of a single declarative sentence. Although they admit this can be hard to accomplish, they predict that a focused thesis enables you to focus your entire text. To further explore thesis statements, as a group, highlight the key sentences from the readings in this chapter. As you read these as representative samples, what varieties of thesis statements do you find? Are they declarative statements or do the authors choose other methods for directing readers to the main point(s) of their works?

The beginning of all discourse is a topic, a question, a problem, an issue. This topic or question or problem or issue can be said to be the *subject* of the discourse. Subject is the *res* of the *res-verba* combination that the Latin rhetoricians talked about. The discovery of the *res* (*what* is said) became the province of that part of rhetoric that dealt with "invention." *Verba* (*how* it is said) was the concern of two other parts of rhetoric, "style" and "delivery." Obviously, we cannot make any sensible decisions about the expression part of our discourse until we have clearly and firmly defined the subject matter.

Frequently, our subject-matter is assigned to us. Our teacher announces in class, "For next Friday I want you to write a 500-word letter to the editor of the school newspaper, giving your views on the proposed increase in tuition." Or the editor of a magazine writes to us and asks us to do a 300-word piece on the demonstrations against the building of a nuclear power plant in our community. Or the president of the company for which we work asks us to prepare a report for the next business meeting on the success of the latest advertising campaign. Occasionally, we choose our own subject, but more frequently when we are engaged in a major writing project, we are dealing with a subject that has been assigned to us.

But the choice or designation of a subject is only a beginning; in fact, it can be a dead-end if something further is not done to define the subject. It is not enough for us to decide that we are going to write on "democracy." Before "democracy" can become a real subject for a discourse, something must be *predicated* of it. The subject must be converted into a thesis; it must, to use a term from logic, be stated in the form of a *proposition,* a complete sentence that asserts or denies something about the subject. So our vague subject "democracy" must be turned into a sentence like "Democracy is the form of government that best allows its citizens to realize their potentialities as human beings" or "A democracy cannot function effectively if its citizens are illiterate." Now we have a theme or a thesis to write about—a precise notion of what we are going to say about the subject of "democracy."

John Henry Newman, in a section called "Elementary Studies" in his idea of a University, points out the importance of stating a subject in the form of a proposition. His fictitious Mr. Black is commenting on a composition written by a boy named Robert:

> "Now look here," Mr. Black says, "the subject is '*Fortes fortuna adjuvat*' [Fortune favors the brave]; now this is a *proposition;* it states a certain general principle, and this is just what an ordinary boy would be sure to miss, and Robert does miss it. He goes off at once on the word '*fortuna.*' '*Fortuna*' was not his subject; the thesis was intended to *guide* him, for his own good; he refuses to be put into leading strings; he breaks loose, and runs off in his own fashion on the broad field and in wild chase of 'fortune,' instead of closing with a subject, which, as being definite, would have supported him.
>
> "It would have been very cruel to have told a boy to write on 'fortune'; it would have been like asking him his opinion 'of things in general.' Fortune is 'good,' 'bad,' 'capricious,' 'unexpected,' ten thousand things all at once (you see them all in the Gradus), and one of them as much as the other. Ten thousand things may be said of it: give me *one* of them, and I will write upon it; I cannot write on more than one; Robert prefers to write upon all."

Hundreds of Roberts and Robertas are defeated every year in their composition classes because they will not or cannot define their subject. The Latin rhetoricians used a formula, referred to as *status* or *stasis,* for determining the point at issue in a court trial, a formula that might help students decide on a thesis. The formula consisted of three questions that were asked about the subject of dispute or discussion:

An sit (whether a thing is)—a question of fact
Quid sit (what is it?)—a question of definition
Quale sit (what kind is it?)–a question of quality

In a murder trial, for instance, the case for the prosecution and the defense could turn on one of three issues:

1. Did Brutus, as has been alleged, kill Caesar? (whether a thing is)
2. If it is granted that Brutus *did* kill Caesar, was the act murder or self-defense? (what is it?)
3. If it was in fact murder, was Brutus justified in murdering Caesar? (what kind is it?)

The application of this formula settles the issue in a trial and in turn suggests the topics that lawyers resort to in arguing their case.

The use of this formula will not establish the thesis of a discourse, but it can help students determine what aspect of the subject they are going to treat, and then they are in a position to formulate a thesis. Let us suppose that the teacher has asked her students to write a letter to the editor about the increase in tuition. First of all, they must determine what aspect of the subject they are going to talk about. Is there actually going to be an increase in tuition next term, or has the increase only been proposed or rumored? Some of the students may know that the Board of Trustees has been considering an increase in tuition but has not yet formally voted on the proposal. If so, the burden of the letter they would write would be something like the following: "The students of this university have been in an uproar about something that is not yet a fact. If they had taken the trouble to determine the facts, they would know that they do not yet have any just cause for complaint."

Suppose, however, that the report about the increase in tuition charges per credit-hour has been confirmed. What aspect is there left to discuss? Well, the students could direct their attention to the question of definition. Is the change from $48 to $52 per credit-hour really an *increase* in tuition costs? Not if one considers that the Board of Trustees has also voted to reduce the number of credit-hours that students will be allowed to take in any one semester. So although the cost per credit-hour will go up, the total cost of tuition per semester will remain the same. It is apparent that in this instance, a discussion of the definition of *increase* could turn into a mere quibble about words, but with other subjects, like "democracy" or "socialized medicine," there would be more of an opportunity to deal, in a substantive way, with the definition of key terms.

But suppose that a change in tuition has been approved and that this change does constitute a substantial increase in the cost of tuition. Now the third question (*quale sit*) can disclose the real focus of the discussion. Was the increase necessary? Can it be justified? In comparison with the general rise in the cost of living, does the increase in tuition turn out to be minimal? Will the increase in tuition ensure the continuance of, or even an improvement in, the quality of the education the students receive? Or will the increase prevent many students from continuing their education? The application of the third question turns up a number of significant areas of discussion.

The subject-matter considered in relation to the current situation or occasion and to the audience often dictates which of the three questions is most applicable. In any case, however, the application of the pertinent question of *status* does help to define the aspect of the subject that is to be discussed. Once that aspect has been determined, the students should be prepared to formulate a thesis sentence. Once the subject has been narrowed down, what do individual students want to say about that subject?

The cardinal principle is to *state the thesis in a single declarative sentence.*

It is important that the thesis be formulated in a single sentence. Making use of a second sentence to state the thesis is likely to introduce foreign or subsidiary matter and thereby to violate the unity of the thesis. It is equally important to formulate the thesis in a *declarative* sentence. Hortatory sentences like "Let us fight to preserve the integrity of our democracy" and interrogatory sentences like "Is democracy a feasible form of government?" leave the subject fuzzy; both kinds of sentence have a tentative or uncertain air about them. The thesis will be clearly and firmly stated if the predicate *asserts* or *denies* something about the subject: "The integrity of our democracy can be preserved only if we fight to maintain it"; "Democracy is (is not) a feasible form of government."

The thesis sentence is a good starting-point in the composition process because it forces the writer to determine at the outset just what it is that he or she wants to say about the chosen or the designated subject. Moreover, it lays the foundation for a unified, coherent discourse. Then, too, it often suggests some of the *topics* that can be used to develop the subject.

Say, for instance, that for a paper you were going to write for a political science course, you settled on the thesis "Democracy is a feasible form of government for the newly emergent countries of South Africa." That statement precisely defines the proposition that you want to argue for in your paper: a democratic form of government will work in South Africa. If you keep that objective in mind, it is likely that your paper will achieve a tight unity. But the mere verbalization of the thesis also suggests some lines of development. Will you not, for instance, have to define at the beginning of your essay at least two of the key terms in your thesis sentence—*democracy* and *feasible?* Will it not also be advisable for you to specify which countries of South Africa you have in mind? Is there a possibility that you could strengthen your argument about the feasibility of a democratic government in certain countries of South Africa by comparing the situation in these countries with the situation in other countries where democracy has proven successful? As you can see, the statement of your thesis has already suggested the topics of *definition* and *comparison* as possible lines of development and has also suggested a possible organization of your essay that will be conducive to coherence.

Defining the thesis in a single declarative sentence will also help you determine whether you can adequately handle the given or chosen subject within the word limit set for you. The subject "democracy" is so broad that you could not forecast how much development would be necessary to adequately treat that subject. A proposition like "Democracy is the best form of government" is still somewhat broad and vague, but at least it fixes some limits to the subject. You perhaps could not do justice to such a thesis in 500 words, but you might be able to treat it satisfactorily in 1500–2000 words. On the other hand, a proposition like "Representative democracy allows each citizen to exercise some voice in the conduct of the government" might very well be adequately treated in 500 words.

Simple as the principle is, some writers have difficulty in framing their thesis in a single declarative sentence. Part of their difficulty stems from the fact that they do not have a firm grasp on their ideas before they sit down to compose a thesis sentence. Thought and language interact with each other. Hugh Blair, the eighteenth-century Scottish rhetorician, one said, "For we may rest assured that whenever we express ourselves ill, there is, besides the mismanagement of language, for the most part, some mistake in our manner of conceiving the subject. Embarrassed, obscure, and feeble sentences are generally, if not always, the result of embarrassed, obscure, and feeble thought."

It often takes considerable practice before students acquire the ability to define a thesis sharply. They can foster the development of this ability if they will make a habit of formulating a thesis sentence for any formal prose they read. Sometimes the author of the prose they are reading will help them by actually stating the thesis somewhere in the essay, and in that case, their job is to locate that thematic sentence. In some cases, however, the central idea of an essay is nowhere explicitly stated, and the readers must be able to abstract the central idea from the whole essay. The ability to generalize in this way is often the last ability we acquire in learning how to read. If we cannot abstract a thesis from what we read, it is not likely that we will have much success in formulating our own thesis sentences.

We must acquire this ability if we hope to be able to communicate clearly and coherently with others through the medium of written prose. Failure to sharply define one's subject is the chief cause of fuzzy, disunified discourse. Vague beginnings invite chaotic endings. The audience for a discourse, whether written or spoken, can achieve no firmer grasp of the thesis than the writer or the speaker has. As a matter of fact, if we make allowances for what is inevitably lost in the process of transmission, the audience's grasp will always be *less* than the writer's or the speaker's.

So we round back to what was said earlier in this chapter: the beginning of coherent, unified writing is a sharply defined thesis. But as soon as that general principle is enunciated, it invites some qualification. Someone once said, "I don't really know what I want to say until I have said it." And indeed there may be times when it may be advantageous for us to start writing *before* we have a firm, clear idea of what our thesis is. In such cases, the act of writing out our yet unfocused thoughts could become part of the invention process, could lead to the discovery of what we finally want to say about the subject we had chosen, or been delegated, to write on. The articulation of our thesis would not come until *after* we had written our rough draft. We could still say, however, that even in those cases, the articulation of the thesis would be the starting-point, the catalyst, the focusing device for the writing of the final product.

EVANS D. HOPKINS (b. 1954)

Lockdown

CONSIDER THIS:

Evans D. Hopkins is a former Black Panther who wrote for that group's newspaper in the 1970s. He served more than 15 years for armed robbery at prisons in Virginia in the 1980s and 1990s. He frequently writes about his experiences in prison and more generally about criminal justice. His work has appeared in *The New Yorker, The Washington Post,* and the on-line magazines *Nerve* and *Slate.* Hopkins notes, "Years ago I was a most serious poet, but the verse seemed to dry up, though I suppose some of it has informed my prose. I recall what a literary friend wrote to me about this once: 'Poetry is based upon beauty; and you've very little of that in prison.'" As you read, consider Hopkins's aims in "Lockdown." What do you feel he is attempting to accomplish with this essay about life in prison? What do you learn that you didn't know prior to reading his descriptions? What questions are you left with? What terms and events does Hopkins find necessary to define? To compare and contrast? What methods does he employ to emphasize the facts of prison life? What sort of persona does the author create, relying on what sort of persuasive appeals—logical, ethical, or emotional? What do you think as you finish reading the essay, about prison, about lockdown, and about the author's ending argument?

I know something serious has happened when I wake up well before dawn to discover two guards wearing armored vests and riot helmets taking a head count. I'd gone to bed early this August evening, so that I might write in the early morning, as is my custom, before the prison clamor begins. So when I wake up I have no idea what was going down while I slept. But it's apparent that the prison is on "full lockdown status." At the minimum, we will be locked in our cells twenty-four hours a day for the next several days.

While lockdowns at Nottoway Correctional Center in Virginia are never announced in advance, I'm not altogether surprised by this one. The buzz among the eleven-hundred-man prison population was that a lockdown was imminent. The experienced prisoner knows to be prepared for a few weeks of complete isolation.

But I'm hardly prepared for the news I receive later in the day from a local TV station: two corrections officers and two nurses were taken hostage by three prisoners, following what authorities are calling "a terrible botched escape attempt" that included a fourth man. The incident was ended around 5:30 A.M. by a Department of Corrections strike-force team, with the hostages unharmed. However, according to authorities, eight of the rescuers, including the warden, were slightly wounded when a shotgun was discharged accidentally.

Oh, God, I think. Forget a few weeks. No telling how long we'll be on lock *now.* I try to take heart by telling myself, "It's nothing you haven't seen before, might as well take the opportunity to get the old typewriter pumpin', maybe even finish your book."

The idea that most people have of prison life consists of images from worst-case-scenario movies, or from news footage of local jails. Visitors to prison often comment on how surprised they are to see men moving around, without apparent restraint, having believed that prisoners are kept in their cells most of the time. In modern prisons, however, there is usually lots of orderly movement, as inmates go about the activities of normal life: working, eating, education, recreation, etc.

In a well-run institution, long lockdowns—where all inmate movement stops—are aberrations. Yet major institutions lock down regularly, for short periods, so that the prison can be searched for weapons and other contraband. Lockdowns are also called for emergencies, as this one has been at Nottoway, or, in fact, for any reason deemed necessary for security.

By the second week of the lockdown, one of our hot meals has been replaced with a bag lunch—four slices of bread, two slices of either cheese or a luncheon meat, and a small piece of plain cake or, more rarely, fruit. Since counsellors or administrative personnel must do most of the cooking, the lockdown menu usually consists of meals that require minimal culinary skills. Today we have chili-mac (an ungodly concoction of macaroni and ground beef), along with three tablespoons of anemic mixed vegetables and a piece of plain cake—all served on a disposable aluminum tray the size of a hardcover book.

We have not yet been allowed out to shower, so I lay newspaper on the concrete floor and bathe at the sink. There is a hot-water tap, in contrast to the cells at the now demolished State Penitentiary, in Richmond, where I served the first several years of my life sentence for armed robbery, and where I went through many very long lockdowns.

I have endured lockdowns in buildings with little or no heat; lockdowns during which authorities cut off the plumbing completely, so contraband couldn't be flushed away; and lockdowns where we weren't allowed out to shower for more than a month. I have been in prison since 1981, and my attitude has had to be "I can do time on the moon," if that is what's called for. So I'm not about to let this lockdown faze me. (Besides, I am in what is known as the "honor building," where conditions are marginally better.)

Around one o'clock in the morning, the three guards of the "shower squad" finally get around to our building. They have full riot gear on, and a Rottweiler in tow. One by one, we are handcuffed and escorted to the shower stalls at the center of the dayroom area. As I walk past the huge dog, I turn my head to keep an eye on it. The beast suddenly lunges against the handler's leash and barks at me with such ferocity that I actually feel the force of air on my face. I walk to the shower with feigned insouciance, but my heart is pumping furiously. I can forget sleeping for a while.

Back in the cell, I contemplate what's happening to this place. Information about the hostage incident has been trickling in. While the show of force seems absurd to those of us here in the honor building, I have heard reports of assaults on guards in the cell houses of the main compound, where the treatment of the inmates is said to have been more severe. On the night of the original incident, some men in a section of one building refused to return to their cells, and in at least one section there was open rebellion—destruction and burning.

Today a memorandum from the warden is passed out, and the warden himself appears on a video broadcast on the prison's TV system. He announces that there will be no visitation until some time in October—about two months from now.

Other restrictions are to be imposed, he says, including immediate implementation of a new Department of Corrections guideline, stripping all prisoners of most personal property: televisions with screens larger than five and a half inches; any tape player other than a Walkman; nearly all personal clothing (jeans, nongray sweatsuits, colored underwear, etc.); and—most devastating for me—*all typewriters.*

I find this news disquieting, to say the least, and I decide to lie down, to try to get some sleep. This is difficult, as men are yelling back and forth from their cells, upset about this latest development. Many of them have done ten or fifteen years, like me, obeying all the rules and saving the meagre pay from prison jobs to buy a few personal items—items that we must now surrender.

I awaken in the night, sweating and feverish in the humid summer air. Sitting on the edge of my bed while considering my plight, I look at photographs of my family. My eyes rest on the school portrait of my son, taken shortly before he died from heart disease ten years ago, at age twelve. Sorrow overwhelms me, and I find myself giving in to grief, then to great, mournful sobs.

The tears stop as suddenly as they began. It has been years since I've wept so, and I realize that the grief has been only a trigger—that I am, by and large, really feeling sorry for myself. This is no good, if I'm to survive with my mind and spirit intact. I can't afford to succumb to self-pity.

This new day begins shortly after 8 A.M., when three guards come to my cell door. One of them says, "We're here to escort you to Personal Property. You have to pack up everything in your cell, and they will sort out what you have to send out, and what you can keep, over there."

He looks through the long, narrow vertical slot in the steel door and—seeing all the books, magazines, journal notebooks, and piles of papers I have stacked around the cell—shakes his head in disbelief. "Looks like you're gonna need a lot of boxes," he says. I have the accumulated papers, magazines, and books of a practicing freelance writer. The only problem is that my "office" is about as big as your average bathroom—complete with toilet and sink, but with a steel cot where your bathtub would be.

Now the new rules say twelve books, twelve magazines, twelve audiotapes. Period. And "a reasonable number of personal and legal papers." I wonder how much of all this stuff they will say is reasonable, when sometimes even I question the sanity of holding on to so much. But who knows *when* I'll be able to get to any files, manuscripts, books, and notes that I send home? I finish packing after three hours, ending up with twelve full boxes. I sit and smoke a cigarette while waiting for the guards to return, and contemplate the stacked boxes filling the eight feet between the cot and the door. *Where are all the books, plays, and film scripts I dreamed of producing?*

As I walk to the property building, on the far side of the compound, the sun is bright, the sky is cloudless, and the air of the Virginia countryside is refreshing. I look away from the fortress-grey concrete buildings of the prison, and out through the twin perimeter fences and the gleaming rolls of razor wire, to note that the leaves of a distant maple have gone to orange. I realize that the season has changed since I was last out of the building.

I am accompanied by three guards. Two push a cart laden with my boxes, grumbling; the third, an older man I know, walks beside me, making small talk.

"Man, things are really changing here," this guard says. Lowering his voice so that the other two cannot hear him, he tells me that he considered transferring to work at another institution, but that the entire system is now going through similar changes.

Back in my cell, I don't have the energy to unpack the four boxes I've returned with. I am glad to have at least salvaged the parts of the manuscripts I've worked on over the years.

I lie upon the bed like a mummy, feet crossed at the ankle and hands folded over my chest, and try to meditate. However, with my tape player gone (along with my television), I have no music to drown out the sounds coming from the cell house. A wave of defeat settles over me.

I think of what I've often told people who ask about my crime—that I got life for a robbery in which no one was hurt. I'll have to rephrase that from now on. If robbery can be said to be theft by force, I can't help but feel like I've just been robbed. And I've most certainly been *hurt.* Maybe that's the whole idea, I think—to injure us, eye for an eye.

Perhaps I should acknowledge that the lockdown—and, indeed, all these years—have damaged me more than I want to believe. But self-pity is anathema to the prisoner, and self-doubt is deadly to the writer.

I get up quickly, pull out a yellow pad and ballpoint from one of the boxes, and stuff spongy plugs in my ears to block out the noise. I know that if I don't go back to work immediately—on *something*—the loss of my typewriter may throw up a block that I'll never overcome.

Just before Christmas, the lockdown officially ends. The four and a half months have taken their toll on everyone. There have been reports of two or three suicides. Some inmates have become unhinged, and can be seen shuffling around, on Thorazine or something.

Things are far from being back to "normal operations." There is now the strictest control of *all* movement; attack dogs are everywhere and officers escort you wherever you go. The gym is closed, and recreation and visitation privileges have been drastically curtailed. At least the educational programs, which were once touted as among the best in the state's prison system, are to resume again in the new year.

On Christmas Eve, the first baked "real chicken on the bone" since summer is served. But the cafeteria-style serving line has been replaced with a wall of concrete blocks. Now the prisoner gets a standard tray served through a small slot at the end of the wall.

As I hasten to finish my food in the allotted fifteen minutes, I look at the men from another building in the serving line. There is a drab sameness to the men, all dressed in the required ill-fitting uniform of denim jeans, blue work shirts, and prison jackets.

I spot a friend of more than fifteen years, whom I haven't seen in months. I can only wave and call out a greeting, for as we are seated separately, "mingling" with men from another building is nearly impossible in the chow hall. "I'm a grandfather now," he shouts to me, beaming. "I've got some pictures to show you, when we get a chance." Then he remembers the strict segregation by building now, and his smile fades. He knows that I may never get a chance to see them.

I notice a large number of new faces among the men in line. Most of them are black. Many are quite young, with a few appearing to be still in their teens.

Such young men are a primary reason for the new lockdown policies, which are calculated largely to contain the "eighty-five-per-centers"—those now entering Virginia's growing prison system, who must serve eighty-five per cent of their sentences, under new, no-parole laws.

Virginia, like most states and the federal government, has passed punitive sentencing laws in recent years. This has led to an unprecedented United States prison/jail population of more than a million six hundred thousand—about three times what it was when I entered prison, sixteen years ago. In the resulting expansion of the nation's prison systems, authorities have tended to dispense with much of the rehabilitative programming once prevalent in America's penal institutions.

When I was sent to the State Penitentiary, in 1981, I was twenty-six—the quintessential angry young black male. However, there was a very different attitude toward rehabilitation at that time, particularly as regards education. I was able to take college courses for a number of years on a Pell grant. Vocational training was available, and literacy (or at least enrollment in school) was encouraged and increased one's chances for making parole.

In the late seventies, there was a growing recognition that rehabilitation programs paid off in lower rates of recidivism. But things began to change a few years later. First, the highly publicized violence of the crack epidemic encouraged mandatory minimum sentencing. The throw-away-the-key fever really took off in 1988, when George Bush's Presidential campaign hit the Willie Horton hot button, and sparked the tough-on-crime political climate that continues to this day. The transformation was nearly complete when President Clinton endorsed the concept of "three strikes you're out" in his 1994 State of the Union address. And when Congress outlawed Pell grants for prisoners later that year the message became clear: We really don't give a damn if you change or not.

Although the men are glad, after more than four months, to be out of their cells, there is little holiday spirit; it's just another day. Several watch whatever banality is on the dayroom TV screen. Most sit at the stainless-steel tables and listlessly play cards to kill time, while others wait for a place at the table. Some wait to use one of two telephones, while others, standing around in bathrobes or towels, wait for a shower stall to become available.

Most of the men in this section of the building are in their forties or fifties, with a few elderly. It strikes me that for most of them prison has become a life of waiting: waiting in line to eat, for a phone call, the mail, or a visit. Or just waiting for tomorrow—for parole and freedom. For the older ones, with no hope of release, I suppose that they wait for the deliverance of death.

As I record the day in my notebook, I find myself thinking about my aunt's grandnephew—her adopted son. He was rumored to have been dealing drugs, and he was shot dead in the doorway of her home on Thanksgiving Day, just over a month ago; my father, who is seventy-five, was called to comfort her. With violence affecting so many lives, one can understand the desire—driven by fear—to lock away young male offenders. But considering their impoverished, danger-filled lives, I wonder whether the threat of being locked up for decades can really deter them from crime.

I understand the philosophy behind the increased use of long sentences and harsh incarceration. The idea is to make prison a secular hell on earth—a place where the young potential felon will fear to go, where the ex-con will fear to return. But an underlying theme is that "these people" are irredeemable "predators" (i.e., "animals"), who are without worth. Why, then, provide them with the opportunity to rehabilitate—or give them any hope?

Still, what really bothers me is knowing that many thousands of the young men entering prison now may *never* get that "last chance to change," which I was able to put to good use—in an era that, I'm afraid, is now in the past. And more disturbing, to my mind, are the long "no hope" sentences given to so many young men now—they can be given even to people as young as thirteen and fourteen. Although I personally remain eligible for parole—and in all likelihood will be released eventually—I can't help thinking of all the young lives that are now being thrown away. I know that if I had been born in another time I might very well have suffered the same fate.

BRENT STAPLES (b. 1951)

Just Walk on By: A Black Man Ponders His Power to Alter Public Space

CONSIDER THIS:

Brent Staples was born in Chester, Pennsylvania, has taught psychology at various colleges, and has been a reporter for the *Chicago Sun-Times* and the *New York*

Times, where he is currently on the editorial board. He also contributes to magazines, including *Ms., New York Woman,* and *Harper's. Parallel Time* won the Anisfield-Wolff Book Award in 1995.

Staples's vision of his racial identity and its impact on his work is very clear. He writes in *Slate* magazine, "As the great-grandson of a black man born in the waning days of slavery, I am very much conscious of this connection and of what my ancestors endured to propel me to a Ph.D. from the University of Chicago—and a job as an essayist for the most powerful newspaper in the world. I feel that connection strongly. I work to honor it—and I write directly out of it." Staples here underlines one of his frequent editorial topics: the importance of education.

What were your assumptions as you read the opening paragraph of Brent Staples's essay "Just Walk on By"? How does his essay play, intentionally and strategically, on your cultural expectations? What do you feel as you move to the essay's second paragraph? If you are familiar with the issue of racial profiling, how would you connect accusations that police more regularly stop black motorists with Staples's vision of himself as able to "alter public space in ugly ways"? Compare the ways Evans Hopkins and Brent Staples each investigate issues of race, power, and authority in their essays. What does each author suggest—using what organizing techniques—about appearance and reality?

My first victim was a woman—white, well dressed, probably in her early twenties. I came upon her late one evening on a deserted street in Hyde Park, a relatively affluent neighborhood in an otherwise mean, impoverished section of Chicago. As I swung onto the avenue behind her, there seemed to be a discreet, uninflammatory distance between us. Not so. She cast back a worried glance. To her, the youngish black man—a broad six feet two inches with a beard and billowing hair, both hands shoved into the pockets of a bulky military jacket—seemed menacingly close. After a few more quick glimpses, she picked up her pace and was soon running in earnest. Within seconds she disappeared into a cross street.

That was more than a decade ago. I was 22 years old, a graduate student newly arrived at the University of Chicago. It was in the echo of that terrified woman's footfalls that I first began to know the unwieldy inheritance I'd come into—the ability to alter public space in ugly ways. It was clear that she thought herself the quarry of a mugger, rapist, or worse. Suffering a bout of insomnia, however, I was stalking sleep, not defenseless wayfarers. As a softy who is scarcely able to take a knife to a raw chicken—let alone hold it to a person's throat—I was surprised, embarrassed, and dismayed all at once. Her flight made me feel like an accomplice in tyranny. It also made it clear that I was indistinguishable from the muggers who occasionally seeped into the area from the surrounding ghetto. That first encounter, and those that followed, signified that a vast, unnerving gulf lay between nighttime pedestrians—particularly women—and me. And I soon gathered that being perceived as dangerous is a hazard in itself. I only needed to turn a corner into a dicey situation or crowd some frightened, armed person in a foyer somewhere, or make an errant move after being pulled over by a policeman. Where fear and weapons meet—and they often do in urban America—there is always the possibility of death.

In that first year, my first away from my hometown, I was to become thoroughly familiar with the language of fear. At dark, shadowy intersections in Chicago, I could cross in front of a car stopped at a traffic light and elicit the *thunk, thunk, thunk, thunk* of the driver—black, white, male or female—hammering down the door locks. On less traveled streets after dark, I grew accustomed to but never comfortable with people who crossed to the other side of the street rather than pass me. Then there were the standard unpleasantries with police, doormen, bouncers, cab drivers, and others whose business it is to screen out troublesome individuals *before* there is any nastiness.

I moved to New York nearly two years ago and I have remained an avid night walker. In central Manhattan, the near-constant crowd cover minimizes tense one-on-one encounters. Elsewhere—visiting friends in SoHo, where sidewalks are narrow and tightly spaced buildings shut out the sky—things can get very taut indeed.

Black men have a firm place in New York mugging literature. Norman Podhoretz in his famed (or infamous) 1963 essay, "My Negro Problem—and Ours," recalls growing up in terror of black males; they "were tougher than we were, more ruthless," he writes—and as an adult on the Upper West Side of Manhattan, he continues, he cannot constrain his nervousness when he meets black men on certain streets. Similarly, a decade later, the essayist and novelist Edward Hoagland extols a New York where once "Negro bitterness bore down mainly on other Negroes." Where some see mere panhandlers, Hoagland sees "a mugger who is clearly screwing up his nerve to do more than just *ask* for money." But Hoagland has "the New Yorker's quick-hunch posture for broken-field maneuvering," and the bad guy swerves away.

I often witness that "hunch posture," from women after dark on the warren-like streets of Brooklyn where I live. They seem to set their faces on neutral and, with their purse straps strung across their chests bandolier style, they forge ahead as though bracing themselves against being tackled. I understand, of course, that the danger they perceive is not a hallucination. Women are particularly vulnerable to street violence, and young black males are drastically overrepresented among the perpetrators of that violence. Yet these truths are no solace against the kind of alienation that comes of being ever the suspect, against being set apart, a fearsome entity with whom pedestrians avoid making eye contact.

It is not altogether clear to me how I reached the ripe old age of 22 without being conscious of the lethality nighttime pedestrians attributed to me. Perhaps it was because in Chester, Pennsylvania, the small, angry industrial town where I came of age in the 1960s, I was scarcely noticeable against a backdrop of gang warfare, street knifings, and murders. I grew up one of the good boys, had perhaps a half-dozen fist fights. In retrospect, my shyness of combat has clear sources.

Many things go into the making of a young thug. One of those things is the consummation of the male romance with the power to intimidate. An infant discovers that random flailings send the baby bottle flying out of the crib and crashing to the floor. Delighted, the joyful babe repeats those motions again and again, seeking to duplicate the feat. Just so, I recall the points at which some of my boyhood friends were finally seduced by the perception of themselves as tough guys. When a mark cowered and surrendered his money without resistance, myth and reality merged—and paid off. It is, after all, only manly to embrace the power to frighten and intimidate. We, as men, are not supposed to give an inch of our lane on the highway; we are to seize the fighter's edge in work and in play and even in love; we are to be valiant in the face of hostile forces.

Unfortunately, poor and powerless young men seem to take all this nonsense literally. As a boy, I saw countless tough guys locked away; I have since buried several, too. They were babies, really—a teenage cousin, a brother of 22, a childhood friend in his mid-twenties—all gone down in episodes of bravado played out in the streets. I came to doubt the virtues of intimidation early on. I chose, perhaps even unconsciously, to remain a shadow—timid, but a survivor.

The fearsomeness mistakenly attributed to me in public places often has a perilous flavor. The most frightening of these confusions occurred in the late 1970s and early 1980s when I worked as a journalist in Chicago. One day, rushing into the office of a magazine I was writing for with a deadline story in hand, I was mistaken for a burglar. The office manager called security and, with an ad hoc posse, pursued me through the labyrinthine halls, nearly to my editor's door. I had no way of proving who I was. I could only move briskly toward the company of someone who knew me.

Another time I was on assignment for a local paper and killing time before an interview. I entered a jewelry store on the city's affluent Near North Side. The proprietor excused herself and returned with an enormous red Doberman pinscher straining at the end of a leash. She stood, the dog extended toward me, silent to my questions, her eyes bulging nearly out of her head. I took a cursory look around, nodded, and bade her good night. Relatively speaking, however, I never fared as badly as another black male journalist. He went to nearby Waukegan, Illinois, a couple of summers ago to work on a story about a murderer who was born there. Mistaking the reporter for the killer, police hauled him from his car at gunpoint and but for his press credentials would probably have tried to book him. Such episodes are not uncommon. Black men trade tales like this all the time.

In "My Negro Problem—and Ours," Podhoretz writes that the hatred he feels for blacks makes itself known to him through a variety of avenues—one being his discomfort with that "special brand of paranoid touchiness" to which he says blacks are prone. No doubt he is speaking here of black men. In time, I learned to smother the rage I felt at so often being taken for a criminal. Not to do so would surely have led to madness—via that special "paranoid touchiness" that so annoyed Podhoretz at the time he wrote the essay.

I began to take precautions to make myself less threatening. I move about with care, particularly late in the evening. I give a wide berth to nervous people on subway platforms during the wee hours, particularly when I have exchanged business clothes for jeans. If I happen to be entering a building behind some people who appear skittish, I may walk by, letting them clear the lobby before I return, so as not to seem to be following them. I have been calm and extremely congenial on those rare occasions when I've been pulled over by the police.

And on late-evening constitutionals along streets less traveled by, I employ what has proved to be an excellent tension-reducing measure: I whistle melodies from Beethoven and Vivaldi and the more popular classical composers. Even steely New Yorkers hunching toward nighttime destinations seem to relax, and occasionally they even join in the tune. Virtually everybody seems to sense that a mugger wouldn't be warbling bright, sunny selections from Vivaldi's *Four Seasons*. It is my equivalent of the cowbell that hikers wear when they know they are in bear country.

DONNA STEINER

Sleeping with Alcohol

CONSIDER THIS:

Before reading Donna Steiner's essay, consider your own relationship to difficult personal topics. What use do you find in someone writing about addictive and dangerous behavior? How does a writer achieve distance on such a subject, whether discussing the topic as a social issue or as one related to the author or the author's friend, partner, or family member? Do you believe distance or closeness is required? If you think these topics are the writer's subject, what techniques can bring the subject into focus, can allow for useful and moving discussion? When does examination turn into indulgence or "mere" disclosure? What strategies would you suggest to someone intent on sharing such issues? Why are writers and readers drawn to these topics?

Donna Steiner won the *Bellingham Review's* Annie Dillard Nonfiction Award for this essay, "Love Drunk." She is a writing instructor in Tucson, Arizona, and also writes poetry, which has appeared in *The Sun* magazine and *Two Rivers Review*. My initial questions may have set you up to expect certain problems or strategies for this essay. How were those expectations confirmed or confounded?

Start small. The bottle cap. Silver on the underside, green and black on the top. It's fluted around the edge, like a pie crust, and dented in the middle, like a felt hat. The green is the green of grass; beer companies like to associate their products with nature. When I poke the cap with my finger it skitters across the desktop, making a sound that isn't unpleasant. It's a sound I'm accustomed to, for she will often toss the caps onto the kitchen floor—they make great cat toys. We know an artist who creates beautiful, expensive murals using nothing but bottle tops and flip tabs. The murals look like aquariums, all gleam and fluidity, like daydreams of cold liquid.

I study one amber-hued beer bottle. It's slender, nine inches high, and seductive in the way that bottles often are. This one looks to me like a human torso, and my instinct is to hold it, covet it. I don't drink, but I want to experience what the serious drinker experiences. With no one to witness my foolishness, I surrender to the process. Lifting the bottle to my mouth is a small turn-on. My lips fit perfectly around the opening. I feel a charge, a subtle electricity. My throat feels as though it's vibrating: a little air, a little liquid, a little moisture left on the lips. One kisses a bottle mouth—she taught me that.

She refers to herself as a drunk.

When I think about her, I don't think: drunk. I think: runner. I think: artist. I see her dancing around our apartment, mouthing the words to Motown songs but miming disco moves. I consider how her voice deepens when she wants to talk about something serious, how she has no tolerance for indirect conversation or ambiguous language. I remember how my hands trembled when I met her. She wakes up in the morning in the middle of a conversation, asking, "What's the difference between a barnacle and crustacean?" She has a long list of wacky endearments for me, including "my fresh coat of paint" and "my little prize-winning chicken," and she's in the very small group of people who think I'm fun—even when she's sober.

Okay. (Say it!) Sometimes I think: drunk.

I tell her I'm thinking of writing this essay and ask if she'd be okay about it. She says sure. I'd like to conduct an interview, and one night we sit down for about 30 minutes, side by side. I have a notebook and a pen, she has a bottle. She's drunk from start to finish, drinking as we talk; therefore, more drunk toward the end than at the beginning. When we're through she says, "Let's do it again, same questions, when I'm sober." I agree, but I'm not sure my writing schedule and her drinking schedule will allow for that possibility.

I hadn't planned the questions in advance, so again, I start small.

How much does a six-pack of beer cost?

Cheap beer is $2.49 plus tax, which comes to $2.61. Better beer, on sale, is $4.99 plus tax. Really good beer is around $6.00 but I never buy that. Too expensive.

How many beers does it take to get drunk?

Whoa. Tough question. (pause) What do you mean, "drunk"? (pause) It depends on the brew. Microbrews are much stronger than regular brews, and to a real drinker, light beers are like drinking soda. They're like drinking nothing.

Has anyone ever asked you to quit?

Yeah.

Did you quit?

Not at the time she asked. Probably about two years later.

How long did you quit for?

Seven or eight years.

What's the worst thing that ever happened to you while you were drunk?

(She laughs) Well, I got raped, I broke my foot . . . (counting on her fingers) I don't know. I got kicked out of college, I had a car accident, I lost my driver's license. (long pause) That's all.

What would be the best incentive for quitting?

Love. (no hesitation)

Although I am totally into my role as the detached interviewer, my eyes fill with tears.

(After a long pause) But that's never enough.

How come?

(Another long pause) I think because drinking sometimes makes you feel . . . like you're somehow filling your time in a productive way, you know, without it you feel a little at sea, like you wouldn't know what to do with your time.

Do you think you'll ever quit drinking?

No. (silence) I'm sorry I'm so hard to live with.

You're very easy to live with, for the most part.

Yeah, but for that last part I'm a real pain in the ass.

Even in the middle of winter, on the East Coast, she'll bundle up and sit outside, snow falling, late into the night as the temperature drops below zero. I fear she'll fall asleep, that I'll find her in the morning, dead of exposure. The partner of the alcoholic fears many things; some fears are realized and some aren't.

A friend's father fell on New Year's Eve. At the top of the staircase he was drunk. At the bottom he was dead. Five minutes before midnight, five minutes after. Ten stairs.

We have stairs. Our home has hard edges and sharp corners, surfaces that could break a bone or blind an eye. She stumbled into bed the other night. The lights were on. I watched her try to remove her clothes—once, twice, she lost her balance. A painting she'd completed was propped against the wall. I heard the canvas ping each time her ankle struck it. Finally she sat down, wrestling off her pants. You make a choice to live with the fear, or you leave.

I have no intention of leaving. I walk around our apartment, continuing as reporter, looking for evidence. Not evidence of alcohol—that would be easy. If I moved this chair I'd find seven or eight cat-batted bottle caps. There's probably a stray bottle or two under her drawing table. So what? I want evidence of something else, proof of why I stay. Her jacket's tossed on a chair and one of the cats is curled up on it. I lean in and smell the jacket, and the cat's warm fur. The phone number of our favorite pizza place is stuck on the refrigerator, along with the first card she gave me: a picture of a map. Written inside: *Let's go everywhere.*

I like broken things, torn things, tired things. I like old sheets and worn towels. My favorite sheets aren't yet worn enough to be considered perfect, but I know they will become worn—the anticipation is slightly thrilling in itself. They were too stiff when I purchased them, but I've washed them so often that now, four years later, they've become less dangerous, more familiar.

The one who sleeps beside me has become less dangerous and more familiar, too. I didn't know, when I met her, that alcohol was an ongoing chapter in her history. If I'd known from the start, I would not have proceeded differently. I approached the problem from a position of naive compassion, but I've grown self-protective. At times I see her as self-involved, self-indulgent, and see myself as misguided and desperate. That's what alcohol does. It tempers hope, alters perception. It lets the heart roam a little less widely, as though possibilities have become fewer, the world itself somehow less. It forces you to assess, a day at a time, risks versus benefits. The effort wears you out in ways that cannot be judged attractive.

What is the cost, the toll alcohol will take? I can feel our couplehood eroding as though we are standing on a bank that's becoming saturated, our footing steadily growing less stable. I wonder if we're past the point or not yet at the point when I can look into her eyes and say, "Stop; this is killing you." Is the bottle half empty or half full? The question is dramatically beside the point. Always, eventually, it ends up empty.

Three a.m. Moonlight seeps in around the window shades. She's just coming to bed, but she overshoots her mark and ends up near the closet, in a corner. She can't see; it's dark and she's already removed her glasses. But, of course, that's only part of the problem. She's unable to crack the maze of the dark room. Her brain can't hear me silently rooting for her. *Just turn around; a simple 90-degree turn will do it.* It's like watching one of those battery-powered kids' trucks that can't back up so it just spins its wheels. I hear her bumping gently against a wall-mounted mirror. All she has to do is turn, but the smooth glass and her faintly perceived reflection confound her; she's like a bird persisting against a window. Her white T-shirt catches the little light of the night. Beautiful.

Beautiful, and drunk. I get out of bed, and I take her hand.

HAUNANI-KAY TRASK (b. 1949)

Tourist, Stay Home

CONSIDER THIS:

Born in San Francisco to parents of Hawai'ian descent, Haunani-Kay Trask has been a professor of Hawaiian studies at the University of Hawai'i-Manoa since 1986 and is the director of the Center for Hawai'ian Studies there. She founded, along with her sister, Ka Lahui Hawai'i, a movement dedicated to Hawai'ian self-determination. Much of Trask's writing focuses upon the troubles tourism has brought her Hawai'i. Writing in *USA Today,* Trask notes, "While more than 6 million tourists annually vacation in their aboriginal homeland, native Hawaiians fill up the unemployment lines, the prisons and the welfare and homeless lists. They suffer the lowest educational attainment and family income of all ethnic groups in Hawaii." In a *Progressive* magazine interview, she explains, "Our language was banned in 1898. I grew up speaking and reading English, but I never had an opportunity to speak and read my own language. The Hawai'ian language was unbanned for tourist purposes in 1978. So we, the Hawai'ian people, are very close to other native peoples who are trying to recover and teach their native languages." Clearly, Trask's positions are strongly argued. Explore the methods she used in this essay: What techniques does she use to assert her argumentative authority? Which strategies convince you? Which would you challenge? To what other cultures and colonizing moments do you relate her work?

Most Americans have come to believe that Hawai'i is as American as hotdogs and CNN. Worse, they assume that they, too, may make the trip, following the path of the empire into the sweet and sunny land of palm trees and hula-hula girls.

Increasing numbers of us not only oppose this predatory view of my native land and culture, we angrily and resolutely defy it. On January 17, 1993, thousands of Hawai'ians demonstrated against continued American control of our homeland. Marking the 100th anniversary of the overthrow of our native government by U.S. Marines and missionary-descended sugar barons, Hawaiian nationalists demanded recognition of our status as native people with claims to a land base and political self-determination.

For us, native self-government has always been preferable to American foreign government. No matter what Americans believe, most of us in the colonies do not feel grateful that our country was stolen along with our citizenship, our lands, and our independent place among the family of nations. We are not happy natives.

For us, American colonialism has been a violent process—the violence of mass death, the violence of American missionizing, the violence of cultural destruction, the violence of the American military. Through the overthrow and annexation, American control and American citizenship replaced Hawaiian control and Hawaiian citizenship. Our mother—our heritage and our inheritance—was taken from us. We were orphaned in our own land. Such brutal changes in a people's identity, its legal status, its government, its sense of belonging to a nation, are considered among the most serious human-rights violations by the international community today.

As we approach the Twenty-first Century, the effects of colonization are obvious: outmigration of the poor amounting to a diaspora, institutionalization in the military and prisons, continued land dispossession by the state and Federal governments and multinational corporations, and grotesque commodification of our culture through corporate tourism.

This latest affliction has meant a particularly insidious form of cultural prostitution. Just five hours by plane from California, Hawai'i is a thousand light years away in fantasy. Mostly a state of mind, Hawai'i is the image of escape from the rawness and violence of daily American life. *Hawai'i*—the chord, the image, the sound in the mind—is the fragrance and feel of soft fondness. Above all, Hawai'i is "she," the Western image of the native "female" in her magical allure. And if luck prevails, some of "her" will rub off on you, the visitor.

The predatory reality of tourism is visible everywhere: in garish "Polynesian" revues; commercial ads using Hawaiian dance and language to sell vacations and condominiums; the trampling of sacred *heiau* (temples) and burial grounds as tourist recreation sites. Thus, our world-renowned native dance, the *hula,* has been made ornamental, a form of hotel exotica for the gaping tourist. And Hawaiian women are marketed on posters from Paris to Tokyo promising an unfettered "primitive" sexuality. Far from encouraging cultural revival, as tourist industry apologists contend, tourism has appropriated and prostituted the accomplishments of a resurgent interest in things Hawaiian (the use of replicas of Hawaiian artifacts such as fishing and food complements, capes, helmets, and other symbols of ancient power, to decorate hotels).

As the pimp for the cultural prostitution business, the state of Hawai'i pours millions into the tourist industry, even to the extent of funding a private booster club—the Hawai'i Visitors' Bureau—to the tune of $30 million a year. Radio and television propaganda tells locals "the more you give" to tourism, "the more you get."

What Hawaiians get is population densities as high as Hong Kong in some areas, a housing shortage owing to staggering numbers of migrants from Asia and the continental United States, a soaring crime rate as impoverished locals prey on ostentatiously rich tourists, and environmental crises, including water depletion, that threaten the entire archipelago. Rather than stop the flood, the state is projecting a tidal wave of twelve million tourists by the year 2010. Today, we Hawaiians exist in an occupied country. We are a hostage people, forced to witness and participate in our own collective humiliation as tourist artifacts for the First World.

Meanwhile, shiploads and planeloads of American military forces continue to pass through Hawai'i on their way to imperialist wars in Asia and elsewhere. Every major Hawaiian island has lost thousands of acres to military bases, private beaches, and housing areas. On the most populous island of O'ahu, for example, fully 30 per cent of the land is in military hands.

Unlike other native peoples in the United States, we have no separate legal status to control our land base. We are, by every measure, a colonized people. As a native nation, Hawaiians are no longer self-governing.

Because of these deplorable conditions, and despite the fact that we are less than 20 per cent of the million-and-a-quarter residents of Hawai'i, native Hawaiians have begun to assert our status as a people. Like the Palestinians, the Northern Irish, and the Indians of the Americas, we have started on a path of decolonization.

Beginning with the land struggles in the 1970s, and continuing with occupations, mass protests, and legislative and legal maneuvering in the 1980s and 1990s, Hawaiian resistance has matured into a full-blown nationalist struggle.

The contours of this struggle are both simple and complex. We want to control our own land base, government, and economy. We want to establish a nation-to-nation relationship with the U.S. Government, and with other native nations. We want control over water and other resources on our land base, and we want our human and civil rights acknowledged and protected.

In 1921, Congress set aside 200,000 acres of homesteading lands specifically for Hawaiians. We are fighting for control of these lands, as well as approximately 1.2 million acres of the Kingdom of Hawai'i illegally transferred by the white oligarchy to the United States in 1898. Called the "trust" lands because the Federal and state governments allegedly hold them in "trust" for the Hawaiian people, this land base is currently used for all manner of illegal activities, including airports, military reservations, public schools, parks, and county refuse sites, even private businesses and homes. Because of this long record of abuse, and because nationhood means self-determination and not wardship, Hawaiians are organized and lobbying for return of the "trust" lands to the Hawaiian people.

To this end, we have re-created our own political entity, *Ka Lāhui Hawai'i,* a native initiative for self-government. At our first Constitutional Convention in 1987, we devised a democratic form of government, with a Kai'āina or governor, a legislature and judges, elders, and chief advisory councils. We have made treaties with other native nations, and we have diplomatic representatives in many places. We want recognition as a sovereign people.

Sovereignty, as clearly defined by our citizens in 1987, is "the ability of a people who share a common culture, religion, language, value system, and land base to exercise control over their lands and lives, independent of other nations." We lay claim to the trust lands as the basis of our nation.

While we organized in Hawaiian communities, the state of Hawai'i created an Office of Hawaiian Affairs, or OHA, in 1980. Ostensibly for representation of Hawaiian rights by Hawaiians (the only group allowed to vote for its all-native trustees), OHA was powerless as a mechanism for self-government. It had no control over trust lands, and no statutory strength to prevent abuses of native culture. For the next ten years, OHA supported reparations for the overthrow and forcible annexation to the United States, rather than recognition and restoration of our nationhood.

Because OHA is a state agency beholden to the reigning Democratic Party, it has made no claims for a land base against the state. Arguing that they represented Hawaiians rather than the state, OHA trustees made an agreement with the governor—an unprincipled Hawaiian named John Waihe'e—to settle all ceded lands claims. OHA was to receive over $100 million in 1991, then $8.5 million annually. No lands were to be transferred. They would instead be lost to Hawaiians forever.

As a result of humiliating public criticism from the Hawaiian community for OHA's sell-out role in this deal, OHA proposed a kind of quasi-sovereign condition which it would oversee. In direct opposition to the Ka Lāhui model of a "nation-to-nation" relationship with the Federal Government, OHA argued that the governing structure of the Hawaiian nation, landless though it might be, should come under the state of Hawai'i.

There were several problems with this position. OHA was not representative of all Hawaiian communities and never had been, because voting procedures gave too much weight to the most populous island of O'ahu, resulting in a skewed underrepresentation of neighbor island people. Any lands or monies transferred by the Federal Government to OHA would go to the state, not to the Hawaiian people, since OHA was a state agency; this would mean *less*, not more, control by Hawaiians over their future. Giving OHA nation status would be akin to calling the Bureau of Indian Affairs an Indian nation. And finally, state control of Hawaiians, even under an alleged "Office of Hawaiian Affairs," is still wardship, not self-determination.

While the tide of native resistance swelled, a coordinated state strategy emerged. First, Governor Waihe'e came out in favor of a landless model of a "nation-within-a-nation." Speaking as if he invented the concept and never once mentioning Ka Lāhui's leadership, Waihe'e publicly advocated Federal recognition of Hawaiians as a native nation. In his "state of the state" address immediately following the January 17 commemoration, Waihe'e called for Hawaiian sovereignty to be devised by an OHA-led constitutional convention and funded by the state legislature. OHA supported the governor's efforts.

After nearly two decades of organizing, forces for and against sovereignty were clearly drawn: the state of Hawai'i and its Bureau of Indian Affairs clone, the Office of Hawaiian Affairs, supported continued wardship of our people under the tutelage of OHA; Ka Lāhui Hawai'i, a native initiative for self-government, supported self-determination on a definable land base with Federal recognition of our nationhood.

While OHA and the governor submitted legislation mandating the constitutional convention, Ka Lāhui's membership soared to 16,000 enrolled citizens. As the largest sovereignty organization, Ka Lāhui now poses a substantial threat to the legitimacy of OHA. Sensing this danger, and hoping to head off our own efforts in Washington, D.C., Waihe'e traveled to the American capital to float the notion of an OHA-type nation with President Clinton and his Secretary of the Interior. As we pass the midpoint of this centennial year, the state strategy appears to be Federal recognition, but no real "nation-within-a-nation" on the order of the American Indian nations. A land base is out of the question.

For Hawaiians, the stakes are high indeed: self-determination, or the yoke of perpetual wardship. In the meantime, marginalization and exploitation of Hawaiians, our culture, and our lands, continues, while corporate tourism thrives on nearly seven million visitors a year (thirty tourists for every native). In the face of Hawaiian resistance, it's still business as usual.

If OHA is successful, the Hawaiian people will be burdened with yet another agency, non-Hawaiian in design and function, set in place to prevent rather than fulfill native autonomy. Historically, the decline of Hawaiians and our culture is directly traceable to land dispossession. Therefore, any attempt to address Hawaiian sovereignty which does not return control of lands to Hawaiians is doomed to fail.

Like agencies created by the Federal government to short-circuit Indian sovereignty, OHA will be a top-down institution whose architects envision an extension of the state of Hawai'i rather than a native initiative to promote self-government.

Elsewhere in the Pacific, native peoples struggle with the same dilemma.

The Maori, like the Hawaiians a minority in their own land, have been dispossessed through conquest and occupation by a foreign white people, and have suffered psychologically from cultural suppression. They, too, have been demanding a form of sovereignty, seeking identity and cultural integrity by returning to their lands. And they have supported Hawaiian resistance, as fellow Polynesians and as fellow colonized people.

In Tahiti, a strong independence movement has captured the mayorship of the second-largest city while uniting antinuclear, labor, and native nationalist forces to resist French colonialism. With others in the Pacific, Tahitians have spearheaded the nuclear-free and independent Pacific movements.

Aborigines, Kanaks, East Timorese, and Belauans focus world attention on genocide and military imperialism. And for each of these indigenous peoples, there is the familiar, predictable struggle for self-determination.

If Hawaiians are not alone in the Pacific Basin, our struggle for self-determination is certainly unknown across most of the North American continent, particularly to the hordes of tourists who inundate our beautiful but fragile islands. In this United Nations "Year of Indigenous People," a willful ignorance about native nationhood prevails in the dominant society. Given this, and given the collaborationist politics within colony Hawai'i, whatever successes my people do achieve will be won slowly and at great expense.

For those who might feel a twinge of solidarity with our cause, let me leave this final thought: Don't come to Hawai'i. We don't need any more tourists. If you want to help, pass this message on to your friends.

SHERMAN ALEXIE (b. 1966)

White Men Can't Drum

CONSIDER THIS:

Sherman Alexie was born on the Spokane Indian Reservation in Washington and earned a B.A. from Washington State University in 1991. He writes fiction and poetry and won the National Book Award in 1996 for his novel *Reservation Blues*. Most of his writing revolves around his identity as a Native American, a member of the Spokane and Coeur d'Alene tribes. For Alexie, identity is central. "Native

American writing is about survival," he said in an interview with Slipstream Press. "We recently went over 1 million in population, estimated as 75–90 percent less than the population when whites first arrived in America. With that kind of genocidal philosophy prevalent, it is our strongest tradition, our longest dance, to remain alive, to survive."

Naturally enough, iconic Native American elements such as dreams and storytelling figure prominently in Alexie's work. In an interview with *Cineaste* about writing *Smoke Signals* and *The Lone Ranger and Tonto,* he said, "My first form of writing was poetry. While there's certainly a strong narrative drive in my poetry, it was always about the image, and about the connection, often, of very disparate, contradictory images." Alexie continues, "I've always been fascinated with dreams and stories and flashing forward and flashing back and playing with conventions of time. . . . It's all based on the basic theme, for me, that storytellers are essentially liars." To what degree do you find Alexie's background as a writer of fiction and poetry coming to the foreground in this persuasive, investigative, personal essay? Consider how the strategies he uses to consider colonialism differ from those used by Haunani-Kay Trask.

Last year on the local television news, I watched a short feature on a meeting of the Confused White Men chapter in Spokane, Washington. They were all wearing war bonnets and beating drums, more or less. A few of the drums looked as if they might have come from K mart, and one or two men just beat their chests.

"It's not just the drum" said the leader of the group. "It's the idea of a drum."

I was amazed at the lack of rhythm and laughed, even though I knew I supported a stereotype. But it's true: White men can't drum. They fail to understand that a drum is more than a heartbeat. Sometimes it is the sound of thunder, and many times it just means some Indians want to dance.

As a Native American, I find it ironic that even the most ordinary moments of our lives take on ceremonial importance when adopted by the men's movement. Since Native American men have become role models for the men's movement, I find it vital to explain more fully some of our traditions to avoid any further misinterpretation by white men.

Peyote is not just an excuse to get high.

A Vision Quest cannot be completed in a convention room rented for that purpose.

Native Americans can be lousy fathers and sons, too.

A warrior does not necessarily have to scream to release the animal that is supposed to reside inside every man. A warrior does not necessarily have an animal inside him at all. If there happens to be an animal, it can be a parakeet or a mouse just as easily as it can be a bear or a wolf.

When a white man adopts an animal, he often chooses the largest animal possible. Whether this is because of possible phalic connotations or a kind of spiritual steroid abuse is debatable. I imagine a friend of mine, John, who is white, telling me that his spirit animal is a Tyrannosaurus rex. "But John," I would reply gently, "those things are all dead."

As a "successful" Native American writer, I have been asked to lecture at various men's gatherings. The pay would have been good—just a little more reparation I figured—but I turned down the offers because I couldn't have kept a straight face. The various topics I have been asked to address include "Native Spirituality and Animal Sexuality," "Finding the Inner Child," and "Finding the Lost Father." I figure the next step would be a meeting on "Finding the Inner Hunter When Shopping at the Local Supermarket."

Much of the men's movement focuses on finding things that are lost. I fail to understand how Native American traditions can help in that search, especially considering how much we have lost ourselves. The average life expectancy of a Native American male is about 50 years—middle age for a white man—and that highlights one of the most disturbing aspects of the entire men's movement. It blindly pursues Native solutions to European problems but completely neglects to provide European solutions to Native problems. Despite the fact that the drum still holds spiritual significance, there is not one Indian man alive who has figured out how to cook or eat a drum.

As Adrian C. Louis, the Paiute poet, writes, "We all have to go back with pain in our fat hearts to the place we grew up to grow out of." In their efforts to find their inner child, lost father, or car keys, white males need to go way back. In fact, they need to travel back to the moment when Christopher Columbus landed in America, fell to his knees on the sand and said, "But my mother never loved me."

That is where the real discovery begins.

Still, I have to love the idea of so many white men searching for answers from the same Native traditions that were considered heathen and savage for so long. Perhaps they are popular among white men precisely because they are heathen and savage. After all, these are the same men who look as if they mean to kill each other over Little League baseball games.

I imagine the possibilities for some good Indian humor and sadness mixed all together.

I imagine that Lester FallsApart, a full-blood Spokane, made a small fortune when he gathered glass fragments from shattered reservation car-wreck windshields and sold them to the new-age store as healing crystals.

I imagine that six white men traveled to a powwow and proceeded to set up shop and drum for the Indian dancers, who were stunned and surprised by how much those white men sounded like clumsy opera singers.

I imagine that white men turn to an old Indian man for answers. I imagine Dustin Hoffman. I imagine Kevin Costner. I imagine Daniel Day Lewis. I imagine Robert Bly.

Oh, these men who do all of the acting and none of the reacting.

My friend John and I were sitting in the sweatlodge. No. We were actually sitting in the sauna of the Y.M.C.A. when he turned to me. "Sherman," he said, "considering the chemicals, the stuff we eat, the stuff that hangs in the air, I think the sweatlodge has come to be a purifying ceremony, you know? White men need that, to use an Indian thing to get rid of all the pollution in our bodies. Sort of a spiritual enema."

"That's a lot of bull," I replied savagely.

"What do you mean?"

"I mean that the sweatlodge is a church, not a free clinic."

The men's movement seems designed to appropriate and mutate so many aspects of Native traditions. I worry about the possibilities: men's movement chain stores specializing in portable sweatlodges; the "Indians 'R' Us" commodification of ritual and artifact; white men who continue to show up at powwows in full regalia and dance.

Don't get me wrong. Everyone at a powwow can dance. They all get their chance. Indians have round dances, corn dances, owl dances, intertribal dances, interracial dances, female dances, and yes, even male dances. We all have our places within those dances.

I mean, honestly, no one wants to waltz to a jitterbug song, right?

Perhaps these white men should learn to dance within their own circle before they so rudely jump into other circles. Perhaps white men need to learn more about patience before they can learn what it means to be a man, Indian, or otherwise.

Believe me, Arthur Murray was not a Native American.

Last week my friend John called me up on the telephone. Late at night. "Sherman," he said, "I'm afraid. I don't know what it means to be a man. Tell me your secrets. Tell me how to be a warrior."

"Well, John," I said, "a warrior did much more than fight, you know? Warriors fed their families and washed the dishes. Warriors went on Vision Quests and listened to their wives when they went on Vision Quests, too. Warriors picked up their dirty clothes and tried not to watch football games all weekend."

"Really?"

"Really," I said. "Now go back to sleep."

I hung up the phone and turned on the television because I knew it would be a long time before sleep came back to me. I flipped through channels rapidly. There was "F Troop" on one channel, "Dances With Wolves" on another, and they were selling authentic New Mexico Indian jewelry on the shopping channel.

What does it mean to be a man? What does it mean to be Indian? What does it mean to be an Indian man? I press the mute button on the remote control so that everyone can hear the answer.

DIANE ACKERMAN (b. 1948)

Mute Dancers: How to Watch a Hummingbird

CONSIDER THIS:

Diane Ackerman was born in Waukegan, Illinois. She's been a social worker and a government researcher and has taught at Cornell, the University of Pittsburgh, and Washington University. Ackerman is best known for her nature writing. In an interview with Amazon.com, she explained, "I studied biopsychology and philosophy at Boston University, then switched to Penn State, where a computer error made me an English major. After taking a few literature and writing classes, I went to graduate school to get a fine-arts degree in poetry and started working very seriously as a writer. I've been able to keep my childhood interest in nature alive."

Within this context, Ackerman holds out poetry as her source of inspiration. She discussed the differences between poetry and prose in a *January* magazine interview: "If I had my druthers—which is an interesting word—every prose book I wrote would be like inhaling jungle. It would all be at a level of poetic intensity that I would find satisfying word by word. Sentence by sentence. Page by page. But, unfortunately, I've discovered that books have to have transitions. The sun can't always be at noon and there are times when you actually have to explain yourself. Or you have to move people around in the landscape and stuff like that. But I have a poet's heart and a poet's sensibility." As you read "Mute Dancers," consider the degree to which Ackerman achieved these aims and analyze the strategies she uses to create an intensely poetic prose style.

A lot of hummingbirds die in their sleep. Like a small fury of iridescence, a hummingbird spends the day at high speed, darting and swiveling among thousands of nectar-rich blossoms. Hummingbirds have huge hearts and need colossal amounts of energy to fuel their flights, so they live in a perpetual mania to find food. They tend to prefer red, trumpet-shaped flowers, in which nectar thickly oozes, and eat every 15 minutes or so. A hummingbird drinks with a W-shaped tongue, licking nectar up as a cat might (but faster). Like a tiny drum roll, its heart beats at 500 times a minute. Frighten a hummingbird and its heart can race to over 1,200 times a minute. Feasting and flying, courting and dueling, hummingbirds consume life at a fever pitch. No warm-blooded animal on earth uses more energy, for its size. But that puts them at great peril. By day's end, wrung-out and exhausted, a hummingbird rests near collapse.

In the dark night of the hummingbird, it can sink into a zombielike state of torpor; its breathing grows shallow and its wild heart slows to only 36 beats a minute. When dawn breaks on the fuchsia and columbine, hummingbirds must jump-start their hearts and fire up their flight muscles to raise their body temperature for another all-or-nothing day. That demands a colossal effort, which some can't manage. So a lot of hummingbirds die in their sleep.

But most do bestir themselves. This is why, in American Indian myths and legends, hummingbirds are often depicted as resurrection birds, which seem to die and be reborn on another day or in another season. The Aztec god of war was named Huitzilopochtli, a compound word meaning "shining one with weapon like cactus thorn," and "sorcerer that spits fire." Aztec warriors fought, knowing that if they fell in battle they would be reincarnated as glittery, thug-like hummingbirds. The male birds were lionized for their ferocity in battle. And their feathers flashed in the sun like jewel-encrusted shields. Aztec rulers donned ceremonial robes of hummingbird feathers. As they walked, colors danced across their shoulders and bathed them in a supernatural light show.

While most birds are busy singing a small operetta of who and what and where, hummingbirds are virtually mute. Such small voices don't carry far, so they don't bother much with song. But if they can't serenade a mate, or yell war cries at a rival, how can they perform the essential dramas of their lives? They dance. Using body language, they spell out their intentions and moods, just as bees, fireflies or hula dancers do. That means elaborate aerial ballets in which males twirl, joust, sideswipe and somersault. Brazen and fierce, they will take on large adversaries—even cats, dogs or humans.

My neighbor Persis once told me how she'd been needled by hummingbirds. When Persis lived in San Francisco, hummingbirds often attacked her outside her apartment building. From their perspective she was on *their* property, not the other way round, and they flew circles around her to vex her away. My encounters with hummingbirds have been altogether more benign. Whenever I've walked through South American rain forests, with my hair braided and secured by a waterproof red ribbon, hummingbirds have assumed my ribbon to be a succulent flower and have probed my hair repeatedly, searching for nectar. Their touch was as delicate as a sweat bee's. But it was their purring by my ear that made me twitch. In time, they would leave unfed, but for a while I felt like a character in a Li'l Abner cartoon who could be named something like "Hummer." In Portuguese, the word for hummingbird (*Beija flor*) means "flower kisser." It was the American colonists who first imagined the birds humming as they went about their chores.

Last summer, the historical novelist Jeanne Mackin winced to see her cat, Beltane, drag in voles, birds and even baby rabbits. Few things can compete with the blood lust of a tabby cat. But one day Beltane dragged in something rare and shimmery—a struggling hummingbird. The feathers were ruffled and there was a bit of blood on the breast, but the bird still looked perky and alive. So Jeanne fashioned a nest for it out of a small wire basket lined in gauze, and fed it sugar water from an eye dropper. To her amazement, as she watched, "it miscarried a little pearl." Hummingbird eggs are the size of coffee beans, and females usually carry two. So Jeanne knew one might still be safe inside. After a quiet night, the hummingbird seemed stronger, and when she set the basket outside at dawn, the tiny assault victim flew away.

It was a ruby-throated hummingbird that she nursed, the only one native to the East Coast. In the winter they migrate thousands of miles over mountains and open water to Mexico and South America. She may well have been visited by a species known to the Aztecs. Altogether, there are 16 species of hummingbirds in North America, and many dozens in South America, especially near the equator, where they can feed on a buffet of blossoms. The tiniest—the Cuban bee hummingbird—is the smallest warm-blooded animal in the world. About two and one-eighth inches long from beak to tail, it is smaller than the toe of an eagle, and its eggs are like seeds.

Hummingbirds are a New World phenomenon. So, too, is vanilla, and their stories are linked. When the early explorers returned home with the riches of the West, they found it impossible, to their deep frustration, to grow vanilla beans. It took ages before they discovered why—that hummingbirds were a key pollinator of vanilla orchids—and devised beaklike splinters of bamboo to do the work of birds.

Now that summer has come at last, lucky days may be spent watching the antics of hummingbirds. The best way to behold them is to stand with the light behind you, so that the bird faces the sun. Most of the trembling colors aren't true pigments, but the result of light staggering through clear cells that act as prisms. Hummingbirds are iridescent for the same reason soap bubbles are. Each feather contains tiny air bubbles separated by dark spaces. Light bounces off the air bubbles at different angles, and that makes blazing colors seem to swarm and leap. All is vanity in the end. The male's shimmer draws a female to mate. But that doesn't matter much to gardeners, watching hummingbirds patrol the impatiens as if the northern lights had suddenly fallen to earth.

JAMAICA KINCAID (b. 1949)

From *A Small Place*

CONSIDER THIS:

Jamaica Kincaid was born in St. Johns, Antigua, and studied photography at the New School for Social Research. She holds numerous honorary degrees and was a staff writer for 20 years at *The New Yorker* starting in the mid-1970s. Kincaid discussed the origins of her writing life in a *Salon* interview: "I'd written little things for *The Village Voice,* some television criticism. But it was William Shawn who showed me what my voice was. I began to write the stories that became *At the Bottom of the River,* my first book, and he published them. He made me feel that what I thought, my inner life, my thoughts as I organized them, were important. That they made literature. That they made sense. There was a world for them. Not only for mine—but many people's. But I am Exhibit A. Because I am not a man, I am not white, I didn't go to Harvard. The generation of writers from *The New*

Yorker that I was a part of were white men who went to Harvard or Yale. And I was none of those things."

Kincaid thinks her heritage as a West Indian writer is vital but she also observed, "The African-American is often used, and has conspired with the rest of America to be used, as a diversion from America's problems. I wish African-Americans would stop contributing to this sideshow." Kincaid's words might provide another lens for rereading the essays by Evans Hopkins and Brent Staples. In her own piece here, to what degree do you feel she actually is "Exhibit A"? How does her use of "you," second-person singular, compare to Diane Ackerman's use of very limited first person? (Ackerman refers to herself only at the beginning of the fourth paragraph—in the sentence beginning "My neighbor . . . "—within her eight-paragraph essay on hummingbirds.) What is the effect of Kincaid's two-paragraph excerpt? And how might you expect her to respond to Haunani-Kay Trask's strategies (both consider tourists)? What would these authors' prose look like if recast using the other's techniques?

The thing you have always suspected about yourself the minute you become a tourist is true: A tourist is an ugly human being. You are not an ugly person all the time; you are not an ugly person ordinarily; you are not an ugly person day to day. From day to day, you are a nice person. From day to day, all the people who are supposed to love you on the whole do. From day to day, as you walk down a busy street in the large and modern and prosperous city in which you work and live, dismayed, puzzled (a cliché, but only a cliché can explain you) at how alone you feel in this crowd, how awful it is to go unnoticed, how awful it is to go unloved, even as you are surrounded by more people than you could possibly get to know in a lifetime that lasted for millennia, and then out of the corner of your eye you see someone looking at you and absolute pleasure is written all over that person's face, and then you realise that you are not as revolting a presence as you think you are (for that look just told you so). And so, ordinarily, you are a nice person, an attractive person, a person capable of drawing to yourself the affection of other people (people just like you), a person at home in your own skin (sort of; I mean, in a way; I mean, your dismay and puzzlement are natural to you, because people like you just seem to be like that, and so many of the things people like you find admirable about yourselves—the things you think about, the things you think really define you—seem rooted in these feelings): a person at home in your own house (and all its nice house things), with it nice back yard (and its nice back-yard things), at home on your street, your church, in community activities, your job, at home with your family, your relatives, your friends—you are a whole person. But one day, when you are sitting somewhere, alone in that crowd, and that awful feeling of displacedness comes over you, and really, as an ordinary person you are not well equipped to look too far inward and set yourself aright, because being ordinary is already so taxing, and being ordinary takes all you have out of you, and though the words "I must get away" do not actually pass across your lips, you make a leap from being that nice blob just sitting like a boob in your amniotic sac of the modern experience to being a person visiting heaps of death and ruin and feeling alive and inspired at the sight of it; to being a person lying on some faraway beach, your stilled body stinking and glistening in the sand, looking like something first forgotten, then remembered, then not important enough to go back for; to being a person marvelling at the harmony (ordinarily, what you would say is the backwardness) and the union these other people (and they are other people) have with nature. And you look at the things they can do with a piece of ordinary cloth, the things they fashion out of cheap, vulgarly colored (to you) twine, the way they squat down over a hole they have made in the ground, the hole itself is something to marvel at, and since you are being an ugly person this ugly but joyful thought will swell inside you: their ancestors were not clever in the way yours were and not ruthless in the way yours were, for then would it not be you who would be in harmony with nature and backwards in that charming way? An ugly thing, that is what you are when you become a tourist, an ugly, empty thing, a stupid thing, a piece of rubbish pausing here and there to gaze at this and taste that, and it will never occur to you that the people who inhabit the place in which you have just paused cannot stand you, that behind their closed doors they laugh at your strangeness (you do not look the way they look); the physical sight of you does not please them; you have bad manners (it is their custom to eat their food with their hands; you try eating their way, you look silly; you try eating the way you always eat, you look silly); they do not like the way you speak (you have an accent); they collapse helpless from laughter, mimicking the way they imagine you must look as you carry out some everyday bodily function. They do not like you. *They do not like me!* That thought never actually occurs to you. Still, you feel a little uneasy. Still, you feel a little foolish. Still, you feel a little out of place. But the banality of your own life is very real to you, it drove you to this extreme, spending your days and your nights in the company of people who despise you, people you do not like really, people you would not want to have as your actual neighbor. And so you must devote yourself to puzzling out how much of what you are told is really, really true (Is ground-up bottle glass in peanut sauce really a delicacy around here, or will it do just what you think ground-up bottle glass will do? Is this rare, multicoloured, snout-mouthed fish really an aphrodisiac, or will it cause you to fall asleep permanently?). Oh, the hard work all of this is, and is it any wonder, then, that on your return home you feel the need of a long rest, so that you can recover from your life as a tourist?

That the native does not like the tourist is not hard to explain. For every native of every place is a potential tourist, and every tourist is a native of somewhere. Every native everywhere lives a life of overwhelming and crushing banality and boredom and desperation and depression, and every deed, good and bad, is an attempt to forget this. Every native would like to find a way out, every native would like a rest, every native would like a tour. But some natives—most natives in the world—cannot go anywhere. They are too poor. They are too poor to go anywhere. They are too poor to escape the reality of their lives; and they are too poor to live properly in the place where they live, which is the very place you, the tourist, want to go—so when the natives see you, the tourist, they envy you, they envy your ability to leave your own banality and boredom, they envy your ability to turn their own banality and boredom into a source of pleasure for yourself.

BARRY LOPEZ (b. 1945)

My Horse

CONSIDER THIS:

Barry Lopez was born in Port Chester, New York, earned an advanced degree from Notre Dame in the 1960s and now lives in Oregon. He won the National Book Award in 1986 for *Arctic Dreams* and a Guggenheim Fellowship in 1987, among many other awards and honors throughout his career. Lopez expounded upon the differences between fiction and nonfiction in an interview with *January* magazine: "Fiction is a different animal from nonfiction short or long, essay or long book. Over here with nonfiction the linchpin is factual truth. What's going on has got to be based in a factual world that is shared by everyone. So if you say: 'The Prime Minister did this,' then you've got to be able to look that up at the library and see that that's what he did, otherwise it falls apart. The basis for fiction is emotional truth. It's got to be the case that the reader reading the work of fiction says: 'This is plausible, this could happen. I know this.'" How does Lopez adhere to his own distinctions concerning fact and fiction in this selection? What is original and/or expected to you about his use of the comparison/contrast pattern of organization? In this pattern, one side of the comparison is often the backdrop to the other. How does that play out in this essay? How does the thesis function in an organization of this sort?

It is curious that Indian warriors on the northern plains in the nineteenth century, who were almost entirely dependent on the horse for mobility and status, never gave their horses names. If you borrowed a man's horse and went off raiding for other horses, however, or if you lost your mount in battle and then jumped on mine and counted coup on an enemy—well, those horses would have to be shared with the man whose horse you borrowed, and that coup would be mine, not yours. Because even if I gave him no name, he was my horse.

If you were a Crow warrior and I a young Teton Sioux out after a warrior's identity and we came over a small hill somewhere in the Montana prairie and surprised each other, I could tell a lot about you by looking at your horse.

Your horse might have feathers tied in his mane, or in his tail, or a medicine bag tied around his neck. If I knew enough about the Crow, and had looked at you closely, I might make some sense of the decoration, even guess who you were if you were well-known. If you had painted your horse I could tell even more, because we both decorated our horses with signs that meant the same things. Your white handprints high on his flanks would tell me you had killed an enemy in a hand-to-hand fight. Small horizontal lines stacked on your horse's foreleg, or across his nose, would tell me how many times you had counted coup. Horse hoof marks on your horse's rump, or three-sided boxes, would tell me how many times you had stolen horses. If there was a bright red square on your horse's neck I would know you were leading a war party and that there were probably others out there in the coulees behind you.

You might be painted all over as blue as the sky and covered with white dots, with your horse painted the same way. Maybe hailstorms were your power—or if I chased you a hailstorm might come down and hide you. There might be lightning bolts on the horse's legs and flanks, and I would wonder if you had lightning power, or a slow horse. There might be white circles around your horse's eyes to help him see better.

Or you might be like Crazy Horse, with no decoration, no marks on your horse to tell me anything, only a small lightning bolt on your cheek, a piece of turquoise tied behind your ear.

You might have scalps dangling from your rein.

I could tell something about you by your horse. All this would come to me in a few seconds. I might decide this was my moment and shout my war cry—*Hoka key!* Or I might decide you were like the grizzly bear: I would raise my weapon to you in salute and go my way, to see you again when I was older.

I do not own a horse. I am attached to a truck, however, and I have come to think of it in a similar way. It has no name; it never occurred to me to give it a name. It has little decoration; neither of us is partial to decoration. I have a piece of turquoise in the truck because I had heard once that some of the southwestern tribes tied a small piece of turquoise in a horse's hock to keep him from stumbling. I like the idea. I also hang sage in the truck when I go on a long trip. But inside, the truck doesn't look much different from others that look just like it on the outside. I like it that way. Because I like my privacy.

For two years in Wyoming I worked on a ranch wrangling horses. The horse I rode when I had to have a good horse was a quarter horse and his name was Coke High. The name came with him. At first I thought he'd been named for the soft drink. I'd known stranger names given to horses by whites. Years later I wondered if some deviate Wyoming cowboy wise to cocaine had not named him. Now I think he was probably named after a rancher, an historical figure of the region. I never asked the people who owned him for fear of spoiling the spirit of my inquiry.

We were running over a hundred horses on this ranch. They all had names. After a few weeks I knew all the horses and the names too. You had to. No one knew how to talk about the animals or put them in order or tell the wranglers what to do unless they were using the names—Princess, Big Red, Shoshone, Clay.

My truck is named Dodge. The name came with it. I don't know if it was named after the town or the verb or the man who invented it. I like it for a name. Perfectly anonymous, like Rex for a dog, or Old Paint. You can't tell anything with a name like that.

The truck is a van. I call it a truck because it's not a car and because "van" is a suburban sort of consumer word, like "oxford loafer", and I don't like the sound of it. On the outside it looks like any other Dodge Sportsman 300. It's a dirty tan color. There are a few body dents, but it's never been in a wreck. I tore the antenna off against a tree on a pinched mountain road. A boy in Midland, Texas, rocked one of my rear view mirrors off. A logging truck in Oregon squeeze-fired a piece of debris off the road and shattered my windshield. The oil pan and gas tank are pug-faced from high-centering on bad roads. (I remember a horse I rode for a while named Targhee whose hocks were scarred from tangles in barbed wire when he was a colt and who spooked a lot in high grass, but these were not like "dents." They were more like bad tires.)

I like to travel. I go mostly in the winter and mostly on two-lane roads. I've driven the truck from Key West to Vancouver, British Columbia, and from Yuma to Long Island over the past four years. I used to ride Coke High only about five miles every morning when we were rounding up horses. Hard miles of twisting and turning. About six hundred miles a year. Then I'd turn him out and ride another horse for the rest of the day. That's what was nice about having a remuda. You could do all you had to do and not take it all out on your best horse. Three car family.

My truck came with a lot of seats in it and I've never really known what to do with them. Sometimes I put the seats in and go somewhere with a lot of people, but most of the time I leave them out. I like riding around with that empty cavern of space behind my head. I know it's something with a history to it, that there's truth in it, because I always rode a horse the same way—with empty saddle bags. In case I found something. The possibility of finding something is half the reason for being on the road.

The value of anything comes to me in its use. If I am not using something it is of no value to me and I give it away. I wasn't always that way. I used to keep everything I owned—just in case. I feel good about the truck because it gets used. A lot. To haul hay and firewood and lumber and rocks and garbage and animals. Other people have used it to haul furniture and freezers and dirt and recycled newspapers. And to move from one house to another. When I lend it for things like that I don't look to get anything back but some gas (if we're going to be friends). But if you go way out in the country to a dump and pick up the things you can still find out there (once a load of cedar shingles we sold for $175 to an architect) I expect you to leave some of those things around my place when you come back—if I need them.

When I think back, maybe the nicest thing I ever put in that truck was timber wolves. It was a long night's drive from Oregon up into British Columbia. We were all very quiet about it; it was like moving clouds across the desert.

Sometimes something won't fit in the truck and I think about improving it—building a different door system, for example. I am forever going to add better gauges on the dash and a pair of driving lamps and a sunroof, but I never get around to doing any of it. I remember I wanted to improve Coke High once too, especially the way he bolted like a greyhound through patches of cottonwood on a river flat. But all I could do with him was to try to rein him out of it. Or hug his back.

Sometimes, road-stoned in a blur of country like southwestern Wyoming or North Dakota, I talk to the truck. It's like wandering on the high plains under a summer sun, on plains where, George Catlin wrote, you were "out of sight of land". I say what I am thinking out loud, or point at things along the road. It's a crazy, sun-stroked sort of activity, a sure sign it's time to pull over, to go for a walk, to make a fire and have some tea, to lie in the shade of the truck.

I've always wanted to pat the truck. It's basic to the relationship. But it never works.

I remember when I was on the ranch, just at sunrise, after I'd saddled Coke High, I'd be huddled down in my jacket smoking a cigarette and looking down into the valley, along the river where the other horses had spent the night. I'd turn to Coke and run my hand down his neck and slap-pat him on the shoulder to say I was coming up. It made a bond, an agreement we started the day with.

I've thought about that a lot with the truck, because we've gone out together at sunrise on so many mornings. I've even fumbled around trying to do it. But metal won't give.

The truck's personality is mostly an expression of two ideas: "with-you" and "alone". When Coke High was "with-you" he and I were the same animal. We could have cut a rooster out of a flock of chickens, we were so in tune. It's the same with the truck: rolling through Kentucky on a hilly two-lane road, three in the morning under a full moon and no traffic. Picture it. You roll like water.

There are other times when you are with each other but there's no connection at all. Coke got that way when he was bored and we'd fight each other about which way to go around a tree. When the truck gets like that—"alone"—it's because it feels its Detroit fat-ass design dragging at its heart and making a fool out of it.

I can think back over more than a hundred nights I've slept in the truck, sat in it with a lamp burning, bundled up in a parka, reading a book. It was always comfortable. A good place to wait out a storm. Like sleeping inside a buffalo.

The truck will go past 100,000 miles soon. I'll rebuild the engine and put a different transmission in it. I can tell from magazine advertisements that I'll never get another one like it. Because every year they take more of the heart out of them. One thing that makes a farmer or a rancher go sour is a truck that isn't worth a shit. The reason you see so many old pickups in ranch country is because these are the only ones with any heart. You can count on them. The weekend rancher runs around in a new pickup with too much engine and not enough transmission and with the wrong sort of tires because he can afford anything, even the worst. A lot of them have names for their pickups too.

My truck has broken down, in out of the way places at the worst of times. I've walked away and screamed the foulness out of my system and gotten the tools out. I had to fix a water pump in a blizzard in the Panamint Mountains in California once. It took all day with the Coleman stove burning under the engine block to keep my hands from freezing. We drifted into Beatty, Nevada, that night with it jury-rigged together with—I swear—baling wire, and we were melting snow as we went and pouring it in to compensate for the leaks.

There is a dent next to the door on the driver's side I put there one sweltering night in Miami. I had gone to the airport to meet my wife, whom I hadn't seen in a month. My hands were so swollen with poison ivy blisters I had to drive with my wrists. I had shut the door and was locking it when the window fell off its runners and slid down inside the door. I couldn't leave the truck unlocked because I had too much inside I didn't want to lose. So I just kicked the truck a blow in the side and went to work on the window. I hate to admit kicking the truck. It's like kicking a dog, which I've never done.

Coke High and I had an accident once. We hit a badger hole at a full gallop. I landed on my back and blacked out. When I came to, Coke High was about a hundred yards away. He stayed a hundred yards away for six miles, all the way back to the ranch.

I want to tell you about carrying those wolves, because it was a fine thing. There were ten of them. We had four in the truck with us in crates and six in a trailer. It was a five hundred mile trip. We went at night for the cool air and because there wouldn't be as much traffic. I could feel from the way the truck rolled along that its heart was in the trip. It liked the wolves inside it, the sweet odor that came from the crates. I could feel that same tireless wolf-lope developing in its wheels; it was like you might never have to stop for gas, ever again.

The truck gets very self-focused when it works like this; its heart is strong and it's good to be around it. It's good to be *with* it. You get the same feeling when you pull someone out of a ditch. Coke High and I pulled a Volkswagen out of the mud once, but Coke didn't like doing it very much. Speed, not strength, was his center. When the guy who owned the car thanked us and tried to pat Coke, the horse snorted and swung away, trying to preserve his distance, which is something a horse spends a lot of time on.

So does the truck.

Being distant lets the truck get its heart up. The truck has been cold and alone in Montana at 38 below zero. It's climbed horrible, eroded roads in Idaho. It's been burdened beyond overloading and made it anyway. I've asked it to do these things because they build heart and without heart all you have is a machine. You have nothing. I don't think people in Detroit know anything at all about heart. That's why everything they build dies so young.

One time in Arizona the truck and I came through one of the worst storms I've ever been in, an outrageous, angry blizzard. But we went down the road, right through it. You couldn't explain our getting through by the sort of tires I had on the truck, or the fact that I had chains on, or was a good driver, or had a lot of weight over my drive wheels or a good engine, because it was more than this. It was a contest between the truck and the blizzard—and the truck wouldn't quit. I could have gone to sleep and the truck would have just torn a road down Interstate 40 on its own. It scared the hell out of me; but it gave me heart, too.

We came off the Mogollon Rim that night and out of the storm and headed south for Phoenix. I pulled off the road to sleep for a few hours, but before I did I got out of the truck. It was raining. Warm rain. I tied a short piece of red avalanche cord into the grill. I left it there for a long time, like an eagle feather on a horse's tail. It flapped and spun in the wind. I could hear it ticking against the grill when I drove.

When I have to leave that truck I will just raise up my left arm—*Hoka hey!* —and walk away.

WENDY BISHOP (b. 1953)

It's Not the Heat, It's the Humidity—It's Not the Cold, It's the Darkness

CONSIDER THIS:

Born in Japan during the Korean War, Wendy Bishop grew up in southern California, and attended college in northern California, taught in Nigeria, Northern Arizona, and Alaska before moving south. She teaches writing at Florida State University and writes poetry, nonfiction, fiction, and textbooks on writing. Though Bishop lives in Tallahassee, she spends time at Alligator Point, Florida as often as she can. Long an advocate of writing teachers writing the same assignments as their students, Bishop composed "It's Not the Heat, It's the Humidity" while teaching a class in which each writer attempted assignments that were difficult for him or her. Two students who preferred looser organization patterns decided to self-assign the five-paragraph form. Bishop joined them because, like the speaker in Lenora Smith's poem "The Five Paragraph Essay," she knew the five-paragraph organization pattern had been assigned so regularly that many view it as purely a school form. Bishop says that many writing students are tired of forming their thoughts this way and see this format as a limiting rather than an enabling one. Investigating these assumptions, she did find the form to be a challenge. Particularly when she added the additional constraint of comparison-and-contrast organization.

As you'll see, the five-paragraph limitation forced Bishop's essay into a different pacing and rhythm than you find in Barry Lopez's comparison essay. Is hers a "true" five-paragraph theme? You might want to decide for yourself, particularly after discussing characteristics of the format and after reading Lenora Smith's poem.

FIRE AND ICE

Some say the world will end in fire,
Some say in ice.
From what I've tasted of desire
I hold with those who favor fire.
But if I had to perish twice,
I think I know enough of hate
To say that for destruction ice
Is also great
And would suffice

—ROBERT FROST

This is my first and last five-paragraph, comparison-and-contrast essay. With a few twists, the twist of key lime in a Florida gin and tonic, the twist of an ankle on ice outside the front door in Alaska, and the twist that I'm a Californian in a continuous state of displacement. Just as everyone else drifted toward that golden state—overpricing the real estate and bankrupting the public schools—I went the other way, north, then south. I'm composed of California's irreproducible coastal mornings, light fog burning off into evenhanded Mediterranean afternoons on patios with potted red geraniums. I never saw snow until I was eighteen—this on a church-camp snow trip—and I never saw snow *falling* until a year after that in a square in Salzburg during the gray, unfamiliar gloom of a real fall afternoon. Then again, I never felt true tropical heat and persistent humidity until my Uncle Bill sent my girlfriend JoAnn and me on a cruise to the Bahamas the year we visited him in Sarasota as college girls. In fact, until a few years ago, I never experienced warm midwinter storms, hurricane-force winds, and Spanish moss flying through the air like displaced witches' wigs. Now I live in Tallahassee and just before that in Fairbanks, Alaska, and both seem times of elected service abroad, across land and landscapes, into and out of cultures and climates—meeting Athabascans and Apalachicolans. At the same time, bringing these places together through interweavings of present and immediate-past memory produces an unexpected symmetry, a yin and yang of dark and light, dry and cold, heat and humidity. What's winter cabin fever in Fairbanks but summer–air-conditioning lockdown in Tallahassee? At a northern All Indian Dance or a Seminole Indian Days celebration, fry bread is fry bread. Salmon and halibut at the Alaska Salmon Bake tastes as vividly as barbecue at Sonny's. And maybe, as Robert Frost suggests in his poem "Fire and Ice," fire is just the flip side of ice. And ice is just the backside of fire.

In early October, sandhill cranes that have been summering here gather in the Creamer's Dairy fields on College Road. Everyone goes down to the split-rail roadside fences to watch the cranes mass in the furrows of already harvested fields. They do what large birds do when on the ground, hunch and lurch, fold and unfold awkward lanky wings. One day they're gone, heading south to New Mexico. The Tallahassee Democrat announces the arrival of the monarch butterflies. They cluster like glistening globs of marmalade on low bushes at Saint Marks Wildlife Refuge. Near me, a nuclear family in coordinated pastel shorts and polos and a biker gal and guy stroll along the grassy earth mounds at Gulf's edge, taking pictures, catching and releasing a monarch, wings and hand waving at imminent departure. *On November 1, I push in the button to engage the four-wheel drive on my Honda station wagon. Snow has been sticking for two weeks, and by winter's end (May)—when I push the button a second time to disengage the four-wheel drive—the snows will have collected up to ten solid feet deep, before melting to dirty fringes, brown earth, and a late-June spring. Winter fun is placing a bet on the date when the Tanana River ice will break up near Nenana.* On November 1, I sense a slightly crisper day, risk turning the air-conditioning off, crack the sunroof in my Honda Civic, and drive with the windows down: if I've miscalculated, the sunroof's thick, tinted plastic will act as a giant lens, refracting the remaining fall heat onto my shoulders. It's still a frog night, but I try the hot tub and find it warmer, finally, than the air outside. Steam rises and seems to float across the stars that are clearer now than when under summer's broad caul of white humidity. Each star winks because my steamed-up glasses are off and the palm-tree fronds wave in a light breeze. Wind chimes clink like iced-tea spoons in glasses of sweet tea. This, I think, is the life. *The aurora borealis is out as I drive to teach a night class at the university on the hill; I skid across an unseen slow-motion mile of black ice, but once out of that danger, I angle my head to see the lights better through the scraped-off windshield. I plug my car-battery cord into the socket in the lower parking lot, hurry up some icy steps, and then throw my head back again to get a better view around the fox fur that lines my jacket hood. I'm arrested by the swirling pea greens and muted reds that veil the stars. Then I notice others, lying on heir backs in parkas on a snow-covered lawn, gazing into the swirling Van Gogh night sky. I join for a moment until the cold snakes into my bones.*

Halloween arrives in a gasp of autumn heat, maybe my children can wear their synthetic Walmart costumes, but more likely, they'll run too hot under a beaming moon and sweat will ruin their vampire-face makeup. Suburban parents hover like a pod of gamekeepers in a wildlife park. Cherokees, Blazers, and Explorers with parking lights on trail small herds of children up just-darkened streets. There are offers to scan candy at the police station for needles or razor blades, and the week commenced with a spate of annual letters to the editor about fundamental fears of witchcraft and demonology. There is something demonic to me about the swamps and cypress trunks, the bats flying out of the moss-strewn live oaks, the uncanny way I can perspire—as if with fear or guilt—at any time of the year. Who but a demon would invent insects that grow the size of horror-movie props? Who but a witch could guarantee that anything planted will grow so rampantly and then mold so insidiously? There's an impressive breaking down going on here that has to do with an invoked earthiness beyond my understanding. Halloween can end in a tumult of eggs drying on stucco houses or Batman in shorts finding himself stung into silliness by red fire ants. *Outside the Fairbanks Safeway, half the parking lot is filled with empty locked cars and trucks, all engines idling. The sky fills with exhaust—this is a dark sky, mind you—now dark from about 4 P.M. to 9 A.M. and losing six minutes of daylight each and every day. Commuting to the preschool with a three month old in his baby seat and a three year old in her child's seat takes on a sense of a transarctic journey. Frankly, I'm terrified. There are vehicles in slow motion negotiating the ice-fog—particulate exhaust that obscures vision and hurts the chest like inhaling a sharp poison. Overall, each day's (night's) drive feels like I'm stranded in a bumper-car concession filled with metal dinosaurs that loom up into sudden vision. Headlights fracture into disorienting diamond-cold facets. One car skids around me, pirouettes three times through a gloomy, fog-filled, street-lamp-illuminated intersection and skitters to the side of the road. I pass, then eye the school buses coming toward me in an eerie procession, strobe lights seeming to make emergency where there is not, as yet, any. Each passes, each driver in her dark maw, looks intent. Eighty below and a spare sleeping bag and gallon of emergency water that will freeze in the parking lot today make me feel less than secure. The baby is oblivious, bundled into the shape of a basketball for the five-yard dash into the preschool. Two years later, the children are, respectively, a white rabbit in a one-piece rabbit suit and Wonder Woman in her outfit from the Fred Meyers store. It's five P.M. on the way home, and we decide to trick-or-treat in town, away from our isolated street of two houses on a mile of dirt road. In a random housing track, we prepare, then, leaving the car idling, run together to the house, enter the first door, hit the marginally warmer chill of the snow porch, fumble with zippers; the parka comes off, the rabbit hood goes up, the sweater is unbuttoned, the gloves—attached by strings—are pulled off long enough to grasp a bag, the doorbell is rung, the homeowner flings open the door in a rush of hot air. Trick or treat. We manage five houses before our heat exchange results in a net loss. Later than evening, the only two neighbor boys from the other house down the road plunge and play their way down to ours at 8 P.M., delighting my five-year-old daughter who heaps candy into their pillowcases. The boys whoop away, their feet leaving great holes in the snow on the front porch that are healed over by morning by new snow.*

Enough sun to grow all year long. Ground that can be dug. By July the tomatoes are rotting in the heat. In September, time for a winter garden. Over time, I plant twelve cabbage palms, five rose bushes, eight pampas grass, twenty-two Mexican-heather plants, assorted crepe myrtle and oleander, holly and wax myrtle, azaleas and more azaleas. I dig small holes in warm red dirt for more than three hundred daylilly roots in a frenzy of expectation. I have two cats, a dog, a swimming pool, two children who play outside until late in the warm evening dusk. Ready or not, everything grows. I learn to put tulip bulbs in the refrigerator to fool them into thinking there has been a winter. *Even in July, ice shards remain in the shadowed banks of streams and road cuts going north out of the Tanana Valley. Spring is brown mud. Late spring is first fast grass. Midsummer, flowers—wild iris; wild rose; vetch, purple and white; dandelions and fireweed, and more fireweed flaming away. Emerald-green grass and garden vegetables grow by leaps and bounds in twenty hours of summer daylight, like time-lapse photography. This short but fierce growing season produces elephantine squash for judging at the Tanana Valley Fair. Potlucks always feature someone's experiment with moose or bear stew, dark dark meat in broth. Pots of beans and vegetables, lots of carbohydrates and brutally heavy home-made deserts. Alys and Pete and other friends who live in unplumbed cabins on little money experiment endlessly with whole grains. And lots of beer and cheap wine. Coats shed inside a too small apartment or cluttered house take up more room off than on, become part of a wall-to-wall quilt where, once served, we sit on parkas, mittens, seven-foot-long bulky knit mufflers, rock back on Sorrel's or Bunny Boots used by workers on the Alaska pipeline and found in the Salvation Army stores. Teddy Bears' Picnic writ large—eating commences immediately and continues until every pot is licked clean; then we trundle out, talked out, not 'et out, into the cold.* Covered dishes arranged with care on long tables. Everyone waits before arriving and before eating, tastes, shares recipes, greetings. There is order. There is a silver set out. Children are dressed up and shooed outside to the humid, leafy oak-tree shade in summer or to dash through a few fall leaves in winter. The reason to gather is to share food but seemingly not to eat. At the end of all the talk, knives chink on porcelain, food is scraped into the trash. We find our dish, cover it, and leave. The evening air is lovely, sixty-five degrees. I twirl in my long skirt. Want to drink another glass of wine. At home, I dig into the leftovers like an animal. On a brilliant eighty-degree day, after Thanksgiving dinner, we take a walk around the neighborhood, swimming against kids on rollerblades, the couple with two schnauzers, the woman with the blond French braid who runs seriously every day all year long. Returned, light sinking lower in the late afternoon, we watch football games to see snow on the fields up north. *Up north, far north, we watch football games to see grass left on the ground, and a sudden interest in golf tournaments is a sudden interest in seeing the earth—seeing if it is still under the snow, where we'll find it in some months, everything lost found again, garden tools, one mitten, tattered notepaper caught in the rotting stalks of plants. Every month, for six months, I resolve to start running again. Put on long underwear, sweats, another set of sweats, inner and outer mittens, wool face mask and cap, glasses, walk outside at forty below and move twenty pounds of clothes very slowly down the driveway. At the end of the Thanksgiving dinner I cook my first year, pregnant and nauseous, I watch Susan crack open the turkey bones and suck out the marrow. Each bone, each marrow. Twelve people are wedged around the table, and the house perspires inward on the glass windows like a turkey glaze; we (they) eat turkey, cranberries, potatoes, bread, and four pies, without once leaving the table until Susan gets up to bus her turkey shards; we settle into more darkness while Lynn plays flute and Ken plays fiddle.* On the first shopping day of Christmas, I see a woman in Gayfer's trying on a Christmas sweater embroidered with winter scenes. *Sweaters are ordered out of L. L. Bean catalogs, all wool, cable-knot, layered one over the other so some are never even seen. On the first day of December, we visit the ice carvings on the Chena River downtown. At high noon, there is finally enough sun to trap light and refract it through blocks of blue ice carved into life-sized moose, bear, and wolves. A stage coach the kids can sit in. Strolling on the festive, frozen river, we warm up enough to shuck down to down vests and wiggle our toes in sock-filled snow boots.*

On the first day of December, the Festival of Lights—spring, summer, fall, and winter leftovers of light fill thousands of small bulbs on the downtown trees in Tallahassee, arc from the excited eyes of my children as they help wrap presents in bright foil, leap from roadside decorations and reflect upside down in fenders and hubcaps; Christmas beams from the miniature bells on sweaters. Friends—Elise, Lizanne, and Devan—join hundreds of men, women, and children dressed as elves, Santa's helpers, and ma-and-pa 'Clauses, for the Jingle-Bell run. Christmas in Leon County can't come soon enough and can't stay long enough. *In Fairbanks, Christmas trees shipped north from Seattle are stored in a huge heated warehouse. If an outdoor tree is brought in from the cold, all the needles fall off.* In Tallahassee, we ransom our tree from a tree farm up Havana way; Bonnie takes me and Morgan and Tait on an energetic trip of misdirection along highways and around false corners until we wade with others into the long grass and choose our own. By the second week, the tree is dropping hundreds of tiny dead black insects on the presents; I Dust-Bust until Christmas Day.

For my friend Don in Pennsylvania, I collect moose stories—urban legends of slaughter and silliness and awe. Moose maimings or moose being maimed, moose ambling where they ought not to amble given this North Star Borough of ornery 1960s individuals who have floated up from the Lower Forty-eight, each to have the inalienable right to keep fifteen snarling, barking sled dogs outside their houses. A man tries to ward off a moose charge with a machete and ends up "riding" the moose through town. A moose cow and calf spend six months in the leafless woods outside our house; we the zoo animals on that empty slice of their land. I send Don a series of incriminating alligator stories from the newspaper to tell him I have arrived south. Alligators with many shades of the same personality—overly friendly, terrifying, hoary. Alligators who walk into houses through the open back door like an unwanted neighbor bumming some sugar. Alligators who when killed disgorge six dog collars. Alligators who gaze at me complacently half submerged in the marshes of the wildlife refuge, having been here longer and adapted better. As I near the end of my essay, I start to see that the long AlCan highway—ten days times twelve hours of steady insistent driving, two adults, two toddlers in the front seat of a U-haul towing all their cold memories and a car without air-conditioning toward all their hot hopes along an endless interstate—provides a concrete link between these two landscapes. They are part of the same whole. The cup is half empty *and* half full. The football field is half full of snow and half full of grass. *On certain days, we can see Denali from Fairbanks, and the whole Alaska range;* on certain days, Tallahassee has the highest mountains on earth in the tumbling, building, vast cumuli that gather before summer storms. Closed-window seasons and hot, window-open seasons; growing seasons and waiting seasons. Armadillo, opossum, gray heron, bass, manatee, owl, hummingbird. *Moose, musk ox, brown and black bear, crane, owl, hummingbird. Spruce, fir, tundra, and fireweed.* Cabbage palm, magnolia, and daylily. Hurricanes, tornadoes, heat lightning, tropical depressions. *Volcanoes, earthquakes, blizzards, and ice storms.* Crane balances with butterfly, and moose partners alligator. To have hot we have to have cold. I see how my

Mediterranean self has been taken to extremes. Fire and ice will both suffice. I bind them together into one life. And luckily so.

LEONORA SMITH (b. 1945)

The Five Paragraph Essay

CONSIDER THIS:

Leonora Smith teaches in the Department of American Thought and Language at Michigan State University and writes poetry and short stories. Reading and writing work together in a specific way in her composition classes. "I use writing with every reading assignment, and then use the assignment to segue into discussion. Often it's very short." Here's an example exercise: "Pick out a quote that puzzles you and describe what you find puzzling." What's next? "We then write these on individual pieces of paper and pass them around, commenting in writing for ten minutes or so, then move into the discussion." Here are some follow-up exercises: "Under what circumstances do you envision the author coming to write this article?" "What—in the text and in your experience—makes you form this vision?" "Create a short (five-minute) writing assignment for the rest of the class which asks them to think through a major implication of the argument or perspective the article presents." Clearly Smith finds "assignments" to be generative. After reading her poem, explore why she finds the "five-paragraph essay" assignment so problematic. Compare her experiences with yours (and decide whether you find her metaphor effective, offensive, silly, sublime, etc.).

A five paragraph essay
reminds me of a blind date
with an ex-seminarian—
that long opening paragraph
of boring foreplay,
then the thesis: one, sterile,
over-emphatic thrust

not . . . awful, just . . . wearying.
And it goes on
with its three, dull interminable reasons
why I should take off my clothes,
each with its own turgid point:
he bought me steak, God said so,
we might die young.
His right hand, with its chilly fingers
trying to snake up my skirt,

the left fumbling—inept, but unrelenting—
trying to unhook my brassiere,
the strange medicinal smell
of his hard lipped kisses.

Each topic sentence with its own—
not very persuasive—support:
whispers that I'd love it,
grow huge breasts, be cured
of acne (I guess his scent—it's Clearasil).

Until, desperate,
approaching my curfew
or the end of the assigned 250 words,
he protrudes what he feels to be
his strongest argument into my ear
with his tongue—if I don't "do it"
his "things" will turn blue.

Not one real reason,
not one thing to remind me
why it's called "the body."

Then, the windows all fogged up,
and me wanting anything but this—
to read the comics, chew gum, nap—
we have to do the whole first part
all over again
because it's required that you have a conclusion—
a sad replay I am already forgetting
as the naugahyde scree-screes
under my garters
as I stare at the movement of my own shadow
in the foggy glass:

nothing worth remembering
nothing written here
worth taking home from school.

5

Classroom Authors

MAGGIE GERRITY

In Capital et Caritas

CONSIDER THIS:

When she composed this essay, Maggie Gerrity was a graduate student pursuing a degree in fiction writing. In her process narrative, she notes, "I believe every writer—every person, really, though writers tend to be more sensitive to it—has one event that shaped him or her significantly." Before you read Gerrity's "event," think back through the texts you've already read in this chapter. Can you identify crucial events in these writings that validate Maggie's observation? Think, too, about your own life. What event, or events, have been crucial in your maturation? Now, if you were to write about the most important of these, what method of development might you choose? What comes to mind immediately as your most likely writing strategy for this topic? As you read Gerrity's essay, compare the decisions she made for presenting her topic to those you might employ yourself to explore a similar set of issues.

I thought I'd die when he showed up for my confirmation in a green sport coat. In the basement of Saint Gregory's, my classmates tracked down their sponsors before the service: godparents in brown, older siblings in navy, aunts and uncles in gray. Wasn't it bad enough that I had to ask a teacher to be my sponsor, a sign to God and even worse to Deacon Wentzel that my family was a bunch of heathens? No, in front of my classmates, in front of kids I didn't know from CCD at Saint Mary's and Saint Cyril's, in front of all their families, in front of nearly every priest in the county—basically everyone good and holy within a twenty-mile radius—the Lucky Charms leprechaun was going to place his hand on my shoulder and vouch for the bright future of my spirituality.

Nine years later, I still believe in God thanks in large part to the man in the green sport coat—"Brother," I'll call him, since he insisted we're all brothers and sisters in Christ—but I certainly wouldn't call myself a Catholic anymore. It will be six years in November since we huddled around his open grave at Holy Cross Cemetery, me with his family under the green tent. I was his daughter, after all, not literally but in spirit, the daughter he knew he'd never have. His brothers were my uncles, his sister my aunt. I still have a purple flower from his funeral pressed between two pages of the Book of Job, those words I turned to so frequently in the months after his death. The Church had failed him. If we didn't talk about something, it was supposed to go away. God was supposed to absolve our sins. Brother wasn't supposed to die at fifty-six of complications to AIDS.

It made sense to me even in junior high why Brother's classroom and Deacon Wentzel's were at opposite ends of the two-story brick building and on different floors. Deacon Wentzel's God was the enforcer, the almighty warden, the giant hand that extended from a puffy cloud above the altar at Saint Mary's, the one that terrified me until I realized it looked like a one-legged man mooning the congregation. For Deacon Wentzel, I regurgitated psalms and the sayings of Jesus the way I did state capitals for Sister Maryann and the Our Father in Latin for Frau Vojkto—*Pater noster, qui est in coelis . . . .*

Brother introduced me to the God I still know today: protective, jubilant, and above all else, forgiving. He taught me I should carry God *in capital et caritas* (in head and heart) because He loved me always in all ways. Each year I contributed my favorite Bible verses to the paper chain that circled Brother's classroom. I can't remember the ones I chose, but when I flipped through the Good News Bible during sunny afternoons, he let me dawdle in the psalms or in John's gospel as long as I wanted. He told me if I wanted to learn how to write, I needed to read every book of the Bible. In ninth grade, Deacon Wentzel made the class clap for me because I'd been the first to read the entire New Testament.

I remember the day Brother came into class sophomore year, scrawled *dungarees* on the chalkboard, and said, "There are ninety-six words in dungarees. See if you can find them all." Then he sat at his desk and rested his head on his folded forearms, the gray of his thick Irish wool cardigan blending with the gray and black of his beard (suddenly more gray than black—when had that happened?). Not long after that, he hung a small black and white poster on a bulletin board in the back of the room: *What to do if someone you know has AIDS.* He never discussed it. He retired that August and started going to mass every day.

A year later, he was gone, dead at nine p.m. on Halloween, three hours after I'd gone to the hospital to see him, still disbelieving that he wouldn't recover from a two-week bout with double pneumonia. His sister said she could never let me see him that way, that I should keep the memory of him I always had—in front of a classroom or at mass, maybe in that green sport coat again. I missed several days of school, sat with his family at the funeral, then sulked in the back row of classrooms for the rest of the semester, speaking only when called on, sleeping through *The Merchant of Venice* or explanation of the respiratory system, a ghost of who I once was, irritable, rushing home every day after school just to cry. The guidance counselor and several concerned teachers put me on suicide watch, though at the time I wanted to move on with my life somewhere faraway from those claustrophobic hallways, not take it with my own hands.

I didn't learn the truth for eight months, a sunny July morning when my parents sat me down in the living room as soon as I woke. My mother did all the talking. It's two or three hours I've blocked out completely, except for small flashes—*gay, AIDS, didn't want anyone to know.* His retirement hadn't been his choice, exactly, she said; a kid hit him, and he lost his temper and hit the kid back (Joey Shay, my best friend would later tell me—that kid deserved to get knocked around a little). The county investigated such incidents, not the diocese, and if Brother wanted to keep teaching, he'd have to reveal his illness and expose the school to that scrutiny. He retired instead and told me once that after I graduated, he had a lot he wanted to tell me.

I've never seen Joey Shay since then, but if I ever do, at a high school carnival or in the grocery store down the street from his house, I can't say I won't lunge at him. No, that's not the Christian thing to do, but teaching had been everything to Brother, and he took that away from him when he mouthed off or pushed a smaller kid in the hallway and got caught. I hope God was watching that.

In college, I tried grief counseling, rainy afternoons in a too-quiet basement office with a soft-voiced man, but it felt too much like confession. What did I have to be sorry for? When the AIDS Quilt came to campus, I spent hours on my hands and knees on the wood floor of the gym, careful not to miss a single hand-sewn panel. I couldn't make a panel for Brother, couldn't tell that secret. Instead, I spent a year volunteering for a local AIDS organization, doing paperwork and writing their client newsletter. This, I told myself, was how I was supposed to move on.

But four years after Brother's death, I was still ashamed to admit I'd known someone who'd died of AIDS. I knew the stigma attached to the illness, and I wasn't brave enough to announce I'd loved a dying gay man like a father, bought him sweaters at Christmas and tacky ties on Father's Day, that he'd given me a sweet sixteen brunch and the claddagh necklace that rarely left my neck, the Irish symbol for friendship, loyalty, and love. What thirteen years of Catholic school had left me with was the delusion that if I remained silent about my grief, it would dissolve.

Now that I'm a teacher, I think of Brother almost every day. This semester, in a classroom with a chalkboard for the first time, I swear sometimes I smell his sweet cologne mixed with the chalk dust at the front of the room. I want to tell my students the same things Brother told me—"Load your brain before you shoot off your mouth," and "Silencio!" I grade their papers in green ink.

Brother wouldn't be ashamed that I've given up Catholicism. He refused to live in the shadow of Deacon Wentzel's God, too. My God teaches inclusion rather than exclusion, celebration rather than guilt, forgiveness rather than damnation. Secrets are safe with Him. In John's Gospel, Jesus proclaims: "One day you will know the truth, and the truth will set you free." I *am* free now, finally—of guilt, of embarrassment, of shame—and the truth I've found is that I don't need to have someone else's beliefs forced on me. I know my own now, thanks to Brother. He's still with me *in capital et caritas.* I'll never be ashamed to tell people that again.

WRITING PROCESS NARRATIVE FOR "IN CAPITAL ET CARITAS"

This is an essay I've been trying to write for two or three years but have never been able to focus enough. I believe every writer—every person, really, though writers tend to be more sensitive to it—has one event that shaped him or her significantly. For me, it was Brother's death. All my work deals in one way or another with my feelings surrounding his death: loss, abandonment, betrayal, trust.

What I like so much about the final product is that I don't talk about my writing but rather my faith. I'd never worked out in such a small space my reasons for giving up on Catholicism. This essay forced me to do that, to confront those old fears of Deacon Wentzel's version of damnation.

In the professional draft, I said Brother helped me understand why I needed to give up my Catholicism, but I never went back to it. My chronology was jumbled, in large part because I wanted to end with what I thought was a powerful image, those green Doc Martens. My group (Jay, Juli, and Ed) helped me to see that that image isn't all that powerful, and we discussed where the essay needed to go. They helped me to see it had to end with me as a teacher. It's a far more organic ending, and one I like far more. The style exercise in which we had to create more affirmative and ambiguous endings helped a lot, because it forced me to make tough statements and not back away from them.

Jay and Juli, in our final workshop, pushed me to open up a particularly puzzling section. They couldn't quite understand why Brother's illness had to be a secret. I talked to them about the circumstances of his retirement, and they said that information needed to be in my essay. Well, it is now, though I don't think it can stay when I revise a final time before sending the piece out.

I'm quite pleased with the final draft of this essay. I plan to send it to several journals focusing on faith and the arts, *Image* and *Mars Hill Review.* I think this piece has helped me to finally close that chapter of my life and start looking forward in a far more meaningful way, both as a writer and a person.

SANDRA GILES

"The Mediums, Their Message" (and earlier version, "The Medium")

CONSIDER THIS:

When drafting this essay, Sandra Giles, a graduate student studying fiction, composition, and rhetoric, conducted primary research by attending a meeting hosted by a chapter of the Foundation for Spiritual Knowledge to listen to a British medium, Libby Clark. Besides hoping to write an essay on a local event, Giles is also interested in spirituality; these twin interests led to a complicated initial draft, "The Medium," as she worked to find the appropriate form for sharing her observations and impressions. After a workshop in revising, Giles decided to narrow her paper's focus, thereby composing "The Mediums, Their Message." She says, "The story of my own spiritual search is a separate essay . . . well, book." How did refocusing the form and direction of her essay allow her to improve her work?

On a Thursday evening in May in Tallahassee, Florida, Libby Clark, a medium from England, spoke at the Unity Church on Crowder Road, near the Indian Mounds. At ten minutes past the announced starting time, the audience was as big as it was going to get, less than fifty people, mostly middle-aged, except for the three teenagers toward the back of the crowd, which was actually the middle of the room. Marilyn ___________ , head of the Tallahassee chapter of the Foundation for Spiritual Knowledge, introduced her, and she walked down the center aisle toward the stage from the back. She was forty-ish with blonde-colored hair, wearing a knee-length, sleeveless lavender dress. She looked like someone who would be seen working at a department store in the mall. Or someone in church. As she walked, the tail of her lavender scarf floated behind her like a silky, diaphanous cloud, but she walked like she was ready to get to the stage and begin, like her feet touched the ground firmly.

She walked up the three steps to the stage and turned toward the podium that had been pushed far to the right, as if she would speak from there, but instead, she lifted the microphone, took a sip of water from a glass that had been placed there for her, and walked to the center. She chatted a bit at first, amiably, establishing a rapport with the audience by discussing the hot, humid Florida weather, her voice soft and breathy, her accent British.

When it was time to begin the reading proper, she stood straight, feet together, and seemed to pull inward for a moment. She walked stage right and pointed to the far end of the second row. "I need to be in this area." She paused. "Does anyone have a middle-aged woman who passed? Maybe breast cancer? There was a time when the doctors cut something out, but it was too late." Libby continued, "She's very chatty, this one." Then she pointed to a woman named Sissy and said, "I'm with you, dear, the lady in the purple shirt. Do you know this woman? She's saying you do." Sissy answered in the affirmative, knowing the unwritten rules of being in the audience at this type of event: let the medium do most of the talking, filling in information only when specifically asked. "She's saying you talk to her daughters so they'll remember her, you show them photos and things. Who is she?" Sissy answered that the woman must be her late sister-in-law, her husband's sister.

Libby paused again before continuing, pulled inward again. "She's talking about dogs. She's calling them handbag dogs. Do you know what this means?" She looked confused, bending down to gesture that the dogs were small. Sissy nodded, saying that her sister-in-law used to joke about the number of dogs Sissy and her husband collected, strays, most of which were small enough to fit in a handbag. Libby nodded, pacing slowly from side to side. "She's also talking about the bird. The one who rings the telephone." Sissy was getting excited then, barely able to keep from blurting out too much information. She squirmed in her seat. Yes, she said, she has a parrot that mimics the telephone, causing the dogs to start barking and any people in the room to run for the phone. The bird gets a huge kick out of it, and so do Sissy's nieces. Libby said that the sister-in-law's message was one of gratitude to Sissy for keeping her memory alive to her daughters. "She wants you to keep doing it. Will you?" Sissy put her hand over her mouth and nodded, her eyes filling with tears. But the medium had one last request for Sissy: to tell her husband that his sister came through. And to tell him about the parrot. "He'll drop his teeth!"

The messages were like that, reassuring, full of thanks and encouragement for the living, full of reassurances that the departed ones were just fine on the other side. Happy. One woman received a message from a son who had died a decade before, in his late teen years. During this last year, she had apparently endured health problems and problems with surviving children, and a divorce. His message: these were experiences that would make her stronger. That she was doing fine and he was proud of her. That he was perfectly fine and happy, and still with her, and that there was nothing more she could have done to prevent his death.

After the reading, that woman stood in the back of the sanctuary surrounded by a small circle of her friends. "I'm so relieved," she said. "I've been so worried. So guilty I didn't do more." She breathed a long, deep sigh as her friends patted her on the shoulders and hugged her.

Marilyn patted her on the shoulder. "That's what it's all about," she said.

THE MEDIUM

I had expected her to look like a gypsy, I guess. I had found out about her from Sissy, a friend of mine: Libby Clark, a visiting spiritualist medium from England, in Tallahassee to give a public reading at the Unity Church on a Thursday evening in May. I suppose I should have had Jonathan Edwards in mind, the quite normal-looking guy on television, calmly and oh, so credibly relaying messages to people in his audience sitting on black platforms like bleachers. He wears Docker-like pants and sweaters.

Still, as I waited in line to pay the $10 fee, I looked around the small sanctuary for an obese woman in gypsy skirts, with hundreds of bangles on her wrist and rings on every finger. With a red or purple bandana covering her hair. As I sat waiting for the reading to begin, thumbing through the hymnal from the shelf under the chair in front of me, I searched for a costume like I'd dressed up in for Halloween, when I was a kid. Or like the get-up of the fortune teller I visited at a school carnival when I was ten, who looked into a big eight ball and announced in a quivering falsetto, "Your life will be changing soon." Then she'd taught me how to jiggle the eight ball and get a different pre-fab message.

Sissy, sitting beside me, asked if there was anybody who had passed, from whom I wanted to receive a message. I nodded. I wasn't sure I really wanted to receive a message, though. I wasn't sure I believed any of this could be real. I was still thinking of gypsy skirts.

At ten minutes past the announced starting time, the audience was as big as it was going to get, less than fifty people, mostly middle-aged, all quite normally dressed except for the three band-member-looking teenagers toward the back snickering. At that point, a middle-aged woman named Marilyn, head of the Tallahassee chapter of the Foundation for Spiritual Knowledge, introduced Libby Clark, the medium from England. Down the center aisle walked a forty-ish woman with blonde-colored hair. She wore a knee-length lavender dress, sleeveless, with white strappy heels. She looked like someone who would be seen working at a department store in the mall. Or someone in church. As she walked, the tail of her lavender scarf floated behind her like a silky, diaphanous cloud, but she walked normally, like she was ready to get to the stage and begin, like her feet—in the impossibly narrow white straps—touched the ground firmly. My heart leapt into my throat. I thought maybe I might get a message after all. Surely someone would. This could be real, couldn't it?

As it turned out, I didn't hear from anybody, but several people from the audience did, including Sissy. Libby Clark walked stage right and pointed in our direction. She said, "I need to be in this area now." She paused. "Does anyone have a middle-aged woman who passed? Maybe breast cancer? There was a time when the doctors cut something out, but it was too late." Sissy poked me with her elbow. Libby continued, "She's very chatty, this one." Then she pointed to Sissy and said, "I'm with you, dear, the lady in the purple shirt. Do you know this woman? She's saying you do." Sissy answered in the affirmative, knowing the unwritten rules of being in the audience at this type of event: let the medium do most of the talking, filling in information only when specifically asked. "She's saying you talk to her daughters so they'll remember her, you show them photos and things. Who is she?" Sissy answered that the woman must be her late sister-in-law, her husband's sister.

Libby paused again before continuing. "She talking about dogs. She's calling them handbag dogs. Do you know what this means?" She looked confused, bending down to gesture that the dogs were small. Sissy nodded, saying that her sister-in-law used to joke about the number of dogs Sissy and her husband collected, strays, most of which were small enough to fit in a handbag. "She's also taking about the bird. The one who rings the telephone." Sissy was getting excited then, barely able to keep from blurting out too much information. She squirmed in her seat. Yes, she said, she has a parrot that mimics the telephone, causing the dogs to start barking and any people in the room to run for the phone. The bird gets a huge kick out of it, and so do Sissy's nieces. Libby said that the sister-in-law's message was one of gratitude to Sissy for keeping her memory alive to her daughters. "She wants you to keep doing it. Will you?" Sissy put her hand over her mouth and nodded, her eyes filling with tears. But the medium had one last request for Sissy: to tell her husband that his sister came through. And to tell him about the parrot. "He'll drop his teeth!"

The messages were like that, reassuring, full of thanks and encouragement for the living, full of reassurances that the departed ones were just fine on the other side. Happy. One woman received a message from a son who had died a decade before, in his late teen years. During this last year, she had apparently endured health problems and problems with surviving children, and a divorce. His message: these were experiences that would make her stronger. That she was doing fine and he was proud of her. That he was perfectly fine and happy, and still with her, and that there was nothing more she could have done to prevent his death.

After the reading, that woman stood in the back of the sanctuary surrounded by a small circle of her friends. "I'm so relieved," she said. "I've been so worried. So guilty I didn't do more." She breathed a long, deep sigh as her friends patted her on the shoulders and hugged her.

Marilyn caught my eye. "That's what it's all about," she said.

I still didn't know what I thought about these "readings." But what I felt was comforted, about the welfare of my loved ones, both on the other side and here. And if it wasn't real, then what was the harm, really? I suppose someone absolutely desperate to hear from a departed one could be ten-dollared to bankruptcy, but as Libby had explained at the end of the reading, we don't really need mediums. We have our dreams, and our vague intuitions when we suddenly think of Grandma or Great-Aunt Sis. "You don't need people like me, not really," she had said. "Trust yourselves."

As I walked through the parking lot, I saw the group of three teenagers snickering and sneering amongst themselves, probably on a hunt for faults or contradictions.

I gave them a wide berth.

WRITING PROCESS FOR "THE MEDIUMS, THEIR MESSAGE"

This will eventually be part of a longer piece which will explore the Foundation for Spiritual Knowledge in Tallahassee, Florida, which is a group of local people in training to be mediums and spiritual healers. These two goals are intertwined.

The essay started this way: as a class prompt, we were to describe ourselves as an article of clothing, and I wrote that I'd like to be a fuchsia scarf worn with a black wool coat. Later, as I was sorting through the freewrites from that day, trying to come up with an idea for a "Brief" essay, the scarf immediately reminded me of Libby Clark (thus, I guess, the emphasis on her scarf in draft 1).

In draft 1, "Angels," I really didn't intend to do anything more than report what I had seen. I didn't intend it to be a personal essay, but the last line did remark that I gave the snickering teenagers (who had annoyed me greatly throughout the performance) a wide berth. The peer reviewers picked up on that and asked me to put more of myself in there—why had I gone? Why was I interested? Had it changed me? Etc.

So in the next draft, "The Medium," I explored my own interests and reactions a bit more, but I found myself tempted to slip into this whole big exploration of my own beliefs and my own spiritual search—which is a whole 'nother essay, not this one—so I had to back off on that, and I think I backed off too much. My groupmates still wanted a bit more along those lines.

In the meantime, I'd decided to change this from a brief essay to a *New Yorker* style essay, since it did describe a visit around town. But from the Monday group workshop to the following Wednesday (when drafts were due for the whole class), I didn't have time to do much but change some wording and add a paragraph of description. From that Monday to the Wednesday, I had graded a set of my students' essays, responded to drafts of their next one, and begun individual conferences with them. Phew!

In any case, many whole-class reviewers asked for a longer, deeper piece, and I really liked that idea, so what I have in this current version, "The Mediums, Their Message," will simply be a small part of a larger piece, as described above. I don't want very much of myself at all in there, except as "the reporter." The story of my own spiritual search is a separate ess—well, book.

AMANDA FLEMING

"Not Your Typical Martha Stewart Decorating Tip" and "Girlfriend's Guide: Getting that Trophy Husband"

CONSIDER THIS:

To compose an essay on taxidermy and hunting—two subjects she had some experience with and mixed feelings about—Amanda Fleming, a graduate student in creative writing at the time of completing these essays, researched her topic.

She composed "Not Your Typical Martha Stewart Decorating Tip" as an alternately styled essay that weaves together narrative, double-voice (inserted boxed author's comments), description, satire, lists, and fact sheets in a way that causes readers to reflect on their own attitudes toward this subject. In her second essay, "Girlfriend's Guide," which grew out of the research and writing of the first essay, Fleming writes broad (and inevitably critical) satire by parodying both etiquette and how-to manuals as she suggests, in an unexpected reversal, how women might hunt . . . men. With this strategy, her text takes its place within a long tradition of literary satire and echoes Jonathon Swift's "Modest Proposal." The course assignment for Amanda Fleming's class was to intentionally create two essays from the same initial research. As you read these pieces, and before you read Fleming's process narrative, speculate on how she composed these texts; given these products, what steps do you think this writer followed to arrive at two very different locations after leaving from the same starting point?

"You wouldn't hear a redneck say deer heads detract from the decor."

—Jeff Foxworthy

When I was eleven my mother would haul me over to her friend's house so she could drink pot after pot of coffee. Meanwhile, the lady's Chihuahua and I sat together and watched TV. The Currys placed their television set just off to the side of the chimney, and during commercials my eyes kept shifting to the deer above the mantle, its placid gaze surveying people enter and exit through the front door—the Watch Deer.

In the privacy of the living room, I put the dog on the floor and stepped up onto the brick fireplace. As if I were petting a live horse, I took a single finger and slid it with the flow of hair back between its two ears. The hair felt stiff, coarse. And when I pressed down on it I felt resistance, not like a cat's head where the skin floats along the bone. The antlers reminded me of hard celery, with ridges running up through the various branches of the rack. 6 points. I looked in its eyes. Shiny and dark. No pupil. Just black.

"You like my deer?" Mr. Curry caught me red-handed, getting sentimental over his decoration. "I shot him last winter, up at Moore's Pasture."

"Don't you ever dust him?" I smart-assed.

"I saw him at daylight," Mr. Curry went on, "eating corn off of a food plot about 100 feet long and 15 feet wide. He was a pretty deer, standing there in the morning dew."

"Not so pretty now, hanging up here, dead. Collecting dust."

"I sat in that deer stand for two years before I sighted him." Mr. Curry walked up to me. With a tight fist he knocked on the deer's neck. He sounded like hollow plastic.

"At least if he were still alive he could clean himself."

He left the room and came back with a feather duster, when what I needed was a vacuum cleaner with a hose attachment. I didn't want to brush over the deer's eyes, afraid the animal could still feel, and might flinch.

"They aren't real. And neither is that nose." Mr. Curry knocked on the nose with a knuckle. "Just the hide."

"You took out its eyes?" I thought, astonished. *"Don't you know it can still see?"*

Mental Note: One thing you'll always hear from behind you as you stare up toward someone's dusty deer head: "Yep, there's a long story behind that." Prepare yourself.

Thomasville, Georgia, is home to George and Louie's Restaurant, Pebble Hill Plantation, Myrtlewood Hunting Plantation, and Harden's Taxidermy on East Jackson Street. Harden's provides their customers with standard mounting services but also provides creative custom mounts. Boyfriend (my darling hunter/fisher extraordinaire) and I walked Jackson Street and were taken in by the front window of Harden's.

Item #1: Turkey.

Entire turkey gutted, cleaned, and mounted in this manner: upside down, hanging from its claws by a rope attached to a tree limb. From time to time the a/c or a ceiling fan will hopefully produce enough of a breeze to allow the turkey to turn around, enabling the viewer to see all sides of the bird. (The owner might need to live in a museum to properly display this mount.)

Item #2: Bass.

Four bass, one bream, all gutted, cleaned and mounted on the bottom magazine laying area of a coffee table below the glass. Add some fake grass, some sand and rocks. Then PRESTO! The river comes to your living room.

Item #3: Rattlesnake.

Entire body of diamondback rattlesnake, cleaned and positioned in a coil, head erect, fangs open to the public. Good to scare burglars. Good to scare unwanted kids.

Item #4: Deer.

A buck and a doe, both cleaned and positioned side by side on a double wood head and neck mount, gazing toward each other. Some of Boyfriend's friends call it the "Romeo and Juliet" mount.

Item #5: Triceratops.

Head mount, displayed over front doorway. Only noticeable when customers leave display area to the outside. It takes a few steps before they really *notice* what the hell it is.

On this day, Boyfriend could not be pulled away from his conversation with one of the processors, so I wandered around, poking at the displays with animal bone tactically placed in patterns along the various mounts. "Honey," he said when he'd finished trading numbers, figures, opening and closing dates, "don't you just love this place?"

"Yeah. I never knew dead stuff could keep my attention so long."

"Yeah, this is exactly how I want our house to look."

Once you've killed it . . .

Sailfish 80"	$559.95
Turkey	$400–500
Barracuda	$329.95
Goose	$250–300
Bass 21"–27"	$199.95
Deer	$150–300
Duck	$160

Not too long ago I helped Boyfriend move into his new apartment, one where we could be alone. We unpacked turkey decoys. We unpacked jumbo-sized bottles of deer urine. Scent-A-Way. Wild hog's teeth. Four pair of boots. Three boxes of t-shirts (exclusively for hunting and fishing). Three tackle boxes. One television (to watch the Outdoor Network). A grill (to cook his fish). I could tell this new apartment wasn't going to be the romantic weekend get-away spot I'd imagined. I searched his boxes for a picture to hang on one of the bare walls, a candle to decorate the stale bathroom, a plant to liven up the bedroom, its walls dungy and dirty white. He shook his head when I actually found air freshener. "Not this close to hunting season."

I found it charming that he was the one to suggest we check out the flea market, and I deemed it promising that he actually bought two framed prints of deer in the wild. When he got them back and hung them on the wall of the living room, he got quiet. "You know, one of my deer mounts would look good centered on that wall between the two pictures." He was thinking hard about how soon he'd get his deer mount back from the taxidermist. I was thinking, *My goodness, if I marry this guy my whole house may be decorated with dead stuff. What does Martha Stewart say about decorating with dead animals? Would she want me to sell out to the "Rustic Lodge" look?*

"I don't know honey. You'd have to hang it up about right here." I pointed to the spot in the wall about shoulder level. "The antlers are going to hit the ceiling if you hang it any higher. But, you're going to bang your head into it, you know."

"Hey," he said, grinning. "It's going to look huge in here." He was right. His apartment was small. He kissed my cheek. "You are so smart. That's why I love you."

Except from: "Spouses may not see eye-to-eye over where to put the hunting trophy"

—BY MICHAEL H. HODGES

> At Rooftop Landing in Lewiston, owner Dave Aldrich displays about 30 heads, a number of which, he says, were donated by aggrieved husbands. But his favorite is the moose. Some poor fellow, it seems, was going through a bitter divorce and, as Aldrich tells it, was heaved out by his wife with nothing more than the van, a sack of clothes and his moose head to his name.
>
> When the guy showed up at Rooftop Landing offering his moose head, Aldrich couldn't understand why he'd want to part with it.
>
> The answer was painfully simple. When the moose was in the van, the homeless fellow explained, there wasn't any room left for him to sleep.

Mental Note: One winter morning, around 2 a.m., take one of the preserved deer hooves off the shelf and mark tracks around your favorite hunter's truck. Go back to sleep. Wake up in time to see the look on your hunter's face.

I was waiting for Boyfriend to finish getting ready to go out to eat, flipping through channels on his television, trying to avert my eyes from staring at the new treasures he'd found while walking in the woods. On top of the television lay two rattles (one from a diamondback rattlesnake), a deer skull positioned comically atop a wild boar jaw (a wild mental image if you were trying to figure out what animal it was alive), and an assortment of tortoise shells. I saw the videotape: *Teach Yourself Taxidermy.* On the cover was a stuffed fox, a mounted duck and a walleyed raccoon waving one paw.

"Honey?" I held the video in my hand and waited for him to come out of the living room. "I think there's something you need to explain."

"Do you want me to put it in for you?" he asked.

"No. And I don't want to find out you're gutting raccoons on the front porch."

"Do you know how much money I'll save? I may start a new career."

"I know what a mess you'll make. The answer's *no.*"

Mental Note: Buy film on his credit card. Splurge on the camera *you* want. Justify it by putting on a smile when he comes in at midnight and wants a picture of him beside the 8-point on his tailgate.

I won't lie. I met men who hunted, men who fished. But their wives stayed home. I made myself almost enjoy the feel of worm and cricket guts, though I can't cast a bait-caster without getting backlash to save my poor pitiful life. I know it would impress some hunters if their beloved could nail a 10-point, bag a 20 lb. turkey, or reel in a 15 lb. large-mouth wall hanger.

I confess. I made Christmas bow ties for his 2 deer mounts one year.

I watched him gut a young male deer in the driveway of his parents' house, the water hose washing the fresh blood out into the street. He cut a t-slice in its abdomen with his buck knife, careful as he removed the sac as not to break it, which would cause a foul odor of entrails. "I don't waste the meat," he told me. Hunting didn't seem as cruel after that.

I ate venison, the spike's meat. And liked it. He cooked it in spaghetti in the place of hamburger meat. He packed a good argument, that deer wasn't considered red meat, and it was healthier than most kinds of meat because it has less fat. He knew a guy who had a heart attack last year and now eats deer meat because his doctor recommended it. I brought several packages of deer sausage back to college with me and placed the white butcher shop waxed paper packed in the freezer with the stamped word DEER staring back at me each time I grabbed a handful of ice.

Venison—365 Days a Year

Old Texas Settlers Venison

Chicken Fried Venison

Quick Venison Chili

Venison Picadillo

Venison, Sausage, and Rice Supreme

Venison Scallopini

Venison Meatballs Teriyaki

Venison Wok Melange

—TAKEN FROM *BEST OF THE BEST FROM TEXAS COOKBOOK*

Mental Note: Never, ever ask the attendant to spray "new car" scent into your favorite hunter's truck during hunting season. It takes approximately four bottles and two months to make the truck deer-friendly again.

I won't lie. It has crossed my mind. It still does. Waking up at four a.m., hiking two miles through mosquitoes and dark wood just to sit in a "condo" and wait. Waiting. Waiting. Waiting. Holding the gun steady. Taking aim through the scope.

I spent $300 on a Minolta 100–300 zoom lens to see if *that* would get me into the woods, both to find out for myself and to satisfy some craving of my lonely hunter, who wanted his beloved to share in the experience of being quiet enough ("Don't you cough, or sneeze, or whack at any mosquitoes"), patient enough ("You better bring one of your books"), and lucky enough ("Don't even think of washing your hair with scented shampoo or spraying on perfume") to see a deer in the wild come into view. In the early morning we waited, listening for hooves brushing through palmettos, but instead we heard a symphony of crickets and frogs, sometimes pausing for an interlude, tall pines waving their needles down to earth, and a dove whooping out into the cold air.

We hoped that any minute a buck, maybe even a doe, would strut out of the brush and into the clearing. If it were a buck, it would proudly hold its rack high. He wouldn't know we were there—me and my beloved, crouched in a green and brown spray-painted tree house, our bodies pushed together, our breathing halted, our hearts beating out of our chests and vibrating three layers of clothing for something you don't see everyday.

Mental Note: Bears can climb deer stands. If you "deer watch," at least know how to shoot.

When a weary hunter comes in from a long day at the mill, and upon taking off his work shoes he catches a glimpse of his very own mount over the chimney, what comes to mind probably isn't, "Me big hunter. Me kill deer." I can't vouch for every hunter, but according to Boyfriend, it's the memory of the deer, unaware, poised and majestic, that comes to mind.

The hunter doesn't necessarily remember all the long, cold winter mornings spent just sitting, doesn't necessarily remember the money spent on equipment or the time spent fine tuning each piece and part, doesn't necessarily remember how heavy all the clothing felt, how many afternoons after work he spent throwing out corn, or how frustrated he felt, two days before hunting season was over, that maybe, just maybe, he'd wasted another five-hundred dollars on a stupid hunting lease claiming to have deer. The hunter will have long forgotten about the taste of the deer's meat, the excited feeling searching for the fallen deer through thorn vines and poison ivy, and how it felt like the taxidermist would never finish the mount.

Quick Itemized List of Basic Necessities:

Rocky 800 Gram Bear Claw Hunting Boots	$159.99
Cabela's Thermax Blister-Free Socks	$7.99
Cabela's Rain Suede Packable Rainwear	
Pants	$84.95
Parka	$99.95
Mossy Oak Break-Up Ensemble:	
Jeans	$29.95
100% cotton denim uninsulated shirt	$34.95
Denim hat	$12.95
Blaze Gear Vest	$34.95
Ruger Bolt Action Rifle	$469.95
Pentax 3X9 scope	$399.95
Bolistic Tipped Bullets 30.06	$24.95
Break-up Thumb Loop Sling	$15.99
Buck Knife, Vanguard Wood Design	$69.99
Hunters View Timber Ghost Stand	$79.99
Ameristep Step-up Pegs, 20-pack	$39.99
Econo-Feeder Kit (Deer Feeder)	$29.99
Scent Killer, 8 Ounce Bottle	$5.49
Trophy 3-Call Deer Kit	$27.99
1-year Hunting Lease (Moore's Pasture)	$300.00
Bumper Buddy (42 pounds of crafted aluminum)	$189.99
Tasco 60X70 binoculars	$299.99

And lastly . . . .

Windstopper Gloves (with the half-finger design and mitten that flips back when you need your trigger finger; has a Windstopper lining for low heat loss and 150-gram Thinsulate Lite Loft insulation)	$24.95
TOTAL:	Way Too Much

> Mental Note: Good news. If he spends $160 on a pair of Maui Jim film-coated for fewer scratches, polarized sunglasses, then you get a pair, too!

I won't lie. I didn't just think about it. A January afternoon we drove out to Allentown, Florida, out past the shanty houses and the eight-pew churches, through a tunnel of long leaf pine trees, out to the intra-costal waterway. He propped up a beer flat with a bulls eye drawn in Sharpee in the middle. We inserted our ear plugs, he took aim, leaning his body against the bed wall of the truck, his feet flat for stability, and fired. Even through the earplugs I felt a ringing in my ears.

"Your turn," I heard his muted voice. I held the rifle (not so light), began to take aim (felt his hands moving mine in a new position), took aim again (felt his feet kick my feet apart and his voice saying, "farther apart,"), took aim again and this time took a deep breath. I could barely see the bull's eye through the scope. It looked fuzzy, often times shifting out of view then back in again. I could not hold it still. "How can you shoot a deer if you can't even shoot a tree?" I knew when I fired the recoil would make me jump. I'd miss the target. I'd drop the gun. I'd ruin the gun. Now that I was closer to the chamber, it would hurt my ears. It would make me jump. I took aim, because I was always a tomboy. Because I was always the one leading the other tent mates into the dark tent at Girl Scout camp, the one to not turn down the dare of eating an entire jalapeno pepper. But I could not pull the trigger.

Q. Before you got started with this paper, did you know you wanted to use so many fractured narratives and lists?

A. Yes, but I could never find the backbone I wanted. In researching deer heads and taxidermy, I found more information on taxidermy in general, and the facts I found out about deer heads involved the gutting and mounting, and how fun is that? When I chose the layout for this paper, I had already written two pages. I decided to use my own personal experience about deer heads and dead animals as decoration, but without focusing too solidly on these objects I tried to veer off toward my views on hunting. After the paper went to workshop, I felt like I had not accomplished what I set out to. I felt like I had not focused close enough.

Q. When you wrote this paper, what other sources did you use besides the factual information you found in newspapers and on the Internet?

A. To be honest, I tried to use my memory and past experiences. Luckily, I am the type of person who tries to have an exciting life, one exciting enough to write about. Sadly, this does pose a problem, for I tend to get in over my head at times, but I always have something to write about. I originally watched the gutting of the spike with the intention of writing about it one day. Sometimes I feel like a cheat, living just to write. But I forgive myself.

Q. Did you use all the information you wanted to?

A. No. I have never shot and mounted my own doe/buck/creature. However, if I had, that would be a nice way to show how I have come to appreciate hunting as a sport and deer meat as a new breakfast food. I did leave out so much information, as I expected I would, but again, the information was not as easy to find as I thought. And what I found was not so easy to mold into any sort of paper.

Q. When you wrote this, did you become preoccupied with the subject?

A. Yes. I started stopping by hunting stores, talking to hunters, ordering hunting catalogs, and looking for deer heads in interior decoration. By focusing so tightly on "deer heads" I had to be consumed, to some degree. I looked for information everywhere, looked for parallels in everything.

Q. Would you use this information to write a short story?

A. Yes. Actually, I started one a while back but could never keep it going because I did not have enough information, I did not know what it was like to mount a deer.

GIRLFRIEND'S GUIDE: GETTING THAT TROPHY HUSBAND

> Supplement to Girlfriend's Guide: "How to Make a Fabulous French Clutch out of your Neighbor's Noisy Dachshund"

Let me get this out in the open. I like men—fried. I have numerous human activist groups protesting outside my house, carrying signs advocating the preservation of men, and shouting, "Men have feelings, too! Men have feelings, too!" From time to time one of them gives my BMW a flat tire. They mail me convincing letters about how men should be preserved for society, for the love of nature. And many letters ask something along the lines of, "How could you harm such a creature and live with yourself? What if you were a man?" They mail them on "green" scented stationary (which works just dandy for livening up your lingerie drawer). They send professional photographs taken of men during their daily routine, sleeping soundly, sauntering along a river looking for food, and one photograph I felt particularly schmaltzy about—a man standing over his young as they watched snow fall for the first time. Whenever I bite into a tender, perfectly marinated piece of thigh muscle, I admit, I tend to feel a bit devilish.

In my favor, I never waste a man. I make sure I use every last piece of him. The neck meat is best used for stew beef or chop beef. I usually save the loins for special occasions, like when I have friends over and can break out the chops for the grill. If it's wrapped in bacon and grilled over an open flame, honey, hold me down. Although I don't use the hands, I found a taxidermist who can mount them, palms up, and I give them as Christmas presents to my girlfriends. They make nifty little key holders to sit on the kitchen counter. What those activists do not understand is that butchering a man is no easy job. Cutting up one hindquarter is fairly easy, but it usually takes me five to six days to package the entire creature, so I spread it out. Each day I have to drain the blood and add new ice into the cooler. It's really a mess! (For more information, see Girlfriend's Guide: "101 Ways to Butcher Your Man Once You Get Him Home.")

Trophy men. Let me be the first to inform you, there's more to bagging a trophy man than just setting up camp in his front yard, waiting for him to walk out unbeknownst, bludgeoning him (or whatever your choice of slaying) and dragging him into your trunk. I've put hours and hours into this hobby, slaving over a hot caffe latte many a late hour planning my strike.

The first thing I learned was when to make your move. Daylight is so definitely out of the question if he lives in a highly populated neighborhood—for obvious reasons. But if you get into your stand about 4 a.m. and wait, trophy man will walk out the front door to get his morning newspaper, still groggy and donned in his tattered bathrobe. A loose robe belt is a good sign he's not fully awake. Men are creatures of habit. He will walk straight to the newspaper, pick it up, and walk back inside. Some men have variations in their routine: wave to neighbor Louie, pull out the trashcan, turn on a sprinkler, and so on. Be wary. Take notes. Leave food where he'll see it. Leave *good* food. Here is my foolproof list of the top 5 food items that attract men:

1. Thick Steak
2. Beer
3. Pork Rinds
4. Ice Cream
5. Pizza

Remember to leave food out for men during the non-hunting season. Don't be greedy and only leave food when you are hoping to capture them. That's just not fair.

As one hunter to another, I am going to give you a valuable piece of information I acquired waiting too many hours for one man to strike at a hot box of pizza. Here's your million dollar tip: power tools. A simple Craftsman (has to be a Sears Craftsman) power drill at the end of an extension cord does just the trick when you need to lure your prey into some shrubbery.

Your lookout post may be as simple as an already built tree house or as complex as a camouflaged shrubbery domicile. The idea is not to be seen coming, going, or waiting, so consider where you are going to park your car. Once in the stand, your fanny may tell you that wood stands are cumbersome, so consider a lightweight pillow with closures that snap onto the rump of your pants. This gives you less to carry with you. (I found I could sew just about anything to my camouflage jump suit: flashlights, hair scrunchies, nail files.)

I do not wish to sway you one way or the other in regards to the act of taking down your kill. Sport hunters like the quick response they get from a rifle, and hunters who have developed their talents choose to bow hunt for a greater challenge. I personally like to load four run-of-the-mill bricks in my alligator purse and approach my prey from behind. Once unconscious, I can drag the man to the trunk. Once he gains consciousness, I apologize profusely and offer him a glass of water, to which I have added arsenic. Other sport hunters do not look fondly on my strategy. For one, it's risky. I lost two men already once they gained consciousness, and I lost one when my alligator purse strap snapped and the whole thing went flying through the air during the swing. Not only was he unhappy I tried to kill him, but he wasn't too keen I'd taken out his entire front picture glass window.

I chose a BMW as my vehicle as choice. What man in his right mind would suspect a woman who drives a powder blue Bavarian auto of stalking? I also wear something along these lines: a tan mini skirt, sheer hose, alligator moccasins, pair of gold hoop earrings, white v-neck sweater (no sleeves), and an alligator headband (so my bangs don't fall in my eyes). I try to dress casual, yet elegant. What you choose to wear is up to you, but the more you look like you are about to snare your prey the worse chance you have of doing so. Although perfume helps your self-esteem, ladies, please refrain from smelling like a perfume counter when you take down your kill. Your victim may smell you before he sees you, and therefore he may be on guard.

Trophy men are butchered like any other wild game, but their elegance is preserved through the hanging of their heads on the wall next to your faux Renoir with the gold ornate frame. If you've gone through all the motions of trapping your man, you don't want to wait three years to get him back again from the taxidermist. If you've ever called your local taxidermist and felt like you knew their answering machine intimately you might have told yourself there has to be a better way. If you've been thinking about teaching yourself the art of butchering and preserving your kill, I'm here to tell you: It isn't that hard. Remember, you may handle your mount 30 times before he ever gets to your living room wall. Skinning. Cleaning. Preserving. Gluing. Drying. Brushing. Gelling. Drying some more. It's a mess that only Avon Skin-So-Soft can fix. Give yourself about four months, maybe more, from start to finish. Know that good mounts take time and patience. (For more information, see Girlfriend's Guide: "Turning Your Man into a Decoration.")

Men are killed for trophies everyday. Some end up on walls. Some end up mounted, full body forms. Some fall into the hands of crafty taxidermists who are clever enough to create a mount of the man jumping out of a wall. The mounts can be crafted into shoulder mounts looking right, looking left, or in a creeping stance for lower ceilings. Some mounts end up in competitions where artists feature their mounts in various facial expressions (happy, serene, angry, macho). Consider your surroundings. Ask yourself what kind of tone you want to set for your guests. As a rule, I always display men of a series together (e.g., The men I landed at Howard's Creek boat landing made a fine addition to the "fishing" motif in my guest room). I feel it gives consistency to a room without being the dominant fixture.

Sadly, even some of the top sport hunters have had spousal disputes as to where (or if) the mount gets hung in the house. Mandy Seitz, owner of Seitz's Tavern, has a longstanding agreement with her customers to hang any mounts that they bag in her bar. A half dozen mounts grace the walls of the trendy Chelsea watering hole. One of the items is road kill, Seitz explained, but the rest were trophies bequeathed by women who "were probably happy their husbands didn't have to make the decision" about exhibiting them at home. When asked whether her husband would let her display a trophy in their home, Seitz, speaking from behind the bar, answered carefully: "I can hang one up here any time I like."

Seitz's husband, John, explained that he had come "full circle" in regards to the hunting issue. Early in their courtship, he gladly accompanied his wife on a hunting trip. Once his wife shot the "man," John extended his arm to touch the creature and wish it farewell. However, the "man" lunged upward and tried to stand. "I jumped like two feet," he said, "and

Mandy had to shoot that man in the neck at point-blank range. It's soured me for all time." He explained that when he sees a man mount ("And we've got a whole slew in the bar") he just feels downhearted. He understood his wife's need to "tromp through the [neighborhoods] and destroy living things," he says, "but when I look at the mounts now, I just think they need to be vacuumed. And from a man's point of view, that's probably the bottom line."

When you finally have your man mounted and ready to go onto your wall, you'll probably want to display it right away and in the middle of the action: above the television, in view of the front door, in the central room of the house. However, you've gone through the work of stalking, planning, bagging, cleaning, butchering, and preparing your mount. You may have four months, maybe more, behind you. Your mate has not had this experience. He has not swung an alligator purse loaded with four bricks. He was not there when you put the last staple in the mount. Understand your mate may have the same passion for collecting stamps as you do for your own hobby. Be patient. Courteous hunters not only know how to show respect to their partners but also to the prey they have taken down. Dust your mount regularly. Use a horse grooming brush and hair gel to preserve the man's hair style, and wipe your mount with a warm damp rag once a month to keep your mount looking as good as the day you bagged it. Be sure to read my supplement ("Turning Your Man into a Decoration") with *unwavering* attention. Follow each step. Do not get impatient! It's just like having your nails painted; don't walk into the kitchen before it's set. Store your meat properly under the appropriate conditions. Remember to package the meat in the appropriate wrapper. Do not *waste* the meat. You killed it. You have to eat it. Do not push the meat to the rear of the freezer. Do not continue to buy ground beef when you have perfectly good meat at home. Lastly, be fair. Be humane. Show your mount the respect it deserves. And show it off every chance you get!

WRITING PROCESS NARRATIVE FOR "GIRLFRIEND'S GUIDE"

STAGE 1

I wish I could say this one just came to me in a flash, that I'd had the idea brewing for days, weeks even, but I did not. In fact, I made a TOTAL revision two days before it was due. My original idea was simply to explore the topic of "taxidermy," perhaps give a run down on how to skin and mount your own deer head, and maybe even turn it (eventually) into an awesome article/interview of a taxidermist I know.

First thing I did before either paper was research magazine articles and "weird" news to get an angle. I found tons of info, but what I lacked was a structure. What I ended up with on "Not Your Typical" was the result of many (many) lunges toward a common ground. What I came up with on "Not Your Typical" is truly opposite my views in "Girlfriend's Guide" (or whatever I call it).

STAGE 2

I stopped by the taxidermist and discussed various aspects of taxidermy with Gerald Hammock, and I even got a grand tour of his facilities (cutting room, cooler, display area, drying room). I have to say Gerald doesn't have a "thing" for cleanliness. I mean, he had everything where he could get to them, and he had LOTS of examples of trophies, manikins, skins, horns/antlers, and other animal carcasses. The room had the aroma of Au De Rotten Wild Hog. I took notes, and afterwards I called him and interviewed him on the process of the actual "mounting." I was not happy with this because I did not get to "watch" a mounting. The full process takes anywhere from several days to several weeks (and with Gerald, several MONTHS). So I was ready to ditch the idea, but I gave it a try.

What I found was that giving the reader a list four pages long regarding the cutting up and preservation of a deer was probably not going to fly, *after all.* What I would have to do is never mention "meat," "skin," "blood," or "death." Not so good.

STAGE 3

So, I took a mini-vacation and didn't touch it for about two days. I let it simmer. I watched what was going on in the world, watched format, looked for structure, and searched for some radical way I could present my material.

STAGE 4

As I turned onto HWY 20 from HWY 231 I headed back from my vacation (exactly 20 miles from home) it hit me in a flash. I had not expected to have a vision of men heads, but I did! At first I drove along thinking how I could make it work, what angles I could take, how I could make it funny. When I got in, before I unpacked, I wrote. What I came up with was a not-so rough draft of my finished copy.

STAGE 5

Once I drafted this essay, I have to admit, there wasn't a tremendous amount that I could do with it but tightly edit it. I had a few members of my group mention expanding on a few things, but overall my MAJOR task was to create this PERSONA. I am still working toward this, chipping away at some personality. Here and there I see ways to add information about our narrator, and before I am done completely with this I hope to have more of her experiences in here, more of her humorous fiascos and so forth.

Right now I am pleased with what I ended up with despite the fact this paper did not go where I wanted it to go. Ha ha Thank Goodness. My original idea was horribly boring.

CONNECTING TO READING

A. Create a series of journal entries as you complete readings for this chapter, to compile a "form and topic journal." Define these patterns of organization (by yourself or as a group, using the dictionary and writing handbooks, and good guesses). Illustrate each entry by pointing to specific lines, paragraphs, passages, or entire works in this chapter (or by skimming readings in other chapters that catch your eye). If you've kept a number of your own past writings, find illustrative samples there, too. In a sense, you're making your own handbook of patterns and options that another writer could use to help write a paper:

Sample:

Narration: telling a story, usually in chronological order. One of my teachers once explained it [by] using the writer E. M. Forester: "The King died and then the Queen died." = Plot. "The King died and then the Queen died of grief." = Story. Example from this chapter: "A friend's father fell on New Year's Eve. At the top of the staircase he was drunk. At the bottom he was dead. Five minutes before midnight, five minutes after. Ten stairs" ("Sleeping with Alcohol").

Example from my writing: "I left for college in August, bound for a city with deep southern roots. From a city where yucca and platanos were as common as the palm trees that grew on every corner, to chicken and greens. Salsa and merengue rang in my ears as I entered a dorm room that sheltered Garth Brooks and Tim McGraw. It was a culture shock for me and after a few days, withdrawal took over, but inevitably, I began to adapt. I started saying chicken and rice instead of *arroz con pollo. Caramelos* became candy and *bistec,* steak."

—Classroom author

B. Continue with your choice of—description; narration; cause and effect; analogy; example and illustration; classification and division; process analysis; comparison and contrast; definition; persuasion: logical appeals, emotional appeals, ethical appeals; relationships of antecedent and consequence (what came before and what followed from that), contraries, contradictions; circumstances such as the possible and impossible or past fact and future fact; testimony from authority, testimonials, statistics, maxims (sayings), law, precedent (examples). Aim for 10 entries, over a two-week period.

C. Rewrite an author's paragraph, using different options and organization. Do this together in a group with a single short work of your choice taken from this chapter. To choose a paragraph, it will be profitable to look at the way the entire essay is organized and the way individual paragraphs are developed within that essay. It is worth considering what tone and force these choices appear to give the text, to speculate on why the author made these choices, to explore what other options might have been available, and finally, to consider what choices you might have made in the same situation. You could repeat this exercise using one of your own paragraphs.

D. As a group, decide which essay in this chapter wins your award for using the greatest number of the methods of organization under discussion. Which follows a single, classic strategy the most single-mindedly?

E. In a journal entry, or in a class discussion list posting, analyze two authors' writing strategies and organizational choices. Choose two authors' works that are distinctly different and, with your peers, compare these authors' strategies and choices. Several authors in this reader discuss the same theme yet from very different standpoints, choosing different modes of development (and even different genres). For instance, Haunani-Kay Trask and Jamaica Kincaid talk about tourists. Plan to present your observations to a small group or your class as a whole.

F. In a small group discussion, return to Chapter 2 and consider how the strategies under discussion in this chapter were employed by authors when composing their literacy narratives. Take notes on your observations and share them with the class so that, together, you can review the patterns found in the entire set of readings.

CONNECTING TO WRITING

A. Try post-outlining one of your papers to practice making declarative thesis statements. To do this, read each paragraph and summarize the focus of the paragraph in a single sentence. You may already find you've stated a thesis and you can pull that out. Or you may discover an implied thesis that you can declare more specifically after the fact. Post-outlining can also allow you to investigate the overall organization of your paper: When you list all these sentences and then read across them, what do they say about the points you made in this text? Some software will do this for you. Compare your post-outline to thesis statements marked in the same text by your word processor.

B. Complete a journal entry in which you review several papers you've written. Identify some of your "tried and true" patterns of organization and development and then try to improve a section of one of these by imitating one of the patterns you've identified in one of this chapter's selections. In your paper, did you have a hard time arguing a point? Consider how Sherman Alexie uses story, dialogue, and dark humor in his argument. What can you learn from Haunani-Kay Trask's use of statistics? What about switching to second person, "you"? Write a summary of your observations after completing this analysis suitable for sharing in a small group (approximately one page).

C. As a journal exercise, choose a method of stating a thesis that you find in these chapter readings and recast a paragraph from one of your previous papers using that technique. Share the two versions with a writing group without telling them which you began with. Which do they prefer and why? After sharing these versions, discuss how each of you identifies the thesis in any of the chapter selections you agree to review together. How explicit or implicit a statement do you find? Equally, share any patterns of thesis making you've begun to notice within your own writings.

D. Define a pattern of organization and parody it a bit by using that pattern in an unexpected way and/or by shifting to an unexpected genre. For instance, write a poem about comparison and contrast by using that pattern. Write a prose sketch that defines definition. Write an argument that boldly parodies or exemplifies logical, ethical, and pathetic appeal.

E. In an on-line e-mail exchange, write to a partner and explain which piece of writing from this chapter you like best, and why. Forget patterns of organization for a moment (if you can). On what grounds other than organization have you chosen it? Explain your preference to your correspondent in some detail, quoting passages, pointing to sections. Is it possible or useful to separate content from organization? Why and when might a writer choose to do so? A teacher of writers? When and why might each insist on *not* doing so? Respond to each other's e-mail and then bring printed copies of the exchange to class for discussion with another pair of readers (and paste entries into your class journal).

WRITING PROJECTS

1. Ask each member of a writing group to compose an essay on the same topic, developed from the same, community negotiated thesis. Together, in class, generate a list of topics that you all agree might be worth investigating in a short essay of approximately 1,000 words. In small groups, choose three of these topics and compose possible declarative thesis statements on each of these subjects. Agree on one thesis for your group; each group member writes a draft using the agreed-upon thesis. When you share these drafts in a subsequent group response session, consider which methods of organization you each chose for your essay. Post your "variations on the same theme" essays in an on-line chapbook or 'zine.
2. Self-assign a form for your paper. If you already have a topic you want to explore, choose a method of development for that topic that would challenge you personally and combine topic and method to create your next class essay. First, look through several handbooks for advice on using this method. Next, find several essays that you like which use this method. If possible, find one of these in a contemporary literary magazine or news magazine that you enjoy reading. Finally, write on a topic you already had in mind, using this form. Keep composing notes about the ways the pattern aids and/or seems to alter the direction of your text. Note any ideas you borrow from the models you collected. Use these observations to write a writing process narrative to accompany your essay.
3. Write a second essay using the same topic and a different method of development (Amanda Fleming's essays model this process to a degree). Share both drafts with a group and have them respond to each. Which do they prefer and why? Which do you prefer and why?
4. Imitate one of the essays in this chapter. Instead of comparing your truck to a horse, compare it to . . .; instead of comparing life in Florida to life in Alaska, compare . . .; instead of examining how tourists have colonized

Hawaii, examine how tourists have colonized . . .; research and describe not hummingbirds but . . .; instead of arguing against church policies and doctrine, argue against . . .; don't examine, illustrate, or illuminate the policy of lockdown in U.S. prisons but examine the effects of the policy of . . . , and so on.

5. Rebut one of the chapter readings in an argumentative or persuasive essay of your own. Research the questions/issues raised in the chapter reading that you choose and form your own, opposing or contrasting thesis. Speak back to the positions taken in the essay you choose to contest. Quote from it and find other sources to support your views and claims.
6. Compose an essay on a controversial topic of importance to you. If your first draft is cast in first-person voice, recast the first page in second person (as in Jamaica Kincaid's text). Next, recast the first page in third-person singular. That is, present three versions of at least the first page of your essay in three voices: I, you, she (or he). What choices did each force you into as a writer? What effect do these choices have on readers in your writing group? Decide to retain the original voice or to continue revising into one of these other voices.
7. Write an essay about your understanding of and relation to rules, particularly rules for patterning and organizing essays and for developing paragraphs using your own previous essays as evidence and your experience as a writer in school to date. When do rules profit a writer? When do they hinder a writer? You might choose to use the quotes from Agatha Christie or Frank D'Angelo that end this chapter to prompt your exploratory draft.
8. Turn a personal journal entry into an essay. As you do so, decide who your ideal reader is and what your aims are in your piece. How important is your reader? To what degree do you imagine him or her or them as you draft? Draft a thesis statement. How will this imagined reader respond to that thesis? As you draft, consider the changes that you make for your imagined reader. Keep (journal) notes as you draft this essay "with the reader in mind." Or print the essay with a wide right-hand margin and talk back to it in the manner of the double-entry journal. If keeping an audience in mind in this manner is different from your normal drafting habits, comment on how this change feels: does it help or hinder your work to envision your reader?
9. As a group, choose an essay test topic, answer it, and compare the strategies group members chose to develop their essay answer. To do this, have each group member collect some sample exam essay topics (and responses if you have them). Consider writer's strategies for these topics. How did writers formulate a thesis for such a focused, timed-response assignment? What methods of organization worked best with which test prompts and why? Summarize your findings and share them with other groups. Next, choose a topic generic enough for your entire group and complete a timed, 20-minute response, posting these if you have that option on a class discussion list. Now, respond to your responses, noting what was effective and least effective in

each case. To what degree did you each rely on traditional patterns of organization? Which is the best piece of writing? What criteria do you use to decide?

10. Take your timed essay and expand it into a longer draft. What strategies did you employ? Did you stick with your original thesis? Did you conduct primary or secondary research? Did you use more than one method of organizing and generating text? Is your timed essay a blueprint for the larger essay, or did your larger essay wander farther afield? Why or why not?

* * * *

If you were a carpenter, it would be no good making a chair, the seat of which was five feet up from the floor. It wouldn't be what anyone wanted to sit on. It is no good saying that you think the chair looks handsome that way. If you want to write a book, study what sizes books are, and write within the limits of that size. If you want to write a certain type of short story for a certain type of magazine you have to make it the length and it has to be the type of story that is printed in the magazine. If you like to write for yourself only, that is a different matter—you can make it any length, and write it in any way you wish; but then you will probably have to be content with the pleasure alone of having written it.

—AGATHA CHRISTIE

As I read, take notes and think about what I have read, I find my mind ranging over a wealth of ideas, a veritable thesaurus of words and concepts, looking for some sort of ordering principle, some way to see one thing in terms of another. Although I do not self-consciously go through a formal checklist of inventional devices, I find myself more or less consciously using analogy, etymology, definition, and division into parts in my reading, my note taking, and my thinking.

—FRANK D'ANGELO

Drafting, Responding, and Revising

Thinking About Your Methods for Drafting, Responding, and Revising

> What I'm writing now is not literature, but it could be if I spent a lot of time editing, and rewriting; it would probably sound a whole lot different. I think that student literature can be considered literature if the student perfects the piece through revision.
>
> —ANONYMOUS CLASSROOM AUTHOR

Classroom authors on revision:

- Revising is like putting a fine-honed edge on a blade.
- Revising for me is like a kind of control that I don't get anywhere else. I can change the words, erase them, create others. It's a chance to polish and perfect ideas before someone else sees them.
- Revising is like a secret; I hide all the stupid things I wrote (when I was obviously not myself) the first time.
- Revising is like cleaning the house; everything is there in front of you just not in an order you're satisfied with. It takes valuable time and effort to get it just like you want it.
- Revising is like improving what I have, putting on the finishing touches.
- Revising is like a challenge—to sort things in a logical order and make them a pleasure to read.

Most of us are proud of our final written products, but we're often more ambivalent about the drafting and revision it took to produce them. That is, many of us like to prepare to travel but even more of us like to arrive. However, we know there's a process involved—choosing a destination, preparing, packing, financing, being in motion, and arriving. It should come as no surprise then to realize that to journey from ideas to final written products, writers plan, practice, try and try again. They draft, gather responses from readers, and revise. Consider, for instance, the following drafting levels:

- *Full breath draft:* A full breath draft is a piece of writing in process; it will be readable and comprehensible to the writer. It will be accessible to an outside reader (typed), but the writer may envision the paper taking a different direction in the next draft. It is more complete than a rough draft, being blocked out enough to make it worth a reader's response and full discussion.

  Possible readers: writer, writer's friends, writing tutor

- *Professional draft:* A professional draft probably has gone through several revisions. It will be carefully developed, formatted, and proofread, but the writer will expect to improve the piece after receiving revision suggestions.

  Possible readers: classmates, instructor, writer's friends or tutor

- *Portfolio draft:* A portfolio draft will have gone through several drafts. It will present a writer's best effort at that point in time. It will be carefully developed, formatted, and proofread and will be presented according to class requirements.

  Possible readers: classmates; instructor; other instructors (if used in other courses with permission); others online; employer; eventually, perhaps, an editor at the place of publication and general readers

When we draft, we re-see, re-view, re-envision, and re-fashion our work; we move from early to late versions. We try out one new ploy or 10 new ploys. We move from thinking about our aims to considering how potential readers will understand those aims. But this kind of journey isn't only about moving from big to small, messy to focused (although some texts do follow that trajectory). Revising is about opening up a draft, about holding out ideas for inspection and improvement, before, eventually, closing down again, then polishing, editing, and presenting.

Some writers begin to revise before putting words to paper; for instance, while taking a walk or while working at a part-time job. This sort of writer raises and rejects or accepts various openings in her mind before placing text on the screen. Other writers begin revision work in earnest only after they have an initial draft, when they can see what they've already said. In fact, different writing tasks often require different sorts of revision practices.

While it's easy to talk about drafts in a temporal sense—first, second, third; early, middle, late; or full, professional and portfolio, as described above—it's wise to keep in mind that we redraft because we revise our thoughts and understandings as well as our text. And when we do turn to the text, we revise globally (idea, thesis, full draft) as well as locally (paragraphs, sentence, words). Some research suggests that expert writers tend to revise at *all* of those levels. On the other hand, less expert writers procrastinate and barely get enough words on the page. Because they often have shorter, more meager texts, when they finally do consider the words before them, they find those words overly precious, so hard to have come by that they can't bear to see them go. Less expert writers fix only the small problems in a text—correct a misspelling, substitute one word for another word, fiddle with a verb tense. They don't have enough invested to make the grander, meaning-enhancing experiments of deep revision.

Before you share with others, you need a readable draft, one worth their time and consideration. After you get down your first ideas, particularly if you had trouble exploring your ideas, try a fat draft. To do this, create a text that is arbitrarily twice as long as the first one. If you push to double your text, soon there's bound to be enough material to work with, enough words that some can be given up on the way to improving the quality of what you're saying and how you're saying it. If you already have sufficient material—and this is the rarer case—you can complete a memory draft, as described below. A memory draft can help you identify what is most important in what you've written.

- *A fat draft:* Arbitrarily double your text. Turn a one-page poem into a two-page poem. Turn a 5-page essay into a 10-page essay. Tell two stories or provide two examples or arguments instead of one. The fat draft doesn't have to be good or better or finished; it simply has to be honestly twice as long.
- *A memory draft:* Read your text carefully. Once silently. Once aloud. Then put it away. Immediately sit down and write another text of at least the same or longer length; recreate portions of your text, go off on a tangent, or do both. This is a memory draft; it may closely shadow the original or strike off in a new direction. Again, this does not have to be good or better or finished; it simply has to be as long or longer and written without a reference to the original, except for what you have retained in memory.

Now you're ready to share your thoughts because all writers—novice and experienced writers, published and unpublished writers alike—need response.

You should share your initial drafts with classmates or other readers to get a general reaction and suggestions for change. You should not expect such readers to correct your spelling or help you decide on a final title. In fact, it may help most if they simply listen to your draft, or even to your ideas about your draft. To accomplish this, ask readers of early drafts what they liked, where they got lost, what stood out to them, and note their responses. Gather the opinions of several readers (or listeners), but remember that you are in charge of making the changes that best suit your aims for your work.

In later drafts, you may want to ask for written comments from your readers. At this point, most writers find it valuable to have readers offer both a running commentary on the text and an endnote or summary comment. It's important to writers to hear what is working *and why,* as well as what isn't working *and why.* The why is important. If you don't learn why your text affected someone, you have to guess. Was the reader just feeling tired that morning, does the reader *never* like essays about the environment, or did you actually make some missteps and thereby lose credibility with your reader?

The more mature your draft, the more attention you'll want to pay to audience. As this happens, a reader's strong ideas may come into conflict with your own. Readers may ask you to revise your piece to meet their expectations more closely. Also, they may have particular genre expectations. It's not bad to have an audience like this at all, particularly if your readers can clearly discuss their expectations for and reactions to your text. As you respond to their readings, their expectations, and their ideas, you refine your own ideas and defend and improve your choices. Doing this makes you a more confident writer.

- I think your introduction is professional and complete. Quotes serve as strong supports in an introduction and this quote serves as the perfect stepping stone. (Reader 1)
- You open your paper with a Bible verse but don't further elaborate on it. Why? By using that as an opening, I expected to see a Christian theme running through your paper. (Reader 2)
- The first paragraph showed the reader that this would be a story of accomplishment right away. It might be even more intriguing if you didn't foretell the ending so soon. Let readers build that up as they read. (Reader 3)

I really enjoyed reading the responses to my paper. They helped me see what my paper is missing. I plan to revise by rereading every response and will try to make the most important revisions suggested. These will add more depth to specific scenes. I don't expect this to be easy because there were so many revision options that I agree will make my paper well rounded and full.

—Classroom Author

Writers have some natural hesitations about sharing their work with others. First, they may have set themselves high standards and worry that others will judge them as not having met those standards. Also, they may be intimidated by the power of those who evaluate their work, fearing readers may be tempted to judge them along with their texts. Other writers lack the confidence to set the standards that help themselves improve. These writers may not know what to ask from their readers. Classroom authors, in particular, are working toward course requirements. To know how well they've succeeded, they need to know what constitutes a successful response for an assignment.

After you've had your writing reviewed by several readers, after you've revised again, you are ready for a more analytic response on your draft. If you are trying to do X, Y, and Z (or your assignment was to do X, Y, Z), then you'll now want readers to tell you if you have accomplished those goals. Not just if, but *how well.* You'll expect at this point to have your writing ranked against other writings. Of the three essays your reader has on this subject, you're ready to know if yours is strongest, in the middle, or weakest, *and why.* Or, you may want your writing ranked against your own writing, asking "Of my three essays, which is the strongest and weakest and why?"

At this point, your writing effectiveness can be linked to specific criteria. You don't want to know the relative strengths of your three papers; instead, you want to know if each accomplishes certain things. This is when you may confirm your suspicion that two of the papers are strong and one is excellent. You may also learn that the two strong papers are equally strong, but for different reasons. That is, you can have two B-level and one A-level essays, but the B-level essays, may each be B-level for different reasons.

Although criteria for writing may appear to be clear, how readers apply them is less clear. Say your teacher told you that "B papers are those that have a strong voice; a clear development; inform readers about your topic by using details, examples, and illustrations; and exhibit few surface-level, usage problems." One of your papers, according to this teacher reader, is a B-level essay because it does most of these things—despite a few proofreading errors—but he also rates it highly because the essay has a striking topic and your strong sentences and word choice created an engaging authorial presence.

Now, your second B-level paper is more consistent in all areas of evaluation. It has fewer proofreading errors, but the voice you constructed is also less sure, less impressive to your evaluator. This paper is more evenly written and has fewer highs and lows. Both papers are equally effective but for different reasons. This explains why readers can look at the same paper and arrive at the same grade but for different reasons and how they can apply the same criteria but appear to do so differently.

Your next evaluator may not value your strong voice as much as she does error-free prose, so your first B-level paper now merits a B–. She may also value consistency of performance so much that she thinks your second paper merits a B+. As authors in this chapter will explain, evaluating writing is a subjective art although negotiated criteria can be applied more consistently when readers are trained to respond to those criteria and have had a hand in developing the criteria. That is, when your readers are reasonable and involved in the evaluation process and you can talk to them about their evaluations, both reader and writer benefit.

For most of us, reasonable readers include friends, family members, writing teachers, tutors, and classroom peers. Most classroom authors get the greatest amount of feedback and response from other classroom authors—their peers—and expect to be evaluated by their teachers. Your teacher will probably have guidelines for workshops and have you respond to each other in pairs, in small groups, online, and as a full class.

Without exception, writers feel that critiquing the work of peers is difficult but ultimately rewarding. For instance, there are tense moments at first: "It felt like everyone was waiting to start and I felt like I had to talk because I'd feel terrible if no one talked about my essay," said one writer to explain why she made herself break the ice and start to respond in a workshop setting. Another observed, "I like the workshop because getting other readers' opinions helps me understand where I should go next with my draft." Clearly, the more responses you receive, the more your ability increases to understand audience(s) and discover revision directions. Equally, the more practice you gain responding to other authors, the more skillful you become at responding to your own writing.

Most of us prefer a respondent who is a coach rather than a critic, an ally rather than an evaluator. While teachers will ultimately provide you with a course grade, that's not the best moment for learning how to improve as a writer. To improve, writers need formative response and evaluation more than they need summative response and evaluation. *Formative response tells you how you're doing so you can change your performance and do it better or differently.* This is the response you get from peers on a draft, from your teacher at mid-term, or from a tutor who is helping you work on a new ending for your paper. *Summative response and evaluation tells you what you accomplished and is received after you've completed your work and set it aside by submitting it.*

To improve at revision, you have to give yourself the time to draft. That's why I often ask for a writer's revision plan (after students have responded to each other's work in a workshop) and assign a radical revision for the last paper of a term.

> *Radical revision:* Choose a class essay from early in the term that is already retired; it's easier to radically revise an essay you're at least temporarily finished with or don't feel close to. You'll revise the paper in a way that challenges you to take risks and try something you've never tried before. The revision can end up less effective than the original because there's no real risk without the possibility of failure. The core of the exercise, then, is to write a process narrative where you recount what you chose to do, and why—why was this a risk or challenge for you as a writer, how did this revision work, and what did you learn? Radical revisions might include trying one or more of the following:
>
> - *Voice/tone changes:* Use double, multiple, meta-voice or interrupting voice; change from first to third person or try second singular or third plural; write as a character; change tone (serious to comic, for example); try a question-and-answer format; write a dialogue; change ethnicity; use the point of view of something inanimate; use a second voice to question the authority of the text, and so on.
>
> - *Syntax changes:* Alternate sentence length in planned patterns; make sentences of arbitrary lengths (all very short; all very long; or all 10 words long); translate into another language (and maybe translate back again); remove all adverbs, all adjectives, and so on.
>
> - *Genre changes:* Change from essay to poem to song to bumper sticker; try fables, letters, sermons, journals, fairy tales, comic books, recipes, prayers, and nontext genres, such as dolls, origami, games, and so on.
>
> - *Audience changes:* Write for different magazines, different members of your family, different members of the community; write from the point of view of

two participants; change from adult to child to alien; try parody, imitation, and so on.

- *Time changes:* Try flashbacks, flash forwards; use the continuous present; describe an event backwards; situate a text in a different era; change the expected climax point of a narrative to a new and unexpected place, and so on.
- *Typography/physical layout:* Use different fonts for different speakers, compose in hypertext for a Web page, and so on.
- *Multimedia/art piece:* Try performance, a play, audio, and/or videotape; a Web page; an art installation; conduct a sing-along; write on unexpected objects (shirts, shoes, walls); mime; push your text off the page, and so on.

Revision is hard work, but successful revision also provides writers with a striking sense of control and accomplishment. In the readings that follow, Anne Lamott reminds you to give yourself the space to revise by accepting your drafts. Gail Godwin explores the problems of perfectionism (perfection is no friend to revision). Toby Fulwiler illustrates the way an assigned revision sequence can show writers the possibilities of their work. Essayist Annie Dillard discusses her revision process. Think of the authors in this chapter as your allies in thinking through issues of revision, response, and evaluation. Richard Straub offers advice on how to respond to the writing of your peers and illustrates that advice. Peter Elbow and Pat Belanoff provide a typology of response possibilities. Using five categories of response—from sharing to criteria-based response—they indicate when such techniques are useful to writers.

In an illustrated assignment sequence, "The Executive Summary," I share an exercise designed to help you evaluate the merits of differing peer responses and to decide how to use these formative evaluations to improve your draft. The class handout is followed by one classroom author's executive summary, drawn from a set of peer responses that I reproduce in part (I've included copies of the first and last pages of four of the responses that this author has summarized in her executive summary). Next, Gerald Locklin's poem humorously addresses the confusing response comment. Like most of us, this poet has squinted at the poorly scribbled response to a piece of writing, trying to puzzle out the meaning of a cryptic evaluation comment. A second poem, by Linda Pastan, suggests that more than papers are evaluated in life. Finally, Jay Szczepanski illustrates the rich complexity of a drafting process and self-analysis and Thomas Harmon took up the challenge of the radical revision by translating his essay on comics into a comic book format.

Chapter Readings

ANNE LAMOTT (b. 1954)

Shitty First Drafts

CONSIDER THIS:

Anne Lamott's book, *Bird by Bird,* offers some wonderfully straightforward advice about the writing process: "The very first thing I tell my new students on the first day of a workshop is that good writing is about telling the truth." But where does one start? "Start with your childhood, I tell them. Plug your nose and jump in, and write down all your memories as truthfully as you can." Born in San Francisco and educated at Goucher College, she received a Guggenheim fellowship in 1985. Her fiction is noted for its close observation about domestic affairs and its sharp sense of humor.

And how does one really become a writer? Lamott continues: "You sit down. . . . You try to sit down at approximately the same time every day." Obviously, then, revision is part of Lamott's writing process and in this essay she lets you in on one of the secrets of that process: poor first drafts. We all write them. You may have been surprised at Lamott's title. Is there anything else that she says about writers that surprises you in this essay? Does Lamott's discussion of her own drafting habits echo or amplify or contradict any of the advice offered at the beginning of this chapter?

Now, practically even better news than that of short assignments is the idea of shitty first drafts. All good writers write them. This is how they end up with good second drafts and terrific third drafts. People tend to look at successful writers, writers who are getting their books published and maybe even doing well financially, and think that they sit down at their desks every morning feeling like a million dollars, feeling great about who they are and how much talent they have and what a great story they have to tell; that they take in a few deep breaths, push back their sleeves, roll their necks a few times to get all the cricks out, and dive in, typing fully formed passages as fast as a court reporter. But this is just the fantasy of the uninitiated. I know some very great writers, writers you love who write beautifully and have made a great deal of money, and not *one* of them sits down routinely feeling wildly enthusiastic and confident. Not one of them writes elegant first drafts. All right, one of them does, but we do not like her very much. We do not think that she has a rich inner life or that God likes her or can even stand her. (Although when I mentioned this to my priest friend Tom, he said you can safely assume you've created God in your own image when it turns out that God hates all the same people you do.)

Very few writers really know what they are doing until they've done it. Nor do they go about their business feeling dewy and thrilled. They do not type a few stiff warm-up sentences and then find themselves bounding along like huskies across the snow. One writer I know tells me that he sits down every morning and says to himself nicely, "It's not like you don't have a choice, because you do—you can either type or kill yourself." We all often feel like we are pulling teeth, even those writers whose prose ends up being the most natural and fluid. The right words and sentences just do not come pouring out like ticker tape most of the time. Now, Muriel Spark is said to have felt that she was taking dictation from God every morning—sitting there, one supposes, plugged into a Dictaphone, typing away, humming. But this is a very hostile and aggressive position. One might hope for bad things to rain down on a person like this.

For me and most of the other writers I know, writing is not rapturous. In fact, the only way I can get anything written at all is to write really, really shitty first drafts.

The first draft is the child's draft, where you let it all pour out and then let it romp all over the place, knowing that no one is going to see it and that you can shape it later. You just let this childlike part of you channel whatever voices and visions come through and onto the page. If one of the characters wants to say, "Well, so what, Mr. Poopy Pants?," you let her. No one is going to see it. If the kid wants to get into really sentimental, weepy, emotional territory, you let him. Just get it all down on paper, because there may be something great in those six crazy pages that you would never have gotten to by more rational, grown-up means. There may be something in the very last line of the very last paragraph on page six that you just love, that is so beautiful or wild that you now know what you're supposed to be writing about, more or less, or in what direction you might go—but there was no way to get to this without first getting through the first five and a half pages.

I used to write food reviews for *California* magazine before it folded. (My writing food reviews had nothing to do with the magazine folding, although every single review did cause a couple of canceled subscriptions. Some readers took umbrage at my comparing mounds of vegetable puree with various ex-presidents' brains.) These reviews always took two days to write. First I'd go to a restaurant several times with a few opinionated, articulate friends in tow. I'd sit there writing down everything anyone said that was at all interesting or funny. Then on the following Monday I'd sit down at my desk with my notes, and try to write the review. Even after I'd been doing this for years, panic would set in. I'd try to write a lead, but instead I'd write a couple of dreadful sentences, xx them out, try again, xx everything out, and then feel despair and worry settle on my chest like an x-ray apron. It's over, I'd think, calmly. I'm not going to be able to get the magic to work this time. I'm ruined. I'm through. I'm toast. Maybe, I'd think, I can get my old job back as a clerk-typist. But probably not. I'd get up and study my teeth in the mirror for a while. Then I'd stop, remember to breathe, make a few phone calls, hit the kitchen and chow down. Eventually I'd go back and sit down at my desk, and sigh for the next ten minutes. Finally I would pick up my one-inch picture frame, stare into it as if for the answer, and every time the answer would come: all I had to do was to write a really shitty first draft of, say, the opening paragraph. And no one was going to see it.

So I'd start writing without reining myself in. It was almost just typing, just making my fingers move. And the writing would be *terrible.* I'd write a lead paragraph that was a whole page, even though the entire review could only be three pages long, and then I'd start writing up descriptions of the food, one dish at a time, bird by bird, and the critics would be sitting on my shoulders, commenting like cartoon characters. They'd be pretending to snore, or rolling their eyes at my overwrought descriptions, no matter how hard I tried to tone those descriptions down, no matter how conscious I was of what a friend said to me gently in my early days of restaurant reviewing. "Annie," she said, "it is just a piece of *chicken.* It is just a bit of *cake.*"

But because by then I had been writing for so long, I would eventually let myself trust the process—sort of, more or less. I'd write a first draft that was maybe twice as long as it should be, with a self-indulgent and boring beginning, stupefying descriptions of the meal, lots of quotes from my black-humored friends that made them sound more like the Manson girls than food lovers, and no ending to speak of. The whole thing would be so long and incoherent and hideous that for the rest of the day I'd obsess about getting creamed by a car before I could write a decent second draft. I'd worry that people would read what I'd written and believe that the accident had really been a suicide, that I had panicked because my talent was waning and my mind was shot.

The next day, though, I'd sit down, go through it all with a colored pen, take out everything I possibly could, find a new lead somewhere on the second page, figure out a kicky place to end it, and then write a second draft. It always turned out fine, sometimes even funny and weird and helpful. I'd go over it one more time and mail it in.

Then, a month later, when it was time for another review, the whole process would start again, complete with the fears that people would find my first draft before I could rewrite it.

Almost all good writing begins with terrible first efforts. You need to start somewhere. Start by getting something—anything—down on paper. A friend of mine says that the first draft is the down draft—you just get it down. The second draft is the up draft—you fix it up. You try to say what you have to say more accurately. And the third draft is the dental draft, where you check every tooth, to see if it's loose or cramped or decayed, or even, God help us, healthy.

What I've learned to do when I sit down to work on a shitty first draft is to quiet the voices in my head. First there's the vinegar-lipped Reader Lady, who says primly, "Well, *that's* not very interesting, is it?" And there's the emaciated German male who writes these Orwellian memos detailing your thought crimes. And there are your parents, agonizing over your lack of loyalty and discretion;

and there's William Burroughs, dozing off or shooting up because he finds you as bold and articulate as a houseplant; and so on. And there are also the dogs: let's not forget the dogs, the dogs in their pen who will surely hurtle and snarl their way out if you ever *stop* writing, because writing is, for some of us, the latch that keeps the door of the pen closed, keeps those crazy ravenous dogs contained.

Quieting these voices is at least half the battle I fight daily. But this is better than it used to be. It used to be 87 percent. Left to its own devices, my mind spends much of its time having conversations with people who aren't there. I walk along defending myself to people, or exchanging repartee with them, or rationalizing my behavior, or seducing them with gossip, or pretending I'm on their TV talk show or whatever. I speed or run an aging yellow light or don't come to a full stop, and one nanosecond later am explaining to imaginary cops exactly why I had to do what I did, or insisting that I did not in fact do it.

I happened to mention this to a hypnotist I saw many years ago, and he looked at me very nicely. At first I thought he was feeling around on the floor for the silent alarm button, but then he gave me the following exercise, which I still use to this day.

Close your eyes and get quiet for a minute, until the chatter starts up. Then isolate one of the voices and imagine the person speaking as a mouse. Pick it up by the tail and drop it into a mason jar. Then isolate another voice, pick it up by the tail, drop it in the jar. And so on. Drop in any high-maintenance parental units, drop in any contractors, lawyers, colleagues, children, anyone who is whining in your head. Then put the lid on, and watch all these mouse people clawing at the glass, jabbering away, trying to make you feel like shit because you won't do what they want—won't give them more money, won't be more successful, won't see them more often. Then imagine that there is a volume-control button on the bottle. Turn it all the way up for a minute, and listen to the stream of angry, neglected, guilt-mongering voices. Then turn it all the way down and watch the frantic mice lunge at the glass, trying to get to you. Leave it down, and get back to your shitty first draft.

A writer friend of mine suggests opening the jar and shooting them all in the head. But I think he's a little angry, and I'm sure nothing like this would ever occur to you.

GAIL GODWIN (b. 1937)

The Watcher at the Gates

CONSIDER THIS:

"The most serious danger to my writing," Godwin says in the *New York Times,* "is my predilection for shapeliness. How I love that nice circular Greek shape or a nice, neat conclusion, with all the edges tucked under. This sometimes leads me to 'wrap up' things, to force dramatic revelations at the expense of allowing the truth to reveal itself in slow, shy and often problematical glimpses." Before you read Godwin's essay, think of your anti-muse. The muse is the goddess writers believe helps them write. Who or what is the devil, demon, or evil genie that keeps you from drafting and revising? As you read, decide if your anti-muse, devil, don't-write-now-genie, resembles Godwin's "watcher."

Gail Godwin was born in Birmingham, Alabama, and raised in North Carolina. She has worked as a reporter, and has taught at Iowa, the University of Illinois, Vassar, and Columbia. Godwin credits her mother with inspiring her to become a writer. In an interview with the National Book Foundation, she said, "One of my first perceptions was of my mother as a writer, because she was writing stories when I was very little and I would watch her type them up and send them out. Then she'd get a check back, and we'd go out and spend it. I saw she got a lot of pleasure and satisfaction out of making up stories, and she would discuss them with me all the time, asking what I thought should happen next, so I felt very involved from the first."

I first realized I was not the only writer who had a restraining critic who lived inside me and sapped the juice from green inspirations when I was leafing through Freud's "Interpretation of Dreams" a few years ago. Ironically, it was my "inner critic" who had sent me to Freud. I was writing a novel, and my heroine was in the middle of a dream, and then I lost faith in my own invention and rushed to "an authority" to check whether she could have such a dream. In the chapter on dream interpretation, I came upon the following passage that has helped me free myself, in some measure, from my critic and has led to many pleasant and interesting exchanges with other writers.

Freud quotes Schiller, who is writing a letter to a friend. The friend complains of his lack of creative power. Schiller replies with an allegory. He says it is not good if the intellect examines too closely the ideas pouring in at the gates.

> In isolation, an idea may be quite insignificant, and venturesome in the extreme, but it may acquire importance from an idea which follows it. . . . In the case of a creative mind, it seems to me, the intellect has withdrawn its watchers from the gates, and the ideas rush in pell-mell, and only then does it review and inspect the multitude. You are ashamed or afraid of the momentary and passing madness which is found in all real creators, the longer or shorter duration of which distinguishes the thinking artist from the dreamer . . . you reject too soon and discriminate too severely.

So that's what I had: a Watcher at the Gates. I decided to get to know him better. I discussed him with other writers, who told me some of the quirks and habits of their Watchers, each of whom was as individual as his host, and all of whom seemed passionately dedicated to one goal: rejecting too soon and discriminating too severely.

It is amazing the lengths a Watcher will go to keep you from pursuing the flow of your imagination. Watchers are notorious pencil sharpeners, ribbon changers, plant waterers, home repairers and abhorrers of messy rooms or messy pages. They are compulsive looker-uppers They are superstitious scaredy-cats. They cultivate self-important eccentricities they think are suitable for "writers." And they'd rather die (and kill your inspiration with them) than risk making a fool of themselves.

My Watcher has a wasteful penchant for 20-pound bond paper above and below the carbon of the first draft. "What's the good of writing out a whole page," he whispers begrudgingly "if you just have to write it over again later? Get it perfect the first time!" My Watcher adores stopping in the middle of a morning's work to drive down to the library to check on the name of a flower or a World War II battle or a line of metaphysical poetry. "You can't possibly go on till you've got this right!" he admonishes. I go and get the car keys.

Other Watchers have informed their writers that:

> "Whenever you get a really good sentence you should stop in the middle of it and go on tomorrow. Otherwise you might run dry."

> "Don't try and continue with your book till your dental appointment is over. When you're worried about your teeth, you can't think about art."

Another Watcher makes his owner pin his finished pages to a clothesline and read them through binoculars "to see how they look from a distance." Countless other Watchers demand "bribes" for taking the day off: lethal doses of caffeine, alcoholic doses of Scotch or vodka or wine.

There are various ways to outsmart, pacify or coexist with your Watcher. Here are some I have tried, or my writer friends have tried, with success:

- Look for situations when he's likely to be off-guard. Write too fast for him in an unexpected place, at an unexpected time. (Virginia Woolf captured the "diamonds in the dustheap" by writing at a "rapid haphazard gallop" in her diary.) Write when very tired. Write in purple ink on the back of a Master Charge statement. Write whatever comes into your mind while the kettle is boiling and make the steam whistle your deadline. (Deadlines are a great way to outdistance the Watcher.)
- Disguise what you are writing. If your Watcher refuses to let you get on with your story or novel, write a "letter" instead, telling your "correspondent" what you are going to write in your story or next chapter. Dash off a "review" of your own unfinished opus. It will stand up like a bully to your Watcher the next time he throws obstacles in your path. If you write yourself a good one.
- Get to know your Watcher. He's yours. Do a drawing of him (or her). Pin it to the wall of your study and turn it gently to the wall when necessary. Let your Watcher feel needed. Watchers are excellent critics after inspiration has been captured; they are dependable, sharp-eyed readers of things already set down. Keep your Watcher in shape and he'll have less time to keep you from shaping. If he's really ruining your whole working day sit down, as Jung did with his personal demons, and write him a

letter. On a very bad day I once wrote my Watcher a letter. "Dear Watcher," I wrote, "What is it you're so afraid I'll do?" Then I held his pen for him, and he replied instantly with a candor that has kept me from truly despising him.

"Fail," he wrote back.

TOBY FULWILER (b. 1942)

A Lesson in Revision

CONSIDER THIS: (See Author's Introduction in Chapter 3)

In this essay, Toby Fulwiler lets you see a revision sequence along with student writing derived from that sequence. Before you begin reading, think about your own attitudes toward "assigned revision." Have you been asked to produce a certain number of drafts? If so, how did that work? Did you complete the drafts or did you fabricate some after the fact? Did you give yourself enough time to learn from the process? Compare and contrast any drafting sequences you've been assigned to the multiple draft sequence presented here. Consider your own response to the "Potatoes" essay. What might you suggest the writer do in her next draft?

The real secret to good writing, for most writers, is rewriting. It's true that a few gifted writers compose, understand, and edit all in one draft—but neither I nor my students seem to do our best writing that way. Even when writers are pleased with their first drafts, those drafts don't usually tell the whole story that could be told—the one revealed only in second- and third-draft writing. In other words, it's the act of writing itself that explains the whole story to the writer. There are no shortcuts to full understanding, even for good writers.

There are no shortcuts, either, to careful writing. Just as first drafts seldom tell the whole story or make the best case, so too are first words and sentences seldom as polished, careful, and precise as they could be. What makes words and sentences more polished, careful, and precise is returning to them over and over again, each time with a little more distance, a little more clarity, and a little more rigor, and editing them until they create just the effect the writer hopes to achieve.

As the result of teaching writing and writing professionally over the past two decades, I have come to believe that knowing when, where, and how to revise is the greatest difference between my own good and bad writing as well as between the practices of experienced and inexperienced writers. This essay will try to explain in some detail that difference.

The following story describes the effect of systematic revision on twenty-five first-year college students in a writing class at the University of Vermont. All were required by their various majors to take this course; none who entered claimed to enjoy writing. My job was to change this attitude and, in the bargain, help them become better writers.

DRAFT I

The first assignment, a common one for first-year writing classes, is to write about a recent personal experience of some importance to the writer—a good place to start a composition course because it starts with what writers already know best, their own experience. While I asked that these first drafts be typed, I specified no particular form or length. Students brought their papers to class, read them out loud in groups of four or five, and commented on each other about "what interested them" and "where more information would help." After class, I took copies home with me to read. Let me show you some of the paragraphs of these first papers.

- This probably is the most heroic event of my childhood. Everyone has their moments, but I believe that this episode is indeed commendable.
- In everyday life there are so many things that frustrate us, annoy us or make us upset that when we find something that makes us truly happy we should take advantage of it at every opportunity. For me, that thing is chocolate. The experience that I had which helped me to form this philosophy was one that will remain forever in my mind as a beautiful memory.
- Life—it definitely has its ups and downs. Most people don't need to think about what to do with themselves for amusement during life's livelier moments, but have you ever considered the things people do when life seems to be getting quite dull? Well, every so often I realize just what stupid, mindless things I've caught myself doing to fill time.
- Last summer my mother and I flew to Ireland. I've traveled there four times before. I thought it would be the normal three week tedious venture of traveling the countries visiting relatives and seeing the sights. This action-packed vacation turned out to be more than I could handle. From recalling old memories, to falling in love, I helped discover a new side of myself.

Most of the twenty-six papers were variations of these four, where the writers told us of forthcoming heroism, frustration, ups and downs, and action. Nothing is really wrong with any of these beginnings, except that they are slow, foreshadowing excitement to come and summarizing the writer's point before the paper demonstrates it. Would you rather have action promised or delivered? Would you like to be told the meaning of a story before hearing it? While I can't answer for you, I want the story to start fast, and I want to figure out its meaning for myself.

Further on in some of the same papers, however, I found both fast and interesting writing. Here is a passage from Avey's paper, exploring the story of a boarding-school friendship:"

- Let me draw a picture for you. My first day of boarding school, the first person I see was a girl with black, starchy hair and face was as white as a clown. She wore huge black combat boots (which I never knew existed until I went to the Cambridge School) and a dangling cross earring protruding from her nose.

Avey draws a picture with words, allowing us to see the girl she's talking about "with black starchy hair," and "combat boots," and "a dangling cross earring protruding from her nose." When I read this, I can make my own judgment—that this girl is bold, fashionable, weird, whatever. And the writer shows me the character, asking me to evaluate it myself; I am drawn further into the story and want to see whether my judgment will be confirmed or not. (More on Avey's story later.)

In a different paper, John writes about spending eleven months in Equador and includes the following dialogue:

> "You mean in America people live together before marriage?" she asked me in a childish voice.
>
> "Well, yes. I guess so. Once in a while, it's a pretty common thing," I said back in a casual voice. I had to think a lot before responding because I hadn't learned much of the Spanish language yet. She looked at me stunned as I looked at her and giggled.

I especially enjoy hearing John and his Ecuadorian friend talk with each other—a conversation I imagine taking place in halting Spanish. Hearing people speak, overhearing them actually, puts me in the story and lets me make of the conversation what I will. In this case, because the writer doesn't summarize for me, I infer the difference between a liberal North American culture and a more conservative one in South America.

Look at one more sample from these first papers, this one written by Amanda, a student from Scotland attending college in the United States.

> For most of this summer I again worked on the farm where I removed rotten, diseased potato shaws from a field all day. But I was in the sun all the time with a good bunch of people so it was quite good fun. . . . Later on I signed up with an employment agency and got a waitressing job in Aberdeen, a city thirty-five miles north of our farm. It was only for one week, but I didn't mind—it was the first job I got myself and I felt totally independent.

Amanda cannot quite make up her mind what her story is about: the paper's title is "Waitressing," and we see here some of the details ("Aberdeen, a city thirty-five miles north of our farm") and importance of this first "job I got myself." In addition, however, she also describes in brief but wonderful detail the potato field "where I removed rotten, diseased potato shaws . . . in the sun . . . with a good bunch of people." In other words she includes descriptive rather than summary detail about two possible directions her paper might take: she could focus on either her week as a waitress or her life picking potatoes on her father's farm.

It turns out that a lot of students were in the same situation as Amanda, trying to write one story that had embedded within it the seed of several others, each of which, if told fully, would itself be substantial and complete. Remember Amanda, we will keep tabs on her throughout this essay.

For their second drafts, I suggested that each writer create (recreate) as much action, dialogue, and detail as possible, while keeping summary comments and judgments to a minimum. I concluded by telling the class: "If you want to switch topics, please do. Your topic needs to be interesting enough to endure several more weeks of attention and experimentation!"

DRAFT II

I asked the students to meet again in their same small groups to share the second drafts. This time each writer brought enough copies to share with his or her groupmates, read a draft aloud while the others followed along, received comments on it, then left a copy for me to take home and read. Please look at these paragraphs from different parts of Amanda's second draft:

Waitressing

> "Hey Muriel, how much are the chili-burgers and chips?"
>
> "Two pounds ten pence" came the reply.
>
> "Okay . . . . oh heck, Muriel, I've done it AGAIN! I'm never going to get it right. Blimming tills!"
>
> This was a common conversation between me and the cook with whom I worked in a small snack bar during the summer holidays this year. It was the first time I had worked outside a farm. Normally during my holidays—Easter, Summer or October I would work on neighboring farms or on our own in the North East of Scotland, which is a large agricultural area.
>
> I have also worked on potato fields, where I either picked them in a squad of about fifty to sixty people. We would bend over collecting the "tatties" till there were none left on our "bit" only to have a tractor drive past and dig up some more. This job was always in October, so the weather was never very good. It either rained or was windy, often both. Some days it would be so cold that we would lie in between the drills of undug potatoes to protect ourselves from the wind.

Amanda still can't decide what to focus on; however, she now includes good lively dialogue about waitressing (first paragraph) and specific details of farming (second paragraph). Look especially at the details of the potato field, where Amanda describes herself as [lying] in between the drills of undug potatoes to protect ourselves from the wind." Her concrete, specific language puts us with her in that freezing October potato field, all the while allowing us to be safely warm vicarious observers—which good writing does—and we want more. Lying between those potato rows to keep warm is the kind of detail that it's hard to fake or imagine—only the writer who's been there would think to include it, and so we believe her completely.

I also want you to see the second draft of a paper by a nursing major named Dawn who had spent the previous summer as a nurse's aide in a nursing home. Here are two paragraphs from her story, the first early in the paper, the second later on:

> Well, I walked into the first room, expecting to see women, but no there were two men lying in their beds. My face turned red with embarrassment, I didn't expect that I would have to take care of men. So Charlene gave me a washcloth and towel and told me to wash them up and dress them. As I washed them I thought to myself, I can handle this, I mean these people don't know what is going on and I am just here to help them survive.
>
> It was this year when I got my last surprise. It was on a Saturday when a dear patient of mine died. His name was Frank, he was my first death. I sat there and watched him go on his journey to heaven. The time was 12:45 p.m. when I heard his wife yell to me. I ran as fast as I could. I kept thinking, "Oh my god, what do I do?" When I got to his bed, Frank's eyes were rolled back and he was breathing with difficulty. I yelled to the nurse and stood by Frank, making him as comfortable as I could. The nurse ran to call the doctor and the rest of his family. As all this was going on, I just stood their applying cold compresses to his face and wondering what happened. Earlier that morning he was smiling and laughing, and now here he was dying. All of a sudden Frank stopped breathing. I felt for a pulse but couldn't get one.

Dawn now includes the reader with her on the hospital floor as she begins work. Her surprise at finding "men" in the room ("My faced turned red with embarrassment") is another of those telling details; few writers who haven't worked in a nursing home would invent that anxious insight, which, like Amanda lying in the potato field, is entirely convincing. I now want to see even more details of the washing of the men. How did she get over her anxiety? How does she actually dress and shave them?

You might also notice in her second paragraph both some tense action ("I felt for a pulse and couldn't get one") and some fanciful summary ("I sat there and watched him go on his journey to heaven"—How does she know?). Note the differences between what a writer can authentically know (the data supplied by her senses) versus that she cannot (what goes on in someone else's mind). In recounting personal experiences, writers create the strongest belief when they record what they experience and know firsthand, rather than their guesses, speculations, and judgments.

By now, in draft two, at least a dozen other papers also include rich and specific details that make the writing exciting to read. Many are shared in the small groups, and I read as many of these passages as I can to the whole class, knowing they will encourage still other students to reconsider their own next drafts. They do. I found the following entry about these second drafts in John's journal (Figure 6-1).

Figure 6-1

9/12 Today in english Toby took
parts of some peoples papers to teach
us how to write better. I think I
am starting to feel my writing coming
together ~~It's very hard to tell a
story and not show.~~ you begin to
totally reshape the actual incident when
you want to get down to the littilest
detail to give the reader the feeling
you have. I really think the idea of
having all the diff't drafts really
helps. You totally can get to the root
of your topic. It makes you feel
like a surgeon. Tonights assignment is
to focus on a very short time span.
I think this one is going to be
the toughest.

Then, a few days later, in another journal entry, John assesses his own second draft before beginning a third. The story he set out to tell covered one whole season when he coached an eighth-grade basketball team. John, a business major, now understands that to recreate a truly believable narrative, he must write with careful detail—a kind of writing he has never done before (Figure 6-2).

John's problem has changed from the novice writer's dilemma of filling enough pages to fulfill the assignment to the working writer's dilemma of selecting from among "SO MUCH MATERIAL." He now sees that he has stories within stories and must decide which one to tell and in how much detail.

Draft III

Many writers are now beginning to see that the more they write, the more their stories grow, develop, and evolve into tales they didn't at first intend to tell. However, most still need coaching about how to actually make this evolution happen and their stories continue to grow. In the spirit of play and experimentation, I placed two new limitations on draft three: (1) that the time covered in the narrative be limited to a single day or less and (2) that the setting be limited to one specific place. With this draft everybody's writing really took off. Students had more material than could be shared in one period. Look at what Dawn's paper has become, an internal monologue inside her head written in present tense with few specific details:

Figure 6-2

I'm going to try to use more dialogue in my paper. That is what I really think I was missing.

The second draft is very dull. As I read it, it has no life. I should have used more detail.

I'll try more dialogue, lot's more, in draft #3

• I'll have it take place at one of my practices, Giving a vivid description of what those practices were like when the kids showed up.

I have SO MUCH MATERIAL. But I have a hard time deciding what seems more interesting.

My Job as a Nursing Aide

Up the steps I go, through the big white door again. The fowl odor of urine strikes my nose. Sounds quiet. . . . for now anyway. Of course it is quiet, it's 6:30 a.m. in the morning. Got to get on this elevator that creeks when it moves. Time to punch in already! Seems like I just got out of here. Another eight hours for a small paycheck. I hope my feet stay under me.

It is my last day, YEAH, tomorrow is a day off. Oh no! I've got to listen to this report, it takes too long and what do I care about who gets what medications anyway.

"Dawn, you have assignment five!" yells Terry while laughing at me.

"Gee thanks, why do I get stuck with the mens end? Oh I get it, just because I'm younger than all of you, so I have more time on my hands!"

Well, stuck with the men again. I kind of figured I would, but it would have been nice to get a different assignment. Report is finally over, now I have to hurry and get my bucket filled . . . let's see powder, soap, gloves, bags for the laundry, shaving cream, after shave cologne, razors and medicines for my patients treatments. Yup, I've got everything. First I should do my rounds to make sure everyone is still breathing. Then I will start to get up at least two people.

"Dawn, breakfast trays are here!"

"Already, I only got up two people and nine more to go!"

Amanda, meanwhile has dropped the waitress story and elected to go with the potatoes. Look at the first full page of her third draft:

Potatoes

Potatoes, mud, potatoes, mud, potatoes, that was all I saw in front of me. They moved from my right side to my left, at hip level. A conveyor belt never stopping. On and on and on.

I bounced and stumbled around as the potato harvester moved over the rough heath, digging the newly grown potatoes out of the ground, transporting them up a conveyor belt and pushing them out in front of me and three other ladies. Two on either side of the belt.

The potatoes passed fast, a constant stream. My hands worked deftly, pulling out clods of dirt, rotten potatoes, old shaws and anything else I found that wasn't a potato. They were sore, rubbed raw with the constant pressure of holding dirt. They were numb, partly from the work, and partly from the cold. It was October, the ground was nearly frozen, the mud was hard and solid. Cold. Dirt had gotten into my yellow and yet brown rubber gloves, had wedged under my nails, increasing my discomfort.

On and on the tractor pulled the harvester that I was standing in, looming high above the dark rich earth, high above the potatoes.

My back ached right at the bottom of my spine. A searing, nagging pain. I stooped over the belt unlike the other ladies who were short and able to lean their hip's and waist's on the side of the belt, resting their bodies as they worked. "Oh to be short."

A bump and a shuggle, all movements hurt as the harvester moved. My feet throbbed, tired from lack of support in welly boots and standing all day. My eyes blurred as they moved over the potatoes in front of me, guiding my hands to the dirt and noting the difference of a rotten or dirty potato.

My brain is dead, dormant. Boredom, tediousness and pain. I was tired, tired of thinking, looking at and picking at potatoes. My mind wandered to the old days, before I went to boarding school seven years ago. Where potato picking was with your friends, and families would turn up at the field early on the cold October mornings to labor all day and make some extra cash.

I was there, lines up, waiting for the tractors to start. A bunch of men passed, red baskets fell in front of me ready to be filled. The sky was still duskey, it was seven in the morning, the sun was beginning to rise. A hush is on the field. The squad are silent remembering the feel of their warm beds and the personalness of their dreams.

A whirr and clatter, an engine starts. A sigh escapes my body, I watch the pattern of the hot air condense in the cold. A buzz is felt on the field. The day has begun. It is work, but the fifty of us are experiencing it together, as a team.

Nobody in class had yet written like this, making the rhythms of sentences match the rhythms of the experience ("Potatoes, mud, potatoes, mud"). When Amanda read this draft out loud to the class, the students sat in awed silence.

Here was their classmate, eighteen-year-old Amanda, to whom her Scottish teachers had said she could not write, demonstrating new and exciting techniques, writing an interior monologue complete with sentence fragments, flashbacks, made-up words, colloquial language, and compelling details. In the comments that follow I could hear the admiration for a classmate's work well done and an unspoken resolve to try still more experiments with next drafts: "I could really feel your work!" "Good job, Amanda!" "Nice going!" "Good writing!"

DRAFT IV

What next? Actually, more of the same. Revision, when taken seriously, is a process that generates ever more and deeper thought, telling the writer that "Yes, you're on the right track. It's getting better," or "No, I think I've exhausted what I have to say on this subject. Better start something else." I wanted to give my writers one more shot at discovering still more about the story they were trying to tell, so for draft four I suggested writing from still another perspective: "Change either your TENSE (from the past to present), POINT OF VIEW (from first to third), or FORM (from essay to drama, letters, or diary)—or all three."

Some students, especially those who were pleased with the shape of their writing, resisted "new" drafts, but only because their old ones were developing in pleasing directions. In a journal entry I find later, Dawn takes me to task (Figure 6-3).

At this point in the course, these student writers had been trying out new and different approaches to telling their personal stories. Now, with virtually everyone accepting the idea that good writing was the result of intensive exploration, frequent and frank feedback, risk taking, and seeing good models, I felt it was time to slow down and see what the whole might look like.

So, during the fifth week of the term, I scheduled conferences where we talked one-on-one about each writer's several drafts: What did the writer like

Figure 6-3

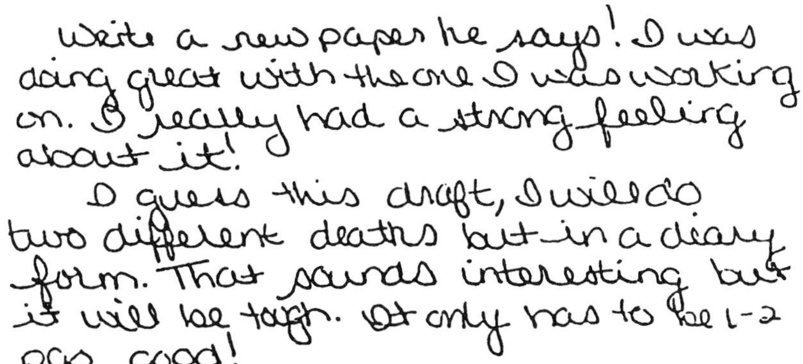

Write a new paper he says! I was doing great with the one I was working on. I really had a strong feeling about it!

I guess this draft, I will do two different deaths but in a diary form. That sounds interesting but it will be tough. It only has to be 1-2 pgs good!

best or least? What story was emerging? Where would the next draft lead? We conducted each conference with plans for a fifth more focused and comprehensive draft, which would give shape to each experience.

With these last drafts, virtually every one of the twenty-six students had arrived at a pleasing story of self. Dawn's story in the nursing home finally took the form of "a day in the life," where she invited readers to accompany her throughout her whole eight-hour shift. Had I space here, I would share with you Jon's recreated journal of eleven months in Ecuador as an exchange student which is how he solved the problem of writing in detail yet still covering a long span of time. Or I would show you Avey's portrait of a deteriorating relationship with her boarding school best friend over a four-year period, which she finally told as a series of telephone conversations each a few months later—and more distant—than the previous one. Or John's decision to capture his basketball coaching season by focusing on a three-minute talk with the rival coach sitting in the bleachers before one game began. As you can see, some writers, such as Dawn, found their stories early on and stayed close to it, while others, such as Amanda, kept moving their pieces outward, adding ever newer dimensions to what they started with, finding out ever more about their own stories.

Let me conclude this study of one writing class with excerpts from Amanda's last draft, for which she invented a narrative in three scenes, to tell the story of her work in the potato field. In Part One, Amanda described her most recent season (1988) working on the farm before coming to college, working in her father's newly purchased mechanical harvester so now only four people are needed to complete the entire season's harvest. As she explained in our conference: "The last year when I worked there, it was only four of us and the relentless machine." This was the experience she recounted in the "Potatoes, mud, potatoes, mud" draft.

In Part Two—separated by white space and a new date (1983)—Amanda flashed back to when she was younger and one of sixty local people who handpicked the potatoes—the origin of the passage about lying "down among drills of undug potatoes."

For Part Three Amanda wrote only a single paragraph, set off from the other sections by white space and dated in parallel fashion to the other parts (1989). Here is the whole of her third and last section:

> 1989. October 17th
> This year the potato harvester is still working, the same women on board, with the same bored expressions on their faces. Soon this job will probably not need anyone to work or help the machinery. Labor is an expense farmers cannot afford. There are no tattie holidays anymore, no extra pocket money for the small children of the district. Change, technology, development is what they say it is, I say that it is a loss of a valuable experience in hard work, and a loss of good times.

Do you remember that I said at the start of this chapter that it is important for writers to hold off telling readers exactly what to think about their stories?

That readers need to be invited in and allowed to make meaning for themselves? Well, Amanda has done that right up until the end, showing us the different versions of potato picking on her father's farm. In the beginning she didn't know which story to tell, waitressing or potatoes. In draft three she found the story behind her other stories, and that's what that last paragraph is about—but it only emerged in the sixth week of writing. By then, of course, she didn't need it, having understood her point by the way she ordered her dialogues, and monologues. But I think Amanda needed that last paragraph for herself. I would not have wanted it earlier, but it closes her paper.

By now I think you understand the story I wanted to tell about revision. But just in case, let me do as Amanda did and suggest some ideas that might help you when you return to your own drafts—so long as you understand these to be suggestions and not commandments. Although writing gets better by rewriting, there are no guarantees. I know of no formula for revising that works every time or for everyone—or every time for anyone. Revision is a chancy process: Therein lies both the excitement and the frustration.

IDEAS FOR REVISION

The story I just told you involves personal experience writing. However, the premises about the generative power of writing and even many of the specific revision strategies apply, with some modifications, to reports, reviews, research papers, and arguments as well. In argumentative papers, for instance, try writing one draft from the opposite point of view, one as if you were a politician, and maybe one as a newspaper editorial. To that end, the following ideas are sound for virtually any substantial writing task you are called upon to undertake.

Attend to Matters of Conception First

Focus on what you want and need to say, try to get that out, and worry later about how it looks. Keep rereading and keep asking yourself: What is my story? What else should be included? What's no longer necessary? Worry about sentence-level matters, including correct spelling and punctuation, and precise word choice, only after these larger purposes are satisfied. (It's not an efficient use of your time to carefully edit a paragraph that you later delete because it's part of a story you no longer want to tell.)

Allow Time

If a paper is due next week, start it this week, no matter if you have all your data and ideas or not, no matter if the big chem test is on the horizon. Beginning to write, even for ten concerted minutes, will start the incubation process in your own mind, and you'll actually be working on the paper in your subconscious. Plan, at the outset, to do more than one draft—as many more as you need to find and tell your story.

Start Over

Even when you return to a draft that you think just needs a conclusion, reread the whole thing all over, from start to finish, with an eye toward still other possible changes. Every time you read your own paper you create yet another dialogue with it, from which could emerge still a better idea. The conclusion may be all the old paper needed—when last you read it. But that was then and this is now, so don't stand pat; keep looking for what else could happen to the story you are telling.

Compose on a Word Processor

Computers make all the difference when it comes to making changes easy. Save early drafts by relabeling files so that you always have a paper trail to return to or old copy to restore in case you change your mind. If you don't have access to a computer, try to make at least one typed draft before the final one: typed words give you greater distance from your own ideas and invite more possibilities of change. (When Amanda entered my class, she had never typed a paper before and had to learn keyboarding while she learned to revise.) One more hint: For early drafts, start a new file each time and see what else your paper can become. The new file guarantees that you generate new language and, therefore, new thought. You can always merge files later on and synthesize your several insights.

Seek Response

As soon as you have enough copy in reasonable shape, read it or show it to someone you trust and get their reaction. Another pair of eyes can always see what you cannot. Most good writers ask others to read and react to their work *before* the final copy is due. And, of course, you needn't feel obligated to take all the suggestions you're given.

Imagine a Real Audience

Keep your teacher or several skeptical classmates in mind as you write and especially as you reread. Of course whatever story, essay, or report you write is clear to you; it's your story, essay, or report. Ask What information do *they* need to know that I already take for granted? Then put it in because they'll understand you better.

Play with Titles, Introductions, and Conclusions

These are emphatic, highly visible points in any paper. Provocative titles catch readers' attention. Good introductions keep readers going. Strong conclusions leave strong memories in readers' minds. But these same elements work on the writer as well as the reader, as a good title, introduction, or conclusion can suggest changes for what follows (or precedes). Sometimes these elements come first—as controlling ideas—sometimes later, but in any case they can capture (or recapture) the essence of your paper, telling you what to keep and what to cut.

Imagine Other Points of View

Whether the paper is based on experience, data, or opinion, try to see it from another point of view: your job as seen by your boss or a customer; the pro side of the gun control debate even though you are arguing con; how other reviewers have interpreted a movie, play, poem, etc. Seeing and acknowledging other points of view is especially helpful for anticipating questions and objections to your own and therefore allows your writing to present a more complete case.

Let Form Follow Content

Be aware that writing can be and do anything you can make it do, that there are no real rules that all writers *must* follow. There are, however, conventions of genre (writing a twenty-inch book review for the local paper) and discipline (the voice, form, and style of a laboratory report). To violate conventions is to risk not being taken as seriously as you might wish. But, more often than not, so long as your content is substantial and your style clear, the actual form of your writing is more open than you may imagine. Is your paper best written as a report? As an essay? As an exchange of letters? As drama? The point is this: Changing form is not cosmetic; it causes you to see your subject differently.

MY STUDENTS RESPOND

When time came to hand in the midterm portfolios, week seven, we (the class and I) agreed to call these personal experience papers done. Meanwhile, they had started on their second writing assignment, a collaborative research essay on a local issue or institution—which would also be a many-draft process, this time with both the research and the writing shared among group members. At this point, I asked my students to comment anonymously on the process of writing and rewriting this first assignment (see Figures 6-4, 6-5, and 6-6).

At the beginning of the term, I believed that people learned to write by some combination of provocation and nourishment. I set out, dutifully, to provoke these twenty-six student into as many experimental drafts as they would tolerate, reminding them often that the more they tried, the more they would grow. I allowed no one to stand pat and only write what he or she was already good at. Then when someone took a risk and tried something new, I, along with the others in the class, would say "Wow! Good job." In fact, it was amazing how much improvement the word *Wow* seemed to engender. Of course, not everything worked, but everything counted, and the class understood that good writing meant, in the words of one, being "involved," but not being "attached." In the end, however, I learned something else: When students write well, they teach writing teachers to teach well. Thanks, class, for a wonderful lesson.

Figure 6-4

I have a lot different attitude towards writing now, than I did during the first Class. At the beginning of the year. I was scared to write. I've written more papers in these first few weeks, than I did all of last year in English. As we have gone on this year, I feel the ~~#~~ writing has gotten easier. It isn't taking me so long to start a paper and once I am started there is no stopping me. This early writing has also drastically improved my typing abilities as well.

I am hoping that this class will break me out of this writing shell and help me enjoy writing on my own. I don't want to just write when it is required.

Figure 6-5

writing has changed for me. I'm beginning to realize how much you can do with a single idea. I ~~#~~ like the idea of writing 5 pages about a single hour, day or afternoon. On the first day of class I wasn't really sure what to think it seemed like such an odd way to start class. Yet, maybe one of the best ways considering the type of class this is I still find writing very difficult I never seem able to get the way I feel down on paper My goals are to be able to do this by the end of the semester. I want there to ~~#~~ be some of me in the paper also.

Figure 6-6

Writting: I'm more involved in it. But not as attached. I used to really cling to my writing, and didn't want it to change. Now, I can see the usefulness of it. I just really like my 3rd draft. But for the final draft I am thinking of struggling with it. I feel like I have to let go of my third draft, but that's not what it's all about. I can still really enjoy my third draft and create another exciting paper.

Writing is more than just pen to paper or hands to key board. It is also reading, rereading and getting some criticism on it. I have improved my papers so much after getting feedback from Ed Kelley, Dawn, Gavin, Kelley, Lance Amy and Toby, and Amanda.

ANNIE DILLARD (b. 1945)

"Transfiguration" and "How I Wrote the Moth Essay—and Why"

CONSIDER THIS:

Annie Dillard was born and raised in Pittsburgh. She has taught at Wesleyan University in Middletown, Connecticut, and won the Pulitzer Prize in 1975 for *Pilgrim at Tinker Creek.* Dillard has some passionate words to say about revision in the passionately entitled "Write Till You Drop" from the *New York Times:* "Every book has an intrinsic impossibility, which its writer discovers as soon as his first excitement dwindles. The problem is structural; it is insoluble; it is why no one can ever write this book. Complex stories, essays and poems have this problem, too—the prohibitive structural defect the writer wishes he had never noticed." Should the writer give up, then? No! says Dillard. "He writes it in spite of that. He finds ways to minimize the difficulty; he strengthens other virtues; he cantilevers the whole narrative out into thin air and it holds. Why are we reading, if not in hope of beauty laid bare, life heightened and its deepest mystery probed? Can the writer isolate and vivify all in experience that most deeply engages our intellects and our hearts? Can the writer renew our hopes for literary forms?"

Dillard's passion for writing translates into care about the writing process. In the essay and commentary shared here, Dillard provides one model for the writing process narratives that writing students compile. You can find the essay she comments on, "Death of a Moth," in any number of essay anthologies. In this essay on her essay, you find a discussion of her composing process and even a reprint of a manuscript page, adorned with doodles and drawings and illustrating the very physical nature of hand revision: words are crossed off and others inserted. To what degree does this page resemble a page from one of your own drafts? From any writer's drafts?

I live on northern Puget Sound, in Washington State, alone. I have a gold cat, who sleeps on my legs, named Small. In the morning I joke to her blank face, Do you remember last night? Do you remember? I throw her out before breakfast, so I can eat.

There is a spider, too, in the bathroom, with whom I keep a sort of company. Her little outfit always reminds me of a certain moth I helped to kill. The spider herself is of uncertain lineage, bulbous at the abdomen and drab. Her six-inch mess of a web works, works somehow, works miraculously, to keep her alive and me amazed. The web itself is in a corner behind the toilet, connecting tile wall to tile wall and floor, in a place where there is, I would have thought, scant traffic. Yet under the web are sixteen or so corpses she has tossed to the floor.

The corpses appear to be mostly sow bugs, those little armadillo creatures who live to travel flat out in houses, and die round. There is also a new shred of earwig, three old spider skins crinkled and clenched, and two moth bodies, wingless and huge and empty, moth bodies I drop to my knees to see.

Today the earwig shines darkly and gleams, what there is of him: a dorsal curve of thorax and abdomen, and a smooth pair of cerci by which I knew his name. Next week, if the other bodies are any indication, he will be shrunken and gray, webbed to the floor with dust. The sow bugs beside him are hollow and empty of color, fragile, a breath away from brittle fluff. The spider skins lie on their sides, translucent and ragged, their legs drying in knots. And the moths, the empty moths, stagger against each other, headless, in a confusion of arching strips of chitin like peeling varnish, like a jumble of buttresses for cathedral domes, like nothing resembling moths, so that I should hesitate to call them moths, except that I have had some experience with the figure Moth reduced to a nub.

Two summers ago I was camping alone in the Blue Ridge Mountains in Virginia. I had hauled myself and gear up there to read, among other things, James Ramsey Ullman's *The Day on Fire,* a novel about Rimbaud that had made me want to be a writer when I was sixteen; I was hoping it would do it again. So I read, lost, every day sitting under a tree by my tent, while warblers swung in the leaves overhead and bristle worms trailed their inches over the twiggy dirt at my feet; and I read every night by candlelight, while barred owls called in the forest and pale moths massed round my head in the clearing, where my light made a ring.

Moths kept flying into the candle. They would hiss and recoil, lost upside down in the shadows among my cooking pans. Or they would singe their wings and fall, and their hot wings, as if melted, would stick to the first thing they touched—a pan, a lid, a spoon—so that the snagged moths could flutter only in tiny arcs, unable to struggle free. These I could release by a quick flip with a stick; in the morning I would find my cooking stuff gilded with torn flecks of moth wings, triangles of shiny dust here and there on the aluminum. So I read, and boiled water, and replenished candles, and read on.

One night a moth flew into the candle, was caught, burnt dry, and held. I must have been staring at the candle, or maybe I looked up when a shadow crossed my page; at any rate, I saw it all. A golden female moth, a biggish one with a two-inch wingspan, flapped into the fire, dropped her abdomen into the wet wax, stuck, flamed, frazzled and fried in a second. Her moving wings ignited like tissue paper, enlarging the circle of light in the clearing and creating out of the darkness the sudden blue sleeves of my sweater, the green leaves of jewelweed by my side, the ragged red trunk of a pine. At once the light contracted again and the moth's wings vanished in a fine, foul smoke. At the same time her six legs clawed, curled, blackened, and ceased, disappearing utterly. And her head jerked in spasms, making a spattering noise; her antennae crisped and burned away and her heaving mouth parts crackled like pistol fire. When it was all over, her head was, so far as I could determine, gone, gone the long way of her wings and legs. Had she been new, or old? Had she mated and laid her eggs, had she done her work? All that was left was the glowing horn shell of her abdomen and thorax—a fraying, partially collapsed gold tube jammed upright in the candle's round pool.

And then this moth-essence, this spectacular skeleton, began to act as a wick. She kept burning. The wax rose in the moth's body from her soaking abdomen to her thorax to the jagged hole where her head should be, and widened into flame, a saffron-yellow flame that robed her to the ground like any immolating monk. That candle had two wicks, two flames of identical height, side by side. The moth's head was fire. She burned for two hours, until I blew her out.

She burned for two hours without changing, without bending or leaning—only glowing within, like a building fire glimpsed through silhouetted walls, like a hollow saint, like a flame-faced virgin gone to God, while I read by her light, kindled, while Rimbaud in Paris burnt out his brains in a thousand poems, while night pooled wetly at my feet.

And that is why I believe those hollow crisps on the bathroom floor are moths. I think I know moths, and fragments of moths, and chips and tatters of utterly empty moths, in any state. How many of you, I asked the people in my class, which of you want to give your lives and be writers? I was trembling from coffee, or cigarettes, or the closeness of faces all around me. (Is this what we live for? I thought; is this the only final beauty: the color of any skin in any light, and living, human eyes?) All hands rose to the question. (You, Nick? Will you? Margaret? Randy? Why do I want them to mean it?) And then I tried to tell them what the choice must mean: you can't be anything else. You must go at your life with a broadax. . . . They had no idea what I was saying. (I have two hands, don't I? And all this energy, for as long as I can remember. I'll do it in the evenings, after skiing, or on the way home from the bank, or after the children are asleep. . . .) They thought I was raving again. It's just as well.

I have three candles here on the table which I disentangle from the plants and light when visitors come. Small usually avoids them, although once she came too lose and her tail caught fire; I rubbed it out before she noticed. The flames move light over everyone's skin, draw light to the surface of the faces of my friends. When the people leave I never blow the candles out, and after I'm asleep they flame and burn.

HOW I WROTE THE MOTH ESSAY—AND WHY

It was November 1975. I was living alone, as described, on an island in Puget Sound, near the Canadian border. I was thirty years old. I thought about myself a lot (for someone thirty years old), because I couldn't figure out what I was doing there. What was my life about? Why was I living alone, when I am gregarious? Would I ever meet someone, or should I reconcile myself to all this solitude? I disliked celibacy; I dreaded childlessness. I couldn't even think of anything to write. I was examining every event for possible meaning.

I was then in full flight from success, from the recent fuss over a book of prose I'd published the previous year called *Pilgrim at Tinker Creek.* There were offers from editors, publishers, and Hollywood and network producers. They tempted me with world travel, film and TV work, big bucks. I was there to turn from literary and commercial success and to rededicate myself to art and to God. That's how I justified my loneliness to myself. It was a feeble justification and I knew it, because you certainly don't need to live alone either to write or to pray. Actually I was there because I had picked the place from an atlas, and I was alone because I hadn't yet met my husband.

My reading and teaching fed my thoughts. I was reading Simone Weil, *First and Last Notebooks.* Simone Weil was a twentieth-century French intellectual, born Jewish, who wrote some of the most interesting Christian theology I've ever read. She was brilliant, but a little nuts; her doctrines were harsh. "Literally," she wrote, "it is total purity or death." This sort of fanaticism attracted and appalled me. Weil had deliberately starved herself to death to call attention to the plight of French workers. I was taking extensive notes on Weil.

In the classroom I was teaching poetry writing, exhorting myself (in the guise of exhorting my students), and convincing myself by my own rhetoric: commit yourself to a useless art! In art alone is meaning! In sacrifice alone is meaning! These, then, were issues for me at that time: dedication, purity, sacrifice.

Early that November morning I noticed the hollow insects on the bathroom floor. I got down on my hands and knees to examine them and recognized some as empty moth bodies. I recognized them, of course, only because I'd seen an empty moth body already—two years before, when I'd camped alone and had watched a flying moth get stuck in a candle and burn.

Walking back to my desk, where I had been answering letters, I realized that the burning moth was a dandy visual focus for all my recent thoughts about an empty, dedicated life. Perhaps I'd try to write a short narrative about it.

I went to my pile of journals, hoping I'd taken some nice, specific notes about the moth in the candle. What I found disappointed me at first: that night I'd written a long description of owl sounds, and only an annoyed aside about bugs flying into the candle. But the next night, after pages of self-indulgent drivel, I'd written a fuller description, a description of the moth which got stuck in candle wax.

The journal entry had some details I could use (bristleworms on the ground, burnt moths' wings sticking to pans), some phrases (her body acted as a wick, the candle had 2 flames, the moth burned until I blew it out), and, especially, some verbs (hiss, recoil, stick, spatter, jerked, crackled).

Even in the journals, the moth was female. (From childhood reading I'd learned to distinguish moths by sex.) And, there in the journal, was a crucial detail: on that camping trip, I'd been reading about Rimbaud. Arthur Rimbaud—the French symbolist poet, a romantic, hotheaded figure who attracted me enormously when I was sixteen—had been young and self-destructive. When *he* was sixteen, he ran away from home to Paris, led a dissolute life, shot his male lover (the poet Verlaine), drank absinthe which damaged his brain, deranged his senses with drunkenness and sleeplessness, and wrote mad vivid poetry which altered the course of Western literature. When he was in his twenties, he turned his back to the Western world and vanished into Abyssinia as a gunrunner.

With my old journal beside me, I took up my current journal and scribbled and doodled my way through an account of my present life and the remembered moth. It went extraordinarily well; it was not typical. It seemed very much "given"—given, I think, because I'd asked, because I'd been looking so hard and so long for connections, meanings. The connections were all there, and seemed solid enough: I saw a moth burnt and on fire; I was reading Rimbaud hoping to rededicate myself to writing (this one bald statement of motive was unavoidable); I live alone. So the writer is like the moth, and like a religious

Jan B.

while R sun sent his beams

Kindling

Two summers ago I ~~was camped~~ was camping alone in the Blue Ridge mountains in Virginia. I had hauled myself and gear up there to read, among other things, ~~in peace~~, James Ramsey Ullman's The Day on Fire, a novel about Rimbaud that had made me want to be a writer ~~of~~ when I was sixteen; I was hoping it would do it again. So I read every day sitting under a tree by my tent, ~~pausing to eat four or five times and walk once or twice, and I read every night~~ while warblers swung in the leaves overhead and bristleworms trailed their inches over the fuzzy dirt at my (side) feet; and I read every night by candlelight, while the barred owls called in the forest and pale moths massed in the clearing. ~~...~~ when my light made a ring.

~~The moths flew in~~ Moths kept flying into the candle. They would hiss ~~and spatter~~ and recoil, lost upside down in the shadows among my cooking pans. Or they would singe their wings and fall, and their hot wings would stick, as if melted, to whatever they touched, the first thing, a pan, a lid, a spoon, so that the snagged moths could struggle only in tiny arcs, unable to flutter free. These I could release by a quick flip with a stick; in the morning I would find my cooking stuff embossed with torn flecks of moth wings, little triangles of shiny dust here and there on the aluminum. So I read, and boiled water, and replenished candles, and read on.

One night one female moth flew into the candle, was caught, burned dry and held. ~~and burned so fast~~ sizzled, dropped her abdomen into the wet wax, stuck, flamed and fried in a second. Her wings burnt right off and disappeared in a thin, foul smoke; her legs spattered and curled, her head (crackled and jerked) (like small arms fire)

~~Her wings, fan wings~~ I must have been staring at the candle, or maybe I looked up when a shadow crossed my page; at any rate, I saw it all ~~the whole thing~~.

contemplative: emptying himself so he can be a channel for his work. Of course you can reinforce connections with language: the bathroom moths are like a jumble of buttresses for cathedral domes; the female moth is like an immolating monk, like a hollow saint, a flame-faced virgin gone to God; Rimbaud burnt out his brains with poetry while night pooled wetly at my feet.

I liked the piece enough to rewrite it. I took out a couple of paragraphs—one about why I didn't have a dog, another that ran on about the bathroom spider. This is the kind of absurdity you fall into when you write about anything, let alone about yourself. You're so pleased and grateful to be writing at all, especially at the beginning, that you babble. Often you don't know where the work is going, so you can't tell what's irrelevant.

It doesn't hurt much to babble in a first draft, so long as you have the sense to cut out irrelevancies later. If you are used to analyzing texts, you will be able to formulate a clear statement of what your draft turned out to be about. Then you make a list of what you've already written, paragraph by paragraph, and see what doesn't fit and cut it out. (All this requires is nerves of steel and lots of coffee.) Most of the time you'll have to add to the beginning, ensuring that it gives a fair idea of what the point might be, or at least what is about to happen. (Suspense is for mystery writers. The most inept writing has an inadvertent element of suspense: the reader constantly asks himself, where on earth is this going?) Usually I end up throwing away the beginning: the first part of a poem, the first few pages of an essay, the first scene of a story, even the first chapter of a book. It's not holy writ. The paragraphs and sentences are tessarae—tiles for a mosaic. Just because you have a bunch of tiles in your lap doesn't mean your mosaic will be better if you use them all. In this atypical case, however, there were very few extraneous passages. The focus was tight, probably because I'd been so single-minded before I wrote it.

I added stuff, too, to strengthen and clarify the point. I added some speculation about the burning moth: had she mated and laid her eggs, had she done her work? Near the end I added a passage about writing class: which of you want to give your lives and become writers?

Ultimately I sent it to *Harper's* magazine, which published it. The early drafts, and the *Harper's* version, had a different ending, a kind of punch line that was a series of interlocking statements:

I don't mind living alone. I like eating alone and reading. I don't mind sleeping alone. The only time I mind being alone is when something is funny; then, when I am laughing at something funny, I wish someone were around. Sometimes I think it is pretty funny that I sleep alone.

OPPOSITE: *"With my old journal beside me, I took up my current journal and scribbled and doodled my way through an account of my present life and the remembered moth." Page from the first draft of "Transfiguration."*

in these were quickly, too.

The rip in thigh seam is 10" long. Oh, dear jeans.

Last night moths kept flying into the candle. They would hiss & spatter & recoil, lost upside down & flapping in the shadows among the pans on the table. Or — and this happened often, & again tonight — they'd burn their wings, & then their wings would stick to the next thing they'd touch — the edge of a pan, a lid.... These I could free with a quick flip with a spoon or something.

Some, of course, burnt badly & couldn't get away. One moth flew in the near candle. Her wings burnt right off, her legs & head crackled and jerked. Her body was stuck upright in the wax; it must have been dry. Moths are dry. Because it acted as a wick; without burning itself, it drew up wax from the pool, and gave off a steady flame for two hours, until I blew ~~the candle~~ it out. That one candle had two flames. Brightened up my whole evening.

I was screaming to them last night. I got upset, & it was in my voice. Wonder what the neighbors thought: no! don't do it! please — no! So tonight I read in the lodge. After the B & B, I read upstairs on the couch.

Talked to Steve, at Cortes w/ KK; talked to Richard twice, at noon, & now.

I don't know what those firm segmented multilegged invertebrates are, but they're all over the place up here. Bristleworms? They're hard on the outside, chitinous I guess. Anyway. One on the path today was on its side, struggling. A big spider of the harvestman sort, but w/ a big grey body, was all over it doing I know not what, & so was a fly.

I took this ending out of the book version, which is the version you have. I took it out because the tone was too snappy, too clever; it reduced everything to celibacy, which was really a side issue; it made the reader forget the moth; and it called too much attention to the narrator. The new ending was milder. It referred back to the main body of the text.

Revising is a breeze if you know what you're doing—if you can look at your text coldly, analytically, manipulatively. Since I've studied texts, I know what I'm doing when I revise. The hard part is devising the wretched thing in the first place. How do you go from nothing to something? How do you face the blank page without fainting dead away?

To start a narrative, you need a batch of things. Not feelings, not opinions, not sentiments, not judgments, not arguments, but specific objects and events: a cat, a spider web, a mess of insect skeletons, a candle, a book about Rimbaud, a burning moth. I try to give the reader a story, or at least a scene (the flimsiest narrative occasion will serve), and something to look at. I try not to hang on the reader's arm and bore him with my life story, my fancy self-indulgent writing, or my opinions. He is my guest; I try to entertain him. Or he'll throw my pages across the room and turn on the television.

I try to say what I mean and not "hide the hidden meaning." "Clarity is the sovereign courtesy of the writer," said J. Henri Fabre, the great French entomologist, "I do my best to achieve it." Actually, it took me about ten years to learn to write clearly. When I was in my twenties, I was more interested in showing off.

What do you do with these things? You juggle them. You toss them around. To begin, you don't need a well defined point. You don't need "something to say"—that will just lead you to reiterating clichés. You need bits of the world to toss around. You start anywhere, and join the bits into a pattern by your writing about them. Later you can throw out the ones that don't fit.

I like to start by describing something, by ticking off the five senses. Later I go back to the beginning and locate the reader in time and space. I've found that if I take pains to be precise about *things*, feelings will take care of themselves. If you try to force a reader's feelings through dramatic writing ("writhe," "ecstasy," "scream"), you make a fool of yourself, like someone at a party trying too hard to be liked.

I have piles of materials in my journals—mostly information in the form of notes on my reading, and to a lesser extent, notes on things I'd seen and heard during the day. I began the journals five or six years after college, finding myself highly trained for taking notes and for little else. Now I have thirty-some journal volumes, all indexed. If I want to write about arctic exploration, say, or star chemistry, or monasticism, I can find masses of pertinent data under that topic. And if I browse I can often find images from other fields that may fit into what I'm writing, if only as metaphor or simile. It's terrific having all these

OPPOSITE. *First encounter with the flaming moth: a page from Annie Dillard's journal, August–October 1974.*

materials handy. It saves and makes available all those years of reading. Otherwise, I'd forget everything, and life wouldn't accumulate, but merely pass.

The moth essay I wrote that November day was an "odd" piece—"freighted with heavy-handed symbolism," as I described it to myself just after I wrote it. The reader must be startled to watch this apparently calm, matter-of-fact account of the writer's life and times turn before his eyes into a mess of symbols whose real subject matter is their own relationship. I hoped the reader wouldn't feel he'd been had. I tried to ensure that the actual, historical moth wouldn't vanish into idea, but would stay physically present.

A week after I wrote the first draft I considered making it part of the book (*Holy the Firm*) I had been starting. It seemed to fit the book's themes. (Actually, I spent the next fifteen months fitting the book to *its* themes.) In order to clarify my thinking I jotted down some notes:

moth in candle:

the poet—materials of world, of bare earth at feet, sucked up, transformed, subsumed to spirit, to air, to light

the mystic—not through reason
but through emptiness

the martyr—virgin, sacrifice, death with meaning.

I prefaced these notes with the comical word "Hothead."

It had been sheer good luck that the different aspects of the historical truth fit together so nicely. It had actually been on that particular solo camping trip that I'd read the Rimbaud novel. If it hadn't been, I wouldn't have hesitated to fiddle with the facts. I fiddled with one fact, for sure: I foully slandered my black cat, Small, by saying she was "gold"—to match the book's moth and little blonde burnt girl. I actually had a gold cat at that time, named Kindling. I figured no one would believe it. It was too much. In the book, as in real life, the cat was spayed.

This is the most personal piece I've ever written—the essay itself, and these notes on it. I don't recommend, or even approve, writing personally. It can lead to dreadful writing. The danger is that you'll get lost in the contemplation of your wonderful self. You'll include things for the lousy reason that they actually happened, or that you feel strongly about them; you'll forget to ensure that the *reader* feels anything whatever. You may hold the popular view that art is self-expression, or a way of understanding the self—in which case the artist need do nothing more than babble uncontrolledly about the self and then congratulate himself that, in addition to all his other wonderfully interesting attributes, he is also an artist. I don't (evidently) hold this view. So I think that this moth piece is a risky one to read: it seems to enforce these romantic and giddy notions of art and the artist. But I trust you can keep your heads.

RICHARD STRAUB (1956–2002)

Responding—Really Responding—to Other Students' Writing

CONSIDER THIS:

Richard Straub, from Dunmore, Pennsylvania, earned his Ph.D. at Ohio State. He taught courses in writing, composition and rhetoric, and literature at Florida State University for 15 years. Much of his work revolved around response to and evaluation of students' writing as discussed in *Twelve Readers Reading,* a study of the ways composition teachers respond to student texts. As you read his essay, consider which of his pieces of advice for responding to students' writing you already follow and which are new to you. You might find yourself considering the types of advice you would offer if responding to the sample student paper in this essay.

Okay. You've got a student paper you have to read and make comments on for Thursday. It's not something you're looking forward to. But that's alright, you think. There isn't really all that much to it. Just keep it simple. Read it quickly and mark whatever you see. Say something about the introduction. Something about details and examples. Ideas you can say you like. Mark any typos and spelling errors. Make your comments brief. Abbreviate where possible: *awk, good intro, give ex, frag.* Try to imitate the teacher. Mark what he'd mark and sound like he'd sound. But be cool about it. Don't praise anything really, but no need to get harsh or cut throat either. Get in and get out. You're okay, I'm okay. Everybody's happy. What's the problem?

This is, no doubt, a way of getting through the assignment. Satisfy the teacher and no surprises for the writer. It might just do the trick. But say you want to do a *good* job. Say you're willing to put in the time and effort—though time is tight and you know it's not going to be easy—and help the writer look back on the paper and revise it. And maybe in the process learn something more yourself about writing. What do you look for? How do you sound? How much time do you take up? What exactly are you trying to accomplish? Here are some ideas.

HOW SHOULD YOU LOOK AT YOURSELF AS A RESPONDER?

Consider yourself a friendly reader. A test pilot. A roommate who's been asked to look over the paper and tell the writer what you think. Except you don't just take on the role of The Nice Roommate or The Ever-faithful Friend and tell her what she wants to hear. *This all looks good. I wouldn't change a thing. There are a couple places that I think he might not like, but I can see what you're doing there. I'd go with it. Good Stuff.* You're supportive. You give her the benefit of the doubt and look to see the good in her writing. But friends don't let friends think their writing is the best thing since *The Great Gatsby* and they don't lead them to think that all is fine and well when it's not. Look to help this friend, this roommate writer—okay, this person in your class—to get a better piece of writing. Point to problems and areas for improvement but do it in a constructive way. See what you can do to push her to do even more than she's done and stretch herself as a writer.

WHAT ARE YOUR GOALS?

First, don't set out to seek and destroy all errors and problems in the writing. You're not an editor. You're not a teacher. You're not a cruise missile. And don't rewrite any parts of the paper. You're not the writer; you're a reader. One of many. The paper is not yours; it's the writer's. She writes. You read. She is in charge of what she does to her writing. That doesn't mean you can't make suggestions. It doesn't mean you can't offer a few sample rewrites here and there, as models. But make it clear they're samples, models. Not rewrites. Not edits. Not corrections. Be reluctant at first even to say what you would do if the paper were yours. It's not yours. Again: Writers write, readers read and show what they're understanding and maybe make suggestions. What to do instead: Look at your task as a simple one. You're there to play back to the writer how you read the paper: what you got from it; what you found interesting, where you were confused; where you wanted more. With this done, you can go on to point out problems, ask questions, offer advice, and wonder out loud with the writer about her ideas. Look to help her improve the writing or encourage her to work on some things as a writer.

HOW DO YOU GET STARTED?

Before you up and start reading the paper, take a minute (alright, thirty seconds) to make a mental checklist about the circumstances of the writing, the context. You're not going to just read a text. You're going to read a text within a certain context, a set of circumstances that accompany the writing and that, you bring to your reading. It's one kind of writing or another, designed for one audience and purpose or another. It's a rough draft or a final draft. The writer is trying to be serious or casual, straight or ironic. Ideally, you'll read the paper with an eye to the circumstances that it was written in and the situation it is looking to create. That means looking at the writing in terms of the assignment, the writer's particular interests and aims, the work you've been doing in class, and the stage of drafting.

- *The assignment:* What kind of writing does the assignment call (or allow) for? Is the paper supposed to be a personal essay? A report? An analysis? An argument? Consider how well the paper before you meets the demands of the kind of writing the writer is taking up.
- *The writer's interest and aims:* What does the writer want to accomplish? If she's writing a personal narrative, say, is she trying to simply recount a

past experience? Is she trying to recount a past experience and at the same time amuse her readers? Is she trying to show a pleasant experience on the surface, yet suggest underneath that everything was not as pleasant as it seems? Hone in on the writer's particular aims in the writing.

- *The work of the class:* Try to tie your comments to the concepts and strategies you've been studying in class. If you've been doing a lot of work on using detail, be sure to point to places in the writing where the writer uses detail effectively or where she might provide richer detail. If you've been working on developing arguments through examples and sample cases, indicate where the writer might use such methods to strengthen her arguments. If you've been considering various ways to sharpen the style of your sentences, offer places where the writer can clarify her sentence structure or arrange a sentence for maximum impact. The best comments will ring familiar even as they lead the writer to try to do something she hasn't quite done before, or done in quite the same way. They'll be comforting and understandable even as they create some need to do more, a need to figure out some better way.
- *The stage of drafting:* Is it an early draft? A full but incomplete draft? A nearly final draft? Pay attention to the stage of drafting. Don't try to deal with everything all at once if it's a first, rough draft. Concentrate on the large picture: the paper's focus; the content; the writer's voice. Don't worry about errors and punctuation problems yet. There'll be time for them later. If it's closer to a full draft, go ahead and talk, in addition to the overall content , about arrangement, pacing, and sentence style. Wait till the final draft to give much attention to fine-tuning sentences and dealing in detail with proofreading. Remember: You're not an editor. Leave these sentence revisions and corrections for the writer. It's her paper. And she's going to learn best by detecting problems and making her own changes.

WHAT TO ADDRESS IN YOUR COMMENTS?

Try to focus your comments on a couple of areas of writing. Glance through the paper quickly first. Get an idea whether you'll deal mostly with the overall content and purpose of the writing, its shape and flow, or (if these are more or less in order) with local matters of paragraph structure, sentence style, and correctness. Don' t try to cover everything that comes up or even all instances of a given problem. Address issues that are most important to address in this paper, at this time.

WHERE TO PUT YOUR COMMENTS?

Some teachers like to have students write comments in the margins right next to the passage. Some like to have students write out their comments in an end note or in a separate letter to the writer. I like to recommend using both marginal comments and a note or letter at the end. The best of both worlds. Marginal comments allow you to give a quick moment-by-moment reading of the paper. They make it easy to give immediate and specific feedback. You still have to make sure you specify what you're talking about and what you have to say, but they save you some work telling the writer what you're addressing and allow you to focus your end note on things that are most important. Comments at the end allow you to provide some perspective on your response. This doesn't mean that you have to size up the paper and give it a thumbs up or a thumbs down. You can use the end comment to emphasize the key points of your response, explain and elaborate on issues you want to deal with more fully, and mention additional points that you don't want to address in detail. One thing to avoid: plastering comments all over the writing; in between and over the lines of the other person's writing—up, down, and across the page. Write in your space, and let the writer keep hers.

HOW TO SOUND?

Not like a teacher. Not like a judge. Not like art editor or critic or shotgun. (Wouldn't you want someone who was giving you comments not to sound like a teacher's red pen, a judge's ruling, an editor's impatience, a critic's wrath, a shotgun's blast?) Sound like you normally sound when you're speaking with a friend or acquaintance. Talk to the writer. You're not marking up a text; you're responding to the writer. You're a reader, a helper, a colleague. Try to sound like someone who's a reader, who's helpful, and collegial. Supportive. And remember: Even when you're tough and demanding you can still be supportive.

HOW MUCH TO COMMENT?

Don't be stingy. Write most of your comments out in full statements. Instead of writing two or three words, write seven or eight. Instead of making only one brief comment and moving on, say what you have to say and then go back over the statement and explain what you mean or why you said it or note other alternatives. Let the writer know again and again how you are understanding her paper, what you take her to be saying. And elaborate on your key comments. Explain your interpretations, problems, questions, and advice.

IS IT OKAY TO BE SHORT AND SWEET?

No. At least not most of the time. Get specific. Don't rely on general statements alone. How much have generic comments helped you as a writer? "Add detail." "Needs better structure." "Unclear." Try to let the writer know what exactly the problem is. Refer specifically to the writer's words and make them a part of your comments. "Add some detail on what it was like working at the beach." "I think we'll need to know more about your high school crowd before we can understand the way you've changed." "This sentence is not clear. Were *you* disappointed or were *they* disappointed?" This way the writer will see what you're talking about, and she'll have a better idea what to work on.

DO YOU PRAISE OR CRITICIZE OR WHAT?

Be always of two (or three) minds about your response to the paper. You like the paper, but it could use some more interesting detail. You found this statement interesting, but these ideas in the second paragraph are not so hot. It's an alright paper, but it could be outstanding if the writer said what was really bothering her. Always be ready to praise. But always look to point to places that are not working well or that are not yet working as well as they might. Always be ready to expect more from the writer.

HOW TO PRESENT YOUR COMMENTS?

Don't steer away from being critical. Feel free—in fact, feel obliged—to tell the writer what you like and don't like, what is and is not working, and where you think it can be made to work better. But use some other strategies, too. Try to engage the writer in considering her choices and thinking about possible ways to improve the paper. Make it a goal to write two or three comments that look to summarize or paraphrase what the writer is saying. Instead of *telling* the reader what to do, *suggest* what she might do. Identify the questions that are raised for you as you read:

- Play back your way of understanding the writing:

  This seems to be the real focus of the paper, the issue you seem most interested in.

  So you're saying that you really weren't interested in her romantically?

- Temper your criticisms:

  This sentence is a bit hard to follow.

  I'm not sure this paragraph is necessary.

- Offer advice:

  It might help to add an example here.

  Maybe save this sentence for the end of the paper.

- Ask questions, especially real questions:

  What else were you feeling at the time?

  What kind of friend? Would it help to say?

  Do you need this opening sentence?

  In what ways were you "a daddy's little girl"?

- Explain and follow up on your initial comments:

  You might present this episode first. This way we can see what you mean when you say that he was always too busy.

How did you react? Did you cry or yell? Did you walk away?

This makes her sound cold and calculating. Is that what you want?

- Offer some praise, and then explain to the writer why the writing works:

  Good opening paragraph. You've got my attention.

  Good detail. It tells me a lot about the place.

  I like the descriptions you provide—for instance, about your grandmother cooking, at the bottom of page 1; about her house, in the middle of page 2; and about how she said her rosary at night: "quick but almost pleading, like crying without tears."

HOW MUCH CRITICISM? HOW MUCH PRAISE?

Challenge yourself to write as many praise comments as criticisms. When you praise, praise well. Think about it. Sincerity and specificity are everything when it comes to a compliment.

HOW MUCH SHOULD YOU BE INFLUENCED BY WHAT YOU KNOW ABOUT THE WRITER?

Consider the person behind the writer when you make your comments. If she's not done so well in class lately, maybe you can give her a pick-me-up in your comments. If she's shy and seems reluctant to go into the kind of personal detail the paper seems to need, encourage her. Make some suggestions or tell her what you would do. If she's confident and going on arrogant, see what you can do to challenge her with the ideas she presents in the paper. Look for other views she may not have thought about, and find ways to lead her to consider them. Always be ready to look at the text in terms of the writer behind the text.

Good comments, this listing shows, require a lot from a reader. But you don't have to make a checklist out of these suggestions and go through each one methodically as you read. It's amazing how they all start coming together when you look at your response as a way of talking with the writer seriously about the writing, recording how you experience the words on the page and giving the writer something to think about for revision. The more you see examples of thoughtful commentary and the more you try to do it yourself, the more you'll get a feel for how it's done.

Here's a set of student comments on a student paper. They were done in the last third of a course that focused on the personal essay and concentrated on helping students develop the content and thought of their writing. The class had been working on finding ways to develop and extend the key statements of their essays (by using short, representative details, full-blown examples, dialogue, and multiple perspectives) and getting more careful about selecting and shaping parts of their writing. The assignment called on students to write an essay or an autobiographical story where they looked to capture how they see (or have seen) something about one or both of their parents—some habits, attitudes, or traits their parents have taken on. They were encouraged to give shape to their ideas and experiences in ways that went beyond their previous understandings and try things they hadn't tried in their writing. More a personal narrative than an essay, Todd's paper looks to capture one distinct difference in the way his mother and father disciplined their children. It is a rough draft that will be taken through one or possibly two more revisions. Readers were asked to offer whatever feedback they could that might help the writer with the next stage of writing (Figure 6-7).

This is a full and thoughtful set of comments. The responder, Jeremy, creates himself not as a teacher or critic but first of all as a reader, one who is intent on saying how he takes the writing and what he'd like to hear more about:

> Good point. Makes it more unlikely that you should be the one to get caught.
> Great passage. Really lets the reader know what you were thinking.
> Was there a reason you were first or did it just happen that way?
> Would he punish you anyway or could you just get away with things?

He makes twenty-two comments on the paper—seventeen statement in the margins and five more in the end note. The comments are written out in full statements, and they are detailed and specific. They make his response into a lively exchange with the writer, one person talking with another about what he's said. Well over half of the comments are follow-up comments that explain, illustrate, or qualify other responses.

The comments focus on the content and development of the writing, in line with the assignment, the stage of drafting, and the work of the course. They also view the writing rhetorically, in terms of how the text has certain effects on readers. Although there are over two dozen wording or sentence-level errors in the paper, he decides, wisely, to stick with the larger matters of writing. Yet even as he offers a pretty full set of comments he doesn't ever take control over the text. His comments are placed unobtrusively on the page, and he doesn't try to close things down or decide things for the writer. He offers praise, encouragement, and direction. What's more, he pushes the writer to do more than he has already done, to extend the boundaries of his examination. In keeping with the assignment and the larger goals of the course, he calls on Todd in several comments to explore the motivations and personalities behind his parents' different ways of disciplining:

> Maybe you could say more as to why you think your mom is like this.
> Did your dad get into trouble as a kid so he know what it's like? Explain why he reacts as he does.

He is careful, though, not to get presumptuous and make decisions for the writer. Instead, he offers options and points to possibilities:

> Perhaps more on your understanding of why your parents react as they do.
> What other things did you do to get into trouble? Or is it irrelevant?

From start to finish he takes on the task of reading and responding and leaves the work of writing and revising to Todd.

Figure 6-7

Jeremy

Todd
ENG 1
Rick Straub
Assignment 8b

"Uh, oh"

When I called home from the police station I was praying that my father would answer the phone. He would listen to what I had to say and would react comely, logical, and in a manner that would keep my mother from screaming her head off. If my Mother was to answer the phone I would have to explain myself quickly in order to keep her from having a heart attack.

When I was eleven years old I hung out with a group of boys that were almost three years older than me. The five of us did all the things that young energetic kids did playing ball, riding bikes, and getting in to trouble. Because they were older they worried less about getting in trouble and the consequences of there actions than I did.

My friends and I would always come home from school, drop our backpacks off and head out in the neighborhood to find something to do. Our favorite thing to do was to find construction cites and steal wood to make tree forts in the woods or skateboard ramps. So one day, coming home from school, we noticed a couple new houses being built near our neighborhood. It was a prime cite for wood, nails, and anything else we could get our hands on. We discussed our plan on the bus and decided that we would all meet there after dropping our stuff off at home. I remember being a little at hesitant first because it was close to my house but beyond the boundaries my parents had set for me. Of course I went because I didn't want to be the odd man out and have to put up with all the name calling. I dropped my bag off and I headed to the construction cite.

I meet my friends there and we began to search the different houses for wood and what not. We all picked up a couple of things and were about to leave when one of my friends noticed a what looked to be a big tool shed off behind one of the houses. It looked promising so we decided that we should check it out. Two of the boys in the group said that they had all the wood they could carry and said they were going home. The rest of us headed down to the shed to take a look.

Once there we noticed that the shed had been broken in to previously. The lock on it had been busted on the hinges were bent. I opened the door to the shed and stepped inside to take a look around while my friends waited outside. It was dark inside but I could tell the place had been ransacked, there was nothing to take so I decided to leave. I heard my to friends say some thing so turned back around to site of them running away. I thought that they were playing a joke on me so I casually walked

A I like this pargraph. It thoroughly lets the reader relate to you and also produces a picture in the reader's mind
B Good point, makes it more unlikely that you should be the one to get caught
C What other things did you do to get into trouble? Or is it irrelevant?
D Great passage really lets the reader know what you were thinking
E was there a lesson you were first or did it just happen that way

Jeremy's response is not in a class by itself. A set of comments to end all commentary on Todd's paper. He might have done well, for instance, to recognize how much this paper works because of the way Todd arranges the story. He could have done more to point to what's not working in the writing or what could be made to work better. He might have asked Todd for more details about his state of mind when he got caught by the policeman and while he was being held at the police station. He might have urged him more to make certain changes. He might even have said, if only in a brief warning, something about

Figure 6-7 (continued)

Jeremy

Todd
ENG 1
Rick Straub
Assignment 8b

"Uh, oh"

When I called home from the police station I was praying that my father would answer the phone. He would listen to what I had to say and would react comely, logical, and in a manner that would keep my mother from screaming her head off. If my Mother was to answer the phone I would have to explain myself quickly in order to keep her from having a heart attack.

I like this paragraph. It immediately lets the reader relate to you and also produces a picture in the reader's image

When I was eleven years old I hung out with a group of boys that were almost three years older than me. The five of us did all the things that young energetic kids did playing ball, riding bikes, and getting in to trouble. [Because they were older they worried less about getting in trouble and the consequences of there actions than I did.] Good point, makes it more unlikely that you should be the one to get caught

My friends and I would always come home from school, drop our backpacks off and head out in the neighborhood to find something to do. Our favorite thing to do was to find construction cites and steal wood to make tree forts in the woods or skateboard ramps. So one day, coming home from school, we noticed a couple new houses being built near our neighborhood. It was a prime cite for wood, nails, and anything else we could get our hands on. We discussed our plan on the bus and decided that we would all meet there after dropping our stuff off at home. [I remember being a little at hesitant first because it was close to my house but beyond the boundaries my parents had set for me. Of course I went because I didn't want to be the odd man out and have to put up with all the name calling.] I dropped my bag off and I headed to the construction cite.

what other things did you do to get into trouble? Or is it irrevalent?

great passage really lets the reader know what you were thinking

I meet my friends there and we began to search the different houses for wood and what not. We all picked up a couple of things and were about to leave when one of my friends noticed a what looked to be a big tool shed off behind one of the houses. It looked promising so we decided that we should check it out. Two of the boys in the group said that they had all the wood they could carry and said they were going home. The rest of us headed down to the shed to take a look.

Once there we noticed that the shed had been broken in to previously. The lock on it had been busted on the hinges were bent. I opened the door to the shed and stepped inside to take a look around while my friends waited outside. It was dark inside but I could tell the place had been ransacked, there was nothing to take so I decided to leave. I heard my to friends say some thing so turned back around to site of them running away. I thought that they were playing a joke on me so I casually walked

was there a reason you were first or did it just happen that way

A What else happened. At the police station? How long were you there?
B Maybe you could say more as to why you think your Mom is like this
C Did your Dad get into trouble as a kid So he knows what it's like? Explain why he reacts as he does.
D Would he punish you anyway or could you just get away with things
E I like the way you use dialogue in this section to illustrate how each of your parents would react and then explain to the reader what each of them are like. It works well.

the number of errors across the writing. But this is moot and just. Different readers are always going to pick up on different things and respond in different ways, and no one reading or response is going to address everything that might well be addressed, in the way it might best be addressed. All responses are incomplete and provisional—one reader's way of reading and reacting to the text in front of him. And any number of other responses, presented in any number of different ways, might be as useful or maybe even more useful to Todd as he takes up his work with the writing.

Figure 6-7 (concluded)

```
     I called home.  Sweet beading on my lip.

     "Hello", my mom said.  Oh geez, I'm dead.

     "Mom can I talk to dad?"

     "Why, what's wrong?"

     "Oh, nothing, I just need talk to him," yes, this is going
to work!

     "Hold on," she said.

     "Hello," my father said.

     "Dad, I'm at the police station,"  I told him the whole
story of what happened.  He reacted exactly as I expect he would.

     "Uhhmmm(long pause). You're at the police station...........
```

I really like the ending, it tells the reader what is going to happen without having to explain it step, by step. Good paper, I like the use of dialogue, Perhaps more on your understanding of why your parents react as they do.

I really like the ending, it tells the reader what is going to happen without having to explain it step, by step. Good paper. I like the use of dialogue. Perhaps more on your understanding of why your parents react as they do

All this notwithstanding, Jeremy's comments are solid. They are full. They are thoughtful. And they are respectful. They take the writing and the writer seriously and address the issues that are raised responsibly. His comments do what commentary on student writing should optimally do. They turn the writer back into his writing and lead him to reflect on his choices and aims, to consider and reconsider his intentions as a writer and the effects the words on the page will have on readers. They help him see what he can work on in revision and what he might deal with in his ongoing work as a writer.

PETER ELBOW (b. 1935) AND PAT BELANOFF (b. 1937)

Summary of Ways of Responding

CONSIDER THIS:

Peter Elbow was born in New York City and educated at Williams College and Exeter. He has taught at M.I. T., the State University of New York at Stony Brook, and recently retired from the English Department at Amherst. Pat Belanoff is an associate professor of English at the State University of New York at Stony Brook where she teaches composition and literature, medieval literature, and history of the language. In his *Writing Without Teachers,* Elbow reverses the traditional model of the writing process: "Instead of a two-step transaction of meaning-into-language, think of writing as an organic, developmental process in which you start writing at the very beginning—before you know your meaning at all—and encourage your words to gradually change and evolve. Only at the end will you know what you want to say or the words you want to say if with." Belanoff underlines the importance of writing in college this way: "Writing needs to be a part of all classes because it generates thought; students spend far too much time in school being receptors. They cannot struggle through to their own place in or out of the academy if they do not produce discourse of some kind. Talking is good, of course, but it is not enough. Writing is doing." Whereas Richard Straub suggests ways you might respond to other writers' texts, Peter Elbow and Pat Belanoff overview and chart the ways you can encourage readers to respond to your work. Here you're reversing the roles a bit: instead of thinking about how to respond to others, you're thinking about how they might best respond to you. Some of the techniques these authors share may be new to you. For those that are, try to imagine how such requests would work with a particular piece of writing that you actually have at hand.

THE TWO PARADOXES OF RESPONDING

First paradox: The reader is always right; the writer is always right.

The reader gets to decide what's true about her reaction: about what she sees or what happened to her, about what she thinks or how she feels. It makes no sense to quarrel with the reader about what's happening to her (though you can ask the reader to explain more fully what she is saying).

But you, as the writer, get to decide what to do about the feedback you get: what changes to make, if any. You don't have to follow her advice. Just listen openly— swallow it all. You can do that better if you realize that you get to take your time and make up your own mind—perhaps making no changes in your writing at all.

Second paradox: The writer must be in charge; the writer must sit back quietly too.

As the writer, you must be in control. It's your writing. Don't be passive or helpless. Don't just put your writing out and let them give you *any* feedback. You need to decide what kind of feedback (if any) you need for this particular piece of writing. Is your main goal to improve this piece of writing? Or perhaps you don't really care about working any more on this piece—your main goal is to work on your writing in general. Or perhaps you don't want to *work* at anything—but instead just enjoy sharing this piece and hearing what others have to say. You need to make your own decision about what kind of feedback will help you. Don't let readers make those decisions.

Therefore ask readers for what you want or need—and insist that you get it. Don't be afraid to stop them if they start giving you what you don't want. (Remember, for instance, that even after you are very experienced with all kinds of feedback, you may need to ask readers to hold back *all criticism* for a piece that you feel tender about. This can be a very appropriate decision; stick up for it.)

Nevertheless, you mostly have to sit back and just listen. If you are talking a lot, you are probably preventing them from giving you the good feedback they could give. (For example, don't argue if they misunderstand what you wrote. Their misunderstanding is valuable. You need to *understand* their misunderstanding better in order to figure out whether you need to make any changes.)

Let the readers tell you if they think you are asking for inappropriate feedback—or for feedback they can't give or don't want to give. For example, they may sense that your piece is still unformed and think that it doesn't make sense to give judgment. They may think sayback or descriptive feedback would be more helpful. Or they may simply hate giving judgment. Listen to them. See whether perhaps you should go along: they may be right.

If you aren't getting honest, serious, or caring feedback, don't just blame your readers. It's probably because you haven't convinced them that you really want it. Instead of *blaming* the readers, simply *insist that they give you what you need.*

What follows is a summary of the kinds of feedback we have earlier described.

I. NO RESPONDING: SHARING

How to Use It	*When It's Useful*
Just read your words out loud; see what they sound like. You probably learn more from the act of *reading in the presence of listeners* than from any kind of feedback.	When you don't have much time. Or at a very early stage when you're just exploring or feeling fragile about what you've written and don't want criticism. It's also useful when you are completely finished with a piece: you've finally got it the way you want it or you don't have the time or energy to make any changes—so it's time to celebrate by *sharing* it with others and not getting feedback at all.

II. DESCRIPTIVE RESPONDING

Sayback

How to Use It	*When It's Useful*
Ask readers: "Say back to me in your own words what you hear me getting at in my writing. But say it more as a question than as an answer—to invite me to figure out better what I *really* want to say."	At an early stage when you are still groping, when you may not yet have been able to write what you are really trying to say. If readers say back to you what they hear—and invite you to talk—this often leads you to *exactly* what you want to write.

Pointing

How to Use It	*When It's Useful*
Ask readers: "Which words or phrases stick in mind? Which passages or features did you like best? Don't explain why."	When you want to know what is getting through. Or when you want a bit of confidence and support.

Summarizing

How to Use It	*When It's Useful*
Ask: "What do you hear as my main point or idea (or event or feeling)? And the subsidiary ones?"	When you want to know what's getting through. If a reader says she disagrees with you, you need to know what she thinks you are saying.

What's Almost Said or Implied

How to Use It	*When It's Useful*
Ask readers: "What's *almost* said, implied, hovering around the edges? What would you like to hear more about?"	When you need new ideas or need to expand or develop what you've written—or when you feel your piece isn't rich or interesting enough. What you *don't* say in a piece of writing often determines the reactions of readers as much as what you do say. If this is an important piece of writing for you, you had better look to feedback about the implications.

Center of Gravity

How to Use It	*When It's Useful*
Ask readers: "What do you sense as the source of energy, the focal point, the seedbed, the generative center for this piece?" (The center of gravity might well *not* be the "main point" but rather some image, phrase, quotation, detail, or example.)	Same as for "What's Almost Said," above.

Structure; Voice, Point of View, Attitude Toward the Reader; Level of Abstraction or Concreteness; Language, Diction, Syntax

How to Use Them:	*When They're Useful*
Ask readers to describe each of these features or dimensions of your writing.	At any stage. When you need more perspective.

Metaphorical Descriptions

How to Use Them	*When They're Useful*
Ask readers: "Describe my piece in terms of weathers, clothing, colors, animals. Describe the shape of my piece. Give me a picture of the reader-writer relationship. What's your fantasy of what was on my mind that I *wasn't* writing about ('substitute writing')?"	At any stage. When your writing feels stale and you need a fresh view. If readers learn to give this kind of feedback, their other feedback tends to improve. Sometimes young, inexperienced, or naive readers can't give you other kinds of feedback but give very perceptive metaphorical feedback.

III. ANALYTIC RESPONDING

Skeleton Feedback

How to Use It	*When It's Useful*
Ask readers to tell you about these three main dimensions of your paper: • Reasons and support. ("What do you see as my main point and my subpoints—and the arguments or evidence that I give or could give to support each?") • Assumptions. ("What does my paper seem to take for granted?") • Audience. ("Who do I imply as my audience? How would my reasons work for them? How do I seem to treat them in general?")	When writing a persuasive essay or any essay that makes a claim. At an early stage when you have a lot of unorganized exploratory writing, skeleton feedback is a way to get help from your readers in adding to and organizing your material. At a late stage, readers help you analyze strengths and weaknesses. It's also helpful for giving *yourself* feedback.

Believing and Doubting

How to Use It	*When It's Useful*
Ask readers: "Believe (or pretend to believe) everything I have written. Be my ally and tell me what you see. Give me more ideas and perceptions to help my case. Then doubt everything and tell me what you see. What arguments can be made against what I say?"	The believing game alone is good when you want help and support for an argument you are struggling with. Together they are useful at any stage. They provide strong perspective.

Descriptive Outline

How to Use It	*When It's Useful*
Ask readers: "Write me *says* and *does* sentences—for my whole essay and for each paragraph or section." *Does* sentences shouldn't mention the content of the paragraph— i.e., shouldn't slide into repeating the *says* sentences.	Descriptive outlines make most sense for essays—and are particularly useful for persuasive pieces or arguments. They give you the most *perspective.* Only feasible when the reader has the text in hand and can give a lot of time and care. Particularly useful for giving feedback to yourself.

IV. READER-BASED RESPONDING: MOVIES OF THE READER'S MIND

How to Use It	*When It's Useful*
Get readers to tell you frankly *what happens inside their heads* as they read your words. Here are ways to help them: • Interrupt their reading and have them tell their interim reactions. • Get them to tell reactions in the form of a story (first . . . then . . .). • Get them to give subjective "I statements" about what is happening in them, not allegedly objective "it statements" about the text.	Movies of the reader's mind are useful at any stage—but they depend on a relationship of trust and support with readers. They can lead to blunt criticism. They're most useful for long-range learning: they may not give you direct help in improving this particular draft.

- If they are stuck, ask them questions (e.g., about where they go along and where they resist, about their feelings on the topic before and after reading).

V. CRITERION-BASED OR JUDGMENT-BASED RESPONDING

How to Use It	*When It's Useful*
Traditional criteria for imaginative or creative writing: • Description, vividness of details. (Do we *experience* what's there?) • Character. (Do we find characters real or interesting?) • Plot. (Is it believable, interesting, or meaningful?) • Language. (Not just "Is it clear?" but "Is it alive and resonant with meaning?"—perhaps through imagery and metaphor.) • Meaning; so what? (Is there a meaning or impact that makes it seem important or worthwhile?) Traditional criteria for expository or essay writing: • Focus on task. (Does it squarely *address* the assignment, question, or task?) • Content. (You might want to distinguish three dimensions: ideas, details or examples, reasoning.) • Clarity. • Organization. • Sense of the writer. (Voice, tone, stance toward the reader.) • Mechanics. (Spelling, grammar, punctuation; proofreading.)	When you want to know how your writing measures up to certain criteria. Or when you need a quick overview of strengths and weaknesses. This kind of feedback depends on experienced and skilled readers. And still you should always take it with a grain of salt. Of course, you can specify whatever criteria you think right for a given piece of writing: what the particular writing task demands (e.g., persuading the reader) or what you are currently working on (e.g., voice). Or you can let *readers* specify the criteria that they think are most important.

FEEDBACK FROM YOURSELF

Certain of these feedback procedures particularly increase your perspective and thus improve your feedback from yourself.

- Certain kinds of *descriptive feedback* sharpen your eye, help you see things about your text you hadn't noticed (e.g., summarizing; describing the structure; the voice and point of view; level of abstraction/concreteness; language, diction, syntax).
- *Descriptive outline* and *skeleton feedback* are particularly powerful analytic structures that help you see what's strong and weak in any essay.
- *Criterion-based feedback* can help you zero in on features you know *you* need to be careful about, for example, "Is it organized?" "Enough details or examples?" "Quotation mark problems?"
- Don't forget that if you do *process writing* about what you have written, you will probably come up with helpful suggestions for yourself. Talk about what pleases you and where you are troubled; spell out your frustrations.

Classroom Handouts

The Executive Summary

CONSIDER THIS:

How do you feel when you share the same paper with several readers? What do you do when you receive contradictory or conflicting revision advice? Some of us, I think, get even more insecure about our text and try to defend our choices or agree to change everything or simply get irritated with the whole process, particularly the subjectivity inherent in evaluating writing. Other writers seem simply to ignore advice and continue on their way. In the first case, we give the reader too much control of our text. In the second, we ignore our reader and possibly make choices that assure we never have another. To discover a middle ground, I ask writers to try the assignment you are about to read. The executive summary of classroom author Clarissa Evans catalogs the responses of 17 peers. I've provided samples of these comments. Explain the negotiations you see Clarissa make as she tabulates and analyzes these responses and develops her revision timetable.

Those who read a number of large and complicated reports each day rely on the digest at the opening of the report—called an executive summary—which distills the essence of the information that is to follow. In the same way, you need to distill the sometimes conflicting interpretations readers offer of your work, to evaluate their revision advice in light of your own aims for the piece you are writing, and then to come up with a work plan. The executive summary in this instance is composed for you, the writer in charge of the project. It is the cover sheet that summarizes the detailed annotations to your draft provided by workshop readers.

After the workshop, when you have received this response and advice from 10 to 20 readers, you need to make decisions, sort out emotional reactions, and draw energy from what was said and suggested. You should aim to compose your summary and revision plan within 24 hours of the workshop, in writing, in case you don't have the opportunity to undertake a revision immediately. In fact, it's useful if you have a break from your writing and even if the paper is due very soon after the workshop, the executive summary process itself offers a tool for gaining needed distance from the workshop situation. Some writers need to follow this process once, in order to internalize and formalize their own best method of sorting and weighing advice. Other writers will find this a useful sequence to follow after each workshop. If revision is delayed for any reason, the executive summary can keep workshop ideas fresh and well-ordered.

Remember that it's the thinking process involved in compiling an executive summary that proves valuable for writers. Develop a version of the following steps that works for you.

After each workshop, complete the first three steps within 24 hours.

1. Read all the written responses and write an executive summary by listing and tabulating comments and the numbers of times you received them:

Example:

Suggested Changes

- Find an organization plan that lets readers know I intend to talk about two issues (two people).
- Consider revising conclusion (one person).
- Lots of small punctuation changes (16 people marking different spots—check which I agree with).
- Confusion about why I have a stake in the city's rental housing policy that restricts the number of students per rental unit (four people).

Strengths

- Liked the way I used an interview with a landlord and with two sets of student renters (five people).
- Thought the piece should be submitted as a letter to the editor or as an article for the campus newspaper (three people).

- Liked the title (one person—what am I supposed to do?).
- Would have liked to read even more, didn't think it was too short (seven people).
- Felt I had addressed both sides of the issue and that they could form their own opinion (three people).
- Thought my single-sentence paragraph in the middle was effective (one person).

(Note: There are various ways to present these summary lists, but it should be easy to skim to get a general impression of agreement and contradictions since you'll receive both.)

2. Write a brief, one- or two-paragraph response to the workshop and then discuss what you think about contradictory suggestions.
3. Write a detailed one-page revision plan and revision timetable (calendar).
4. Revise.

Remember, this is a revision *plan*. Use it if it helps. It's an aid and not a straight jacket. It's a practice session that pays off with a better performance. Just as musicians or athletes practice their art, writers review their options and daydream and plan what they'll do in their next draft. Then, when you write (perform) you enter the flow of revision intent on producing your next best version.

CLARISSA E.

Executive Summary

Part 1

Suggested Changes:

- Complete the ending, make it more final (10 people)
- Leave out sentence that mentions other best friend (6 people)
- Tell Dee's race (3 people)
- Suggestions for better word choice (10 people)
- Too much repetition of words (5 people)
- Use more emotion, description, and details (8 people)
- Develop story about Internet guy (6 people)
- Show more of the story, tell less (7 people)
- Go into more detail about middle school (4 people)
- Tell why I didn't like Rachel (4 people)

Strengths

- Good use of dialogue (8 people)
- Specific stories made paper interesting (1 person)

Part 2 I liked the workshop because most of the suggestions that were made were ideas that I had for revision or things that I had thought about while writing, but had some reservations about putting them into my paper. A lot of the suggestions that were given were for me to expand on certain ideas in some areas, such as the McDonald's scene with the Internet guy that I hadn't thought much about. This is one particular scene that I'm worried about expanding on. I'm afraid that if I talk too much about him and the McDonald's, that it might take away from the focus at hand, my best friend. One of the major things that the workshop did for me was confirm ideas that I had, but was not too sure how well they would work. After hearing so many others suggest the same ideas, I am confident that the ideas will work.

Part 3 I think the first thing that I need to do in the line of revising this paper is to add description to a large part of the paper. I need to describe the settings and the people involved in the story. There were also particular parts of the story that many said that they wanted to know more about. I am going to attempt to add more details about meeting the guy offline at McDonald's and why was I meeting guys online. Many people also suggested that I add more dialogue to the paper. One area that it was most suggested was the part that discussed the arguments. I am going to try to talk to the teacher that gave the *To Kill A Mockingbird* lecture and see if my memory can be jogged about what was said as far as the lecture and the argument between Dee and me. Also, I am going to get some of the notes that Dee and I passed during high school and middle school, if I still have them, and see how I can incorporate them. I also plan to add onto the ending of the paper. I am not sure exactly what I'm going to do yet because I had planned on telling about how Dee and I are still friends, but it was suggested that I include some of what was written in the journal. Right now, I think that I will try both ideas. It was also said that the paper format is too formal, so I'm going to try out other formats, possibly making it seem as if it's just random memories. The one that was suggested that I like most was the journal entry format.

Timeline

10/26–10/30—Talk to teacher and get notes passed in high school. Work this information into paper.

10/31–11/5—Work on details that need clarification and add description of the schools and characters.

11/6–11/12—Work on ending.

11/13–11/19—Add dialogue and try out different formats.

11/20–(due date)—Look for anything else that can be done to make the paper better. Complete process cover sheet.

DANIEL'S RESPONSE: 1ST & LAST PAGES OF CLARISSA'S DRAFT
CLARISSA E.
ENC4311-04
PAPER 2
PUBLICATION POSSIBILITIES: YM OR *SEVENTEEN*
POTENTIAL AUDIENCE: PEOPLE PREPARING TO GO AWAY FOR COLLEGE AND LEAVING FRIENDS BEHIND

BEST FRIENDS

When I graduated from high school, I had two best friends, one that I had known since first grade and one that I had known since seventh grade. *I don't really know what's going on with the friend that I've had since first grade, but my best friend that I've had since seventh grade is still my best friend and thanks to the Internet, I get to talk to her almost everyday.* We don't have any wild and crazy adventures share, but we went through puberty together and that's an adventure in itself.

This is a really long sentence

Dee and I met each other in seventh grade in math class. She *was* friends with the people that took me in when I started going to James Weldon Johnson Middle School. Most everybody had been there since sixth grade and all of their cliques *had been* formed and there *was* no room for a quiet, shy, new student. I started there the beginning of seventh grade, but there just *wasn't any room for outsiders.* For most of the year, I scrambled for friends, bouncing from one group to another; that usually came to the same decision that the previous group had, I acted like a white girl. Nobody wanted to be friends with the new black *girl that tried to act white.* Eventually, I came upon a group of people that *is* probably the most unique group of friends that a person could ever meet. I told them of all that

Be careful of the passive voice (ex: is, are, was, were)

repetitive

; each

how do you act white?

Why? How?

DANIEL'S RESPONSE: 1ST & LAST PAGES OF CLARISSA'S DRAFT

maybe use some dialogue here

and

awkward

I had been through and they decided that didn't see anything wrong with me. They took the criticisms of others and teased me, once when they finally helped me to get enough confidence to start telling people off.

did she confide in her other friend in the same way?

explain

show, don't tell

Dee *was* the person that I connected with most, but not until eighth grade. Dee already had a best friend, but that *didn't stop her from confiding in me and I in her.* We shared some of the same general problems, *but not under the same* circumstances. Dee and I both *had a lack of self-confidence*

QUESTIONS

1. Is the dialogue during the break up scene senior year angry enough?
The dialogue is believable. I'm not sure that you want it to be too angry, because I don't see it as the focus of the story.

2. Are there any parts that need clarification or more detail?
I've marked some places where it would be better to "show," instead of "telling" the reader.

3. Is the morning trip to McDonald's scene too long or too much?
I think we need more of these little scenes in the story.

4. Does the ending have enough closure?
Yes, I like the ending, but I don't really see a change in the narrator.

5. Do you have any other suggestions?
I think all writings has to have a change occur in a character. I don't think I see this change. You start off talking about how the narrator "acts white" and I thought this would be your focus, but it didn't follow through. The dialogue is strong, but I wanted to see more of it. What is the character/narrator yearning for? Where is the climax in the story? There are several places where I think you could do a lot more showing than telling. Overall, I like this. It's a good "coming of age" story, but I need to see the change in these people more developed.

Thank You and Good Luck,
Daniel

GARETH'S RESPONSE: 1ST & LAST PAGES OF CLARISSA'S DRAFT
CLARISSA E.
ENC4311-04
PAPER 2
PUBLICATION POSSIBILITIES: YM OR *SEVENTEEN*
POTENTIAL AUDIENCE: PEOPLE PREPARING TO GO AWAY FOR COLLEGE AND LEAVING FRIENDS BEHIND

BEST FRIENDS

This is irrelevant because there is no other mention of this person

When I graduated from high school, I had two best friends, one that I had known since first grade and one that I had known since seventh grade. *I don't really know what's going on with the friend that I've had since first grade,* but my best friend that I've had since seventh grade is still my best friend and thanks to the Internet, I get to talk to her almost everyday. We don't have any wild and crazy adventures to share, but we went through puberty together and that's an adventure in itself.

Dee and I met each other in seventh grade in math class. She was friends with the people that took me in when I started going to James Weldon Johnson Middle School. Most everybody had been there since sixth grade and all of their cliques had been formed and there was no room for a quiet, shy, new student. I started there the beginning of seventh grade, but there just wasn't any room for outsiders. For most of the year, I scrambled for friends, bouncing from one group to another that usually came to the same decision that the previous group had, I acted like a white girl. Nobody wanted to be friends with the new black girl that tried to act white. Eventually, I came upon a group of people that is probably the most unique group of friends that a person could ever meet. I told them of all that

GARETH'S RESPONSE: 1ST & LAST PAGES OF CLARISSA'S DRAFT

they

Try rewording this sentence, It's confusing

I had been through and they decided that didn't see anything wrong with me. (They took the criticisms of others and teased me, once when they finally helped me to get enough confidence to start telling people off.)

Dee was the person that I connected with most, but not until eighth grade. Dee already had a best friend, but that didn't stop her from confiding in me and I in her. We shared some of the same general problems, but not under the same circumstances. Dee and I both had a lack of self-confidence

GARETH'S RESPONSE TO "BEST FRIENDS"

Let me start by saying that I really like these types of stories. In fact, my paper is also about recalling past school experiences. They are hard to do, because there is so much information to pack into such a long timeframe. The problem that I saw with this paper is that you cover a span of 6 years with a little over a page per year. That is not enough. You are telling more than you are showing. At times, you just make statements, brush past them, and move on to the next thing. For instance, on page 3, you write, "Dee felt like the teacher was calling people bigots, but I felt like the teacher was right on target." That is a big statement to make, but the next paragraph doesn't capitalize on it at all. Other parts need more info as well. Concerning your History teacher in the 11th grade, you state that you hated the class and didn't like the teacher, but you didn't give adequate reasons as to why. You need to concentrate less on the number of recollections you can fit into your paper. It would help to concentrate more on adding depth to your strongest points, which I think are the prom scene on page 5, and your experimentation with dialogue on the same page. The ending needs a little work. It feels rushed. What did the journal mean to you? What were some of the passage that she wrote in it? Make it more personal.

RACHEL'S RESPONSE: 1ST AND LAST PAGES OF CLARISSA'S DRAFT
CLARISSA E.
ENC4311-04
PAPER 2
PUBLICATION POSSIBILITIES: YM OR *SEVENTEEN*
POTENTIAL AUDIENCE: PEOPLE PREPARING TO GO AWAY FOR COLLEGE AND LEAVING FRIENDS BEHIND

BEST FRIENDS

3 mentions of "best friends" in one small ¶

Introduce their names here—why wait?

If there is nothing to tell, why bring it up?

When I graduated from high school, I had two best friends, one that I had known since first grade and one that I had known since seventh grade. **I don't really know what's going on with the friend** that I've had since first grade, but my best friend that I've had since seventh grade is still my friend and thanks to the Internet, I get to talk to her almost everyday. We don't have any wild and crazy adventures to share, but we went through puberty together and that's an adventure in itself.

You already told us this

who where?

Dee and I met each other in seventh grade in math class. She was friends with the people that took me in when I started going to James Weldon Johnson Middle School. Most everybody had been there since sixth grade and all of their-cliques had been formed and there was no room for a quiet, shy, new student. *I started there the beginning of seventh grade, but there just wasn't any room for outsiders. For most of the year, I scrambled for friends, bouncing from one group to another that usually came to the some decision that the previous group had, I acted like a white girl.* Nobody wanted to be friends with the new black girl that tried to act white. Eventually,

RACHEL'S RESPONSE: 1ST AND LAST PAGES OF CLARISSA'S DRAFT

I came upon a group of people that is probably the most unique group of friends that a person could ever meet. I told them of all that I had been through and they decided that didn't see anything wrong with me. They took the criticisms of others and teased me, once when they finally helped me to get enough confidence to start telling people off.

You get a slight bit repetitive w/ Dee— use she

Dee was the person that I connected with most, but not until eighth grade. Dee already had a best friend, but that didn't stop her from confiding in me and I in her. We shared some of the same general problems, but not under the same circumstances. Dee and I both had a lack of self-confidence

QUESTIONS

1. Is the dialogue during the break up scene senior year angry enough?
   Not really, I got the sense you were sad, not angry

2. Are there any parts that need clarification or more detail?
   I think detail could be added everywhere!

3. Is the morning trip to McDonald's scene too long or too much?
   Liven it up some. It wasn't too long, but I got bored.

4. Does the ending have enough closure?
   No. Where are you guys w/ your friendship now? That is important.

5. Do you have any other suggestions?
   Clarissa-
   I think this story is a very sweet dedication to your friend Dee. I don't think you need to go so much into all the "guys" so much. You mention too many of them, I couldn't keep it straight. Make Dee talk more; let us get to know her.

RACHEL'S RESPONSE: 1ST AND LAST PAGES OF CLARISSA'S DRAFT

ADD DETAIL! You don't describe much. I have no idea what anything looks like, smells like, etc. This is an essential. I mean, you don't even let us know what she looks like. Also, watch for repetition on such words as best friends, Dee, close, guys.

Good Luck,
Rachel

MIKE'S RESPONSE: 1ST AND LAST PAGES OF CLARISSA'S DRAFT
CLARISSA E.
ENC4311-04
PAPER 2
PUBLICATION POSSIBILITIES: YM OR *SEVENTEEN*
POTENTIAL AUDIENCE: PEOPLE PREPARING TO GO AWAY FOR COLLEGE AND LEAVING FRIENDS BEHIND

BEST FRIENDS

I graduated from high school, I had two best friends, one that I had known since first grade and one that I had known since seventh grade. (I don't really know what's going on with the friend that I've had since first grade,) but my best friend that I've had since seventh grade is still my best friend and thanks to the Internet, I get to talk to her almost everyday. We don't have any wild and crazy adventures to share, but we went through puberty together and that's an adventure in itself.

maybe give them a name

Not really important, throws the reader off to what your really going to talk about here

Dee and I met each other in seventh grade in math class. She was friends with the people that took me in when I started going to James Weldon Johnson Middle School. Most everybody had been there since sixth grade *and all* of their cliques had been formed *and there* was no room for a quiet, shy, new student. I started there the beginning of seventh grade, but

MIKE'S RESPONSE: 1ST AND LAST PAGES OF CLARISSA'S DRAFT

Why did you act this way?

there just wasn't any room for outsiders. For most of the year, I scrambled for friends, bouncing from one group to another that usually came to the same decision that the previous group had, I acted like a white girl. Nobody wanted to be friends *with the new black girl that tried to act white.* Eventually, I came upon a group of people that is probably the most unique group of friends that a person could ever meet. I told them of all that I had been through and they decided that didn't see anything wrong with me. They took the criticisms of others and teased me, once when they finally helped me to get enough confidence to start telling people off.

Dee was the person that I connected with most, but not until eighth grade. Dee already had a best friend, but that didn't stop her from confiding in me and I in her. We shared some of the same general problems, but not under the same circumstances. Dee and I both had a lack of self-confidence

QUESTIONS

1. Is the dialogue during the break up scene senior year angry enough?

2. Are there any parts that need clarification or more detail?

3. Is the morning trip to McDonald's scene too long or too much?

4. Does the ending have enough closure?

MIKE'S RESPONSE: 1ST AND LAST PAGES OF CLARISSA'S DRAFT

5. Do you have any other suggestions?

Dear Clarissa,

Congrats on doing a great job of getting together a lot of different aspects to paint the picture of you and dee's friendship. You really do well with the dialogue and I am glad you used a lot of specific stories about your times together. Well done too on putting down a good progression of your friendship through the years. I felt like the dialogue of the senior year was a good turning point to the story of when you had a roadblock in your relationship (good transition from good times to bad. I felt like your ending could use a little bit more closure and that you could maybe do some reflection on your friendship.

Mike

GERALD LOCKLIN (b. 1941)

Amphibians Have Feelings Too

CONSIDER THIS:

Gerald Locklin was born in Rochester, New York. The author of many collections of poetry, Locklin has taught at California State University, Long Beach since 1965. He contributes frequently to periodicals including *Poetry* and *The Wormwood Review.* Locklin discusses his career in his essay "The Education of a Writer," by explaining "I started out to be a fiction writer and only began writing poetry because I'd read somewhere that it would improve one's prose style. I've ended up better known as a poet but have continued to write stories and novellas also, as well as academic articles and reviews." His inspiration comes from various places. "I try to remain open to all sources of possible writing ideas: childhood, travel, relationships, overheard conversations, reading, music, humor, satire, the complications of daily life." What do you notice about the way Locklin tells his story? What surprises you about his analysis of response? His approach to writing poems? What story would you immediately tell in response to this one?

There was this fine guy named Steve Odin
and I haven't seen him for many years
but we taught together fifteen years ago
when we were just starting out in graduate school.

The other day I was correcting a freshman paper
which contained many sentence fragments
and I thought of Steve,
because that year he had a kid who kept writing
sentence fragments, and so Steve kept scrawling
FRAG in the margin of the papers,
and the kid never came in for a conference,
he just kept writing sentence fragments
and Steve kept scrawling FRAG in the margin.

Then the last day of the semester rolled around
and after everyone else had left
this student came up to the desk and said,
"Mr. Odin, there's just one thing I'd like to ask you."

"Sure. What is it?"

"Why have you been writing FROG on my paper all semester?"

LINDA PASTAN (b. 1932)

Marks

CONSIDER THIS:

Do you grade yourself? Think of the ways you move through your day evaluating your own success. How do you set goals for yourself? How do you decide how you meet them? As a long-time student, do you tend to see the world in terms of grades? Do you grade others? Based on what criteria? Linda Pastan lets us see the exasperating absurdity and pervasiveness of grades. Perhaps her poem will remind you of a time you've felt graded or felt like a grader of others. Share the story of that time.

Linda Pastan was born in New York City and earned degrees from Radcliff College and Brandeis University. The winner of numerous awards and a lecturer at the Breadloaf Writer's Conference in Vermont and a teacher at the American University, Pastan's work has appeared in many journals and magazines, including *Atlantic Monthly, New Yorker,* and the *Paris Review.* Pastan's poetry often deals with domestic life and is noted for its accessibility. "The writing of a poem, then," says Pastan," becomes a search for meaning, an attempt to solve what I have called 'the mystery of the ordinary.' It is a journey between the world we see and the world we suspect lies just out of sight. It is a journey with many signposts, many stopping-off points, but no final destination." In an interview session for *Preview Port,* the interviewer asks: "Does writing come easily to you?" "Not usually." Pastan replies, "Occasionally after working hard on one poem, there will be a residue of energy floating around in my head, and another poem will just come to me. But in general, it is very hard, though often exhilarating, work." Question: "Do you revise much?" Answer, "Yes. Compulsively."

My husband gives me an A
for last night's supper,
an incomplete for my ironing,
a B plus in bed.
My son says I am average,
an average mother, but if
I put my mind to it
I could improve.
My daughter believes
in Pass/Fail and tells me
I pass. Wait 'til they learn
I'm dropping out.

9

Classroom Authors

JAY SZCZEPANSKI

"On a Blackslick Road in Winter" (and two earlier drafts)

CONSIDER THIS:

It's easier to "see" revision changes across small sections of a draft or with a short text. As you read each version of Jay Szczepanski's draft, in the margins, make your own best reader's responses, following Richard Straub's advice. Close reading of this sort will better allow you to see the changes that Jay undertook. You can read his writing process narrative at the end of his drafting sequence, which is printed in the order of composition. For a fourth, preliminary, version of a portion of this essay, turn to Szczepanski's "Story Told Simply" in Chapter 8. That earlier draft evolved into the section of this essay subtitled "Elizabeth." You can create a detailed draft trail of your own to study by saving each draft and using the "track changes" function on your word processing software. On each subsequent draft, your deletions, additions, and reorderings will be highlighted in color. Jay Szczepanski was a graduate student in composition and rhetoric when he composed this sequence.

PURPLE PURPLE PURPLE

Ohio is a strange place in winter. You need to know this because this story takes place in Ohio (in February).

My friend Elizabeth drives a van whose purple is so deep that it's plum. It's an attractive color, and I often tell her so. Her eyes are green, and this provides a nice contrast—green and purple are secondary colors, after all.

It's late as she drives the van (late for the winter, that is; it's 10 p.m. and has been dark for hours). Sulfur lights give off just enough orange to make the sky an Easter sort of violet.

Because it's Ohio and it's February and it's late, I can commit myself to talking to her in a stray, lazy sort of way (she's driving me home after a movie—this is what awkward teenagers do in the Middle West when their houses rest amongst the fallow winter wheat fields and city access comes through federal interstates and state roads).

Dialogue isn't important very often. I said to her, as she smiled-drove-smiled, I said, "You know, you know I'm gay," like it was something that yes, she did know, but had been politely waiting for me to bring up.

She didn't know, naturally (and how could she; it's shameless, those people whom we use to cover up our queerness), and she almost coaxed her lovely purple van into the pylons of an overpass.

Make-up is ridiculous, but she wore it anyway, and against the red and green dimness of the dashboard and instrument panel, her mascara turned a purply-black as it fell from around her eyes.

I had cried like this many times on my own. I used to whisper to myself, "I'm gay, I'm gay," to try and get used to it, but I whispered so low I purposefully couldn't hear it. I knew that my breath slipped up my trachea (which I assume is purple) from diaphragm, that it was hot but wasn't there.

Elizabeth drove me home and we sat in the driveway, the dry heat of the van's duct system crusting us over, and she finally knew that I was purple—so purple I could no longer kiss her.

NO TITLE, DAMMIT

My friend Elizabeth drives a van whose purple is so deep that it's plum. It's an attractive color, and I often tell her so. Her eyes are green, and this provides a nice contrast—green and purple play well together.

It's late as she drives the van, late for the winter. As we pass the Ohio turnpike, the orangish sulfur lights give off just enough light to make the sky an Easter sort of violet. There are no stars because the clouds hide them all, keep the heat in, place us together.

Because it's Ohio and it's February and it's late, I can commit myself to talking to her in a stray, lazy sort of way. We have watched a movie in Elyria, and she's driving me home.

I love her because she can drive and I cannot. We are awkward teenagers in the Middle West, gliding on a road between two fallow winter wheat fields, the snow blowing stutteringly in wispy breaths across the grey pavement on county road nine.

I said to her, as she smiled-drove-smiled, I said, "You know, you know I'm gay," as if it were something that yes, she knew, but was politely waiting for me to bring up.

I am often amazed when I remember this scene, the first in a long line of repeated utterances to my friends, my family, slowly becoming more confident statements, less iffy, less naked.

She didn't know, naturally (and how could she; it's shameless, those people whom we use to cover up our queerness), and she almost coaxed her lovely purple van into the pylons of an overpass. This actually happened.

Make-up is ridiculous, but she wore it anyway, and against the red and green dimness of the dashboard and instrument panel, her mascara turned a purply-black as it fell from around her eyes, slowly, slowly. It's an unfortunately sharable burden.

I had cried like this many times on my own. I used to whisper to myself, "I'm gay, I'm gay," an attempt to get used to it, understand it, but I often whispered so low so that I purposefully could not, would not hear it. I understood the mechanics of it: I knew that my breath slipped up my trachea from my diaphragm, past my alveolar ridge, past my teeth and across my tongue. I also understood its heat was borne from somewhere also deep inside, a place that I could not locate.

Elizabeth drove me home, and we sat in the driveway, nothing, spent, relieved and nervous, the dry heat of the van's duct system crusting us over.

ON A BLACKSLICK ROAD IN WINTER

My friend Elizabeth drives a van whose purple is so deep that it's plum. It's an attractive color, and I often tell her so. Her eyes are green, and this provides a nice contrast—green and purple play well together.

It's late as she drives the van, late for the winter. As we pass the Ohio turnpike, the orangish sulfur lights give off just enough light to make the sky an Easter sort of violet. There are no stars because the clouds hide them all, keep the heat in, place us together.

Because it's Ohio and it's February and it's late, I can commit myself to talking to her in a stray, lazy sort of way. We have watched a movie in Elyria, and she's driving me home.

I love her because she can drive and I cannot. We are awkward teenagers in the Middle West, gliding on a road between two fallow winter wheat fields, the snow blowing stutteringly in wispy breaths across the grey pavement on county road nine.

I said to her, as she smiled-drove-smiled, I said, "You know, you know I'm gay," as if it were something that yes, she knew, but was politely waiting for me to bring up.

I am often amazed when I remember this scene, the first in a long line of repeated utterances to my friends, my family, slowly becoming more confident statements, less iffy, less naked.

She didn't know, naturally (and how could she; it's shameless, those people whom we use to cover up our queerness), and she almost coaxed her lovely purple van into the pylons of an overpass.

This actually happened.

Make-up is ridiculous, but she wore it anyway, and against the red and green dimness of the dashboard and instrument panel, her mascara turned a purply-black as it fell from around her eyes, slowly, slowly. It's an unfortunately sharable burden.

I had cried like this many times on my own. I used to whisper to myself, "I'm gay, I'm gay," an attempt to get used to it, understand it, but I often whispered so low so that I purposefully could not, would not hear it. I understood the mechanics of it: I knew that my breath slipped up my throat from my gut, past my teeth and across my tongue. I also understood its heat was borne from somewhere also deep inside, a place that I could not, cannot locate.

Elizabeth drove me home, and we sat in the driveway, nothing, spent, relieved and nervous, the dry heat of the van's duct system crusting us over.

WRITING PROCESS NARRATIVE FOR "A BLACKSLICK ROAD IN WINTER"

The infamous color exercise inspired this one. I was pleased with the freewrite—I tend to write an amazing amount in only a little time (and this makes me wonder how much of a freewrite I could do if I used a word processor).

The initial exercise was a bunch of ramblings—they often are. What I tended to do after I got home from class everyday was to type my freewrites as I had them, then retype those to see what I could get out of them. I very often got a first draft, but not always.

You and I have talked about my transition from poetry to prose—this brief essay was a quasi-prose-poemish thing that I was happy with. The original draft had too much refrain, too much "music," I guess. I tried to tone it down for number two, not because I necessarily felt it would make the piece better, but because one of my goals is to try to write in prose (but then again, who says poetry can't be nonfiction).

Number two was a little more stable—I removed much of the refrain language and tried to give it a more linear feel. I kept it in present tense because I think it gives the piece more immediacy, something I wanted to take from draft one to draft two (and draft three, and draft four . . .).

I also have this thing with narrator-like sentences where I tell the reader what to do/think. I've been experimenting with it all of my life, and I'm still not close to making it work. I don't even know if it's possible, but I'll keep working on it. Maggie and Juli helped me edit these areas out so I was less expositive and more descriptive.

Between drafts two and three I went wild and tried to overdo the description in each line to see what I would get out of it. I cut about half of what resulted, but that's fine with me—what I was able to keep (see the parts about driving on the road, the title) added some depth to the piece.

I see this one as more of a transition piece than anything else—sort of my move into prose-land.

I also used an older part of this piece for a part in my "longer" essay. I think it fits fairly well and was a sort of inspiration for the larger work. It's nice how all of my work seems to fit together.

THOMAS HARMON

"Watch," "Radical Revision Guy," and "Radical Revision Process Narrative"

CONSIDER THIS:

Most of us have read comic books at some point in our lives. For Thomas Harmon, an undergraduate writing student, acknowledging his passion for comic books felt somewhat awkward. He thought he had to hide or justify his pleasure in the genre. Whereas Tom's essay offers an "adult" discussion of his interests and connects them to his development as an English major, his comic-book-radical-revision of that essay demonstrates the lure of the form. He also found that composing a comic book was harder to do than enjoying one. Tom describes his life with comics in his essay "Watch" and translates that life into a radical revision by translating himself into the little-known superhero "Radical Revision Guy." What would you have to do to translate one of your essays into a comic book? What do you suspect was the challenge for Harmon of revising his essay into that format?

WATCH

"We in this country, In this generation, are by destiny, rather than choice, the watchmen on the walls of world freedom."

—JOHN F. KENNEDY, FROM THE SPEECH INTENDED TO BE GIVEN IN DALLAS, NOVEMBER 22ND, 1963

It's a bit awkward, growing up a comic book reader, especially growing UP a comic book reader. The older you get, the more you feel the need to justify the hobby. You start to mature, and you start to be a little more critical of your arts; you figure out that "Major League" isn't an Oscar-quality movie, just as "Saved by the Bell" isn't quality television. Along with this creeps the growing stigma; comics are for kids, comics have nothing to say, and that had better be one of your dad's porno mags when I come back in the room, young man, or you're grounded.

Like most aging comic book fans, I deal with this every time I slip, shoulders hunched just a little bit, into a comic store, or every time I sit in my room and flip through a few back issues to pass the time. I'm not always sure how to deal with this; I know it's silly to still let something like that bug me, but it does, nonetheless. At this point in my life, I should be self-assured enough that what other people think of my hobbies shouldn't matter at all, much less enough to make me ashamed to enjoy the things I enjoy.

Still, I feel I can justify my comics fix to my more literary side. Offhand, I can name just about a dozen comics that have garnered enough mainstream critical acclaim to combat the notion that comics are only for children. The best of these, in my opinion, is Alan Moore's *Watchmen.*

I first read *Watchmen* about a year after I started high school. Reading comics and reading about comics, you hear a lot about it, so I picked up a trade paperback that collected the twelve-issue series. It was originally presented in 1987 by DC Comics, the company most famous for Superman and Batman, both important characters in American pop culture, and, to many people, important characters in American literary history. (Somebody else's paper to write, trust me.) So, the company who invented superheroes let a writer reinvent them.

Watchmen is a story about superheroes, not so different from Superman and Batman, in that what they do is help people in trouble. What's so different about it is the close scrutiny of the personal lives of the heroes, presenting them as real people who just happen to fight wrongdoers. In keeping with this, the main theme (and ultimately, the main conflict in the story) deals with the question of how people with these powers and these moral obligations to do "right" really react to something as morally ambiguous as the Cold War, still the most relevant political topic of the 1980s in which the series was conceived.

In reading, my eyes were opened to what the comics medium could do. Moore's collaboration with artist Dave Gibbons is a masterpiece from the first word bubble to the last, on a level far denser than the standard newsstand superhero fare. The ramifications of costumed heroes on the general populace is seen up close, and it's never as cut and dry as "Look, up in the sky! It's (insert hero here)!" The most original trick of *Watchmen* is its non-suspension of disbelief, a totally realistic universe set on the same shelves as books in which it MUST be assumed that people can have unbreakable skeletons, lift semis, and still lead normal lives while jumping muggers at night. Moore plays with and on superhero conventions and transcends the genre in doing so, creating a post-modern work of fiction that takes everything that longtime readers of spandex-clad crimefighters have taken for granted since elementary school and distorting them in the lens of our own lives and history.

The story of *Watchmen* wraps a subplot about the elimination of the few costumed heroes that remain after the government outlawed them after a police strike in the 70s around the larger plot of impending nuclear war by the antagonized Soviet Union. By the mid-eighties, most of the heroes have retired, and the ones left in commission work for the United States government, one of whom is the only true Superhuman in the book, Dr. Manhattan, a man with godlike abilities given to him in a nuclear accident. His presence changes the path of American history; in the words of one of the characters, "God exists, and he's American." With the help of a being whose abilities are limited only by his imagination, the U.S. wins the Vietnam War and lives in a world of electric cars and other results of Dr. Manhatten's powers. His presence frightens the Soviet Union to the brink of war; the story, while jumping around in time, is constantly overshadowed by the constant news headlines telling of oncoming atomic destruction.

Throughout the story, the collective psyche of the society in which these heroes exist is examined through the use of everyday reoccurring characters like the news vendor and the retired 1940s costumed hero. At the same time, the lives of characters such as the vigilante Rorshach (a brilliant combination of "Taxi Driver"'s Travis Bickel and the Batman) and the Silk Spectre (a retired second-generation hero, and the wife of Dr. Manhattan) are given close scrutiny, showing not just how they're combating these problems, but how they're dealing with them personally. Even the psychology of Dr. Manhattan, whose humanity seems to be slipping from him with every decision, is explored and tied into the story.

Where nuclear war and a seemingly remote plot to kill or frame costumed heroes tie in together becomes clearer and clearer towards the end; even the near-omnipotent Dr. Manhattan, already becoming isolated from everyday humanity, is targeted with a media smear claiming he's responsible for the cancer of several people close to him. These two threads tie up in the form of another former costumed hero who makes the saving of his world from nuclear destruction his moral duty, at the cost of his conscience and of the lives of anybody who stands in his way.

I won't give you more than that. I've said too much already.

Moore purposefully plays the characters and themes of *Watchmen* against comic book clichés; in a realistic setting, the power of Dr. Manhattan would indeed have a huge effect on the way people live their lives, but in any normal comic on the racks, there might be three people with those kinds of abilities lounging around unnoticed by the rest of the world. In *Watchmen,* however, Dr. Manhattan has a legion of spin doctors trying to make sure that he remains an all-American symbol of righteousness, and at the same time trying to keep him content with his life and his work, fearing the consequences should his world be rattled too much. In the early days of comics, during the Second World War, superheroes such as Superman and Batman were seen fighting Nazis in Europe and the Japanese in the Pacific, and this was all accepted, that our nation's heroes would fight for truth, justice, and the American Way. Moore's use of Dr. Manhattan plays on this notion, and puts it in a realistic light.

Superhero stereotypes such as the Golden Boy and the intense vigilante are also explored in Ozymandias and Rorshach, respectively. Ozymandias is blonde-haired, blue-eyed, in perfect physical condition, and is known as "The World's Smartest Man." He is popular, a celebrity, even. This pokes a little fun at the notion of the superhero as the nation's sweetheart ala Superman or Captain America, a boy-next-door quality. Rorshach, however, takes the role of the Batman or the Punisher to contrast Ozymandias' public adoration; he dresses in a ratty old trenchcoat and a hat, looking more like a homeless bum than anything else. He is more feared than respected, a scourge of the underworld, and an extremist.

The political views of the characters are explored and are symbolic of the politically charged times of the Cold War. Rorshach is conservative to the point of extremism, vowing to "Never surrender, never compromise, even in the face of Armaggedon." (This is mirrored in this mask of flowing black shapes on a white background; no grey areas, just well-defined areas of good and evil.) His views of other people and even of the Cold War are reflected in this "never compromise" attitude. Other characters, such as the Silk Spectre, take a less extreme view, almost confused in comparison, constantly questioning and reevaluating their places.

Moore's writing is intricate, with the various subplots being supplemented by constant shifts in time and place. It's written almost like a movie, with plenty of cutaways and simultaneous action. His dialogue is darkly funny at times, and he portrays each character with a level of personality and individuality not usually seen in comics. The action in the story is also mirrored in a young man's reading of a comic within the comic, expertly weaved through most of the main story, that tells the tale of a shipwrecked sailor on a bloody quest for revenge, which at times seems to symbolize one or even all of the characters of *Watchmen.* Shifts back into the 1940s, when the first costumed heroes began appearing in *Watchmen's* world, are common, to help give background and detail to the story taking place in the eighties. The level of precision with which Moore ties all of these elements together into the plot is simply mind-boggling.

On the surface level, *Watchmen's* art (supplied by Moore's collaborators, artist Dave Gibbons and colorist John Higgins) is very comic-book simple, all standard, symmetric grids. The characters are realistically drawn, to complement Moore's very realistic story, and the pages are viewed as from a movie. Upon inspection, the view and color of each panel take on a significance, with color changes and characters' stances (and even their facial expressions) having relevance to the overall plot of the story. Some examples: color lighting schemes switch at important moments; the constantly shifting shapes on Rorshach's mask repeat themselves at ironic places in time; a blood stain is referred to again and again by ketchup stains, spilled water, etc.

Despite this very traditional layout, the graphic novel is ambitious in that it uses other forms of written media as bookends. Letters, newspaper and magazine articles, and excerpts from one of the characters' "biography" are all used to ground the story, almost giving it a documentary feel at times. Moore's multimedia approach demands that the reader be immersed in the culture of this book; it's impossible to fully understand the story without having read the entirety of the documents given to the reader as bookends. In all, the reading of *Watchmen* is a total experience, and a rereading is almost required to fully understand all the symbols and self-referencing that happens and re-happens throughout the story.

One of the most amazing things about *Watchmen* is its historical importance as a work of fiction. While I believe that it's a piece of fiction that people will still be reading years from now, it's really a piece that speaks volumes about the decade in which it was written, the 1980s. I think a lot of people in my generation feel a bit sheltered from the true feeling of the decade, and many of the pieces of literature regarding the eighties ("Less Than Zero" comes to mind) are more kitsch now than anything. Many of the ideas the series explores are stereotypically eighties, such as the detached fear at the end of the Cold War, the grey moral politics that came along with it, and the burgeoning Information Age. I think that it could be argued that *Watchmen* is one of quintessential artistic pieces of the eighties, capturing the mindset and the atmosphere of the times in an interesting way by distorting it in a comic book mirror.

For me, this has plenty of personal importance. In the eighties, when the world was aligning and realigning itself politically, faking free elections and building bombs, I was reading comic books, four-color fistfuls of underwear-clad muscle-bound boneheads spending more time punching each other than noticing the ridiculously unpractical costumes their female counterparts wore. Nothing really overtly political or ominous happened, at least nothing that affected my life to any extent; I was no more terrified of Dr. Doom than I was of Brezhnev. At least Doctor Doom was fun to watch in action, hellbent on world domination that he was. The Russians didn't wear capes, just those furry hats. No wonder the Fantastic Four never invaded.

In reading the wacked-out version of the eighties *Watchmen* portrays, I've been better able to understand the decade in which I grew up, through a medium I spent a lot of that decade enjoying. A larger plot, with a smaller plot wrapped around, no doubt.

In the presence of college students, especially English majors who have read a lot of "classics" and a lot of "important" books, it's a little weird to talk about a comic book in such hushed terms, like a literary achievement. *Watchmen* justifies the comics medium as a true artform the way only a true classic can, and its arrival marked a turning point in the way graphic fiction portrayed society. The dizzying variety of literary techniques used in *Watchmen* transcends the written novel and even makes a case for the superiority of the comics medium as a storytelling device. In motion pictures, the story is limited by what can be filmed and put on a screen. On the written page, the story is limited by the way in which the author can present the material. In the comics medium, however, the limitations of both are minimized; the author can specifically bring his or her vision to the page, provided the artist can portray the scene correctly. Camera "views" are limitless, just as internal thoughts can be shown in the use of "clouds." *Watchmen* uses these elements to their fullest, creating an engaging, thought-provoking story without sacrificing any of its power to make it easier to read.

The effect that *Watchmen* has had upon me as a reader has been strong. Gradually, as a comics reader, I had begun to discern between the well-written and the ridiculous, the cheap-thrill versus the thought-provoking, and the artistic from the overtly commercial. Moore and Gibbon's masterpiece shines because it celebrates the comic book as an artform, rather than try to make it as movie-like or novel-like as possible.

Justifying comics as an artform will always be a bit of a problem, as long as the stereotype that comic books are only for children interested in seeing big guys hit each other is prevalent. Gradually, as more mature graphic classics such as *Watchmen* are

written, comics will see more and more mainstream acceptance as not only a form of entertainment, but as a way in which life is expressed and observed. One day, hopefully, that slump in my shoulders will fade just a little.

Sources:

Moore, Alan, and Dave Gibbons. *Watchmen.* 1986, DC Comics, New York.

"Watching the Detectives: An Internet Companion for Readers of Watchmen"

http://raven.ubalt.edu/staff/moulthrop/hypertexts/wm/

Script for *Radical Revision Guy*[1]

A COMIC COMPOSED BY TOM HARMON

FRAME 1: GUY

Hi, everybody! This is my radical revision! I'm gonna make a really crude comic book to talk about comic books with!

FRAME 2: GUY

. . . and yea, I realize this is crude. That's what makes it "radical"
Text box in frame: Meanwhile, as the readers groan, let's begin this paper with a short interlude. Here to set the mood is a licensed character.

FRAME 3: SKELETAL COMIC CHARACTER IN TRENCH COAT AND HAT FROM DC COMICS

What a way to summarize most people's attitudes towards comic books in general. Comics? Like the funnies, right? Joking

FRAME 4: ADULT GUY AND YOUNG GUY (LABELED AS SUCH)

Adult Guy: It's always a bit awkward, growing up a comic book reader, especially growing UP a comic book reader. The older you get, the more you feel the need to justify the hobby.
Young Guy: Hi, everybody.

[1]Harmon's original cover drawing for "Radical Revision Guy" is followed by this script, the text he created based on his initial class essay. Because he imported a wide array of copyrighted materials into his project, it couldn't be reproduced here in full. If you plan to share your work beyond the classroom, which is to be hoped, consider relying on public domain images or your own photos and art.

FRAME 5: NBC WEB IMAGE OF YOUNG PEOPLE IN SHADES IN A CONVERTIBLE. GUY IN THE UPPER CORNER

You start to mature, and you start to be a little more critical of your arts; you figure out that "Saved by the Bell" isn't quality television.

FRAME 6: GUY MAKING A CONSTRUCTION PAPER IMAGE

When you're really young, it doesn't matter that much. Fun is fun. Vacant lot wiffleball games and construction paper and the walk up and down Ramsey Street to school all take up about the same social energy as reading comics. Later, though, boys play ball, girls skip rope, and the rest of us geeks keep putting our money on the drug-store counter for a fistful of four-color excitement.

FRAME 7: GUY WITH OFFSTAGE SECOND VOICE AND IMAGE OF THE ATOM.

Guy: So, while the rest of the world was worrying about getting atomized and the better part of my grade and middle school were hitting each other in the arm

Off-stage yoice: Ow! You Dweeb!

FRAME 8: GUY WITH COMIC IN FRONT OF FACE

. . . I was reading comic books. Yup.

FRAME 9: GUY STILL READING; SHADOW IMAGE OF GUY HITTING OFF-STAGE SPEAKER WITH A HAMMER

See at least nobody was really getting hurt in comics (unlike on the playground).

FRAME 10: DOCTOR DOOM—MARVEL COMICS WITH INSERT SMALL FACE OF GUY

And when people WERE getting hurt in comics, at least it was by cool people like doctor Doom, who had much more inventive ways of destroying us than with nuclear weapons. (Besides, who's more fun? Khrushchev banging a table with a shoe or ol' Vic Von Doom shooting lasers from his fingers?)

FRAME 11: CIRCLE FRAME WITH GUY LECTURING

SO, this was how I entertained myself for a pretty good portion of my younger years. And, as I got older and hence more critical of my diversions, I discovered that comics aren't just about morons in skintight suits beating each other senseless while dizzy heroines gasp and faint. A lot of people don't know this, but there's a lot of pretty heady stuff out there.

FRAME 12: GUY COMMENTING ON A SHORT COLLAGE OF DC SERIES *WATCHMEN*

One of my most favorite of these heady comics is Alan Moore's *Watchmen* stories that was originally published in 1986. Say hello guys. Watchmen's just about the pinnacle of what a comic book should be and what a writer, an artist, and the collaborators can do with the almost limitless possibilities presented by the format.

SMALL FRAME 13: GUY WITH LARGE HEAD OF ALAN MOORE

And Alan Moore, he's scary

FRAME 14: GUY WEARING A UNIVERSITY LETTER SWEATER

But before all you literary types jump bully-style on my hide for talking so reverently about a comic book, lemme point out that I've seen Watchmen in course text listings. So you might be able to use this as a reference some day.

FRAME 15: GUY, THINKING: STORY ON BOTH SIDES OF CAMEO

Where to start? Watchmen's a story set in and about an alternate Earth in which superheroes really existed. It's based around the lives of these superheroes and the ways they deal with life in a 1980s still threatened with nuclear Armageddon. Against this backdrop is set a plot to save the world by one of these super heroes, but it raises the question, "What does salvation cost?" This pushes Watchmen past standard superhero moral dilemma ("How do I beat up Professor Bomb and not mess up my hair?") and into the deeper issue of "If somebody wielded "super" power, how do we judge their ends?"

FRAME 16: TWO IMAGES OF GUY LOOK TOWARD EACH OTHER, TEXT BETWEEN

The characters are all portrayed realistically, with the man who fights crime in the owl suit being just as unsure about his life as the newspaper vendor, and the atomic-powered man ruminating about the worth of human life.

FRAME 17: SKETCH OF MAN IN THE OWL SUIT WITH SMALL IMAGE INSET

Generally in superhero comics, the good guys end up doing what is generally considered to be the "right" thing. In Watchmen, nobody really makes an undeniably right decision; heroes cheat on their spouses, go mad, and take broken bottles to pregnant women.

Man in Owl Suit: Don't tell the blue guy, 'kay??

FRAME 18: GUY TALKING

And the ART! Dave Gibbons is simple, yet effective as a storyteller, providing well-developed figures and perfect atmospheres.

FRAME 19: 3 FRAME STRIP FROM WATCHMEN, DC COMICS

Copyrighted strip

FRAME 20: GUY POINTING AT A ROUGH DRAWING OF A HERO

And so, with no limits, a good story, and a body of great work out there, what is there to keep comics from respectability? Why still a joke?

FRAME 21: GUY IN "ACTION POSE!!" LABELED

Probably because people aren't willing to risk a few chuckles from the peanut gallery and try something new. How's this: go by a comic store, and go buy a comic. Grow up already.

FRAME 22: SKULL IMAGE IN A HAT

The End. (Joking, of course.)

WRITING PROCESS NOTE FOR "RADICAL REVISION GUY"

Thomas Harmon
is gonna tell y'all
about his fab plan
to do something weird
to one of his compositions.

Well, to be honest, I was planning on doing a turn on my first paper, "Spider Stories," maybe to do another point of view, or, as Wendy suggested, to rewrite it in a five-star essay manner, very formal and dry. I had begun to reblock the spider paper, and to tweak out a lot of the more flowery parts, those that would be inappropriate for the paper. BUT . . .

. . . during workshop, Sam made an off-comment about turning my paper we were workshopping ("Watch") from the essay format into a comic-book format. This sounded like a pretty radical way to: a) make use of the fact that my printer's working and b) to be pretty radical, 'cos it's not like I haven't written enough five-star papers in my life. (God bless you, Mr. Buytart.)

So, I spent about a bazillion hours on the Clarisworks Drawing Program, and yeesh, am I lousy at it. (Getting better, though!) I think it turned out just okay . . . still, it looks pretty funny. I wish my roommate hadn't made so much fun of it, though. (He has the right; he's an art major, and a good one, too.) I think it looks a bit rushed, except for page 2, which looks really great, if you ask me. I'm goddamn PROUD of that page.

Still, it's "radical," right? *whew*

I'd be remiss if I didn't thank Mr. Larry Bonk for DJing on V89 that night and making me laugh. Brought out the crazy cartoonist in me, just a bit.

CONNECTING TO READING

A. In class, compose your own metaphors for revising. "For me, revising is like . . ."? How do your metaphors change when you change the prompt: "For me, revising (insert different genres: poetry, fiction, nonfiction, school essays, personal essays) is like. . . ." To date, what have been your drafting habits and strategies? Your revising habits and strategies? What would you like to know about revising but don't yet know how to accomplish? Share your drawings and observations in a class discussion.

B. For a sequence of four journal entries on drafting and revising, complete the following activities. First, consulting the readings in this chapter, make a list of (1) new information, (2) good advice, (3) questions about response and evaluation these authors make you curious about, and (4) points that confuse you or that you don't agree with. Second, write informally to connect two essayists. For instance, compare the advice offered by Anne Lamott and Gail Godwin. Which essay is most useful to you and why? Third, consider Toby Fulwiler's advice for revising. How much is old news and how much is new to you? What have been obstacles to following this sort of advice in the past? How could you change your revision habits? Finally, apply Toby Fulwiler's advice to Annie Dillard's essay. Does she appear to follow any or many of his points? Conversely, does she observe anything about her drafting process that would lead you to add a point or two to Fulwiler's advice? In class groups, pool your insights from the first day (consulting/summarizing chapter readings in a list) and post your list to a class discussion board. Use the other three entries as notes for class discussions.

C. In a class discussion, share your ideas on the following: What do you know about how others revise their writing? If you've ever watched others revise, tell some stories of what they did and how it worked. Consider the ways "revision" works in areas of life other than writing? How does a dancer revise a dance? How does an artist revise a drawing? A musician revise a song? How do other practitioners revise (if you think or know they do): athletes, doctors, scientists, engineers, and architects? Consider as well the discussions of revision in the writing process narratives in this book; doing so, what do you learn about classroom authors' revision practices? As the class ends, freewrite for ten minutes on one aspect of this discussion that interests you.

D. In an e-mail letter to a class partner, reflect on your preferred readers. Who do you trust to read your writing and under what conditions? Whose advice about revising and evaluation(s) of your writing do you trust most and why? Whose advice would you never follow and why? Why (and where) might you seek out more response to your writing? Tell two stories that describe the least useful and the most useful response to your writing you've ever received. If you can, trace the influence of those responses or response situations to who you are as a writer today and how you approach response. After an exchange and a response with a partner, copy the exchange to your journal. If you've kept essays with peer comments, review some of these using Richard Straub's advice. Did the peers responding to you follow his advice? To what degree? Bring a peer-annotated essay to class to share in a group discussion.

E. In a class group, identify your favorite chapter reading on revision, response, and evaluation. Which elements did you respond to and why? Next, share some stories of small or large writing groups that you've experienced: how did your readers' responses help or not help you? How could responses in those situations been improved? Share some stories about you and the grading of your writing. Plan to share with the class the group's choice of what was most interesting or what was illustrative of a member's story of response and grading (one story related to each issue).

CONNECTING TO WRITING

A. To compose your own two- to three-page informal position statement on "How I Revise," compare an early draft to a later draft of one of your texts much as you did when you analyzed Jay Szczepanski's or Thomas Harmon's revisions. Make a list of all the changes you made. What, if anything, kept you from making more changes than you did? Were you dealing with a watcher (or writing behaviors like procrastination and avoidance) that kept you from digging deeper? Did you ever expand your text, take risks? If so, name the risks or challenges of the draft and think of others you could have taken if you had more time.

B. After reading Gail Godwin's essay, draw your watcher. Then write a "Wanted Dead or Alive" caption to go with it.

C. Try a revision exercise. Get a feel for one of the steps in Toby Fulwiler's drafting sequence. Freewrite about a recent personal experience of some importance to you; don't leave the computer or your notebook until you've captured the full arc of the experience, a full rough draft. Do this for three days running, each day choosing a different topic. On the fourth day, take one of those rough drafts and revise it by limiting the time covered in that narrative to one day and the setting to one specific place. What happened to your draft when you revised it using those two constraints?

D. Revise a draft—or a portion of a draft—by rewriting it from another point of view. If you're writing about school, write from a teacher's or an office staff person's perspective. If you're writing about family, choose another member's viewpoint. If you're writing about politics, explore the other side of the discussion. If you're writing about science, write from the point of view of the patient, the animal, or the plant under study; you can even speak for the cosmos. What shifts when your narrative point of view shifts? What lessons about revision are encoded in such an exercise? Write an analysis of or response to this exercise to accompany the drafts.

WRITING PROJECTS

1. Compose a disciplinary-specific "Revising [or Drafting] in . . ." essay. That is, research the ways writers in your discipline revise. Read published interviews if they're available and interview professional writers in your field. Using the essays in this chapter for ideas, you may want to compile a set of questions that lets the individuals you interview share how they draft and revise, under what conditions, and with what results? For your audience, consider a group of possible majors in that field. You're composing, say, "Drafting a Biology Report" or "Lawyers Revising." Be sure in this essay to focus on drafting and revision processes as you learn about them from your interviewees. You could also research "College Students and Revision" by reading across the writing process narratives in this book.
2. Write an essay where you extend the idea of revision, metaphorically, to some other aspect of your life. In fact, you could write about "Revising a Life" or "Revising a Love Affair." Or compose a poem or a short story on revision.
3. Complete an entire essay using Toby Fulwiler's revision sequence. Take the practice writing you undertook in "Connecting to Writing," application E, and continue with that topic through the entire drafting sequence or take another essay on a new topic through Fulwiler's sequence.
4. Revise a piece of writing nearly out of existence. That's right. Take a piece that you care about enough to play with it further and, using your intuition or some of the suggestions for radical revision found in this chapter, compose as many drafts as you can until the text falls to pieces. This works best with a shorter initial draft and with one that you care about but not crucially (that is, you have to be willing to drive this text to some crazy dead ends). Now, number/title the drafts and compose a writing process narrative that takes a reader on a brief tour of what happened between the drafts. What did you decide to do with each draft, why, and with what result? If

you like, reassemble the best pieces into a new, final version. You might want to post this on a class discussion board or share it as a class power point demonstration or make it into a website. Consider drafts that include other media.

5. Compose an essay (or class lecture/PowerPoint demonstration) or Web page on the topic of the art of editing. Teach your classmates how to distinguish between drafting, revising, and editing. Find someone who edits other writers' texts for a living. Interview that individual and share what you learn. Consult handbooks at the library or bookstore. If possible, find editors of two distinctly different sorts of texts and interview them both to share the similarities and differences. End with editing advice for students in a writing course.
6. Shape an essay on revision based on the work of expert, published writers. Find the published drafts of a writer you admire and compare two versions of one of his or her works. For instance, it may surprise you to learn that Anne Frank revised sections of her famous diary and that you can find copies of those revisions and discuss them. Editions of other writers' texts are available in your library. Your challenge is to illuminate the drafting process without boring your reader with page after page of drafts that exhibit few or difficult-to-discern revisions.
7. In the spirit of Annie Dillard, compose a "How I Wrote" [or choose your own title] essay that allows you to explore and share your revision process; include samples of your drafts.
8. Complete a radical revision and writing process essay. Like Thomas Harmon, pick an earlier piece of your writing and complete a radical revision. Compose an essay considering the lessons of that revision (You're writing a process essay whereas Tom wrote a process *note*.)
9. Compose a self-portrait as a reader of peer writing. What should those who submit their writing to you expect to receive in response? To understand yourself as a reader, respond to another writer's paper—choose a work by a classmate or any of the classroom authors' drafts in this book. Analyze your written responses. What types of comments do you make? What sort of role do you tend to play: critic, coach, ally, cheerleader, or other? Looking at your comments, are there places where these could be misinterpreted? What about your handwriting? Are you about to have FRAG read as FROG? After conducting an honest self-audit, you might use Richard Straub's essay to generate ideas about how and where you'd like to grow as a reader of peer work.
10. Write an essay about response and/or grading. Choose from two options.

    Option A: Sometimes classroom authors tell me they don't like to respond to peer texts because they don't feel qualified or skilled enough to do so. Others argue that it's the teacher's job not the student's job. Write an essay that argues both sides. What are the benefits of peer readers and what are the weaknesses of peer readers? Do the same with teachers as readers. Be fair to both sides of the argument and then decide which view you favor or, if you can, mediate a middle ground. For instance, are there times when peers are better readers and other times when teachers are better readers? Or, write an essay about the advantages or disadvantages of competition. That is, do you think we should or shouldn't have grades in school?

Option B: Consider the ways evaluation works in another area of your life. Do you feel responded to, graded, evaluated as an athlete? As a dancer? As a law student? Or, as Linda Pastan's poem suggests, as a lover, sibling, and so on?

* * * *

Well, very often, once I get to the revising, at least two or three words per line just give me grief; they won't budge because they say, "No, I'm staying here," and I say, "Yeah, but you're not right!"

—June Jordan

One of the few things I know about writing is this: spend it all, shoot it, play it, lose it, all, right away, every time. Do not hoard what seems good for a later place in the book, or for another book; give it, give it all, give it now. The impulse to save something good for a better place later is the signal to spend it now. Something more will arise for later, something better. These things fill from behind, from beneath, like well water.

—Annie Dillard

Chapter 7

Research and the Writer: Joining Voices

Thinking About the Ways All Writers Are Researchers

> I don't find a difference when writing expository prose and when doing "creative writing." To me, it's all essentially writing. To me, they're very similar, just the writing research comes from two different areas: internal source or external source.
>
> —JUAN, WRITING STUDENT

> Researchers who never manage to narrow their subjects produce drafts that are a lot like blurry landscape shots. While they manage to cover a lot of territory, their reader never gets a very good look at anything. The picture lacks details and often provides an ambiguous or vague sense of emphasis. It includes so much information, it's hard to figure out what's most important.
>
> —BRUCE BALLENGER, WRITING TEACHER

> Writing a research paper about literature is like watching *The Wizard of Oz;* it's a yearly obligation.
>
> —JIMMY, WRITING STUDENT

> Research papers become more appealing when you make them a reflection of yourself, when you tailor them around your own interests or your own curiosities.
>
> —WENDY MCLALLEN, WRITING TEACHER

It's no secret, research papers are one of the most frequently assigned exercises in American schools, and it's even less of a secret that writing students often don't like these projects. I think this is so often the case because writers in school rarely have the chance to learn the pleasures of research. They see research as something they're told to do rather than something they want to do. Perhaps this has been your experience? Under these conditions, it is a real challenge to think of research as it really is—a process of finding out; that is, learning, as well as finding support for your ideas and presenting your thinking and arguments in the company of the thinking and arguments of others. Still, once you learn how research can, does, and should work for your writing aims and purposes, you've won half the battle in learning how to convert assigned research into a satisfying process in service of your work. Once that happens, you've started to view research like a writer.

Think of it this way: you're a writer and all writers research. They do this because they love to learn about the world in ways that inform their writing. Writers study the world: they observe it, they interview its inhabitants, they record the results of their studies and thoughts. Books are printed. Libraries are built. On-line databases are developed. Then, other writers read and respond to the records that have been left, even as they spend time developing their own insights and deepening their own thinking.

Whether consulting your memory or an on-line database, you're searching for information and voices to strengthen your own voice. When you quote an authority, you show that you've considered the thoughts and positions of others. You also align yourself with that individual in an ongoing, community discussion which you may just at that point be entering or seeking to enter. Connection and entry occur when you consolidate your thinking with the help of others. When readers realize you're grounded and connected—that you've done your researcher's homework—they begin to listen to your points with less resistance. You gain a hearing and your views are respected.

Writers' research is often so well integrated into their texts that readers take it for granted. Notice how a writer explains how to choose the best medicine to administer to a child who has an ear infection, offers a discussion of the symbolic complexities of a Shakespearean sonnet as argued by several critics, or shares a meditation on his past and the culture of the town or region where he was raised. In each case, the writer is connecting information, aggregating thought, and using and amplifying authoritative data. And the invested writer checks and rechecks facts, whether writing nonfiction or fiction. A writer researches to augment memory and observation and to increase her personal storehouse of knowledge, no matter the genre of writing.

It's taken me many years as a practicing writer to understand just how deeply research is part of every writing project I undertake. From my perspective, there's never a moment when I "just sit at the computer and write from thoughts in my head," that old-fashioned image many of us hold about creative writers. Instead, I have learned how to organize data—the material, facts, images, information I need or may need—all the time. And while organization alone won't get the writing done for me, it's an important part of my composing process. That's why I hold on to my personal notebooks, lining them up together on a bookcase shelf for future reference. That's why, with their permission, I keep students' writing, by class, in file drawers, in case I want to write a textbook like this one that cites some of their learning. That's why I read and take notes on my reading whenever I'm writing.

If writers are always learning (in fact, that's why most like to write) then the research essay, argument, or paper assignment can be reconceptualized as an agreement to focus such learning: to work at it intently for a time and for a particular project. The research paper assignment is at its most tedious (makes you, me, most writers groan) when presented as a static way to teach a certain limited kind of inquiry: go to the library, look up three sources, cite these to support your argument by paraphrasing or quoting accurately, beware of plagiarizing, and so on. That's not the research most writers know, though. Research for writing can produce well-documented scholarly reports and articles, but those articles shouldn't (in fact can't) be created unless the writer engages in a complex and stimulating world of textual thinking: a search and a discussion both.

Let me put it this way, research is methodical, perhaps, but rarely boring. Humans organize and catalog data so we can find it again and use it; so the amazing wealth of information available to thinkers in our world can be retrieved, examined, evaluated, shared. Databases are now as important to researchers as physical libraries once were. I'm willing to guess that in your university library as in mine, the banks of PCs now line the first floor and the books and periodicals fill the higher stories. To those who have been visiting libraries for 40 years, like I have, it's clear that the atmosphere of libraries has changed dramatically. Owing to the amount of information shared on the World Wide Web and the development of powerful search engines, more people than ever are searching for and finding the information they need at a distance from the library, although the physical entity "campus library" still provides both data and book storage and houses information technology specialists (a.k.a. librarians).

Research—on-line, in print or in person—still raises the same questions for writers that it always has:

- What topic do I want to investigate and why? Or how do I discover a topic?
- For what aims and what audience?
- What information is available and how reliable is it?
- How can I join the voices that I find to my voice?
- How do I avoid appropriating information?
- How do I cite my findings?
- How do I limit my search yet make sure I've searched rigorously?
- How do I share the excitement of my search and convince my reader of the credibility of my findings?

If you don't yet see yourself as a researcher, one way to change that attitude is to think about yourself (and your brain) as data collection central. In the course of a day, how do you accumulate information? For instance, when dressing to go out, do you consult the Weather Channel? Well, then you've researched. In your chemistry class, do you take notes? Do you organize and save the notes to prepare for the mid-term exam? In practice, you're researching particular aspects of chemistry, consolidating that information, and preparing to share it again. Before you decide to go to the football game, do you talk about the teams? Read the sports page? Predict outcomes with your peers? Think back through previous years' statistics to make these predictions? Listen to a radio announcer talk about the game? You've shored up your guesses, you've joined your thoughts to those of other thinkers, and thus you've researched. When you write an informed letter to the editor concerning the coverage of the game you attended, citing your differing experience of events, citing the opinions of those who sat with you, and citing some of the team statistics, you've written a certain sort of research argument.

Now the idea of "life as a research process" may not seem very connected to academic research and school-assigned research writing assignments, but I believe both types of research lead us to the issue of engagement. Often, school research papers are stultifying to writer and assigned because the writer has failed to become engaged with the research process. In my experience, writers have to make the research assignment *their own* to see the possibilities of research. If you feel research is something being done *to* you, it's certain that you'll conceive of research as dry as dust, formulaic, and no fun. If you see yourself as an active agent, someone looking for information, shaping ideas, forming impressive textual persuasions, then the experience changes radically. Soon you come to understand that research supports personal actions (such as how to buy the right car, how to find out how to get a job after graduation, what steps are involved in starting a small business) as well as scholarly discussions (results of recent scientific experiments; results from an anthropological dig; an academic essay arguing the provenance of a painting). Conference papers and calls for proposals and journals themselves in full-text format are now available on-line.

The essayists in the chapter reintroduce you to research by helping you see the goals, processes, and procedures that best allow you to talk in an informed way in your writing. They encourage you to enjoy research because they're convinced that enjoyment and engagement are keys to your success as a research writer. Peter Elbow and Pat Belanoff do some contrasting, as I just have, of traditional attitudes and practices and assumptions about the research process while showing why research doesn't have to conform to those received stereotypes. Elbow and Belanoff ask you to move from personal reflection to writing that includes both primary research (interviewing and observing) and secondary research (reading); they offer ideas for generating your own topics and developing a drafting sequence for your project. Gay Lynn Crossley explains the place of reading in researched writing. By illustrating the way she researches when writing poetry, Melissa Goldthwaite presents research as a creative act. In a similar manner, Catherine Wald shows that novelists and biographers rely on accurate historical detail to support their constructed worlds.

Stuart Greene argues that we all use argument on a regular basis. He believes writing in school is a process of entering into critical conversation, and he discusses how you might position yourself in these sorts of discussions by examining the way his writing students have done so. Classroom authors, like Leah Marcum in "Storm Surge" (found in Chapter 8), use Web sources to inform their writing as do Rachel Harrington and Margaret Steele in this chapter, who were investigating the history of Iowa blizzards and mirrors, respectively, in their essays. Two additional essays are drawn from student essays published on a writing program website as strong examples for peers to consider as they write their own (http://writing.fsu.edu/oow/index.htm). In discussing any of the essays in this chapter, you'll want to investigate the benefits of traditional methods of research and how new technologies can enlarge your research abilities.

Chapter Readings

PETER ELBOW (b. 1935) AND
PAT BELANOFF (b. 1937)

Writing a Research Paper

CONSIDER THIS (See Authors' Introductions in Chapter 6):

Before you read, brainstorm a list of all the topics you'd really like to know more about, if you weren't too busy to learn about them because you're in school. My quick list includes composting, why I subscribe to the daily newspaper even though I don't read it, how anyone thought to invent the paper clip, how to lay tile, what it will be like to die, and how anyone used to live in Florida in the summer without air conditioning. You may not have thought of brainstorming or freewriting as a way of helping you conduct research. We seem to think of invention as disorderly and the presentation of research as an exceedingly orderly process. Peter Elbow and Pat Belanoff help you consider the research process as a more flexible and friendly activity than you may have thought—one that can help you answer questions you really care about. They can't give you a topic, because they don't know you or your writing situation, but the discussion that follows allows you to think systematically about the research journey you may be about to embark upon.

DECIDING ON A TOPIC

Mainly, in the assignments we've given you so far, we've asked you to write material out of your own head with input from your teacher and classmates in your writing class and in other classes. We think it highly likely that you found—while writing on some of these topics—that you wished you knew more about them. This is your chance to revise an earlier report on the basis of research: interviewing, observing, reading.

Set aside some time for looking back over all the pieces you've done for this writing course. (We hope that, in itself, will prove to be valuable.) As you read, jot down a list of possibilities for research. Perhaps you wrote your narrative about the neighborhood, town, or city where you grew up. Maybe you wrote a description of a frightening dream. We've read quite a few persuasive and argumentative papers on the subjects of college food plans, campus security, and the pros and cons of ungraded courses. And we've read many, many analyses of newspaper editorials, advertisements, and all varieties of literature: poems, plays, novels, and so forth. All of these subjects can be developed into research topics.

To arrive at a topic, try setting up a question for yourself. For example, the student who wrote the argument paper on the college food plan (see readings for Workshop 11) might ask: "What kinds of food plans are provided by college campuses, and what are the benefits and problems of each?" The student who wrote "Collage about Human Differences" (Workshop 3) might ask "What kinds of differences are there among the students, faculty, and staff on campus?" The students (in the same workshop) who wrote about collaborative writing might ask "How much collaborative writing is there on this campus (or some other site) and who does it?" The student who interviewed his brother for Workshop 8 might ask "What kinds of writing do high school students do and how do they feel about it?"

FIRST ROUND OF FREEWRITING

Once you've selected a topic and framed a question for your research to answer, reread what you've already said about the topic and do some focused freewriting or clustering about what else you'd like to know. It's quite likely that you'll have more than one topic that seems promising and interesting to you. If so, do some more freewriting or clustering on all of them as a way to discover which presents the greatest complexity and richness for you. If you still can't decide, share this freewriting with others in and outside the class. Their responses will help you decide on your final topic.

When you settle on your final research question, do more freewriting. Push yourself as much as you can to get down on paper what you already know and what your opinions on the subject are. Don't worry about whether what you write is "right" or not. The point is to make clear to yourself exactly where you're starting from. You may be surprised to discover that you actually know more than you think you do and have more opinions about your subject than you're aware of—or, not so positively, you may find out that you have strong opinions and nothing to back them up.

For instance, our meal-plan writer surely knows college regulations: the costs of various plans, the restrictions and privileges of each, his own experience with the food and the experiences of his friends, and his observations of others in the cafeteria. He probably also knows something about changes in the plan, both those that have already occurred and others being discussed by students and administrators. But he may discover that although he thinks the food and the service are awful, when he tries to find specific examples of that, he comes up short.

As you do this freewriting, interject questions as they come up: "Have the prices gone up recently? How much?" "What kinds of plans do other schools have?" "What provisions are made for those on special diets?" "Is there a profit? Who gets it?" "What are the students really complaining about?" Later you can reread and highlight these questions.

DESIGNING A RESEARCH PLAN

For the purposes of this workshop, we ask you to design a research plan that requires you to do several kinds of research: library, individual, and possibly electronic. This may seem arbitrary to you (it is), but we want you to get some sense of the full range of research strategies and the ways these strategies complement one another. And perhaps it's not as arbitrary as it might seem at first since most subjects can probably be profitably researched in all three ways.

To get started on a plan, make a list of questions you've thought up, starting with your major research question. If you have a chance to share your freewriting and your list, others will probably come up with additional questions. Decide which can best be answered by library research, which by observation and interviews, and which by electronic resources. Since we're asking you to do all of these activities, make sure you have questions in all categories. Again, your classmates can help here.

Following through on one of our examples, the student who wrote about "Human Differences" might list the following questions:

For interviewing:

1. Do you see yourself as a minority of any kind? Because of your race? Your ethnic group? Your gender? Your religion? Your physical appearance? Your intellectual or social interests? Your age? Your status as a full-time or part-time student? As a commuting student? As a parent?
2. Do you tend to associate mainly with those who are part of this same minority?
3. In what other ways do you see yourself as different from students here?
4. Do you feel the same difference in your home neighborhood? In your job?
5. Do you think others (students, teachers, staff, colleagues at work, neighbors) treat you differently from the way they treat others? Why?
6. Does your sense of being different in some way affect how you behave? How?

For observation:

1. What sort of differences are visible on your campus? In your neighborhood? At your job?
2. In each of these settings, do people spend most of their time with those who seem to be most like themselves? In which of these settings is that most true? least true?
3. Do people behave differently depending on whether they're interacting with those most or least like themselves?

4. How do students group themselves in your classes?
5. Do your teachers interact with all students the same way? Do you notice any differences?

For the library:

1. Are statistics available about the make-up of the student body on your campus? On campuses across the country?
2. What information can I find about changes in the make-up of college students over the past 100 or so years?
3. Are there books written by people who describe what it's like being a member of a minority group? For example, what's it like to be handicapped in some way? What's it like to go back to college when you're 45? What's it like to be a woman in a mostly male setting? Or vice versa?
4. Are there articles about the ways colleges (or businesses or neighborhoods) deal with human differences among their members? What seems to work? Not work?

For the Internet:

1. What can I find out about the make-up at particular colleges by seeking out their home pages?
2. Are there special sites for students who see themselves as belonging to minority groups? That is, sites for blind students? For older students?
3. Is there a government site that has information about current college students? A break-down by ethnic group? By age? By gender?
4. Is there some site I can use to disseminate some of my interview questions and thus get input from students on other college campuses?

Once you have this bare-bones list of questions, you'll profit from talking them over with others. Get them to help you devise more questions and refine those you already have. And most important, get them to help you with questions for interviewing and observing. Then you're ready to decide more specifically how to go about your research: what to do first, next, and last.

For example, a student who wanted to find out more about the writing students do in high school might go to the library and look for research studies specifically about this, or for more general articles that describe particular teachers' experiences teaching writing in high school. She could then design interview questions that seek to validate or extend this research. She might want to design a questionnaire for students and teachers to see how similar their reactions or experiences are to the conclusions of the writers of these articles. Or she could reverse these tasks and observe and interview first, perhaps get permission to sit in several high school classes and see what kinds of writing occur there—or even sit in a meeting of teachers as they discuss the place of writing in the high-school curriculum. On the basis of these observations, she could design a questionnaire soliciting information from both students and teachers about their experiences with writing. She could then go to the library and see whether what she has observed and found out is substantiated by other research.

All topics are not alike; some may require that you do a particular kind of research first. The main thing for you in this workshop is to learn to have comfortable traffic back and forth between your own thinking and observing and the thinking and information that others have published. In most workshops we emphasize collaboration with fellow students. Here we want you to understand that you can also collaborate with people you know only through their published works, through interviewing them, or through the words they post on the Internet. What you'll probably realize as you work through this assignment is that you'll need to move back and forth between all these varieties of research.

Before you actually begin to do the research you've laid out for yourself, we suggest that you write a brief list of some of the things you suspect your research will uncover. This may seem odd to you, but it often makes your research more exciting if you've already got some possible conclusions in mind. This list can be very sketchy—just fantasize that you already know all there is to know about your topic.

A note of caution: Students often think that research papers have to prove something. One of the lessons we stressed in Workshop 10 is that we can seldom prove things: All we can do is get people to listen. Except in rare cases, you're not going to get a final answer to whatever question you pose for yourself. The best you can do is gather data that give you insight into a possible answer, one that will be valid within the limits you set for yourself. You can't come to any conclusions about what American college students think about campus food, but you can reach some conclusions about what undergraduates (or perhaps only freshmen or just male freshmen) on your particular campus think about campus food in particular cafeterias right now. You set up the limits, the context, in which you are doing your research. When you report it, you then let your readers know what that context is.

You can't claim anything beyond what your research shows, but that doesn't mean you can't make suggestions or hypothesize about larger issues. It means you have to acknowledge what your data and information apply to and what they don't. Nor does it mean that your research isn't useful; we suspect that this sort of particularized research would be more interesting to the administrators at your school in charge of food services than more generalized research that might not apply so directly to the decisions they have to make.

INTERVIEWING AND OBSERVING

Observing and interviewing are skills; you'll want to make sure you're doing them as well as possible. Before you begin your research through observing, map out where to observe and what sorts of activities to look for. The questions you draw up to further your research will be mainly questions to yourself while you're observing. After a practice run, you may need to alter those questions. Most researchers build a practice run directly into their research plans, knowing that they can't always decide what to look for until they've started looking.

If you're going to design a questionnaire, make sure you try it out on friends or classmates first to uncover whatever glitches it may have. Researchers in the social sciences almost always do this. When you plan your interviewing, it's important to prepare a set list of questions if you're going to draw valid conclusions. You can also do these activities in tandem: first ask your informants to respond to a written questionnaire and follow that up by interviewing a random sample of those who responded. This is also an established research practice, performed, for example, by the U.S. Census Bureau. Also, before you start on your interviews, you may want to look back at some of the advice we gave in Workshop 8.

Your subject may be quite different from those we've been using as examples. We cannot include all possibilities here. Strategies for research are as varied as the questions that can be asked. But you should be able to lay out a plan of action for yourself with the help of your teacher and your classmates. The important thing is to keep your task manageable, to make it into something you can handle within the time you have. Your teacher will let you know how much time that is.

USING THE LIBRARY

If you're not familiar with your campus library, you'll want to set aside some time to become comfortable finding your way around it. Check whether there's a handout or some other printed introduction available. Many campus libraries set up group tours for students unacquainted with the facility. Sometimes writing teachers or teachers of other introductory courses set aside class time for a visit to the library.

Obviously you cannot "master" a college library on the basis of this one task, but the trick is not to feel intimidated. Few people who use libraries ever master them. Realize that it's legitimate to ask librarians for help—and don't be afraid to ask "dumb" questions. Most librarians are happy to help as long as you treat your own questions as occasions for learning, not as requests for them to do the work for you. Also, remember that libraries classify books by subject, so once you've located a book on the shelves, look at the books surrounding it. Libraries are ideal places for wandering and browsing; people who like libraries let themselves pause and glance at books or documents that they are passing. Read a few titles, pick up a book, look at the table of contents, and read a page. Libraries are good for serendipitous finds. Don't give in to the feeling that many people have: "I don't belong here if I don't know where to find what I want."

Here are some of the most promising places to look for information in a library:

- General encyclopedias (e.g., *Encyclopedia Americana* or *Encyclopedia Britannica*).

- Specialized encyclopedias (e.g., *McGraw-Hill Encyclopedia of Science and Technology, International Encyclopedia of Higher Education,* or *The New Grove Dictionary of Music and Musicians*). There are specialized encyclopedias in many areas. Ask the librarian about encyclopedias in your field of interest.
- Almanacs (e.g., *Universal Almanac* or *Facts on File*).
- Biographical dictionaries (e.g., *Dictionary of American Biography* or *International Who's Who*).
- General periodical indexes to short articles (e.g., *Reader's Guide to Periodical Literature* or *Book Review Digest*).
- Specialized periodical indexes (e.g., *Education Index* or *United States Government Publications*). There are many such specialized indexes.
- Abstracts. An abstract is a summary of a scholarly work. Reference rooms in libraries offer online, CD-ROM, or print volumes in various subject areas that include abstracts of articles that appear elsewhere, usually in periodicals. For example, there is a series titled *Psychological Abstracts.* Using this series saves you time because you can usually tell from the abstract whether a particular article is relevant to your research. Abstracts are also sometimes included at the beginnings of articles in certain journals and essay collections. These too can save you time by pinpointing which articles would help your research and which would not.
- Book catalogs. Online Public Access Catalogs (OPAC) are computerized catalogs that have replaced or are replacing card catalogs at most libraries. Almost all are easy to use, and printed instructions are usually available. If not, ask for help from a librarian. Computerized catalogs cut research time immensely. Many libraries' online catalogs also provide access to other libraries' holdings, as well as to such resources as reference works, periodical indexes, and digital text collections.
- CD-ROM and online searches. Most libraries are now equipped with an array of electronic resources ranging from *The Oxford English Dictionary* or *Newspaper Abstracts* on CD-ROM to dedicated computer terminals providing access to the Internet. (Many of the print resources listed above are now available online or in CD-ROM form and will in some cases be available *only* in this form in the future.) Access to electronic sources makes it possible for researchers to probe an immense store of material relatively quickly. Generally, this is done by isolating the key terms relevant to your project and plugging these terms into a search engine. Finding the terms that each search engine recognizes and that will yield useful "hits" requires careful study of the user guidelines but also some trial and error. You will want to give yourself plenty of time to investigate the electronic resources your library offers and to become skilled at using them.

Our list of reference sources is, of course, only illustrative. There are far too many to list here. (A full writing handbook or a textbook devoted to research papers will give more.) To see what more specific resources might be available in your area—and you will often find a reference book that is just what you need—consult a guide like Eugene P. Sheehy's *A Guide to Reference Books* or ask the help of a librarian. The value of reference books is that they give you an overview of your topic and a range of books and articles you can track down.

The essential skill for doing library research is to learn a *different relationship to the printed (or electronic) word.* We tend to feel we have to *read* articles and books, but in research you need to learn to *glance, browse,* and *leaf* through material. You have learned the main thing if you can tell in a few seconds from a title or an abstract whether something is worth tracking down, then tell in a minute or two whether an article or website is worth reading, and in two or three minutes whether a book is worth spending an hour trying to "mine" (not necessarily read). To do this makes you feel insecure at first, but give yourself permission to keep on until you feel more comfortable with the process. Instead of feeling intimidated by the weight or mass of what might seem like everything that's ever been written, change gears and think of it as a vast collection of meeting rooms. In each room people are talking about a topic. Imagine that you have an invitation to poke your head into as many rooms as you want for just a moment or two. No one will be disturbed by your coming in for a few minutes or by your leaving in the middle of the discussion. Be sure to jot down a few notes about the conversation you've heard in each room after you leave it.

Of course you have to do some *careful* reading too. Think of it this way: You don't have much time for this research assignment, so you'll want to end up having browsed and dipped into a number of books, articles, and online sources, and having found 50 to 100 pages worth reading carefully for the light they throw on your topic. The main task is to *find* the best 50 to 100 pages to read carefully and not waste time reading the *wrong* 50 to 100 pages. Inevitably, however, you will do some reading you won't use. This procedure should make you more skilled and comfortable when you have something you want to investigate further. Your goal is to feel that from now on you can wade in and make use of a library whenever you have something that merits the search, whether it's a school assignment or simply something you need to know.

Remember too that you cannot say *everything* about any topic. You always need to limit what you say in some way. Your research is always more convincing and valid to the degree that you realize—and show your reader that you realize—that you are not claiming to have read everything on the subject. This means that you can feel fine about acknowledging what you haven't done. One of the most interesting parts of a research paper can be a section that talks about questions or material you would pursue if you were able to carry on with more research or your suggestions for others who might want to do so. Good researchers almost always do this.

As you read the 50 to 100 pages you've identified as best dealing with your topic in some central way, keep a dialectical notebook as we describe in Mini-Workshop B.

USING THE INTERNET

This section assumes that you have access to a computer with a connection to the Internet and that you have used a World Wide Web browser, such as

Netscape Communicator or Internet Explorer. If you have never used a browser, ask your teacher about computer labs at your school that are staffed by a consultant. Once a consultant has helped you open a Web browser and shown you its navigational tools, you probably will have very little trouble getting around the Internet. You will quickly learn to navigate both by clicking on links and by entering an address, or URL (Universal Resource Locator), into the address box. Indeed, the Web's merit lies in its simplicity of navigation and design: Not only can anyone learn to cruise the Web fairly quickly, but practically anyone can learn to make a Web page. Since the Web eliminates virtually all costs of publication and distribution, many people turn to it to publish their work.

Yet the ease of access and distribution also causes problems for the researcher. Because anyone can make a Web page cheaply and with relatively little labor, academically suspect information often masquerades as authoritative research. You can find informed, intelligent discussions of academic subjects, but these pages are in no way distinguished from less reliable pages. Nor is there any conveniently organized card catalog to all academically sound resources on the Internet. In short, when researching on the Web, you have to spend more time discriminating between what is useful and what is useless. For a detailed discussion of finding and evaluating sources on the Internet, please consult Mini-Workshop F, "Doing Research on the Web."

WRITING AN EXPLORATORY DRAFT

Once you've done whatever tasks you set for yourself for the first segment of your research (observing/interviewing, library study, and/or surfing the Internet), you're ready to write an exploratory draft. Before beginning, we recommend that you lay out all the notes and writing you've done so far and read through everything. After this perusal, do some freewriting to record what you've learned and how you react to seeing all the material. Think particularly about whether you've discovered any patterns or recurrent themes in your writing and notes.

You may discover at this point that you're not so interested in your original question any more, but in some other question that has arisen as you worked on this project. If this were a rigid assignment, you'd have to continue with your original question, but we're not being rigid here. If you have come up with a more interesting question or discovered something more thought provoking than what you started out to discover, we hope you'll change your project to follow up on it. (And we suggest that if, in other classes, you come up with something slightly different from the assignment, you ask your teacher whether you can adjust the assignment to what you've discovered. The worst your teacher can say is no. Many teachers will say yes.)

As you write this draft or after you've finished it, jot down questions for yourself to use as the basis of your next round of research, which may include a return to what you've already done to refine it or a move to another form of research—either in or out of the library.

One of the fallacies about research is that researchers always use everything they find and all research notes they write up. This is simply not true. Remember that research is finding out about something. If you knew what that was going to be at the outset, you wouldn't need to do the research. But since you don't know, you'll read and write a great deal that won't be relevant to your finished research. Researchers almost always throw away more than they use.

MOVING TOWARD A FINAL DRAFT

Whenever you decide you have done as much research as necessary, you are ready to write a full draft of your paper. Before beginning, you'll benefit from laying out the writing you've done so far and looking through it again. You may discover—perhaps for a second time—that you're not so interested in your original question any more. Your data may point to something far more intriguing to you. That will probably be fine with your teacher, but you should check with him.

Because the research process gives you lots of notes and rough writing, you may lose direction or perspective. Thus, you may want to make an outline before you start your full draft. Or you may decide instead to make an outline *after* you've written your draft. This can also work well. You could do both. Just don't agonize so long over your outline that you have little time and energy left to write the paper itself. You don't need to spend a lot of time on an outline. It can be as simple as this:

> I'll start by stating why I was interested in my subject and what my original thinking was, move to how I went about doing the research, lay out some of what I found, and end with my conclusions.

Or you may want something as detailed as this:

1. Statement of question.
2. Statement of methods of research.
3. Recounting of observations.
   a. Engineers.
   b. Classrooms.
4. Recounting of interviews.
   a. Engineers.
   b. Undergraduates.
5. Recounting of information gleaned from books and magazines.
6. Reflections on the way the interviews, observations, and printed sources confirm one another, if at all.
   a. Similarities.
   b. Differences.
7. Conclusions.
8. Possible explanations of conclusions.
9. What I learned and what it means to me.
10. What I'd still like to know.

An important thing to remember about outlines—whether generalized or specific—is that they're only outlines. You need not follow them like a robot. As you begin to write, you may discover some better structure. That may cause you to go back and revise your outline, although you needn't do this if you feel that the structure you're working with is satisfactory.

You can get help from others at this stage. Read or describe your bits of information and data to them and ask them for suggestions about what they see as central and organizing. There are no "right answers" as to how a paper should be organized; it's a question of what works best for readers. You may want to try out two or three organizations.

A little aside: One way to structure your final paper is to present the story of your search. Tell how you started (including false starts), your original writing and thinking, early hypotheses, what was going on in your head as you worked through the series of steps we've led you through, the order in which you discovered things, what you did, partial conclusions you drew, and what you concluded. In other words, your paper could end up being a mixture of process writing and the results of that process. But to do this, you'll need to do process writing throughout. So we suggest that at the end of each piece of your search, you do some writing in your process journal. Even if you don't decide to use it in your paper, it will be a valuable record for you.

DOCUMENTATION

You'll need to make sure that you know how to document the information you've used in your paper. If you've used interviews, you must document these interviews. Your teacher will tell you what style of documentation she wishes you to use. She may also want to go over some of that technical information in class. If you've used a questionnaire, you should include it plus a tabulation of the answers. If you used the Internet, you'll also need to document that as a source.

Documentation of sources is particularly important in research papers—just as important for personal research as for library research. None of us has the right to claim credit for the ideas and words of others regardless of whether we read them or heard them in an interview. And, from a pragmatic point of view, documentation lends authority to your research paper. If people know that you feel safe in revealing your sources, thus giving readers the opportunity to check their validity, they're far more likely to give your words credit.

Quotations

It is possible to do a considerable amount of research and learn from the information and opinions of interviewees and published works—and write a terrific paper of your own without a single quotation or footnote. (Joyce has no footnotes in *Ulysses* for all the details he checked up on.) But for this assignment we are asking for some quotations and footnotes. You should integrate and internalize what you learn into your own thinking, but this is also an assignment in showing to readers that others have said things about your topic. Your reader should not feel he is in a closet with you having a dialogue, but that he is in a large room with a number of people—other voices—involved in the issue. Quotations that allow these voices to come through to your readers will give them a feel for the texture of research on your issue.

For the format and use of quotations in your text, see Mini-Workshop J.

Footnotes Aren't Footnotes Any More

"Footnote" is the word that probably springs to mind when you think of how to document your sources: a *note* at the *foot* of the page. But we are following the recent Modern Language Association (MLA) guidelines for citing sources *without* footnotes. The new MLA citation system makes life easier for both writers and readers and is now standard for academic writing in most of the humanities. (You can still use footnotes for an aside to the reader, but try not to use too many since they can make a reader feel bumped around.)

The citation system that fits the social or natural sciences is the American Psychological Association (APA) system. Some of the essays in the readings in this book, as you've probably noticed, use the APA documentation style. At the end of our listing of examples in the MLA style, we'll list the major differences between MLA and APA.

Documentation procedure has two elements: the *parenthetical citation* in your text as you go along, and the *list of works cited* at the end. When you want to document a source—that is, to tell readers what article, book, or interviewee you are referring to—add a small parenthetical citation. Parentheses show readers where to look for the full information about the article or book in the final list of works cited.

Parenthetical Citations

In parentheses place only the information that readers need for finding the article or book in your list of works cited. Thus:

- Give *only* the page number(s) in your parentheses if you mention the author in your text. For example, your text might read as follows:

> Hammond writes that early jazz recordings contain little if any improvisation, contrary to popular conceptions (87).

Note that the parenthesis is *inside* the sentence's punctuation.

- If the author's name is not in your sentence, then add the name to the parenthesis. For example:

> Historians of jazz have pointed out that early recordings contain little if any improvisation (Hammond 87).

Note that there's no comma between the author's name and the page number. The last name alone is sufficient unless you are using two authors with the same name.

- If you cite more than one work by Hammond in your essay, add the title (or shortened title) to your parenthesis; for example, (Hammond, *"An Experience"* 87). But you can skip the title if you mention it in your text. Note the comma after the author's name but not after the title.

Other conventions:

- Titles of articles or chapters are in quotation marks; book titles are underlined with no quotation marks.
- If the work has more than one volume, specify which one you are citing, followed by a colon and the page number—for example, (1:179).
- If citing a passage from a poem, give line numbers. If citing a passage from a play, give act, scene, and lines—for example (4.5.11–14).
- If there are two or three authors, list them; for more than three, cite only the first author and add "et al."

In APA style, always give the date of the work, but don't give page numbers unless it's a direct quotation. Thus our first example above, if changed to APA, would be simply: (1970). The second example would be (Hammond, 1970). Note the comma before the date.

Works Cited

This is a list of outside sources you cite in your paper. Place it at the end of your research paper on a separate sheet. Here are examples of the most common kinds of citations.

Print and Other Traditional Sources The items are alphabetized by author and follow this general sequence: author, title, publisher. Here's the order in more detail:

- Author (last name first).
- Full title of the work you're citing. If this is part of a larger work, the title will be in quotation marks.
- The title of any larger work, magazine, or journal—if the work you're citing is part of a larger work. This title will be underlined or italicized.
- Name of the editor or translator, if any (first name first).
- Edition.
- Number of the volume(s) used. For example, if the work consists of 5 volumes, and you used only volumes 2 and 3, you need to make that clear.
- City of publication.
- Publisher.
- Year of publication.
- Page numbers (if the work you're citing is only a portion of the larger publication).

Note: If the work you cite is unsigned (e.g., an article in an encyclopedia or newspaper), begin with the title. Thus its place in your alphabetized list would be determined by the first letters of the title. If it is an unsigned U.S. Government publication, however, begin with "United States," then the agency that puts it out (e.g., Bureau of the Census), and then the title of the piece—as though the government were the author.

Book

Cameron, Julia. *The Right to Write: An Invitation and Initiation into the Writing Life.* New York: Putnam-Penguin, 1999.

Note that if Cameron had been the editor rather than the author, her name would be followed by a comma and "ed."

Article in a periodical: newspaper

Campbell, Paula Walker. "Controversial Proposal on Public Access to Research Data Draws 10,000 Comments." *Chronicle of Higher Education* 16 Apr. 1999: A42.

Article in a periodical: monthly magazine

Gardner, Howard. "Who Owns Intelligence?" *Atlantic Monthly* Feb. 1999: 67–76.

Article in a periodical: scholarly journal

Gillette, Mary Ann, and Carol Videon. "Seeking Quality on the Internet: A Case Study of Composition Students' Works Cited." *Teaching English in the Two-Year College* 26 (1998): 189–95.

Note that the second author's name is not reversed. Because the pages of this journal are continuously numbered throughout the year, we have "26 (1998): 189–95." If it were a journal where each issue started with page 1, the note would read "26.2 (1998): 189–95." (The "2" here means the second issue of that year.)

Article or other work in an anthology

Gioia, Dana. "My Confessional Sestina." *Rebel Angels: 25 Poets of the New Formalism.* Ed. Mark Jarman and David Mason. Brownsville, OR: Story Line, 1996. 48–9.

Hammond, John. "An Experience in Jazz History." *Black Music in Our Culture: Curricular Ideas on the Subjects, Materials, and Problems.* Ed. Dominique-René de Lerma. Kent: Kent State UP, 1970. 42–53. Rpt. in *Keeping Time: Readings in Jazz History.* Ed. Robert Walser. New York: Oxford UP, 1999. 86–96.

Here we provide citation formats for a poem in an anthology and for a scholarly essay reprinted in a current anthology. The facts of the original publication must be provided for scholarly articles subsequently reprinted: note the abbreviation "rpt." (reprint), which clarifies the relation between the two sources.

Letter or personal interview

Fontaine, Sheryl. Letter to the authors [or "Telephone interview" or "Personal communication"]. 14 Apr. 1999.

Review

O'Neill, Peggy. Rev. of *Reflections in the Writing Classroom,* by Kathleen Blake Yancey. *Teaching English in the Two-Year College* 26 (1998): 202–204.

Electronic Sources The documentation of electronic sources, like these sources themselves, is in a state of constant flux. The general principles mirror those governing the documentation of print sources, but the information itself is necessarily somewhat different. One key difference is the requirement in many cases to include the *date you accessed* a particular site. The general pattern for online sources runs as follows (with each piece of information required only *if applicable* to the particular source and available):

- Name of author(s).
- Title of the work, underlined or italicized. (If the piece you're citing is part of a larger work, then the title would be in quotation marks.)
- Name of editor(s), compiler(s), or translator(s).
- Publication information for any print version of the source.
- Title of the larger work (scholarly project, database, or periodical) in which the cited work appears.
- Name of the editor of the scholarly project or database.
- Version number of the source or, for an electronic journal, the volume number, issue number, or other identifying number.
- Date of electronic publication or of the latest update.
- Name of any sponsoring institution or organization, such as a museum or university.
- Date of access and network address.

For a professional or personal site, the information is less complicated. This is the general pattern:

- Name of author.
- Title of site. If there is no title, use a generic term such as "Home page" (without underlining or quotes). If the page has an official title (for example, *Italo Calvino Page*), it would be underlined or italicized.
- Name of sponsoring organization, if any.
- Date of access and network address.

CD-ROM, Magnetic Tape, and Diskettes These sources are handled somewhat differently; they are closer to traditional print sources in format:

- Name of author(s).
- Title of publication.
- Name of editor, compiler, or translator.

- Publication medium (CD-ROM, diskette, or magnetic tape).
- Edition, release, or version.
- Place of publication.
- Name of publisher.
- Date of publication.

Examples of some of the most common entries follow:

An online database, scholarly project, or personal or professional website

Novosel, Tony. *The Great War.* 27 Apr. 1999 <http://www.pitt.edu/~pugachev/greatwar/ww1.html>.

THOMAS: Legislative Information on the Internet. 9 Apr. 1999. Lib. of Congress, Washington. 25 Apr. 1999 <http://thomas.loc.gov/>.

Voice of the Shuttle: Web Page for Humanities Research. Ed. Alan Liu. 22 Apr. 1999. English Dept., Univ. of CA, Santa Barbara. 28 Apr. 1999 <http://humanitas.ucsb.edu/>.

Material from an online database or scholarly project

Bimber, Bruce. "The Death of an Agency: Office of Technology Assessment & Budget Politics in the 104th Congress." *Voice of the Shuttle: Web Page for Humanities Research.* Ed. Alan Liu. 22 Apr. 1999. English Dept., Univ. of CA, Santa Barbara. 28 Apr. 1999 <http://humanitas.ucsb.edu/liu/bimber.html>.

Article in an online periodical

Herbert, Bob. "The Other America." *New York Times* on the Web 9 Apr. 1999. 25 Apr. 1999 <http://www.nytimes.com/library/opinion/herbert/040899herbert. html>.

Material from a CD-ROM

Whiting, R.M., and Ignace J. Gelb. "Writing." *Microsoft Encarta 98 Encyclopedia Deluxe Edition.* CD-ROM. 1998 ed. Redmond, WA: Microsoft, 1997.

The format of these citations can be hard to remember; we ourselves have to look it up again and again. You could make a photocopy of these pages to keep handy. And we've printed an abbreviated version of this information inside the back cover for ready reference.

Note how citations have "hung margins"; that is, the first line of each citation is "flush left" (all the way to the left margin of type on the page), and succeeding lines of each citation are indented five spaces—as we have shown them. Our examples are double-spaced (as you should type your manuscripts), but citations are usually single-spaced in published or printed matter.

If you are using APA style, you will call the list of sources "References" rather than "Works Cited." The chief differences in style are that initials rather than first names are used, the date of the work appears immediately after the author's name, only the first word of the source is capitalized (although journal titles are capitalized in the conventional manner), and no quotation marks are used for journal articles. Thus, you would have the following:

Cameron, J. 1999. *The right to write: an invitation and initiation into the writing life.* New York: Putnam-Penguin.

Gillett, M.A., and C. Videon. 1998. Seeking quality on the internet: a case study of composition students' works cited. *Teaching English in the Two-Year College,* 26: 189–95.

You'll also notice some minor differences in punctuation.

We have shown here only the most common kinds of citations. You will need to consult a good handbook for more complicated ones, especially for works from unusual sources (such as a television advertisement, record jacket, or map). Truth be told, few readers will care too much about deviations from correct form when it comes to seldom-cited kinds of sources. Still, these must be cited in a consistent manner.

SUGGESTIONS FOR COLLABORATION

Most researchers know they need to pool their work to begin to think about definitive answers. You and another student or even your whole group may decide to focus on one topic, which you can research together. You can then integrate what you've done and turn this workshop into a collaborative writing task. This sort of project will give you a feel for the kinds of collaborative work so prevalent in the scientific and business world today.

If you decide to make this into a major collaborative project, you may want to go back and read over the sections on collaborative writing in Workshop 3.

GAY LYNN CROSSLEY (b. 1964)

Making Peace with the Research Essay—One Teacher's History

CONSIDER THIS:

Gay Lynn Crossley teaches in the Department of English and Communications at Marian College. She has been the president of the Indiana Teachers of Writing Association. Commenting on her own history with research, she explains, "By the time I was in fourth grade, I had made the discovery that books held power. The knowledge to become anything I wanted to be could be found in books. So when I wanted to become an astronomer, I turned to books on the solar system. When I wanted to become an architect, I checked out books from the public library on house design." Before reading Crossley, make a few mental notes about your personal history with the school research paper assignment. What stories would or could you tell?

Here's what I remember: After spending 10 or so weeks of spring semester 1983 writing what my teacher wanted to hear about assigned literature, she introduced the research assignment—and introduced the topic that every member of the class would have to study: Alaska. Then, each of us was given a slip of paper telling us what we would have to research, specifically, about Alaska. The fates were not smiling on me that day. My slip read: the economic repercussions of the Alaskan pipeline. A minimum of ten pages, with a minimum of twelve sources, on the economic repercussions of the Alaskan pipeline. Yes, the economic repercussions of the Alaskan pipeline.

I assumed that I was supposed to report on them somehow. Not that I knew why, or who would care—that is, until the class before the essays were due. Our teacher was moving to Alaska that summer, and students in her composition class were to provide her with a crash course on her new home. I imagine that explanation helped some students, those lucky ones researching the settling of Alaska or the impact of the gold rush. For me, though, her explanation felt hollow as I read transcripts from the state legislature and any article I could find on the Alaskan pipeline, so desperate I no longer cared if they addressed economic repercussions. I had to find twelve sources on a topic that seemed a last ditch effort on my teacher's part to come up with as many slips of paper as she needed for the number of students in her class. The essay I submitted was the biggest cut-and-paste job you've ever seen. I threw together the outline and note cards *after* I'd given a handwritten copy of my essay to a typist (in the days before the personal computer). Then, friends took me out (it was a Thursday night, I believe) so that I could forget the last few sleepless nights, the stress and strain. The next morning, I dragged myself to class (late) and turned in the assignment, remembering as I did that I'd never written the conclusion. To this day, as you may gather, I resent that teacher.

When I began teaching, I was determined to handle the research assignment differently. Everything I was learning about the teaching of writing confirmed what I had intuited as a student. The outline and note card routine was flawed in that it imposed a linear "think-then-write" process on student writers, and was motivated more by a need to police us than a desire to teach us anything about writing. By throwing a ten-page, twelve-source minimum at writers, teachers encourage a hatchet job since we are understandably more concerned with finding a source, any source, than with learning from that source. If we are limited to citing books, reputable magazines, and academic journals, we experience only one narrowly defined version of research. Furthermore, if we are not encouraged to think rhetorically about researched writing, we'll more than likely produce "schooled" writing, just as I did. And Alaska as an assigned topic, not to mention the economic repercussions of the Alaskan pipeline? Bad, just bad. The student I was, the student you are, should be encouraged to research topics that are important to us, or to find our own reasons for researching an assigned topic.

During my early years as a teacher, it was my mission to persuade writers to find something worthwhile in research and, simultaneously, to prevent them from remembering me with resentment (or at least the same kind of resentment that I felt). With the zeal of a used car salesperson, I emphasized the freedom to choose topics and purposes for research that grew from their own interests. I argued passionately that research was not about reading the index of a book in order to find the few pertinent pages, that research was not about pasting together quotes, that research was not about masquerading our personal perspectives in the name of objectivity (all the things I thought I had to do). Research was about learning and discovering the joy of learning. Let freedom ring.

And that's what it was about for me: freedom. It makes sense; it's the very thing I wished I'd had. Freedom to write without faked note cards, without the obligatory references to books I hadn't read, without that horrible, stilted feeling of quoting for the sake of quoting. Freedom to write about anything but the Alaskan pipeline. Still, during my first years teaching, I found myself reading stilted essays, butchered prose, awkwardly placed quotations. Over time I realized that these students were teaching me a lesson: encouraging writers to use their freedom isn't enough. They showed me that I was spending so much time teaching what research wasn't that I never got around to teaching what it could be. The freedom to choose our own topics, to consider alternative sources, to find our own reasons for researching a topic matters little until we learn that research, first and foremost, is about reading—about reading fully and actively, in both the most traditional and the broadest sense. Here's what I've learned.

READING YOUR TOPIC TO LIFE

At its root, research (it's a verb, too, you know) means to *re-search*—to search again, within ourselves and in the company of others. It's the work of a reader searching into—questioning, challenging, qualifying, borrowing—what others have to say and a writer searching for words that will shape what has been discovered. However, for many of us, our work as a researcher takes a back seat from the get go. The "topic" sits squarely in the driver's seat and with it the perception that the success or failure of a research essay hinges on the topic. I've found this perception to be not only largely untrue, but also harmful. The topic is important in that it should somehow inspire us, but it's our questions, interest, passion, and inquiry that drive a research essay. A writer makes or breaks a topic, not the other way around.

But how do we "make" a topic, especially if we didn't get to choose it? We read life into it by reading ourselves into it—our interests, questions, passions. Rarely do we find ourselves researching a subject that we know nothing about. (How many subjects do we know absolutely nothing about?) Yet, it never dawned on me to consider what I knew about the French Revolution when my history professor assigned the term paper. It didn't seem to matter, in my mind, that my favorite novels in high school were Dickens' *A Tale of Two Cities* and Hugo's *Les Miserables.* Or that, like many adolescent girls, I was captivated by biographies of Marie Antoinette. Or that I had sought out every film and mini-series related to the French Revolution. I didn't consider what I found compelling about the French Revolution, so my research essay for that history course was basically a string of quotations from historians, rehashing what I pretty much already knew about the causes of the Revolution. Had I considered what fiction had already taught me, or the very reason I was drawn to novels and films about the French Revolution, I could have come up with a much more interesting, focused essay about ideas that I'd found exciting since childhood. Maybe I could have explored the romanticism associated with the French Revolution and why it resonated so powerfully for me growing up in the United States. Maybe I could have learned something.

From what I gather, my experience is not unique. Take some time to think about your own past as a researcher:

1. Do you recall a time when you were encouraged to share research for an audience other than your teacher? If you do, what kind of research did you do? Was that research experience different from others you've had? How or how not?
2. What have been acceptable sources for your research projects? Have you been free to draw on alternative sources that were perhaps more familiar to you? What value did you find in working with those sources?
3. Have you *ever* researched a topic that started out interesting to you but, in the process, became dull and stale? Why do you think that happened?
4. Did you ever learn what your classmates were doing for their research projects and find them more interesting than yours? What made theirs different?

If our teachers assign a topic or limit our choice of topics, we're not doomed. Perhaps a topic does seem foreign and unfamiliar at first, but once we read ourselves into it, we tap into the potential of that topic to motivate writing that is worthwhile to us and to our readers. So consider when you first heard about that topic, who you've heard talking about that topic, where most of your knowledge about that topic comes from, the questions you had about it, how your interest in that topic has changed over time. Connecting ourselves in these ways to an assigned topic can help us personalize it, give us a chance to do something interesting with it.

We often think that an "open topic" assignment would solve all our troubles. If only we could choose to write about what we want. However, choosing our own topics can lead to writing just as stale as my essay about Alaska. We can feel the pressure to choose a weighty, significant topic; it is for an academic research essay after all. Again, we are not reading ourselves into our research projects. If you are able to choose your own topic, make a list of topics that interest you, the concerns that have been occupying your mind lately, the questions that run through your mind as you watch the news, talk to family, and think about your boyfriend or girlfriend. Don't dismiss any possible topics on your list, and more importantly, don't edit your thinking as you're jotting them down. Once you have your list, then read yourself into each topic. That is, beside each, pose the specific questions that make that topic alive for you or note the particular motivation to learn that each holds. In my experience, few topics are trivial or inappropriate. More likely, they have been treated in a trivial or inappropriate way. If you aren't sure about a topic, or how to research that topic, talk with your teacher, who can help you discover how to pursue that subject appropriately for the assignment.

WRITERS IN CONTEXT: READING OUR PURPOSES AND AUDIENCES

Even if we've found a topic, a focus for our research, that reflects our sincere interests, the essay we write can still seem forced if we see no real reason for sharing our research other than to complete a requirement. Without a rhetorical context for research, we can be just as unsure about our role as research writers, about what we're supposed to do as researchers. Transforming the research process from a passive process of quoting to an active process of reading requires a transformation in how we see ourselves as writers. And again, this transformation requires us to read—this time our goals and intentions as writers. Rather than students trying to get an assignment "right," we are writers with a job to do—a job that's important to us.

Once you've identified some topics you are interested in researching, list your possible answers to the following questions:

1. What do you want to research about this topic? (Your answers to this question can help you focus your project.)
2. Why are you interested in researching these specific areas? (Your answers to this question can help you imagine a purpose for your research and name possible audiences.)
3. Who could you imagine sharing this research with (in a letter, for example) and why? (Your answers to this question can help you sharpen your purpose, or consider another focus or purpose for your research.)

Our answers to these questions work together, feeding off one another, to help us arrive at a research project. For some writers, a topic and purpose doesn't really gel until they begin thinking about an audience. One student, Cary, wanted to research "something about the health-care profession." But she struggled to name a focus or purpose until she considered audience. She imagined writing this research as a letter to the children she planned on having someday so that they could see that she was making professional decisions with them in mind, even as an 18-year-old, first-year student. That "something" about the health-care profession was really her need to understand the risks and benefits of choosing nursing as a career. She read (or reread, more specifically) her goals and intentions as a researcher, and her project fell into place from then on.

Once we identify our purposes as researchers, possible contexts for our research emerge, and we can often arrive at rich and productive research projects that we find worth our time—and that inspire us to assume more active roles as researchers. Furthermore, we find a reason to reconsider what we think research is about.

First, we can see through Cary's example that research is not just an academic task. We research, on some level, every time we integrate new understandings with old, every time we seek to learn something from others. Sometimes this integration is prompted by something we experience: our parents kept telling us about the dangers of driving too fast on icy roads, but it wasn't until we slid off into a ditch the morning we were late for school that we consider the truth in their warnings. So we accept that icy roads are dangerous, but that's all we know. We then enhance that knowledge when we relate what we learn in science class—traction is difficult on icy roads—to our parents' warnings and our experiences. In this sense, we've been researching—at the most basic and fundamental level—most of our lives as we have worked to make sense of people and the world around us by asking questions, reading, and watching TV.

Second, not only is the researcher active, but the research itself is also active. It's a part of what Bruce Ballenger (and others) call "an ongoing conversation" (Ballenger 1999). This analogy is familiar to those of us working at colleges and universities. Your professors are expected to publish papers so that they will remain current on what's being said, learned, and challenged in their fields. Oddly enough, though, I hadn't heard of this analogy until research became a likely part of my job. Nevertheless, thinking of research as an ongoing conversation seems applicable to research of all kinds. If the analogy is a good one, why aren't undergraduate students (as well as high school and middle school students) taught to view their work this way? Research teaches us what people have been saying about a subject, the different perspectives they bring to a subject, and, at times, what remains to be said. When we read our sources or conduct an interview, we are entering into a conversation about a subject with a history, a base of common knowledge, and a desire to address the questions and issues that motivate the discussion. Good researchers do not merely eavesdrop on that conversation; they contribute something to it.

The impact of context on creating a worthwhile research project doesn't end with tailoring topics and audiences or with thinking about research as an active and familiar process. Context is crucial in helping us clarify our purposes for writing and make decisions about sources. Consider the following scenarios:

A. In an English Composition course, you decide to research diabetes because you're concerned about your grandmother's declining health.
B. In a nursing course, your professor assigns you to research diabetes as a part of a case study on a diabetic patient.

Each of these situations will impact your purpose as a researcher and the kind of research you will conduct. For your English Composition class, you will probably be most interested in learning the symptoms of diabetes so that you can convince your grandmother to see the doctor. In the nursing class, you find that your research should focus on the treatments for diabetes, more specifically the side effects of those treatments because, as a future nurse, you are concerned with patient care.

Furthermore, these situations will help you decide what kinds of sources you should examine. In the English Composition class, you may have more freedom to draw from popular sources such as the article you find in *Healthy Woman* about the warning signs of diabetes for women in their fifties. However, this source will probably be unacceptable for your nursing class. The nursing instructor will think medical and nursing journals more appropriate. As we advance in our course work, our research is often expected to be more specialized.

Use the following questions to help you begin your research process and to help you determine the expectations of your research and your options as a writer:

1. What is my purpose for reading about this topic and sharing my research with a particular audience?
2. What does my audience and purpose suggest about what I need to learn and share through research?
3. What is the "common knowledge" associated with this topic? Is there a place for this common knowledge in my research? Why?
4. How specialized should my sources be in light of my purpose and audience (as well as the requirements of the assignment)? What are useful and appropriate sources?

These questions help us to read our context and determine the expectations for our research—for example, the sources we can draw from, the form and tone of our essay, the role of personal narrative in our essay—and name our goals as research writers. Our purpose will likely sharpen or modify as we continue our research, but imagine how much more productive—how much less overwhelming—our first trip to the library will be if we can run a search on "diabetes, women, symptoms" rather than just "diabetes."

THE SEARCH

Beginning the Search

We begin our research into a topic before we ever set foot in the library, visit the women's shelter, surf the Internet, interview the diabetic, or write to the Environmental Protection Agency for information. Our work starts when we begin searching our own minds for what we know about a subject and what remains to be known, given our purposes and audiences as researchers. We carry sources around with us: conversations with our parents about "flower power"; an MTV special on 1960s rock and roll bands; reruns of *The Wonder Years.* We've gathered information one way or another our entire lives. We're the place to begin searching, and this beginning place automatically encourages us to take on a more active role. Take some time to list the sources of your knowledge about the topic you are researching. While all of the sources you list may not be appropriate for your essay, list them anyway because they may trigger new ways of looking at your topic.

Collecting Sources

I almost titled this part of the discussion "Finding Sources," the term we commonly use. However, we can "find" four-leaf clovers, but I hope we don't associate (only) luck with conducting research. I can "find" my dog's stuffed elephant once I stumble over it, but I don't trust that I'll stumble on the right journal article when I go to the library. Yes, we might very well feel lucky or unlucky depending on the day, or might trip over the perfect book on the way to the copy machine. But good research asks us to leave less to chance.

I prefer to think of "collecting" sources. This term implies more control on the part of the writer, and seems more accurate. When we "collect" Nolan Ryan baseball cards, we aren't just satisfied with what we "find." We're more discriminating. We're not as interested in the common cards as we are with his rookie card. We're not looking for cards we already own. We're looking for the card that will add something to, or complete, our collection.

We should bring this same discriminating mindset to the research process. Not every article we find on boarding horses, for example, will suit our purposes as researchers when we're searching, specifically, for ways to maintain good nutrition for the horses we board. We can't leave the library with the first three articles we find. If we do, we usually face big problems when we start writing.

Evaluating Sources

Researchers need strategies for evaluating the sources they find so that they can collect the best sources for their project, those sources that will contribute something to their specific discussions on a topic and will be appropriate for context. These strategies involve another, more traditional form of reading. The following questions can help you identify suitable sources:

1. *Is the publication credible for your purposes?* Certain publications are known for a particularly liberal or conservative bias, for example. Some publications are written for a general audience (glossy magazines with pictures, by and large) and some for a specialized audience of knowledgeable peers (the seldom glossy, rarely illustrated journals with plain covers, containing articles with colons in the titles). You can make early decisions at the computer terminal or in the reference section by paying attention to the publication in which possible sources are located. Noting the type of publication is especially important when running an Internet search. If you are unfamiliar with the publication, scan the entire journal (even a couple of back issues) so that you can identify its bias and can begin thinking about how you will work with or against that bias in your own writing. If all else fails, ask around.
2. *Is the writer credible for your purpose?* If you are researching the need for stable family structures to an audience of single mothers, it can work against you to use Dan Quayle's definition of family, especially if you don't address

the controversy surrounding his definition. Likewise, Richard Simmons might not be the nutritional expert you want for a nursing class project, unless your purpose is to survey popular advice on nutrition.

3. *Is the discussion appropriate for, or applicable to, your project?* Scan the content of the source, primarily for the main point or purpose of the discussion. The article you find may be about Daisy Buchanan's character in *The Great Gatsby,* but if it concentrates on her as a representative of the upper class, it might not pertain much to your analysis of "pink clouds" as a window into her inner life.

Realize that while scanning might serve your purposes early on, you'll eventually need to read and reread sources, especially those you end up using.

Recording the Search

For any source that you are seriously considering, use the following suggestions to help you organize and save time during the rest of the research process:

1. Record all bibliographic information that you'll need. If you don't end up using the source, you haven't wasted much time. More importantly, if you decide to include the source at the last minute, you'll be able to without another trip to the library.
2. Make copies of the serious contenders.
3. Use a highlighter and annotations during initial and subsequent readings of a source in order to guide you when you return to it—but be selective when highlighting. If you highlight everything, you are probably not reading closely enough and may be in danger of plagiarizing your source.

   Annotation strategies:

   a. Star the main point of your source and restate it in the margin.
   b. Underline all subpoints or arguments made in support of the main point. (Distinguish subpoints and arguments from examples.)
   c. Record in the margins questions that you have about what's being said.
   d. Box key terms.
   e. Star conclusions, if reached.
   f. Write your questions/observations in the margins so that you can record your train of thought while reading the source.
4. If a source has "made the cut" after your evaluation process, write a summary paragraph for that source and a paragraph in which you explain what this source can offer your discussion. The more effort you put into the summary at this point, the more prepared you'll be to introduce your source in your essay later on.

   Suggestions for writing the summary:

   a. It is customary to refer to the writer and the title of the source in the first sentence.

b. Identify the main point of the article—not just the subject of the article, but also (and more importantly) the purpose of the article.
c. Record how the writer achieves the main point.
d. State conclusions, if reached.

Revising Purpose

An initial search can be full of frustrating and pleasant surprises. Be prepared for the frustrating ones (the perfect book that someone else checked out) and leave yourself open to the pleasant ones. Depending on the sources we find, it may be necessary to modify our research projects. Perhaps we set out to research the environmental problems associated with overflowing landfills, but research led us to some articles about what some communities are doing to address this problem and we wonder if our own college campus could implement some of these measures. Now we may be more interested in researching a proposal for a recycling plan to be submitted to our student government association. In short, the sources we "read" (whether they are magazine articles, interviews, documentaries, etc.) can prompt us to respond in ways we may not have anticipated. They can take our thinking in new directions, help us arrive at more focused discussions. As you read your sources, pay attention to how they are pushing you to reconsider what can be done with your topic.

MORE THAN QUOTING: READING FOR A PURPOSE

Our past experiences may have taught us that research is about quoting experts on a subject in order to support the assertions we want to make. We get the impression that we need a quote from Georgia Newman to support our claim that child-care costs are skyrocketing (even though that comes as little surprise to us as single parents). Consequently, we often see research as a matter of finding those sources that agree with us, then quoting them a "respectable" number of times, often determined by how much our writing "looks" like research.

There is a role for the expert source in research. Earlier in this piece, I made reference to Bruce Ballenger's *Beyond Note Cards* (1999). It is important, in my mind, to demonstrate a familiarity with Ballenger's work since he has published two books on the research essay. Expert sources lend credibility to our discussions. Furthermore, as we advance in course work, our teachers may expect us to be familiar with the key sources and scholars in that field.

We reduce the purpose of research if we see it only as a process of reporting and quoting sources. With this view, the research we conduct merely covers "old ground" or echoes the positions we held before we even started the research process. Ideally, research should be a discovering and deepening process, and as we enter college, teachers increasingly expect research to enhance thought, not just to restate original positions. We begin by reading more closely.

Introducing Sources

Typically, the first time we use a source, we should mention the author (by first and last name) and, if appropriate, the title (from that point on we can just refer to the source by the author's last name). If the source is especially comprehensive (a government study on television viewing habits or a book on education reform), if a source is particularly credible but known only to people in that field, or if a source plays a primary role in our research, we should introduce our readers to the general scope and perspective of that source. That is, we should include summary paragraphs or sentences about the source. For example: "In 'No Wonder Johnny Can't Read,' Debra Keevan examines the educational standards of high schools in seven large American cities and concludes that standards, especially in reading and writing, have dropped dramatically in the last decade." Then we can begin using specific parts of Keevan's discussion for our purposes.

If it is important to establish the credibility of a source (especially to an audience who may not be familiar with that source), we should do so as part of our introduction of that source. Some sources require us to do very little: we only have to mention Roger Ebert if we are researching trends in independent film making, and his credibility is understood. However, many very credible sources do not have such name recognition. We'd need to point out that Debra Keevan is a 35-year veteran teacher, recently appointed by the President to a Department of Education Task Force.

Beyond "S/He Says": Taking Our Cue from Verbs

One of the features that distinguishes experienced research writers from less experienced research writers is the way that they represent and integrate quoted or paraphrased passages. Inexperienced writers have a tendency to rely on "s/he says" when referring to the content of a source. This tendency is often viewed as an indication that we are not as familiar with our sources as we should be. But there might be other reasons. Our early educational experiences emphasize reporting and quoting sources, which make us practiced in the kind of neutral stand with our sources that "s/he says" implies. Furthermore, this emphasis on reporting and quoting, on reading with little or no judgment of the content, has prevented us from developing our authority as readers.

As we pay closer attention to what our sources are saying in particular, and accomplishing in general, it becomes necessary to find a language that will help us accurately refer to a source. Our sources are likely doing something far more specific than merely "saying." Writers claim, argue, and challenge. Just as we are trying to accomplish a purpose when we write, so are our sources. Perhaps, too, expanding the language we have to talk about sources will also prompt us to read more closely. Finally, the language we use will often direct us in determining how else we need to work with a source once we've quoted or paraphrased a passage. Below is a list of some of the most common verbs used when integrating quoted or paraphrased material. It is not a complete list by far. The point is to choose verbs that say something meaningful about what we find in our sources and/or how we are using sources to advance our discussion.

States, Maintains, Claims,

Asserts:	Your reader expects you to specifically and accurately represent what is being asserted, etc.
Explains:	Your reader expects you to provide the explanation offered.
Suggests/Implies:	Your reader expects you to explain how you see your source suggesting or implying a particular meaning.
Reasons:	Your reader expects you to detail that reasoning.
Complicates:	Your reader expects you to explain how your source complicates the discussion.
Questions:	Your reader expects you to explain what your source is questioning and the basis for that questioning.
Argues:	Your reader expects you to summarize the argument(s).

What other verbs can you think of and how would they direct your work?

Once we move beyond "s/he says," we position ourselves to do more with sources than report from them. We can begin to talk confidently with our sources because we are better aware of what they are "saying." We can take exception with a conclusion they reach more easily if we realize that they are reaching a conclusion. We can add to their discussions if we notice that the reasons they provide for something are incomplete, and so on. When we begin talking confidently with our sources, using them to accomplish our purposes as writers, then we distinguish ourselves from inexperienced research writers. (See also Hint Sheet 5.)

CONCLUSION

Largely because of the research essay, I ended up with a C+ in my second semester Freshman Composition course. I was an English major at the time, and some people are surprised that I remained one. But I did because I'd had many more writing experiences before that spring semester that were positive, enlightening, and invigorating. I knew, on some level, to separate my writing abilities from my performance on that assignment, and on another level, I knew that I hadn't done the job of a writer to begin with; I merely lived through an assignment. It remains an experience that influences my work as a teacher today.

So, here's what I believe. The power to transform a writing experience (even about the economic repercussions of the Alaskan pipeline) lies not just with our teachers, but also, and more importantly, with us as writers. And that power rests in our authority as readers—to read an assignment, a topic, a context, and our sources, actively, specifically, and with our goals informing our every step.

Come to think about it, I never understood the big deal about the Alaskan pipeline anyway—the debates, the controversy, the high expectations. Who was involved? How did native Alaskans think differently than this girl who grew up in Texas? Were some of these economic repercussions tied to (more interesting to me) environmental repercussions? Whose lives were affected? (People are always more interesting to me than corporations.) There's a beginning.

MELISSA GOLDTHWAITE (b. 1972)

This, Too, Is Research

CONSIDER THIS:

Melissa Goldthwaite teaches creative nonfiction, poetry, and composition at St. Joseph's University. When asked to comment on her own research processes and practices, she explained, "I research for many reasons: to learn, to add specificity and texture to my work, to understand other points of view, to find and question authority. Often, I research just so I don't embarrass myself. My most recent and consuming research interest is a qualitative and historical study of the place of the personal essay in composition studies."

Thinking of Goldthwaite's comments, consider the times you've researched to shore up your authority and to question authority. In her essay, Goldthwaite considers why individuals research. Even if you don't consider yourself inclined to research, try to make a list of your own before you read. Ask yourself what prompts researchers? Who researches more, those who write fiction and poetry or those who write essays and articles? Support your claims and compare them with the responses of your peers.

Research is a creative process. And just like other creative processes, research gets hampered when we close down its possibilities, narrow too much our definitions.

—Bill Roorbach

I am writing about when I was fourteen years old, the first time I flew on an airplane. Somewhere between Boston and Monterey, probably in Chicago, we had a layover. I remember standing in an airport bathroom, washing my hands, and looking into the mirror above the sink. The effect was dizzying. The walls, both in front of and behind me, were lined with mirrors, and when I looked into the one in front of me, I saw an eternity of reflections, my own flight-weary face framed in mirror inside of mirror as far as I could see. Today, as I write these sentences, I begin to doubt my own memory, so I test it: get out a handheld mirror, stand with my back to the mirror above my dresser, hold the small mirror in front of me, and look in. When the angle is right, it works—reflection inside reflection. This is research.

Think of all the ways you research in a given day: reading a map for directions, studying labels at a grocery store, or asking a friend which professor you should take next term. I line up boxes of cereal on the table while I'm eating breakfast to compare nutritional values, read online reviews before purchasing books, watch cooking shows on PBS to learn new recipes and techniques. Now consider all the kinds of research you do when you're writing—whether you're writing a critical paper or a creative piece. Perhaps you start in the library or with an Internet search to survey information on your topic, but it's not likely that you stop the process of research there. Writers, especially creative writers, do more than consult books and journals for quotations. We ourselves (our memories and experiences) and the world around us are sources, and it's likely that most anything we write will involve some form of research: research for inspiration, for details, for enriching memories, for learning.

RESEARCH FOR INSPIRATION

Researching the familiar is often inspiring. The world—newspaper headlines, overheard conversations, and even the local phone book—is a writer's muse, her best inspiration. Poet David Citino (2000) encourages writers to see intersections between themselves and what they read; he writes, "Writing poems from the news keeps poets in the world, where we belong. Everything is a text, we learn these days in theory classes. Of course, our reading—the way we let the world in—can include, in addition to newspapers and magazines, tabloid rags and *Scientific American,* catechisms and physics texts, billboards and gravestones."

No source is too trivial or beyond the writer's reach. Look, for instance, at newspaper headlines. Citino lists some: "Amish Busted for Buying Cocaine from Biker Gang"; "Man Charged After Corpse Is Left in Van at Strip Joint"; "Parish Priest in Italy Struck Dead by Easter Bell." And I keep a file of my own. Here's one of my personal favorites: "Wine Tasting for Homeless." When I read this headline in the *Columbus Dispatch* just before Christmas, I mistakenly thought the wine tasting was actually *for* the homeless and imagined lines of people in tattered winter coats, sipping wine from crystal glasses. The true story wasn't any less ironic: dinner (in addition to cheese and crudités) and jazz music followed by an auction of a fur coat, a diamond ring, a lease on a car from Byers Imports, among other high-ticket items—all in the name of helping the homeless. At times these newspaper gems are *found poems* complete with perfect details; many times, though, the headlines spark thoughts and can be transformed by imagination and experience into something far removed from the initial "source."

Research for creative writers—indeed, for any writer who cares about the richness and texture of her work—involves a great deal of freedom and imagination; often we're not constrained by context. A phrase from an overheard conversation on the bus may become a line in a poem; the outfit a woman in the grocery store is wearing may become inspiration for the description of a character in a novel; one line from an Emily Dickinson poem may spark the idea for an entire essay. Our sources are everywhere; we only need to be open to them. Fiction writer Juliet Williams, for instance, turns to the phone book for help with creating characters:

> Many times I can't think of jobs that might fit well with the idea of the character I have in mind, so I look through the index in the yellow pages to find something that seems to fit. If I don't know much about a particular occupation, the advertisements themselves help give me an idea of the basics of that work, and its language. Also, if I'm having trouble coming up with a name that fits my character, I use the regular phone book. Names go a long way to convey character to a reader. Often I'll have only an idea that I'd like my character's last name to start with an H, say, but I can't come up with something that doesn't sound too snooty or too bland. So I open the phone book to the H's and start browsing. Works every time.

Where else could you find such a choice of professions—from chimney sweep to soil tester—or names—Denny Dickensheets and Aladar Zipser? Like the phone book, many other items around the house can become sources too: cookbooks, music collections, old letters, even garbage. I once read a list poem about what a soon-to-be-married woman was throwing away. This makes me want to ask you: What's in your garbage? (Or medicine cabinet or pantry or closet?) What do those items say about you as a person? If a stranger were to find your credit card bill, what would she know about you or be able to interpret? The details of your life—and the lives of those around you—are rich sources; attention to those sources is an invaluable form of research.

RESEARCH FOR DETAILS

Several years ago, I was writing a poem about trillium, Dutchman's-breeches, and the fragility of relationships. As I was writing, a tree outside my office window captured my attention, found its way into the poem. I searched my *Peterson First Guide to Trees* to find the name. All I knew was that its leaves were heart-shaped, that the flowers were purplish pink, that it drew me in. *Redbud.* This detail, which I discovered through research and attention to my surroundings, has it own significance in the poem, but the field guide also made its way in as a point of contrast:

> [T]he redbud is in bloom, its pink
> flowers clusters bright before dull, heart
> leaves bud. We've not been talking.
> Flowers, I know, are easier to predict,
>
> And a field guide will tell
> what a lover can't: when flowers pass
> and fruits appear, when the season ends
> and it's time to give up or in.

When my students hand in poems or essays about trees or birds, I pen in the margins, What kind? Can you be more specific here? I want to picture a quaking aspen or Lombardy poplar. I want to hear the song of a yellow warbler or eastern meadowlark as I read. What I'm really asking them to do is research, to find out, to let the details change them and their writing. Sometimes an apparently minor point—a name, date, color—can change the focus and impact of the piece. For one writer I know, finding out where a word came from helped reinforce the effect of her poem. Sandee McGlaun writes about a time when she researched the etymology of a word:

> I actually don't know what made me decide to look up the name of the flower—impatiens—that the woman in the poem was planting on a loved one's grave, but I did. Amazingly I found that it came from a Latin term meaning "not enduring" or "unable to endure," and so I incorporated the definition directly into the last line of the poem:
>
> no one told this grief:
>
> shovel lifting red clay, the itch
> of sweat, and a mound
> of lace-white *impatiens,*
> Latin, unable to endure.

Since language is the primary focus for writers, researching words (especially with the *Oxford English Dictionary,* which is now available on CD-ROM) can be illuminating for both writer and reader, making symbols more powerful and suggestive.

And while books (field guides, dictionaries, and textbooks) can be great assets to a writer, there are also other resources available for finding the perfect detail. If you're looking for the right color, for instance, head to the local home-improvement store and gather a collection of paint swatches or (to learn the difference between blue and cerulean) buy a Crayola 96 Big Box of crayons. Start searching online catalogs, not to buy products, but to get ideas for what tools a character might have in her garage or what books she might have on her shelf. Interview experts to learn what you don't already know. While doing research for a short story, McGlaun called a funeral home and spoke to a funeral director:

> I asked him what must have seemed, to him, grotesque and bizarre questions: How large would a person have to be to not fit into a regularly sized casket? How large to be too large to cremate? I of course prefaced the questions with the explanation that I was writing a short story, and, as it turned out, the man who took the call was thrilled to help me out. He had such a good sense of humor about it, in fact, that I even ended up using bits and pieces of our conversation as dialogue in the story.

Observations, interviews, and other forms of collecting data (even if that data is paint swatches or crayons) are all forms of research from which creative writers, all writers, can benefit. In addition, a wealth of information can be found in public records: court records, driving records, birth and death records, probate records, police records, property records, and so on. Many of these records are available online (see, for instance, <http://www.ancestry.com>) and contain the kinds of details that can be especially useful if you're writing about a particular person or place. Although there are times when details come to us unbidden, there are plenty of other times when we need to search them out, and research—broadly conceived—is one of the best ways of doing so. Seeking details out often calls forth memories, bids the unbidden, leaving you with a wealth of information—some you'll use, some you'll set aside. Remember to give yourself time to sort through and process all you gather.

RESEARCH FOR ENRICHING (AND SUPPLEMENTING) MEMORIES

Often, creative writing grows out of the personal, and experience and memory are our primary sources. Yet we can enrich and supplement those sources in a variety of ways. Search the attic or junk drawers of your house (or your parents' house) to find old toys you once played with, your old lunch box, letters received a dozen years ago. Interview family members, read old journals, look through photo albums, find school papers and report cards, travel to your elementary school, drive past the house your mom grew up in: Discover the archives of your life.

Many times, those who base their writing on personal experience are accused of self-indulgence or "navel-gazing," but the truth is that writing personally—and doing it well—often requires looking outside of oneself for the material to create a self in and through language. In "Afterword: Writing 'The Greece Piece,'" a reflection on the process of writing her memoir *That Shining Place,* Simone Poirier-Bures (1999) discusses her use of memory and old letters (ones she had sent and received) as sources; she writes about the personas evident in the letters she sent and the self created by writing: "I was making a manuscript, but I was also making a self." The material we use to create and represent selves in writing need not come exclusively from memory. There are multiple sources that inform even the most personal writing, and sometimes we need those sources to make sense of the experience for ourselves and to interpret it for others.

The research that informs our writing is often a means of reconstructing our lives, helping us see our experiences within a broader context. And it's often in prologues, introductions, afterwords, and acknowledgment pages that we see a glimpse of the many kinds of research creative writers do. In *Refuge: An Unnatural History of Family and Place,* Terry Tempest Williams (1991) dedicates several pages of her acknowledgments to detailing the books, lecturers, friends, scientists, anthropologists, teachers, and others who informed her memoir. And in her prologue, she reflects beautifully on the ways physical and emotional landscapes are connected, reminding her reader of the ways her knowledge and experience of the natural world is vital to the personal story she's telling:

> I sit on the floor of my study with journals all around me. I open them and feathers fall from their pages, sand cracks their spines, and sprigs of sage pressed between passages of pain heighten my sense of smell—and I remember the country I come from and how it informs my life.

Williams comes from Utah and works as a naturalist at the Utah Museum of Natural History. The titles of each chapter of *Refuge* are the names of birds, and she charts the level of the Great Salt Lake even as she charts the events of her own life. In her memoir, Williams braids together stories of her mother's death from cancer, stories of the environment, stories of love and loss and healing.

What are the sources that inform your life and the events most memorable to you? I've studied old journals and phone bills to reconstruct the details of relationships, called family members to get names and anecdotes, and once even asked a friend to climb the mountain I was writing about (756 miles away) to make sure I'd gotten the names of the trees along a certain trail right. A student in the creative nonfiction class I'm teaching, Theresa Hammond, points to the importance of valuing the sources particular to your own life—those resources that are out of the ordinary. She spent the summer of 1998 in Jordan and Israel and researched the Israeli occupation, drawing from foreign newspapers and books in other languages. What unique collections or specialized knowledge do you have? How might you draw from those sources?

Maureen Stanton, writing a memoir that deals with a boyfriend's death from cancer, demonstrates the important role of research in her own work:

> I obtained Steve's medical records and then had to interpret them with a medical dictionary, and also went to the med school library to get various articles so that I understood the physiology of the experience, and could then translate that into lay language and hopefully, lyrical language. I'm also researching various forms of grieving (Tibetan, Bali, etc.), mythology (Native American mythology of the Sleeping Bear Dunes where I hiked many times, and others), have had to research holistic and alternative treatments for cancer, both legitimate and not, and fact check incidents from that time period (i.e., *Detroit Free Press* headlines, meteorological records for a long spell of sunless days I remembered).

Through the work of interpreting and researching, Stanton makes her own experience more accessible to others. She sets her individual story within a social and historical context, giving it a fullness by interpreting the sources around her through the lens of her personal experience. The connections she's able to make ground the memoir, make it more powerful.

While it may seem obvious that writers of creative nonfiction would use research to enrich and supplement memories, other writers do the same, adding specificity and nuance to their work. Poet Aimee Nezhukamatathil writes about her parents' homelands (India and Philippines), and since she's only visited, never lived in either of those places, her research expands her knowledge, even as it helps her present her own experiences more vividly to others; she writes:

> I search the Web, collect cookbooks, find zoology and biology books, and buy all kinds of field guides . . . to cull these specifics. If I can't remember what my grandmother cooked for me in her old copper pot (but I knew it had cardamom and a white flower's leaves) while I was sick with a cough, I'll look up home medicines, botanical guides, even cookbooks of southern India.

Recalling a memory of a lizard climbing the wall of her aunt's house in the Philippines, Nezhukamatathil writes, "I assume the reader has never had that experience, never seen that particular sheen of the lizard's blue (yes, blazing blue!) eyes and its pale tail the color of bread." From a reptile book of Asia, she's able to "gather what exactly that lizard was looking for to eat, where they live, what they do in the daytime. All those details seem too terribly important to leave out." As wonderful and full as many experiences and memories are, they can almost always be enhanced by searching for further details, and the discovery of those details has a dual effect—it makes the writing more powerful to others, and the writer and reader learn something in the process.

RESEARCH FOR LEARNING

These categories, these reasons for and strategies relating to research, certainly overlap and inform one another. What they have in common relates to our desire to learn, to see the world and ourselves in new and interesting ways—and to present that learning to others through whatever form we choose. Often the forms we use as creative writers—poems, stories, and essays—make research invisible, partly because such forms don't require traditional citations. However, many of the specifics and details that constitute creative writing are only available through research—through informal interviews, consulting books or newspapers, being aware of one's surroundings, reading personal journals, or searching one's memory for temporarily forgotten details.

Research can be vital to a writer's work at any stage of the writing process—providing inspiration and material for invention, even as it helps you revise your thinking about a particular topic or experience. Maureen Stanton, writing about her experience of working at a nuclear plant, found information on earthquakes and explosion-detecting devices, nuclear power plants (by accessing the USGS Web site), and how paint colors are named (by calling the manufacturer); she even researched and obtained a copy of the psychological test that was given to potential employees. "Through research," she writes, "I know more about the plant now than when I worked there." As this example demonstrates, research can add to—and sometimes change—what we already know. It can also help us take a closer look at what most people ignore.

According to creative nonfiction writer Kristina Emick, "If art is the act of paying attention, researching is one method of such tuning in, noticing, and exploring." And she accomplishes this tuning in by giving herself a focused topic, one she can explore in considerable detail, allowing the research to drive the essay. Research lends energy to her writing because she's always learning something new. Emick explains:

> In "Of Hangnails," I thought I'd give myself an assignment inspired by Montaigne and write a short piece on what seemed at first a fairly insignificant part of the body (Montaigne wrote *Of Thumbs,* so I was going a step further in triviality). I researched the OED to find out how the word *hangnail* developed, how

> it gets used in idioms, and how its meaning changed over time. I searched beauty books for information on what causes hangnails and how to take care of them. I researched newspapers to find out if hangnails had shown up in recent news (they had, and both instances ended up in the essay).

Emick includes the anecdotes she culled from the news: computer users in Los Angeles blaming hangnails on El Nino and a second grader in Colorado who struggled through a penmanship contest with a hangnail. Emick even researched herself, closely observing her own painful and stubborn hangnail. In doing so she realized the role the hangnail plays in her life, and she made the seemingly insignificant interesting to herself and her readers. Research became a kind of magnifying glass for Emick, who writes, "For just a moment, and not once since, the hangnail was the center of my world."

Go ahead: immerse yourself in research, allow your chosen topic to become, for a time, the center of your world. If you're writing about oranges, peel one, taste it, examine it, let the scent of it fill the room. If you remember running barefoot as a child, try it as an adult. Try it after a rainstorm. Frequent antique stores and yard sales. Borrow a fondue set. Read everything you can. You may not use all the information you gather, but the details you discover and the connections you make will surely expand your perspective, influence your thinking, and give you much to draw from.

RESEARCH FOR WRITING

Start writing things down. Carry a small notebook every place you go. Keep a commonplace book for quotations and observations. Start a file for your research. I have an old shoebox full of newspaper clippings, scraps of paper and restaurant napkins with ideas written on them, and countless ticket stubs from concerts, movies, the ballet. When I can't think of something to write, I dig through the shoebox for inspiration. It's full of details: I know from one ticket stub that I saw Savion Glover dance on Sunday, November 16, 1997. Seeing the ticket brings forth memories (how we sat in the second row, how my watch broke that night) and makes me want to look for the program from that evening's show. If I decide to write about that night, I'll look for Web sites, try to learn more about Glover and his dancing. If someone walks into my study, sees me on the floor, shoebox by my side, and asks what I'm doing, you know what I'll say: "Research."

"This, too, is research," I've said to myself throughout the process of writing this essay. My own process of research mirrors the advice I've given here, and all of the details and examples come from practicing the very strategies I encourage others to recognize. That is, for inspiration, I asked other writers for examples of the ways they do research. For details, I consulted a map to remind me how many miles it is from Columbus, Ohio, to Jaffrey, New Hampshire; I looked through my own file of newspaper clippings, checked out the phone book and field guides for particular names. I got out a box of crayons and went to the Crayola Web site <http://www.crayola.com/>. To supplement my memory, I looked through my own poems and essays for examples, stood in front of a mirror to test what I thought I knew. And throughout the process, I've learned things I didn't know before. The examples used to illustrate these claims about research came from books, newspapers, experience, e-mails—from the many sources around me.

There are multiple sources surrounding you too. Take them in, allow them to circulate through you, transform those sources in your own writing—even as they transform you. In "I Stand Here Writing," Nancy Sommers (1993) explains her wish for her own students, one I share:

> If I could teach my students one lesson about writing it would be to see themselves as sources, as places from which ideas originate, to see themselves as Emerson's transparent eyeball, all they have read and experienced—the dictionaries of their lives—circulating through them.

Creative writing is not a solitary activity of the mind; rather, it is informed by the world around us, by the experiences we hold in our memory, by the connections we make, by the details and small treasures we find through research.

CATHERINE WALD (b. 1954)

Research and the Fiction Writer: Perils, Pleasures, and Pitfalls

CONSIDER THIS:

Catherine Wald is a novelist, essayist, journalist, and translator. She has published in *Woman's Day, Readers' Digest,* and the *New York Times,* among other newspapers and magazines. She also runs a popular website called Rejection.com, "The Writer's and Artist's On-line Source for Misery, Commiseration, and Inspiration." She spoke to AbsoluteWrite.com about her far-flung research process for her novel *Women in Flames:* "During the five years I spent writing this book" she writes, "I was constantly conducting research. Of course I read incessantly: everything by any Indian writer that I could get my hands on, whether contemporary or going back to the time period I was writing about. . . . I also watched a lot of films, especially those of Satyajit Ray, the Bengali film genius who was a student at Tagore's school, and of Merchant/Ivory, who are both great admirers of both Ray and Tagore. . . . I also spoke to many people, listened to music and ate lots of Indian food. Many, many people were extremely kind and helpful with my research." Are you surprised at all to find watching films, listening to music, and eating food listed as research? Does Wald's article on writers researching offer any further surprises or contradictions for your image of *researcher*? Is Wald's article in your mind a research essay?

Research: It can be tedious, time-consuming, tantalizing, and even traumatizing. Sometimes it leads the writer down unexpected pathways, revealing new directions for characters or plot. Sometimes it becomes so engrossing that it turns into a dangerous distraction from the fiction writer's real work: writing that novel.

When I began my second novel, I thought I had a good handle on the research process. After all, I'd already completed a 500-page narrative set in India in 1904, having followed trails of information that led to everywhere from New York's Columbia University Law Library's Bengali Codes of the 1800s, to a translator living in California who specialized in the poetry of Rabindranath Tagore, to an expert on Ayurvedic medicine whom I found on the Internet. Surely when it came time to conduct research about life in Paris in 1911, the skills I'd already developed would help me do the same kind of work faster and more efficiently.

As if! In making that assumption, I'd conveniently forgotten that research is more than just a skill; it's a calling and an obsession that often takes on a life of its own, much like the writing process itself. As such, it's bound to be slow and unpredictable. And yet, I couldn't help wondering if more experienced writers could offer me some practical tips. How do they rein themselves in when they feel they're getting too carried away? Do they have any shortcuts? To find out, I spoke with three prominent novelists whose works focus on different time periods and cultures, as well as a biographer who teaches research techniques to fiction writers.

If anyone could answer my questions, I figured, it would be Arthur Golden, whose painstaking research for *Memoirs of a Geisha* (Knopf, 1997) led to a hugely successful novel in which the author crossed gender, culture, and time boundaries to create a realistic picture of life in a closed Japanese subculture. Because the universe of the geisha is shut off, even to Japanese, and because it has no written tradition, Golden found that even after years of living in Japan, reading, and conducting interviews, he hadn't gotten his main character quite right. By the time he was finally able to interview a geisha from the era and locale of his story line, he'd already written an 800-page draft, which ended up in the wastebasket.

So part of research, it seems, is knowing when to give up and start over. But wasn't it hard to throw all that work out?

"You wouldn't believe how easy it was for me," Golden said. "Because I very much wanted to present a portrait of this world that was accurate, intriguing, and intimate. I didn't realize when I started how much work it would be to figure out what that world was really like. I had done what research I could with books and interviews. The things I didn't know, I was making up, and it turns out they were all wrong. So when I finally interviewed this geisha and found out the reality, I felt like I was sitting on top of the world."

Although the novel he is now working on is not set in Japan, Golden does notice a similar dynamic interplay between his research and writing processes. "You are drawn to a subject because it interests you. Then as you begin to learn about things through research, you begin to imagine moments and aspects of your character, and you find your imagination sparked."

In the beginning, he finds it impossible to move forward without doing research, because "you're looking for the character and learning who might be possible and who might not be possible in that world. In the world of the geisha, certain personalities or views of the world just don't exist." Then, as the writer begins to understand the time period and culture, he said, "You reach a point when you recognize a kind of internal logic to the world, and you know you can improvise and still have a reasonable chance of getting it right. Before you get there, you can't do too much."

Later, Golden feels compelled to write rather than study. "I get excited, and I don't want to do research, I want to get working." Then, as specific scenes and themes are developed, the need for research reemerges. For example, at one point while writing *Memoirs,* he found he needed to know more about the precise details of kimono materials and designs. That was when he realized that "kimonos were terrifically important in that world. A fourteen-year-old geisha going out for her debut is going to be wearing some of the most expensive clothes she'll ever wear. She has no earning power, yet she can't become a geisha unless she has access to those kimonos. That's a formula for indentured servitude. So given how important they are in this world, I realized my character would really notice them."

For Golden, one of the rewards of research is that "reality is always so much more interesting than what I would try to imagine." In one *Memoirs* scene, he needed to get his main character, Sayuri, onto a roof in order for her to notice a possible escape route. Originally, he had her go up to wash the roof tiles. But a Japanese friend nixed the idea, saying that people don't wash roofs, but they might go up to pull weeds. "That's so much more interesting," he said. "And that's the kind of thing research will always yield."

He added that no matter how meticulous your research, you're bound to get some things wrong. "Unless you have actually lived in that world, there are going to be things you screw up." Golden avoided some of these problems with *Memoirs* by asking people knowledgeable in Japanese culture to review his manuscript. In the end, though, creating characters consistent with their time and culture was far more important to him than minor details. So when a reader criticized Sayuri's choice of subway routes, Golden was relieved rather than perturbed. "If that's all you get wrong, it's okay. Obviously I would have rather had it right, but that sort of thing is not going to hamper the novel in any way."

I asked Golden if his experience with *Memoirs* has made the research process for his second novel any easier. "I think that I know a lot more about what I'm doing now than I did ten years ago, in every respect—about research, about writing, and about creating a character," he said. "But of course there's no substitute for the work you have to do, which involves heading down the wrong road lots of times."

Can a really experienced researcher avoid those wrong roads? I hoped Patricia O'Toole would know. An award-winning journalist and author of *The Five of Hearts* (Clarkson N. Potter, 1990), a biography of Henry Adams and his friends that was short-listed for the Pulitzer Prize, and *Money and Morals in America: A History* (Clarkson N. Potter, 1998), O'Toole is currently working on a book about Theodore Roosevelt's post–White House days. She also teaches research techniques to fiction and nonfiction writers in Columbia University's MFA program

For O'Toole, one of the keys to recapturing a lost time period is to get as much information as possible about the sensory experience of everyday life. "I want to know what things looked like, what they smelled like, what colors they were, what they felt like, what they sounded like," she said. For that reason she is always delighted when she turns up voice recordings or museum exhibits that give a sense of the colors and textures of clothing, furniture, and other daily items. She's also studied Roosevelt's dinner menus. "I've always wanted to taste terrapin, because they're always having that."

O'Toole urges fiction writers to take advantage of the plethora of multimedia sources that are available online. "Since we're writing books, we always think of printed sources, but it's wonderful to be able to look at visual things," she said. As part of her own research, O'Toole recently visited the "American Memories" section of the Library of Congress Web site (www.americaslibrary.gov), where she found "all these incredible film clips of Theodore Roosevelt that I can watch while sitting at my laptop. I even found a video of William Howard Taft's visit to the Panama Canal in 1910."

O'Toole recommends that writers venture beyond standard online services and search engines to proprietary databases that are available through big research institutions and libraries. "Lots of universities are putting together electronic bibliographies, and sometimes they post the full text of their sources. It's just amazing what I've accumulated in the way of World War I stuff from the Web." For example, to get a sense of the wartime experiences of Roosevelt's son, Quentin, she visited a military database called Air University Library, where she found memoirs by World War I aviators posted in their entirety.

Many universities, specialized research libraries, and municipal libraries have card catalogues online. O'Toole recommended the RLIN Archives and Manuscript Files in the Library of Congress, which is a guide to archives, manuscripts, and oral history collections, and a database called Dissertation Abstracts, which lists abstracts of doctoral dissertations. "The most important thing to know is that databases exist for practically everything under the sun," she said. (For a sampling of what's out there, go to Columbia University's Libraries page—www.columbia.edu/cu/libraries—and then click on Electronic Reference Tools & Indexes. Every listing with a globe icon is available to the public.)

O'Toole is also a fan of good old-fashioned newspaper clips, which are relatively easy to locate, thanks to new databases and electronic archives. For a scene in which Roosevelt sets off for Africa by ship, O'Toole gleaned details—"how many people turned out to say good-bye, what his cabin looked like, what went on at the piers"—that would have been impossible to find in secondary sources.

Still, all the articles and databases in the world can't prevent you from getting sidetracked in your research. When that happens to O'Toole, she doesn't try to fight it. "I'm so curious about everything under the sun, and I like to think that I get more payoff from meandering than I would get from just plunging ahead and not peeking my head down that side corridor. Always with research, when you get it all done, you think, 'Geez, I read one hundred things, and there were probably only ten that really helped.' But the only way you knew how helpful those ten things were was because you did read the other ninety."

"So that's the price you have to pay?"

"Or the joy," she replied, "depending on how you think about it. It turns out to be a price because everyone is always working with limited time and limited money. But if high speed is what you're looking for, I think you ought to be doing something else. Wasting time is an occupational hazard. It's part of what life as a writer is all about."

Wasting time on research is not a major concern for Anne Perry, whose fictional oeuvre—some 30 mystery novels—is deeply rooted in Victorian England. Perry, whose most recent book is *Half Moon Street* (Ballantine Books, 2000), is such a regular habitué of that culture that her research process is relatively efficient. She will typically begin a first draft of a new novel with very little preliminary digging. "Obviously I need to conduct research to make sure key elements of the plot are viable for the time period. But after that, I write from what I know to make sure I've got the story and the drama right." It's only after completing the first draft, she says, that "I tend to go through and put in what I don't know."

Perry, who lives in Scotland, does not spend much time in libraries or museums. For one thing, that "would take me a great deal of time." For another, she finds remnants of that time period woven into the architecture of contemporary British life. "There's Victoriana all around," she said. When she does need more detail about daily domestic life, she pores through old hardware or domestic goods catalogues. She also likes to read back issues of the *London Illustrated News*, not for the articles so much as for the advertisements, whose descriptive terminology and illustrations she finds very helpful. "They show how things were used, how much something cost compared with something else, and whose budget it would be within, which is very important." And she makes good use of an inexpensive British book series called Shire Books, which describes in detail various Victorian-era professions—everything from ironmongers to chimney sweeps.

Another way Perry absorbs the cultural climate of the middle to late 1800s is by studying the arts. Occasionally she listens to popular ballads, but she focuses on poetry and painting. "I find poetry of the time to be very interesting, because so much of it is symbolic. It's not really about what people were thinking, but about what they dared and dared not say." As for visual art, "There are quite a few paintings that have whole stories in them, often showing women in disgrace, with quite a bit of melodrama. It's very different from today."

When it comes to differences in values, mores, and lifestyles, Perry said, she treads a fine line between portraying an earlier culture's attitudes and judging them by today's standards. "There are some things that we would find extraordinary, but that the main characters would not, and therefore we shouldn't write it as if it were extraordinary—which is really easy to do."

Cleanliness, she said, is a good example. "We would probably find the body odor and so forth of Victorian people very offensive. But the people at the time would have found it completely natural. If you were to describe it accurately—let's say when the heroine meets the hero for the first time—the reader would think, 'Ew!' The reader wouldn't be able to empathize with their feelings for each other, which must be rooted in their time, not ours. If you put the body odor in as part of an accurate description, you've got a literal truth, but an artistic untruth." The same thing applies to the position of women in society. "You have to make sure you don't have your characters incensed or outraged about something that really was perfectly acceptable at the time."

For Perry, the greatest pitfall regarding research is not how to conduct it, but how to weave it naturally into the writing. She struggles to resist the temptation of "getting so sidetracked with the fascination of research that you put in things that clog up the story. Because you think, 'I've researched this, I've got to get it in somewhere.' It may be really fascinating to you, and there may be the odd reader who is interested, but it has to matter to the characters in the story, or be something that would pass through their thoughts. If it isn't, or if it slows the story down, it has to go."

Early in his career, Frederick Busch gave in to the temptation to cram too much research into a novel. He told me that in his 1979 novel *Rounds* (Farrar, Straus & Giroux), he was so proud of what he'd learned about pediatric medicine that he ended up with "too much research littering my pages." Nearly 20 fictional works later, he no longer makes that mistake. "Now I remind myself that my book is about characters and not about the research. My job is to serve and tantalize the reader, not to educate the reader."

Busch relishes research, even though he knows from the outset that only a small portion of what he learns will actually appear on the printed page. For the historical novel *The Night Inspector* (Harmony Books, 1999), which features a character based on Herman Melville, Busch read everything from 1850s government manuals on customs inspections to antique books on cargo and the Port of New York. He also spent hours poring over maps of the Hudson River. "I got so much information that was useless, but I had it as ballast. It was the seven-eighths of the iceberg that stays underwater. This gave my characters the ability to talk with some sense of authority and experience, even though they did not specifically address every single detail."

For more general background on New York life in the late 1800s, Busch read newspapers, focusing, as Perry does, on advertisements. "Ads," he said, "give a sense of what mattered to people and how much money was worth, which is one of the hardest things to learn. And when you read ads, you're reading the subconscious of a culture, the junk and detritus and the commercial instincts, which is very useful."

Another tool for Busch is photographs. "I lived with photos of New York City at the end of the century. Every day before work I would put a new photo on my desk. I'd lean my head on my hands and fall into the picture, and try to imagine from visual elements what might have been available to the other senses."

To develop his Melville character, Busch also visited the master's farm in Pittsfield, Massachusetts, sat at the desk where Melville wrote *Moby Dick,* and strolled through the Hancock Shaker Village, which Melville enjoyed touring. In his forays, Busch had his eye out for an object that he had come to see as a metaphor for Melville's struggles as an artist: the tin badge the author wore later in his life when he was forced to earn his living as a customs inspector. When Busch finally located that badge in the Pittsfield public library, the librarian refused to take it out of its case for him. "I guess I looked a little lust-crazed," he recalled ruefully. Still, seeing was believing. "It confirmed my sense that the badge owned Melville, not that he owned the badge, that he had a sense of being captured by it."

When possible, Busch uses interviews to fill in his knowledge of a time and culture. For a novel-in-progress set during World War II, he plans to speak with a prisoner of war interned in England, as well as with a woman who ran a boardinghouse for the officers in charge of the prison. "I will probably use none of that information directly, but I will have it as part of the psychological weather in which my characters lived," he said. Busch agreed that no matter how rewarding it is, all research must come to an end. If it goes on too long, it can be "a way to stall, to keep you from having to write the damn book. It's a wonderful blanket to pull over your head. The trick is to know when to pull it down again."

"But how *do* you know?"

One way, he said, is "when you suspect you're having too much fun. That's a good sign that you're hiding behind the research, and not doing what you're supposed to be doing at that moment."

But there was another answer, too. Years ago, Busch said, he invited the English novelist Sir Angus Wilson (1913–1991) to teach at the Iowa Writers' Workshop. One afternoon the eminent older writer was stretched out on a lawn chair, and Busch asked, "Sir Angus, how do you know when you've done enough research?"

I could hear Busch's smile through the phone lines as he relayed Wilson's response. "He patted his stomach and said, 'When I feel full, my dear boy.'"

STUART GREENE

Argument as Conversation: The Role of Inquiry in Writing a Researched Argument

CONSIDER THIS:

Stuart Greene is the O'Malley Director of the University Writing Program, associate professor of English at the University of Notre Dame, and an avid runner, so he devotes a fair amount of time finding out about the causes of his aches and pains, the best ways to remain healthy, and what new gear he can purchase. He teaches courses on composition theory, literacy, rhetoric, and writing. He has coedited *Teaching Academic Literacy* and is working on a four-year study of writing across the disciplines and an argument textbook. I've stated that research is part of every writer's life and Greene, in this essay, suggests that argument is equally woven into the fabric of every life. It's not surprising then to see him discussing the researched argument. What are the attributes of this sort of writing, and where have you encountered writing like this in your own academic life?

Argument is very much a part of what we do every day: We confront a public issue, something that is open to dispute, and we take a stand and support what we think and feel with what we believe are good reasons. Seen in this way, argument is very much like a conversation. By this, I mean that making an argument entails providing good reasons to support your viewpoint, as well as counterarguments, and recognizing how and why readers might object to your ideas. The metaphor of conversation emphasizes the social nature of writing. Thus inquiry, research, and writing arguments are intimately related. If, for example, you are to understand the different ways others have approached your subject, then you will need to do your "homework." This is what Doug Brent (1996) means when he says that research consists of "the looking-up of facts in the context of other worldviews, other ways of seeing."

In learning to argue within an academic setting, such as the one you probably find yourself in now, it is useful to think about writing as a form of inquiry in which you convey your understanding of the claims people make, the questions they raise, and the conflicts they address. As a form of inquiry, then, writing begins with problems, conflicts, and questions that you identify as important. The questions that your teacher raises and that you raise should be questions that are open to dispute and for which there are not prepackaged answers. Readers within an academic setting expect that you will advance a scholarly conversation and not reproduce others' ideas. Therefore, it is important to find out who else has confronted these problems, conflicts, and questions in order to take a stand within some ongoing scholarly conversation. You will want to read with an eye toward the claims writers make, claims that they are making with respect to you, in the sense that writers want you to think and feel in a certain way. You will want to read others' work critically, seeing if the reasons writers use to support their arguments are what you would consider good reasons. And finally, you will want to consider the possible counterarguments to the claims writers make and the views that call your own ideas into question.

Like the verbal conversations you have with others, effective arguments never take place in a vacuum; they take into account previous conversations that have taken place about the subject under discussion. Seeing research as a means for advancing a conversation makes the research process more *real*, especially if you recognize that you will need to support your claims with evidence in order to persuade readers to agree with you. The concept and practice of research arises out of the specific social context of your readers' questions and skepticism.

Reading necessarily plays a prominent role in the many forms of writing that you do, but not simply as a process of gathering information. This is true whether you write personal essays, editorials, or original research based on library research. Instead, as James Crosswhite suggests in his book *The Rhetoric of Reason*, reading "means making judgments about which of the many voices one encounters can be brought together into productive conversation."

When we sit down to write an argument intended to persuade someone to do or to believe something, we are never really the first to broach the topic about which we are writing. Thus, learning how to write a researched argument is a process of learning how to enter conversations that are already going on in written form. This idea of writing as dialogue—not only between author and reader but between the text and everything that has been said or written beforehand—is important. Writing is a process of balancing our goals with the history of similar kinds of communication, particularly others' arguments that have been made on the same subject. The conversations that have already been going on about a topic are the topic's historical context.

Perhaps the most eloquent statement of writing as conversation comes from Kenneth Burke (1941) in an oft-quoted passage:

> Imagine that you enter a parlor. You come late. When you arrive, others have long preceded you, and they are engaged in a heated discussion, a discussion too heated for them to pause and tell you exactly what it is about. In fact the discussion had already begun long before any of them got there, so that no one present is qualified to retrace for you all the steps that had gone before. You listen for a while, until you decide that you have caught the tenor of the argument; then you put in your oar. Someone answers; you answer him; another comes to your defense; another aligns himself against you, to either the embarrassment or gratification of your opponent, depending on the quality of your ally's assistance. However, the discussion is interminable. The hour grows late, you must depart, with the discussion still vigorously in progress.

As this passage describes, every argument you make is connected to other arguments. Every time you write an argument, the way you position yourself will depend on three things: which previously stated arguments you share, which previously stated arguments you want to refute, and what new opinions and supporting information you are going to bring to the conversation. You may, for example, affirm others for raising important issues, but assert that they have not given those issues the thought or emphasis that they deserve. Or you may raise a related issue that has been ignored entirely.

ENTERING THE CONVERSATION

To develop an argument that is akin to a conversation, it is helpful to think of writing as a process of understanding conflicts, the claims others make, and the important questions to ask, not simply as the ability to tell a story that influences readers' ways of looking at the world or to find good reasons to support our own beliefs. The real work of writing a researched argument occurs when you try to figure out the answers to the following:

- What topics have people been talking about?
- What is a relevant problem?
- What kinds of evidence might persuade readers?
- What objections might readers have?
- What is at stake in this argument? (What if things change? What if things stay the same?)

In answering these questions, you will want to read with an eye toward identifying an *issue*, the *situation* that calls for some response in writing, and framing a *question*.

Identify an Issue

An issue is a fundamental tension that exists between two or more conflicting points of view. For example, imagine that I believe that the best approach to educational reform is to change the curriculum in schools. Another person might suggest that we need to address reform by considering social and economic concerns. One way to argue the point is for each writer to consider the goals of education that they share, how to best reach those goals, and the reasons why their approach might be the best one to follow. One part of the issue is (*a*) that some people believe that educational reform should occur through changes in the curriculum; the second part is (*b*) that some people believe that reform should occur at the socioeconomic level. Notice that in defining different parts of an issue, the conflicting claims may not necessarily invalidate each other. In fact, one could argue that reform at the levels of curriculum and socioeconomic change may both be effective measures.

Keep in mind that issues are dynamic and arguments are always evolving. One of my students felt that a book he was reading placed too much emphasis on school-based learning and not enough on real-world experience. He framed the issue in this way: "We are not just educated by concepts and facts that we learn in school. We are educated by the people around us and the environments that we live in every day." In writing his essay, he read a great deal in order to support his claims and did so in light of a position he was writing against: "that education in school is the most important type of education."

Identify the Situation

It is important to frame an issue in the context of some specific situation. Whether curricular changes make sense depends on how people view the problem. One kind of problem that E. D. Hirsch identified in his book *Cultural Literacy* is that students do not have sufficient knowledge of history and literacy to communicate well. If that is true in a particular school, perhaps the curriculum might be changed. But there might be other factors involved that call for a different emphasis. Moreover, there are often many different ways to define an issue or frame a question. For example, we might observe that at a local high school, scores on standardized tests have steadily decreased during the past five years. This trend contrasts with scores during the ten years prior to any noticeable decline. Growing out of this situation is the broad question, "What factors have influenced the decline in standardized scores at this school?" Or one could ask this in a different way: "To what extent have scores declined as a result of the curriculum?"

The same principle applies to Anna Quindlen's argument about the homeless in her commentary "No Place Like Home," which illustrates the kinds of connections an author tries to make with readers. Writing her piece as an editorial in the *New York Times*, Quindlen addresses an issue that appears to plague New Yorkers. And yet many people have come to live with the presence of homelessness in New York and other cities. This is the situation that motivates Quindlen to write her editorial: People study the problem of homelessness, yet nothing gets done. Homelessness has become a way of life, a situation that seems to say to observers that officials have declared defeat when it comes to this problem.

Frame a Good Question

A good question can help you think through what you might be interested in writing; it is specific enough to guide inquiry and meets the following criteria:

- It can be answered with the tools you have.
- It conveys a clear idea of who you are answering the question for.
- It is organized around an issue.
- It explores "how," "why," or "whether," and the "extent to which."

A good question, then, is one that can be answered given the access we have to certain kinds of information. The tools we have at hand can be people or other texts. A good question also grows out of an issue, some fundamental tension that you identify within a conversation. Through identifying what is at issue, you should begin to understand for whom it is an issue—who you are answering the question for.

FRAMING AS A CRITICAL STRATEGY FOR WRITING, READING, AND DOING RESEARCH

Thus far, I have presented a conversational model of argument, describing writing as a form of dialogue, with writers responding to the ways others have defined problems and anticipating possible counterarguments. In this section, I want to add another element that some people call framing. This is a strategy that can help you orchestrate different and conflicting voices in advancing your argument.

Framing is a metaphor for describing the lens, or perspective, from which writers present their arguments. Writers want us to see the world in one way as opposed to another, not unlike the way a photographer manipulates a camera lens to frame a picture. For example, if you were taking a picture of friends in front of the football stadium on campus, you would focus on what you would most like to remember, blurring the images of people in the background. How you set up the picture, or frame it, might entail using light and shade to make some images stand out more than others. Writers do the same with language (see also Chapter 4).

For instance, in writing about education in the United States, E. D. Hirsch uses the term *cultural literacy* as a way to understand a problem, in this case the decline of literacy. To say that there is a decline, Hirsch has to establish the criteria against which to measure whether some people are literate and some are not. Hirsch uses *cultural literacy* as a lens through which to discriminate between those who fulfill his criteria for literacy and those who do not. He defines *cultural literacy* as possessing certain kinds of information. Not all educators agree. Some oppose equating literacy and information, describing literacy as an *event* or as a *practice* to argue that literacy is not confined to acquiring bits of information; instead, the notion of literacy as an *event* or *practice* says something about how people use what they know to accomplish the work of a community. As you can see, any perspective or lens can limit readers' range of vision: readers will see some things and not others.

In my work as a writer, I have identified four reasons to use framing as a strategy for developing an argument. First, framing encourages you to name your position, distinguishing the way you think about the world from the ways others do. Naming also makes what you say memorable through key terms and theories. Readers may not remember every detail of Hirsch's argument, but they recall the principle—cultural literacy—around which he organizes his details. Second, framing forces you to offer both a definition and description of the principle around which your argument develops. For example, Hirsch defines *cultural literacy* as "the possession of basic information needed to thrive in the modern world." By defining your argument, you give readers something substantive to respond to. Third, framing specifies your argument, enabling others to respond to your argument and to generate counterarguments that you will want to engage in the spirit of conversation. Fourth, framing helps you organize your thoughts, and readers', in the same way that a title for an essay, a song, or a painting does.

To extend this argument, I would like you to think about framing as a strategy of critical inquiry when you read. By critical inquiry, I mean that reading entails understanding the framing strategies that writers use and using framing concepts in order to shed light on our own ideas or the ideas of others. Here I distinguish *reading as inquiry* from *reading as a search for information*. For example, you might consider your experiences as readers and writers through the lens of Hirsch's conception of cultural literacy. You might recognize that schooling for you was really about accumulating information and that such an approach to education served you well. It is also possible that it has not. Whatever you decide, you may begin to reflect upon your experiences in new ways in developing an argument about what the purpose of education might be.

Alternatively, you might think about your educational experiences through a very different conceptual frame in reading the following excerpt from Richard Rodriguez's memoir, *Hunger of Memory.* In this book, Rodriguez explains the conflicts he experienced as a nonnative speaker of English who desperately sought to enter mainstream culture, even if this meant sacrificing his identity as the son of Mexican immigrants. Notice how Rodriguez recalls his experience as a student through the framing concept of "scholarship boy" that he reads in Richard Hoggart's 1957 book, *The Uses of Literacy.* Using this notion of "scholarship boy" enables him to revisit his experience from a new perspective.

As you read this passage, consider what the notion of "scholarship boy" helps Rodriguez to understand about his life as a student. In turn, what does such a concept help you understand about your own experience as a student?

Motivated to reflect upon his life as a student, Rodriguez comes across Richard Hoggart's book and a description of "the scholarship boy."

For weeks I read, speed-read, books by modern educational theorists, only to find infrequent and slight mention of students like me. . . . Then one day, leafing through Richard Hoggart's *The Uses of Literacy,* I found, in his description of the scholarship boy, myself. For the first time I realized that there were other students like me, and so I was able to frame the meaning of my academic success, its consequent price—the loss.

His initial response is to identify with Hoggart's description. Notice that Rodriguez says he used what he read to "frame the meaning of my academic success."

Hoggart's description is distinguished, at least initially, by deep understanding. What he grasps very well is that the scholarship boy must move between environments, his home and the classroom, which are at cultural extremes, opposed. With his family, the boy has the intense pleasure of intimacy, the family's consolation in feeling public alienation. Lavish emotions texture home life. *Then,* at school, the instruction bids him to trust lonely reason primarily. Immediate needs set the pace of his parents' lives. From his mother and father the boy learns to trust spontaneity and nonrational ways of knowing. *Then,* at school, there is mental calm. Teachers emphasize the value of a reflectiveness that opens a space between thinking and immediate action.

The scholarship boy moves between school and home, between moments of spontaneity and reflectiveness.

Years of schooling must pass before the boy will be able to sketch the cultural differences in his day as abstractly as this. But he senses those differences early. Perhaps as early as the night he brings home an assignment from school and finds the house too noisy for study.

Rodriguez uses Hoggart's words and idea to advance his own understanding of the problem he identifies in his life: that he was unable to find solace at home and within his working-class roots.

> He has to be more and more alone, if he is going to 'get on.' He will have, probably unconsciously, to oppose the ethos of the hearth, the intense gregariousness of the working-class family group. . . . The boy has to cut himself off mentally, so as to do his homework, as well as he can.

In this excerpt, the idea of framing highlights the fact that other people's texts can serve as tools for helping you say more about your own ideas. If you were writing an essay using Hoggart's term *scholarship boy* as a lens through which to say something about education, you might ask how Hoggart's term illuminates new aspects of another writer's examples or your own—as opposed to asking, "How well does Hoggart's term *scholarship boy* apply to my experience?" (to which you could answer, "Not very well"). Further, you might ask, "To what extent does Hirsch's concept throw a more positive light on what Rodriguez and Hoggart describe?" or "Do my experiences challenge, extend, or complicate such a term as *scholarship boy?*"

Now that you have a sense of how framing works, let's look at an excerpt from a researched argument a first-year composition student wrote, titled "Learning 'American' in Spanish." The assignment to which she responded asked her to do the following:

> Draw on your life experiences in developing an argument about education and what it has meant to you in your life. In writing your essay, use two of the four authors (Freire, Hirsch, Ladson-Billings, Pratt) included in this unit to frame your argument or any of the reading you may have done on your own. What key terms, phrases, or ideas from these texts help you teach your readers what you want them to learn from your experiences? How do your experiences extend or complicate your critical frames?
>
> In the past, in responding to this assignment, some people have offered an overview of almost their entire lives, some have focused on a pivotal experience, and others have used descriptions of people who have influenced them. The important thing is that you use those experiences to argue a position: for example, that even the most well-meaning attempts to support students can actually hinder learning. This means going beyond narrating a simple list of experiences, or simply asserting an opinion. Instead you must use—and analyze—your experiences, determining which will most effectively convince your audience that your argument has a solid basis.

As you read the excerpt from this student's essay, ask yourself how the writer uses two framing concepts—"transculturation" and "contact zone"—from Mary Louise Pratt's article "Arts of the Contact Zone." What do these ideas help the writer bring into focus? What experience do these frames help her to name, define, and describe?

The writer has not yet named her framing concept; but notice that the concrete details she gathers here set readers up to expect that she will juxtapose the culture of Guayabal and the Dominican Republic with that of the United States.

Exactly one week after graduating from high school, with thirteen years of American education behind me, I boarded a plane and headed for a Caribbean island. I had fifteen days to spend on an island surrounded with crystal blue waters, white sandy shores, and luxurious ocean resorts. With beaches to play on by day and casinos to play in during the night, I was told that this country was an exciting new tourist destination. My days in the Dominican Republic, however, were not filled with snorkeling lessons and my nights were not spent at the blackjack table. Instead of visiting the ritzy East Coast, I traveled inland to a mountain community with no running water and no electricity. The bus ride to this town, called Guayabal, was long, hot, and uncomfortable. The mountain roads were not paved and the bus had no air-conditioning. Surprisingly, the four-hour ride flew by. I had plenty to think about as my mind raced with thoughts of the next two weeks. I wondered if my host family would be welcoming, if the teenagers would be friendly, and if my work would be hard. I mentally prepared myself for life without the everyday luxuries of a flushing toilet, a hot shower, and a comfortable bed. Because Guayabal was without such basic commodities, I did not expect to see many reminders of home. I thought I was going to leave behind my American ways and immerse myself into another culture. These thoughts filled my head as the bus climbed the rocky hill toward Guayabal. When I finally got off the bus and stepped into the town square, I realized that I had thought wrong: There was no escaping the influence of the American culture.

The writer names her experience as an example of Pratt's conception of a "contact zone." Further, the writer expands on Pratt's quote by relating it to her own observations. And finally, she uses this frame as a way to organize the narrative (as opposed to ordering her narrative chronologically).

In a way, Guayabal was an example of what author Mary Louis Pratt refers to as a contact zone. Pratt defines a contact zone as "a place where cultures meet, clash, and grapple with each other, often in contexts of highly asymmetrical relations of power." In Guayabal, American culture and American consumerism were clashing with the Hispanic and Caribbean culture of the Dominican Republic. The clash came from the Dominicans' desire to be American in every sense, and especially to be consumers of American products. This is nearly impossible for Dominicans to achieve due to their extreme poverty. Their poverty provided the "asymmetrical relation of power" found in contact zones, because it impeded not only the Dominicans' ability to be consumers, but also their ability to learn, to work, and to live healthily. The effects of their poverty could be seen in the eyes of the seven-year-old boy who couldn't concentrate in school because all he had to eat the day before was an underripe mango. It could be seen in the brown, leathered hands of the tired old man who was still picking coffee beans at age seventy.

The writer provides concrete evidence to support her point.

The moment I got off the bus I noticed the clash between the American culture, the Dominican culture, and the community's poverty. It was apparent in the Dominicans' fragmented representation of American pop culture. Everywhere I looked in Guayabal I saw little glimpses of America. I saw Coca-Cola ads painted on raggedy fences. I saw knockoff Tommy Hilfiger shirts. I heard little boys say, "I wanna be like Mike" in their best English, while playing basketball. I listened to merengue house, the American version of the traditional Dominican merengue music. In each instance the Dominicans had adopted an aspect of American culture, but with an added Dominican twist. Pratt calls this transculturation. This term is used to "describe processes whereby members of subordinated or marginal groups select and invent from materials transmitted by a dominant or metropolitan culture." She claims that transculturation is an

The writer offers an illustration of what she experienced, clarifying how this experience is similar to what Pratt describes. Note that Pratt's verb *clash,* used in the definition of *contact zone,* reappears here as part of the author's observation.

identifying feature of contact zones. In the contact zone of Guayabal, the marginal group, made up of impoverished Dominicans, selected aspects of the dominant American culture, and invented a unique expression of a culture combining both Dominican and American styles. My most vivid memory of this transculturation was on a hot afternoon when I heard some children yelling, "Helado! Helado!" or "Ice cream! Ice cream!" I looked outside just in time to see a man ride by on a bicycle, ringing a hand bell and balancing a cooler full of ice cream in the front bicycle basket. The Dominican children eagerly chased after him, just as American children chase after the ice-cream truck.

The author adds another layer to her description, introducing Pratt's framing concept of "transculturation." Here again she quotes Pratt in order to bring into focus her own context here. The writer offers another example of transculturation.

Although you will notice that the writer does not challenge the framing terms she uses in this paper, it is clear that rather than simply reproducing Pratt's ideas and using her as the Voice of Authority, she incorporates Pratt's understandings to enable her to say more about her own experiences and ideas. Moreover, she uses this frame to advance an argument in order to affect her readers' views of culture. In turn, when she mentions others' ideas, she does so in the service of what she wants to say.

CONCLUSION: WRITING RESEARCHED ARGUMENTS

I want to conclude this chapter by making a distinction between two different views of research. On the one hand, research is often taught as a process of collecting information for its own sake. On the other hand, research can also be conceived as the discovery and purposeful use of information. The emphasis here is upon *use* and the ways you can shape information that enable you to enter conversations. To do so, you need to demonstrate to readers that you understand the conversation: what others have said in the past, what the context is, and the direction you anticipate this conversation might take. Keep in mind, however, that contexts are neither found nor located. Rather, context, derived from the Latin *contexere,* denotes a process of weaving together. Thus your attempt to understand context is an active process of making connections among the different and conflicting views people present within a conversation. Your version of the context will vary from others' interpretations.

Your attempts to understand a given conversation may prompt you to do research, as will your attempts to define what is at issue. Your reading and inquiry can help you construct a question that is rooted in some issue that is open to dispute. In turn, you need to ask yourself what is at stake for you and your reader other than that you might be interested in educational reform, homelessness, affirmative action, or any other subject. Finally, your research can provide a means for framing an argument in order to move a conversation along and to say something new.

If you see inquiry as a means of entering conversations, then you will understand research as a social process. It need not be the tedious task of collecting information for its own sake. Rather, research has the potential to change readers' worldviews and your own.

Classroom Authors

MARGARET STEELE

"Reflecting on Mirrors" and "Surviving with a Mirror"

CONSIDER THIS:

To compose these essays, Margaret Steele undertook a particular research challenge. Authors were asked to investigate the origin of a common object: dice, spoon, paper clip, playing cards, and so on. Using this research, which included looking at on-line and library holdings of secondary texts and conducting primary research, looking at the objects in use, interviewing those who relied on them (bridge players, for example, or cataloging the types of paper clips sold in office supply stores), the writer composed two essays growing out of the same matrix of information: a research-filled, informational essay and a more imaginative text or literary essay. Margaret Steele, a reentry college student, decided to write about mirrors: "I asked my teenage daughter whether she would prefer to read an essay about perfume or mirrors. I was surprised when she immediately said mirrors. So mirrors it was." Before you read this essay, think about the common objects that you surround yourself with and make a list of several that you'd like to know more about. After you read, think about how you might have approached Steele's topic of mirrors, and which of her versions you preferred (and why).

REFLECTING ON MIRRORS

INTRODUCTION

Mirrors surround us in our daily lives. After arising in the morning, we look in a mirror to see how to wash our face, shave our face, brush our hair, apply our makeup and check out our outfits in order to achieve that desirable perfect look. However, it was once believed that if you looked into a mirror too long, you were sure to see the devil one day. And, if a child looked into a mirror before the age of one, he would die young or be cross-eyed. Since it was bad luck for a bride to look in a mirror after she was completely dressed, she would leave one article of clothing, such as a glove, to put on after that last look (Opie, 249–253). But, is vanity the only purpose of mirrors? Absolutely not. In fact, mirrors serve many other purposes, not just today, but in ancient times also.

POLISHED SURFACE

The definition of mirror in *The New Encyclopedia Britannica* is "any polished surface that diverts a ray of light according to the law of reflection." Where the ancient Roman and European mirrors were polished "convex disks" of metal, the modern mirror is in fact glass with a backing of silver or aluminum. A mirror's surface is perfectly smooth so that it may reflect as much light as possible. Mirrors are either flat or curved, concave or convex.

HISTORY

Douglas Low recounts "The History of Mirrors" in his article entitled *Mirror Resilvering.* The first mirror was probably a pool of water in which one could see a reflection. Low theorizes that about 2000 B.C. ancient cultures were polishing the semitransparent, black obsidian stones, also known as volcanic glass, to be used as mirrors. He also states that the oldest record of a brass mirror is recorded in the Bible about 1500 B.C. (Exodus 38:8); "And he made the laver of brass, and the foot of it of brass of the looking glasses of the women assembling, which assembled at the door of the tabernacle of the congregation" (qtd. Low 1).

Mirrors as we know them today came into existence about 1500 A.D. and coincided with the production of flat glass upon which the "reflecting surface" was added in a process which mixed tin and mercury. Before this time flat glass was very expensive and scarce. Skillful labor was required to make one of these mirrors and took weeks to complete (Low). During the Renaissance, mirror production centers were established in Nurnberg and Venice and in London and Paris by the 17th century. These mirrors were very expensive, therefore the largest and most exclusive could be found in places like the palace at Versailles, built in the mid-1600s (*The New Encyclopedia Britannica*). The mirror we know today is called a silver mirror and was invented in 1835 by a German, Justus Von Liebig. Of all the metals, silver is the best-known reflector of light.

USES

- *Starting Fires*—Along with other glass items, mirrors can deflect the sun's bright rays onto grass or twigs in order to start a fire. A third century B.C. scientist, Archimedes, used his knowledge of physics against the Romans when they tried to take Syracuse. Besides constructing weapons, he was credited with using large mirrors to direct the sun's rays on the Roman ships in order to set them on fire. Whether this actually happened is debatable but it tells us they were aware of this characteristic of mirrors (Gale "Archimedes").
- *Signals*—Another very important use for mirrors is as a device for signaling. This use is documented in history, beginning with the use of polished metals. In *Hellenica,* a work by the Ancient Greek soldier and writer Xenophon, reference is made to the Athenian ships' order "to signal with a shield when they were halfway across the straits" (Holzmann 1). Professor Carl Friedrich Gauss invented a device

for survey work in 1810, which used silvered and unsilvered mirrors to relay messages between stations. British and American armies later used this as a telegraph means (Holzmann 2). A list of the items that were included in a Vietnam pilot survival vest included a survival mirror. An advertisement for a signal mirror relates the story of three men who were stranded on ice and unconscious. They were rescued because a ship saw the flash from the mirror that was around one of the men's neck. A flash can be seen from a mirror up to 100 miles away (Survival "Ultimate").

- *Trade Goods*—When the early Europeans came to North America they traded goods with the native Indians. Beginning with Columbus, this was essential to the interaction between the two cultures. In exchange for fur skins, the Europeans gave the natives cloth, glass beads, metals and mirrors. These items were also given to the Indians as a sign of good faith (Riordan "Native Americans Overview"). Archeologists have found European trade items, including mirrors, as far as a thousand miles from where the items were originally exchanged (Gale "Native Peoples").
- *Decoration*—Mirrors became a very important decoration item in the late 17th century. The frames were wonderfully crafted of material such as ivory, silver, or tortoiseshell or made from splendid woods such as walnut or olive. The frames were cheaper to make than the mirror itself, and so were replaced as decorating tastes changed (*The New Encyclopedia Britannica*). In modern times, mirrors are fairly cheap and we would keep the wonderfully crafted frame and replace the mirror.
- *Lighting Homes*—Many of the homes in Natchez, Mississippi predate the Civil War and are historically preserved. A guide at one of the homes explains why there are long mirrors throughout the house. The home was built before electricity or even gaslights and the only sources of light were candles and the sun. The mirrors were positioned so as to capture the sun's rays coming through the many, long windows and thereby light up the room.

SUPERSTITIONS

- *Breaking a Mirror*—Most of us were told that it was bad luck to break a mirror and a few of us might even have believed it. But, as *A Dictionary of Superstitions* tells us, it was a serious matter in earlier times. One reason goes back to the fact that mirrors were once very expensive. Some of these superstitions have existed since at least the 1700s. Breaking a mirror foretold the death of a family member or the loss of a best friend within one year. The person who would die corresponded to the person who broke the mirror: if a child broke a mirror, one of the children would die and if a servant broke a mirror, one of the servants would die. It was believed to be the unluckiest thing that could happen. As late as 1960, an account is told of two mischievous boys in Yorkshire who broke everything they could in some railway cars, except the mirrors, because they were superstitious (Opie 240–250).

- *Looking into When Sick*—While we do not think twice about looking into a mirror, there was a time when doing so at the wrong moment would bring dire consequences. Mirrors in a room where someone was sick were once covered. It was thought unlucky for a sick person to look into a mirror and see his/her face (Opie 250–251).
- *Death*—Sometimes, all the mirrors were covered with white cloths or turned to face the wall when someone died. There were different reasons for this:

> the looking-glass is muffled, to intimate that all . . . vanity . . . is over with the deceased . . . a dread is felt of some spiritual being imaging himself forth in the blank surface of the mirror . . . if you look into the mirror in the death-chamber, you will see the corpse looking over your shoulder . . . It is not good for a corpse to be reflected in a glass or mirror . . . because the dead will not rest . . . It is feared that the soul, projected out of the person in the shape of his reflection in the mirror, may be carried off by the ghost of the departed, which is commonly supposed to linger about the house till the burial. (*A Dictionary of Superstitions* 250)

- *Thunderstorms*—Mirrors were also covered during a thunderstorm because it was thought dangerous to look at lightning through a mirror (Opie 251).
- *Foretelling the Future*—It was once believed that if you set a candle in front of a mirror and ate an apple with one hand and combed your hair with the other hand, you would soon see the face of your future husband looking over your shoulder (Opie 249–253).

Many of these superstitions probably arose from people believing that the mirror could capture their soul. Other superstitions have their origins in Greek mythology. In Ancient Greece, the gods sentenced an arrogant young man, Narcissus, to look at his own handsome image in a pool of water. Falling in love with his own face, he couldn't move and wasted away, eventually leaving only a flower where his body once was. Humans have always been fascinated with their own images and constantly seek ways to perfect them.

WORKS CITED

Gale Group. "Archimedes Makes Scientific Discoveries, c. 250 B.C." *Discovering World History.* Gale Research, 1997. http://www. galenet.com/servlet/HistRC/

Gale Group. "Native Peoples and Early European Contacts." *Encyclopedia of American Social History* 3 vols. Charles Scribner's Sons, 1993.

Gilson, Simon. *Medieval Optics and Theories of Light in the Works of Dante.* UK: Edwin Mellen, 2000.

Holzmann, Gerald J. and Pehrson, Bjorn. "Mirrors and Flags." *The Early History of Data Networks.* http://www.it.kth.se/docs/ early_net/ch-2-1.2.html

Low, Douglas A. "The History of Mirrors." *Mirror Resilvering.* Syracuse, NY, 1996 http://web.syr.edu/~aslow/mirror.html

"Mirror." *The New Encyclopedia Britannica.* Vol. 8. Chicago, 1998.
Opie, Iona and Tatem, Moira. "Mirror." *A Dictionary of Superstitions.* NY: Oxford UP, 1989.
Riordan, Patrick. "Native Americans Overview (1600–1754)." *American Eras.* 8 vols. Gale Research, 1997–1998. http://www. galenet.com/servlet/HistRC/
Sindlinger, Albert. "Common Sense Survival Guides." A & U Specialty Publications, 2001. http://members.tripod.com/~Sidlinger/
Survival Inc. *Ultimate Survival.* 1999. http://www.sharplink.com/ jkits/index.html

SURVIVING WITH A MIRROR

The *Survivor* TV series has been a run away hit. For those of you who missed it, sixteen people are taken to a desolate area, divided into two tribes, and left for up to thirty-nine days. Every three days, the contestants go to tribal council. At this meeting one of them is voted off the show by the other players. They compete in a series of challenges for immunity from being voted out. The survivor left at the end of the show receives one million dollars. These sixteen people are average citizens from all walks of life who have applied to be on the show. Currently, a casting call has gone out for the next installment of the series. Although the destination for this one is still a secret, previous participants have been placed on a deserted island, the Australian outback and Africa.

Maybe you are thinking about applying for the next show. After all, even the people who haven't ended up in first place have been given instant celebrity status. Many of their careers have been changed by the show. Some are doing commercials and some have parts in other TV shows. What would you need to do to prepare? Well, of course, you need to get into the best shape that you can. Most of the immunity challenges are physical, but not geared just to male participants. Some require stamina and balance, like standing the longest on a beam. If you can win the immunity challenge, then you won't be voted off at the council that night. But, even if you go into the game in good physical condition, the elements you will face can soon wear down your strength. You will lose a lot of weight because your main diet will be rice. Searching for food is one big part of the survival game. But, how will you cook it? And, how will you stay warm at night if the temperature falls?

The participants arrive at the destination with the clothes on their back and one personal item of their choice. If you are serious about wanting to endure this hardship for the possibility of a personal reward, begin thinking about what you would take. What would be the most helpful? Surely a book could keep you from being bored and also be used to start a fire if necessary. A comb or brush would be almost impossible to live without. Lip balm would save your lips if you are in a very hot environment. And there's nothing like a deck of cards or a board game to pass the long, boring days ahead of you.

Let's go back to that fire you made with pages from the book. How did you start the fire? "A lighter," you say. That's probably not an item that is allowed since it would give an unfair advantage. Even if matches are allowed, they would get wet if you are dropped in the water and made to swim to shore, like the contestants on the first show. But, what about a mirror? With a mirror, you can deflect the sun's rays onto those torn pages or some straw and leaves and start a fire. This has been done for centuries. After the Greeks developed glass, they used the lenses to focus sunlight on objects such as sticks to start a flame. A third century B.C. Greek scientist, Archimedes, was credited with using large mirrors to direct the sun's rays on the Roman ships in order to set them on fire. Whether this actually happened is debatable but it tells us the ancient Greeks were aware of this characteristic of mirrors. Now, of course, you can spend all day rubbing two sticks together in hopes of producing a spark. It's been done on the show before, usually with only a little smoke for the effort, and a lot of blisters.

Thinking about taking a razor for your beard? Or, if you're a woman, make-up in case there's a good-looking guy with you? How will you see without a mirror? The truth is that you can probably find a good facsimile. The first mirrors were in effect pools of water in which one could see a reflection. Hopefully, the water won't be too dark, or green, or murky. Any of these would distort the image, of course. If the water is not clear, then a shiny metal object makes a good mirror. The oldest record of a brass mirror is recorded in the Bible about 1500 B.C. The ancient Roman and European mirrors were polished convex-shaped metals. Mirrors as we know them today came into existence about 1500 A.D. and coincided with the production of flat glass to which a mixture of tin and mercury were added on the surface. There weren't many mirrors around though because the glass was so expensive and skillful labor was required to make one. The mirror that we know today is called a silver mirror and was invented in 1835. Of all the metals, silver is the best-known reflector of light.

Let's suppose for a minute that you left the Survivor camp to go searching for food. You found some small tracks and followed them. Failing to find the food and realizing that you were due back in camp an hour ago, you head back and get lost. You're scared. How will anybody find you? Find a safe place to stay put for a while and pull out your mirror. You did bring it with you, didn't you? A mirror can be used as a signaling device. When aimed at the sun's rays, a flash can be seen from a mirror up to 100 miles away. This use is documented in history, beginning with the use of polished metals. In *Hellenica,* a work by the Ancient Greek soldier and writer Xenophon, the Athenian ships signaled with a shield when they had reached the desired destination. A device using mirrors to send messages was used for survey work in 1810. Later, British and American armies used this same device to send telegraphs. A list of the items that were included in a Vietnam pilot survival vest included a survival mirror. Recently, three men were stranded on ice and were rescued because a ship saw the flash from the mirror that was around one of the men's neck.

So relax. You know that a camp is set up in the area to handle any emergency the survivor contestants might get in. They have been notified by now that you are missing and probably already have the search plane in the air. Just keep flashing that mirror at the sun.

Let's say you've gotten on this show and you are now one of the last three contestants remaining in the survival competition. There are only a few days to go. You are keeping a raging fire going at all times now so there is no need to start a new one. But the days have gotten cold and you and your tribe are not able to venture far from the fire because of the lack of warm clothing. You are unable to go hunt for food. Suddenly, an uncivilized native from the area that you are in shows up. He's wearing a long fur covering around his body and carrying some freshly killed meat. He looks friendly enough and you are starving and cold. Take out your mirror and begin bartering with him for his fur garment and the meat. He has probably never seen a mirror before and may think it is magic and worth more than the furs and meat. Trading goods with the native Indians of North

America was essential for the early Europeans. In exchange for their furs, the Europeans gave them cloth, glass beads, metals, and of course, mirrors. The natives must have prized those mirrors because archeologist have found them as far as a thousand miles from where they were originally exchanged. You have your fire and, with that meat, you won't have to venture from camp for the remaining few days, so trade the mirror.

A word of caution about that mirror. I was assuming that you were not the superstitious type. If you are, you might want to take a different object. You're going to have a hard thirty days ahead of you. If you break that mirror and are superstitious, you will probably resign yourself to seven years bad luck, or even worse. This was a serious matter in the 1700s. Breaking a mirror foretold the death of a family member within one year of the breakage. Many people still believe today that it is unlucky to break a mirror. In 1960, two boys in Yorkshire broke everything in some railway cars except—because they were superstitious—the mirrors. Some people believed that this association with mirrors began because, as you remember, mirrors were once so expensive.

You probably don't want to spend a long time looking in that mirror either. It was once believed that if you looked into a mirror for too long that you would see the devil one day. You're going to have enough danger ahead of you without having the devil along for the trip. People must have believed that a mirror could capture your soul because they covered all the mirrors in a house with a white cloth when someone died. They believed the dead would not rest if the corpse was reflected in a mirror. They also thought that the soul of the person looking into the mirror could be snatched out of the person by their reflection and carried off by the ghost of the deceased.

If there is a thunderstorm, cover the mirror. Some believe it's dangerous to look at lightning through a mirror. But suppose you are a female and meet that special guy on this adventure. It wouldn't hurt to place a candle in front of the mirror, comb your hair with one hand and eat an apple with the other hand. It was once believed that in doing this, you would soon see the face of your future husband looking over your shoulder. Of course, you stand the chance of the face being the devil that was going to show up if you looked in the mirror too long. Probably not a good idea to do this.

I really don't think you need to worry about having bad luck if you break the mirror. Even broken, you can still use the pieces to start a fire or signal for help. You're going to have enough bad luck as it is with starvation, thirst, sleepless nights, boring days, wild dangerous animals, pesky bugs, etc. But, the reward can be big. The clue to surviving to the end is to be an invaluable member of your tribe. They will not want to vote out the member with the mirror. The fire that can be created with it will be necessary for warmth, cooking food, and frightening off dangerous animals. You will be invaluable in the Survivor game as long as you choose to take your mirror.

WRITING PROCESS NARRATIVE FOR "MIRRORS"

The assignment for this essay was to research and write about an object. I still had no idea what I was going to write on when I came to class on July 2. Wendy wrote idea after idea on the board as students came forth with many splendid ideas. I even offered several suggestions myself, but I left class without a definite idea. At that point I was thinking about safety pins or bobby pins.

A few days later, I searched the Internet for information on safety pins or bobby pins. There was not enough information for even a one-page report. I'm sure if I had weeks to research, I would eventually find enough information for a decent essay, but that was not the case. I looked once again at the list Wendy had made in class. I have a small collection of bells and decided to do that. I searched the Internet again and found lots of information on bells. After over an hour of searching and printing out information I was already getting bored. I thought about perfume. There was plenty of information on that but I wasn't hooked on the subject. I looked around my living room at other objects. My mirrored wall that gives the illusion of a larger room caught my attention. There were a lot of Internet sites about mirrors. Still undecided, I asked my teenage daughter whether she would prefer to read an essay about perfume or mirrors. I was surprised when she immediately said mirrors. So, mirrors it was.

The next day I searched for information about mirrors on the Internet and also went to the local library near my house. There was practically nothing at the library. The following day I spent two hours at the university library doing research. The problem with choosing an object that can also be a verb is that you have to sort through hundreds of titles that are about the verb, not the object. There was only one encyclopedia that had sufficient information on mirrors and that was *The New Encyclopedia Britannica.* Between using the Gale Net database and locating several books, I finally had enough information.

On July 7, I spent four hours compiling my information and writing my paper. Fridays and Saturdays are my best days to write because I have the whole day to sit at my computer. I had chosen to do the formal version first in order to become knowledgeable with my subject. July 10—I didn't feel like I had enough information. When I had spoken to Wendy about my subject, she had mentioned mirrors being used as trade goods. I spent two hours searching the Internet for information about mirrors as trade goods and also as survival equipment. This really added to my paper.

The use of a mirror as a survival tool had gotten my interest and I thought about making this the main theme of my informal paper. I proposed to my small group the idea of writing an essay about the importance of a mirror for a contestant on the *Survivor* TV show. They all liked the idea. Since a few of them had not seen the show, they said they would also need information about the show. I was interested in this paper and sat down at my computer that night and wrote for three hours. We also discussed my formal version and they suggested that I mix up the historical facts about mirrors with the superstitions to make it more interesting.

I spent six hours at my computer on July 13, working on my professional draft of the formal essay. I rearranged several subtopics, wrote an introduction and compiled my Work Cited page. All of this time was not spent writing. My printer decided to go crazy on me, refusing to print more than one page at a time. After working on it for a long time, I gave up. Thankfully, I was ahead of schedule on this assignment and had the time to sit and patiently print each page, one copy at a time.

I had an hour before class began on July 18th and spent this time writing on my second version. July 21st was a good writing day for me. I was interested in my paper and wrote for six hours. The small group workshop on Monday liked my paper and had some small revision suggestions but nothing major. I was concerned because I needed a revision for my final draft. I set up a conference with Wendy, telling her that this was the one that I needed the most help with. She said that my group was correct and only small revisions were necessary. It read well as it was. She also said that it was much stronger than my formal version because my own voice was in it. There's definitely a lot to be said for being interested in what you are writing.

Wednesday's full class workshop on my formal draft was very helpful and they gave me a lot of good suggestions. They didn't like the superstitions and history intermingled because it didn't flow well. I spent three hours that night and three hours the next day revising the paper, incorporating many of their good suggestions.

My informal version was easy to revise since basically I corrected some grammar errors and added a few explanations.

RACHEL HARRINGTON

Blizzard Baby

CONSIDER THIS:

To better understand how culture shaped her life, even as it was just beginning, Rachel Harrington completed her own version of an assignment that asks authors to research the year they were born. Secondary resources for this project include newspapers and magazines (which have interesting advertisements that can be read to better understand contemporary consumer values), movies and music, and general histories of the era. Primary resources include parents and other relatives who were around for the big event. Rachel, an undergraduate when she composed this essay, notes that, "The general story of my birth was about the same coming from both my mom and my dad. But, they each remembered specific details that the other did not. Between the two of them, I gathered the most vivid description of my birth and the weather that surrounded it." Reviewing a scrapbook in the presence of a parent who compiled it with a tape recorder running will help a memoirist gather insights and quotes for this sort of paper.

Some classroom authors organized their paper month by month; others used newspaper headlines and events as the backdrop for talking about family events. Rachel decided to research the weather that year since she was born in Iowa—blizzard country. Before you read her narrative, jot down what you know or have been told about the year of your birth: family stories, political events (who was president?), world events. Note, too, possible sources you could consult when composing a paper of this sort.

Rachel Harrington
Professor Bishop
ENC 4311 Article and Essay Workshop
6 October 1999

Blizzard Baby

> There is no soft nonsense about the seasons in Iowa. Winter is a savage season; blizzards out of the west rattle the teeth in your skull. Frost goes deep in the fallow ground; snow piles up and when the ice comes, impenetrable, squirrels scamper over it hungrily.
>
> —Paul Engle, 1956

The first snowfall creeps in while people are tucked into their beds under handmade patchwork quilts, sleeping to the rhythmic hum of the heater kicking on and off. The exterior glass panes of the windows are frosted over, creating grids of intermingling frost lines from the thin layer of ice that encloses the house. The small Iowa town awakes to a world of ashen and gentle snowflakes falling to the ground and covering the grays and browns that ended the fall season. It is early November, and the tips of the fallen, ginger-colored maple leaves stick through the first white of winter. The first snow is anticipated and met with excitement and energy. Children anxiously stuff themselves into bulging snowsuits and fur-lined boots. Mittens and scarves and stocking caps cover the remaining inches of flesh, leaving only a pair of eyes and red cheeks and noses to peer out into the brightness. Car engines are revved up, their faithful owners leaving them running to bring warmth to the frozen steel while they shovel and scrape the ice and snow off of the windshields. Hands are cold and noses are running. The first evident signs of winter are here. Snow, the final descent into a four-month freeze and smoking brick chimneys. Amidst the bustle of the community, my mom sits at her kitchen table sipping her decaffeinated coffee, the glare from the fallen snow permeating into the small, blue and white-checkered tile room. She watches Peter, her three-year-old son, roll in the drifts outside, laughing as he throws his arms into the iciness. She looks down at her swollen belly, so bloated that she can hardly reach her coffee mug from the unborn baby situated between her and the lacquered pine table.

This first light and placid snowfall is part of the beauty of winter in the Midwest. The holiday atmosphere kicks in, persuading people out into the bitter cold to cut their ideal Evergreen down, strap it to the hood of their station wagons, and then trim and decorate the drooping limbs with tinseled garlands and polished ornaments. Children flock out into desolate yards, throwing themselves onto the frozen ground while stretching and fanning their arms and legs in uniform patterns creating snow angels. Winter mentality begins, bringing up canned vegetables from the cellar and the hope of a snowed-in day off from busy lives. People bustle through the malls in snow boots, their hands gripping Sears shopping bags and tattered wish lists. Winter is here in all its glory.

In all the flurry, the harsh aspects of winter are almost forgotten. The excitement of the season change masks the realities of an Iowa winter. And when the darker face of

Rachel Harrington
Page 2

winter surfaces, nothing but the atmosphere with its relentless aggression is seen outdoors. Snowstorms with gusting winds sweep through the prairie lands of Iowa, forcing people inside their homes, where they pray that the electricity will hold to heat their homes in the below-zero temperatures. These storms may start to form hundreds, even thousands of miles away, as temperate low-pressure systems travel east from as far as Asia, across the mighty Pacific Ocean. When the conditions are right, the strongest of these low-pressure systems make it over the Rocky Mountains and then build momentum after their long journey over rugged terrain (Angel, 2). Other storms start brewing due to dry Canadian air flowing south (Ruffner, 359). Crossing over the huge Great Lakes decreases the temperatures, and the storms from the north gain more speed. Whatever their origin, impending storms develop upper atmospheric winds over Iowa. These winds determine what will come with the winter weather.

Blizzards are more exciting than frightening, bringing temperatures in the teens and heavy loads of snow, blanketing towns and fields in a layer of white dust. In Iowa, the snowfall is usually moderate averaging twenty to twenty-four inches from the months of November through April (Ruffner, 360). There is always the possibility of an unusually bad snowstorm that closes down roads and whips through towns dumping masses of snow, leaving people stranded in their homes. If the temperature is near freezing, the snow will fall gently and evenly. It is when the temperature is extremely cold, inching below zero, that the snow will drift (Angel, 3). Depending on the strength and duration of the winds, the snow may continue to blow and drift. When the snow stops and the snowplows come out and clear the roads, life goes back to its normal pace.

The heavy snow is not the worst gift that winter gives. In fact, its beauty is worth the worrying and stockpiling of water and food and firewood. The ice is what Iowans fear. Sleet and freezing rain are the products of winter that bring ugliness and danger. This collision of warm and below freezing air levels cause extremely cold liquid, almost frozen, to plummet to the earth where it freezes on contact and creates ice (Angel, 3). Ice can be heavy and causes severe damage where it accumulates, knocking down power lines, communication towers, even caving in roofs of homes. Coats of ice on roads cause the surfaces to be impossible to travel, creating transportation difficulties and complete chaos when emergencies arise.

During the winter of 1978, a near emergency situation was brewing in my parents' home. Iowa was plagued with an extreme winter season, and by the first week of December, Cedar county residents were prepared for the worst. Snow and ice had fallen numerous times, starting in small doses in late October. My parents lived in Mechanicsville, a very small community that was tucked into the farming hills of western Iowa. There were a few nearby towns, such as Lisbon where my grandmother lived, only fifteen miles away, but they were only slightly larger with about the same attributes: a small grocery store, a gas station, a bank, and a fire station. Cedar Rapids, thirty miles away, was the closest town that offered any glimpse of a larger community. My mom was nine months pregnant with me, and St. Luke's Hospital of Cedar Rapids was to be my first home; thirty miles away from our house and reachable by only two major roads.

In the first week of December, my mom went into false labor at the same time that her son Peter was scheduled to have tubes put in his ears. After a day at the hospital, my dad switching his post from the labor area to the pediatric ward, they returned home with a miserable Peter and an exhausted—and still pregnant—mom. Two days later, the air-waves and televisions were exploding with news of an oncoming storm that was moving too quickly for forecasters to know what it was bringing along with it. Considering the severity of the recent weather and my due date approaching, my parents were at a cross-road. What were they to do if my mom went into labor during this unpredictable storm, thirty miles away from her physician and the nearest hospital?

With no time to spare, they quickly devised a plan of action. After numerous fretting episodes and the help of the local fire department (all three of the men who volunteered), they had a plan of action that was the only logical solution if I decided to enter this world when the winter was at its most ruthless stage. It happened that there was a small clinic in downtown Mechanicsville, operating to treat the common cold and minor injuries. A doctor from the hospital lived nearby and agreed to be ready in case my mom needed him. No deliveries had ever taken place here before, but they took the precautions of preparing the office for a birth and brought in the necessary equipment. My dad would pull my mom two blocks on a sled, a wooden shuttle designed for a small child, to the clinic where the doctor and an underqualified nurse would meet them. If there were any complications, Mechanicsville's fire engines would be standing by to battle the icy roads to Cedar Rapids. With what they had to work with, it was a good plan.

The storm came through, bringing some of the worst ice and freezing rain my parents had ever seen. All the roads were unfit for travel and not an establishment was open for business. The entire town and county shut down, people captive in their houses. For seven hours, my mom and dad sat in our living room, the electricity coming and going and the wind sucking our house in various directions. Forty mile-per-hour gusts of wind roared through the small town, cracking off dead tree branches and ripping power lines. My mom, huddled with my dad and Peter on the living room floor in a pile of blankets, sat still, afraid to move, thinking any motion would bring the onset of my birth closer.

Maybe I had a premonition of the callous ways of an Iowa winter storm. Maybe I just wasn't ready to be born into that frigid night. Whatever the reason, my mom did not go into labor; nor did the occasional contractions occur that she had been having the preceding week. The storm passed and the town's people eventually emerged from their houses with bags of salt and shovels, attempting to forget the fear that had possessed them.

The new week started, and the mildest of snow flurries came and went. My parents, although anxious for my arrival, continued on and laughed about the idea of them braving the ice sheets on a wooden sled, my dad pulling a swollen-bellied woman through ripping winds.

Saturday, December 9 was a picturesque seasonal day. The temperature was in the mid-twenties, with small flakes occasionally cascading down from the spruce and fir trees that lined our Main Street property. Although my due date was the following day, my parents decided to go about the day as planned. They were piling on the layers of clothes

Rachel Harrington
Page 4

to brave the Christmas tree farm that was only miles away. By tradition, they always went with my grandmother and picked out the perfect tree amid a sea of towering pines and human boot imprints. As Peter was getting his final layer of wool, my mom felt a sharp pain in her abdomen. I was finally ready. My mom looked out the kitchen window to see the snow that was lightly falling blowing around the yard, creating tiny tornados of blur.

Being that the weather was just gaining momentum, my parents threw Peter in Betsy, our sky blue Dodge station wagon. My dad raced to Lisbon and dropped Peter off at my grandmother's. No questions asked. The rushed phone call from my dad had her waiting in her driveway in the increasingly thrashing winds. She opened Betsy's back door and grabbed Peter who was bawling because he wanted the Christmas tree excursion instead of me. They were off to Cedar Rapids and slid across Highway 30 as the wind blew old Betsy from side to side on the ice-patched road.

After arriving to St. Luke's, shaken and relieved, the normal processes of a birth were expected. The only obstacle that remained in their way was the absence of the doctor. Just a small glitch in the situation. The only available staff was an intern who had never delivered a baby before and insisted that my mom resist the contractions until the doctor arrived, and an experienced nurse who served as my mom's sanity for the next two and a half hours. Needless to say, contractions are hard to withstand. The nurse and my dad delivered me, an anxious life that came out shivering. The doctor, held up by the wrath of an Iowa winter storm, walked in at the last minute, his wool coat still covered with a thin layer of white dust.

WORKS CITED

Andrews, Clarence A. *This Is Iowa, A Cavalcade of the Tall Corn State.* Iowa City, IA: Midwest Heritage Publishing Company, 1982.

Angel, Jim. Illinois State Water Survey, *The Cold Hard Facts About Winter Storms.* Illinois: 1999. www.sws.uiuc.edu/atmos/statecli/ winter/coldhard.htm

Erickson, Lori. *Iowa, Off the Beaten Path: A Guide to Unique Places, Second Edition.* Old Saybrook, CN: The Globe Pequot Press, 1990.

Ruffner, James A. *Climates of the States, Third Edition,* Volume 1. Detroit: Gale Research Company, Book Tower, 1985.

Wall, Joseph F. *Iowa, A History.* New York: W. W. Norton, 1978.

WRITING PROCESS NARRATIVE FOR "BLIZZARD BABY"

Dear Wendy,

This was a very interesting project as far as the research that it entailed. When you first assigned this paper, I went out and did lots of research on my birth year. I found information on the major events of 1978, such as the cult suicide or political situations with Jimmy Carter. I gathered advertisements in order to see the styles and differences to the present. I had so much information, but still was not sure where I was going. After talking to several classmates, I decided to do something different. Since we basically were given the freedom to take this paper in any direction, I wanted to narrow my paper down to facts and research that parallels my birth and is fascinating to me: weather patterns, specifically winters in Iowa.

While the majority of the class was jamming as much general facts into their papers, I put away all my research and delved into learning about the patterns of Iowa weather. I lived there for eight years and visit family frequently, so I have had some firsthand experience with the winters, the beautiful aspects and the scary aspects. I wanted to concentrate on my birth as well, because my individual history is an interesting story to me. I went to two libraries and looked up information in climate-related books and checked out several books that catered to just Iowa and its history. I sorted through it all and found a lot of research about the winters in this state.

I was born during a bad snowstorm, something that I know from family stories. But, I hadn't heard this story for quite some time. So, I interviewed both of my parents which was the most helpful research pertaining to the personal aspect of the paper. My parents have been divorced for seventeen years, and it is amazing what memories and details have been lost or morphed in that time period. The general story of my birth was about the same coming from both my mom and my dad. But they each remembered specific details that the other did not. Between the two of them, I gathered the most vivid description of my birth and the weather that surrounded it.

I put together a first draft based primarily on my birth. I then went back and inserted research where I thought it fit best. It seemed to lack research in comparison to other classmate's papers, which concerned me. But I realized that this paper is written by me and that I may not need as much research due to the personal nature of my topic.

After half-class workshop, I felt much better about the quantity of research that I had. Actually, many members of my group felt that the research took away from the personal approach of my paper. Many of them said it was even boring to read. But I still felt that the majority of the research needed to remain in the paper, mainly to follow the guidelines of the assignment. I did cut quite a few weather information pieces out, but I left the ones that seemed the most effective in explaining how brutal Iowa winters could be. And despite that they may not have found the storm research interesting, I kept it. I find weather patterns to be very fascinating myself, especially in a climate where I am not as familiar considering I have lived in the south for fourteen years.

I revised the paper, removing some of the research that did not directly relate to my birth. I also wanted to really locate the readers to rural Iowa during the winter. It is a place that most people know little about, and is very interesting. Location is a big focus for me in most of my writings. I like to feel out a location when I read someone else's work, so I try my hardest to create the same vivid images within my own writing.

Thanks,
Rachel Harrington

ANDREA VACCARO

What Exactly Is a Guide Dog?

CONSIDER THIS:

Andrea Vaccaro was a first year student when she wrote this essay in her composition course. As you read Andrea's essay, consider how this sort of project differs from a traditional research paper. Try completing a post-outline for this paper, noting the conventions of the form, called an "I-Search." Why do you think this project is named I-Search? What sort of voice is used? What author/audience relationship is developed? What are the divisions of the I-search? What do you learn by reading the I-search? What sorts of sources—primary and secondary—are consulted and how are they cited? Now, do the same with a traditional research paper provided by one of your class members. Consider the differences and similarities between these two sorts of research. In particular, note the way each writer handles and presents sources.

As I look around, it seems as though it is raining puppies and dogs. Can you guess where I am? No, it is not the humane society. Give up? I am at a training facility for guide dogs, where everywhere, including the office, there are dogs being played with, spoiled with love, and working hard with their trainers.

Now that I have given you a mental picture of what a guide dog training facility looks like, you might like to know what they actually do there. At least that is what I wanted to know. I was amazed after seeing a student on campus with his guide dog, and watching the two interact together. I stared as the dog helped his master avoid people and stopped at the bottom of each series of steps leading up to the Love Building. I had never seen anything like this before. I believed this showed people how smart dogs are and how humans and dogs can intelligently interact together. This incident is what intrigued me to want to know more about dogs as guides. I wanted to know how guide dogs are chosen and trained. Is there a particular breed that is easier to train? These are the questions we will find the answers to.

I began my search on the Internet. I was very surprised to see how many guide dog training schools have their own websites. Some only talked about how to volunteer or make contributions to their program, but others were very helpful in my search for information. One of the very first sites I visited gave me a great definition of tasks a guide dog is trained to do. According to the Assistance Dogs International website, guide dogs are provided to assist blind and visually impaired people in avoiding obstacles, stopping at curbs and steps, and negotiating traffic. Yet, this is only a small list of what guide dogs are taught. Everything that goes into training a guide dog starts when they are born.

My first question was how are guide dogs chosen? When I asked this question, I believed that the trainers went to people who were selling puppies and performed a few simple tests to see if they would qualify for their program. Little did I know that they have their own little "puppy factory." At each facility, they breed their own dogs. After the puppies are born, the trainers have a larger selection of candidates. This is obviously a more efficient way to have puppies. This answer led me to ask how the schools raise all of those puppies. I found my answer at the Southeastern Guide Dogs Inc. (SEGDI) website. At SEGDI, and all other facilities, the puppies are given to volunteer families who raise the dogs for the first twelve to sixteen months of their lives. These volunteer families are expected to provide love, attention, socialization, and exposure to the surrounding environment. They are also expected to include the dog as a part of the family, taking them to as many places as possible (SEGDI Homepage). This list of responsibilities fails to note the little things. For example, house training the dog, teaching the dog to sit and obey commands, and making sure the dog does not beg for food.

Although it is very hard for volunteer families to give up the dog, they know their sacrifice is helping disadvantaged people live a more normal life. After the twelve to sixteen month time period, the volunteer families return the dogs to the school for evaluation. According to Guiding Eyes, "Only half are deemed suitable for a career as a guide dog" (Burros C1). At Guide Dogs for the Blind, Inc., testers working outdoors note puppies' reactions to pedestrians, stairways, street gates, and cars approaching them from various directions. They also test for "intelligent" responses, such as "following objects readily," "showing curiosity about unfamiliar objects and people," and "adjusting to the tester and the environment" (Harrington 38). A trainer at SEGDI said, "there is no specific test to determine which dog will make a guide" and that they "look for soundness, friendliness, willingness, and confidence level." As you can see, different schools have different procedures.

For the next four months, the chosen dogs go through extensive training. Three of the four months is spent learning everything the dogs will need to know in order to serve their master. The Guide Dog Association says that after the three months of training is complete, the guide dog will be able to walk in a straight line without sniffing, walk on the left hand side slightly ahead of the trainer, stop at all curbs, wait for a command before crossing roads, stop at the top and bottom of stairs, avoid head high obstacles and spaces too narrow for a dog and a person, board and travel on all forms of public transport, take the trainer to lift a button, learn about twenty basic commands, lay quietly in restaurants or at work, and intelligently disobey commands which may lead the handler into danger (Guide Dog Assoc. homepage). As you can see, this list is quite extensive. The fourth month is spent training the dog and its master together as a team. At The Seeing Eye, Inc., handlers spend three or four weeks in The Seeing Eye's training course, living in dorms, taking lectures at night, and working with their dogs during the day (Green 48). This is a very thorough process that can end up costing a lot of money. According to Katherine Ulrich, the approximate amount of money spent is about $10,000 per team. The person who receives the dog has to pay nothing except the food and veterinarian bills for his newly adopted dog. At SEGDI, they receive no help from the government and completely rely on private donations. Yet it is worth all the work and money because these dogs help people live more independent lives. This lifestyle wouldn't have been possible without the dog.

Well, what happens to the dogs that do not pass the school's examination? According to an article in *The New York Times,* some of them join the Bureau of Alcohol, Tobacco and Firearms, where they are trained to sniff out drugs and bombs (Burros C9). As the article said, "Not that those who don't become guide dogs are bums" (Burros C9). Because others become some of the best behaved pets anywhere. Of course, the puppy raisers have the first choice in keeping the dog. Approximately 50 to 60 percent end up deciding to adopt the dog. If they do not adopt the dog, the Guiding Eyes training school screens a long waiting list of applicants (Burros C9).

Because I am a dog lover, I wanted to know which breeds were considered smart enough to do this kind of work. I was hoping, of course, that my dog would be one of them. According to every website, newspaper article, and book I read, Labrador Retrievers, Golden Retrievers, and German Shepherds are the most commonly used dogs in this profession. Rarely are other types of dogs used. I was happy to see that my dog, which is a Golden Retriever, was on the list. Yet I later read an article in which a man named Mr. Abbot, vice president of Guiding Eyes, said, "It is really unusual to find a Golden Retriever . . . They are so affectionate and distractible. But a good one can be really good" (qtd. in Burros C9). At first I was kind of upset. Then I realized that this man was right on target. That is exactly how Goldens are. I know my Golden Retriever never can resist the temptation of chasing a squirrel or ignoring free food. These temptations cannot be indulged if they intend to be a guide dog. Mr. Abbot also talked about German Shepherds, stating that, "German Shepherds are very fast dogs. If there's not a lot for them to do they get bored quickly" (qtd. in Burros C9). So, in this case, Labrador Retrievers made up 90% of this class and were the most used breed at Guiding Eyes (Burros C9).

This about covers the part of my question concerned with how guide dogs are chosen, what they will learn and when they begin training, how long they train for, and what types of breeds are better qualified. But what exactly is entailed in the training process? What do the trainers do in order to teach the dogs how to stop at the bottom of stairs and intelligently disregard an order that may put the team in danger? To find the answer I knew I needed to talk with someone who actually worked with guide dogs. I decided the best place to start was by calling the Florida Division of Blind Services. I was surprised to find out there was only one training center in Florida. I realize now that Florida is lucky to have one because there are only ten guide dog schools in the country. The school is called Southeastern Guide Dogs, SEGDI for short, and it is located in Palmetto. The school is very close to Sarasota, my home town. I had already heard of SEGDI because my mom had said something about it when I told her the topic for my paper. I contacted them through their website. They had an address where e-mail could be sent to ask for more information and questions. I told them about my paper and asked for an interview with one of their trainers. They responded very quickly and said one of their trainers would be happy to have an e-mail interview. I would have rather met the person, but this was better than nothing.

The trainer at SEGDI, Katherine Ulrich, has spent nine years training guide dogs. Katherine has trained approximately 143 dogs. When I asked what made her want to become a guide dog trainer she said, "to help people improve the quality of their life." Guide dogs will provide a new sense of freedom for their masters, and people like Katherine are the ones who will help them achieve this.

How do the trainers teach the dogs to intelligently disobey a harmful order and to stop at the bottom of stairs? According to Katherine Ulrich, it takes, "repetition and consistency." Katherine also said, "Intelligent disobedience is based on self-preservation."

This makes sense, doesn't it? What human or animal wouldn't want to save themselves from harm? Yet Katherine tells us that it is more than that, stating, "the dog must have the confidence to make these decisions" and that, "this develops during the training process." After receiving these responses, I learned a lot of new information that I couldn't find in any books or articles.

Katherine told me that the average working life of a guide dog is eight to ten years. When a guide dog has fulfilled its purpose and can no longer perform its job requirements, there are several different options for them. Most schools have a guide dog retirement program. Once again, the volunteer family who raised the dog as a puppy has the option of adopting the dog first. If not, the dog could be placed in another program. For example, they can help the police in searches for drugs. If the dogs do not go to another program, they are placed in a loving home where they can relax and take a deserved vacation. At SEGDI, some of their older dogs become therapy dogs or demonstration dogs for the school. As you can see, the dogs are well taken care of even after their job is done.

After writing this paper, my view on guide dogs changed completely. I now know just how much hard work and dedication goes into training just one dog. How a family has to put aside its feelings of love and attachment for the dog they have raised for the first year of its life. And how appreciative all the people are when they receive their dog, knowing that so many people sacrificed to give them a new sense of freedom. Hopefully, after reading my paper, you will be more informed about what went into that one well behaved guide dog you may have seen in the grocery store or somewhere else.

WORKS CITED

Assistance Dogs International. 27 Sept. 1998 <http://www. assistance-dogs-intl.org/service.html>.

Green, Kathleen. "You're What? Dog Guide Instructor." *Occupational Outlook Quarterly* VOL # (1996): 47–49.

Guide Dog Association of N.S. Wales and A.C.T. 28 Sept. 1998 <http://www.guide-dogs.com.au/>.

Harrington, Paula. *Guide Dogs for the Blind: Looking Ahead.* San Rafael: Guide Dogs for the Blind, Inc., 1990.

Southeastern Guide Dogs. 27 Sept. 1998 <http://www.guidedogs. org/segd-home.htm>.

Ulrich, Katherine. E-mail to A. Vaccaro. 22 Oct. 1998.

Witchel, Alex. "Teaching Man's Best Eyes to See." *New York Times* 6 Mar. 1996: C1+.

MICHAEL TORRALBA

Radiohead's *OK Computer*

CONSIDER THIS:

Michael Torralba was a first year student when he wrote this essay in his composition course. As you read Michael's essay, consider the way this writer organizes his review/critical response to a popular culture text—a record album. How does this presentation differ from that found in a traditional research paper? How does Michael Torralba build his argument? How convincing is he? Why? Now consider a more traditional research paper provided by a member of your class. Is this paper also presenting an argument? Again, explore the methods used by each author for presenting sources. Why might Internet sources be particularly useful for a research paper like this? Are there potential problems with such sources? Consider some of your own essays in this genre. How do they compare to Torralba's? Given a choice of a personal or a scholarly research project, which do your prefer? Among scholarly genres, which are your favorite? Among informal research genres (I-search, consumer reports, researched essay, and so on), which are your favorites? To write? To read? Why?

In the mid-1990s, rock and roll experienced another of its many transitions. During the early '90s, the "grunge" scene, emanating from Seattle and its surrounding area, enthralled the youth of the time with the music of such acts as Soundgarden, Pearl Jam, and Nirvana. This surge in high-distortion, high angst rock snapped the genre out of the doldrums of glam-metal, which, for a long time, dominated the "rock music" racks of record stores across America.

By 1997, grunge was dead, its end spurred by the death of Kurt Cobain, the impending breakup of Soundgarden, and the increasing vapidity of Pearl Jam. At the same time, bubble gum pop made its comeback, thanks to acts like Hanson and the Spice Girls (even today, irritatingly saccharine acts like the Backstreet Boys and their seemingly infinite clones dominate pop charts). Fortunately, in the summer of 1997, the British rock band Radiohead released *OK Computer,* which received both critical acclaim and commercial success, a rare combination in today's music scene. The album caught enough attention in both respects that it was later nominated for both best alternative album and album of the year and received the former award (Hilburn C-6).

OK Computer is important because it is one of the few albums released in this decade that has an underlying message; Radiohead, while never coming out and stating it, does an excellent job of blending subtlety with clarity.

By both its lyrical and musical complexity, *OK Computer* covers a broad emotional range, evoking, as David Cheal puts it, "gloom and alienation; but you also get warmth and yearning" (15). Dimitri Ehrlich adds that, as a whole, the album is "unglossy, unhandsome, and every bit as complex as modern life" (56).

"Paranoid Android" expresses this complexity at a level in which frustration and alienation come hand in hand. The song, clocking at nearly seven minutes, begins with the elegant plucking of an acoustic guitar and lead singer Thom Yorke's statement of bitterness: "When I am king, you will be first against the wall." After a brief guitar break, the song begins its tremulous diatribe on the loss of identity: "Why don't you remember my name? /Off with his head now, off with his head." The song abruptly changes tempo from a restrained pace to one that is uninhibited and furious. Toward the end of the song, the listener hears another change in pace as it moves to a slow, dirge-like melody as Yorke calmly lists a series of phrases that evoke negative feelings, including "panic" and "vomit"; and then ties them to the phrase "the yuppies networking," which, it can be argued, symbolizes unfettered materialism. As a final statement to the extreme bitterness of "Paranoid Android," Yorke sarcastically sneers, "God loves his children, yeah."

One of the most unique songs on *OK Computer* is "Exit Music (For a Film)." For nearly three minutes, the song consists of the strumming of an acoustic guitar, a synthesized background choir, and, again, Thom Yorke's vocals, which, this time, are delivered much more softly, almost whispered, although delivered with a cold, distant overtone: "Sing us a song/A song to keep us warm/There's such a chill." Then, a drum beat kicks in, accompanied by a low-pitch, synthesizer-generated drone; Yorke's voice becomes more forceful, building to a crescendo, and the softness dematerializes into hard spitefulness. "We hope that you choke," Yorke spits. At this point, it is obvious that *OK Computer* has no chance at turning out to be a happy album.

The next track, "Let Down," best exemplifies the overall bleakness of the album. A relatively simple, Beatles-style guitar riff opposes the depth of the lyrics, which are enunciated with a peculiar slur. The first words Yorke utters relate to "Transport/Motorways and tramlines/Starting and then stopping/Taking off and landing." The marvel of transportation, usually associated with progress, is, in this case, placed in the same context of "the emptiest of feelings." Put simply, the song paints a picture of modern urban life gone horribly wrong; the message is isolation in exchange for utility and comfort. The result is a feeling of existential disappointment, of being "Crushed like a bug in the ground."

"Don't get sentimental," the song warns. "It always end up drivel."

"No Surprises" is another track that stands out. This song takes a stab at suburban idealism. Musically, the song lacks the aggressiveness inherent in "Paranoid Android" and "Exit Music (For a Film)"; it makes up for this through its particularly vicious lyrics. Ironically, the words are delivered in as concise a manner as possible; it is therefore easy not to pick up on their message if one does not pay careful attention. In fact, some of *OK Computer's* most vicious imagery lies in "No Surprises." From the get-go, Thom Yorke delivers thoroughly depressing imagery: "A heart that's full up like a landfill/A job that slowly kills you/ Bruises that won't heal." The phrase "no surprises" is used in a context that implies that life in our sanitized, cushioned world, where everything is comfortable, does not offer emotional fulfillment. The only option that would result in some semblance of peace is "a hand shake and some carbon monoxide."

OK Computer ends on a quiet note. "The Tourist" features a slow, relaxing melody with minimal guitar work. Thom Yorke's vocals are, once again, soothingly delivered, although for one, brief period at the end, they reach a yodel-like climax. "It barks at no one else but me/Like it's seen a ghost/I guess it's seen the sparks a-flowin'/No one else would know." The words seem to be spoken from the point of view of a person who sees something wrong with society, something that no one else seems to notice. "The Tourist" then winds down quickly, with the cryptic warning, "Hey, man, slow down/Idiot, slow down."

The best way to briefly describe *OK Computer* would be a combination of Beatles melodies with Pink Floyd pessimism. The album is great not just because it is a collection of very good songs, but also because the songs, when looked at as a whole, come together to convey a single, underlying theme. This theme, from what can be observed at this point, is the alienation that comes with our increasingly sheltered and computerized world. Musically, *OK Computer* is among the most well executed and creative rock albums of the 1990s. The inventive work of Radiohead's three guitarists, Jonny Greenwood, Ed O'Brien, and Thom Yorke gives the album a solid foundation, and, as Aiden states, "Yorke's swooping tenor voice ties the material together" (27).

WORKS CITED

Aiden, Vaziri. "Radiohead: British Pop Aesthetes." *Guitar Player* Oct. 1997: 27.

Cheal, David. "The Arts: Radiohead Take Off From Planet Mud." *The Daily Telegraph* 30 June 1997: 15.

Ehrlich, Dimitri. "Why Intimacy Matters." *Interview* June 1998: 56.

Hilburn, Robert. "Tuned to Their Own Frequency; A Grammy Nomination Caps a Year as Iconoclastic Radiohead Joined the Resurgence of British Rock." *Los Angeles Times* 22 Feb. 1998: C-6.

CONNECTING TO READING

A. With group members, share some stories of you as a researcher (defined broadly). Gay Lynn Crossley notes that she was a curious child, going to the library to find out about astronomy or architecture. At any age before this year, where did your curiosities lie? What did you ask about? Did you research informally or formally? What types of books did you tend to read? What types of TV shows did you watch? What sort of questions did you ask about the world? Consider the research you actually have wanted to (or have) undertaken at previous ages. What were you terribly curious about in elementary, middle, high school, and as you began (or are beginning) college? Do any of those subjects still hold your interest? Be prepared to share one *brief* story per member with the class as a whole.

B. In a journal entry, considering your past life as a research assignment author, what advice from Peter Elbow and Pat Belanoff and/or Gay Lynn Crossley do you wish you had received? Or if you already had received it, what advice do you wish you had followed? What, if anything, are these authors still not telling you that you need to know to be a successful research writer? Start with a list and end with a 10-minute freewrite that develops from your listing. Post two paragraphs of reflective writing from this journaling on the class discussion list and respond to two postings by classmates.

C. In a discussion group, brainstorm as many humorous, outlandish, ironic, and/or absurd ways a writer could do research based on your reading of Melissa Goldthwaite's and Catherine Wald's essays.

D. Practice responsible Web research with this exercise. Choose a working topic and find six Internet sources: three that appear solid and three that appear dubious. Share these with a group and discuss your evaluation criteria to determine if they agree with you and why. Take home one partner's list—check the citations for bibliographic accuracy and the sites for quality. Return to class and continue your discussion (or complete the assignment on-line in class if you are studying writing in a computer classroom). Since all of us spend much of our research time (consumer as well as scholarly) consulting the Internet, it's important to ascertain whether these sources are valuable, reliable, and current enough to be useful. Remember, too, that websites come and go. If you want your text to endure, rely on sources that you are sure will have a shelf life. Often that means going to the shelves and consulting print texts and reference sources housed in your public or college library. Also, you need to learn to share these citations accurately. Consult the *Columbia Guide to Online Style* (by entering this title in your favorite search engine or go to http://www.columbia.edu/cu/cup/cgos/idx_basic.html for basic directions or information on obtaining a complete guide).

E. In a journal entry that you'll use for speaking notes in class and then submitting to your teacher, analyze the research conducted by the four classroom authors shared in this chatper. If you've written essays similar to theirs, describe what you found most challenging about such assignments. If you haven't undertaken similar work, which sort of text would you be most likely to choose to write? Finally, in some detail, describe what each author does well when conducting and sharing research. Your response to these essays will likely run two or more pages in length and include a list and a narrative.

CONNECTING TO WRITING

A. As a group, compile a class handout, "Top Ten Hints For Research Writers." Consider the elements that have proved crucial to your own success as a researcher. Begin by writing down all the best advice you have for yourself and others as you conduct research. Now, amplify that advice by gleaning tips from each of the authors in the chapter and, if you can, consulting handbooks for research. Groups may choose to work on-line to draft their best version of this handout together. Make copies for your entire class which will analyze the group lists and compile a class advice list of the 20 most useful pieces of advice that could be shared with another writing class or with high school authors.

B. In an exploratory writing, retrieve a memory from your early years and then, sharing copies with peers, decide how you could use research to clarify and augment that memory. Think of a childhood experience that is important to you but about which the exact details are a bit hazy. If you want to *remember* more about that time you went to the Niagara Falls with your middle school, where could you turn to get more vivid and more exact details to vivify your descriptions? (For instance, you could check your yearbook to remember what a friend looked like and what clothes everyone was wearing. Photos or postcards of Niagara Falls also come to mind.)

C. Explicate a literary work using dictionaries, encyclopedias, thesauruses, and common reference texts, as you write informally to understand the text you've chosen, defining words, untangling and paraphrasing, guessing at meanings. Compile a Works Consulted page with accurate citations to accompany this informal writing. As you share this in a group, note which reference books helped your reading. Now, as a writer, reread one of your own texts: a poem or a portion of a story or literary essay. Using Melissa Goldthwaite's and Catherine Wald's essays, choose a poem or short prose text and share with a reader all the influences on it. Some will be evident to readers; some only to you as the author can reveal. This exercise can take the form of double-entry notebooks: in the margins of your text, annotate your writer's research decision process.

D. In an informal position paper, share your understanding of the differences in citation systems. Why do you prefer to cite in one way or the other (if you do), and what influence do you think the Web is going to have on how we track down, trace, and share information (if you think it is having an influence or will have an influence)? What's your position on citing sources? Think about citation systems. How do authors of poems cite research? How do authors of magazine articles—like Wald—cite their sources? How do authors of scholarly works, like those shared in class by classmates or found in handbooks, cite their references? What influences the way sources are used and shared? How does an author know whether to cite sources internally, informally, not at all, or in a Works Cited page? Post this writing on the class discussion board and respond to two peer position papers.

E. In the form of a narrative journal entry, consider your relationship to the literary essay. How is the scholarly essay in your field similar or different? Make a chart that explores these similarities and differences. Now, think of five works of art (literary text, painting, film, CD, etc.) that you care about passionately enough to research and write about. What distinguishes these from those you've been assigned to write on in the past? Do the same with subjects in your field of study (if different than English or the humanities). Use this entry to speak from during a class discussion.

WRITING PROJECTS

1. Research some aspect of your own life. Two of my favorite research essay projects include studying the meaning(s) of your name(s) and investigating local and global events occurring on the day you were born or that took place during your first year of life (see Rachel Harrington's essay). For names, consider who named you. What does your name mean? What notable individuals in history have had a similar name? Interview others with the same name and add their stories to your exploration, and so on. For the day you were born, consult family members but quickly move on to printed sources: newspapers and magazines of the time. What was happening in the world that year? How did the public events around your birth affect your family? Explore, speculate, predict: how does the past influence your present? For either paper, use a mix of primary (interview) and secondary (printed) sources, including *both* library and Internet sources.

2. Research some aspect of a community you have lived in or the community you live in now. That is, you may want to evoke and recreate an environment, landscape, region, city, community you grew up in or around, or you may want to investigate what it is that makes your current community tick (invention handouts in Chapter 4 may provide useful starting prompts for this activity). Think of communities broadly; for instance, you're a member of your major department, your university, your town and your state, as well as the communities you chose to affiliate with (sports, hobbies, religious, service) and so on. In this instance, you may want to introduce, define, or describe this community for those who don't know it. Equally, you may want to create a researched argument about some aspect of community life. For the latter, you'll find ideas in Stuart Greene's essay.
3. Like Andrea Vaccaro, conduct an I-search and share your learning in a personal essay directed to an audience of peers. Kenneth Macrorie developed the I-search project, which is really a process report consisting of three main sections. In the first section, before you search, you explain everything you knew about a topic of your choice before you commenced your formal research process. In the second section, you recount your search for information on that topic. In the final section, you reflect on what you've learned by searching. How well did Andrea Vacarro's essay follow this general outline? You can I-search the practical (what graduate school to attend; what car to buy) or the more esoteric (what independent filmmakers operate out of your city? Who are they and what do they do?). You can write an "I-search a Word" paper: exploring the derivation and meaning of a word and how it has been used through history. Consider an "I-search a Place" paper (think of the vignettes in guide books) and other variations of the I-search format.
4. Research the history of a common object or practice. Where do things (objects, expressions, rituals, habits) we use, need, and take for granted come from? *Panati's Extraordinary Origins* is a book devoted to exploring origins. Choose one of these categories of items to research. Consider what you take for granted in life: superstitions, friction matches, potato chips, lawn mowers, zippers, holidays. For instance, by knowing that the inventor of air-conditioning lived in a nearby Florida town, I might investigate the development of this device since I can't imagine surviving local summers without it. Choose your topic. Research. Share what you learn. For inspira-

tion, reread Margaret Steele's essays in this chapter and return to Amanda Fleming's essays on hunting and taxidermy in Chapter 5.

5. Research for a magazine article suitable for submission to a magazine of your choice. Survey your favorite magazines for samples of research. "Assign" yourself a subject for one of those magazines and write a researched essay or argument that you could submit to the editors. Consider Michael Torralba's music review. Where would you expect to see his essay published? For what reading audience? Now, consider the magazines you like and read. For instance, from surveying the magazines on my table, I could choose to write about higher education for a special issue of *Harpers.* About the artist on show in a downtown museum for *The New Yorker.* About my travels and teaching in Africa for *Doubletake.* About an interview with my favorite poet for *Poets & Writers Magazine.* About new medications for depression or where to eat in the South for *More* and about the fallout from the dismantling of Napster for *Rolling Stone.* To complete my assignment, I'll have to read articles similar to the one I hope to write to see how I should use sources, address my audience, and shape my report. Consider your own aims, audiences, and publishing venues.
6. There's nothing wring with perfecting your technique. Study a literary text, consult critics, and put your voice in dialogue with those voices. You'll find help for completing this often-assigned research task in Edward Corbett's essay on "Formulating a Thesis" found in Chapter 5 and in Peter Elbow and Pat Belanoff's essay which opens this chapter. With your instructor's encouragement, you might benefit from rewriting a paper that you liked but felt was less than successful, using some of the information in this chapter to help you. Equally, work with your teacher who will have advice on the research process. You can find quite a bit of research assistance these days at your campus writing center and through on-line sources using a search engine.
7. Research your future. If you are choosing between majors or heading into a more lengthy course of study in your chosen field, research what it means to be a member of good standing in that community. Combine primary and secondary research: interview those holding your future job, look up government statistics on that occupation, review necessary courses of study that will take you where you want to go. Create a guide for others like you who want to know more about a future career as X, Y, or Z.
8. Create a Web page on a subject of your choice. Research and share your research via links. To design your Web page you'll want to collect more material than you hope to share and then you face the same challenges as any researcher as you sort, evaluate, arrange, and share materials according to the best Web page standards.
9. Make technology and how it's changing our understanding of plagiarism, copyright, intellectual property, or any related issue the subject of your research. Prepare a researched position paper on one of these topics.

10. Use the resources of this chapter to help you complete a research paper assigned in any other course you are taking at this time.

* * * *

I also always get hold of experts and use them. One expert working with deaf children put me in touch with a boy who was also a very good mime artist, and what he showed me about being a mime artist went into the book.

—ALLAN BAILLIE, WRITER

[W]henever I feel that I'm losing my voice in research writing, I go back to earlier pieces I've written (pieces I feel good about, that I like) and reread them. Although they don't all "sound" exactly the same, there's something about the collection as a whole that I identify as "mine": a certain way of phrasing statements, a particular manner of using colons or hyphens, a preference for using some words instead of others. . . . Think about what you like most about your work and how you can incorporate those elements into your research writing.

—CINDY MOORE, WRITING TEACHER

Chapter 8

Examining Experience: Story, Memory, and the Essay

Thinking About Story, Narrative, and the Essay

> I had so many grand ideas about writing that I had forgotten that you have to write to be a writer. . . . [Now,] instead of pondering over ideas and waiting for the perfect one, the one to make me famous, I take small ideas and make them good ones.
>
> —FRANK, CLASSROOM AUTHOR

In the beginning was a story. You listened to your mother and two friends telling stories as they highlighted each other's hair in the kitchen. You listened to three older cousins describing the way each had the biggest car crash *ever* in three different high schools. You listened to your best friend tell about a family trip to the coast. You, in turn, like to tell what happened the year you backpacked for the first time. Eventually, you add this previously rehearsed story to the ones two new college roommates are telling. As you narrate, your story develops more drama and detail. Some facts you cling to—the mountains *were* in Colorado—some facts you change—you went with your family but it seems *more effective* for the story-telling occasion and your story-sharing aims to present the experience as if you were traveling on your own and, in a way, . . . you did since your experiences are *your* experiences.

Next time you tell that story, you work it into an essay investigating your relationship to the environment, focusing on the campground you came upon midday on your first day of hiking and how the sight of four empty cans of Hormel beans and a tattered plastic Wonder hotdog bun wrapper half-buried in a still smoldering campfire in an area restricted to camp stove use only made you wonder about the campers who preceded you and their reasons for having traveled to wilderness territory. Would you see them in the days ahead? Would you be willing to confront them about their abuse of the campground facilities?

Does it matter that it was your father who made that observation about other campers that day? Or does it matter more that you can now use the memory of the way the sun felt warming your shoulders or the way the half-stamped-out, smoking unseasoned ponderosa pine branches and the plastic wrapper seemed to make a blue-skied Colorado morning suddenly tawdry and ominous as you explore the statement you want to make about the world ecology you are inheriting?

Most writers argue that you should make the most of your experiences. Anyone who has ever been involved in a fight with another family member knows that her "true story" of the fight represents only one version of the event: hers. And anyone who has tried to create a totally fictional world without any reference to his past and his life experiences finds that sort of world impossible to achieve, sterile, and unimportant to his readers. Truth and fiction don't start and stop but shade into each other. Is literature fact shaped by the imagination? And, to what extent can nonfiction ever remain unshaped, uncolored by the author's views and opinions, imaginings and real-life situations? Although some fiction relies very little on real events and some fact may be presented with very little apparent personal coloring, most of the time our work declares its facticity or fictionality primarily through accepted literary devices such as "Once upon a time" or "On June 2, 2003." And most writers know that they work in the undefined territory between fact and fiction most of the time.

You'll want to use this overlap to the best of your abilities: To make a point, you may need to leave out some facts. To shape an argument, you may have to overemphasize others. What matters the most will be your understanding of these processes and your own ethical stance. You should know where you stand. If you think it's important to get to the truth behind the event, you'll want to make your way there by the best available means. If you manipulate or shape the facts to deceive the reader, harm other individuals, or bring undeserved glory on yourself . . . well, you know that's not the best course, the moral course, the way you and the readers you respect should be traveling. Whereas you can choose to be an unreliable narrator for a strategic reason or out of ignorance, if you fabricate out of malice, you'll quickly lose your credibility, your readers, and your own sense of learning through writing.

In *The Essay* (National Council of Teachers of English, Urbana, IL 1996), Paul Heilker suggests that the contemporary essay has three primary attributes: it is skeptical—examining and exploring the world from multiple angles and viewpoints; it is antischolastic—considering subjects high and low, sacred and profane, global and local (that is, the essayist takes the *entire* world of lived experience as her subject); and it is organized through associative chains as much as or more than through formal patterns of logic, like those discussed in earlier chapters. The informal essay often offers its readers a thoughtful, wandering, speculative stroll through issues. This does not mean the essay lacks organization and structure, just that essayists may realize their aims and organization through methods other than the "if A then B" sorts of structure demanded by formal essays. Often, essayists organize by emphasizing repetition, metaphor, circularity, analogy, and so on. The thesis/support writer aims for certainty, perhaps writes out of certainty. The informal essayist writes to learn and then shares that learning.

Writers and readers tend to distinguish between formal and informal essays. Formal essays regularly rely on thesis and support organization, may use an impersonal voice, and often appear in scholarly journals across academic disciplines: law, biology, literature, management, medicine. The informal essay is used by scholars, too, generally to reach wider audiences. However, we most often associate the informal essay with personal writing, with memoir, autobiography, analyses of life experiences, observations, and reflections which utilize literary techniques such as dialogue, description, story and vignettes, personal illustrations, metaphor, description, and so on. Often, the informal essayist seems to do what Frank, in the opening quote for this chapter, observes: take small ideas and make them good ones, Authors of essays undertake a philosophical or lyrical investigation of the world. You'll find their (generally) first-person, informal essays in your Sunday newspaper, in literary and national magazines, on best-seller lists, and in college writing courses (you'll find formal essays in college writing courses, too). The personal essay has a long pedigree, but its most important ancestors are Francis Bacon and Michel Montaigne.

During the last half of the twentieth century, in particular, the personal, the informal, the creative, the literary essay challenged the dominance of the novel and short story, and essays now appear regularly alongside fiction and poetry in both popular and literary magazines. A trip through your local bookstore will unearth a number of collections by the contemporary practitioners found in this book who join other well-regarded essayists including Joan Didion, Joseph Epstein, Gretel Erlich, Vickie Carr, Henry Louis Gates, Jr., Judith Ortiz Cofer, and Nancy Mairs, to name only a few.

Because the essay so defined is an investigation, in this chapter authors discuss the possibilities and limits of memory and the uses of story when undertaking personal investigations. They help you think like an essay writer thinks about the relationship of fact to fiction. They encourage you to consider the ways narrative structures and techniques can inform your writing. To do this, you have to explore *how* stories mean as well as *what* they mean. In fact, writing from memory and from experience and then sharing the meaning of those experiences with the world is such a rich endeavor, you'll have to pick and choose, shape and connect, investigate and examine. "So when you're writing about yourself, the problem is what to leave out. . . . You wouldn't want everything; it would be like reading the *Congressional Record*," says journalist Russell Baker. In a manner of speaking, writers use truths to fish for other truths. Most of us rehearse the stories of our lives and to do this, some things are left out so others can advance, take center stage, and help us explore the meanings of all human life.

Possible lives. Possible topics. Possible readers. Improvisation. Writer and teacher Lynn Bloom claims that nonfiction is jazz. And, in a personal essay, novelist Barbara Kingsolver reminds you that writing, at times, is both meditative and personally redemptive:

> In my own worst seasons I've come back from the colorless world of despair by forcing myself to look hard, for a long time, at a single glorious thing: a flame of red geranium outside my bedroom window. And then another: my daughter

> in a yellow dress. And another: the perfect outline of a full, dark sphere behind the crescent moon. Until I learned to be in love with my life again. Like a stroke victim retraining new parts of the brain to grasp lost skills, I have taught myself joy, over and over again.

This may have happened to you. By concentrating on your experiences you come to know them better and begin to understand the world and your place in it. By doing this work through essay writing, you allow writers to undertake such a journey with you.

Why do stories matter? In his essay, Scott Russell Sanders explores 10 reasons and argues that stories are central to human experience. Narratives are told in all cultures and often follow similar patterns: A scene is set and listeners are oriented. Something happens and events are complicated. The storyteller evaluates the action, holding up the events for you to examine with him. There is a result or a resolution, and together, writer and reader share meaning. Dean Newman's narrative illustrates one such sequence: event, complication, evaluation, resolution. Patricia Hampl, Lynna Williams, and Barbara Kingsolver follow with essays that explore the complicated connections between fact and fiction, memory and family, narrative and representation. Donald Murray orients you to aspects of the essay form. In "Try This," I offer possible essay invention topics, illustrating each topic-cluster with brief excerpts from writing students who undertook work in those areas.

Topics similar to those I suggest are explored by a number of classroom authors in this chapter. Leah Marcum uses a sequence of stories to write an essay investigating her love of storms and hurricanes, she examines experience—as you may in your own personal essay—using many of the writing strategies discussed in this chapter. Marcum's essay is followed by that of Keith Gawrys who explores childhood memories. In her essay, Carlyn Maddox also investigates family, honoring and sharing her grandfather's life but doing so in a way that is dramatic yet avoids the dangers of sentiment. While Keith Gawrys explores one childhood location and memory and Carlyn Maddox focuses on one family member, Jay Szczepanski's essay "Story Simply Told" roams more broadly and molds a number of explorations into a multifaceted investigation of self.

Chapter Readings

SCOTT RUSSELL SANDERS (b. 1945)

The Most Human Art: Ten Reasons Why We'll Always Need a Good Story

CONSIDER THIS:

Scott Russell Sanders is a master of the personal essay. "When I started writing essays 20 years ago, I didn't have a name for them," he told *The Kenyon Review.* "At the time I was working on a novel called *Bad Man Ballad.* But I got stuck—I couldn't get the narrator's voice right. So I decided to take a break from the novel and write something else, which turned out to be a simple account of a walk I had taken the previous weekend while carrying my 1-year-old son in a backpack. That piece became 'Cloud Crossing' in *The Paradise of Bombs.* It was my first personal essay, although at the time I probably would have called it a story from life."

Sanders has taught at Indiana University since 1971 and his work often appears in journals and periodicals, including *Harper's* and *Audubon* magazines, and he has received fellowships from the National Endowment for the Arts and the Guggenheim Foundation. Many of Sanders's stories and essays share a common theme. "No matter how much I write about the possibility of peace and commitment and love," he said in an interview in *The Sun* magazine, "I bear in mind the threat of cruelty, the certainty of pain and loss. I write always in the face of grief. I write about hope because I wrestle with despair." Also, as a major concern of Sanders's is the troubling state of our ecosystem, he sometimes feels as if he's "digging a hole in the sand, in which sand keeps running back in." The title of this selection is eye-catching; most of us like to make lists (think of how central lists are to the *Late Show with Dave Letterman*). As you read, note the way Sanders turns a list into an essay. Analyze the way he organizes his exploration of the importance of story to humans.

We have been telling stories to one another for a long time, perhaps for as long as we have been using language, and we have been using language, I suspect, for as long as we have been human. In all its guises, from words spoken and written to pictures and musical notes and mathematical symbols, language is our distinguishing gift, our hallmark as a species.

We delight in stories, first of all, because they are a playground for language, an arena for exercising this extraordinary power. The spells and enchantments that figure in so many titles remind us of the ambiguous potency in words, for creating or destroying, for binding or setting free. Italo Calvino, a wizard of storytelling, described literature as "a struggle to escape from the confines of language; it stretches out from the utmost limits of what can be said; what stirs literature is the call and attraction of what is not in the dictionary." Calvino's remark holds true, I believe, not just for the highfalutin modes we label as literature, but for every effort to make sense of our lives through narrative.

Second, stories create community. They link teller to listeners, and listeners to one another. This is obviously so when speaker and audience share the same space, as humans have done for all but the last few centuries of our million-year history; but it is equally if less obviously so in our literate age, when we encounter more of our stories in solitude, on page or screen. When two people discover they have both read *Don Quixote,* they immediately share a piece of history and become thereby less strange to one another.

The strongest bonds are formed by sacred stories, which unite entire peoples. Thus Jews rehearse the events of Passover; Christians tell of a miraculous birth and death and resurrection; Buddhists tell of Gautama meditating beneath a tree. As we know only too well, sacred stories may also divide the world between those who are inside the circle and those who are outside, a division that has inspired pogroms and inquisitions and wars. There is danger in story, as in any great force. If the tales that captivate us are silly or deceitful, like most of those offered by television and advertising, they waste our time and warp our desires. If they are cruel, they make us callous. If they are false and bullying, instead of drawing us into a thoughtful community they may lure us into an unthinking herd or, worst of all, into a crowd screaming for blood—in which case we need other, truer stories to renew our vision. So *The Diary of Anne Frank* is an antidote to *Mein Kampf.* So Ralph Ellison's *Invisible Man* is an antidote to the paranoid yarns of the Ku Klux Klan. Just as stories may rescue us from loneliness, so, by speaking to us in private, they may rescue us from mobs.

This brings me to the third item on my list: Stories help us to see through the eyes of other people. Here my list overlaps with one compiled by Carol Bly, who argues in "Six Uses of Story" that the foremost gift from stories is "experience of *other.*" For the duration of a story, children may sense how it is to be old, and the elderly may recall how it is to be young: men may try on the experiences of women, and women those of men. Through stories, we reach across the rifts not only of gender and age, but also of race and creed, geography and class, even the rifts between species or between enemies.

Folktales and fables and myths often show humans talking and working with other animals, with trees, with rivers and stones, as if recalling or envisioning a time of easy commerce among all beings. Helpful ducks and cats and frogs, wise dragons, stolid oaks all have lessons for us in these old tales. Of course no storyteller can literally become hawk or pine, any more than a man can become a woman; we cross those boundaries only imperfectly, through leaps of imagination. "Could a greater miracle take place than for us to look through each other's eyes for an instant?" Thoreau asks. We come nearer to achieving that miracle in stories than anywhere else.

A fourth power of stories is to show us the consequences of our actions. To act responsibly, we must be able to foresee where our actions might lead; and stories train our sight. They reveal the patterns of human conduct, from motive through action to result. Whether or not a story has a moral purpose, therefore, it cannot help but have a moral effect, for better or worse.

An Apache elder, quoted by the anthropologist Keith Basso, puts the case directly: "Stories go to work on you like arrows. Stories make you live right. Stories make you replace yourself." Stories do work on us, on our minds and hearts, showing us how we might act, who we might become, and why.

So we arrive at a fifth power of stories, which is to educate our desires. Instead of playing on our selfishness and fear, stories can give us images for what is truly worth seeking, worth having, worth doing. I mean here something more than the way fairy tales repeat our familiar longings. I mean the way *Huckleberry Finn* makes us want to be faithful, the way *Walden* makes us yearn to confront the essential facts of life. What stories at their best can do is lead our desires in new directions—away from greed, toward generosity; away from suspicion, toward sympathy; away from an obsession with material goods, toward a concern for spiritual goods.

One of the spiritual goods I cherish is the peace of being at home, in family and neighborhood and community and landscape. Much of what I know about becoming intimate with one's home ground I have learned from reading the testaments of individuals who have decided to stay put. The short list of my teachers would include Lao-tzu and Thoreau and Faulkner, Thomas Merton, Black Elk, Aldo Leopold, Rachel Carson, Gary Snyder, and Wendell Berry. Their work exemplifies the sixth power of stories, which is to help us dwell in place.

According to Eudora Welty, herself a deeply rooted storyteller, "the art that speaks most clearly, explicitly, directly, and passionately from its place of origin will remain the longest understood." So we return to the epic of Gilgamesh, with its brooding on the forests and rivers of Babylonia; we return to the ancient Hebrew accounts of a land flowing with milk and honey; we follow the Aboriginal songs of journeys over the continent of Australia—because they all convey a passionate knowledge of place.

Native American tribes ground their stories in nearby fields and rivers and mountains, and thus carry their places in mind. As the Pueblo travel in their homeland, according to Leslie Marmon Silko, they recall the stories that belong to each mesa and arroyo, and "thus the continuity and accuracy of the oral narratives are reinforced by the landscape—and the Pueblo interpretation of that landscape is *maintained.*

Stories of place help us recognize that we belong to the earth, blood and brain and bone, and that we are kin to other creatures. Life has never been easy, yet in every continent we find tales of a primordial garden, an era of harmony and bounty. In *A God Within,* René Dubos suggests that these old tales might be recollections "of a very distant past when certain groups of people had achieved biological fitness to their environment." Whether or not our ancestors ever lived in ecological balance, if we aspire to do so in the future, we must nourish the affectionate, imaginative bond between person and place.

Mention of past and future brings us to the seventh power of stories, which is to help us dwell in time. I am thinking here not so much of the mechanical time parceled out by clocks as of historical and psychological time. History is public, a tale of influences and events that have shaped the present; the mind's time is private, a flow of memory and anticipation that continues, in eddies and rapids, for as long as we are conscious. Narrative orients us in both kinds of time, private and public, by linking before and after within the lives of characters and communities, by showing action leading on to action, moment to moment, beginning to middle to end.

Once again we come upon the tacit morality of stories, for moral judgment relies, as narrative does, on a belief in cause and effect. Stories teach us that every gesture, every act, every choice we make sends ripples of influence into the future. Thus we hear that the caribou will only keep giving themselves to the hunter if the hunter kills them humbly and respectfully. We hear that all our deeds are recorded in some heavenly book, in the grain of the universe, in the mind of God, and that everything we sow we shall reap.

Stories gather experience into shapes we can hold and pass on through time, much the way DNA molecules in our cells record genetic discoveries and pass them on. Until the invention of writing, the discoveries of the tribe were preserved and transmitted by storytellers, above all by elders. "Under hunter-gatherer conditions," Jared Diamond observes, "the knowledge possessed by even one person over the age of 70 could spell the difference between survival and starvation for a whole clan."

Aware of time passing, however, we mourn things passing away, and we often fear the shape of things to come. Hence our need for the eighth power of stories, which is to help us deal with suffering, loss, and death. From the Psalms to the Sunday comics, many tales comfort the fearful and the grieving; they show the weak triumphing over the strong, love winning out over hatred, laughter defying misery. It is easy to dismiss this hopefulness as escapism, but as Italo Calvino reminds us, "For a prisoner, to escape has always been a good thing, and an individual escape can be a first necessary step toward a collective escape."

Those who have walked through the valley of the shadow of death tell stories as a way of fending off despair. Thus Aleksandr Solzhenitsyn tells of surviving the Soviet gulag; Toni Morrison recounts the anguish of plantation life; Black Elk tells about the slaughter of the buffalo, the loss of his Lakota homeland. Those of us who have not lived through horrors must still face losing all that we love, including our own lives. Stories reek of our obsession with mortality. As the most enchanting first line of a tale is "once upon a time," so the most comforting last line is "and they lived happily ever after." This fairy-tale formula expresses a deep longing not only for happiness, but also for ever-afterness, for an assurance that life as well as happiness will endure, that it will survive all challenges, perhaps even the grave. We feel the force of that longing, whether or not we believe that it can ever be fulfilled,

The ninth item on my list is really a summation of all that I have said thus far: Stories teach us how to be human. We are creatures of instinct, but not solely of instinct. More than any other animal, we must *learn* how to behave. In this perennial effort, as Ursula Le Guin says, "story is our nearest and dearest way of understanding our lives and finding our way onward." Skill is knowing how to do something; wisdom is knowing when and why to do it or to refrain from doing it. While stories may display skill aplenty, in technique or character or plot, what the best of them offer is wisdom. They hold a living reservoir of human possibilities, telling us what has worked before, what has failed, where meaning and purpose and joy might be found. At the heart of many tales is a test, a riddle, a problem to solve; and that, surely, is the condition of our lives, both in detail—as we decide how to act in the present moment—and in general, as we seek to understand what it all means. Like so many characters, we are lost in a dark wood, a labyrinth, a swamp, and we need a trail of stories to show us the way back to our true home.

Our ultimate home is the Creation, and anyone who pretends to comprehend this vast and intricate abode is either a lunatic or a liar. In spite of all that we have learned through millennia of inquiry, we still dwell in mystery. Why there is a universe, why we are here, why there is life or consciousness at all, where if anywhere the whole show is headed—these are questions for which we have no final answers. Not even the wisest of tales can tell us. The wisest, in fact, acknowledge the wonder and mystery of Creation—and that is the tenth power of stories.

In the beginning, we say, *at the end of time,* we say, but we are only guessing. "I think one should work into a story the idea of not being sure of all things," Borges advised, "because that's the way reality is." The magic and romance, the devils and divinities we imagine, are pale tokens of the forces at play around us. The elegant, infinite details of the world's unfolding, the sheer existence of hand or tree or star, are more marvelous than anything we can say about them.

A number of modern physicists have suggested that the more we learn about the universe, the more it seems like an immense, sustained, infinitely subtle flow of consciousness—the more it seems, in fact, like a grand story, lavishly imagined and set moving. In scriptures we speak of God's thoughts as if we could read them; but we read only by the dim light of a tricky brain on a young planet near a middling star. Nonetheless, we need these cosmic narratives, however imperfect they may be, however filled with guesswork. So long as they remain open to new vision, so long as they are filled with awe, they give us hope of finding meaning within the great mystery.

DEAN NEWMAN (b. 1949)

Becky's Mirror

CONSIDER THIS:

Dean Newman works as an editor for the Florida Department of Education and has taught writing at Tallahassee Community College and Florida State University. A musician and storyteller, he reads for the literary journal *Apalachee Review* and has published fiction in *Sundog, West Wind Review,* the on-line journal *Kudzu Quarterly,* and other magazines. Think about this piece of flash (very short) nonfiction in light of Scott Russell Sanders's 10 reasons humans tell stories. Which of these reasons seem to have prompted Newman? How many of the reasons Sanders lists do you find applicable to this narrative? Of what story of your own, from your own life, does this essay most remind you? Tell that story to your peers.

I know I had on those heavy, steel-toed boots—my legs felt like lead on each step up to the front porch of the house. I must have been working with logs—cutting lodge pole pines—peeling them with a drawknife—laying them out—notching them—rolling them up an incline with a kant hook—bone tired. So it must have been '79 or '80, and my legs were lead, and I sat on the top step and began to unlace the boots and struggle them off my tired feet.

Then I heard my daughter's voice behind me—Leah—two or three then. Probably three. When I turned around and looked, I could see her through the sliding glass door—sitting on the floor and talking to herself. It was that adult, mother voice she used with her dolls.

Watching a child play when they don't know you're watching is better than stopping to smell any roses I've ever smelled. It's a sweet, sweet, painful moment because we're grown up, and we know.

In my stockinged feet, carrying my heavy boots, I moved slowly toward the door so I could see her better without catching her attention.

She sat splay-legged on the floor with a doll sitting between her legs. Leah was brushing Becky's hair. Becky had on a brown, gingham dress—but no shoes—eaten by the dog. Becky's hat, a wide brimmed sun hat with a ribbon hanging down the back, lay on the floor beside her. Leah was telling her what pretty hair she had. She told Becky more sternly, "Try to stay clean for ten minutes and don't wipe your nose on your new dress."

Then she sensed me watching.

She leapt up and ran to the door with Becky tucked tightly under her arm, leaned hard against the glass to help me push the sliding door open, then threw her free arm around one of my legs and, now in her wounded child voice, said, "Dad, one of the boys took Becky's meer, and they won't tell me where it is." Jesse and Jeremy—her two older brothers.

At that moment—I don't know why—I decided I should correct my daughter's pronunciation. I said, "Honey, it's mirror—the word is mir-ror."

I don't know what I expected from such a little girl, but when she stopped hugging my leg and looked up at me—without speaking—looking me in the eyes—gauging something, I think—I felt doubt and said, "It's pronounced mir-ror."

Leah's mouth opened slightly—in a look that I swear was grown up doubt. With a bit of a sneer, she said, "No it's not."

Feeling very sure of myself about this, I said "Yes it is. It's mir-ror."

She sighed a deep, bothered sigh and took me by my free hand and led me, still carrying the heavy boots, across the living room and down the hall to the bathroom. She pulled me inside and shut the door behind us. She stepped up to the full length mirror on the back of the door—looked at her reflection for a moment—a long moment—then she looked up at me and said, "See that? That's me. It's a Me-er."

PATRICIA HAMPL (b. 1946)

Memory and Imagination

CONSIDER THIS:

Patricia Hampl was born in St. Paul, Minnesota, received her MFA from the University of Iowa, and has taught at the University of Minnesota since 1979. Her work has appeared in *The American Poetry Review,* the *New Yorker,* and the *Paris Review,* among many other publications, and she has received a number of awards for both poetry and prose.

Hampl does not like to pigeonhole literature. "Memoir still is in the wet-cement stage," Hampl said in a *Pioneer Press* interview. "I like its mongrel nature. There is something culturally healthy about literature not being cordoned off with fences around it." Hampl's teaching statement also reflects her rounded views about writing: "I came to teaching after working as an editor and freelance writer so I may have a tendency to see my students as colleagues. I think of us as working on their writing in order to get it ready for an imaginary magazine I'm editing. I like that moment when a student sees that sentences have sinew; that language is as physical in its way as paint is for an artist. Then we're cooking." Hampl's essay "Memory and Imagination" seems to illustrate her beliefs as shared in these interviews. What do you think she means when she claims memoir is a "mongrel" form? As you read the essay, consider its mongrel nature. How does Hampl use story? Exposition or exploration? What is the effect of the essay and how do you respond to it? What do you think she's "cooking"?

When I was seven, my father, who played the violin on Sundays with a nicely tortured flair which we considered artistic, led me by the hand down a long, unlit corridor in St. Luke's School basement, a sort of tunnel that ended in a room full of pianos. There many little girls and a single sad boy were playing truly tortured scales and arpeggios in a mash of troubled sound. My father gave me over to Sister Olive Marie, who did look remarkably like an olive.

Her oily face gleamed as if it had just been rolled out of a can and laid on the white plate of her broad, spotless wimple. She was a small, plump woman; her body and the small window of her face seemed to interpret the entire alphabet of olive: her face was a sallow green olive placed upon the jumbo ripe olive of her black habit. I trusted her instantly and smiled, glad to have my hand placed in the hand of a woman who made sense, who provided the satisfaction of being what she was: an Olive who looked like an Olive.

My father left me to discover the piano with Sister Olive Marie so that one day I would join him in mutually tortured piano-violin duets for the edification of my mother and brother who sat at the table meditatively spooning in the last of their pineapple sherbet until their part was called for: they put down their spoons and clapped while we bowed, while the sweet ice in their bowls melted, while the music melted, and we all melted a little into each other for a moment.

But first Sister Olive must do her work. I was shown middle C, which Sister seemed to think terribly important. I stared at middle C and then glanced away for a second. When my eye returned, middle C was gone, its slim finger lost in the complicated grasp of the keyboard. Sister Olive struck it again, finding it with laughable ease. She emphasized the importance of middle C, its central position, a sort of North Star of sound. I remember thinking, "Middle C is the belly button of the piano," an insight whose originality and accuracy stunned me with pride. For the first time in my life I was astonished by metaphor. I hesitated to tell the kindly Olive for some reason; apparently I understood a true metaphor is a risky business, revealing of the self. In fact, I have never, until this moment of writing it down, told my first metaphor to anyone.

Sunlight flooded the room; the pianos, all black, gleamed. Sister Olive, dressed in the colors of the keyboard, gleamed; middle C shimmered with meaning and I resolved never—never—to forget its location: it was the center of the world.

Then Sister Olive, who had had to show me middle C twice but who seemed to have drawn no bad conclusions about me anyway, got up and went to the windows on the opposite wall. She pulled the shades down, one after the other. The sun was too bright, she said. She sneezed as she stood at the windows with the sun shedding its glare over her. She sneezed and sneezed, crazy little convulsive sneezes one after another, as helpless as if she had the hiccups.

"The sun makes me sneeze," she said when the fit was over and she was back at the piano. This was odd, too odd to grasp in the mind. I associated sneezing with colds, and colds with rain, fog, snow and bad weather. The sun, however, had caused Sister Olive to sneeze in this wild way, Sister Olive who gleamed benignly and who was so certain of the location of the center of the world. The universe wobbled a bit and became unreliable. Things were not, after all, necessarily what they seemed. Appearance deceived: here was the sun acting totally out of character, hurling this woman into sneezes, a woman so mild that she was named, so it seemed, for a bland object on a relish tray.

I was given a red book, the first Thompson book, and told to play the first piece over and over at one of the black pianos where the other children were crashing away. This, I was told, was called practicing. It sounded alluringly adult, practicing. The piece itself consisted mainly of middle C, and I excelled, thrilled by my savvy at being able to locate that central note amidst the cunning camouflage of all the other white keys before me. Thrilled too by the shiny red book that gleamed, as the pianos did, as Sister Olive did, as my eager eyes probably did. I sat at the formidable machine of the piano and got to know middle C intimately, preparing to be as tortured as I could manage one day soon with my father's violin at my side.

But at the moment Mary Katherine Reilly was at my side, playing something at least two or three lessons more sophisticated than my piece. I believe she even struck a chord. I glanced at her from the peasantry of single notes, shy, ready to pay homage. She turned toward me, stopped playing, and sized me up.

Sized me up and found a person ready to be dominated. Without introduction she said, "My grandfather invented the collapsible opera hat."

I nodded, I acquiesced, I was hers. With that little stroke it was decided between us—that she should be the leader, and I the side-kick. My job was admiration. Even when she added, "But he didn't make a penny from it. He didn't have a patent"—even then, I knew and she knew that this was not an admission of powerlessness, but the easy candor of a master, of one who can afford a weakness or two.

With the clairvoyance of all fated relationships based on dominance and submission, it was decided in advance: that when the time came for us to play duets, I should always play second piano, that I should spend my allowance to buy her the Twinkies she craved but was not allowed to have, that finally, I should let her copy from my test paper, and when confronted by our teacher, confess with convincing hysteria that it was I, I who had cheated, who had reached above myself to steal what clearly belonged to the rightful heir of the inventor of the collapsible opera hat. . . .

There must be a reason I remember that little story about my first piano lesson. In fact, it isn't a story, just a moment, the beginning of what could perhaps become a story. For the memoirist, more than for the fiction writer, the story seems already *there,* already accomplished and fully achieved in history ("in reality," as we naively say). For the memoirist, the writing of the story is a matter of transcription.

That, anyway, is the myth. But no memoirist writes for long without experiencing an unsettling disbelief about the reliability of memory, a hunch that memory is not, after all, *just* memory. I don't know why I remember this fragment about my first piano lesson. I don't, for instance, have a single recollection of my first arithmetic lesson, the first time I studied Latin, the first time my grandmother tried to teach me to knit. Yet these things occurred too, and must have their stories.

It is the piano lesson that has trudged forward, clearing the haze of forgetfulness, showing itself bright with detail more than thirty years after the event. I did not choose to remember the piano lesson. It was simply there, like a book that has always been on the shelf, whether I ever read it or not, the binding and title showing as I skim across the contents of my life. On the day I wrote this fragment I happened to take that memory, not some other, from the shelf and paged through it. I found more detail, more event, perhaps a little more entertainment than I had expected, but the memory itself was there from the start. Waiting for me.

Or was it? When I reread what I had written just after I finished it, I realized that I had told a number of lies. I *think* it was my father who took me the first time for my piano lesson—but maybe he only took me to meet my teacher and there was no actual lesson that day. And did I even know then that he played the violin—didn't he take up his violin again much later, as a result of my piano playing, and not the reverse? And is it even remotely accurate to describe as "tortured" the musicianship of a man who began every day by belting out "Oh What a Beautiful Morning" as he shaved?

More: Sister Olive Marie did sneeze in the sun, but was her name Olive? As for her skin tone—I would have sworn it was olive-like; I would have been willing to spend the better part of an afternoon trying to write the exact description of imported Italian or Greek olive her face suggested: I wanted to get it right. But now, were I to write that passage over, it is her intense black eyebrows I would see, for suddenly they seem the central fact of that face, some indicative mark of her serious and patient nature. But the truth is, I don't remember the woman at all. She's a sneeze in the sun and a finger touching middle C. That, at least, is steady and clear.

Worse: I didn't have the Thompson book as my piano text. I'm sure of that because I remember envying children who did have this wonderful book with its pictures of children and animals printed on the pages of music.

As for Mary Katherine Reilly. She didn't even go to grade school with me (and her name isn't Mary Katherine Reilly—but I made that change on purpose). I met her in Girl Scouts and only went to school with her later, in high school. Our relationship was not really one of leader and follower; I played first piano most of the time in duets. She certainly never copied anything from a test paper of mine: she was a better student, and cheating just wasn't a possibility with her. Though her grandfather (or someone in her family) did invent the collapsible opera hat and I remember that she was proud of that fact, she didn't tell me this news as a deft move in a childish power play.

So, what was I doing in this brief memoir? Is it simply an example of the curious relation a fiction writer has to the material of her own life? Maybe. That may have some value in itself. But to tell the truth (if anyone still believes me capable of telling the truth), I wasn't writing fiction. I was writing memoir—or was trying to. My desire was to be accurate. I wished to embody the myth of memoir: to write as an act of dutiful transcription.

Yet clearly the work of writing narrative caused me to do something very different from transcription. I am forced to admit that memoir is not a matter of transcription, that memory itself is not a warehouse of finished stories, nor a static gallery of framed pictures. I must admit that I invented. But why?

Two whys: why did I invent, and then, if a memoirist must inevitably invent rather than transcribe, why do I—why should anybody—write memoir at all?

I must respond to these impertinent questions because they, like the bumper sticker I saw the other day commanding all who read it to QUESTION AUTHORITY, challenge my authority as a memoirist and as a witness.

It still comes as a shock to realize that I don't write about what I know: I write in order to find out what I know. Is it possible to convey to a reader the enormous degree of blankness, confusion, hunch and uncertainty lurking in the act of writing? When I am the reader, not the writer, I too fall into the lovely illusion that the words before me (in a story by Mavis Gallant, an essay by Carol Bly, a memoir by M. F. K. Fisher), which *read* so inevitably, must also have been *written* exactly as they appear, rhythm and cadence, language and syntax, the powerful waves of the sentences laying themselves on the smooth beach of the page one after another faultlessly.

But here I sit before a yellow legal pad, and the long page of the preceding two paragraphs is a jumble of crossed-out lines, false starts, confused order. A mess. The mess of my mind trying to find out what it wants to say. This is a writer's frantic, grabby mind, not the poised mind of a reader ready to be edified or entertained.

I sometimes think of the reader as a cat, endlessly fastidious, capable, by turns, of mordant indifference and riveted attention, luxurious, recumbent, and ever poised. Whereas the writer is absolutely a dog, panting and moping, too eager for an affectionate scratch behind the ears, lunging frantically after any old stick thrown in the distance.

The blankness of a new page never fails to intrigue and terrify me. Sometimes, in fact, I think my habit of writing on long yellow sheets comes from an atavistic fear of the writer's stereotypic "blank white page." At least when I begin writing, my page isn't utterly blank; at least it has a wash of color on it, even if the absence of words must finally be faced on a yellow sheet as truly as on a blank white one. Well, we all have our ways of whistling in the dark.

If I approach writing from memory with the assumption that I know what I wish to say, I assume that intentionality is running the show. Things are not that simple. Or perhaps writing is even more profoundly simple, more telegraphic and immediate in its choices than the grating wheels and chugging engine of logic and rational intention. The heart, the guardian of intuition with its secret, often fearful intentions, is the boss. Its commands are what a writer obeys—often without knowing it. Or, I do.

That's why I'm a strong adherent of the first draft. And why it's worth pausing for a moment to consider what first draft really is. By my lights, the piano lesson memoir is a first draft. That doesn't mean it exists here exactly as I first wrote it. I like to think I've cleaned it up from the first time I put it down on paper. I've cut some adjectives here, toned down the hyperbole there, smoothed a transition, cut a repetition—that sort of housekeeperly tidying-up. But the piece remains a first draft because I haven't yet gotten to know it, haven't given it a chance to tell me anything. For me, writing a first draft is a little like meeting someone for the first time. I come away with a wary acquaintanceship, but the real friendship (if any) and genuine intimacy—that's all down the road. Intimacy with a piece of writing, as with a person, comes from paying attention to the revelations it is capable of giving, not by imposing my own preconceived notions, no matter how well-intentioned they might be.

I try to let pretty much anything happen in a first draft. A careful first draft is a failed first draft. That may be why there are so many inaccuracies in the piano lesson memoir: I didn't censor, I didn't judge. I kept moving. But I would not publish this piece as a memoir on its own in its present state. It isn't the "lies" in the piece that give me pause, though a reader has a right to expect a memoir to be as accurate as the writer's memory can make it. No, it isn't the lies themselves that makes the piano lesson memoir a first draft and therefore "unpublishable."

The real trouble: the piece hasn't yet found its subject; it isn't yet about what it wants to be about. Note: what *it* wants, not what I want. The difference has to do with the relation a memoirist—any writer, in fact—has to unconscious or half-known intentions and impulses in composition.

Now that I have the fragment down on paper, I can read this little piece as a mystery which drops clues to the riddle of my feelings, like a culprit who wishes to be apprehended. My narrative self (the culprit who has invented) wishes to be discovered by my reflective self, the self who wants to understand and make sense of a half-remembered story about a nun sneezing in the sun. . . .

We only store in memory images of value. The value may be lost over the passage of time (I was baffled about why I remembered that sneezing nun, for example), but that's the implacable judgment of feeling: *this,* we say somewhere deep within us, is something I'm hanging on to. And of course, often we cleave to things because they possess heavy negative charges. Pain likes to be vivid.

Over time, the value (the feeling) and the stored memory (the image) may become estranged. Memoir seeks a permanent home for feeling and image, a habitation where they can live together in harmony. Naturally, I've had a lot of experiences since I packed away that one from the basement of St. Luke's School; that piano lesson has been effaced by waves of feeling for other moments and episodes. I persist in believing the event has value—after all, I remember it—but in writing the memoir I did not simply relive the experience. Rather, I explored the mysterious relationship between all the images I could round up and the even more impacted feelings that caused me to store the images safely away in memory. Stalking the relationship, seeking the congruence between stored image and hidden emotion—that's the real job of memoir.

By writing about the first piano lesson, I've come to know things I could not know otherwise. But I only know these things as a result of reading this first draft. While I was writing, I was following the images, letting the details fill the room of the page and use the furniture as they wished. I was their dutiful servant—or thought I was. In fact, I was the faithful retainer of my hidden feelings which were giving the commands.

I really did feel, for instance, that Mary Katherine Reilly was far superior to me. She was smarter, funnier, more wonderful in every way—that's how I saw it. Our friendship (or she herself) did not require that I become her vassal, yet perhaps in my heart that was something I wanted; I wanted a way to express my feeling of admiration. I suppose I waited until this memoir to begin to find the way.

Just as, in the memoir, I finally possess that red Thompson book with the barking dogs and bleating lambs and winsome children. I couldn't (and still can't) remember what my own music book was, so I grabbed the name and image of the one book I could remember. It was only in reviewing the piece after writing it that I saw my inaccuracy. In pondering this "lie," I came to see what I was up to: I was getting what I wanted. At last.

The truth of many circumstances and episodes in the past emerges for the memoirist through details (the red music book, the fascination with a nun's name and gleaming face), but these details are not merely information, not flat facts. Such details are not allowed to lounge. They must work. Their work is the creation of symbol. But it's more accurate to call it the *recognition* of symbol. For meaning is not "attached" to the detail by the memoirist; meaning is revealed. That's why a first draft is important. Just as the first meeting (good or bad) with someone who later becomes the beloved is important and is often reviewed for signals, meanings, omens and indications.

Now I can look at that music book and see it not only as "a detail," but for what it is, how it *acts.* See it as the small red door leading straight into the dark room of my childhood longing and disappointment. That red book *becomes* the palpable evidence of that longing. In other words, it becomes symbol. There is no symbol, no life-of-the-spirit in the general or the abstract. Yet a writer wishes—indeed all of us wish—to speak about profound matters that are, like it or not, general and abstract. We wish to talk to each other about life and death, about love, despair, loss, and innocence. We sense that in order to live together we must learn to speak of peace, of history, of meaning and values. Those are a few.

We seek a means of exchange, a language which will renew these ancient concerns and make them wholly and pulsingly ours. Instinctively, we go to our store of private images and associations for our authority to speak of these weighty issues. We find, in our details and broken and obscured images, the language of symbol. Here memory impulsively reaches out its arms and embraces imagination. That is the resort to invention. It isn't a lie, but an act of necessity, as the innate urge to locate personal truth always is.

All right. Invention is inevitable. But why write memoir? Why not call it fiction and be done with all the hashing about, wondering where memory stops and imagination begins? And if memoir seeks to talk about "the big issues," about history and peace, death and love—why not leave these reflections to those with expert and scholarly knowledge? Why let the common or garden variety memoirist into the club? I'm thinking again of that bumper sticker: Why Question Authority?

My answer, of course, is a memoirist's answer. Memoir must be written because each of us must have a created version of the past. Created: that is, real, tangible, made of the stuff of a life lived in place and in history. And the down side of any created thing as well: we must live with a version that attaches us to our limitations, to the inevitable subjectivity of our points of view. We must acquiesce to our experience and our gift to transform experience into meaning and value. You tell me your story, I'll tell you my story.

If we refuse to do the work of creating this personal version of the past, someone else will do it for us. That is a scary political fact. "The struggle of man against power," a character in Milan Kundera's novel *The Book of Laughter and Forgetting* says "is the struggle of memory against forgetting." He refers to willful political forgetting, the habit of nations and those in power (Question Authority!) to deny the truth of memory in order to disarm moral and ethical power. It's an efficient way of controlling masses of people. It doesn't even require much bloodshed, as long as people are entirely willing to give over their personal memories. Whole histories can be rewritten. As Czeslaw Milosz said in his 1980 Nobel Prize lecture, the number of books published that seek to deny the existence of the Nazi death camps now exceeds one hundred.

What is remembered is what *becomes* reality. If we "forget" Auschwitz, if we "forget" My Lai, what then do we remember? And what is the purpose of our remembering? If we think of memory naively, as a simple story, logged like a documentary in the archive of the mind, we miss its beauty but also its function. The beauty of memory rests in its talent for rendering detail, for paying homage to the senses, its capacity to love the particles of life, the richness and idiosyncrasy of our existence. The function of memory, on the other hand, is intensely personal and surprisingly political.

Our capacity to move forward as developing beings rests on a healthy relation with the past. Psychotherapy, that widespread method of mental health, relies heavily on memory and on the ability to retrieve and organize images and events from the personal past. We carry our wounds and perhaps even worse, our capacity to wound, forward with us. If we learn not only to tell our stories but to listen to what our stories tell us—to write the first draft and then return for the second draft—we are doing the work of memoir.

Memoir is the intersection of narration and reflection, of story-telling and essay-writing. It can present its story *and* reflect and consider the meaning of the story. It is a peculiarly open form, inviting broken and incomplete images, half-recollected fragments, all the mass (and mess) of detail. It offers to shape this confusion—and in shaping, of course it necessarily creates a work of art, not a legal document. But then, even legal documents are only valiant attempts to consign the truth, the whole truth and nothing but the truth to paper. Even they remain versions.

Locating touchstones—the red music book, the olive Olive, my father's violin playing—is deeply satisfying. Who knows why? Perhaps we all sense that we can't grasp the whole truth and nothing but the truth of our experience. Just can't be done. What can be achieved, however, is a version of its swirling, changing wholeness. A memoirist must acquiesce to selectivity, like any artist. The version we dare to write is the only truth, the only relationship we can have with the past. Refuse to write your life and you have no life. At least, that is the stern view of the memoirist.

Personal history, logged in memory, is a sort of slide projector flashing images on the wall of the mind. And there's precious little order to the slides in the rotating carousel. Beyond that confusion, who knows who is running the projector? A memoirist steps into this darkened room of flashing, unorganized images and stands blinking for a while. Maybe for a long while. But eventually, as with any attempt to tell a story, it is necessary to put something first, then something else. And so on, to the end. That's a first draft. Not necessarily the truth, not even a truth sometimes, but the first attempt to create a shape.

The first thing I usually notice at this stage of composition is the appalling inaccuracy of the piece. Witness my first piano lesson draft. Invention is screamingly evident in what I intended to be transcription. But here's the further truth: I feel no shame. In fact, it's only now that my interest in the piece truly quickens. For I can see what isn't there, what is shyly hugging the walls, hoping not to be seen. I see the filmy shape of the next draft. I see a more acute version of the episode or—this is more likely—an entirely new piece rising from the ashes of the first attempt.

The next draft of the piece would have to be a true re-vision, a new seeing of the materials of the first draft. Nothing merely cosmetic will do—no rouge buffing up the opening sentence, no glossy adjective to lift a sagging line, nothing to attempt covering a patch of gray writing. None of that. I can't say for sure, but my hunch is the revision would lead me to more writing about my father (why was I so impressed by that ancestral inventor of the collapsible opera hat? Did I feel I had nothing as remarkable in my own background? Did this make me feel inadequate?). I begin to think perhaps Sister Olive is less central to this business than she is in this draft. She is meant to be a moment, not a character.

And so I might proceed, if I were to undertake a new draft of the memoir. I begin to feel a relationship developing between a former self and me.

And, even more compelling, a relationship between an old world and me. Some people think of autobiographical writing as the precious occupation of a particularly self-absorbed person. Maybe, but I don't buy that. True memoir is written in an attempt to find not only a self but a world.

The self-absorption that seems to be the impetus and embarrassment of autobiography turns into (or perhaps always was) a hunger for the world. Actually, it begins as hunger for a world, one gone or lost, effaced by time or a more sudden brutality. But in the act of remembering, the personal environment expands, resonates beyond itself, beyond its "subject," into the endless and tragic recollection that is history.

We look at old family photographs in which we stand next to black, boxy Fords and are wearing period costumes, and we do not gaze fascinated because there we are young again, or there we are standing, as we never will again in life, next to our mother. We stare and drift because there we are . . . historical. It is the dress, the black car that dazzle us now and draw us beyond our mother's bright arms which once caught us. We reach into the attractive impersonality of something more significant than ourselves. We write memoir, in other words. We accept the humble position of writing a version rather than "the whole truth."

I suppose I write memoir because of the radiance of the past—it draws me back and back to it. Not that the past is beautiful. In our commercial memoir, in history, the death camps *are* back there. In intimate life too, the record is usually pretty mixed. "I could tell you stories . . ." people say and drift off, meaning terrible things have happened to them.

But the past is radiant. It has the light of lived life. A memoirist wishes to touch it. No one owns the past, though typically the first act of new political regimes, whether of the left or the right, is to attempt to rewrite history, to grab the past and make it over so the end comes out right. So their power looks inevitable.

No one owns the past, but it is a grave error (another age would have said a grave sin) not to inhabit memory. Sometimes I think it is all we really have. But that may be a trifle melodramatic. At any rate, memory possesses authority for the fearful self in a world where it is necessary to have authority in order to Question Authority.

There may be no more pressing intellectual need in our culture than for people to become sophisticated about the function of memory. The political implications of the loss of memory are obvious. The authority of memory is a personal confirmation of selfhood. To write one's life is to live it twice, and the second living is both spiritual and historical, for a memoir reaches deep within the personality as it seeks its narrative form and also grasps the life-of-the-times as no political treatise can.

Our most ancient metaphor says life is a journey. Memoir is travel writing, then, notes taken along the way, telling how things looked and what thoughts occurred. But I cannot think of the memoirist as a tourist. This is the traveller who goes on foot, living the journey, taking on mountains, enduring deserts, marveling at the lush green places. Moving through it all faithfully, not so much a survivor with a harrowing tale to tell as a pilgrim, seeking, wondering.

LYNNA WILLIAMS (b. 1951)

We Told You This, Didn't We?

CONSIDER THIS:

Lynna Williams is a professor of English and former director of the creative writing program at Emory University. She has been a journalist and a speechwriter and earned degrees from the University of Missouri and George Mason University. Her short stories have appeared in *The Atlantic, Lear's,* and *The Oxford American,* as well as other periodicals. *Things Not Seen and Other Stories* was a *New York Times* Notable Book in 1992.

Williams calls herself "a new Southern writer," which she defines as "urban, rootless and riddled with unbelief." She said in an interview with *The Fresno Bee,* "I write about outsiders who are inside of a culture where people believe in God, but they themselves don't . . . . My stories are set in the South. But I have a hard time calling myself a Southern writer." You might use this story to decide for yourself how much of Williams's self-description as a writer seems to hold true in this essay. Also, how is this essay organized? By what means does the author forge connections between her sections? Along the way, you might want to make your own list of "1) Things my parents reveal. 2) Things they do not."

My mother and father were married fifty years ago today. The anniversary brunch my brother and I hosted at the country club down the highway has been over for hours, but my mother and father happen to be the Astaire and Rogers of serial undressers: their party clothes are coming off slowly, one piece at a time, and all over the house. It's not seductive, this routine; instead it makes me think of dinner at a magician's house: *Apple in the hand. Apple vanishes. Apple turns up in the souvenir spoon rack.* My parents disappeared when we got home, but in the last hour I've found my father's dinner jacket underneath an ancient white poodle; his cummerbund is folded in thirds, like a napkin, on the kitchen counter. My mother's pearl earrings, the easiest things to shed, I find in a coffee cup on the fireplace mantle. I am deciding how interested I am in pursuing this search when I notice that my brother still hasn't moved from the living room couch. He wept during the anniversary toasts, which only made it clear how much prettier his eyes are than mine. Now he looks thoughtful, the way he did in childhood, suggesting I eat a bug for his science project. As I pass in front of him, he suddenly shifts his weight, puts his hand under his leg, and comes up with my mother's halfslip. His wife, who only married into this family, says, "You guys," which wakes up the poodle. The two of them leave the room together.

They've always done it this way, my parents, getting out of their work clothes, or changing for lunch after church when I was little. I was a second grader, I think, when I started going through the house before bedtime, first gathering up what my mother had worn on a particular day, then hunting down my minister-father's suit coat, his dress shirt, his slacks. When my arms were full I lugged everything to the dining room, where I reassembled the outfits on side-by-side chairs, black wingtips to the left, navy pumps to the right. My parents saw me doing it, of course, but they let it go. My hunch is that my mother—in 1959, on Fitzgerald Street, the only mother with a job downtown, and a closetful of seriously straight skirts—assumed that Clothes Wrangling was one of the lesser badges in Brownies. Without saying a word about it, she and I had worked out a deal about Brownies. She stopped calling Troop 118 "your little brown shirt friends," and I let her send me to PTA bake sales bearing Hostess Cupcakes, cut into quarters and rewrapped.

I'd been carrying my parents' clothes around for a week when my mother finally asked about it at breakfast one morning, as she stooped to clear the dining room chairs. "What are you actually doing?" she said; grown-up, I hear in that "actually" most of my mother's true voice: precise, ironic, not unhappy, most of the time. Before I could lie, my brother splashed his spoon in his Cheerios, and it came out then: the scary story he'd told me about a family named Pendergrast who'd lived in our house before us, and whose little boy had discovered his parents' clothes were all that held their bodies together. We were in my bedroom when my brother told me all this, and he leaned over me, his face as white as the moon. "The mom took off her jacket, and her arms fell off," he whispered. "The cleaners lost his father's pants and, well, you've seen the wheelchair ramp out back."

Now, some thirty-five years later, he has the halfslip balled in his fists, high above his head, and his mouth is opening. He wouldn't really joke about what part of my mother her discarded lingerie has put at risk, but I am jumping for his hand when we hear my mother's voice from the den downstairs. She's calling for my father to come, for all of us to come. It is not her tragic voice, I am almost sure it isn't, but my brother drops the slip, instantly; the two of us collide with his wife at the door to the stairs. My father, wearing exactly half a tuxedo, is right behind us, saying my mother's name.

Shoving into the den, the four of us see her, leaning back in the recliner, her ankles crossed, the television remote in her hand. Automatically I notice she has made it all the way out of her party clothes, into slacks and a Braves starter jersey I sent from Atlanta. "Tommy, look," she says to my father. "Look right there." Her fingernail, two-coated in fire engine red, points to the TV. "That's where your father and I have our funeral plots," she says to me. "In fact, you can see where we'll be; just look to the left of where all those people are standing."

"Rose Hill." This from my father. "We bought the plots when we still lived in Fort Worth."

My brother and I are staring at the television, at the sobering rows of headstones, and the twenty or so people who apparently are not there to visit my parents' graves. In the edge of the shot, I see a motor coach. My head bobs up and down, and it's my brother who says it first. "Mom, why is your cemetery on PBS?"

But I know the answer. I went back to Fort Worth after journalism school, for a reporting job at *The Star-Telegram.* "Lee Harvey Oswald," I say. "That's Lee Harvey's Oswald's grave.

My mother points again. "We'll be just down there," like she's telling us where to meet her for lunch if we get separated at the Grand Canyon. Then she sees my face, my brother's face. "We told you we'll be buried near Oswald," she says. "We'd had the plots three years when Kennedy was shot. I'm sure we've told you this."

1) The whereabouts of my parents' clothing. 2) The whereabouts of what will one day be their graves. These are categories. 1) Things my parents reveal. 2) Things they do not.

The five of us watch the rest of the documentary on Oswald, my Royalist parents and yellow-dog Democrat sister-in-law arguing back and forth about Zapruder, the arc of history, even, at one point, the Stamp Tax. My brother and I are silent, watching for the documentary's jump cuts back to the cemetery, to the sloping path that leads away from Oswald's grave. When the credits roll, my parents thank us again for their party, and disappear upstairs; they're on the bottom stair when I see their fingertips touch, just their fingertips, like those junior high science experiments on conducting electricity. When we hear the door close behind them, my sister-in-law punches my brother on the arm. "My theory is they're cousins," she says. "Don't you remember? They're sure they told you about it."

My best friend is a New Yorker by birth, but we met in a first-grade classroom in Fort Worth. She was in Calcutta for a while, and Liberia, and now she's in rural Iowa, teaching English as a Second Language. None of this moving around has improved her mood. But that night, after everyone else is asleep, I call her anyway, because she's known my parents forever. I can't tell this to someone who requires a backstory.

When I'm finished with the whole Fiftieth-Anniversary-Gala-with-Bonus-Cemetery-Plot-Revelation, my friend produces an eerily perfect imitation of Jack Webb in the opening moments of Dragnet. "A quiet ranch house on a quiet street in Quiet Town USA," she says. "But inside, true crimes are happening. Happening every day." Her voice deepens, and she comes down hard on each word. "Crimes. Against. Narrative."

I know what she means. She means that if my mother and father were Mr. and Mrs. Anton Chekhov, the play's original title would have been, "Trees in Rows." And only later, years later, would they think to tell their children, "Yeah, it was a cherry orchard; didn't we say that?" But I ask my friend, "What? What are you talking about?" because I want her to say it out loud. I'm better when people say things out loud.

But she's already telling me a story of her own, about a blind date on Christmas Eve. "The Dean's secretary had seen him around, and when he called he said he had two tickets to Handel's *Messiah* at a little church out in the country. He said he went every year, and it was beautiful. So he picks me up, and it's snowing a little, and then it's snowing a lot, and then we can't see the road very well. We couldn't find the turnoff to the church; we drove around for hours, and we never did get to the *Messiah*."

I tell her I hope his car heater worked. We both know that, ordinarily, the subtext would be, "Tell me you didn't sleep with a guy who can't find the Messiah in a snowstorm." But now, clearly, what I'm really saying is, "Can we talk about me some more, please?"

"Wait, I'm not finished," she says. "So I get to school after New Year's and I'm telling some women at coffee about Christmas Eve, and suddenly they're all laughing. It turns out this guy's dated everyone at the college, but only once, and only on Dec. 24. And he never finds the church where the concert is, because there isn't one. He made the whole thing up, and now it's his very own Christmas tradition."

I position a length of phone cord above my upper lip, and look in the mirror. With a twisty black moustache I could almost be a great-aunt, on my father's side, we visited at the Eastern Star Home when I was small. Suddenly I want to know where the blind date lives in Iowa, and how long his parents have been married. I imagine their anniversary parties, everyone on the dance floor spinning out these elaborate, detailed, *textured* lies. I see the blind date's mother, dipping in her husband's arms, inventing a long-ago meeting with Orville Redenbacher on a night plane to Memphis. I hear her describe his bow tie, the faint smell of popcorn salt on his skin, the shared cab to the Peabody Hotel, the gift packages of popcorn that still arrive now and then at her office address, always without a card. Not a single word is true, but she doesn't leave anything out. I love this woman.

"Lynna," my friend says, and then again, more urgently.

I drop my moustache. The two of us are grown women, with jobs and mortgages and boxed sets of Marvin Gaye CDs, but right this minute we're in fourth grade again, standing three kids apart in the line our class formed to march back inside after recess. We were the tallest girls, which made it possible to yell over the other kids' heads.

"It's not true," my friend told me then. "No way is it true."

"It could be," I said. "It could be true."

Now, right in my ear, she says exactly what she said then, just before Mrs. Richards came and took us out of line for talking. "You are not adopted," she says. "Say it. Say, 'I'm not adopted.'"

I am not adopted. But in fourth grade all the girls in Mrs. Richards' class believed we were. The adoption craze was what we did, after the boys stopped letting us play kickball with them, and before Mrs. Richards gave us the band room for spelling bee practice. For weeks, we snuck pictures out of family albums and brought them to school, huddling by the chainlink fence at recess to check out the noses of our alleged grandmothers, turning the evidence this way and that in sunlight so bright we blinked back tears. We argued about which parts of ourselves were visible in the faces, the bodies, of ranchers photographed outside little country churches, of Woolworth's clerks teetering above platform shoes, of sailors waving from battleships pulling out to sea. The frenzy ended when Jane Martin went to the nurse's office, crying that she didn't care if her ears were huge and suspicious, she didn't want some other family. Our parents were summoned to an emergency PTA meeting: birth certificates passed around like party favors, a little homily from the principal about communication in the home, cookies and lime punch for everyone. We found out that night that Marsha Lester, a fourth grader from another class, really was adopted. She and her family were special guests at the PTA meeting, and Marsha recited a poem her mother had written just for her: *I am chosen, special as can be; I am chosen, forever family.*

I was pretty sure that if I was adopted, I'd have a better poem. But part of me never stopped worrying. I knew my parents couldn't forget bringing me home from the Lottie Moon Home in a donated pink blanket, but I could easily see them mixing up a talk they'd really had with me, with one they just thought they'd had. We had had a sex talk, sort of, after my father found me reading Harold Robbins' *A Stone for Danny Fisher,* a dictionary open to a page of "c" words. But still I could see that, with all the talk about how wonderful it was to make a baby, they might have left something out: Yes, I was born when a miracle happened between a man and a woman, but what if, somehow, it was some *other* man and woman?

I couldn't prove it, though. My birth certificate was in the cherry secretary in the living room, which my father's parents bought on their wedding day in 1902, and my mother's nose was above my mouth. But fourth grade was when I started having dreams that Walter Cronkite was my father. Walter Cronkite gave a person the whole story.

Eventually I graduated from the University of Missouri School of Journalism—the Cathedral of the Whole Story, Midwestern Diocese—but before I ever went to college, I worked for two years as a reporter in Abilene, Texas. We'd left Fort Worth a couple of years after Kennedy was killed in Dallas, and I finished high school in Abilene. I was editor of the school paper, and a week before I was due to leave for college, I went down to *The Reporter-News* for an interview. I didn't tell anyone at home where I was going. Almost any of the paper's regular editors would have known my parents, known that technically I was college material, known enough to ask just what I thought I was doing, an eighteen-year-old girl applying for a grown-up job. But the city editor I talked to was new in town, a native of that place West Texans call Somewheres Else; he not only didn't know my family, he seemed a little vague on the difference between Texas and Oklahoma. But one thing he did know was that the tone in his newsroom needed raising, and by chance I'd worn a white dress to the interview, a white dress and thrift shop pearls. Before I left the house I'd dipped the pearls in a dish of vinegar to make them shine.

The new editor hired me on the spot, and immediately laid out the job requirements: for $2 an hour, I was to show up on time, go pink at swear words, type, answer the city desk phones, call the funeral homes around town for obits, and flutter my hands when the copy desk guys got out of control.

My parents weren't happy when I didn't leave for college, but they didn't say much. Once or twice I heard my mother on the phone, saying she didn't know what the story was with me. "Unless she tells us, we never know what's going on with her," she said, and I was careful to close the door to my room before I started to laugh.

I loved the paper. The newsroom was the filthiest place I had ever seen, and when I came to work at 2:00 P.M. for the nightshift, I always thought of visiting day in prison movies: it was just me and the guys. For a while I didn't mind that my job was to be a girl, a nice girl, not a reporter at all. But one night, a couple of months after I started work, I stopped after a call to the third mortuary on the list, and took my dinner break early. When I got back, I did some more typing, and the story I dropped into the copy tray on the city editor's desk was my own: a baby dead, a two-year-old girl face down in a newly paved road in a little country subdivision. The funeral director at Reed's had told me about it, and I went down the back stairs and drove to Buffalo Gap. The light was fading when I pulled up in front of a green house with a two-seater swingset in the front yard, and a dozen or so people in shifting patterns, like a kaleidoscope. The ambulance had already taken the body away, but it still took me forever to get out of the car. But when I did, somehow I knew the baby's mother wasn't the keening woman in a Mack Eplen's uniform; the mother was the girl a year or two older than me, alone in the grass, wearing pedal pushers and a man's striped Arrow shirt.

It was all there in the story I wrote, the tiny beaded moccasin in the mother's left hand, the way her voice jumped and skittered, the other mothers twisting on the balls of their feet, whispering, *"Hush now, Ricky. Did Stephanie see it happen? Ricky saw it. He came inside and said 'Mama, that little girl's dead.'"*

I put in every detail. The only thing I left out was how I talked my way inside the house, and the ocean of sweet tea I drank sitting on the wagon-wheel couch in Alice Lang's living room. The mother's full name was in the story, Alice Caroline Lang, but not the seven times I said, "I understand, oh, I understand," when her voice died away to nothing. When it was almost over—when there was nothing more I could do or say to stay a little longer—I asked to use the restroom. When the door closed behind me, I leaned in close to stare at the mirror above the sink. There was no color in my face, and a voice behind my eyes was saying the words the city editor did not want used in his newsroom. I said them, over and over, because I knew then, I knew what my childhood was for. I had grown up in my parents' house and I knew what stories were—I knew; they didn't—and why it mattered to tell them right. That night in Alice Lang's tiny house, I felt what I never had in my father's church on Sunday mornings. I felt the call; I felt worshipful, and dedicated, and *true.* I saw myself sitting on a million couches, patting a million hands, saying a million times, "You can tell me; you might feel better if you told me." I saw myself telling the stories right every time.

I wrote the story of Cassie Elizabeth Lang, age two years, four months, running into the street after the ice cream bell, in my head, before I ever walked into the newsroom. It was a good enough story, even after the guys on the copy desk took out the adjectives, that they asked me to come to the Red Rooster after the paper was out. I had never gone with them before, and I sat nearest the wall in a booth with cracked red-leather seats. Over the noise and the juke box, I told the city editor that the stories I wrote were going to be true stories. He was fifteen years older than I was, a former reporter in Vietnam who had come back to a job at the best newspaper in Texas, and immediately started to work his way down—smaller cities, each paper a little worse than the paper before. Even now I don't like thinking about how I must have looked to him: a kid in a plaid skirt talking about truth. What I remember is that he bought the beers, and the sun was coming up when he drove me up College Hill to my parents' house. I wanted to give him something, because my life finally was beginning, and he was there. When he kissed my forehead to say goodnight, I said into his shoulder, "My mother had a mastectomy. It was in the summer and I was gone for a weekend, and when I came home, it was over. Nobody told me until it was over."

"I'm sorry," he said, and I knew from his face he was going to ask me questions. I got out of the car, and I went into the bathroom at the front of the house.

I didn't throw up; I sat cross-legged on the tile floor, and thought about what I had done to Alice Caroline Lang in taking her story, what my mother had done to me in keeping hers.

I did go to college, and I did become a reporter. But I never told the truth, not the way I wanted to; I just told whichever parts of the story I could get, however I could get them. Now I write fiction. I invent the characters, where they live, what they eat, who they love, how much and for how long. Babies die in my stories, but no one gets hurt. And almost every day, about dinnertime, I dial my parents' number. My mother answers, and we talk about the Atlanta Braves, or our cats and dogs, or how much better the weather is where I live. We were on the phone a few months ago when my mother told me they were selling their plots at Rose Hill. I told her about grad students in Oxford, Mississippi, making love on Faulkner's grave, and she said primly that she and my father would cross that cemetery off their list of possibilities.

And then, last week, my mother called me from Texas, where she was visiting her sister in Waco. I told her how many days before baseball season started; she told me she and my aunt were off the next day to the Hill Country to retrieve their mother's Depression-era cakeplate from a second cousin.

My mother's mother died years before I was born. I had never heard of the second cousin, or the cakeplate. "Why would he have it?" I said. "And why are you going to get it now?"

"It was our mother's cakeplate," she said, and asked if I'd remembered to have my gutters cleaned.

Sure, I said, but what I wanted to know was how the cakeplate disappeared, how my mother knew where it was now, why it mattered, if it had been the prettiest thing in my grandmother's house, what kind of cakes she served on it on Sundays after church, where she bought it, and how, when there was no money, and whether she let the kids take turns bringing it to the table when company came.

What I said was, "Be careful driving down there," and my mother said, "It's been so long now, but I think the glass was pink."

BARBARA KINGSOLVER (b. 1955)

In Case You Ever Want to Go Home Again

CONSIDER THIS:

Novelist Barbara Kingsolver was born in Annapolis, Maryland, and grew up in Kentucky and the Congo, now Zaire (her father practiced medicine there for a time). Kingsolver's work, including nonfiction and poetry, has appeared in numerous publications including *McCall's, Nation,* and the *New York Times Book*

Review. Kingsolver spoke of how her early nonfiction writing influenced her other work in a *Salon* interview. "I was working as a journalist in the '80s and spent a lot of time in the little mining towns of southern Arizona, covering this mine strike. Spending all those hours talking to people in their living rooms, I learned the language. I just got it in my ear—the wonderful way that Spanish inflects on the English and the way people turn phrases around and say, 'Don't go sticking your neck out on a limb.' After a while, I started to hear it. I found I could write *Animal Dreams* after that, because I understood how people talked."

It's one thing to go home again (anyone who has ever returned to a home town after an absence or attended a high school reunion knows the feeling), it's another thing entirely to go home again as a writer who has turned the facts of a town into the fictions of novels and short stories. As you read Kingsolver's narrative, consider the degree to which you're willing to share your versions of family life with your family and your versions of friendship with your friends. Should writers draw heavily on their relationships with those around them? How? What, in Kingsolver's essay, are some of the ramifications of such decisions?

I have been gone from Kentucky a long time. Twenty years have done to my hill accent what the washing machine does to my jeans: taken out the color and starch, so gradually that I never marked the loss. Something like that has happened to my memories, too, particularly of the places and people I can't go back and visit because they are gone. The ancient brick building that was my grade school, for example, and both my grandfathers. They're snapshots of memory for me now, of equivocal focus, loaded with emotion, undisturbed by anyone else's idea of the truth. The schoolhouse's plaster ceilings are charted with craters like maps of the moon and likely to crash down without warning. The windows are watery, bubbly glass reinforced with chicken wire. The weary wooden staircases, worn shiny smooth in a path up their middles, wind up to an unknown place overhead where the heavy-footed eighth graders changing classes were called "the mules" by my first-grade teacher, and believing her, I pictured their sharp hooves on the linoleum.

My Grandfather Henry I remember in his sleeveless undershirt, home after a day's hard work on the farm at Fox Creek. His hide is tough and burnished wherever it has met the world—hands, face, forearms—but vulnerably white at the shoulders and throat. He is snapping his false teeth in and out of place, to provoke his grandchildren to hysterics.

As far as I know, no such snapshots exist in the authentic world. The citizens of my hometown ripped down the old school and quickly put to rest its picturesque decay. My grandfather always cemented his teeth in his head, and put on good clothes, before submitting himself to photography. Who wouldn't? When a camera takes aim at my daughter, I reach out and scrape the peanut butter off her chin. "I can't help it," I tell her, "it's one of those mother things." It's more than that. It's human, to want the world to see us as we think we ought to be seen.

You can fool history sometimes, but you can't fool the memory of your intimates. And thank heavens, because in the broad valley between real life and propriety whole herds of important truths can steal away into the underbrush. I hold that valley to be my home territory as a writer. Little girls wear food on their chins, school days are lit by ghostlight, and respectable men wear their undershirts at home. Sometimes there are fits of laughter and sometimes there is despair, and neither one looks a thing like its formal portrait.

For many, many years I wrote my stories furtively in spiral-bound notebooks, for no greater purpose than my own private salvation. But on April 1, 1987, two earthquakes hit my psyche on the same day. First, I brought home my own newborn baby girl from the hospital. Then, a few hours later, I got a call from New York announcing that a large chunk of my writing—which I'd tentatively pronounced a novel—was going to be published. This was a spectacular April Fool's Day. My life has not, since, returned to normal.

For days I nursed my baby and basked in hormonal euphoria, musing occasionally: all this—and I'm a novelist, too! *That,* though, seemed a slim accomplishment compared with laboring twenty-four hours to render up the most beautiful new human the earth had yet seen. The book business seemed a terrestrial affair of ink and trees and I didn't give it much thought.

In time my head cleared, and I settled into panic. What had I done? The baby was premeditated, but the book I'd conceived recklessly, in a closet late at night, when the restlessness of my insomniac pregnancy drove me to compulsive verbal intercourse with my own soul. The pages that grew in a stack were somewhat incidental to the process. They contained my highest hopes and keenest pains, and I didn't think anyone but me would ever see them. I'd bundled the thing up and sent it off to New York in a mad fit of housekeeping, to be done with it. Now it was going to be laid smack out for my mother, my postal clerk, my high school English teacher, anybody in the world who was willing to plunk down $16.95 and walk away with it. To find oneself suddenly published is thrilling—that is a given. But how appalling it also felt I find hard to describe. Imagine singing at the top of your lungs in the shower as you always do, then one day turning off the water and throwing back the curtain to see there in your bathroom a crowd of people, rapt, with videotape. I wanted to throw a towel over my head.

There was nothing in the novel in incriminate my mother or the postal clerk. I like my mother, plus her record is perfect. My postal clerk I couldn't vouch for; he has tattoos. But in any event I never put real people into my fiction—I can't see the slightest point of that, when I have the alternative of inventing utterly subservient slave-people, whose every detail of appearance and behavior I can bend to serve my theme and plot.

Even so, I worried that someone I loved would find in what I'd written a reason to despise me. In fact, I was sure of it. My fiction is not in any way about my life, regardless of what others might assume, but certainly it is set in the sort of places I know pretty well. The protagonist of my novel, titled *The Bean Trees,* launched her adventures from a place called "Pittman, Kentucky," which does resemble a town in Kentucky where I'm known to have grown up. I had written:

"Pittman was twenty years behind the nation in practically every way you can think of except the rate of teenage pregnancies. . . . We were the last place in the country to get the dial system. Up until 1973 you just picked up the receiver and said, Marge, get me my Uncle Roscoe. The telephone office was on the third floor of the Courthouse, and the operator could see everything around Main Street square. She would tell you if his car was there or not."

I don't have an Uncle Roscoe. But if I *did* have one, the phone operator in my hometown, prior to the mid-seventies, could have spotted him from her second-floor office on Main Street square.

I cherish the oddball charm of that town. Time and again I find myself writing love letters to my rural origins. Growing up in small-town Kentucky taught me respect for the astounding resources people can drum up from their backyards, when they want to, to pull each other through. I tend to be at home with modesty, and suspicious of anything slick or new. But naturally, when I was growing up there, I yearned for the slick and the new. A lot of us did, I think. We craved shopping malls and a swimming pool. We wanted the world to know we had once won the title "All Kentucky City," even though with sixteen-hundred souls we no more constituted a "city" than New Jersey is a Garden State, and we advertised this glorious prevarication for years and years on one of the town's few billboards.

Homely charm is a relative matter. Now that I live in a western city where shopping malls and swimming pools congest the landscape like cedar blight, I think back fondly on my hometown. But the people who live there now might rather smile about the quaintness of a *smaller* town, like nearby Morning Glory or Barefoot. At any rate, they would not want to discover themselves in my novel. I can never go home again, as long as I live, I reasoned. Somehow this will be reckoned as betrayal. I've photographed my hometown in its undershirt.

During the year I awaited publication, I decided to calm down. There were other ways to think about this problem:

1. If people really didn't want to see themselves in my book, they wouldn't. They would think to themselves, "She is writing about Morning Glory, and those underdogs are from farther on down Scrubgrass Road."
2. There's no bookstore in my hometown. No one will know.

In November 1988, bookstoreless though it was, my hometown hosted a big event. Paper banners announced it, and stores closed in honor of it. A crowd assembled in the town's largest public space—the railroad depot. The line went out the door and away down the tracks. At the front of the line they were plunking down $16.95 for signed copies of a certain book.

My family was there. The county's elected officials were there. My first-grade teacher, Miss Louella, was there, exclaiming to one and all: "I taught her to write!"

My old schoolmates were there. The handsome boys who'd spurned me at every homecoming dance were there.

It's relevant and slightly vengeful to confess here that I was not a hit in school, socially speaking. I was a bookworm who never quite fit her clothes. I managed to look fine in my school pictures, but as usual the truth lay elsewhere. In sixth grade I hit my present height of five feet almost nine, struck it like a gong, in fact, leaving behind self-confidence and any genuine need of a training bra. Elderly relatives used the term "fill out" when they spoke of me, as though they held out some hope I might eventually have some market value, like an underfed calf, if the hay crop was good. In my classroom I came to dread a game called Cooties, wherein one boy would brush against my shoulder and then chase the others around, threatening to pass on my apparently communicable lack of charisma. The other main victim of this game was a girl named Sandra, whose family subscribed to an unusual religion that mandated a Victorian dress code. In retrospect I can't say exactly what Sandra and I had in common that made us outcasts, except for extreme shyness, flat chests, and families who had their eyes on horizons pretty far beyond the hills of Nicholas County. Mine were not Latter-day Saints, but we read Thoreau and Robert Burns at home, and had lived for a while in Africa. My parents did not flinch from relocating us to a village beyond the reach of electricity, running water, or modern medicine (also, to my delight, conventional schooling) when they had a chance to do useful work there. They thought it was shameful to ignore a fellow human in need, or to waste money on trendy, frivolous things; they did not, on the other hand, think it was shameful to wear perfectly good hand-me-down dresses to school in Nicholas County. Ephemeral idols exalted by my peers, such as Batman, the Beatles, and the Hula Hoop, were not an issue at our house. And even if it took no more than a faint pulse to pass the fifth grade, my parents expected me to set my own academic goals, and then exceed them.

Possibly my parents were trying to make sure I didn't get pregnant in the eighth grade, as some of my classmates would shortly begin to do. If so, their efforts were a whale of a success. In my first three years of high school, the number of times I got asked out on a date was zero. This is not an approximate number. I'd caught up to other girls in social skills by that time, so I knew how to pretend I was dumber than I was, and make my own clothes. But these things helped only marginally. Popularity remained a frustrating mystery to me.

Nowadays, some of my city-bred friends muse about moving to a small town for the sake of their children. What's missing from their romantic picture of Grover's Corners is the frightening impact of insulation upon a child who's not dead center in the mainstream. In a place such as my hometown, you file in and sit down to day one of kindergarten with the exact pool of boys who will be your potential dates for the prom. If you wet your pants a lot, your social life ten years later will be—as they say in government reports—impacted. I was sterling on bladder control, but somehow could never shake my sixth-grade stigma.

At age seventeen, I was free at last to hightail it for new social pastures, and you'd better believe I did. I attended summer classes at the University of Kentucky and landed a boyfriend before I knew what had hit me, or what on earth one did with the likes of such. When I went on to college in Indiana I was astonished to find a fresh set of peers who found me, by and large, likable and cootie-free.

I've never gotten over high school, to the extent that I'm still a little surprised that my friends want to hang out with me. But it made me what I am, for better and for worse. From living in a town that listened in on party lines, I learned both the price and value of community. And I gained things from my rocky school years: A fierce wish to look inside of people. An aptitude for listening. The habit of my own company. The companionship of keeping a diary, in which I gossiped, fantasized and invented myself. From the vantage point of invisibility I explored the psychology of the underdog, the one who can't be what others desire but who might still learn to chart her own hopes. Her story was my private treasure; when I wrote *The Bean Trees* I called her Lou Ann. I knew for sure that my classmates, all of them cool as Camaros back then, would not relate to the dreadful insecurities of Lou Ann. But I liked her anyway.

And now, look. The boys who'd once fled howling from her cooties were lined up for my autograph. Football captains, cheerleaders, homecoming queens were all there. The athlete who'd inspired in me a near-fatal crush for three years, during which time he never looked in the vicinity of my person, was there. The great wits who gave me the names Kingfish and Queen Sliver were there.

I took liberties with history. I wrote long, florid inscriptions referring to our great friendship of days gone by. I wrote slowly. I made those guys wait in line *a long time.*

I can recall every sight, sound, minute of that day. Every open, generous face. The way the afternoon light fell through the windows onto the shoes of the people in line. In my inventory of mental snapshots these images hold the place most people reserve for the wedding album. I don't know whether other people get to have Great Life Moments like this, but I was lucky enough to realize I was having mine, right while it happened. My identity was turning backward on its own axis. Never before or since have I felt all at the same time so cherished, so aware of old anguish, and so ready to let go of the past. My past had let go of *me,* so I could be something new: Poet Laureate and Queen for a Day in hometown Kentucky. The people who'd watched me grow up were proud of me, and exuberant over an event that put our little dot on the map, particularly since it wasn't an airline disaster or a child falling down a well. They didn't appear to mind that my novel discussed small-town life frankly, without gloss.

In fact, most people showed unsurpassed creativity in finding themselves, literally, on the printed page. "That's my car isn't it?" they would ask. "My service station!" Nobody presented himself as my Uncle Roscoe, but if he had, I happily would have claimed him.

It's a curious risk, fiction. Some writers choose fantasy as an approach to truth, a way of burrowing under newsprint and formal portraits to find the despair that can stow away in a happy childhood, or the affluent grace of a grandfather in his undershirt. In the final accounting, a hundred different truths are likely to reside at any given address. The part of my soul that is driven to make stories is a fierce thing, like a ferret: long, sleek, incapable of sleep, it digs and bites through all I know of the world. Given that I cannot look away from the painful things, it seems better to invent allegory than to point a straight, bony finger like Scrooge's mute Ghost of Christmas Yet to Come, declaring, "Here you will end, if you don't clean up your act." By inventing character and circumstance, I like to think I can be a kinder sort of ghost, saying, "I don't mean *you,* exactly, but just give it some thought, anyway."

Nice try, but nobody's really fooled. Because fiction works, if it does, only when we the readers believe every word of it. Grover's Corners is Our Town, and so is Cannery Row, and Lilliput, and Gotham City, and Winesburg, Ohio, and the dreadful metropolis of *1984.* We have all been as canny as Huck Finn, as fractious as Scarlett O'Hara, as fatally flawed as Captain Ahab and Anna Karenina. I, personally, am Jo March, and if her author Louisa May Alcott had a whole new life to live for the sole pursuit of talking me out of it, she could not. A pen may or may not be mightier than the sword, but it is brassier than the telephone. When the writer converses privately with her soul in the long dark night, a thousand neighbors are listening in on the party line, taking it personally.

Nevertheless, I came to decide, on my one big afternoon as Homecoming Queen, that I would go on taking the risk of writing books. Miss Louella and all those football players gave me the rash courage to think I might be forgiven again and again the sin of revelation. I love my hometown as I love the elemental stuff of my own teeth and bones, and that seems to have come through to my hometown, even if I didn't write it up in its Sunday best.

I used to ask my grandfather how he could pull fish out of a lake all afternoon, one after another, while my line and bobber lay dazed and inert. This was not my Grandfather Henry, but my other grandfather, whose face I connected in childhood with the one that appears on the flip side of a buffalo nickel. Without cracking that face an iota, he was prone to uttering the funniest things I've about ever heard. In response to my question regarding the fishing, he would answer gravely, "You have to hold your mouth right."

I think that is also the secret of writing: attitude. Hope, unyielding faith in the enterprise. If only I hold my mouth right, keep a clear fix on what I believe is true while I make up my stories, surely I will end up saying what I mean. Then, if I offend someone, it won't be an accidental casualty. More likely, it will be because we actually disagree. I can live with that. The memory of my buffalo-nickel grandfather advises me still, in lonely moments: "If you never stepped on anybody's toes, you never been for a *walk.*"

I learned something else, that November day, that shook down all I thought I knew about my personal, insufferable, nobody's-blues-can-touch-mine isolation of high school. Before the book signing was over, more than one of my old schoolmates had sidled up and whispered: "That Lou Ann character, the insecure one? I know you based her on me."

DONALD MURRAY (b. 1924)

Trying on the Essay

CONSIDER THIS:

Donald Murray, Professor Emeritus of English at the University of New Hampshire, publishes novels, poetry, a newspaper column, and textbooks on writing and teaching writing. As a journalist, Murray has won a number of awards, among them the Pulitzer Prize for editorial writing in the *Boston Herald* in 1954, and he writes a weekly column entitled "Over Sixty," for the *Boston Globe.* He has published two novels, poetry, and a number of books on the craft of writing and teaching writing; recent work includes *My Twice Lived Life: A Memoir.*

Murray begins his essay with a bulleted list explaining why he values the personal essay. How does this 10-bullet list compare and contrast with Scott Russell Sanders's reasons for valuing story? Try reworking Murray's essay into a version of Sanders's; that is, what are the 10 reasons you find that Murray would use to explain why we'll always need good essays? What does he seem to value most about the form? He also gives advice for writing essays: What are the 10 best pieces of advice you derive from this essay on essay writing?

EXPLORING PERSONAL EXPERIENCE

When I was in college my professors preached an aesthetic pyramid of literature: poetry at the peak, fiction and drama below, nonfiction at the bottom. I bought it. I wrote nonfiction, essays and articles, and aspired to write poetry and fiction. I undervalued the essays I wrote, thinking they were not literature. But fashions change and today the genres seem more equal; in fact, the personal essay seems to be achieving artistic equality. This change is due largely to the political climate in which literature is published and taught. The women's movement and the encouragement of diversity invited personal experience, personal opinion, and personal voices. Those voices often speak in essays that explore what had been secret, unspoken emotional and intellectual responses to life. I have many reasons to write the personal essay.

- The artist's answer, nothing less: to give voice to those without a voice, to articulate the unspoken feelings and thoughts of the reader.
- To give myself voice. I am heard when I write; I vote in the human community, registering my opinions, what I stand for, what I fear, what I stand against, what I celebrate.
- To discover who I am. Writing the personal essay celebrates my difference, authenticates who I am, justifies my existence.
- Hearing myself allows me to hear others. The farther I go into myself, the more I can enter into the lives of others; the more I enter the lives of those different from me, the more I understand myself.

- The personal essay allows me to report the important news of the human condition, the stories rarely covered on page one, on radio news, on television.
- I discover how much I know that I didn't know I knew. Writing educates me.
- Writing the personal essay allows me to make use of my experience. I explore the lives I have lived and am living, even those I may live in the future.
- Donald Barthelme told us to "write about what you're most afraid of." When I do, I survive the terrors that silence me. While writing, the dark clouds rise, the monster shadows retreat. Graham Greene explains, "Writing is a form of therapy; sometimes I wonder how all those who do not write, compose or paint can manage to escape the madness, the melancholia, the panic fear which is inherent in the human situation." Writing is my therapy.
- Writing the personal essay is a favorite form of play. I laugh as a sentence turns toward an unexpected meaning, chuckle as the wrong word becomes the right word, grin as the lie becomes the truth.
- I write the personal essay because I will never learn how to write the personal essay, an art that—blessedly—can never be learned. As I grow old, I am forever a young apprentice to my craft.

These are reasons to write in any genre but I think it is important to recognize how the writer's—and the reader's—needs are satisfied by the essay. I think of my columns as essays, a private conversation with each reader. It is a form I love to write, and after publishing nearly four hundred of these conversations I still find the essay provides me with a great variety of forms and voices. In the essay of personal experience, an individual writer speaks to an individual reader, imagines a reader's response and responds to it. Writer and reader explore the topic together. Writing the essay is an intimate art that can include the entire range of human conversation.

Essays can argue, mourn, describe, analyze, make fun, propose, persuade, record, entertain, irritate, inspire, discourage, confide, share, explain, document, criticize, celebrate. In the essay, the writer sits on a bench beside the reader and comments on the life they share.

I was taught a distinction between the formal and the informal essay, but today almost all essays are written in an informal voice. Many of the essays I studied in school—especially those by Emerson and Stevenson—discussed intellectual or moral issues from a distance. I was far more serious, and far more interested in imposing my morality on others, when I was young; and I liked these essays then. I still respect them but I grew to love the essays of Montaigne, Orwell, E. B. White and Didion because they were personal. They made themselves their own subject, placing personal experience in a wider context. These essays seemed written for themselves, then shared with others; they seemed written not to argue some position that had already been taken but were written to explore experience and discover a potential meaning.

At first, most writers just write personal narratives—the fishing trip with father, the birth of a child, the divorce, the death of a grandparent. These are not essays; they are simple, chronological accounts. The material can make these narratives moving, especially to the teacher or friend with whom they are shared, but the writer needs to make the next step, turning this narrative into a personal essay. The essay looks at narrative experience critically—empathetically but evaluative—putting experience in a larger context, trying on the patterns of meaning hidden within the experience. This is critical thinking; the essay takes a broad experience and narrows it down so that it can be examined, or takes a narrow experience and discovers the broader issues that lie within it. These explorations are good therapy for the writer and, if shared or published, for the reader.

The essay is usually the best way for a beginner to enter the writer's world, for it allows the writer to relive a personal experience of importance to the writer and discover a context and pattern of meaning that will make it significant to a reader.

The Hint of a Topic

The essayist is constantly alert to the world and to the writer's personal reaction to that world. As one who publishes a weekly essay, I am never bored. I remember Henry James' counsel: "Try to be one of those people on whom nothing is lost." I observe, overhear, remember, imagine, but equally important, I am alert to my own reaction and respect it even if it makes me uncomfortable. Most people seem to suspect their individual reactions, particularly if they seem to disagree with those around them, but writers know their difference is their strength.

That difference is sparked when a clue for an essay comes from an image caught out of the corner of the eye, a fleeting half-thought, an almost feeling that is not yet understood. I catch a glimpse of myself in the reflection of a black, night window and see my mother's aging, heavy step. I feel the killing violence I used in war rise within me when a car cuts me off in traffic. I see a high-school rebel in purple, spiked hair and myself in the zoot suit that so satisfyingly worried my parents. I wonder, during Christmas dinner when everyone appears happy, why I remove myself psychologically and observe the festivities from a great distance.

The Instigating Line

What I see—and what I think and feel about it—often scares, contradicts, amuses, angers, intrigues me so that I write to discover its meaning. This tension between what I expect to think or feel and what I actually think or feel is usually caught in a line, the fragment of language filled with potential that we discussed in the last chapter. The line is so important that it must be emphasized here again. The line may be overlooked by the inexperienced writer because the words seem ordinary.

These lines are hardly topics. They are not as developed as that. The development comes in the writing. The line, "Tell me a story, Daddy" reminds me that my daughters always wanted to hear the old, familiar stories and that sparks a column on how I like to read series of mysteries in which the detectives, their worlds, and the crimes they solve are familiar. The word *consultant* pops into my head as during a Christmas visit by a daughter, her husband and their two boys. I write a column defining the role of grandparent by comparing it to the role of corporate consultant I played in another life. "I was born in the laxative age" gave me a black-humor column on the medical world of the aging.

Sometimes the line is an image. I see myself sledding down Wollaston Hill, a small boy held between an uncle's knees; I see Michelle, the little girl who played with her dolls at my side, during street combat in Belgium fifty years ago; I see the trees bent by the prevailing wind that I remember from my first visit to the island of Nantucket. Each of these images contains the seed of writing.

The Lead

Sometimes the line is the lead or first sentence of the essay, the one that sets the tone for all that follows. The beginning of the essay should contain—or strongly imply—a central tension (contradiction, irony, surprise, or problem) that will be explored in the essay The lead is a promise to readers that they and the writer will discover something during the reading that will make them view the world differently from the way they have in the past.

George Orwell is the master of the essay I most often turned to for inspiration and instruction when I began to write editorials almost half a century ago. I copied out some of the things he said about essay writing:

> So long as I remain alive and well I shall continue to feel strongly about prose style, to love the surface of the earth, and to take a pleasure in solid objects and scraps of useless information.
>
> Good writing is like a window pane.
>
> (i) Never use a metaphor, simile or other figure of speech which you are used to seeing in print.
> (ii) Never use a long word where a short one will do.
> (iii) If it is possible to cut a word out, always cut it out.
> (iv) Never use the passive where you can use the active.
> (v) Never use a foreign phrase, a scientific word or jargon word if you can think of an everyday English equivalent.
> (vi) Break any of these rules sooner than say anything barbarous.
>
> A scrupulous writer, in every sentence that he writes, will ask himself at least four questions, thus: What am I trying to say? What words will express it? What image or idiom will make it clearer? Is this image fresh enough to have an

effect? And he will probably ask himself two more: Could I put it more shortly? Have I said anything that is avoidably ugly?

In preparing to write this chapter I started searching for Orwell's opening lines which I admired. I remembered them as being unexpected but true to what happens in the essay. They tease—and deliver. I hear Orwell's voice invite the reader to stand beside him and see the world as he sees it—with an uncomfortable honesty, a biting wit, and a skepticism that is balanced by compassion, but when I went through his collected works I was surprised at how the first sentences of hundreds of his essays were quite ordinary. My surprise made me want to explore the subject and the result is the following column that, I believe, offers a special comfort to the beginning writer.

The other morning, when my words lay sodden on the page, I once more apprenticed myself to George Orwell. I search through the pages of my *Collected Essays, Journalism and Letters of George Orwell* by Sonia Orwell and Ian Angus [Harcourt, Brace & World, 1968] seeking instruction and inspiration from such essays as:

England Your England
"As I write, highly civilized human beings are flying overhead, trying to kill me."

Marrakech
"As the corpse went past the flies left the restaurant table in a cloud and rushed after it, but they came back a few minutes later."

Reflections on Ghandi
"Saints should always be judged guilty until they are proved innocent."

Shooting an Elephant
"In Moulmein, in Lower Burma, I was hated by large numbers of people—the only time in my life that I have been important enough for this to happen to me.

I was instructed and inspired, but not in the way I expected. In tracking down the famous openings of these essays in the 2,014 pages of the collection, I read dozens of beginnings that were as limp or clumsy as mine. I'm no George Orwell, but neither was George Orwell most days.

We need to remember that our friend's house, neat for company, was ripe with old newspapers, dog hair and a cardboard pizza coffin the night before. Most of us measure our worst against another's best.

A friend of mine once played golf with Ben Hogan in his prime and was surprised that their score was close. It was after the game that he noticed the difference between them. Hogan took four hundred golf balls and hit a hundred on each of four key shots he had missed.

George Orwell not only wrote great essays because of talent honed by craft, but because he wrote. He filled the page, day after day, year after year, practicing his craft so that he was prepared for inspiration when it dropped by.

He also submitted and published the worst while waiting for the best.

Many of us in retirement have the time to pursue our dreams, but we have to relearn the lessons of the crafts that are paying for our retirement.

We have to remember the miles of visits that produced no sales as well as the few visits that paid off; we have to remember the loaves of bread that did not rise before the one that did.

These days I am the poet I wanted to be at eighteen. Now I write the poems I imagined for most of the decades between college and retirement, but not many get in the mail. And if they are not in the mail, they are not rejected—or published.

In retirement I wanted to become the artist I never was. I have shelf after shelf of books on art; drawers filled with pens, pencils, brushes, paints, crayons, charcoal, watercolors, oils; stacks of sketchbooks, paper, canvas.

What I do not have is stacks of drawings and paintings. I haven't found—made—the time.

And as a writer I know that talent depends on abundance, the accumulation of work that is good and bad.

In fact, Orwell may not have liked the essays I most admire and been most proud of some of those I pass as ordinary.

The artist often does not know what the world will like. The symphony the composer sees as a failure because it did not achieve his ambition for it, may be the one that is played long after he is gone.

The painting, the play, the book, the newspaper column the maker likes the best may be ignored while the work that is struck off in haste—after a lifetime of apprenticeship to the maker's craft—may be the one that is remembered.

That used to disturb me, but now it offers comfort. The true satisfaction is in the making of the work.

At the moment of making, the writer, painter, composer, golfer, fisherman, baker, quiltmaker enjoy the gift of concentration. And as we age, that gift increases in importance.

We are fortunate when we are lost to the world and too old to suffer the ambition of fame. We are blessed, as Orwell was, when we focus on the small, immediate demands of the work at hand.

This stitch, this dough, this cast, this drive, this melody, this line, this word becomes our momentary universe.

Orwell wasn't, with such a moment, the famous writer, but simply a writer trying to find the right word and fit it into a line that made meaning clear.

And I do not have to be George Orwell any more than he had to be George Orwell. All I have to do is to concentrate on this line, then the next.

Length

That column was 793 words long, just under the ideal length for a newspaper essay that might be published on the op ed page (eight-hundred words), the page that is opposite the editorials in most newspapers. The op ed page editor often buys freelance articles, and it is an ideal place for writers to have their voices heard. Essays in magazines can run two or three times as long, but brevity is an advantage in getting an essay published.

The writer must make sure every word, and every pause between words, contributes to the essay. For years I had the following quotation from William Strunk as reported by E. B. White above my desk until it was tattooed inside my forehead:

> Vigorous writing is concise. A sentence should contain no unnecessary words, a paragraph no unnecessary sentences, for the same reason that a drawing should have no unnecessary lines and a machine no unnecessary parts. This requires not that the writer make all his sentences short, or that he avoid all detail and treat his subjects only in outline, but that every word tell.

Selection

Brevity is achieved by selection. In an essay, the writer focuses on one dominant issue, and everything—each statistic, quotation, fact, anecdote, reference, idea, paragraph, sentence, clause, word—must move the essay forward, contributing to its meaning.

The professional limits the subject far more radically than the amateur: not *"education,"* not *"education in the United States,"* not *"English education in New Hampshire,"* not *"writing in Dick Tappen's classroom,"* but *"why Dick Tappen's students write what they fear."* The essay's limited focus allows the writer to explore one topic in depth and give the reader a full and satisfying development of the essay's meaning.

Specific Information

The essay is written like poetry, technical writing, fiction, science writing—with specific information. The tone may be conversational but the reader will not read it unless there is an adequate delivery of information to satisfy the reader's hunger for specifics.

The Common World

In an essay, writer and reader meet in a common world, a familiar country of experience or ideas that they already share but becomes new during the essay. The writer creates this common world with specific details they share, what they do when they are talking on the telephone that the other person cannot see, how they behave in the false privacy of their car in a traffic jam, what they eat in their laps while watching television. The essay writer deals in the commonplace but, then, because of the writer's point of view, the reader sees it anew.

The writer observes and responds to the shared world—what you really think at the funeral, what you think of people who look like their pets, how you can tell when a marriage won't last. The writer weaves a new vision of this shared world by seeing, as if for the first time, what has become ordinary. The essay articulates thoughts and reactions the reader was not previously conscious of; but when read, strike the reader as true.

Trust

The writer's authority is established by the accuracy of the revealing details and the insight and perception of the writer's vision. The reader believes this person sees their common world in such a way that the reader had better pay attention.

In all writing, even technical or scholarly writing, authority may be supported by citations from external sources, but the reader trusts the authority that comes internally from the writer who delivers information or commentary that sparks the shock of recognition within the reader who says, "Yes. That's the way it is. The writer knows what I have been through, how and what I think and feel about it. I'll read more."

Voice

An essay is a conversation, so the reader should hear the individual voice of the writer. The writer should put this heard quality in the writing by writing out loud, tuning the draft by ear to the purpose and meaning of the text. This doesn't mean that all essay writing should be informal or colloquial; it does mean that the music of the text should support the meaning of the draft.

Self-Exposure

In effective writing and, especially in personal-essay writing, the author exposes himself or herself, revealing thoughts and feelings that the reader has also experienced but may have denied. The writer articulates these hidden or suppressed thoughts and feelings, and that is the strength of many essays. It is, however, a problem for the writer who is usually uncomfortable about this self-exposure.

After the death of my daughter, the doctor who had treated her urged me to write about this experience, and my family agreed. I didn't think I would. It was too private, but with their support I have written about it when it seemed necessary or appropriate. Early on, when writing in public during a teacher workshop, a professor accused me of exploiting my daughter's death. This was both a horrible and liberating experience. His charges somehow freed me of the suspicion that I was doing just that. When I have written an essay about my daughter, the response of readers tells me that I am helping them by articulating what they have not been able to say about their own losses.

Editing

Economist John Kenneth Galbraith once said, ". . . when I'm greatly inspired, only four revisions are needed before, as I've often said, I put in that note of spontaneity which even my meanest critics concede." The essay should be edited out loud, with the writer pacing the writing so the essay builds to points of emphasis and then slows down so the reader can absorb what has been said and be prepared for what will be said.

The final editing should make the draft spontaneous: the murderer carefully raking the ground where the body is buried to hide any sign of struggle. The writing should be deceptively easy to read.

Closing

The ending of an essay should not preach, telling readers what to think—or summarize what the writer thought or discovered—but invite readers to do their own thinking, inspired by the voyage of meaning writer and reader have just shared.

FINDING A CONTEXT

The primary reason we write—and read is to find what Robert Frost described as "a momentary stay against confusion." We tolerate a great deal of conflict, disorder and contradiction in our lives, but we turn to art to discover meaning (maybe not *the* meaning, but at least a meaning). It is the primary task of the writer to find a significant meaning or pattern that neither oversimplifies nor confuses.

The search for meaning in experience through writing is essential for all forms of writing, but it is especially appropriate for the personal experience essay. Let me take a snapshot from the memory of my childhood that has produced published writing and see how meaning can grow from experience.

This is what passed through my head and might have been written in my daybook:

> When I was a kid, we once lived in a neighborhood where the guy next door, he was a butcher I think, used to chase his wife around the block waving a cleaver.

If I stop there, you will ask, "So what?" My story isn't a story—yet. It's not an anecdote, not a parable, not a narrative, not an essay, not a poem, not a news story. It is a fragment from a writer's experience inventory, just a note that has action and the potential for drama, even for many meanings. It is a serving of prose without a context. It has no history, no future, no meaningful connection to the writer—or a reader, yet.

Readers often think material comes to the writer pure and complete. They imagine that my memory of the butcher next door instantly becomes a novel that could be described in a listing similar to one in the *TV Guide*: "The Butcher's Wife," the story of a woman who butchered her husband and found God.

The process of making meaning from memory is complex and mysterious. We sit down to write, and instead of what we planned, an image—the light glinting off the cleaver—passes in front of our eyes sixty years after it happened. Graham Greene said, "When I construct a scene, I don't describe the hundredth part of what I see; I see the characters scratching their noses, walking about, tilting back in their chairs—even after I've finished writing—so much so that after a while I feel a weariness that does not derive all that much from my effort of imagination but is more like a visual fatigue: My eyes are tired from watching my characters."

Before writing and during writing I see far more than I can record. And the more I see, the more there is to see as I pass from this world to the remembered or imagined world. We may have forgotten that place, that time, that event, those people, but during writing it is all recreated in enormous detail. Here is something of what appears in my mind's eye when the light glints off that butcher cleaver. These are not clarified thoughts, just fragments in which meaning may be found.

The fragments need a context that surrounds a fragment of writing and gives it meaning. The writer most often begins with the specific rather than the general. The meaning is organic, it grows from the seed of memory.

WENDY BISHOP (b. 1953)

Try This

CONSIDER THIS (See Author's Introduction in Chapter 5):

As you read through the topics proposed in this piece, list other topics that these suggestions bring to mind. For instance, when I suggest writing about language, you might suggest writing about silence. When I suggest you write about weather, climate, or landscape, as a physics major you might suggest that essayists consider the cosmos, planets, time, space, and so on. Try suggesting reversals, analogies, opposites, and slight changes to my topics in order to complete this exercise about making exercises. In addition, next to each of the topic categories, I provide (and the ones you develop), note those you're interested in most, as a writer and as a reader. If you like, use a 1–10 scale, with 10 indicating strongest interest. Do you find any pattern in your interest levels? In your response as reader and writer to these topics?

Try this:
Write about your voice(s), when you had it, didn't have it, how many you have, who you borrow from, what you sound like, inside, outside, alone, with others, when you had none, what you'd like to say but haven't yet:

> I've never experienced anything. Someone called Devan has experienced a lot, but she's not me, exactly: I've made up her life. (Devan)
>
> This is a story I have had published, and for some reason I find the "voice" of the piece to be truer to my personality than many nonfiction essays I write, truer than the nonfiction here. (Ron)

Write about language:

> *Ugly* is a funny word, the way my mom uses it—to describe behavior usually, or language. *Pregnant* is ugly. She prefers *expecting*. . . . when Ellie's only daughter,

Lisa, conceived a child out of wedlock at the age of 15 in our tiny little Tennessee town, she was *expecting* because she had *been tacky.* (Jennifer)

And for me he brings Julius Caesar to life, removes the mist from "Chack-espiri," as *abuela* would say it. And for those in the room not as fascinated by Julius Caesar or Prince Hamlet or poor Willy Loman as I am, those who are—in teacher talk—disruptive, Mr. D. forgoes the pink slip to the principal, meets the disrupter downstairs in the gym, twelve-ounce gloves, the matter settled. He has a broad definition of art. He knows the world—and he understands the block, *el bloque,* what kids today call "the hood." (Victor Villanueva *Bootstraps,* 2)

Write about names, nicknames, given names, imagined names, personas, naming others, naming yourself, place names:

My name—Devan—floated in my mind over a map of North Alabama, looking for a person to land on who could tell me what really happened. Someone told me that it is a name more often used for boys than for girls, which I can believe, and that it is an old name occasionally used by a group of families—a clan of sorts around Birmingham. (Devan)

I named a gerbil "Nibbles." He was cute. He ran up my brother's back and got into his long hair. Nibbles ate Cheerios from my palm. He chewed up toilet paper rolls and died in one too. (Ron)

Some mornings I wake up and I'm Faith Eidse, other mornings I'm Faith Kuhns. I never officially changed my name. Other people did that for me. And I let them. (Faith)

Melanie, which means "black" in Greek (oh, felicitous naming!) is black damask. My middle name, Annette, is French, means "grace" (very nice, yes?), and is angular and the color of magnolia seeds. Black grace. We run to strange nicknames in my family. My family name is Ginny (pronounced with a hard "g"). My dear Aunt Essie used to call me "Goo." My father used to call me "Mudzin." Nicknames bestowed in my family include Boochie, Donnie, Raytee, Michee, Fats-pedly-edly, Boo-hoo-ca-howrie, Pouch, Bugs, Thumper, Tootie, Scooterpoos, Scoot, Bal-Ball, Ari-belle, Kelli-bear, Pud, Pudman, Tammilamb, Nato-potato, Beady, Brown Sugar, and Boo (twice). (Melanie)

Write about weather, climate, landscape:

But first some facts: I have taught for seven years and am a tenured professor at Cal State Northridge, the exact epicenter of California's latest earthquake. Today is day four. We are beginning to dig ourselves out. Even on the Westside of Los Angeles, where I live with my husband and two sons, it has been rocky. (Haake "This is Geology to Us," 3)

Florida has never felt like home, despite its best efforts at grounding me in sand and pastel. North Florida seems an adequate escape—compromise, for the time being. At least primary color exists here in change of season, and in the soil. The

> further inland you get from water, the deeper you find yourself in red clay. (Becky)

Write about architectures, houses you've loved or hated, places you've built, cities, human-made forms and figures, space within and without, materials, meaning:

> Think, for example, of your houses: the one you live in now, if you have one, and the ones you have inhabited before. I am writing a book about your houses. You never lived in a yellow house on the coast of Maine? No matter. You have had such a house, perhaps a long time ago, not perhaps your chief house, the one you spent the most time in, but the one that you return to now most frequently in dreams, whether you remember them or not, a locus for you, inexplicably, of mystery and desire. I will write about the yellow house. You will read about your house. If I do my job, the book I write vanishes before your eyes. I invite you into the house of my past, and the threshold you cross leads you into your own. (Nancy Mairs *Remembering the Bone House: An Erotics of Place and Space,* 11)

> Back door, rusty hinges, the kind of door that stays so wide open even when it's shut that frogs can hop through the crack. Holes torn into the screens, or bitten through by insects. Bare light bulb. Cinder block bookshelves along the baseboards; an occasional roach. Blue tortilla chips, pretzel rings on the wood table next to the antique typewriter. Everyone asks if Michael writes his poetry on it; "it makes me feel poetic," he says. "That's when it *comes* to me." (Ron)

Write about scars:

> I wonder sometimes if all women hate their noses. I hated mine till I spent a few years living in Los Angeles. When I saw what some people go through to alter their noses, I embarked on a difficult journey—to the land of loving my nose. (Jennifer)

> Somewhere on my head, growing into my scalp-line, is a curved scar from a window casing in St. Joe, Missouri, that I ran into on October 25, 1952, the day after I turned 5. Bright cool day, leafy bushes surrounding a damp poured concrete walk, house-like, high-ceilinged motel with long corridors. (Devan)

> I remember my mother's body in death. Open, naked. I could not look for very long at it, anymore than I can look at my own in the light, except in pieces. Never from the waist down, except in the shower when I have to shave, and always avoiding glimpsing my abdomen. I put my face on with a towel around my waist. Mother learned shame from her mother, from her generation and cultural—and from my father. I, too, learned in much the same way. (Becky)

Write about your inner worlds—illness, death, healing, dreams, wishes, lies, religions, values:

> Marty is changed. She doesn't leave the hostel anymore unless she has to. She won't eat, says her breasts are too big, she's on a diet. After school and before

bedtime, she walks endless laps around the living room and ping pong table, her eyes dull. Her bubbly laugh is gone, her cheeks hollow, elbows pointed. She sheds twenty pounds, forty. She catches hepatitis and is sent home, skeletal and yellow. (Faith)

In the years following my uncle's death I always imagined him sitting in a green, winged chair in an empty room. My aunt stood behind him, looking down with concern. I'm not sure where this vision came from, I suspect from stories I overheard at home. There was no funeral, and fewer and fewer visits from my aunt and cousin. My Uncle John is still the only person I've lost.

The "truth" of the story is that he didn't need to die. Apparently he felt the heart attack coming on and did not go to the hospital. He took a shower and sat down while my aunt called the ambulance. He died before they got there. (Amy)

Write about time:

It focuses on a memory I have from my childhood, centering specifically on the nature of description as it affects us psychologically—my room, my mother's eyes, what were always powerful instruments of persuasion . . . even now that she is gone. (Becky)

Sundays and holidays are the worst, no mail will arrive, to, perhaps, give me some insight into my future. On these days I feel closed off from the world, my link to the schools is broken. I go to a bookstore to, at least, find more information on the schools, to find out how each one ranks and differs from the other, but all of the books are sold out. Then, I go on-line to see if anybody in the computer world can commiserate with my situation. There is a lot of talk about Law Schools but no one mentions feeling the seemingly eternal wait. (Kathleen)

Write about ancestors—real, imaginary, black sheep, genealogies, present realities, absences, presences:

It's a beautiful Sunday afternoon on that quiet campus in the heart of Atlanta. Glover and Dan, sitting on a wall, are lazing in the sun in the company of some young women. Three more young women walk by, headed in the direction of Spelman's gate.

Says Glover Rawls, "Oooh, man, look at those eyes!"

Dan Rawls looks. And looks and looks.

The young woman with the big eyes sticks out her tongue.

"She had the biggest eyes," Dan Rawls tells his daughters in later years. "Skinny, though. You couldn't see her if she turned sideways! But she had the biggest eyes."

According to Dan, he saw her later standing on the balcony of some building, probably a dorm. He stares some more and she sticks out her tongue before turning to go inside.

When she tells the story, she doesn't mention any sticking out of tongues. (Melanie)

Write about decisions, windows, chances, turns:

> My parents prided themselves on an always unnamed amount of assistance of theirs that allowed Ruthie (who had worked as their maid in Japan in 1953) to come to the United States. . . . When I was in sixth grade, a visit was arranged and this woman who had not seen me since age three months came to Ventura. At some point as I was leaving the living room reminiscences to take a shower before bed, and she asked if she could help me bathe. I went very still. Showers were there for my furtive attention to my own new body, for fingering and feeling and escaping in hot clouds of steam. Not for backward memory but its adolescent equivalent—forward memory, prediction, and dreaming. This time my mother didn't force me. I said yes myself. And Ruthie, gray hair in her black hair, scooped water and laved me with a cloth, saying quiet, singing things, murmuring. (Wendy)

Write about habits, hobbies, obsessions and fetishes—the Comb Museum in Homer, Alaska, the way you gather rocks, the need you have to check—to recheck—the stove burners:

> One thing that lies behind this writing that is absolutely true—I really do come from a family that ate mint and garlic sandwiches, and my grandmother really did win prizes at the Garden Club. (Devan)

> Each spring Strat-O-Matic issued new recreations of the previous baseball season. I thumb through the fresh cards, checking statistics on the Boston Red Sox players. Strat-O-Matic was a game I grew up playing with my brothers. . . .
>
> I remember my brother could not stand to lose when we played Strat-O-Matic. He would scribble fiercely on his score sheets, break pencils, swear. . . .
>
> As I install the new computer Strat-O-Matic software, I think about the old player cards we owned, how fingered, dirty, and soft those cards became. The rubber bands would melt from the teams being stored in a shoe box in the closet, so over time I cut up little white strips of white paper to fold in between the rubber band and the team cards.
>
> I remember the tactile pleasure of Strat-O-Matic playing cards, and the quick flip I would do during games to check that player's home run total, his strikeouts or walks, his batting average. Was this guy living up to his real numbers? Exceeding them? (Ron)

> David and I met on a blind date. Actually, we met over the phone, through a mutual acquaintance, a girl he had dated and that I now worked with. I was hooked from the moment I heard his voice, the voice that now causes my internal cavity to constrict against itself . . . (Becky)

Write about gender:

> The harder I tried to keep out of it, the more pronounced "I" became. . . . Paradoxically, I somehow assumed the attitude that "I" despised, that the personal pronoun "I" was sentimental, sloppy, undisciplined, self-indulgent—all the things that I had been taught not to be both at home and in school, grade one on

up. I had been indoctrinated, as many women in this country continue to be, to deny my own existence as a meaningful, contributing, thinking as well as *feeling,* holistic being. (Becky)

The only time my father shared a highly personal moment with me he was driving with me one night. He spoke into the windshield. He told me he was proud of me for something. (Maybe I had just graduated from Eckerd College.) He wanted me to know that. He told me that he was never able to tell his father "I love you." He had wanted to so badly, but even when Papa was in the hospital, and my father knew he was dying, he still could not say the words. (Ron)

Write about travel—local and distant, returning and remaining, insiders and outsiders, landscapes and peoples, how you see a culture and how you're seen:

Had I included my personal experiences of growing up in this part of the country, the reader might learn about traveling snake shows with specimens that extended from one end of the school gym to the other, summer afternoons melted away by sucking on orange sherbet push-ups, and small town nights in a dry county that boasted a bootlegger with a drive-through window on the side of his mobile home. (Heidi)

So I traveled from steamy North Florida to the cold, rocky northeast coast of Ireland to start over. I wandered along fuchsia and blackberry hedges, past stone fences and cropping herds of Belted Galloways (dairy cows); I listened to Medbh McGuckian amid Thom McCarthy and Joan Newmann as they read poems and talked about them; I know because I wrote these things in my journal. Yet nowhere does the journal tell the real story of the journey . . . (Devan)

Write about taboos:

My first bleeding was copious and happened at school in my plaid dress. I didn't notice it until I got to my room at the hostel and stuck to my chair. I was alarmed. I'd never seen so much blood caked into a dress. I had thought menstruation would be discrete, a small leakage now and then. My dress was ruined, and I didn't have any to spare.

Aunt Nettie showed me how to soak it in cold water and gave me a sanitary belt and pad. Sitting under the twist-barred window in the bathroom, threading my first pad, I wondered at having a body that could produce babies. (Faith)

The day I came out to my mother, at the age of 29 (I'm a late bloomer, or a late confessor), the first thing she asked me, the *very first* thing, was, "Does anyone else know?" Knowing that she meant *anyone else in my hometown,* I told her no, and was surprised to discover that this was immeasurably more comforting to her than the news that two of her nieces—the daughters of her younger sister and her brother—are also lesbians. (Jennifer)

At home the things we did were predictable and orderly, so orderly that by four I had already established my lifelong persona as a rebel by refusing to eat—food came around with a grinding annoying regularity, peas and carrots and

> the unrelieved bland repetitiveness of milk. The only thing I liked to eat was candy orange sections or the lemon drops, peppermints, and gingerbread that my grandfather carried in the pockets of his sweater, and to escape meals I would wander out into the yard without my shoes, which I wasn't supposed to do, either, talk to the neighbors, talk to myself, play in the sandbox with Sharon who lived next door, and eat green apples until I was sick. (Devan)

Write about circles and sets—seasons, elements, four corners of the world, wonders of the world, dream catchers, webs, fates, muses, mysteries and initiates:

> I know my education has made me a better writer and a better thinker in many ways. I fear sometimes, though, that it will make me too self-conscious to be honest. So I write about things I dream about as often as I can. Dreams, my dreams at least, are always honest. I dream my demons. I dream about abandonment and humiliation and failure and food and crying while someone laughs at me. In my dreams, the people I care about the most always turn on me. Whenever I can, I write the dreams down and turn them into poems—talismans or therapy. (Jennifer)

> I look for signs, symbols that reflect and resound, move with a rhythm that is most like the peace that I have glimpsed in the night, lying prone on my back, feeling the pulse of wind through the pines dancing around me. It is there, waiting, hiding in the open. (Becky)

Write about family:

> Wasn't sure what to write about. In a foul, overworked stressed-out, hyperactive mood; chose this story because it was amusing and silly and because it is one of my mother's favorite stories, so she means it to tell something about our family. (Devan)

> I would sit with my Mama, who closed her eyes when she sang. Her eyelids would twitch. My Papa never sat beside her; he was always on the front pew because he was an elder. We always had to be on our best behavior when we sat with her; she'd reach over and pinch a plug out of our arm if we wiggled too much. . . . (Heidi)

Write about you writing:

> My structure throughout has been to tell the story of growing up a Mennonite woman in post-colonial Zaire and Canada, and to do so in a way that evokes the colonizing of the body by religion. (Faith)

> I keep thinking of writing process, that I'm sitting in my new chair from Office Depot, that I'm drinking room temperature Diet Pepsi, and that I put off doing these writings for as long as I could. (Amy)

> I taped photos of my mother and aunt all around my computer. This helped a great deal—helped me get at certain emotions. Finally, I find myself inevitably doing some fictionalizing, however little, in the nonfiction piece. (Jennifer)

What was problematic: How could we write about relatives? Did we have the right to speak for them? Whose stories are our stories? Could we tell their stories even if we tried? What's the difference between truth-telling and self-indulgence? Is it easier (better) to speak only of those who are no longer alive? Or, is it simply better not to send them the texts?

> I don't think we have a responsibility to tell everyone's story. I can only tell my memories, my perceptions, and my truths. What I write is what I remember, and my memories are significant for reasons that other family members might not share . . . I don't believe we can speak for others, that we can imagine or suppose what they might have thought or felt. It is too complicated imagining what we think and feel to presume to do it for another person. But if we do write about our imaginings of their thoughts and feelings, we need to do so carefully, always admitting that they are no more true than the "characters" we create. (Amy)

> I suggested that this term I would send my three sisters my writing. My parents, being dead, freed me to write of them. My sisters, were another issue. "Don't do it," said Faith, "Or at least be prepared for anything to happen."
>
> Of the three, the one portrayed most painfully, has yet to respond. The one who is oldest, most distant, called. I've yet to call back. The one portrayed most lovingly, wrote back—"The piece is so personal, so clear. The phone conversation between Gina (you, me, Nancy or Judy) and mom was IT. We've all experienced it, and you've captured it. My guess is there are others in the world who may have shared a similar experience, but for me it was a snapshot. . . . Thanks again for sharing your writing with me. It is a gift I appreciate more than any other."
>
> Gratifying, but I realize it is the silent sister I most want and fear to reach, at this moment of my writing life. (Wendy)

> "I wouldn't share this with my brother" says Ron.
>
> "I don't think I would either—share mine," says Melanie.
>
> "Oh. Oh. You've got to. You've got to publish this," says Faith.
>
> "My mother's been gone for nearly two years now," says Becky, "and I still worry about her reading my work."

Equally vexing—truthfulness versus artfulness. Does all fiction grow out of a matrix of nonfiction or do the two co-exist and the writer tips the see-saw—changing the percentages of fact to facts-as-they might-or-should-be?

> Unless you don't mind being a "stealer of souls" or don't care if your family and friends never speak to you or trust you again, as a writer of personal essays, you will ask yourself over and over, "How much of a shared experience should I, as only one of the sharing parties, make public?" (Melanie)

> A friend of mine has no sight. I don't know how he host his sight, because he is reticent, reserved; and I don't ask about what he doesn't volunteer. The one time I made an oblique query about the lack of light in his life, he evaded me so

definitively and with such deftness that I, as quickly, dropped the subject. (Melanie)

And I remember and still feel "new" feelings for the characters I created: even though based on real people, they became new then, somehow more tangible and accessible than the real ones. Sometimes it's easier to relate to and love fictional characters than it is real persons. (Ron)

What was fascinating: Setting definitions aside, we jumped in, got our words wet—we wrapped them to dry on the racks of memory, we turned fact to fiction or fiction to fact, intentionally and compared the results. It worked this way:

Great-great-grandma Margareth Isaak (fiction)

I don't often sit for photos, so I feel a little stiff today, every button buttoned, every lace tied, every hair tucked in place. Photos are quite literally graven images and some Mennonites don't believe in them. But my husband Abraham is a thinking man, and he's decided that a photo will mean more than a tombstone to our grandchildren. Besides I don't intend to worship this image when it's developed. We won't put it in a fancy frame like the ones the photographer showed us.

Great-great-grandma Margareth Isaak (fact)

In the photograph my great-great-grandma sits with her hands cupped in her lap. There is a book balanced in her hands, but she is not holding it. It's probably just a prop, placed there by the photographer who has ideas about making his subjects look learned and wise.

So much for bright ideas. My great-great-grandma probably can't read English and she's no faker. But she could probably beat the photographer at the Railroad Studio Car in a Bible drill any day. Especially if she had her own well-thumbed Martin Luther translation. (Faith)

How They Met (fact)

My mother and father met for the first time in the Fall of 1945. She was a first semester freshman at Spelman College in Atlanta, Georgia. He was a second semester freshman at Morehouse College.

He was also fresh from the army—he'd served in Africa and Europe during World War II, and was taking advantage of the GI Bill. He was twenty-eight years old, slim, brown, very very handsome, a cosmopolitan older man. She was just turned seventeen, slim, brown, big-eyed and very very pretty—and as confidant as any pretty young woman can be who was the somewhat spoiled baby of her family and had been away to Hampton Institute. No shyness here.

How They Met: 2 (fiction)

"Oooh, man, look at those eyes!"

You're a first semester freshman in a woman's college adjacent to a men's college positively notorious for its eligible young men. Good-looking men all over the place. Good-looking men only too happy to pay vocally appreciative attention to young women happy to have this attention paid to them, though since they're *ladies,* the cream of the nation's young Negro women, its best and brightest and prettiest and very much LADIES, the young women take pains not to acknowledge the attention too eagerly. (Melanie)

Classroom Authors:

LEAH MARCUM

Storm Surge

CONSIDER THIS (See Author's Introduction in Chapter 4):

As you read Leah Marcum's essay, let it be a test case for the definitions and discussions in this chapter. For instance, you might ask how she draws on memory to construct her piece. How does she use story? Is her narrative chronological or does she interrupt events? Does she mix exposition and narration? Why and to what ends? How does she use a classmate's voice to help structure her essay? How does she use research? How trustworthy do her facts seem? Her memory? After speculating as you read the essay, you'll find Leah's writing process narrative, the story of how she wrote this essay. As you read about some of the struggles she had in structuring and composing her essay, consider how many of those struggles you noticed *before* she pointed them out to you. To what degree does her essay illustrate the definition of the personal essay as Donald Murray presents it?

STORM SURGE

> If you'd been through Hurricane Andrew, you would never think about storms the same way again.
>
> —Carolyn, classmate whose house was destroyed by Hurricane Andrew in 1992.

Not long ago, I went to Austria to visit a friend who was staying there for the summer. We hiked in the Alps on what started out as a beautiful day, but got caught in a sudden, violent storm. We dashed for cover in a little open-sided hay shack, and watched the dark gray tidal wave of rain approach us from across a field. Clusters of lightning spider-legged across the threatening sky, and thunder boomed and echoed off the surrounding mountain peaks. The wind whipped through the trees and debris flew everywhere.

Through some inexplicable sense of trust, I felt perfectly safe, though I had no reason to. The walls of our flimsy shelter rattled and groaned, and my friend crouched down on the hay-covered floor and shielded her head with her arms. Lightning struck closer and closer and the thunder was so loud we could feel the ground shake. My friend started crying, "Oh my God, oh my God," again and again. I stood there in the opening of the hay shack, leaning out so I could see everything. The wind bent the trees so far over I thought they'd break, and the sky looked so powerful and majestic that I was rooted to the spot in awe. A deer suddenly appeared, its head and neck outstretched like a horse heading for the finish line, and raced across the field ahead of the wall of rain. I was thrilled. When hail began to ricochet off the ground, my friend yelled at me to get inside. "Are you nuts?" she screamed at me. "You could get killed out there!"

Maybe I am nuts, but I love storms. David Hoadley, a storm chaser, sums up my feelings in his explanation that he chases partly for "the sheer, raw experience of confronting an elemental force of nature—uncontrolled and unpredictable." Hoadley poetically expands on how it feels to stand in a storm by saying that it is "an experience of something infinite, a sense of powers at work and scales of movement that so transcend a single man and overwhelms the senses that one feels intuitively (without really seeking) something eternal . . ." (qtd. in Davidson 9).

Not everyone, of course, enjoys storms like I do, a fact that became quite evident to me in 1995 when Hurricane Opal was forecast to strike the coast south of Tallahassee (it actually struck further west, instead). I was taking a class at Florida State University at the time and most of my classmates talked excitedly about the advancing storm. Hurricane Opal was fast approaching a Category 4 status, and there was a chance that it might even become a Category 5. We knew the University would have to close, and some of us celebrated by swapping hurricane party stories. Without warning, one young woman, Carolyn, started shaking and crying. She said, "If you'd been through Hurricane Andrew, you wouldn't be talking about parties. I'm scared to death!" She explained that she used to live in Homestead, the area south of Miami where Hurricane Andrew caused the most destruction. Carolyn and her family, like many Florida residents, didn't go to a public shelter because they felt that their house was strong enough to stay in. When the storm tore off part of their roof and windows began to shatter, the whole family took shelter in the bathroom. The wind was so fierce they all had to pile up against the door to keep it from flying open. "We spent hours like that, and the whole time we thought we were going to die," she sobbed. "In the morning . . . there wasn't anything left! . . . just the bathroom we were in. How can you even *think* about having a party?"

Carolyn's profound fear of hurricanes did have a sobering effect on me for the moment, but I soon returned to the excitement of looking forward to a big storm. Even so, every time my pulse picks up about some heavy weather coming my way, I remember that frightened, tearful classmate. I get a little twinge of guilt, and I imagine Carolyn's accusing voice, chastising me for my excitement:

Hurricanes are not something to look forward to. You should do everything you can to get out of the way.

I'm not stupid when it comes to extreme weather; I do take precautions and I don't put myself deliberately in harm's way, but if there's any chance of watching a storm from a safe space, I'll do it, and if I can't get to a safe space I'll watch it anyway.

Believe me—if it gets bad enough, you won't be watching it. You'll be praying that you'll get out alive.

The natural world, and the "bad" weather that sometimes goes with it, has always held a fascination for me. As far back as I can remember, I've spent time outdoors; not just playing in the yard as a child, but also camping, spending time at my grandparents' farm, going on picnics to the many springs around Central Florida, and fishing in the surf at the beach. When I got older, I took up hiking and SCUBA diving, and I continued to go camping until my back just couldn't take sleeping on the ground any more. There's nothing I like better than getting out in the fresh air. It does something for me. I feel grounded, at peace, a part of the whole universe. Of course, being outdoors means contending with all kinds of weather, and while I enjoy a glorious sunshiny day with an infinite blue sky as much as the next person, I have to admit, too, that I like *all* kinds of weather—especially the kind where Mother Nature really shows what she can do.

I think my fascination with violent weather systems began when I was seven years old. My central Florida home of Lakeland was directly in the path of Hurricane Donna, a Category 4 hurricane (Category 3 by the time it got to us) that brought a lot of destruction to our small town. Donna hit during the night, and I can remember being awake part of the time, listening to the relentless rain and to the sound of the wind making the windows creak and rattle in our woodframe house. My parents didn't act like they were afraid, so I never got really worried even though we could hear the thud of trees hitting the ground. In the morning, my sodden neighborhood was a different world. We were lucky that there was very little damage to the houses right around us, but huge old oak trees had fallen everywhere. For the first time, those mighty limbs were accessible for climbing. Spanish moss hung to the ground from the prostrate limbs, making curtained rooms between the branches. It was a wonderful playland for us kids in the neighborhood, and for weeks and weeks we were thoroughly entertained.

Playland!? People died in that hurricane!

Hurricane Donna was extremely destructive, but from my perspective as a child, and because the people we knew didn't suffer any catastrophic consequences, it was just one big adventure. A naive perspective, yes, but that's how it was for me, and that's how my excitement for storms began.

Storms are dangerous, destructive, life-threatening and sometimes devastating to entire regions. I know that. I'm not oblivious to the downside of extreme weather, but I can't help getting juiced up when a squall line of big thunderstorms is making its way across the Panhandle of Florida, or when a tropical storm appears which might turn into a hurricane.

From the moment a hurricane forms off the coast of Africa and starts its trek across the Atlantic, my T.V. stays tuned to The Weather Channel and I start thinking in terms of gathering emergency supplies for a siege. I like the whole process of getting ready for it. There's a survivalist-like challenge in preparing my space for life without electricity, and I try to think of everything that will make me comfortable instead of miserable. Living in the woods like I do means that many trees could be across roads for weeks, and it's worth my peace of mind to know that I could manage if I had to.

I don't actually get my house ready for a hurricane unless one is forecast for my area, but I do think it through ahead of time so I'll know what to do and what to buy if I need to. The most important thing is to pick a safe place, away from windows, to stay in during the storm. A hallway or closet, possibly a bathroom, usually fits the bill. We happen to have a basement now, so that's what I'd use for a safe place. A radio, snacks and flashlights go into that space, as well as two cots so we can sleep in relative comfort. Once the storm has passed, it's inevitable that there won't be any electricity, so light and food take the place of safety as the most important thing. I have lots of candles, several oil lamps, and a couple of flashlights, and I try to create one place where the light will be strong enough to read by. Besides the usual hurricane staples of bottled water, peanut butter and canned tuna fish, I buy gourmet goodies like canned shrimp and crab, marinated artichoke hearts and unusual rices and dried pastas. I figure that if life might be a hardship for a while, I might as well get what pleasure I can.

You can plan all you want to, but it won't do a bit of good if the storm is big enough.

Granted, a Category 4 or 5 hurricane is going to produce major destruction and my preparations won't mean much under those conditions. As a native Floridian who has lived in the state all my life, I've had plenty of experience with the getting-ready process, and most of the time, the erratic hurricanes end up someplace other than where I am. So, usually, the preparations I've made don't get put to use, but I know that sometimes it's worth the effort.

When Hurricane Kate headed for the West coast of Florida in November of 1986, I was living in an apartment in Tallahassee. I watched the news until 5:00 p.m., when the electricity went out, a full seven hours before the eye of the hurricane would pass over. By 6:00 p.m., the strongest gusts had gotten up to about 70 mph, and it was nearly dark outside although it hadn't started to rain. I kept looking out my window and I could see a palm tree with all its palm fronds streaming in the same direction like the tails of a wind sock. The traffic light that hung in the intersection by my apartment was more horizontal than vertical. Suddenly, I felt drawn outside and I just opened the door and went out in the yard and stood in the storm.

What a fool!

The little bit of light that was left was an eerie green and my skin immediately felt slick from the heavy, warm humidity. The wind pushed against me so I could feel what a bully it was. There was a strange metallic smell to the air and my whole body felt charged with electricity and power. I only stayed a moment; I just wanted to be in it, to feel it before it got too rough.

The rest of the night passed without incident, and in the morning I discovered that Tallahassee looked a lot like Lakeland did after Hurricane Donna: enormous oaks had fallen everywhere, and the entire city was without power. I was glad I'd made my storm preparations, because I didn't get my electricity turned back on for five days. But it's not my preparedness that comes to mind when I think of Hurricane Kate—it's the experience of standing in my front yard in the early stages of the storm. It's one of my favorite storm memories.

Favorite storm memories. Some of us will never be able to say that.

The storm chasers and I aren't the only ones with a passion for storms—just look at those nuts on The Weather Channel who spend their working days at storm locations, dressed in flapping rain gear and standing in front of beach hotels so the TV audience can see the pounding waves, the drenching rain, the strength of the wind, and get a taste for the power of a hurricane about to hit. Those on-site weather reporters are so pumped up, they're nearly beside themselves. I completely understand.

I take heart that I'm not really crazy when I see articles like "Storms of the Century" on The Weather Channel's web site. This article was written by six meteorologists who put together a list of the top ten storms in the United States during the past century. The meteorologists' enthusiasm and admiration for the individual storms reads like a wine snob's evaluation of fine wines at a tasting. Superlatives abound: epic, raw intensity, incredible, amazing, ferocious, potent, exceptionally rare, resultant definitive magnitude, intense, awesome, peak intensity, deadly, and unquestionably extreme meteorologically. Mixed metaphors sneak in periodically as their excitement gets away from them: "While the top ten did, we think, shake out rather nicely, that's not to say our decision of which players were not quite ready for prime time was a piece of cake" (Forbes, 1999). Trying to decide which storms would make the top ten proved so difficult that they actually ended up with eleven because two of the storms tied for tenth place. In fact, Carolyn, my former classmate, would probably be disappointed to learn that Hurricane Andrew was one of the tenth place ties—not even close to number one (the Labor Day hurricane of 1935 captured the winning spot). And there were so many "favorites" that an honorable mention list of thirty more storms was compiled, and even then there was angst among some whose pet storms were left out.

One of the top ten in the article was another storm that I went through. The Superstorm of March 12–15, in 1993 was an enormous winter storm that affected most of the Eastern third of the United States. It produced blizzards, tornadoes, rains, high winds, and record freezes. At my house, just south of Tallahassee, our electricity was out for four days. Because we have an electric pump for our well water, we had no running water, and even after the power came back on, we discovered that our pump had broken from the hard freeze. The temperature stayed below freezing for three days, dropping as low as 9 degrees one night. Despite the hardship, my husband and I managed to have a pretty good time. We closed off all the rooms in the house, and moved into the living room where the wood stove is. That wood stove got quite a workout: besides heating the living room, its griddle-like lid served as a stove top, and I was able to heat big pots of water for taking sponge baths. We had enough candles in the room to read by, and we spent some time listening to the radio and playing card games. The cabin-like atmosphere was really pretty romantic, and I loved sleeping in front of the glass-fronted wood stove. I wouldn't want to live like that all the time, but for a few days it was fun to live like we were camping out, and I have the Superstorm to thank for forcing me into the experience.

If you'd ever had a bad experience with a storm, you'd never look at one the same way again.

Once, I did have a miserable time in terrible weather, but part of my misery was due to illness. I'd gone on a scuba trip to the Bahamas with twenty other divers, and shortly after boarding the boat, where we lived for the next four days, I started feeling weird and queasy. Probably a little seasickness, I thought, even though I'd never had it before. My illness turned out to be Hepatitis A, but I didn't know that until I got back to land days later. Meantime, I felt worse and worse, and even though I did go diving, it was a disaster because I completely lost my equilibrium, hyperventilated, and ran out of air ninety feet down. After that, I stayed in my bunk, nauseous and weak. Staying in bed didn't help much, though, because on the trip back home a storm came up and the boat rose and fell so sharply with the ten-foot seas that I was just tossed around in the cabin. Also, the boat had been slowed to an idle, and the diesel fumes were coming into the cabin. My stomach revolted, and I couldn't take it any more. I went up on the deck and sat down with my legs and arms wrapped around a pole to keep from being flung into the ocean, and let the wind and rain beat against me. With each high swell, the boat leaned so far over on its side, I thought it would keel over, and then it would drop with a sickening crash into the valley between the waves.

Please, don't tell me you ended up enjoying it!

I've never been so scared in my life. I just knew we were all going to drown. It was an absolutely wretched experience that I thought would never end, but the storm did finally blow over after a few hours and we all arrived safely back home. The only thing that storm was good for was for storytelling.

At least you learned your lesson.

What I've learned from my encounters with extreme weather is this: experience it all, within reason. If all we had was sunshine and calm weather everyday, no one would even notice it any more. So the next time the wind starts blowing and the sky turns dark, check it out. Sit a little away from a window, and get comfortable. Watch the thunder heads build strength and the wind increase as the clouds get closer. Notice how still and silent the birds get, and how loudly the frogs and crickets sing. The sky will get darker and darker, and you'll hear thunder in the distance. Finally, lightning will flash and crack, and rain will blow against the windows—but don't leave yet! Stay for the whole show. Let the powerful side of nature reveal itself, and feel the surge of the storm.

WORKS CITED

Davidson, Keay. "Our National Passion." *Weather* Vol.11, No. I. 2000: 6–11.

Forbes, et al. "Storms of the Century." The Weather Channel Enterprises. 1999. <http://www.weather.com/weather_center/ special_report/sotc/topten/results.html>.

WRITING PROCESS NARRATIVE FOR "STORM SURGE"

Just like with the first paper, I had several false starts. I intended to write on something else, but when we did the "nature" invention in class, I got such an enthusiastic response from my group that I decided to "ride the horse in the direction it's already going."

This is one of those papers that is unfolding naturally. Even before my first draft, I knew I had plenty of ideas to include in this paper about my love of storms. In fact, I had too many ideas and had to pare it down to a reasonable number. I started the paper early one morning and worked straight through to the end. For once, I got the first draft done early so that I could troubleshoot before sharing it in class.

The first draft got a very positive response from my group. They really liked my descriptions of storms I've been through. I love to describe nature (I'm an Annie Dillard fan), so this part was fun for me and very gratifying to get the class feedback. They also said they liked the background voice, although one person asked for clarification about just who the voice was supposed to represent.

The workshop by the whole class revealed that I should have taken that request for clarification about the background voice as a tip-off. I had put it in as kind of a voice of acknowledgment that storms are dangerous—I had no other motive. However, people wondered if the voice was my subconscious, or someone I knew, or . . . what? Still, they liked it, so I left it in, and tried to think who I wanted the voice to be. Finally, I remembered a former classmate who was completely terrified of storms, and I knew I could use her to personify the background voice. I included a part to explain who the voice is, and I added more places where the voice appears to be responding to my narrative, or, my narrative responds to her voice.

With my Portfolio draft, I felt confident that I fixed the confusion over the voice. Regrettably, my two reader/editors disagreed. It still wasn't clear. I consulted with Wendy, who suggested that I give the voice the name of the former classmate, and reiterate the name throughout the paper so that the reader isn't likely to forget who it is. I do that, and I think it works. I wish I had time for another critique to make sure—but it does look pretty good now. I get my husband to read it, and he says it's great, but he's always my most supportive cheerleader, so as a workshopper, he's nearly useless.

Even though I still can't say that I'd be eager to do research, I have to admit that just doing the little bit of research that I did for this piece expanded my knowledge and my confidence that information is out there for the taking—and enhancing of papers.

KEITH GAWRYS

The Legend of the Swine Creek Monster

CONSIDER THIS:

When he wrote this essay, Keith Gawrys was a first-year writing student. In returning to a childhood scene, Keith uses the memory of family friends and a joyous, unreflective time from his youth to guide you into considering your own childhood myths, mysteries, and moments when—finally—you realized you have grown older, must grow older, and that those feelings will be most vividly tapped in memory. Before reading, think for a moment or two about the outdoor places that drew you as a child. How comfortable did you feel there? Did you ever encounter or make up stories about monsters? How do local myths and family stories of place get started? How do they circulate? Who tells scary stories in your family and when?

The past has a way of pouncing on people like the Bogeyman that lurks within every child's closet. It is the same ghoul that thrives on fear and steals precious sleep. It remains in obscurity, an ominous shadow blacker than darkness itself, quick to disappear at the flick of a switch, only to return again in your dreams. Every child's past holds some fiendish monster—a Freddy Krueger, Frankenstein monster, brain-eating zombie, or rabid beast that awakens only when the bedroom is consumed in darkness—yet my monster lacked the bone-chilling terror of many childhood nightmares.

I met my monster on Swine Creek Road, a long gravel path in northern Ohio that follows the length of a brook with the same name. Like the road and surrounding countryside, Swine Creek remains suspended in time. A towering wall of clay, deposited through centuries of flow, stands on one side of the creek, one of the ramparts surrounding the monster's domain. At the foot of the wall lies the smooth sedimentary rocks, perfect for skipping across the surface of the stream, but much too small to add structural support to the monster's castle. On the opposite side of the creek stands the dense woods that willingly part for the small children that pass through them, but somehow push away any adults that try to enter. Beyond the woods stands the home of Jim and Ester Byler, the small farmhouse where I spent many childhood summers while my parents were at work.

Jim and Ester Byler were not your typical American family. They were what my grandfather referred to as "jerked over Amish." Born to Amish parents, they gave up the group's beliefs soon after they married. The Amish sect lives by a strict moral code that governs all of their actions. In essence, they shun everything Yankee, such as gas powered automobiles and household electricity. Instead they drive horse-drawn carriages and employ kerosene lanterns for lighting. Amish women adorn themselves in unrevealing, long, plain-colored dresses with knee high socks to cover any leg left uncovered by the skirt. The men wear trousers with suspenders and shirts buttoned all the way to the collar to cover their chests. Married men are distinguished by their long beards, which serve to tell how long they have been married.

No longer members of the Amish community, the Byler's quickly adjusted to the Yankee lifestyle. I would have thought that Jim and Ester were born Yankee, if they didn't have traces of the Dutch Amish accent. Like the Amish, they were good-natured, hardworking people who still held fast to traditional values. So instead of allowing us to sit around the house all day, Ester encouraged my brothers and I to venture outdoors. My brothers and I spent most of our days exploring the contours of Swine Creek for ourselves.

Upon arrival at the Byler's house, my brothers and I didn't waste any more time around the house than necessary. We hastily kissed our mother goodbye, greeted Ester with a hug, and raced to the perimeter of the backyard and the woods beyond. We did not have to travel too far into the woods before we came upon the creek, but the path through them held dangerous obstacles. The woods were not very dense with trees, but were overrun with the thorns of blackberry bushes. Only someone who knew the proper path through the woods could make it to the creek unscathed. Most adults reached the creek with at least one good scratch from a blood-thirsty thorn. The only times the vines got the best of me were when I tried to pick their ripe berries. But even then, the risk of injury was outweighed by the sweet taste of purple juices coursing through my mouth, staining my fingers, tongue, and everything else its dark violet dye touched. I always returned home like a proud soldier displaying the berry blotches on my face and clothes like purple heart medals.

We could eat only so many blackberries before we felt the pangs of a stomach ache, so we learned to eat them in moderation. We spent most of our time exploring the creek itself with its hundreds of nooks and bends. My younger brother, Todd, was only three years old at the time and only ventured out when we stayed close to the house. Because he was such a burden to lug upstream to our swimming hole and too uncoordinated to skip rocks across the surface of the water, he spent most of his time playing with dirt and trying to catch the minnows that nibbled at his toes.

I was only six years old, but I was big enough to accompany my two older brothers just about everywhere except up to the summit of the clay wall that overlooked the creek. Occasionally they liked to climb to the top of the hill and follow the railroad tracks to some unknown place. I could never find the courage to actually climb the seemingly vertical incline myself, so I followed them from the lower ground for as long as they stayed in sight. Most of the time, we would all venture upstream together to an area where the creek widened and deepened into a natural swimming hole. Here the water went from ankle deep to four feet deep in a few steps. On especially scorching days when even the clouds took cover because they couldn't stand the heat, we went to this spot to take a refreshing dip. Here the clay was soft and grey, perfect for sculpting into works of art or miniature balls for mudfights.

When we grew tired of these games, we searched for the flattest and smoothest rock to skip across the water. We turned the rock skipping into a competition, trying to see who could skip his rock the most times or the farthest. When our supply of rocks diminished, we took a break from the contest to look for more. Another of our favorite games was to try damming up one part of the creek against the flow of current. I could never seem to build my dams as sturdy as the beaver dams that we occasionally found. When my dams continually failed, I pictured the beavers laughing at me from somewhere in the distance. Nothing in the creek ever changed, but we could always find something new to do. It was as if the creek held us in a magic spell—a spell that only Ester Byler could break.

Each day around noon, Ester stood at the base of the woods that shielded her house from the creek, placed her thumb and forefinger together between her lips, and let out a shrill whistle that we could hear up to a mile away. Upon hearing the whistle, any power that the creek held over us instantly vanished as we rushed back to nourish our appetites. After lunch we hurried back upstream to continue playing. We never ventured downstream though, where the stream narrowed and blackened underneath the canopy of trees that enclosed it. Traveling downstream was like venturing into a bear's den. The entire area took on a cavelike quality.

Jim Byler wove a tale of how children our age would travel downstream and never return. He described a time when he once sighted a monster there, and how he barely escaped its grasp alive. He had scars to prove this. When his tale was finished, he warned us in a gruff voice, "Beware of the monster. It won't get you if you boys stay together. But if you wander apart. . . ." Then he made an inhuman growling sound. His growling soon grew into a startling roar that pushed his bottom dentures completely out of his mouth. Then he began to cough, or maybe laugh (I was too scared to notice). It took me a couple of days to recover from the idea that playing in the creek might be a health hazard. It took the encouragement of my older brothers to venture out to the creek again a few days later. My brothers had heard ghost stories before and learned not to take them seriously. But I was at an impressionable age. I believed every word that Jim said.

From then on, I always played upstream and kept a watchful eye on the surroundings for anything suspicious. I never wandered very far from my brothers. As long as I kept them close, I knew that I was safe. I imagined what the Swine Creek monster looked like. It wasn't a fifty-eyed, tentacled freak that oozed from the pages of a Clive Barker or Stephen King novel. I thought that it might look more like a ten-foot tall man-ape with hair covering every part of its body and a head the size of a watermelon. I hardly ever watched horror movies, but I heard the stories of Bigfoot and the Abominable Snowman that roamed the woods of places not too unlike Swine Creek. I pictured the Swine Creek monster as a sasquatch—an enormous beast with huge fangs and even bigger feet. I became suspicious of every odd marking in the sand. Just about anything could pass as a footprint. My hair stood on end at the sound of a snapping twig or sight of a twisted shadow swaying in the wind. I always entertained the possibility that the creature might decide to appear out of nowhere and chase after me in a fit of hunger and rage. Every time I journeyed beyond another bend in the stream, I hoped that I wouldn't accidently bump into the monster. I constantly stole glances behind me, just in case I was being tracked. I did everything in fear of the Swine Creek monster. But I never let that fear get the best of me.

My fears eventually evolved into a sense of adventure. I became a heroic knight on a quest to slay the beast (if it ever decided to come out and face me). I never found the nerve to actually enter its domain myself. And I certainly didn't want to be left alone with it after dark. Each afternoon at dusk, Ester gave another whistle and I returned with my brothers to the safety of the house. By then Jim had returned home from work, ready for me to relay each day's adventures to him. Then he would share a little bit of history about his own adventures with the monster. Each story added credibility to my exploits. Even though I suspected that Jim might be pulling my leg, I still feared the monster. I wanted to meet it more than ever. This combination of fear and curiosity not only pushed me to explore new areas of the creek, but also to explore new areas of my imagination. At night, I dreamed about the Swine Creek monster. I even won a costume contest one Halloween when I dressed-up as my version of the monster.

Two summers passed without anyone ever catching sight of the Swine Creek monster. With each year, its power over me abated and the fact evolved into myth. I guess my physical growth dictated that real monsters only exist in the minds of small children. But somehow in those early days my monster took on a life of its own. I think the day that I stopped believing in monsters occurred sometime after I moved to Florida in the summer of 1981. Without my daily outings at Swine Creek, I eventually pushed the idea of supernatural creatures completely from my mind.

When I returned to Swine Creek ten years later, Jim told me how the monster had aged. Having lost all of its teeth, it no longer ate children. In our absence, Jim became the sole caretaker of the monster myth. But there were no more children to share the monster with. The once horrible creature now lived a lonely and pitiful existence with Swine Creek as its grave. I couldn't help but feel sorry for both Jim and the monster. Without the vitality of our youth they grew into old men, no longer active physically or mentally. Jim started becoming forgetful and encountered some health complications. Last year, he fell prey to a completely different kind of monster, the kind that eats its victims from the inside out. Cancer finished him off a few months later. Jim's recent death, and the death of my own grandfather, brought back memories that I held buried for years. I have always remembered my own grandfather, but for some reason I pushed every memory from Swine Creek completely from my mind. As more memories rushed back to me I realized that I could no longer distinguish between Jim and the monster. The monster lore is my fondest memory of Jim. When he died, the monster died with him. I can only think of the monster as some projection of Jim's true self. Surely Jim was not a monster, yet the monster would have never drawn breath had it not been for Jim's stories. In a sense, Jim was reliving his youth through our adventures.

Jim and the monster are now both a part of the same myth that I hope to one day pass onto my own children. And if I ever return to Swine Creek, I might just venture downstream and explore a part of the creek that I have never seen before. I may find a few scattered bones or even the grave of the monster. And if I do, I will pay my last respects to the man and the monster by inscribing in one of the large stones that marked their domain, "I believe there is a little monster in all of us."

WRITING PROCESS NARRATIVE FOR "THE LEGEND OF THE SWINE CREEK MONSTER"

I was really happy with the way that essay 2 turned out. It covered a topic that was important to me, and I had an emotional stake involved. I was able to be personal with the paper without actually boring the reader. Everyone who read the paper had positive comments.

I was inspired to write this essay after hearing from my grandmother. Around the time that this essay was assigned, she was making plans to visit my family here in Florida. The last time I saw my grandmother was when I graduated from high school in 1993. I began thinking about the last time I visited Ohio and the last time I saw my grandfather alive. Then I remembered that Jim Byler died a few months later. I thought the essay would be a good way to remember both of them.

My rough draft took several hours to write. It took a while to organize my thoughts, but the words came fairly easily. I thought the draft read well. It outlined my basic story in four pages, and Nicole even thought it was a little long winded. I usually consider "long" texts to be boring. I dreaded having to add six more pages of story in the next fat draft. I was afraid of completely losing the readers' interest halfway through. Nevertheless, I kept the four pages from the first draft, and stretched the paper out for four more. I used more description. I went off on tangents. I did whatever I could think of to draw out the paper. In the end, all of the extra information seemed necessary. I didn't see any way to take it out. My two fat draft readers agreed. They offered few suggestions.

I didn't do much to the text before I turned it in for publication. I played with the wording in a few places and tried to clarify a few points, but I didn't cut back on any of the text that I added in the previous revision. I was happy to see that the people who read the paper during the workshop didn't mind the length. My main goal was to appeal to a general audience. I guess I did. Most of the comments that I received were positive. No one thought I needed radical changes. I took advantage of the negative comments that I did receive and restructured the paragraph that describes the Amish culture. I also corrected a few typos and changed the wording in a few sentences (nothing major). With this done, I can't wait to see how I can radically change the paper in essay 4, but stay with the same theme. I was thinking about changing one of the scenes into a screenplay. Maybe it'll be the movie of the week someday.

CARLYN MADDOX

How He Should Have Died

CONSIDER THIS:

When she composed this family story, Carlyn Maddox was a graduate student, focusing on creative nonfiction and fiction. Like many authors, she wanted to honor family memories, to testify about the lives of those she's lost, in this case her grandfather. Because this is a common impulse, to write about a family member is both compelling and challenging. We feel a need to testify about lives lived, and we seek to do so in our own particular way, dramatizing individual experiences and highlighting our personal vision. Before you read, think of the family members you'd most like to "share with the world" and then think also about the challenges involved in such sharing. For example, your aunt is a true original, but how would you create a portrait of an eccentric aunt that transcends or challenges the stereotype we now hold about "Auntie Mame" type women?

Now, before reading Carlyn's essay about her grandfather, think of your own grandparents. How would you direct a film about their lives? What scenes would you focus on? What actor or actress would be a likely candidate to be cast as your relative? What central point about this person and his or her life do you find crucial to convey? Would you be better off writing in the third person to acquire some distance? Or could you speak in this person's own voice? Maddox describes her own goals this way: "Overall, I wanted to explore his [grandfather's] death in a different way that would inspire me and uplift me from the memory, and I think I am still striving to find this balance."

HOW HE SHOULD HAVE DIED

My grandfather should have died the way I remember him: in his rusted out Chevy pick-up, an 8-track of Glenn Miller blaring loud and scratchy over the rough engine, windows rolled down and the south Georgia sun baking his arm a dark tan. Or in his blue 1970ish Impala, a great boat of a car, gliding down Bubba Kennedy Road and squinting at the sky for clouds or rain. Every day, he'd clock dozens of miles around the fields near his farm, checking the greenness of his corn and tobacco, and he should have gone this way, in the open air like this and inhaling the scent of life around him.

He taught me how to drive this land when I was six. Taking me to the freshly tilled East field in the Impala, he placed my hands on the huge wheel and showed me how to steer. I sat on his lap in the curve of his long body, his boot pushing the accelerator and brake as I guided the wheel. "Driving has a rhythm," he would say, placing a hand over mine. "You gotta listen for it in the car and the land." We spent hours like this in the mornings, turning left and turning right and sometimes driving over 55—a thrill for me at six years old. One day when I was eight, he told me he wanted to show me something good. "I'll take the wheel," he said, a mischievous smile lighting his face. "Let's turn Mr. Miller up." With that, he flicked the dial, pulled the gearshift in reverse, and hit the accelerator. "Chattanooga Choo Choo" blasted from the tape as we flew backwards, dust kicking around the car and wheels spinning the thick brown dirt. "I believe they call this doin' donuts," he grinned, excited with his sudden daredevilry. We churned up the field until a cloud of dry dust surrounded the car. All I could see was dust and sky as the car jerked and spun like a ride at a theme park. "Sure is fun, but don't *you* go doin' it!" He yelled over the engine, laughing with each hairpin curve. His laugh was high and cackly, and it was when he laughed like this that his wrinkles softened, and his lips, so often tight with worry over my grandmother's failing health, lifted in hope. On that day he looked free. Like his life was a giant field, existing only for his play.

When he suffered a massive cerebral hemorrhage in 1986, the doctors couldn't believe he survived. I was a sophomore in college at the time, and the vision of his head ballooned to the size of a basketball shocked me.

"You'll be up in no time," I said, trying to sound strong and adult. He blinked in recognition at us standing around his bed.

"I'll also take you for a drive once you're out of here," I told him, squeezing his hand. He nodded a little and moved his mouth to speak, but no words came. Still, I knew he'd make it back to us after this. He was too vital and lively to leave us yet.

He recuperated for weeks and returned home with a walker. He had only partial use of his arms, but he lifted the steel balls he received from the physical therapist religiously and was insistent upon keeping his mind alert. "I watch *Moneyline* to see about the stocks," he told me when I called days later, "And CBS for what's going on in the world."

Of course his limited mobility didn't keep him inside for long; he hired Melrose Hall, a lady living on a tract of his farm, to make breakfast every day for him and grandma and then take him driving. Promptly at 10:00 and then at 1:00, grandaddy lumbered towards the Impala as Melrose took the driver seat. Once, when I came to visit, I saw them driving in the distance near the East field. Grandaddy's arm stretched across the length of the long seat, pointing Melrose in the right direction, and I imagined him saying to her "Take a right," and "Now—a left." I'm sure she knew which way to turn, but grandaddy was fond of giving directions while driving. On this particular day, I asked my grandmother how long they'd been on their latest jaunt. "It's been awhile," she said. "Don't know what they see, but they see it, all day long."

I'm sure sweet-faced Melrose said "Hmm-Hmm" to everything grandaddy told her. He probably recounted the time he train hopped all the way to Las Vegas in 1933, a loaf of bread nestled in his undershirt, and then how he tried to outrun the train yard cops all the way home. Or how his father wrote him in 1931 when he lived and worked in Toledo during the Depression. "He told me to come home and farm," I imagined him telling Melrose. "And since jobs were tight back then, it seemed like a good opportunity." Certainly she learned the names of each field—the Starlight, the East, and the Strawberry; not to mention where his watermelons grew the best or the location of pecan trees needing pest spray. No doubt he talked about other farmers, too, because granddaddy had a passion for knowing who owned what land and where. "There's the McCleod business," he told me once, pointing to a one-story house surrounded by silos and tobacco barns. "And there's the Kennedy mansion," he'd exclaim when we drove down Kennedy Road. The house stood palatial next to the modest homes of farmers and school teachers, and grandaddy loved to talk about its elevator or its huge brass kitchen. To him, Mr. McCleod and Mr. Kennedy were successes, and he often brought them up with a longing in his voice. He knew he could never farm again, and I'm sure these drives with Melrose were both happy and regretful for him as they toured the land.

During these years after his first stroke, I was totally absorbed with my bodybuilding boyfriend and hardly found time to visit. If I wasn't pushing through one of our elaborate muscle building regimes, I was shopping in Tallahassee malls for workout thongs or sport bras to make myself more desirous and wanted. Forgetting granddaddy and Reidsville became easy, as my focus now lay in keeping my boyfriend from flirting with the throngs of other girls at the gym. I justified this avoidance because he'd recuperated so well and had Melrose and grandma to keep him company; I told myself he was fine, just fine. When I did call, his voice would lift upon hearing mine, and I'd realize with a pang how much he missed me. Immediately he would launch into questions, amazing me with what he remembered about our last conversation.

"You still lifting dumbars?" he'd ask, and I'd laugh and say yes.

"You still working in the state library and thinking of becoming a teacher?" Yes, I'd say, elaborating on a made-up project about documenting Ponce De Leon's historical papers. He never knew that I did little more than shelve books and take messages for my boss.

"Well, I'll be . . .", he would say, wistfulness in his voice. Then he'd give me the latest about current rainfall or the growth of his pine saplings. He'd planted them a year before his stroke, and he always related their thriving to me.

"Me and Melrose went to the pine field today," he would tell me. "They's about knee-high now."

"Great," I would say. I pictured him leaning forward in his chair and jerking his arm outward to indicate how high they were.

"So . . .", he would inhale and wait a beat. "Any idea when you'll be coming home?"

I always told him in a couple of weeks. Back then, my visits always seemed a couple of weeks away. I had work, I explained. And there was still my education application to complete and send out.

"Sounds good," he would say, but disappointment tinged his voice. Then, after the conversation dwindled, I would say I had to go.

Time passed between us in this way until 1994 when he suffered another stroke. This time he arrived at Memorial Hospital in Savannah and the doctors were not encouraged by his condition. My sister called me in Folkston where I was teaching high school at the time and said it was serious, so I left lesson plans for a sub and quickly hit the highway north. When I arrived at the hospital, my grandfather laid lifeless and hooked up to several tubes. His room buzzed and blipped around him, and when he finally woke later that day, he was scared and disoriented. Soothing him, we talked of familiar things he would want to know. Daddy told him that Melrose would bring grandma to visit tomorrow, and Mom reassured him that my brother Stephen was driving down from Atlanta. Together we pieced together a picture of people and relatives and Reidsville for him. "We've gotten some rain," my dad said, louder than usual so he could hear. "And your pond looks like it's ready for fish," my mom added. I tried to think of something to say—anything—but I couldn't stop staring at him. He used to be my grandfather. Where had the stroke taken him?

He smiled a little at hearing these particulars, but his eyes remained milky and distant. Gone was the man who taught me how to drive or smell the wind before a storm, the man who kept up with my jobs and wayward boyfriends. Here was the man who always made me feel special, no matter what, and he was fading to a place I could not follow. Here was the man who always called me on Saturday mornings to ask if I'd come home. Now I was here, and he was dying. I held his bandaged hand, a thin tube snaking around his knuckles, and watched him form words with his useless mouth "Ahh . . .", he gulped, and "Uh . . .", he wheezed.

He decided to die then. He blinked hard into the fluorescent lights and appeared displaced from himself. All he had ever known had distilled into this room into a confusing bubble of voices and fading senses. I rubbed his fingers, thinking only the word NO, and saw willpower flicker in his eyes. "It's time . . .", he said, trying to pull upward from the bed. "It's time to go. . . ."

Though this sounded like a goodbye, I knew he just wanted out of the hospital room. The harsh yellow lights and gray walls of the room probably looked like death to him, and if he was truly saying goodbye, he wanted outside air and open land. His words then slurred, but we tried to answer as if we understood every word.

"Not long now," my father said after we stepped into the hall. "I don't think he's going to last but a few more days."

I looked back into the room where he lay amidst tubes and twisted sheets, some Frankenstein's idea of a man, and thought to myself: This isn't supposed to be happening. Not this way and not now.

Looking back at that moment, I'm grateful my grandfather never knew what the grief after his death did to me. He never saw how loss planted its dark seed in my emotions, numbing me for years after in all my relationships and endeavors. I'm thankful he knew me as strong and adventurous, the girl after his own heart as he would often say. A girl not afraid to do donuts in the middle of a dirt field, a girl not afraid to roll down her window and talk to complete strangers like he often did. This is what he would take with him, I reassured myself that day in the hospital, and this is what I would take with me.

His death was eight years ago, and his death still haunts me because it's not the way I wanted to remember him. He shouldn't have died the day after I went back to teach in Folkston. He shouldn't have died in a cold hospital room with a moon-faced nurse grunting at his vitals, or a birdlike doctor poking around his body and mumbling while scribbling on a metal chart. No—I should have been there. Had I been stronger, more adventurous like him, I would have unhooked him from all those machines and taken him out. We would have driven to an open space outside Savannah where the eye falls only on Loblolly pines or tobacco fields. We would have driven until nightfall, or at least until the sun set and there was no weather to note, and we would have stopped only when there was nowhere else to explore. I would have driven him in my truck wherever he wanted to go—to the Savannah river, to a newly tilled field. To any place where Bobwhites shrill at dusk and where two people, a grandfather and granddaughter, can speculate about pine trees and how long they take to grow old.

WRITING PROCESS NARRATIVE FOR "HOW HE SHOULD HAVE DIED"

In the most literal sense, I wrote this piece in the mornings before 7:00 a.m. I can look out my kitchen window to my newly planted trees and remember my grandfather and his pine fields. I could sense him near me, and this helped write the essay.

Writing "How He Should Have Died" was all about choices for me. It started off as an essay based on freewriting with the *In Brief* essays "Nearing 90" and "Artifacts" It was very punchy and emotional. Everyone loved the immediacy of it, and I wondered later if I shouldn't have kept to that *In Brief* essay length and sensibility But when I started thinking about writing a longer essay, I couldn't shake my grandfather's story and death from my mind and had to write it longer—if only to see where the piece would take me.

Ideas during workshop varied. Some wanted more of my reflection during this time, and some wanted less . . . Several wanted more scenes, so I added the donuts in the field part and stretched out our conversation. A few things stuck out for workshop members: Who was Melrose? What about my grandmother? Why don't we hear more of him talking? And, of course, the ever present "Get more specific" about certain details that I omitted or glossed over. My frustration during this was the fact that each workshop member wanted something different, and finally I had to make my decisions based on a gut feeling I had about the overall tone and feeling of the piece. In each draft I stretched more and embellished material. I took some parts of this and continued freewriting and looping until I had enough. In a sense, I created twice as much material as I used.

The most compelling part for me is the thoughts about his death and how I regretted the way he died. He was such an alive person that the way he died seemed like a cheat and a falsity. I started by writing "He should have died the way I remember him . . ." and went from there, spiraling forth into memory and regret. Again, this was a toss-up with workshop members; some wanted more of my memories and others wanted more of the musings about his death. The most difficult part of rewriting this was trying to leave in what I thought was the most compelling part and taking out extraneous summation or explanation. "Don't project onto your grandfather," Erin said to me during one workshop, and she was right: I projected a great deal in earlier drafts onto him and assumed he thought certain things.

The strength of this piece is in its detail, dialogue, and scenes. I am getting more comfortable adding scenes and learning how to embed action and dialogue in them. The weakness is in its overall form, and I am still struggling to figure out how to piece the memories of my childhood in with his death. My tendency is to become entrenched with reflection that pulls the action away from the reader . . . I found myself doing this even with the final draft. Overall, I wanted to explore his death in a different way that would inspire me and uplift me from the memory, and I think I am still striving to find this balance.

If I had more time on this piece, I would probably take more risks and emulate some of the styles I have seen in the essays we've read. I like "Dust" by Mary Oliver and was taken with this style, and I also liked Barbara Hurd's "Refugium" very much. These two had a similar elegiac tone that I would like to achieve with this piece. I would take apart the memories and distinguish them in some way—using artifacts, perhaps, or a timeline. I could see this published in a journal like *The Sun* or possibly *The Georgia Review.* But I will have to make more choices before that happens and see how the material realizes itself on the page.

JAY SZCZEPANSKI

Story Told Simply

CONSIDER THIS:

When he wrote this story, Jay Szczepanski was studying composition, rhetoric, and American literature and completing his master's degree. Nonfiction novel? Book-length memoir? How much of your experience can and should you share? If you choose the smaller canvas of an essay, which story or stories do you tell? How do you open up a scene (and how many), and what is your most effective balance of observation and reflection?

To create this alternately styled text, a full life shaped into snapshots or linked vignettes, what Winston Weathers calls "crots," loosely associated units of prose, Jay began writing about a key moment. The drafts for "A Blackslick Road in Winter" can be found in Chapter 6. Choosing a broad rather than a narrow focus (hoping to cover years instead of days or months), Szczepanski moved on from that piece and then used thematic subheadings to help organize his narrative. In this essay, a number of stories are linked and juxtaposed and dealt out like a stack of cards, inviting the reader to help create meaning from the hand that has been dealt. Covering territory was an intentional—if risky—choice. In his writing process narrative, Szczepanski explains that the final structure and organization he found helped him accomplish his aims: "I'm happy with this one [text]. I've finally written a creative piece of a not insignificant length that isn't a prose-poem." Before reading, ask yourself what sort of hand you might deal out to a reader from your set of life cards. After you read the essay, consider the author's claim at the end of his first section, "Community." At this point, early in his narrative, he claims: "This story will explain me, but I do not understand it." How do you respond to that observation and to the technique of using short, declarative statements like this throughout the essay so that a rhythm of assertion is set up and maintained?

STORY TOLD SIMPLY

She is screaming singing hymns her thin human wings spread out
From her neat shoulders the air beast-crooning to her warbling
And she can no longer behold the huge partial form of the world . . . if she fell
Into water she might live . . . [T]here they are
there are the waters
Of life

—From "Falling," by James Dickey

COMMUNITY

I am from South Amherst, Ohio. The population is 1,280, and we are a village in the eyes of the state. We have one police officer, a fire station, a general store, a gas station, a pizza place, a stoplight and easy access to Lake Erie. We live along the northern coast of Ohio where life differs from the rest of the state. It reminds me of New England, the houses and people. None of us are close, but we are communal because we have to be. This is a story of my family and me, my friends, none of us close, no longer communal.

I live in Florida now. I intend to die here, and I know I will. I'm not sure when, but it will happen probably in my thirties or forties, when I feel I am middle aged and too frustrated to keep going. When I was thirteen, I had a vision one afternoon as I stood alone after church that this would be the case. I will do my best to see that it comes true.

This story will explain me, but I do not understand it.

MOTHER

My mother and my father are separated. They will be divorced soon, and this is for the best. I am certain that their divorce was a long time in coming. She called me three days before Christmas, one day before I was to leave to see them in Ohio, and told me. I said to her, "I figured this would happen." She asked me how I knew.

I've known for my entire life.

When I was in the fifth grade, I woke up early on a May morning in rural Ohio and made breakfast for my mother. It was Mother's Day, and I was happy. I took her her breakfast at 8:00 a.m. I nudged her sleeping form as she lay next to my sleeping father, and presented her with the blueberry muffins. She told me that she was not hungry, to go back to bed. I did.

It was the last thing I have ever done for her.

FATHER

My father is not an alcoholic, exactly. This is my differentiation, not his. If I were to say that he is an alcoholic, I would have to admit that I have addictive tendencies in my personality, that I have learned from him what I should not have: alcoholics beat their children, cheat on their wives, have low-paying jobs, never graduate from high school, drive drunkenly and kill entire families. My father has done all of these, in varying degrees.

He worked as a machinist making metal parts for industry or amusement parks. He came home in the afternoon, ate the dinner my mother made and spoke little.

When I was eleven or twelve, an early adolescent, I upset him. I do not remember what I did (does it ever matter what we do; we are hit and we know it), but I remember that he slapped me, forcefully, the only forceful thing he has done in his life. When I started crying, he hit me again. He held my wet left cheek in his palm to steady me, and he hit and hit and hit. It happened again, as it always does.

One day I hit him back.

SISTER

I have a sister, Amy. She is 18. She wants to attend culinary school but is neither kind nor smart enough. I visited two years ago and I scolded her for her surly demeanor during a family dinner. I said to her, "Amy, for the love of God, I would like to come home sometimes and not have to listen to you bitch."

Amy told me to go back to Florida because no one likes me, because she hates me, because she wishes I would die and go to Hell. She said these things. I wonder, when I think of it at all, why she is so angry, why she curses and wants me to die. I cannot understand her now, or even when she was a child.

I am five years older than she, and I used to play with her Barbies with her. I always upset her in some way. I might have taken the toy she wanted. I might have raised my voice. I might have asserted myself in some way. When I did these things, she would scream. My father would run up the stairs to take care of it.

She never learned to be quiet like I did.

My mother used to say to me, "Be nice to Amy. How do you think she feels, going to school, getting bad grades? The teachers look at her and see you, but she's not you. You have to be nice to her."

My mother is eloquent when she wants to be.

I tell her, "How do you think it feels for me to have a sister who is delinquent, fights, rebels continuously and has no ambition? How do you think it feels to have a sister who hates you?"

I am not as eloquent.

FATHER'S PARENTS

My father's parents raised him in Grafton, Ohio. He is the third brother among seven, six of whom are now living. His brother Jeremy was killed in a motorcycle accident, and my grandmother grieved hideously, so much that she could not drive her school bus for the Midview School District for two months. When my cousin Kari was killed at the age of 14 in an automobile accident last July, my grandmother stopped driving altogether.

She is a sweet woman; she grows wild strawberries in a patch in the side yard where the blackberries used to fruit. When I visit, I supply a coffee can and collect as many as I can take with me to Florida, though I cannot pass them through airport security any longer.

My father's father is the mayor of Grafton, but not exactly. He sits on the board of commissioners and is popular. He is an auctioneer on the side, directs road maintenance and the water-treatment facility at the edge of Eaton Township, and he was once, beyond my memory, a fireman. He had a quadruple bypass in February and will die soon. He gave me a small novelty plastic Mickey Mouse that dropped its pants and peed when squeezed in the middle. I lost it sometime in the late 1980s and have never told him.

I understand that my father's parents were not good to him. He was horsewhipped once, and he still has the psychic scars.

I did not know that they were genetic.

MOTHER'S PARENTS

This past Christmas I visited my mother's parents' house. I love them more than anything. My grandmother has worked her entire life as a migrant laborer, my grandfather as a plant supervisor for the local Ford plant. The older I get, the older my grandparents get. They deserved more dreams in their lives, more breaks, more of whatever they wanted. We share this.

My Nanny calls me every week. A month ago, she told me about an ectopic pregnancy she had after she gave birth to my mother; I had always known that this had happened, but never from her, only from whispers and innuendo. She wanted to be a nurse. I'm the only one who pays attention to her anymore. She is a sad woman (her eyes are grey), sad that everyone has left, especially me. But if I didn't leave Ohio I would have lost myself, I'm sure—and if I'm lost, where can she go?

My grandfather was born in southern Ohio along the Kentucky border. He has finally, so late in his life at the age of 73, bought a pair of shorts to replace the Dickies and grey and black slacks he has worn all of his life. I am immeasurably proud of him for this. The other day he went into surgery for melanoma. This is typical of his life. He and I golf when I visit, though my visits are rare. I have tremendous guilt concerning this, but he understands why I am in Florida.

I miss them.

ME

I am gay and have been my entire life. I have not snapped out of it, and I won't. I fully realized my homosexuality in the sixth grade, although hints of it appeared much earlier. I looked at Eric Hunsinger sitting across from me in the advanced reading class, noticed that his legs were hairy, his hair was dark, his skin was tanned as much as it could be in Ohio. This is what is sexually attractive to me.

Throughout middle school and high school, I was militant in my manners. Do not allow the stutter that paralyzed your childhood to return. Do not lisp in any measure, and keep careful control of your s's. Watch your hands; put them in your pocket if they roam or become loose. Do not let the softness of your voice creep out into conversation. Look at women. Make more male friends. Stop writing poetry. Play sports whether you like it or not.

It is horrible to be insular, to have to be insular. I looked at my male classmates and felt precisely what I know I should not, a twinge of pleasure, then guilt. I knew that some of them were gay, too, but guessing wrong was not worth discovery; I should imitate their developing post-adolescent masculinity in the name of butchness.

I am disappointed that I could never have the thrill of what I assume love amongst teenagers must be. Disappointing love in strange and dark places, hiding from parents, illicit love-making or plain dirty sex, whatever it was or could have been.

Allegedly, I missed little: the fumbling, clumsy embraces and inept kissing, but I know what I wanted.

I want it still.

JESUS

When I was in the seventh grade I began attending church on my own. I participated in the youth group, went on camping trips to Mohican State Park, went sledding in the winters, canoeing in the summers, prayed earnestly and deftly every night; I felt guilty when I forgot. I kneeled against my bed and genuflected as I thought I should. I thanked God for my grandparents, prayed for peace in my family, the extension of my grandmother's life, prayed for patience and courage, prayed for love and good grades, the retarding of my homosexuality.

In Wednesday school (I am or was Pentecostal) in the evenings, my third-cousin Jennifer played the piano in the Sunday school classrooms. She was a genius. She never took piano lessons, but could play anything she heard by ear. My favorite was "Somewhere Over the Rainbow." My God, she had a beautiful voice, and I cry sometimes when I think of her. I do not know what has become of her, but she soothed me more than she knows, more than I know.

My best friends were members of the Silvieus family. Three girls, Jessie, Sara, and Becky. All three are married now and having children of their own, and this concerns me and leaves me slightly bitter. They are all good women in their own way, but ignorant and happy. When I went to college in Florida, I told Becky that I was gay.

One day later, Lee, the pastor, called me to discuss this. He let me know that he told the prayer group and congregation what Becky had told him, that not to worry, it was a disease, but with God's help I could overcome it. That it was the product of a deficient home life, demons or something, that it would only lead me to a life of corruption and sexual perversion, that he still loved me dearly and I would be all right.

I have never been back to church.

ELIZABETH

I.

In high school, my friend Elizabeth drove a van whose purple was so deep that it's plum. It was an attractive color, and I often told her so. Her eyes were green.

One evening she drove me home after a movie. This is what awkward teenagers do in the Middle West when their houses rest amongst the fallow winter wheat fields and city access comes through federal interstates.

I said to her, as she smiled-drove-smiled, I said, "You know, you know I'm gay," like it was something that yes, she did know, but had been politely waiting for me to bring up.

She didn't know, naturally (and how could she; it's shameless, those people whom we use to cover up our queerness), and she almost coaxed her lovely purple van into the pylons of an overpass.

Make-up is ridiculous, but she wore it anyway, and against the red and green dimness of the dashboard and instrument panel, her mascara turned a purply-black as it fell from around her eyes.

Elizabeth drove me home and we sat in the driveway, the dry heat of the van's duct system blowing us apart.

II.

When I finished my sophomore year of college, I visited her at John Carroll University in Cleveland. It was late April, but it still snows in Ohio then, especially along the snow-belt that girds the eastern third of the lake's shoreline. I only had sandals with me as I had come straight to her from the airport. I wore three pairs of socks with them so I wouldn't freeze. We collected the strangely wet snow as it fell past the orange glow of the street lamps outside of her dormitory.

III.

When I finished my junior year of college, I went to Ohio again, this time in the summer, in the middle of June, the month of strawberries and thunderstorms, and I called her from my parents' house to play in the snow.

She has never called me back.

DRIVING

Three days after my rejection to graduate school at Florida State University, I took a bottle of my boyfriend's muscle relaxants and made a long, quiet drive down the Florida coastline. It is a terrible thing to want to kill yourself, but it is another thing entirely to convince yourself that you should.

I have never had nerve, and when I came back home my boyfriend and roommate had me committed in the local hospital. I was taken in the back of a police cruiser to the emergency room entrance. It felt criminal but shouldn't have. The hospital assigned an elderly guard named Glenn to keep me from running away; he could not have stopped me had I chosen to leave.

He was from Ohio, too. His pension went bankrupt, and in the middle of his retirement he needed to work to survive. We talked for five hours, and he hugged me when I was transferred to the psychiatric ward.

It was 3 a.m., and the night shift was on call. A doctor and nurse escorted me into the ward through a series of elaborately locking doors. Sharon, the nurse, led me to a back room and took my weight, height, blood pressure, and wallet. The rest of the patients were asleep in their dark rooms. It was quiet. Sharon kept asking me how I managed to get there, how a nice boy like me felt so hopeless. I told her that it happens sometimes. She could not understand that, and I knew she was a good person.

I envied her.

SPEAKING

In the morning, the angry a.m. shift was in charge. The lead nurse took me into the breakfast room and told me to come see her later so that she could draw my blood. I told her that since I was involuntarily committed that I could refuse all procedures if I chose. She was not aware that I understood how the Baker Act works. She looked at me as if I were stupid, as if, "your illness gets in my way," and told me to "be that way." As she left the room, she told an elderly schizophrenic black woman who was talking too loudly to shut up.

I think people need more kindness than that.

When I was ready to be discharged, I stood by the reception desk waiting for my boyfriend to collect me. A young doctor looked up from his work and said to me, "Why don't we get you settled into a room so you're not eavesdropping on me, ok?" Earlier he had scolded a young woman for bothering him.

I told the doctor not to treat me as if I were a child, that I was not eavesdropping, that I was waiting there as I was instructed to do, that he was rude, that I could not understand why he even became a doctor if he were so dispassionate about his work, that he should not be in this business because it was plain to me that he could not relate to his patients, that most of the people in his care could not talk back to him like I could.

And then I said, "You take care of these people; do you understand?"

I wasn't sick at all.

RUNNING

I do not understand anything very well. I never have. I do not understand why some people hate me, the dysfunction of my family. I do not understand my homosexuality, why people die or even want to. I look at my parents and my grandparents and my sister and my friends, and I want to say collectively to them, *Run. If you know what is good for you, even if you do not, run. Do not look behind you—you must get to someplace that is better than this, you deserve better than this. You must run as quickly as you can, into the water, forward, deeply. I forgive you, but please, alongside me or in front, you must run.*

But what shall we run toward?

WRITING PROCESS NARRATIVE FOR "STORY TOLD SIMPLY"

I guess I've been feeling the need for therapy lately. Current events are always good fodder for nonfiction essays. I composed this one a little differently than the rest of them. I approached it like I used to approach poems—get in touch with the inside and all of that, force myself to write things I absolutely knew I did not want to see in print. I think this is the white-hot center idea that Bob Butler has—Maggie's been influential in this, and she and I have talked about writing without thinking.

The initial draft of this essay only took three hours—about one thousand words an hour—and I surprised myself with this. Revision work was more difficult, but not tremendously hard. I reordered the paragraphs and relied on theme to give the essay a more tightly knit structure.

I took your suggestion about subtitling, and I decided to leave them there because I think it makes what I'm trying to get across in the essay plainer. Maggie pointed out to me that fact that I shifted tense too often throughout the essay, so I've gone through and edited for consistency in that.

I'm happy with this one. I've finally written a creative piece of a not insignificant length that isn't a prose-poem. For the life of me I never thought I could do it, but I think this one is the one I'm most proud of in the class because it shows growth instead of a reliance on tricks I already know.

I also wanted to play with simple words and complex words (got/have, hate/loathe, etc.). I wanted to see how I could juxtapose them for effect, and I think to a large degree that it works. I especially found helpful the exercise of one-syllable words. I rewrote a few paragraphs (these didn't make it into the final draft) using all one syllable, and on the whole I was pleased with what I saw. I tried to keep the prose as bare as I could. I thought ornate language would take away from this essay's directness, which is something I definitely did not want to do.

Though not finished (is anything ever finished?), I'm most proud of this piece because it's personal. I like its rhythm, so I've satisfied my poetic need while still keeping a prose style. I hope you agree.

CONNECTING TO READING

A. In a small group, discuss the issues of fact and fiction and of an author's gender. Why do we label some works *fiction* and some *fact*? How do you know you're reading either sort of text? When you began Patricia Hampl's work, for instance, what sort of work did you assume you were reading and why? Would you read Lynna Williams's essay differently if it began in third person: "Her mother and father were married fifty years ago today"? Since the informal essayist often chooses to write in first-person voice (I), how important is it to know the essayist's gender? Do you pay attention to gender when you begin reading a text? Certainly some names are gender-neutral like Chris or Morgan. But what happens if you read Paule Marshall (Chapter 1) as a man or Christy Brown (Chapter 2) as a woman? What, if anything, do our misreadings or assumptions (fact or fiction, male or female) say about us as readers? What, if anything, do they suggest to you as an essayist? When reading any of the classroom authors, did you lose track of gender and later ask yourself questions about who was writing?

B. Compose a journal entry exploring your feelings about how stories function in essays and how creative nonfiction is different or similar to fiction. Begin with a quote from Scott Russell Sanders or Donald Murray, if you like. How long does a good story have to be? What's the shortest story you know? What's the longest? What is the relationship between story and essay? What happens or has to happen when the size and scope of a narrative shortens or lengthens? For instance, could Dean Newman's text be developed into a longer essay? What would you emphasize and explore? How would you turn this brief nonfiction narrative into a short story? A novel? Read a classmate's entry and respond to it. If you're working on-line, with a partner or small group, construct working definitions of the following terms: "narrative," "essay," "story," "creative nonfiction."

C. In a class reading group, explore the way essayists such as Barbara Kingsolver alternate narrative and exposition, storytelling and reflection upon the stories or ideas she shares. How do these movements work in her essay and the essays of others (particularly those of Patricia Hampl, Lynna Williams, Leah Marcum, Keith Gawrys, and Carlyn Maddox)? How do writers signal this sort of movement? Would you find such movements surprising in fiction or do you find them there? Identify six clear instances of this sort of movement. During a full class discussion, have your group direct the class to two of these instances and share the results of your group discussion.

D. In a journal entry, explore the way the following strategies are used. What effects do you think the author was aiming for and how well does the technique work for you as a reader? Quote briefly from the readings to support your discussion. (1) Story (compare storytelling in several); (2) Breaks in chronology, including white spaces, asterisks, subtitles; (3) Interior or multiple voices (often italicized materials); (4) Lists, dialogue, and character description/development, quotes from other sources.

E. To prepare for a class discussion on voice in essays, compose a journal entry in the form of notes you can speak from later. Donald Murray claims that he writes essays to give himself voice. What voices do you hear in each of the essays in this chapter? Try to characterize each textually. What sort of topic, sentence structure, tone does each author strike? This is like wine tasting, take a sip—even of those essays you haven't read in full—and characterize the author's voice in a sentence or two. For two texts, one professional and one classroom, follow up with a brief descriptive paragraph describing how you visualize this author based on your reading: What does he or she look like? What do you know about him or her, based on what textual clues? Bring enough copies of this entry for your classmates to refer to when, together, you discuss a few of these textual voices in more analytical depth.

CONNECTING TO WRITING

A. In an informal writing that you share with a class partner via e-mail, explore your experiences as 1) a storyteller, 2) an essayist, or 3) both. You might want to begin with some freewrites, such as: "For me, (telling a story; writing an essay) is like. . . ." What stories do you like to retell? What storytellers in your own experience do you admire? How does one learn to tell a good story? What essays do you read? Where are they published? What are some experiences you've had writing essays? Have you ever been encouraged to/discouraged from telling stories in your essays? Have you ever been encouraged/discouraged from using first person in your essays? Explain at some length; tell a story about this. Respond to your partner's message in some depth and store your correspondence in your journal or share with a group.

B. In a journal entry, narrate a single, dramatic event that you have experienced from the viewpoint of all of the players in that event. For instance, if you're narrating the story of how your friend had an accident during a rainstorm, tell the story from your perspective, the perspective of the driver whose brakes didn't hold on the wet street and found himself rear-ending your friend's car, the witness who stopped and helped you push the car out of traffic, and the crash-weary cop who came to write up the accident report, and so on. Have you ever tried to share a written version of your life with someone who shared that version? Family members always hold multiple versions of family events. Consider one of these events and what each participating member's viewpoint would be (and why). Write a follow-up entry to members of a writing group on what you learn as you read across these versions. Whose story did they find most convincing, interesting, and so forth?

C. Write an informal meditation on "story" or "memory" or "truth" or "the essay" after noting at least 10 statements on your topic by authors in this chapter. Put your voice in dialogue with theirs in an exploratory manner.

D. Write a nonfiction essay of fewer than 500 words. Like Dean Newman or in the manner of Jay Szczepanski in one of the smaller sections of his larger narrative, set scene, introduce characters, use dialogue and detail. See how much you can explore in a small space. Of course, you'll have to "take a small idea and make it good" to do this. In fact, you may want to start by listing 10 possible starts for mini-essays that let you take a small moment and use it to reflect on life in general. Bring your piece to class and have each member read aloud. Discuss the set of essays as a whole.

E. Freewrite on two or more of the writing prompts found in "Try This" for a minimum of 10 minutes each. Let your mind associate freely, forging connections or taking digressing paths. Post these on a class discussion board or bring several copies for group members to respond to, asking them to choose their favorite and say why they prefer this text.

WRITING PROJECTS

1. Imitate Scott Russell Sanders by composing your own version of "The Most Human Art: Ten Reasons Why We'll Always Need a Good Essay."

2. Revise an essay you've written previously to do one or more of the following: (a) Examine the viewpoint of someone else connected to the essay; (b) Include other voices: research, epigraphs, an imagined voice in dialogue with yours; (c) Use first-person voice if you avoided first person or were told to avoid it; and (d) Include several short illustrative or evocative stories.

3. Compose an essay suitable for a literary journal of your choice (you can find these in the campus library or local bookstore or on-line) by expanding on your preferred freewrite from "Connecting to Writing," activity E.

4. Create an essay by observing your world for a week. For seven days, keep a journal of "possible topics." Tear out newspaper articles that interest you, go to a favorite restaurant and observe the other diners, look through a box of family photographs, take a long walk and think about the season, and more. As you "collect" the world around you, make notes about topics you could write about. At the end of the week, review your list and choose an essay topic and begin writing. Or, using some of the combinatory and collage techniques you've seen in others' essays, compose an alternately styled essay or create a Web page.
5. Make an essay out of memory. Take a family story that you and at least one other member remember and tell differently. Do some more research on this event by interviewing other family members, consulting any available records, looking up dates and events from that time period, and so on. Retell the story, this time examining the multiple viewpoints that family members hold; investigate them, speculating on the reasons for divergences.
6. Compose an essay that is not directly an imitation of but is informed—flavored—by your reading of some popular essayists. Skim collections and anthologies. Analyze these essayists' subjects. What are they writing about? Choose a piece that moves or intrigues you. Read it. Put it away. Now write your own essay, informed by the memory of a writer whom you admire.
7. Compose in a humorous vein. Consider the humorists you admire. Collect three humorous personal essays. Look for similarities. Do the authors rely on memory (family is often the source of humor)? Are they telling stories that translate everyday experience into event? What sort of dramatic timing is required from a good humor essayist? Try your own "Ten Reasons We Need to Tell Funny Stories"—an essay that reflects on the art of humor—or just write your own humor column, based on the work of someone you admire.
8. Write a personal essay on a public matter of great importance to you. To do this, think local, topical, and context dependent. Consider an actual audience and place of publication. Where does your voice matter? Talk about the need for traffic calming in your neighborhood; share the reasons you think you're a spiritual person.
9. Use the personal essay to talk about any of the big topics: love, war, death, sex. But do so with a craftsperson's care: investigate the way something small and particular in your life lets you speak largely on the subject at hand. Use the essay as a vehicle for exploring personal philosophy. If you can, avoid using the topical word during initial drafts.
10. Focus on the process of writing in your essay. Using an event in your life, tell the event as fact; tell the event as fiction. Finally, write an essay that explores your writer's decisions in each instance. What did you have to do as an author to make fiction out of a life event? You might want to reflect on which version you liked best and why (and whether the same was true of

your readers) and how you used story, narrative, exposition, and memory in each.

* * * *

I used to spin a globe, placing my finger on a spot and imagining someone of a particular age and occupation, who, by chance, hears this poem. How much does that person need to know? No matter whether that person is a 30-year-old shopkeeper in New Delhi or an 18-year-old in Kotzebue, what's going to grab that person's attention?

—COLLEEN J. MCELROY

If people think any of your fiction is based on our life (and I have to truthfully say yes, a lot of my writing is based on my life), they tend to think it's the facts that are true. For example, they think I lived in Chinatown, that I played chess, that I have twin sisters, or that my mother died. The fact is that my mother didn't die, but I thought at one point that she almost died and that same emotion that propelled me to want to know more about my mother led to my writing the book and is in there. The whole tragedy of not just losing somebody but of losing your whole past and not knowing what your connections were—this is what started the book. The emotions. But in fact, no. I was lucky. My mother didn't die, so I was able to find out more.

—AMY TAN

Chapter 9

Language Matters

Thinking About Writers' Relationships to Language and Style

> If we are to accept the definition of a writer as one who writes, we must accept the fact that writers are not a special type of person. Those who write might be of any age, shape, background or interest. They may produce a technical manual or a provocative essay or a piece of artistic prose. The one thing they hold in common is the use of language.
>
> —ANONYMOUS FIRST-YEAR WRITING STUDENT

I might have titled this chapter literacy *revisited* because the subject of language—who uses it and how it is used—concerns writers so regularly. In this chapter, essayists connect some dots. In Chapter 2, "The Literacy Narrative," we look at the ways home environments, local cultures, and gender construct us as literate individuals. In Chapter 3, "Considering Community and Audience," we address the way humans—as members of a number of communities—are constantly acting on and being acted upon by different persuasive individuals, images, texts, and events. And in Chapter 6, "Drafting, Responding and Revising," we consider the drafting, reading (and responding), and revision cycle as activities in a recursive process: early drafts to explore and find meaning, later drafts to consolidate our writing and prepare it for readers. Readers' responses and evaluations are gathered to revise and improve a text, to fine-tune it. That is, at first as we're figuring out what to write, and later in a drafting sequence, we consider how our texts appear to and are evaluated by others.

In this chapter, I ask you to look at the conventions of published writing and how these affect your work. Discussions about usage—that is, agreement about correctness—inevitably connect to discussions about who we are as writers in communities of readers, the focus of Chapter 3. We may wish it otherwise, but there are occasions when our writing will be judged by its appearance as much or more than by its content. Because of that, authors in this chapter raise questions about the relationship of culture and power, asking whose language matters and what does it mean to write in a multicultural, multilingual country like ours? Further, once you are ready to share your work, you'll want to share it in a manner that best represents the identity you are constructing for yourself as a writer. At this point, you become concerned with style.

Also in this chapter, authors provide advice on developing control of your prose style. This is not simply a matter of considering how you dress up your text to look or feel a certain way but also a matter of considering if you accomplished all you can accomplish to influence how others read your text. Do your readers find your sentences as clear and convincing as you planned to make them? Or metaphor-rich, balanced, and erudite, if that's the tone you're striving for? Or does faulty parallel structure and a rash of misplaced commas and typos the spell-checker didn't catch (they're/their, rain/reign) keep your reader from seeing you as the fine writer you really are? No matter how extensive your vocabulary and how sharp your argument, performance mistakes can dramatically change a reader's impression of your work. Conventions, culture, and style. Three big topics joined by the key word: language.

LANGUAGE CONVENTIONS AND CULTURE

Two writing instructors, Neil Daniel and Christina Murphy, have observed that we are in dangerous territory when we claim one language is superior to another, one dialect to another, one way of organizing thought to another. Neither is superior, each reflects and represents different community conventions, cultural logics and social attitudes, as Daniel and Murphy explain:

> [W]hen we talk about grammar as a writing issue we usually are referring to usage conventions that have little to do with logic or linguistic meaning. Writing conventions are essentially arbitrary and have more to do with class distinction, ethnic difference, apparent educational level, and professional field than they do with effective communication . . . good writing depends on making errors in the presence of those who care about the results . . . no one ever masters good writing once and for all.

I appreciate Daniel and Murphy's conclusion that "good writing depends on making errors in the presence of those who care about the results." We have to understand what it means to judge a text effective or not effective and take care that in so judging, we are not judging the author who is in the process of learning—through practice—the effects of making informed language choices. Writers need safe readers. Readers who look at a writer's attempts and then discuss how those attempts work and don't work make the writing classroom the perfect location for exploring language conventions and the language(s) of writing.

In addition, to make effective choices, the writer has to care. Malcolm X tells such a story in his autobiography:

> I became increasingly frustrated at not being able to express what I wanted to convey in letters that I wrote, especially those to Mr. Elijah Muhammad. In the street, I had been the most articulate hustler out there—I had commanded attention when I said something. But now, trying to write simple English, I not only wasn't articulate, I wasn't even functional. How would I sound writing in

> slang, the way I would say it, something such as, "Look, daddy, let me pull your coat about a cat, Elijah Muhammad—."

Malcolm X wanted to critique the dominant discourse—he wanted to speak out—but he also realized that to be taken seriously—to gain a hearing—he had to be as fluent as possible in that language. He realized that the grammar of letters was not the grammar of the street (although it's also important to remember that the reverse is true; many languages other than academic language have power and currency).

Often we talk about language judgments as matters of *grammar,* but the word *grammar* is not only weighted with associations (who doesn't remember being corrected for making a "grammar mistake") but also has multiple definitions, depending on how the word is used. In his essay "Grammar, Grammars, and the Teaching of Grammar," Patrick Hartwell explored five ways writers and teachers of writing use and define grammar:

1. The set of formal patterns in which the words of a language are arranged to convey larger meanings.
2. Linguistic grammar, which studies these patterns.
3. Linguistic etiquette—usage.
4. School grammar (the grammar of textbooks).
5. Stylistic grammar (grammatical terms used to teach style).

At many institutions, students who through lack of practice or opportunity have not yet become fluent in using standard conventions—definition 3, above—are asked to undertake more instruction in writing. In the past, they were set to work at grammar books—definition 4, above—where they toiled over exercises taken out of the context of their writing. "I wanted to write and I did not even know the English language. I bought English grammars and found them dull. I felt that I was getting a better sense of the language from novels than from grammars. I read hard, discarding a writer as soon as I felt that I had grasped his point of view," explains author Richard Wright whose essay "Library Card" you find in Chapter 2. Wright realized that the dull definitions of grammar books would not do him as much good as working with actual texts and deriving his rules from them. Currently, writers who need to improve their understanding of conventions are asked to study the conventions in the context of their own writing.

This is why it discourages me when a classroom author writes: "Reading your own writing is like watching the same movie over and over again. You really don't want to see it anymore." Students need to learn to *read as writers* (as Richard Wright did), observing the conventions that the writers they admire use, studying usage handbooks at times to have the vocabulary for talking about those conventions, and then exploring (sometimes challenging) those conventions in their own writing. For most of us, most of the time, drafts should be considered *experiments* in usage and style. I think classroom authors become discouraged if they focus on language conventions too early in the drafting process. Because of this, my personal rules include the following: (1) You get a better reading from a well-proofed paper, but (2) don't copyedit your drafts until you're ready to "publish" (because you may want to change something and you'll be loathe to change that something if you've prematurely invested in the work of fine-tuned finishing).

One of my students was enrolled in two different English classes. In poetry class Jo'al felt like a basic, or inexpert, writer because she was learning poetry conventions—conventions as awkward for her to learn at first, perhaps, as for me to learn Malcolm X's street language, but neither learning impossible. She was also taking first-year writing. Jo'al noted that she felt confused by the seemingly contradictory advice she was receiving in each writing course, having been asked at one point to stop using metaphors in her nonfiction prose. Jo'al had to learn to be a different writer under different composing conditions, and when she saw that it was a matter of learning, not a matter of deficiency, she rapidly learned to write more scholarly prose, often enlivened (but not overburdened) by her love of metaphor. Conversely, she learned that logical thinking about a topic really didn't damage her poetry, nor did using standard punctuation and spelling. Her movement from the conventions of one genre to another became that of choice rather than that of confused and potentially debilitating guesswork.

Because language is dynamic, the act of people making meaning together, there are reasons for obeying conventions and for not obeying them. The conventional doesn't exist without the unconventional; you can't please in a predictable way without the possibility of unpredictability (though the unpredictable—the renegade, exciting, transgressive language act—seems too often to get lumped in with the mindless language act). For me, the grammar question is summed up in the observation that those of us who are already native speakers of English are speaking and writing in English far more fluently than we are not. Now we need to learn to control our skills for our own purposes.

Meanwhile, not all of the fine writers in English started out using English as their first language. The list of impressive multilingual writers who have made their name as authors using the English language is long. Writers who move between two languages are often the richer for the resources they can tap, but they also know that adjustments have to be made. Anyone who works with contrastive rhetoric—the way users of each language make meaning with written texts—knows there are many effective and culturally different ways to organize thought and the writing down of thought. The thesis/support organization of the conventional scholarly essay written by native English speakers may not translate well for Japanese or Arabic speakers who agree within those cultures to organize their ideas according to different conventions.

The writer who has the ability to draw on more than one language or more than one dialect has probably long been aware of the power of doing this as well as the dangers of assuming that the conventions of one language should dominate over another. Those who write in only one language need to become equally sensitive. Language may provide indications of a writer's culture and class but it does not create or predict those differences; all languages are rich in possibilities which explains why, over time, the English language has borrowed so freely from other languages. Given time and practice and the chance to make errors "in the presence of those who care about the results," all writers can become more fluent and achieve their writing aims whether they speak English as a first or second language, or were raised in the dominant or an alternate dialect.

LANGUAGE AND STYLE

Writers who want their text to be respected will study their composing processes. They will take risks and learn from those risks. They will draft freely but revise with care. To do this, they need to consult the wide range of style options that are available to them. In Chapter 1, Winston Weathers discusses his own writing style and introduces the idea of grammars of style, arguing that there is a conventional style—grammar A—that is taught in school. He also suggests that there are many other grammars of style available to writers. This is why you notice that your favorite journalists, scholars, authors, and technical writers regularly appear to violate the rules you have been at some pains, perhaps, to commit to memory.

We obey the dominant grammar because it is dominant, "what is socially prestigious, or 'correct,' in (formal) writing depends on which social variety of language, officially or unofficially, gains acceptance with public institutions," explains linguist and writing teacher Rei Noguchi. Form and content are partners. We all get high marks for doing what's expected and doing that well, and there are great benefits and pleasures to be had from mastering conventions. A well-crafted text—speech, poem, essay, research report—offers strong aesthetic pleasures to readers and to writers. And the more comfortable you are with the dominant forms of style, the more comfortable you are with testing and pushing that style. However, I don't think anyone learns to be comfortable without trying, failing, tinkering, experimenting, and evolving into their own preferred writing approach. Stylists are concerned with correctness, at times, but they are equally interested in stylistic options as tools, as possibilities.

Let me return to the story of Jo'al to illustrate this point. Jo'al preferred her poems without punctuation, at first, because she thought such a move signaled artistic freedom. However, when she heard classmates misread her work—stumbling over line breaks, clobbering her rhythm, and changing the poem's apparent meaning because they didn't have the orchestration of Jo'al's punctuation choices to guide them through a reading—she began to get interested in how punctuation could work *for her* in a poem. In fact, writers who are invested in their writing often get very invested in understanding usage options (punctuation, word choice, sentence style) and alternate style options (some of which were illustrated in the radical revision exercise outlined in Chapter 7).

The most important learning concerning style and your writing comes when your experiments are *mindful*. You don't just pour on long sentences and esoteric word choices thinking that these make you sound smart. Instead, you learn that such a move can backfire—making you sound insecure and pretentious—you try out options on readers, carefully. You read your work aloud. You vary this paragraph and that and see what your efforts accomplish. You become a student of style, apprenticed to your own writing and to the writing of others.

To help you consider the interrelated issues of usage, culture, and style, I open this chapter with two poems because each highlights some of the issues I've just discussed. Ken Autrey takes us back to the sixth grade and memorized grammar rules. Julia Alvarez illuminates the way language(s) pulls on the bilingual speaker. Studying writers and the rules that guide their work led Mike Rose to explore how learned rules can block and stifle writers who apply those rules in inflexible ways. He doesn't argue that we reject rules but does show us that we should understand how our internalized rules may be making decisions for us as writers and might need to be more fully considered. Allison Joseph's poem reminds us of the deep and dangerous connection between rules, authority, and cultural power. Richard Marius continues our discussion about the effects of writing rules by asking us to look for the truths within false rules, examining the reasons certain rules developed in the first place. In "Reading, Stealing, and Writing Like a Writer," Wendy Bishop urges you to become a student of sentences, to analyze the writers you read and to keep a sentence style notebook (no surprise here). The classroom handouts that follow this essay allow you to practice some of the techniques discussed, illustrated with the style experiments of classroom authors. Next, novelist Kurt Vonnegut offers his eight basic rules for writing with style, and essayist Pico Iyer praises the comma and, at the same time, illustrates the many ways we rely on this "humble" punctuation mark. Finally, the style self-analyses completed by two classroom authors, Sarah Andrae and Amanda Fleming, only begin to outline the possibilities for this assignment that you can profitably undertake as a journal entry or an essay, at the beginning or at the end of a writing course (or at both times).

9

Chapter Readings

KEN AUTREY (b. 1945)

Prepositions in Alabama

CONSIDER THIS:

Ken Autrey has coordinated the writing program at Francis Marion University in Florence, South Carolina, since 1989 and now serves as coordinator of the writing program. An avid poet, he has been a faculty advisor to the campus literary magazine and teaches composition, poetry, and creative writing. He has published in the periodicals *Poetry Northwest, The Chattahoochee Review,* and *The Texas Review,* among others. Before reading this poem, make a list of all the writing rules you were asked to memorize in elementary and middle school and note how many of those memorized rules you continue to rely on. Then look at the way Autrey uses prepositions to tell his story of memorizing prepositions.

About Columbus Day, 6th grade, I learned the power
of lists when Mrs. Hancock held the grammar book
Above our heads and pointed to the prepositions,
stark and alphabetical. Gesturing
Across the room like an explorer in a painting,
she vowed we'd have them down in order
After a week's daily drills, able
to reel them out as smooth as auctioneers.
Against my instinct that the best way
was to muddle through on guesswork,
Among the others I set my memory to the task,
rhymeless amid this agonizing litany.
Around nine Friday my turn came first
(my patronym begins in "A"). I took my stab
At what I knew, "about" to "if" to "on" to "with"
and didn't drop a syllable.

Upon our shoulders lay the weight of grammar,
our burden—to find the objects for all words.
Under a cloud of chalkdust we fidgeted
over the year amid her ranks of facts
Until our heads knocked with the names
of presidents, rivers, seas, and states.

Toward Easter came the counties of Alabama,
this time in circuitous order—
To list them on that map that mirrors Mississippi:
Baldwin, Mobile, up the left side, around
Through Geneva, Covington, Escambia. Even
our sleep resounded with the catalog
Of Indian tribes—Autauga, Cherokee—and harsher
names for elder patriarchs—Hale, Wilcox, Pike.
On our memories trudged until June brought us all
we'd ever need of who, what, when, and where.

JULIA ALVAREZ (b. 1950)

Bilingual Sestina

CONSIDER THIS:

While many of us have experienced divided loyalties, those moving from one language to another often feel particularly torn, especially when learning a new language and culture means leaving parts of their home culture behind. A writer whose work has won a number of awards and has appeared in *The Kenyon Review, Poetry,* and *The New Yorker,* Julia Alvarez captures that sense of division in her poem. Alvarez was born in New York City and spent most of her early years in the Dominican Republic. When Alvarez was 10 her family had to leave the Dominican Republic, fleeing Trujillo's dictatorship. They settled in New York City. Alvarez told *Frontera* magazine, "It was a time when the model for the immigrant was that you came and you became an American and you cut off your ties and that was that. My parents had that frame of mind, because they were so afraid . . . ." Alvarez resisted this acculturation and embraces the fullness of her heritage. "Now I see the richness. Part of what I want to do with my work is of that complexity, that richness. I don't want it to be simplistic and either/or." In an interview with *NuCity* she said, "As a writer, part of my job is reaching out there to something larger than myself. It's important for me to write things that are for anyone interested in the human heart, not just myself." As you read her sestina, try to discover the pattern of this poetic form and make some guesses about why she chose it for this topic.

Some things I have to say aren't getting said
in this snowy, blonde, blue-eyed, gum chewing English,
dawn's early light sifting through the *persianas* closed
the night before by dark-skinned girls whose words
evoke *cama, aposento, sueños* in *nombres*
from that first word I can't translate from Spanish.

Gladys, Rosario, Altagracia—the sounds of Spanish
wash over me like warm island waters as I say
your soothing names: a child again learning the *nombres*
of things you point to in the world before English
turned *sol, tierra, cielo, luna* to vocabulary words—
sun, earth, sky, moon—language closed

like the touch-sensitive *morivivir* whose leaves closed
when we kids poked them, astonished. Even Spanish
failed us then when we realized how frail a word
is when faced with the thing it names. How saying
its name won't always summon up in Spanish or English
the full blown genii from the bottled *nombre.*

Gladys, I summon you back with your given *nombre*
to open up again the house of slatted windows closed
since childhood, where *palabras* left behind for English
stand dusty and awkward in neglected Spanish.
Rosario, muse of *el patio,* sing in me and through me say
that world again, begin first with those first words

you put in my mouth as you pointed to the world—
not Adam, not God, but a country girl numbering
the stars, the blades of grass, warming the sun by saying
el sol as the dawn's light fell through the closed
persianas from the gardens where you sang in Spanish,
Esta son las mañanitas, and listening, in bed, no English

yet in my head to confuse me with translations, no English
doubling the world with synonyms, no dizzying array of words,
—the world was simple and intact in Spanish
awash with *colores, luz, sueños,* as if the *nombres*
were the outer skin of things, as if words were so close
to the world one left a mist of breath on things by saying

their names, an intimacy I now yearn for in English—
words so close to what I meant that I almost hear my Spanish
blood beating, beating inside what I say *en inglés.*

MIKE ROSE (b. 1944)

Writing Around Rules

CONSIDER THIS (See Author's Introduction in Chapter 3):

Write down some of the images that go through your mind when you read the words "blocked writer" and "writing block." What do you note? What does a blocked writer look like? What does being blocked in your writing feel like? Do you have particular stories to tell about feeling stopped in your tracks as a writer? Share a few and then compare your stories to those of the writers introduced by Rose in his essay: Liz, Tyrrell, and Gary.

I

Here's Liz, a junior English major, at work on a paper for a college course: she has been given a two-page case study and must analyze it using the ideas contained in a second, brief handout. She has about one hour to complete her assignment. As she reads and rereads the handouts, she scribbles notes to herself in the margins. Liz is doing what most effective writers would do with such materials: paraphrasing the main points in the passages, making connections among them, recording associations to other pertinent knowledge. But a closer look at these interpretive notes reveals something unusual: Liz seems to be editing them as she goes along, cleaning them up as though they were final copy. In one of her notes she jots down the phrase "is saying that not having creative work is the . . . ." She stops, thinks for a moment, and changes "is the" to "causes." (Later on, explaining this change, she'll comment that "you're not supposed to have passive verbs.") She then replaces "is saying" with "says," apparently following her directive about passive voice, but later changes it again, noting that "says" is "too colloquial." Liz pauses after this editing and looks up—she has forgotten what she initially was trying to capture in her writing. "That happens a lot," she says.

Liz was one of the many college students I studied over a two-and-one-half-year period (*Writer's Block: The Cognitive Dimension*). The purpose of my study was to try to gain insight into what causes some young writers to compose with relative fluency and what leads others to experience more than their fair share of blocks, dead-ends, conflicts, and the frustrations of the blank page. What I uncovered was a whole array of problems that I would label as being primarily *cognitive* rather than primarily *emotional* in nature. That is, many students were engaging in self-defeating composing behaviors not because they had some deep-seated fear of revealing their thoughts or of being evaluated or because of some long-standing aversion to writing, but rather because they had somehow learned a number of rules, planning strategies, or assumptions about writing that limited rather than enhanced their composing. We saw Liz lose her train of thought by adhering too rigidly to stylistic rules when she should have been scribbling ideas freely in order to discover material for her essay. Let me offer two further vignettes that illustrate some of the other cognitive difficulties I uncovered.

Tyrrell, also a junior English major, says he doesn't like to sketch out any sort of plan or draft of what he's going to write. He'll think about his topic, but his pen usually won't touch paper until he begins writing the one, and only, draft he'll produce. As he writes, he pauses frequently and at length to make all sorts of decisions about words, ideas, and rhetorical effects. In short, he plans his work as he goes along. There's nothing inherently wrong with writing this way, but where difficult assignments involving complex materials are concerned, it helps to sketch out a few ideas, some direction, a loose organizational structure before beginning to write. When a coworker and I studied Tyrrell's composing, we noted the stylistic flourishes in his essay, but also its lack of direction. As my colleague noted, "[His] essay bogs down in description and in unexplained abstractions." Perhaps the essay would have had more direction if Tyrrell had roughed out a few ideas before composing his one and only draft. Why didn't he do so? Consider his comment on planning:

> [Planning] is certainly not spontaneous and a lot of the times it's not even really what you feel because it becomes very mechanical. It's almost like—at least I feel—it's diabolical, you know, because . . . it'll sacrifice truth and real feelings that you have.

Tyrrell assumes that sketching out a plan before writing somehow violates the spontaneity of composing: to plan dooms one to write mechanical, unemotional prose. Yet, while too much planning may sometimes make the actual writing a joyless task, it is also true that most good writing is achieved through some kind of prefiguring, most often involving pen and paper. Such planning does not necessarily subvert spontaneity; in fact, since it reduces the load on the writer's immediate memory, it might actually free one to be more spontaneous, to follow the lead of new ideas as they emerge. Tyrrell's assumption, then, is inaccurate. By recognizing only this one path to spontaneity, he is probably limiting his effectiveness as a writer and, ironically, may be reducing his opportunities to be spontaneous.

Gary is an honors senior in biochemistry. When I observed him, he spent over half of his writing time meticulously analyzing each sentence of the assignment's reading passage on one of the handouts. He understood the passage and the assignment well enough but wanted to make sure the passage was sufficiently broken down to be of use when he composed his essay. As Gary conducted this minute analysis, he wrote dozens and dozens of words and phrases across the handouts. He then summarized these words and phrases in a list of six items. He *then* tried to condense all six items into a thesis sentence:

> I have concepts . . . and my task here is to say what is being said about all of those all at once.

Gary's method was, in this case, self-defeating. He worked in too precise a fashion, generating an unwieldy amount of preliminary material, which he didn't seem to be able to rank or thin out—and he was unable to focus his thinking in a single thesis sentence. Gary's interpretive and planning strategies were inappropriately elaborate, and they were inflexible. It was not surprising that when Gary's hour was up, he had managed to write only three disconnected sentences. Not really an essay at all.

But what about the students who weren't stymied, who wrote with relative fluency? They too talked of rules and assumptions and displayed planning strategies. The interesting thing, though, is that their rules were more flexible; that is, a rule seemed to include conditions under which it ought and ought not to be used. The rules weren't absolutes, but rather statements about what one might do in certain writing situations. Their assumptions, as well, were not absolute and they tended to enhance composing, opening up rather than restricting possibilities. And their planning strategies tended to be flexible and appropriate to the task. Fluent writers had their rules, strategies, and assumptions, but they were of a different kind from those of the blocked writers.

What to do? One is tempted to urge the blocked writers to clear their minds of troubling rules, plans, and assumptions. In a few cases, that might not be such a bad idea. But what about Liz's preoccupation with passive constructions? Some degree of concern about casting one's language in the active voice is a good thing. And Gary's precise strategies? It would be hard to imagine good academic writing that isn't preceded by careful analysis of one's materials. Writers need the order and the guidance that rules, strategies, and assumptions provide. The answer to Liz's, Tyrrell's, and Gary's problems, then, lies in altering their approaches to make them more conditional, adaptive, and flexible. Let me explain further. For the sake of convenience, I'll focus on rules, though what I'll say has application to the assumptions we develop and the planning strategies we learn.

II

Writing is a phenomenally complex learned activity. To write in a way that others can understand we must employ a large and complicated body of conventions. We learn from our parents or earliest teachers that script, in English, goes left to right straight across the page. We learn about letter formation, spelling, sentence structure, and so on. Some of this information we absorb more or less unconsciously through reading, and some of it we learn formally as guidelines, as directives . . . as rules.

And there are all kinds of rules. Some tell us how to format our writing (for example, when to capitalize, how to paragraph, how to footnote). There are grammar rules (for example, "Make a pronoun agree in number with its antecedent"). There are preferences concerning style that are often stated as rules ("Avoid passive voice"). There are usage rules ("*That* always introduces restrictive clauses; which can introduce both restrictive and nonrestrictive clauses"). There are rules that tell us how to compose ("Before you begin writing, decide on your thesis and write it down in a single declarative sentence"). The list goes on and on. Some of these rules make sense; others are confusing, questionable, or contradictory. Fortunately, we assimilate a good deal of the information they contain gradually by reading other writers, by writing ourselves, or by simply being around print. Therefore, we can confirm or alter or reject them from experience.

But all too often the rules are turned into absolutes. And that's where the trouble begins. Most rules about writing should not be expressed (in textbooks), stored (in our minds), or enacted (on the page) as absolutes, as mathematical, unvarying directives. True, a few rules apply in virtually all situations (for example, certain formatting rules or capitalization rules). But most rules do not. Writing rules, like any rules about language, have a history and have a time and place. They are highly context-bound.

Should you always, as some textbooks suggest, place your thesis sentence at the beginning of your first paragraph or, as others suggest, work up to it and place it at the end of the paragraph? Well, the answer is that both injunctions are right . . . and wrong. Students writing essay exams would be well-advised to demonstrate their knowledge and direct the reader's attention as soon as possible. But the writer who wants to evoke a mood might offer a series of facts and events that gradually leads up to a thesis sentence. The writing situation, the rhetorical purpose, and the nature of the material one is working with will provide the answer. A single-edged rule cannot.

How about our use of language, usage rules? Certainly there's a right and a wrong here? Again, not quite. First of all, there's a time in one's writing to worry about such things. Concern yourself with questions of usage too early in your composing and you'll end up like Liz, worrying about the minutiae of language while your thought fades to a wisp. Second, the social consequences of following or ignoring such rules vary widely depending on whether you're writing formal or informal prose. Third, usage rules themselves have an evolutionary history: we aren't obliged to follow some of the rules that turn-of-the-century writers had to deal with, and our rules will alter and even disappear as the English language moves on in time. No, there are no absolutes here either.

Well, how about some of the general, commonsense rules about the very act of writing itself? Certainly, rules like "Think before you write" ought to be followed. Again, a qualification is in order. While it certainly is good advice to think through ideas before we record them for others to see, many people, in fact, use writing as a way of thinking. They make major decisions *as* they write. There are times when it's best to put a piece of writing aside and ponder, but there are also times when one ought to keep pen in hand and attempt to resolve a conceptual tangle by sketching out what comes to mind. Both approaches are legitimate.

I'll stop here. I hope I've shown that it's difficult to make hard and fast statements about the structure, the language, or the composing of an essay. Unfortunately, there's a strong push in our culture to make absolute statements about writing, especially where issues of style and usage are concerned. But I hope by now the reader of this essay believes that most rules about writing—about how to do it, about how it should be structured, about what words to use—are not absolute, and should be taught and enacted in a flexible, context-dependent way. Given certain conditions, you follow them; given other conditions you modify or suspend them. A teacher may insist that a young writer follow a particular dictum in order to learn a pattern, but there must come a time when the teacher extends the lesson and explains when the dictum is and isn't appropriate.

Because I've relied on the writing of college students for my illustrations, it might seem that my assertions—particularly about the connection between inflexible rules and blocking—apply only to young, developing writers. Not so. A professional writer's sense of self is intimately involved in his or her work, so, to be sure, the blocks and resistances such writers experience are often related to emotional factors. But the cognitive dimension we've seen with collegiate writers is present as well. The rules that trip up the professional writer may be different, but the fundamental processes and problems can be quite similar. Let me illustrate this point by coming closer to home and offering an illustration from my own writing, the composition of a poem.

III

Here's the background. My father has been dead for many years now, but he is still very much present in my dreams. In one recent dream, I was standing by his bedside; he was comatose. The dream then shifted—as dreams often do—and I was outside watching him tinker at a workbench. When I woke, I knew I had the central image of a poem, a short elegy. Here is what finally emerged, five or so revisions later:

> The last we knew
> doctors were explaining "aneurysm."
> Father lay in the next room, asleep.
> We were surprised, then,
> to find him at his workbench,
> white oleander at his back
> rustling night music in direct sun.
>
> He set the vise
> on a bar of red metal
> and with thin flame
> pared it into petals.

He cupped them, whispering.
Slipping dowels through his fingers
he made a fist, hard,
opened it,
and handed us two shining roses.

We place them by him
asleep in the next room.

I was happy with the poem—with its images, its compression. But I knew that the abrupt shifts in time and place could confuse readers unless they knew that the poem is a dream vision. Now, I didn't want to wreck the poem's compression or interrupt the reader's movement through the events of the poem by intruding into the lines themselves, by grabbing a reader by the collar and yelling, "Hey! This is a dream. Get it?" I knew that I had to do whatever I was going to do in the title; the reader had to be clued in before the poem began. At this point, I blocked. And for reasons not unlike those that tripped up the students I had observed. Titles, to my mind, did certain things, fit certain conventions that I had either read or heard or somehow absorbed from years and years of reading other people's poems: Titles should add something to a poem, not just state the obvious. Titles should be evocative. Titles take up one line. Titles are direct and declarative. The words in a title should be in one sentence. So went the list. Some of these rules I recall learning from mentors. Others I acquired somehow, somewhere. Some of the rules made sense. Others were nonsense. And some—like the injunctions to be evocative and to be direct—potentially conflicted. I tried titles like "The Dream Answer" and junked them quickly as cliches and as . . . well . . . just stupid. Days passed. And more days. I was stuck. I was working with a whole set of notions about titles that placed certain boundaries on what I could invent and what I would consider acceptable. All writers work within boundaries, but these were proving to be too restrictive.

One afternoon I was talking to my friend Bonnie Verburg—a fine writer—about my dilemma. She thought for awhile and went to get a poem of her own: a dream poem. We made some comparisons and talked about the effects we were trying to get by keeping the dissociated structure of the dream. Then she asked why I didn't try a title that itself was dream-like, that is, that compressed disparate words or ideas or events together. Something clicked. I wasn't sure I was following exactly what Bonnie was asking of me, but I saw that I *could* have a title different from the kind dictated by my various directives and assumptions. The poem's title came quickly:

Dream
My Father's Flowers

Bonnie, in effect, had provided a new direction that I hadn't seen as a possibility. My experience with her made it clear that some of my rules about titles were limiting rather than guiding my thinking. In solving the problem before me, I rejected some rules and recast others into more flexible directives, directives with some play in them that might now lead to the composing of effective titles for what I hope are reams of future poems.

ALLISON JOSEPH (b. 1967)

Rules of Conduct: Colored Elementary School, 1943

CONSIDER THIS:

Before reading, consider the words "rules of conduct." What are the rules of conduct of your life? What and who constrains you? What does it mean to obey or disobey such rules? How do you feel constrained—if you do—by rules (tacit or explicit) relating to your race, your religion, your social class or your gender?

Allison Joseph was born in London to parents of Caribbean descent, and raised in Toronto and New York City. She teaches poetry and creative writing at Southern Illinois University and is the director of the Young Writers Workshop there. Growing up in different countries had a strong effect on Joseph, and her time in the Bronx would influence her writing directly. She told *Dream/Girl* magazine, "I was surrounded by all sorts of different cultures—different types of food, music, languages. And it all seemed equally exciting to me. All of it valid. Being surrounded by such diversity let me know that all of it was worthy material for writing." Joseph, speaking in an interview at Kenyon College said, "Poems are about the things you absorb over time." Some of the images and ideas Joseph absorbed and uses in her writing include "family, girlhood, music, body image." What are the stories behind this poem that you and other readers can construct together? Explore the politics that inform this poem and consider why the villanelle form—which requires a set repetition of lines—might have been chosen as the vehicle for this topic.

Watch your language, say words right.
Use education as your tool.
Keep every anger curled in tight.

You won't achieve through force or might,
won't rise above through being cruel.
Watch your language, say words right.

Avoid forbidden streets at night,
stay far from dope and alcohol.
Keep every anger curled in tight.

Speak only when you're called and act polite;
don't dare to miss one day of school.
Watch your language, say words right.

Don't be the child who aches to fight,
the one who yearns to break the rules.
Keep every anger coiled in tight.

Live proud, although you are not white.
Don't let them see you act a fool.
Watch your language, say words right.
Keep every anger coiled in tight.

RICHARD MARIUS (1933-1999)

False Rules and What Is True about Them

CONSIDER THIS:

Richard Marius was born in Martel, Tennessee, and died in Belmont, Massachusetts. Marius worked as a newspaper reporter, then taught at Gettysburg College, the University of Tennessee, and Harvard, where he also was the director of the expository writing program. His work appeared in many periodicals including *Daedalus, Christian Century,* and *Esquire.* He gave an indication of his writing process in an interview with *Contemporary Authors*: "My work is most influenced by my observation of people. . . . I revise far too much, too compulsively, often by printing out my drafts and filling in revisions by hand and afterwards plugging them back into the computer. . . ." In his essay on rules, Marius makes a number of claims about why we have established rules in English. How many of the rules you write by are on his list of false rules?

English has rules established by centuries of habit. They were not written by the moving fingers of God on tablets of stone. Some of them are irrational—as all habits are. But break them, and you make it hard for readers and yourself. When you violate the rules, readers may think you are ignorant and therefore not worth their time. Yes, that attitude is unfair, but as John F. Kennedy frequently said, life is unfair.

The good news is that the rules of English are much less complicated than most people think. When my students make mistakes, I often find that their minds have been running faster than their hands. They think ahead to the next word, the next phrase, the next sentence while they write. They may lose their concentration and make errors that they can easily catch if they go over their work—especially if they read it aloud. When I work carefully over my own early drafts, I find all sorts of dumb mistakes. I laugh at myself and correct them—although to my horror I discover now and then that some of them make their way into print!

Alas, many people—including too many teachers—complicate matters by making up false rules. I once asked a group of high school writing teachers to tell me the most annoying mistakes made by their students. One teacher said, "I had it when my students use 'pretty' as an adverb." I said, "In English it's pretty hard to avoid doing that." And I long ago lost count of the teachers who have told me proudly that they keep their students from splitting infinitives.

False rules oppress writers and may make prose sound stilted and somehow wrong. Any examination of published prose will show that professional writers break these false "rules" all the time. Yet they have a vigorous life.

Writing is a complicated business, one of the most difficult acts of the human brain. False rules seem to grant security, to reduce writing to a formula that anybody can understand, to make it less threatening, to reduce success to a formula or a recipe that anybody can follow. The people who tout false rules are like astrologers; they can always find an audience even if experience proves them wrong.

Writing is more than obeying the rules. Writing is observation and imagination, order and revelation, style and form. It means making a subject part of yourself. And it always involves risk. To multiply false rules is much like welding armor onto a car; in the end the car may be perfectly safe, but it may also be too heavy to move.

Although the false rules are wrongly expressed, they sometimes have substance buried deep inside them. People have devised them to deal with real problems. We should take this substance into account even as we reject the silliness and the pedantry of the extremes.

COMMON FALSE RULES

Here are some common false rules with a few notes about what may be true about them.

1. Don't Use the First Person.

Every college freshman knows this one because so many high school teachers order their students never to say *I* or *we*. So instead of the first person we get impersonal stiff constructions like these:

It is the opinion of this writer . . .
This writer would be forced to agree . . .
This writer has shown . . .
The reader is made to feel . . .
This writer was hit by a truck when she . . .

The best argument for the first person is that we see it in all kinds of professional prose. It is used in reviews of books and movies to avoid the tedious repetition of phrases such as "the reader" or "the audience." Walter Jackson

Bate, writing about Samuel Johnson, demonstrates the graceful use of the first person without recourse to the tiresome and impersonal form, "The reader."

> Even if we knew nothing of the state of mind he was forced to battle during this psychological crisis, the edition of Shakespeare—viewed with historical understanding of what it involved in 1765—could seem a remarkable feat: and we are not speaking of just the great *Preface.* To see it in perspective, we have only to remind ourselves what Johnson brought to it—an assemblage of almost every qualification we should ideally like to have brought to this kind of work with the single exception of patience; and at least some control of his impatience, if not the quality of patience itself, might have been passable if this period of his life had not been so distressing.

The first person appears in accounts of events the writer has observed or participated in. Here is part of a paragraph from one of the best books I have read about the Vietnam War, an account by an infantry lieutenant named Nathaniel Tripp. (A "slick" is a military helicopter.)

> Now and then a Ninth Division convoy would roar through the village at thirty miles an hour. If I heard them coming in time, I would go out to the street and watch them pass. I would look at the filthy, sad-eyed infantrymen sprawled atop the vehicles, slumped over the machine guns, and feel a great sadness and longing. I would look for the platoon leader or company commander, look for the one with the grease pencils and maps, try to meet his eyes with mine so that I could wish him godspeed. If our eyes met, his would quickly dart away again, like a wild animal. And when, now and then, a line of slicks would come fluttering over our village, infantrymen dangling their legs from the doors, my heart would bob up and down with them.

We may expect any eyewitness narrative to use the first person. But what about more formal writing such as the kind we do in academic books and articles. Even here writers expressing opinions about a controversial subject use the first person to avoid any ambiguity about where they stand or as a means of noting their opinions in a controversial field—an opinion with weight because of the writer's experience and authority. Often nowadays writers enter their own work as conversationalists—as I have done in this book. The writers take positions and announce forthrightly that the positions are theirs and not some vague mass. In his book, *The Origins of Virtue,* Matt Ridley attacks one of the favorite views of romantics in the Western world—that "natives," the Indian peoples of North and South America, are kinder and gentler to the environment than Westerners and that therefore native Americans of various sorts are more virtuous than whites of European origin. He demonstrates that when Indians find a profitable occasion to exploit the environment, they do so as avidly as any of the rest of us. He ponders his finding.

> This is not to castigate Indians. It would be cheap and hypocritical of me indeed, sitting in my comfortable house dependent on immense quantities of fossil fuels

> and raw materials for my everyday needs, to be rude about an Indian just because he has found it necessary to sell some cheap logs for cash with which to buy necessities. He is endowed with vast reserves of knowledge about the natural history of the environment that I could never match—its dangers, its opportunities, its medicinal qualities, its seasons, its signs. He is a better conservationist than me in every conceivable way—simply by virtue of his material poverty. But this is because of the economic and technological limitations within which he lives, not because of some spiritual, inherent ecological virtue that he possesses. Give him the means to destroy the environment, and he would wield them as unthinkingly as me—and probably with more efficiency.

But what about scholars, writing hard-core scholarship? They, too, use the first person, especially in areas where many opinions contest against each other and the writer wishes to show his or her own view while respecting others. Here is Harry Berger, Jr., one of our finest Shakespeare scholars, writing about *Macbeth.*

> I would argue that this view of *Richard III,* which Burckhardt in effect ascribes to Shakespeare, cannot be applied to *Macbeth* in the same manner—that it cannot be ascribed to Shakespeare as *his* view of the play—but that it can be applied. As I suggested earlier, it is the view Shakespeare ascribes to the good Scots, Macbeth's enemies, and it is a view he presents critically as self-justifying, scapegoating, and simplistic. Thus we are asked to see their pietistic restoration view as contributing to the subtler evil that obscures the Scottish air and envelops the loyal thanes as well as the bloody dog and his wife. In developing this thesis I shall be carrying further some readings of the play that in recent years have begun to challenge the orthodox view.

Yet modern writers do not use the first person indiscriminately. When you write, ask yourself this: "Am I writing about myself, or is my subject something else?" Don't get in the way of your subject. Professional writers do not say, "In my opinion, the Middle East is one of the most dangerous places in the world." They say simply, "The Middle East is one of the most dangerous places in the world." No one debates that thought. If a writer signs her name to an article, every reader with common sense will understand that the assertions in it represent the writer's considered opinion and not some universal truth agreed on by all. One needs to say "In my opinion" only when the statement is fiercely debated and evidence abounds on every side of the question.

My inexperienced writers sometimes seem to think that nothing is worth writing unless it demonstrates some powerful emotional transformation in the writer. Sometimes they add an emotional commentary at the end of a paper. They want me to know that their hearts are in the right place. Writing about passion has its place now and then. But most of the time the facts standing alone—sometimes starkly alone—have such weight and power that for the writer to add his or her emotions would be trivial and distracting. In the following text, British historian Martin Gilbert tells the story of a young Jewish boy's experience during World War II as a slave laborer for the Germans. (The initials SS stand for the German word *Schutzstaffel*, signifying special forces in the German army chosen for ruthlessness, unthinking obedience, and cruelty.)

> Roman Halter remembered a moment of supreme danger, such as many of the boys faced, each one coming very near to death in some sudden, bizarre, and cruel circumstance. "One day twelve of us were taken out in Dresden by the SS," Roman Halter recalled, "and placed against the factory wall to be shot. Each of us had an SS man behind him who pointed his rifle at our head. We stood there facing the wall with our hands up. I wept because my hip hurt. Normally before an execution the SS would pick on one victim and brutalize him or her.
>
> As we were led out of the factory down the front steps, which were lined with SS men—and SS women, because among the twelve of us who were led out to be shot, there were ten men and two women—one SS officer pointed me out to another SS man, who turned his rifle upside down and lifted it above his head like an axe. I saw all this, and so did Abram Sztajer who was next to me and said in Yiddish, 'Move' (actually the word means 'slide'—'ritz cech'), and in that split second, when the butt was over me in the air, I turned and hopped down one step. The blow slid down the side of my body and momentarily rested on my hip. I screamed. It hurt terribly.
>
> "There was an SS woman on the opposite side, a couple of steps down. When she saw that her colleague had failed to crush my skull, she pulled me towards her and hit me with a sharp object on the side of my head, which instantly produced a gush of blood.
>
> "We were waiting to be shot, and Sztajer, who was on my left, could see from the corner of his eye, the bloodstained part of my face. 'Cry quietly, don't let them know that they have hurt you,' he whispered. For some reason I did what he told me, and gave out intermittent and suppressed groans."
>
> Suddenly the prisoners who were about to be shot were ordered back to their barracks. There was to be no execution. In a few terrifying moments Roman Halter had twice escaped death.

Almost any normal human being reading this account will feel deep passion, outrage, and simple anger at the cruelty here reported. But Gilbert would have ruined the stark effect of his story if he had interjected his own passion onto the narrative. These cruel details in themselves imply a moral judgment. He trusts us to know what side he stands on, and he does not insult us by assuming that we have to be coached about the correct emotions to have before these horrors. He keeps the focus on his true subject—the story of brutality inflicted on a young Jewish boy. He does not turn it to himself.

Wayne C. Booth's "implied author" should come to mind here. Never write to show readers how noble you are. Don't brag, even about your modesty. Don't show off; avoid drawing unnecessary attention to yourself. Stick to the business of telling readers what you know about the story you tell. When we blatantly insert ourselves into a story about someone else, we are like thoughtless people who talk with each other during a play so that no one around them can follow what is happening on stage. Avoid giving the impression that when you say "I think" or "in my opinion" you install yourself in an impregnable fortress, immune to any counterargument. Many Americans suppose that all opinions are equal and that those who express themselves vehemently enough and sincerely enough deserve respect and even admiration. These people imagine that others are guilty of bad taste or at least discourtesy if they disagree with opinions strongly stated. Many an argument ends with the offhand and sometimes surly remark, "Well, you have your opinion, and I have mine." Implied in a remark like this is often another: "Don't bother me with the evidence."

Thank God we live in a free society where people can say any silly thing they please. But if you are going to influence thoughtful and fair-minded people, you must be able to defend your opinions by reasoning about them. Don't use the first person to avoid an argument. If you command evidence, you can argue your case without using the first person at all.

Follow the example of Harry Berger, Jr., in the section cited above from his work. When you deliver yourself of an "I think" or an "in my opinion" it should reflect your own careful statement of a point of view earned by your disciplined study of the issue and presented humbly, recognizing that others have studied with equal care and come to a similar conclusion. If you get in the habit of saying "I think" or "in my opinion" in an arrogant and challenging tone that does not consider the evidence, people will pay no attention to you.

So the false rule about the first person contains some truth. Avoid using the first person except when it is clearly called for. In the following instances, the first person may be in order. When you deliberately assume a conversational tone as in a regular newspaper column, a letter, or a book like this one, you may use the first person. The conversational tone may help you create intimacy with your readers.

Most books about writing share the assumption that we all perform the same task and that the author has something to share with others who write. Most books like this one are chatty—perhaps too much so. E. B. White, John McPhee, George Orwell, Joan Didion, Ann Tyler, and many other modern essayists use the first person as a matter of course. They write (or wrote) about what happens to them, their reactions, their conclusions. They share their experiences to enlarge our own.

Some subjects lend themselves to informality; some do not. You will not find a chatty medical book on brain surgery or leukemia. For such subjects informality would be in bad taste—unless the author happens to be writing about his or her experiences as a victim of either affliction.

For serious subjects, use the first person only if your experiences are essential to your essay. If you report on research that you have done alone or with colleagues, you may use the first person or the passive, depending on your own taste. Most scientific journals use the passive:

> One thousand people were questioned about their preferences for automobiles. They were asked whether performance was more important than economy,

whether they needed a large back seat, and whether color might influence their choice of a new car. They were asked whether they had more confidence in American cars or Japanese makes.

Some writers prefer the first person in such reports, making their prose more informal and lively. That is the style of *Consumer Reports*, the nation's most popular and most respected consumer magazine. Here is a paragraph from an article about tests on strollers for young children:

> Parents and other adults do the most to keep the perils at bay, of course, but they should have an ally in the manufacturer. Unfortunately, the companies whose strollers we tested for this report don't always bear their fair share of the load. Although baby strollers have been significantly improved in recent years, more than 10,000 babies and children under five are injured seriously enough every year in carriages and strollers to require emergency hospital treatment.

If you sign your name to a formal essay or report, you may venture an occasional comment in the first person. You may wish to assert your own choice among conflicting opinions. You cannot use the first person singular if you have not signed the essay. If you write a memo to represent the views of your university on a controversial issue like hate speech, you may use the editorial *we* to show that your thoughts represent the official policy of your institution. But you cannot say *I* since no one knows who you are if your name is not on the piece.

2. Never Write a Sentence Fragment.

This false rule should be amended to read, "Never write a sentence fragment unless you know what you are doing." If you cannot tell the difference between a sentence and a sentence fragment, get yourself a good English handbook and work on the problem until you beat it. But good writers who know what they are doing use sentence fragments for special effects. We can scarcely read any modern writer without running into sentence fragments, especially in narratives but often also in expositions. They provide a rapid pace, especially effective in the context of a series of events or thoughts or described objects. If the context is clear, fragments are both readable and efficient. They get readers quickly from place to place. Here is an example from *The New Yorker.* Writer David Remnick recalls a meeting with the late Isaiah Berlin, who had written about Joseph Stalin and the Soviet Union:

> Foolishly, I thought Berlin wanted to know what had been going on in Moscow. Not quite.

Negative fragments like this one are common as reversals of something positive said in the previous sentence. Fragments are often used as answers to direct or indirect questions.

> I ask him about crime. Two incidents in two weeks.

Sometimes you can begin with a series of fragments—a rapid-fire collection of facts that set tone and theme for your essay. Most fragments depend for meaning on the sentences that come just before them. That is how David Remnick uses the fragment in the text above. It is a quick negation of the supposition in the sentence that precedes it. Fragments can often be joined to the preceding sentence by a comma, a dash, or a colon.

> Surely the death penalty was meant for this: to extract retribution for a man whose limbs were mangled by an explosion as his mother watched through a window. For a father killed in his kitchen while opening a parcel that had nonchalantly been passed around by his family. For another man blown away by a mail bomb addressed to someone else, the work of a terrorist who would then scribble in his journal, "We have no regret blowing up the wrong guy."

Instead of forbidding you to use them at all, teachers should tell you to use them with care. Care includes being sure that the fragment does not become tiresome because you use it too often or that it does not become confusing because you use it out of a proper context.

3. Don't Split Infinitives.

Before we talk about split infinitives, we should be sure we know what they are. An infinitive can be split only by inserting a word or phrase between the infinitive marker *to* and the verb that makes the infinitive. The split infinitives below are in italics.

Red Sox Manager Stuffy O'Neal begged his team *to really and truly try* not to fold until August this year.

McDougal's daily exercise was to *strenuously and rapidly* lift a four-pound chocolate cake from his plate to his mouth until the cake was consumed.

These are not split infinitives:

To be truly understood, Paul wanted his life to be an open book.

Unfortunately, the pages were far too dull to be read.

Many people who know nothing else about grammar know about split infinitives and don't like them. For their dislike they reckon on a literalistic understanding of the infinitive form. In most languages, the infinitive is one word. *Hacer, faire,* and *facere* are infinitives meaning "to do" in Spanish, French, and Latin respectively. Each is one word. Purists insist that an infinitive in English should be considered one word and that to split an infinitive is barbaric. Their reasoning seems confirmed by our use of infinitives in English, especially by our habit of referring to an infinitive with the pronoun *it*: "To write was everything to her; it was a compulsion that sometimes alarmed her friends." The pronoun *it* refers to the infinitive *to write,* a singular entity used as a noun. The purists believe that to split an infinitive violates an integrity of the noun the infinitive may represent.

Nevertheless, common sense tells us that English infinitives are not one word but two, and even the most casual observation reveals that good writers occasionally split infinitives. Split infinitives appear in almost every issue of the *New York Times* and *Time,* for better or for worse huge influences in the way we think of correct English.

> The anthropologist Laura Betzig, surveying these early civilizations, has rendered the Darwinian opinion that politics has often been "little more than reproductive competition"—men using power *to better spread* their genes.

Writing is governed by flexible standards set by editors. Most editors nowadays publish split infinitives, and I find it futile to rave against split infinitives as if they represented decadence and sloth.

Still moderation is in order. Although professional writers may split infinitives, they do so only occasionally. Several split infinitives in a short essay begin to sound clumsy. They seem to break down the natural rhythms of speech that make for clear writing and easy reading. We rarely split infinitives when we speak. We should be moderate in splitting them when we write.

Beyond rhythm is efficiency. Most split infinitives are not bad because they violate a sacrosanct rule but because the adverb that splits is unnecessary. Suppose you write, "He wanted to really work hard." You can drop the really and have a better sentence. Really here is a pointless intensifier. The same is true of most split infinitives; the adverb that does the splitting is unnecessary, and dropping it makes the sentence stronger.

Remember, too, that many people detest split infinitives with an irrational passion. I once knew a university president who scorned any letter to him that split an infinitive. He never wrote a book in his life. But he was convinced that anyone who split an infinitive was ignorant. People like him are surprisingly numerous in the world, and you should at least know that they exist when you write.

I don't split infinitives. Split infinitives disturb some delicate sentence balance in my head. Perhaps my reluctance arises from the lingering memory from my sweet-tempered seventh-grade English teacher, Mrs. Hattie Simmons Witt, in a rural Tennessee school. She believed firmly in God, brushed teeth, soap, and unsplit infinitives, and we loved her. Whatever caused it, my aversion to the split infinitive is so strong and so habitual that I do not fight it. I revise sentences to eliminate split infinitives, and something old-fashioned (and probably pedantic) in me makes me notice when others split them—although I don't correct them on student papers.

You are much more likely to find split infinitives in journalism—newspaper and magazine writing—than in trade books. The more time editors take with a manuscript, the more likely they are to cut split infinitives. But the split infinitive is so common nowadays in so many things we read that writing teachers become a little foolish when they accuse splitters of high crimes and misdemeanors against the English language.

4. Don't End a Sentence with a Preposition.

Prepositions are short words that never change their form no matter how they are used. They connect nouns or pronouns in prepositional phrases, and these phrases serve as adjectives or adverbs in a sentence. Prepositions allow the strength of nouns and pronouns to modify other elements in a sentence.

> *In the night* he dreamed of horses.

The prepositional phrase *in the night* works as an adverb modifying the verb *dreamed;* so does the prepositional phrase *of horses.* Without prepositions, we could not easily express these ideas. *Nightly he dreamed horsely,* we might say. Some scholar might reveal the meaning of such a sentence, but it would be difficult.

> The dictionary *on my desk* is my favorite book.

The prepositional phrase *on my desk* serves as an adjective modifying dictionary, a noun.

To place a preposition before its object follows the general rule of English syntax that related elements in a sentence should be as close to each other as possible. To end a sentence with a preposition deprives that preposition of a natural object on which to rest, and this apparent disorder may be unsettling. "The committee voted against." Against what? "The hamburger came with." With what?

But often it seems unnatural to be strictly formal in putting prepositions before their objects. We can easily say this: "That was the decision I fought against." We can change the sentence to read, "That was the decision against which I fought." But only a robot or a flight attendant would talk like that. You can revise the sentence to read, "I fought against that argument"; but if you have been talking about several arguments and want to identify the particular one you have fought against, you may wish to say, "That was the argument I fought against."

In developing our style, we choose between alternates that sometimes differ only slightly from each other. I can see a difference in emphasis between the sentences "That was the argument I fought against" and "I fought against that argument." Context would determine which one I used, but I would quickly use the former if I found it convenient.

5. Don't Begin a Sentence with a Conjunction.

I once had an angry letter reproaching me for this sin. Conjunctions join sentence elements—words, phrases, or clauses. The common coordinating conjunctions—*and, but, for,* and *or*—join equal elements. Other conjunctions, such as *if, although, whether,* and *even,* join dependent elements.

I do not know the origin of the false rule that sentences should never begin with a conjunction, but it is quoted to me frequently, usually by men over sixty. Yet any glance at a newspaper or magazine shows that professional writers frequently begin sentences with conjunctions. John F. Kennedy used conjunctions to begin fifteen sentences in his short inaugural address in 1961. E. B. White, one of the finest essayists of our times, uses conjunctions to begin many of his sentences. So did Lewis Thomas, one of our best writers about science. So the false rule would seem to have little validity among those who write English best.

Using a conjunction to begin a sentence emphasizes the connection between the thoughts of two consecutive sentences. With a conjunction to open a sentence, you say something like this: "Pay attention. This sentence is closely related to the thought in the sentence immediately before it. But it is important enough to stand by itself, to begin with a capital letter, so you have to take careful note of it."

As I have pointed out earlier, most sentences develop some thought in the sentence immediately preceding them. Although you may wish to emphasize such connections now and then, your readers will become immune to the effect if you use the device too often. Too many conjunctions at the start of a sentence begin to look like a verbal tic, an eccentricity of style that can become as annoying as the steady kicking of a restless child behind you against your seat at the movies. Used with circumspection, the device of beginning an occasional sentence with a conjunction can make your prose a little more fluid. But remember the implacable habit of most writers: around eighty percent of all sentences begin with the subject.

6. Avoid the Pronoun *You*.

If you have read this far, you know I have violated this false rule again and again—for a reason. I have written these pages in an informal, conversational style, and in conversations we address readers as *you*. We do the same in letters.

In more formal writing, to say *you* may seem out of place. No good writer would produce this sentence in a formal essay on cancer: "If you study cancer long enough, you discover that it is not one disease but a large group of diseases that share certain lethal qualities." It's much better to say this: "Cancer is not one disease but a group of related diseases." Nor do professional historians use the pronoun *you* in essays about history: "You have to sympathize with the Germans in World War I, facing as they did powerful enemies in both the east and the west." Say something like this: "In World War I, Germany faced powerful enemies in both east and west."

Even in informal writing the second person should be used sparingly. I dislike a sentence like this: "To serve in one of the first submarines, *you* had to be brave or foolish or both." Your readers did not serve in one of the first submarines; you cannot meaningfully include them in your sentence. Say this instead: "Crew members on the first submarines had to be brave or foolish or both." Nor can you say this: "When *you* have been a famous athlete most of your life, *you* sometimes feel miserable when the cheering stops." Most readers have not been famous athletes all their lives. Write this instead: "Famous athletes sometimes feel miserable when the cheering stops."

It's all right to say *you* in various informal contexts. Articles that give advice or describe processes often use *you:* "Most automatic cameras give *you* no choice in the exposure. A few, however, have a backlight switch, which lets *you* correct the exposure when strong light is coming from behind a subject."

Personal books or essays often address the reader. But in a formal, academic essay written for the college classroom, a research paper in history or philosophy or literature, you should use the second person sparingly if at all. By the conventions of written English, the second person is too informal for such purposes.

7. Avoid Contractions.

Here much of the advice about the pronoun *you* can be repeated. Contractions do well in informal or semiformal prose—like the prose in this book. You may sometimes loosen stiff prose by using contractions. Most teachers accept contractions in college papers, and contractions serve well enough in letters or personal essays. Contractions also serve well in books and articles about personal experience. Nathaniel Tripp in his fine saga about his experiences in Vietnam writes informally.

> Was he a midnight gardener, trying to get a leg up on the weeding? Either he *didn't* know we were there, or he knew us better than we thought, knew we *wouldn't* shoot him.

Contractions serve less well in formal essays. I feel uncomfortable using them in scholarly books and articles because I find them a little too conversational, a little too informal for a serious subject that I want to be taken seriously by the audience who will read the piece. It comes down to tradition. Serious readers about serious academic subjects are not accustomed to seeing contractions in academic writing and in formal trade books about subjects other than personal experience. I do not see contractions in dissertations, in formal books about history or philosophy or literary criticism, in business reports, or in articles in medical journals. Less formal publications such as *Sports Illustrated* and *Time* use them but not excessively. Of course when you quote a source that uses contractions, you quote exactly as the words were written.

8. Use *That* to Introduce Restrictive Clauses, *Which* to Introduce Nonrestrictive Clauses.

Restrictive clauses add essential information to the core statement of the sentence; nonrestrictive clauses add information that may be parenthetical, interesting, and valuable but not essential to the meaning the writing is trying to convey. You cannot leave a restrictive clause out and preserve the meaning of the core statement; you may omit a nonrestrictive clause without damaging the core statement. The restrictive clause in the following sentence is in italics:

> Of all my teachers, the one *who gave me the lowest grades* taught me more than anyone else ever did.

Leave out the italicized clause, and you do not have the sense that the writer conveys in the sentence as it is. In fact you have little sense at all. Grammarians call this clause *restrictive* because it restricts the noun it modifies. We are not talking about just any teacher; we are talking about the one teacher who gave me the lowest grades.

Here is a nonrestrictive clause, one that does not restrict the meaning of the noun it modifies but merely adds some information.

> My English teacher, *who was also my next-door neighbor,* knew me from the time I was born.

Now we have a clause that can be deleted from the sentence without harm to the main statement. The clause is parenthetical; it adds interesting but unessential information. It does not restrict the noun *teacher.*

Many people, especially those older than sixty-five, believe that restrictive clauses should be introduced with *that* and that nonrestrictive clauses should be introduced with *which.* At times they become irate when anyone suggests that this rule is only a foolish and cumbersome false rule that few writers observe or even think about. We have just seen that in clauses that refer to people, *who* can introduce both restrictive and nonrestrictive types. Why all the fuss?

Back in 1906, the English grammarian H. W. Fowler hit on the idea of using *that* to introduce restrictive clauses and *which* to introduce nonrestrictive clauses. He rightly believed that writers should make a clear distinction between the two types. Fowler wanted people to write sentences like these:

> The song that Sam played in the movie *Casablanca* was called "As Time Goes By."
> The ocean, *which* we could see from our house, changed color according to the shifting light of the sun through the clouds.

Because the distinction between restrictive and nonrestrictive clauses is necessary and because Fowler was an English gentleman, many Americans who would love to be like English gentlemen have taken his suggestion as a law of language. Fowler himself knew better. Calling restrictive clauses "defining" and nonrestrictive clauses "nondefining," he wrote the following:

> If writers would agree to regard *that* as the defining relative pronoun, and *which* as the non-defining, there would be much gain both in lucidity and in ease. Some there are who follow this principle now; but it would be idle to pretend that it is the practice of either most or the best writers.

Fowler was much more charitable than his modern disciples who have turned the *that/which* "rule" into an absurd fetish. After the first edition of this little book appeared, some outraged readers called my office to express their fierce indignation that a writing teacher should be so decadent as to deny the "rule" any authority. The fact remains that few writers and editors care much about it.

We use *that* or *which* according to some indefinable sense of which one sounds better in the sentence. Most writers always have done the same. The rule is impossible to observe in sentences such as the one immediately preceding this one or in common usage such as this: *That which* makes the rule invalid is its impossibility. Neither can the "rule" hold in *who/whom* clauses, and it cannot help us in restrictive or nonrestrictive phrases.

But recall the motive of the "rule": You must make a distinction between the two kinds of clauses. The only sure way is by proper punctuation. Restrictive clauses are not set off by any kind of punctuation; nonrestrictive clauses are usually set off by commas, although you can also use parentheses and dashes.

On occasion the meaning of the sentence changes according to whether the writer uses commas to make a clause nonrestrictive or does not use them to make the clause restrictive. Here is an example:

> The novel, which he wrote in Virginia, sold more than 30,000 copies.

Here is a nonrestrictive clause, one that gives some added information about the novel under discussion. He seems to have written only one novel, or at least in this sentence one particular novel is under consideration. He happened to write it in Virginia. But here now is the sentence with the nonrestrictive clause turned into a restrictive clause by the omission of the commas.

> The novel which he wrote in Virginia sold more than 30,000 copies.

Now we are talking about one novel among many. Other novels not written in Virginia may have sold more or less. The one written in Virginia sold more than 30,000 copies. The restrictive clause marks off this novel from others, and it is therefore not set off by commas.

The *that/which* rule is false, and few writers observe it. But you must be conscious of whether your clauses are restrictive or nonrestrictive, and you must punctuate accordingly. Otherwise you may confuse your readers by obscuring your meaning.

CONCLUDING REMARKS ON FALSE RULES

Don't be seduced by false rules, but don't go to the other extreme and suppose that English has no principles and conventions at all. Consider the motives behind the false rules, and observe the cautions that I have mentioned here. Always be aware of your audience. If, for example, you don't know if your teacher will accept contractions, ask her. Try to be efficient in your writing. That is, always use as few words as possible to express as clearly as you can the meaning you want to convey. I revise again and again, trying to cut out excess verbiage—and I always feel at the end that I have not cut out enough. The principle is a good guide for all of us. It will help you cut needless intensifiers out of prose—

especially those that split infinitives. More important, it will make you reflect on the choices in your writing that we often make unconsciously. The way to good writing is always by reflection on what we do as writers sentence by sentence, phrase by phrase, word by word. Read carefully and thoughtfully to learn the practices of other writers. Use common sense and observation.

WENDY BISHOP (b. 1953)

Reading, Stealing, and Writing Like a Writer

CONSIDER THIS (See Author's Introduction in Chapter 5):

Consider the suggestion at the end of the essay to keep a sentence style journal or commonplace book: find sentences you like in the reading materials that you like, study how they work for those authors, and how similar sentences might work for you. Begin by making a list of the types of writing you read. Make some predictions about what types of sentences your favorite authors in those texts choose. For instance, *Rolling Stone* authors tend to use what you could call rambunctious prose, prose that feels showy, slangy, descriptive. Sentences alternate dramatically, between long and short. The language is rarely stuffy and the sentences often capture a sense of spoken language—as if the reporter is sitting on the couch in your living room talking to you in a fairly organized and knowledgeable, but very hip, manner. Characterize the style of some of the authors or magazines you most like to read. This essay may give you some more precise language for analyzing the styles that you already enjoy and try to emulate.

Recently, I was hired by a local lawyer to be an expert witness on the sentence for an upcoming court case. What he asked me to do, as a writer and teacher of writers, was to give him a "standard" or "customary" reading of a legal statute. Thinking about this, I realized, that when I write poems, I do have to be an expert on words. And I can be an expert witness on the sentence because I'm constantly analyzing the sentences I read to compose the sentences I want to write.

I don't just read and write sentences (nor am I particularly good at analyzing them using conventional grammar), but I find sentences to be sculptural, like clay, sometimes, things that writers bend, shape, and mold to their purposes. I think of sentences as alive, responding here when pushed there, resisting here and obliging there. I've come to understand prose—first on the meaning level of what is being said—but also on the literal, syntactical level, as if touching and counting a string of beads, with all my attention tuned high. Then, I steal like a writer to write like a writer, using sentences to make my variation on the common themes and genres that all writers share—love story to technical report.

It wasn't always this way, this love affair with sentences. When I was an undergraduate in college, like many of my students I felt like I just *read*. It wasn't until I claimed the sentence as my area of desire, interest, and expertise—until I wanted to be a writer writing better—that I had to look underneath my initial readings. Soon, I had to question my emotional or story response to a text. It was no longer enough to report my response—hot, cold, or indifferent—or to ask what happened next as the paragraphs went down the page. I started asking, *how—how* did the writer get me to feel, *how* did the writer say something so that it remains in my memory when many other things too easily fall out, *how* did that writer communicate his/her intentions about genre, about irony?

A few years ago, I read the ideas of reading theorist Louise Rosenblatt who pointed out that we can look at the same texts in different ways and in doing so, read them differently: The texts don't change, our reasons for and attitudes towards reading change. (She also claims that each of our readings—even of the same text—are different because we are different, but that's another discussion). We can read instrumentally—to extract information. We usually do this when reading telephone books, textbooks, and reports. Or efferently, to experience the effects of the text, often aesthetic effects: the pain of a love story, the passion of a fine political speech, the life-transforming power of a religious text.

I'm thinking nowadays that it's good to learn to do both, at will—that is, sometimes you can get around a difficult textbook by trying to enjoy it—analyze the style of the writer, try to figure out how she or he even managed to write that way—and for fun you can read the phone book like a poem by looking at the alliteration of the names and streets—Wanda Wallace lives on Woodbine Way. What I want to do as a reading, stealing, writing writer is both, learning to inhabit, often, the middle ground. I need to cultivate double vision. I need both to feel the effects and also to extract the information about how those effects are achieved. I can enjoy the nursery rhyme rhythm of Wanda Wallace on Woodbine Way, but I can't write it myself—unless I analyze (look at all those Ws, listen to the rhythm) and imitate (steal?!) and put together my own pleasurable prose: Randal Reader lives on Writer Road. Look what I've done here—changed gender, made a play on the subject of my paragraph and the subject of writing. Cheap thrills, but that's how a writer reads to write.

You may not think of yourself as reader and writer. But you are doing both in the broadest sense all the time. You're reading your world every day; you compose your life. In the kitchen each A.M., you read the cupboards and refrigerator for breakfast options, cereal to eggs to bagels. You read the weather and read your closet, choosing your clothes by a complicated writer's formula: what's clean, what represents who I want to be today, what's appropriate for the weather? You read the newspaper, perhaps, choosing quickly which story engages you and which you don't need to read further. You read everyone at work or school. You read the signs and ads and marquees on your way home and write your evening plan in your head: go to the mall, stop in to listen to the band at X, or stay home and watch Y on TV. You steal your daily habits from your family (think about Thanksgiving meals), your friends (there are clothes you borrow, sayings you pick up), your developing age and tastes (as a child you never ate artichokes, but now . . .) You steal the right office or school moves by watching others in the same or similar situations. You see what I mean, I think.

So let's go back to this thing I'll define as reading like a writer—I could call it developing rhetorical fluency—but I won't. Let me show you how sentences are all around you waiting to be understood, stolen, modified, used by you in your writing. What I'm talking about are not the sentences given to you in school writing rules. You already know those, and you've practiced them or not as you've chosen. I can think of a fast few here. Don't start a sentence with coordinating conjunctions *and, so, but,* etc. Don't write single sentence paragraphs. All sentences have a subject and predicate (verb). Generally, don't use first person (I), slang, or profanity. Use exclamation points sparingly! Be clear, concise, and coherent. Argue logically. Etc. Now you may not have heard all these rules or heard them phrased just this way, but I bet you have a lot of writing etiquette packed in your brain somewhere. Try it—just for a minute free-write the rules that come to mind, like I just did.

Included in this list—embedded in this list—is the idea that good writers write right and people who break the rules should know better (don't know better) and should be corrected. Correct? But that's a matter of making our language inflexible, and remember how I mentioned the way—as a writer—I've come to feel sentences are alive, fluid and flexible, wild and tamed at times but not any one thing, always. Did you notice that sentence began with a coordinating conjunction? I didn't until I was done drafting since I was most interested in pursuing this idea, sharing it with you.

My argument: if you start to study sentences as a writer does, you'll see that they're more varied and flexible, a better instrument for exploring and expressing thought, than maybe you ever knew. The rules we're "given" can only address a small part of our language repertoire and are most often constraining and constricting rather than elucidating and explaining. It makes sense to follow the rules to get to where you want to go—especially during initial drafting, *for if you don't know what you're saying, your reader surely won't.* But later, as you revise, the possibilities of language should make you want to play, to match meaning to your own sentence magic, to create what we call style—your own best way of saying.

Here's another analogy. It makes sense that when we sit down together at dinner, we're more comfortable if everyone eats in a fairly civilized way—spoons, forks, food moving from plate to mouth in a compact and regular manner. I don't want spaghetti splashed all over the wood floor and staining the carpet, and it would make me queasy to eat off someone else's greasy plate. Fine. But there are occasions when such an orchestrated eating arrangement may be less than useful (or pleasurable): Don't sit me on the back patio eating a wonderful summer watermelon with a tiny silver spoon and napkin. Let me take a chunk in my fingers and bite into the red meat with my teeth and enjoy the sweet drip down my chin. I'll wash at the hose in a minute.

The same with sentences. If all our sentences, all our prose, followed "the rules" and showed good taste and fine manners . . . we'd lose something. We'd be bored to death. We wouldn't "hear" much from texts. But, luckily, that's not how it works.

Here's my experiment to prove this contention. I went through the house picking up as many different types of texts yesterday as I could find. I wanted to skim the texts and find examples of rule breaking—or we could simply call these flexible sentence strategies—to share with you; to show you how interesting intentional variation can be, how needed, how effective. How common this is in the texts around us. Use good manners when the occasion demands it, but not all occasions do—manners and customs change by time, place, and circumstance (although, too often it seems to be a "school" occasion when you're asked to show you know the rules—a little like you like having your gloves checked at the entrance to the cotillion, but that doesn't mean the most memorable dance of your life will take place there).

Now, I need to show you those sentence patterns I've found around the house, breaking another essay rule—don't list a whole lot of other peoples' writing. But I'm going to. Sharing what I found, first, in the texts around my house. Then, what I found, in a set of my students' texts from last semester which I've stored on my back writing room bookcase for just this sort of occasion.

Around the house, I collected a letter from my daughter's middle school principal, popular magazines (*Rolling Stone, Cosmopolitan, Science News, The New Yorker*), a book on computer technology, a detective novel, an ethnography, a book on how to set tile, the local newspaper, a memoir, and an e-mail printout. Easily, in each text, I found authors breaking rules, manipulating expectations of rules, making fun of the rules, or just head down, working, not worrying about the rules. All writers, not just "creative" writers do this, though certainly novelists, poets, and short story writers do it very well, too.

- Here, a middle school principal uses a dash to join two complete sentences and uses a coordinating conjunction, *but*, to start a sentence (bold face is my emphasis or insert, throughout these examples).

  Of course, every day will be different—many challenges and much hard work are ahead. But, we believe we have an enthusiastic Raa school community focused on providing the best educational experiences for each student. (Letter, September 7, 1995)

- Here, a *Rolling Stone* reporter uses the same coordinating conjunction, *but*, to start a new paragraph.

  Louise Maffeo glances out the window of an organic-food restaurant in New York's East Village and clasps her hands thoughtfully. A strange smile animates her pale, freckled face. "*Mary Poppins* is a movie that's indicative of my life," says Maffeo. "I'm the good girl. I can't pretend. I'm Betty, not Veronica."

But Maffeo, who has released her third album, *Bet the Sky,* on K Records, excels in a sneakier sort of subversiveness . . . . (Manning 38)

- Ah! A sentence without a verb (for a very practical reason—it's the text of a photo caption:

  First divorced—from each other—cohosts: George Hamilton and Alana Hamilton Stewart [star] on the *George and Alana Show.* "We make a dynamic couple" he says. (*Cosmopolitan,* 227)

- In this piece of highly conversational prose, the writer wants to create the effect of directly talking with the reader, which leads him into an I/you relationship, slang (*okay, brat*) and rhetorical questions—asking a question "for" the reader that the author immediately answers.

  Clueless: **Okay,** so you feel no pressing need to spend time in the company of a bubbly Beverly Hills brat whose main goal in life is to perform physical and psychological makeovers on her high school classmates and teachers. Still, this is one flick you can't afford to miss. Why? Simply because it's a fresh . . . . (Flatley, 42)

- Although paragraphs are supposed to have a topic sentence, be three to five sentences long, and be about a single idea, the single-sentence in *Science News* magazine seems to function differently. Here a single sentence paragraph acts as a teaser—following the headline and enticing the reader into the "story."

  Quest for Condensate Turns Up Another Find

  Not long after one group set the theme, another composed a variation.

  In July, researchers in Colorado reported having observed the elusive state of matter known as the Bose-Einstein condensate in the form of a cloud of ribidium-87 atoms chilled to near absolute zero (SN: 7/15/95, p. 36). Now . . . . *Science News,* 164)

- There are a lot of rules about sentence length and complexity, but the usual urge is for sentences that are not too long and not too short and not too complex. Clear, concise, coherent. Here's a rule-breaker, labyrinthine sentence, which includes a sentence within a sentence.

  Gardnar Mulloy, tournament tennis player incarnate at eighty-two—**he is six feet one, thin, and trim, walks with the spectacularly balanced gait of a confident athlete, and has a thick mane of white hair**—came up from his Miami home last week to the US Open to start things off on Opening Day with the traditional hitting, together with Bill Talbert and Frank Parker (still only in their seventies), of tennis balls from the Stadium Court net to the spectators. ("The Talk of the Town," 33)

The labyrinthine sentence, properly handled can be elegantly elaborate. And it sounds quite different from the short, sharp sentences of the detective novel that seems to thrive on what can be damned as "primer prose"—short Subject + Verb + Object sentences. However, this short, hard-hitting sentence remains the building block for creating the terse, self-reliant detective we know and love (and notice another characteristic, the one-sentence paragraph):

> Sayres had gone to Doron White, founding partner, previously my ally, and made his argument: I was doing pro bono work without the firm's consent; Crosetti's controversial politics might offend our corporate clients; and I had again placed the firm under the jeweler's eye of publicity.
>
> **Doron had agreed.**
>
> **I'd made the firm a lot of money. I'd made the firm famous.** But all it took was one refusal to back down and I was out the door.
>
> I'd been forced to choose between what mattered and what looked good. I'd chosen not to become Steven Sayres. (Matera, 8)

And to prove that neither short nor long, simple or complex, can possibly be the rule, sentences can have complicated rhythms and balances, parallel stuctures, teetering and tottering to create an effect:

> I expected this to be an **easy book** to write. To portray the life story of **one woman—why should that** pose any serious writing problems? I also expected this to be a **short book.** The life story of **one woman—why should that** require a **very long book?**
>
> Of course, I ought to have known. Didn't my comadre keep telling me I was bringing back **a big book?** *"Se lleva una historia muy grande, comadre,"* she'd say, and she was absolutely right, my **comadre.** This is a big book. Everything seems to have found its way into these pages, even the kitchen sink. I'm afraid there's nothing I can do. You don't choose to write the books you write, any more than you **choose** your mother, your father, your brother, your children, or your **comadre.** (Behar, ix)

- In fact, in many sentences, you find curled up and waiting for you a sense of the persona the author is trying to create. For instance, the repetition, alliteration, word play, punning—self-conscious, high-spirited writing—in this excerpt seem to be part of the act of reviewing—that is, selling—a new novel but also of "selling" the author's view; reading his style helps you know if you're going to like Nick Hornby's first novel:

> Can a man hope to sustain both a record collection and a relationship? Nick Hornby's first novel, "High Fidelity" (Riverhead; $21.95), turns on this **racking** question. The man on the **rack** is Rob Fleming, ex-d.j., college dropout, "Reservoir Dogs" fan, and owner of a failing London record store, who finds himself alone on his thirty-sixth birthday with a "Robocop 2" video and a phone call from his mom. His girlfriend has gone off within the tenant upstairs, and Rob begins to wonder if his **low-fidelity** relationship isn't a casualty of his devotion to **high fidelity.** "What came first," he asks," the music or the misery?"
>
> In the space of two books, Hornby has established himself in England as a maestro of the male confessional. His first, the autobiographical "Fever Pitch," took readers on an uproarious journey through the **mental wasteland** of the sports bore . . . . (Nixon, 91)

- Which doesn't mean that a persona isn't also created in a less rococo text. Here, the conversational, parenthetical, and rhetorical work of this text seems to suit (wears a suit) the interested technologically inclined reader.

> What does Microsoft Windows 95 mean to you as a participant in the PC software business?
>
> If you are a software developer or entrepreneur, the brief answer is that Windows 95 should make you nervous (**unless you work for Microsoft, or have invested in Microsoft, or both**). At the very least, Windows 95 will change how you sell software and what sort of software you develop.
>
> Windows users (**I mean, consumers**) should welcome Windows 95 as a big improvement over previous versions . . . . (Schulman, 3)

- Sometimes this persona is developed by putting on the cloak of another genre as when this tile-setting expert opens his introduction using storytelling conventions, transposing them to a work setting in a way that actually makes me want to read his primarily how-to book (a tile setter with a heart and a good ear for language, I'm doubly interested as someone needing to set tile but wanting to do it with style).

> **Over 20 years ago,** unable to find any certified training in tile setting and confused by conflicting information, **I set out to find** the best way to install ceramic tiles. **Since boyhood,** I had been attracted to the beauty of tiles, and **as a young man,** I would do whatever was necessary to learn the tricks and secrets of installing tile and mosaics over thick slabs of mud. No mastic jobs for me! **I wanted sand, cement and tradition.** (Byrne, 2)

Now I've wandered from rule-breaking to style-making and no one but the author of these excerpts can tell me if the sentence moves I found and admired were *intentional*—but by studying them, I can steal them and make my sentences more supple, more responsive to my writing desires. Three last examples—a newspaper writer using the coordinating conjunction but to pivot the second half of two paragraphs in a row (is it time to change the handbook rule on coordinating conjunctions yet?); a memoir writer using the staccato fragment, list-like, to make a point within a very conventional, well-mannered (look at the use of *whom*) paragraph; and an e-mail, from an essayist in this book, to me in my editorial capacity, where alternate typography is used to add levels of meaning to this swift but affectively flat medium.

> Deputy District Attorney Marcia Clark urged Ito not to proceed along those lines. **But** the judge was plainly distressed by the string of recent delays that have ground the already sluggish trial to a crawl and have imposed new hardships on the idle, long-suffering jury.
>
> He promised prosecutors he would limit the defense to the single remaining topic—a pledge that presumably would curtail any last-minute effort to put Simpson on the stand. **But** the judge declined to force Simpson formally to waive his right to testify, thus at least theoretically keeping the option open for the time being. (Newton et al., A:l)

> Of all my mama's nine brothers, it was Uncle Earkie with whom I had the most difficult relationship. Not only was he good-looking; he was a sharp dresser and always had a nice new car. **A Riviera, say, or an Impala. Not a Pontiac or a Chevy or an Oldsmobile, like everybody else.** Earkie had style. (Gates, 59)

> Date/Time: Monday, 11 Sept. 1995 16:55:29
> To: wbishop@
> From: Ostrom@
> Subject: on its way
>
> by Federal Express, the **BREAKTHROUGH DRAFT** of "Grammar J."I **hope/think** you'll be pleased. It finally came together & found the appropriate audience, thanks to you and your cadre of readers.

Okay, professional writers in all venues, all genres, play with sentence variation. What happens when you do the same? When I asked my writing students to break rules or to broaden their writing repertoires to include all the interesting variations that professional writers choose to use they were aghast—here they had worked so many years—grade school to college to obey the rules, and I said that wasn't good enough. I primed this discussion by having them read some unconventional writers to begin within: Lorrie Moore in a collection of stories titled *Self-Help* and Terry McMillan in her novel *Waiting to Exhale,* as well as essayists and poets who used alternate sentence strategies. (But, of course, I've gone farther now, arguing that all writers use alternate sentence strategies just as most sonnet writers don't write completely regularly metered sonnets, because they sound clockwork and boring!)

Here are some observations shared in journals. These writers were reading stories, poems, and or a novel in groups and then writing their third class paper on any topic triggered by their discussions.

- Terry McMillan's style of dialog was also new to me. She relies completely on her word choice to convey feeling. Rarely does she write: "'Blah, blah, blah,' she said with verve." She gets verve across in the words somehow. McMillan also uses a lot of profanity, which I am not used to. Profanity was not an option in high school writing. (Rob Adams)
- I'm so used to following the rules, so when I read Lorrie Moore I was shocked. She definitely didn't follow rules. She grew on me, and I decided to challenge myself and tried to write unconventional. To my surprise, this really worked for me. I was actually smiling while I was writing. Usually, I don't like to share my essays, but I wanted everyone to read this one. This essay really taught me that I can still write a good essay without always following all of the rules. (Andree Bacque)
- Since Lorrie Moore's style of writing is so unconventional and different from what we were used to reading, most of the group thought it would be interesting to steal some of her techniques. In the first short story, "How to be an Other Woman" she uses second person. We also liked her repetitiveness. (*Self-Help* reading group)

Like Rob's statement above, this reading group also told me that "my teacher last year would have killed me if I turned in something like this. Sometimes the sentences are incomplete and there aren't real transitions, but we like it." No surprise, then, that these good student, careful rule-learners, were reluctant, at first, to revise away.

For me, this is a matter of coming of age as a writer. I know my student writers are real readers and writers—all the terms, novice and professional, student writer and real writers—are problematic. Like I mentioned earlier, each of us reads and writes our life all day long, every day. I urged them to go ahead. Here are a few simple samples of where they went and where I enjoyed following them as a reader:

- sentence fragment and list to open an essay.

  Parties, girls, guys, beer, no curfew, no parents, and most of all freedom! Yes, these are all wonderful characteristics of college, but along with this new found freedom comes a lot more responsibility and a lot more *stress.* ("Coping within College" by Sarah Minchin)

- a fictional imitation of *Self-Help,* using second person and repetition

  Four years go by and nothing. Then while out with friends one night, finally meet a guy. You like tall, dark and handsome . . . he is tall. After some small talk he gets your phone number and even follows with a call. Give him a chance, you never know what may become of it. What is the worst that can happen? ("Tick-Tock" by Kim Michelle Lapenski)

- an essayist imitation of *Self-Help,* using double-voice (mother's voice and conversational voice of author)

  People will continue to take advantage of you as long as you allow them to; don't forget to take your vitamins; everything you do comes back to you; Sunday mass is imperative; an on and on and on . . . ah, Mom's famous words of wisdom. I hate it when she says these things, and since I've been in college, I don't miss them at all . . . or do I? I swear I'm never going to be like my mother when I grow up. I mean, what does she know anyway?

  She was only high school queen . . . oh, and an honor graduate. Who cares if she had eleven brothers and sister and still managed to go to college. Lots of people do that, right? OK, she's kept her marriage alive for twenty-one years, and I guess I should mention that she raised three children . . . and right now is still raising three more. Maybe she's phenomenal, but I just always thought all mothers were like her. You know, she gets up every morning and has breakfast ready even if it is Pop-Tarts; she always supported my mostly short-term activities (dancing, gymnastics, the clarinet, softball, volleyball, etc.); she would never miss anything that's even slightly important to me; it's all normal mother activities.

  At least this is what I thought until I finally realized that I was totally *WRONG! This is in no way normal!* This is spectacular, amazing, and now that I think about it, maybe even crazy . . . ("Talking to My Mom" by Andree Bacque)

- an ironically reported, autobiographical memory using short sentences, for effect

  Suddenly the flames reached the core. I don't remember if it made a sound or not. I do recall a huge ball of fire coming rapidly toward me. It hit like a hot wind, almost gently. It kissed us for an instant, then vanished. I realized that I couldn't see. We were both screaming. If memory serves, I believe I was bemoaning my loss of sight while Kyle was yelling for his mother. ("You Look Real Funny Without Eyebrows" by Rob Adams)

- imitation of Terry McMillan, using profanity to create authentic character

  She hardly slept a wink. The last time she looked at the clock, it had said 5:36. It was after ten when she woke up. She felt exhausted, more so than when she had gone to bed. She tried calling him, but got his machine. Briefly, she entertained the possibility of leaving a really nasty message, but decide to wait. She wanted to bawl his sorry ass out in person. ("Same Old, Same Old" by Rob Adams)

- creating a persona through sentence variation—typographical, conversational, dialogue, contemporary allusions, and so on

  I AM OBSESSED WITH INDEPENDENCE!! I know you thought it would be more exciting like food, sex, drugs, or my looks, right? Well, every story has its beginnings and mine started in the emergency room. As a newborn, I mimed to the doctor (because of course I couldn't speak) that I would "Slap myself, thank you!" As I grew older I learned not to depend on anyone for help. Independence became my guru; it was the Susan Powter of "Being Your Own Person." People may argue whether or not it's a good trait to possess; I'm just trying to see if it's the root of all my problems or the force that enables me to achieve and make my dreams reality. ("God Helps Those Who Help Themselves" by Kaywana Jemison)

I plan to steal from each of these writers. After reading Sarah, I think about beginning a paragraph or essay with a list. After reading Kim, I see how second person works—actually, I've already borrowed some in this essay, talking as I have to you. Andree's prose reminds me that people have well known ways of saying things; when I want to characterize someone, I can use their actual words, as in Rob's imitation, their speech register. (Remember, high school teachers—like dance teachers and those interested in etiquette—are being asked by society to help inculcate "good manners." Don't knock good manners, sometimes they're the only thing that get us through difficult situations. Just don't think the same manners apply to all situations.)

Characterizing someone in a fictional world often turns on creating versimilitude and that means having people talk like they really talk. From Rob I might also steal the nicely balanced sentences in the middle of his paragraph. I could write, then modify. And write again, and modify. Then continue my prose, using, perhaps, some of Kaywana's humorous and effective analogies. For instance, in my advice giving here, am I maybe trying to turn into a writing guru, a supreme coach, a writing star offering you my autograph and ideas?

Well, here I go then, ending my essays with a bit of advice from this expert witness in the sentence.

First, don't worry about anything I've mentioned until you've drafted and explored, finding out what you want to say about your subject. As I said earlier, if you don't know what you're saying, neither can your reader. It's self-indulgent to substitute style for substance, to use rule-breaking to thumb your nose at readers and reasons for writing.

Second, keep a sentence book. Yes, collect favorite sentences everywhere you go—advertising slogans, overheard conversation, your favorite line from a movie or found in a book (even in your repellent textbook on the dullest subject there's probably a sentence doing it's work in a way worth paying attention to). When you read life and/or look at printed texts, think of what you can steal and write it down. Writers save tidbits of thought on napkins, in formal journals, in jot files on the computer disk. You can save sentences.

Third, read sentences out loud. A lot. Read words in lists, signs on streets, phrases on billboards, the strange translated dialogue on subtitled movies, the pompous editorial in the newspaper, the circulars on bulletin boards, and memos in the workplace. Read your favorite novelists and look at how they open or close a chapter. Go to poetry readings and listen to poets deliver their lines, listen to books on tape. Capture the dialogue and accent of individuals you eavesdrop on in coffee shops and wait in line behind for concert tickets. Become a word, sentence, paragraph musician; develop your ear.

Fourth, when you revise, for fun, try out one of your saved sentences—see if it helps you further discover your meaning. Put it in and if it works, keep it. Take it out if it doesn't work. For all this type of play, the computer for composing, of course, is a blessing.

Fifth, you can't get there from here if you don't challenge yourself, take risks, ruin some writing, go to the edge—sometimes past the edge—and back. Finding your way through sentences is a matter of tinkering, playing, working, and then sometimes, retreating. At the same time, there's no dishonor (quite the reverse) in clear, concise, and coherent prose as long as there's also interest there, first for you, second for your reader.

Sixth, what starts as imitation, forced revision, soon becomes internalized skill. The more you play within sentences, the more you know and understand them. That doesn't mean you know how to define predicate adjectives or to list the coordinating conjunctions. In means you know when you're in control and when you're not quite making it (and again, don't leave it up to the reader to decide this—you should decide).

Style Revision Exercises and Examples

CONSIDER THIS:

These handouts are idea sheets for the sorts of exercises you can complete out of class or in class, using your own work or photocopies of the work of others. You can observe stylistic choices by working with a partner at a computer screen, each of you making the changes suggested in a text and discussing and then noting down your observations about the effects of these changes. You can take a text and use your word-processor editing software to illustrate the changes you make, or you can follow the old-fashioned route (especially when working in a traditional classroom) of copying out alternate passages and placing them side by side for study. When you hand-copy or retype a short passage several times, you obtain an almost sculptural feel for the sentences, and gain additional insight into the varied options in punctuation and syntax available to a writer. Two of these handouts are illustrated with samples by classroom authors taken out of context—not the best situation for understanding how a single stylistic choice can affect the tone and direction of an entire text; nevertheless, these worksheets can provide a place for class discussion that leads to creating worksheets together based on your own peers' work.

A. STYLE REVISION USING YOUR OWN WORK: THE LOCAL LEVEL, SENTENCES, AND PARAGRAPHS COMPLETED OUT OF CLASS

Choose and complete one of the first three exercises:

1. *Sentence combining:* Take one of your paragraphs. Break it down into constituent kernel sentences. Example: *I leaned down nearly horizontally to wedge myself into the red roadster.*

Might become:

I leaned down.
I was nearly horizontal.
I wedged myself into the roadster.
The roadster was red.

Send it to two writing partners (via e-mail) and ask them to recombine the kernels into a paragraph again. Consider the three versions of the following and write your own best version. Post all four.

Carlyn's original
My mother stands at the stove, or she's alone in a double bed with the lights out, or maybe she's driving by all the local bars at 3 am. Either way, she comes to a decision as she wipes up spilt baby formula from the counter, or picks up a novel and crawls back in bed, or unbuckles my sleeping brother from the backseat.

Carlyn's paragraph in kernels
I was eight years old.
My father went on business trips.
My mother took to the kitchen.
She smoked Marlboro lights in the dark.
She also drank a six-pack.
My twin sister and I listened.
We stood at the top of the stairs.
Her sadness in heavy, long sighs.
Her once soothing voice now edgy.
Her voice full of sharp things.
It frightened us.
It made us frozen.
We didn't eat supper that night.
We waited.
We wanted the last pop of the beer tabs.
We wished for the kitchen light to click off.
We wanted Dad to come home.
The night would be long.

Wendy's combining
My father went on business trips when I was eight years old. My mother took to the kitchen, smoking Marlboro lights in the dark, drinking a six pack, her sadness tangible in heavy, long sighs, her once soothing voice edgy and full of sharp things that froze my twin sister and I who stood at the top of the stairs, listening. We didn't eat supper that night. We waited, for the last pop of the beer tabs, for the kitchen light to click off, for Dad to come home, knowing the night would be a long one.

Note: I intentionally tried to make a text that was a bit different from the original—and added one word "tangible"

2. *Options in punctuation*: Remove the punctuation from one of your more complicated paragraphs. Send it to two writing partners (via e-mail) to re-punctuate. Consider the choices they made. And create your own best final version. Post all four.

Sandra's original
When Grandma was about ten years old, she went out to the well to get a drink of water. Her father's false teeth were sitting in a glass on the corner, and she

accidentally knocked them in, almost losing her balance grabbing after them. After a long pause, she heard a tiny, muffled splash. Her mother was furious; the teeth had cost a small fortune. "You go tell your father what you did and see what he says." So Grandma went and told him, afraid he'd be furious as well. But he said here's what she should do. She should just tie a biscuit onto a string, a long sturdy string, and lower it into the well. If it was close to dinner time, the teeth would latch onto the biscuit and she could pull them back up.

Classmate repunctuation
Grandma was about ten years old. She went out to the well to get a drink of water and her father's false teeth were sitting in a glass on the corner. She accidentally knocked them in, almost losing her balance. Grabbing after them, she heard a tiny, muffled splash after a long pause. Her mother was furious: "Those teeth cost a small fortune. You go tell your father what you did and see what he says." So Grandma went and told him, afraid he'd be furious as well. But he said she should tie a biscuit onto a string—a long, sturdy string—and lower it into the well. If it was close to dinner time, the teeth would latch onto the biscuit and she could pull them back up.

Sandra's revision
When Grandma was about ten years old, she went out to the well to get a drink of water. Her father's false teeth were sitting in a glass on the corner, and she accidentally knocked them in, almost losing her balance as she grabbed after them. After a long pause, a tiny muffled splash. Her mother was furious; the teeth had cost a small fortune: "You go tell your father what you did and see what he says." So she went and told him, afraid he'd be furious as well. But here's what he said she should do: tie a biscuit onto a string—a long, sturdy string—and lower it into the well. If it was close enough to dinner time, the teeth would latch onto the biscuit and she could pull them back up.

3. *Options in modification/intensification:* Take a very descriptive passage and remove all the adverbs and adjectives (but leave blanks so a reader knows where they were) and e-mail it to a writing partner. Let the partners create their own versions (fill in the blanks). They don't have to use the same number of adjectives and adverbs and they may add others as they choose, but they should try to fill in 50 percent or more of your blanks. Then they should return the paragraphs to you. Revise using any modifications they like. Post all four.

Amanda's fill-in-the-blank version
My mother stands at the stove, or she's alone in a __________ bed with the lights __________, or maybe she's driving by all the __________ bars at 3 am. Either way, she comes to a decision as she wipes up __________ baby formula from the counter, or picks up a __________ novel and crawls back in bed, or unbuckles my__________ brother from the backseat.

Maggie's stab
My mother stands at the stove, or she's alone in a queen-sized bed with the lights flickering, or maybe she's driving by all the juke joint bars at 3 am. Either way, she comes to a decision as she wipes up dried baby formula from the counter, or picks up a trashy novel and crawls back in bed, or unbuckles my darling baby brother from the backseat.

Sandra's stab
My mother stands at the stove, or she's alone in a canopy bed with the lights blazing, or maybe she's driving by all the honky-tonk bars at 3 am. Either way, she comes to a decision as she wipes up curdled baby formula from the counter, or picks up a romance adventure novel and crawls back into bed, or unbuckles my crying brother from the backseat.

Maggie's impression
Since this was somewhat fabricated [memory], my idea of what must have happened, and because it's so up in the air, it was nice to see how far the passage could stretch. My imagery is not functioning in this piece, but having someone else fill in the adjectives helped me reimagine. Very cool idea.

Now, choose two out of the following five options:

4. *Changing POV:* Take one of your paragraphs and recast it in as many different points of view (POV) as you can (first-, second-, third-person singular, first-and third-person plural). Post all versions.

Juli Hong—changing POV
A. Your father told your mother and Mimi not to tell you. He didn't want what had happened junior year to repeat itself. It was important to him that your mind was clear to study. Yes, you hate secrets. So does your mother, her words soaked with sorrow, small lines folding at the outer corners of her heavy-lidded eyes. Secrets grieve everyone at some point in their lives. But your father used them to protect you.
B. Her father told her mother and Mimi not to tell her. He didn't want what had happened junior to repeat itself. It was important to him that his first child was focused enough to study. Nevertheless, this endeavor to protect only hurt her. She told her mother, "I despise secrets." Her mother looked at her daughter, small lines folding at the outer corners of her heavy-lidded eyes. Sorrow soaked her words: "I hate them, too."

Sandra Giles—original
Libby Clark, the medium from England, walks across the stage to the podium, stage right, to take a sip of clear water from a glass. She's been speaking for about an hour now. As she walks, the tail of her long lavender scarf floats behind her, silky and diaphanous. She wears a knee-length lavender dress, sleeveless, with white strappy heels. Her medium-length fingernails pinkish red. Simple pearls at the throat and the ears. A wedding ring. She looks like a lady you might see in the mall, or at church.

A. I walk across the stage to the podium, stage right, to get a sip of water. My throat is tired; I've been speaking for about an hour now. As I walk, the straps on my shoes cut into my feet, but I feel more confident in heels, and more fashionable in strappy ones. I'm wearing lavender, the color I always wear when I give spiritual readings, the color I identify with matters of spirit. And the pearls my husband gave me. People are usually surprised I'm not wearing gypsy skirts and thousands of bangles.
B. You walk across the stage to the podium which holds the glass of water. Your throat is tired and scratchy; you've been speaking for about an hour. As you walk, you know the tail of your lavender scarf floats behind you. People expect you to be a little bit dramatic, at least. They probably expect you to dress like a fortune-teller at Halloween. They also expect, some of them expect, at least, that your reading will be a hoax, a mere show. You chose your simple dress accented with pearls so you'll be taken a bit more seriously. But the color lavender you chose because you identify it most with matters of the spirit.
C. We see Libby Clark, the medium from England, walk across the stage to the podium, which is stage right, to take another sip of water from a clear glass. She's been "reading" for the audience for about an hour now, linking us with the spirits of our departed loved ones. She must convince us this is for real. We want to believe, we really do . . . .

5. *The impersonal or distanced "I":* Take one of your own paragraphs that uses a lot of first person. Recast without any first person "I." Or, take a first-person paragraph and severely reduce the number of I/me constructions without using passive voice.
6. *Sentence cohesion:* Take two paragraphs (or half of a page) of your prose and put all the connections and repetitions between sentences in different type so readers can "see" them. That is, set off all pronoun repeats, all word repeats, all variations of words (or even metaphors or, say, colors) that seem to be the words that link ideas, images, or grammatical structures for writers. Next, see if you can rewrite to better orchestrate these linkages even more intentionally. Post both versions.
7. *A tale of two sentence types—labyrinthine and fragmented:* Take one paragraph of your prose and recast it as a single sentence. Take the same paragraph and reduce it to fragments (artful and intelligible fragments). Now rewrite the paragraph using whatever sentence structures you find most effective. Post all four.

Maggie Garrity—loooong
But it's a good thing you won't drink with him for ten months, because you'll get honest when you drink, too honest, dangerously honest, the kind of honest you get right before you get hurt, and just look at this humid spring night; it will be almost summer, really, and morning, just before closing time, the longest short walk of your life, the pavement tilting, your feet refusing to fall in even steps, him unlacing his shoes in the street and walking home in his

socks, his white socks, dazzling against the cracked pavement of streets whose residents you both know who might see you, and you know they'll talk if they do.

Fragmented
But it's a good thing you won't drink with him for ten months. You'll get honest when you drink. Too honest. Dangerously honest. The kind of honest you get right before you get hurt. Look at the highlights of this humid spring night. Almost summer, really, and morning. Just before closing time. The longest short walk of your life. The pavement tilting, your feet rising and falling in even steps. Him unlacing his shoes in the street and walking home in his socks. His white socks. Dazzling against the cracked pavement of streets whose residents you both know. You won't care if they see you. But they'll talk if they do.

Sandra Giles—labyrinthine
Libby Clark, the medium from England, walks across the stage to the podium for a sip of water, the tail of her lavender scarf floating behind her like an amethyst cloud, walking a bit unsurely in the white strappy heels which seem to cut into her feet, but they look quite fashionable with the simple sleeveless lavender dress, the pearls at her throat and each ear, the pinkish red, medium-length fingernails; in fact, she looks like someone you might see at the mall or at church.

Fragmented
Libby Clark, the medium from England. Walking to the podium, stage right, for a sip of water. Having spoken for about an hour. Lavender scarf-tail floating behind her like an amethyst cloud. Like a cloud of pure spirit. Spirit, lavender. Pearls. String of pearls at the throat and ears. Wedding ring. Like someone shopping at the mall. Like someone at church.

Revised
Libby Clark, the medium from England, walks stage right to the podium where her glass of water sits, the tail of her lavender silk scarf floating behind her like a cloud of amethyst, the stone, the color she identifies most with spirit. Amethyst and pearl, which she wears at each ear and in a simple strand around her neck. She looks like someone working in a department store in the mall. Or someone in church.

8. *Zoom lens:* Take one paragraph and reduce it by exactly 50 percent. Take another paragraph and increase it by exactly 50 percent. Post each pair.

Maggie Garrity—half
It's good you two won't drink until May. You'll get honest when you drink, the kind leading to hurt. Humid spring, almost summer, really, and morning, closing time, your longest walk, pavement tilting, feet refusing to rise and fall, him unlacing his shoes and walking in white socks, dazzling against cracked pavement of streets whose residents will talk tomorrow.

Double
But it's good you won't drink with him for ten months, though all through the mild autumn and chilly winter you'll call to coax him out for a Friday night Newcastle or gin and tonic. He'll always decline: too much work, other plans, not feeling well, not in the mood. You'll plead, offer to buy drinks. Your other friends will tease you that he's imaginary, or at least that you're imagining the way he feels about you. Beware. You'll get honest when you drink, too honest, dangerously honest, the kind of honest you get right before you get hurt. It's a hurt you know well. Look at the flickering black and white highlight film of this humid spring night; it will be almost summer, really, and morning, just before closing time, the longest short walk of your life, ten minutes turned thirty, the rain-slicked pavement tilting, your feet refusing to rise and fall in even steps, your black flip-flops heavy, him unlacing his beat up brown shoes in the street and walking home in his socks, his white socks, dazzling against the cracked pavement of streets whose residents you both know. You won't care if they see you though you know they'll talk if they do, and it won't take long for that talk to get back to you and to everyone else you know. Will your friends dispel the rumors, or will they start them?

9. *Tone coloring:* Simplify the register or syllabics of one of your paragraphs. Try, for instance, to use only one or two syllable words. Or, take a formal paragraph and make it slangy or vice-versa. Post both versions.

Carlyn—original
When I was eight years old and my father went out of town on business trips, my mother took to the kitchen for hours and armed herself with Marlboro Lights, pots of coffee, and a six-pack of Budweiser beer. My twin sister and I would listen at the top of the stairs with amazing acuity to the sounds of a woman engulfed by a sadness we couldn't understand. We heard her long, heavy sighs after the pop and whisk of beer tabs and the heavy thud of her coffee cup on the table; We heard her murmuring to herself—indecipherable gibbering that sounded tearful and strange. Her once soothing voice now filled with edges and sharp things, and it frightened us. So much so that we froze like this at the top of the stairs, never venturing down for supper when she called, and our night became one of waiting. For the last pop of the beer tabs, for the kitchen light to click off. For the night to be over and Dad to come home.

All one-syllable words
When I was eight years old and my dad went out of town on trips, my mom, armed with cigs and beer, sat in the dark, quiet. My twin and I would wait at the top of the stairs to the sounds of our mom crazed by a pain we could not know. The pop and whisk of the beer tabs told us she was drunk, and her low sighs were strange to us. Her once smooth voice was now filled with sharp things, and it was weird to us . . . So much so that we froze like the dead at the top of the stairs. The night then filled with wait. For the last pop of the beer tabs, for her light to click off. For this night to be done and Dad to come home.

Two syllables or more only
Mother sitting alone, drinking, smoking, crying. Children listening, mother's murmurs indecipherable, tearful, frightening. Mother's gibbering edgy and sharpened and scary. Children waiting atop highest stair step, venturing nowhere, even after mother announces supper. Waiting again, popping of Budweiser bottles signaling unknown moments ahead. Waiting frozen, fearfulness falling around father's absence, children staring into darkness until morning.

In-Class Style Revision/Analysis Using Your Own Essay[1]

1. *Poetic style revision*
   A. Turn one of your paragraphs into a poem (however you define poem); that is, at a minimum, cut it into lines, eliminate unnecessary wording, and so forth.
   B. Return it to prose by collapsing the poem into paragraph form. Add to it slightly, if necessary.
   C. Compare the poem paragraph to the original. What changed, what remained? Swap with a classmate, do the same exercise using his paragraph. Compare both sets of paragraphs. What did you do that was the same or different?
2. *Syllabic style revision*
   A. Write a paragraph—paragraph A—describing the pleasures of your favorite beverage without using words of more than one syllable (*joe* not *java* or *coffee*)
   B. Revise and cast in words of primarily two or more syllables—paragraph B.
   C. Revise paragraph A by loosening up and allowing *a few* multisyllabic words—paragraph C.
   D. What changes across the paragraphs? Which version do you prefer? Swap your paragraph A with a classmate and let her revise it in any way she wants; designate this as paragraph D. Compare paragraph D to your paragraphs A, B, and C.
3. *Repetition and redundancy*
   A. Mark definitional redundancy (key terms are defined); terms are explained.
   B. Mark global organizers—white space, numbered sections, "later in this essay," "as mentioned earlier," subheadings, and any others.
   C. Mark literary repetition, including the extending of metaphor and conceit (extended metaphors)—flowers used throughout, water images, and more.

[1]Exercises 1, 3, and 4 can be completed using a sample essay supplied to the entire class.

D. Mark connective redundancy—tend to use *and*, tend to use *–ing* words.

E. Mark any other redundancy you notice.

F. Mark organization/expectation produced by transitions (*first, second, next*) and genre signals ("late in the summer of 1996"; "it was a dark and stormy night") that indicate genre.

4. Notice cohesion and cohesive ties (five types: reference, conjunction, ellipsis, substitution, and lexical).

A. Mark cohesion produced by *reference*—pronoun/nouns, repetition, alternation, antecedents (I/we/my Mom).

B. Mark cohesion indicated by *conjunctions* (and, or, so, but, for, nor, yet).

C. Mark cohesion indicated by *ellipsis*—words that could have been put in but were left out "as implied." "She had a pile of work. She was in a holding pattern of avoidance" (*of that work*).

D. Mark cohesion pronounced by *substitution*—words repeated to tie previous sentence to past sentence. "We know about *institutional* constraints. But when the *University* functions in this manner . . ." or "The *sea* was striking that day. I walked on the *gulf* and looked at the *waves* . . ."

E. Mark lexical ties—variations on a single word: writer, author, composer of a text, writing, writes, composes, creates; something like gulf, ocean, body of water—same concept is rerepresented but varied for artistic effects and to avoid boredom.

F. Mark any other "connecting" cues I've not mentioned.

B. STYLE REVISION USING YOUR OWN WORK: OPENING AND CLOSING

1. Completed out of class: Take one of your opening paragraphs and recast it in three different versions. Present the original and then the revisions as follows:

Style revision A is preceded with an epigraph or uses a quote and/or a line of dialogue.

Style revision B includes an identifiable claim, assertion, or topic sentence and elaboration.

Style revision C is generated by defining an opening technique used by one or more writers you admire and then using the same technique. Explain who uses the technique and then provide your original and your revision.

Example:

Jeff Canup's original
Eighteen and powering up the beach with my pal Ryan and his half-brother T.J.—a 26 year old guitar playing surf punk—through a stiff nor'easter, the wind biting my face, I listened and laughed as he good-spiritedly described

how he felt as he aged and deteriorated. T.J. talked about how, when he was younger, he could surf for four or five hours in six-foot surf, dropping in on mounds of water bigger than he was, crouching into a ball for stability—compression equals power—while the salubrious lip of the wave pitched over, kissing his back. Now on a mediocre day he needed to run home for an energizing power nap and a baloney sandwich after two or three hours in the salty surf.

Style revision A: with an epigraph
"Young people are in a condition like permanent intoxication, because youth is sweet and they are growing." (Aristotle)

Eighteen and powering up the beach with my pal Ryan and his half-brother T.J.—a 26 year old guitar playing surf punk—through a stiff nor'easter, the wind biting my face, I listened and laughed as he good-spiritedly described how he felt as he aged and deteriorated. T.J. talked about how, when he was younger, he could surf for four or five hours in six-foot surf, dropping in on mounds of water bigger than he was, crouching into a ball for stability—compression equals power—while the salubrious lip of the wave pitched over, kissing his back. "I could go out and party all night long, I mean just get ripped, and still be at the beach by six for a dawn patrol session," he said. Now on a mediocre day he needed to run home for an energizing power nap and a baloney sandwich after two or three hours in the salty surf.

I'm beginning to realize that aging is much like the tide. You can't see the change until you walk away and return a few hours later. The water that was just a short time ago bathing the bulkhead, has receded, much like a hairline, exposing the bleached sands of time.

Modeled on "From the Bend for Home" by Dermot Healy. Technique: Open with a brief scene in present tense with dialogue.

T.J. sees a monster set pushing through about 40 yards to our left. He paddles over, the muscles in his back flexing in a steady rhythm, as if to the beat of a metronome. He catches a pristine, six foot, hollow tube. After emerging from the watery void, he drops to his stomach and rides the wave in. Ryan follows, leaving me alone and loving it. "What's wrong man, why'd you come in? The waves are still firing out there," Ryan says.

"I need a break, man. I'm drained. Go ahead and go back out. I'll just sit here on the beach for a few minutes."

2. Complete one of the following exercises:
   A. Take one of your closing paragraphs and revise it to include (1) a repeat, echo, reference, allusion to something from your opening paragraph and/or (2) an increase in parallelism and/or repetition. Share original opening, original conclusion, and revised conclusion. Label each version.
   B. Make your closing paragraph your opening paragraph. After doing this, write a new closing paragraph. Show both versions: original opening and closing turned to new opening; original closing plus new closing.
   C. Imitate an essayist you admire by recasting an opening or a closing paragraph to resemble that writer's style. (1) Imitate tone alone, or (2)

imitate sentence structure alone, and/or (3) imitate both tone and sentence structure. Share original and one or more additional versions, (1) through (3) above. Include all labeled versions.

D. Take a closing paragraph and make it more explicit and forceful (increase direct closure), and take another closing paragraph that is already fairly explicit and make it more evocative or allusive. Present all four labeled paragraphs.

Samples:

Amanda Fleming—exercise B
Original conclusion of "Watercolors"
Later that week I call mom to make sure he did as he promised. Her gentle hands fit snugly around baby bottles, and her long fingers pluck seeds for collecting from her California Poppies. Now that her only son is dead, her grandchildren in another country, and her daughter still in college, I try to give her projects to fill her time. "I cannot bear to watch another thing fail this month," I tell her, my eyes bubbly with tears. "Well, it's not dead yet, but it's not alive," she tells me. "We keep watching for new growth."

Revised (option 2) conclusion to opening
I call mom, her gentle hands fitting snugly around the receiver and the smell of compost on her long fingers. "I cannot bear to watch another thing fail this month," I tell her, my eyes bubbling with tears. I've transported my zinfandel shaded Mandeville vine 2 hours west in the middle of a work week, desperate. Then I drove the 2 hours back, thinking myself a fool. But if anyone can understand Mother's only son is dead, her grandchildren live in another country, and her only daughter is (still) in college. On Sundays she gets melancholy. Mondays, too.

"We've been watching it every day," she says. "It's not dead yet, but it's not alive," she tells me. "We keep hoping for new growth."

Continued (option 2) new conclusion
I can say I know her now, and those quick subject changes don't represent flightiness like I once thought. She's touched those crisp brown leaves, run her fingers over their skin, and she has sighed both for herself and for me. Behind the garage, dad's lumpy, cow smelling compost pile consists of many things—none of them new. When the house gets quiet on Sundays, I know she has gone upstairs, her head heavy with thinking of children in another country or a boy who asked for help but didn't get the answer he wanted. The shades are drawn. I can barely see her body shape under the covers.

Jeff Canup—exercise B
Original opening
The summer after I graduated from high school—an accomplishment that was a relief to me more than anything else, and a surprise to my parents—I took a job working at a marina nestled in a little canal on the intercostal waterway in Jacksonville, Florida. Sitting in those cold, blue, metallic desks for four years at

Bishop Kenny High School, I heard much of what my teachers said. I heard them say things like, "knowledge is power," "Pythagoras invented the Pythagorean Theory," "Faulkner is the best American writer," and "Mr. Canup, you're in space." Yes, I heard my teachers, but listened only for the bell signaling the end of the school day.

Original conclusion
As I said, I learned a great deal that summer, and as I pulled back into the marina, I heard the shout of the blue, metal piling remover turning into a whisper. I whispered back, "I hear you. I'm listening."

Revised conclusion
I learned volumes the summer after I graduated from high school. I learned much more than I had sitting comatosed in the blue, metallic desks at Bishop Kenny High School. And as I pulled my '88 Pontiac Grand Prix back into the marina, I heard the shout of the blue, metallic piling remover. But this time I was able to respond. I was able to echo back, "I hear you. I'm listening."

Maggie Garrity—exercise D (two samples)
Original closing paragraph
I don't think Brother would be ashamed that I've given up Catholicism. He couldn't live in the shadow of Deacon Wentzel's God, either. My God teaches inclusion rather than exclusion, forgiveness rather than damnation, celebration rather than guilt. In one of my favorite excerpts from John's Gospel, Jesus says, "One day you will know the truth, and the truth will set you free." I am free now, finally, of guilt, of embarrassment, of shame, and the truth I've found is that Brother hasn't really left me. I'll always have him *in capital et caritas* when I need him.

Revised to be more forceful
Brother wouldn't be ashamed that I've given up Catholicism. He refused to live in the shadow of Deacon Wentzel's God, too. My God teaches inclusion rather than exclusion, celebration rather than guilt, forgiveness rather than damnation. In John's Gospel, Jesus proclaims: "One day you will know the truth, and the truth will set you free." I am free now, finally, of guilt, of embarrassment, of shame, and the truth I've found is that I don't need of have someone else's beliefs forced on me. I know my own now, thanks to Brother. He's with me *in capital et caritas.* I'll never be ashamed to tell people that again.

Original closing paragraph
In the morning, you'll wonder how much he remembers. You won't ask him. You'll drink your coffee and leave when the gaps of silence between you get longer and you don't know how to fill them. For once, you'll have nothing to say. Before you leave, you'll wrap him in an awkward hug and tell him you'll call. You'll be halfway home, at the long light at Tennessee and Monroe, before you realize you're still wearing his shirt.

Revised to be more allusive
In the morning, when he stares at the live oaks across the street while you linger over mugs of coffee, you'll wish you knew what he remembered, if he meant his I love you the same way you did yours, or if it had been a kamikaze-induced exaggeration. Your eyes will meet once in a while, until one of you blinks and looks away, outside, into your mug, at the floor. For once you'll have nothing to say, nothing and everything at once, so you'll finish your coffee and stand to leave before you open your mouth and start confessing everything again. Wrap him in an awkward hug. Tell him you'll call. Leave. Drive home slowly, your mind still fogged from sleep and all those Rolling Rocks that had seemed like such a good idea the night before. At the light at Tennessee and Monroe, you'll look down and see you're still wearing his shirt. Wash and fold it and set it aside, then wait for him to come and get it. He will, though you'll have no idea what you'll say when he walks through your door.

C. RESEARCH VOICE REVISION SAMPLES

Discuss the differences between the two paragraphs. Which do you find more effective and why?

Set I

Version 1
The Roman Emperor Constantine I banned tattooing because he felt it went against God's handiwork. The Christian religion in general opposed and repressed body ornamentation. Christianity implies from Adam's sin that we are not to deviate from our God-given appearance at all so that we do not further sin against God. It is the Christian religion that promoted conformity in appearance as well as in behavior. The strictness of Christian standards was in part a repressive reaction against surviving expressions of paganism in the popular culture. Pagan superstitions became distorted by religious-inspired fears that people who deviated from the normal appearance might be in league with the devil. This dominance of Christianity and the fear of religious persecution largely extinguished the practice of tattooing and other forms of body ornamentation in Western Europe.

Version 2
According to tattoo historians, if you are a Christian, it may be your ancestors' beliefs that prompt your parents to warn you not to get a tattoo. Because tattoos were part of many pagan cultures, because Christians as early as the Roman Emperor Constantine forbade tattooing, and because, in general, the developing Christian religion promoted conformity, there was a steady decline of tattooing in Western Europe from Constantine's time on. The thinking seemed to run something like this: clothes weren't provided for Adam, tattoos shouldn't be provided for Adam's descendants (Armitage, Demello, Gell).

Set II

Version 1

During this candle making frenzy, a chemist, Michel Eugene Chevreul, around 1854, was making an important discovery in mass explosion of nonflammable candle making material that prevented the igniting of an out-of-control flame. He realized that tallow was not one substance but a composition of two fatty acids, stearic acid and oleic acid, combined with glycerin to form a neutral non-flammable material.

By removing the glycerin from the tallow mixture, Chevreul invented a new substance called "stearine." Stearine was harder than tallow and burned brighter and longer. Stearic acid greatly led to the improvement of candle quality, and is still used today, known as stearine. Stearine also made improvement in the manufacture of wicks. It put an end to the constant round of snuffing and trimming wicks once they were lit. Instead of being made of simply twisted strands of cotton, wicks were not plaited tightly; the burned portion curled over and was completely consumed, rather than falling messily in the melting wax.

Version 2

It's hard to imagine that candles needed "inventing." If you've ever used an old-fashioned oil lamp though, you may have had the experience of a smoking wick that quickly blackened the clean glass bell covering the flame. Effective, efficient wicks had to be invented and the man who accomplished this around 1854 was chemist Michel Eugene Chevruel. He discovered that tallow was composed of two fatty acids (stearic and oleic) combined with glycerin. Chevreul invented stearine by removing the glycerine from this mixture, thus creating a brighter, longer burning candle. Stearine also improved wicks. "Instead of being made of simply twisted strands of cotton, wicks were not plaited tightly; the burned portion curled over and was completely consumed, rather than falling messily in the melting wax" (source page).

Set III

Version 1

One of the most popular stories begins in China with the discovery of combining syrups and snow to create an early form of sherbet. The Chinese shared this practice with Arab traders and in turn the Arabs taught the Venetians and Romans. The Emperor Nero became especially fond of the frozen delicacy and added his own twist: pureed fruit sweetened with honey was added to the snow. It is rumored that Emperor Nero even built special cold rooms underneath the palace for the purpose of storing snow year round. During hotter months he would send slaves to the mountains to collect ice.

Version 2

Most ice cream histories begin in China where syrups and snow were combined to create an early form of sherbet. The Chinese appear to have shared this practice with Arab traders who in turn taught the Venetians and Romans. The Emperor Nero may be responsible for your after dinner sherbet: he became especially fond of the snowy delicacy and added his own twist of pureed fruit sweetened with honey. It's reported that he had special cold rooms underneath the palace for the purpose of storing snow year round and that in the hotter months he would send slaves to the mountains to collect ice much as you or I might make a run to the corner store on a hot summer's evening.

Set IV

Version 1
Lager is one of the many fine classifications of beer that has become a staple in the human diet all over the world. Beer is said to have been the first alcoholic beverage relished by prominent people in civilization. It has been a beverage of choice among the common people and royalty alike for thousands of years. In today's society it is without a doubt a major part of the adult American diet, and is especially prevalent among college dwellings.

Version 2
Fraternities without beer parties? Football games without beer sellers? Bars without neon beer signs? It's hard to imagine humans without beer. Perhaps they never have been. Some of the earliest written references to beer date back to 4000 B. C. [sentence taken from the next paragraph]. The first alcoholic beverage on record, beer was—and still is—relished by rich and by poor and remains a major component of the adult American diet.

D. REVISING OTHER WRITERS' STYLE[2]

1. Revise the following paragraph in two ways.
   A. Suggest a reordering that includes and keeps all the sentences that are here (with only minor changes of a clause or a connector to improve logic).
   B. Rewrite the paragraph to be the strongest version you can create. You can delete or repeat. You can break into more than one sentence. You can reword, combine, and so on.

      His breath always smelled of beer, or tequila. He told me about the worm at the bottom of the bottle, how he was part Indian and lived some time in Mexico. On weekends when I stayed with her the three of us slept in the same bed, me in the middle. Someone bought me a

[2]You can create a revision exercise like this as a class by contributing "revisable" sections from your own essays, challenging each other to revise the texts, and comparing and discussing the revisions.

Dallas Cowboy's Cheerleader outfit, size 6X. I wore that outfit and cheered my lungs out on the weekends I stayed with grandmother. That was his nickname for me. "My Dallas Cowboy's Cheerleader. Hook 'em horns, Texas." I learned how to hold my hand, Texas horn-style. He once showed me a hundred dollar bill, a real one. I thought it was a fake, but it wasn't. I learned much later it was very real. It was the money my grandmother got when Charlie died. I also learned it went pretty quick, on tequila or six-packs of beer. Sometimes grandmother would run Doug off, and sometimes it was my uncle who ran him off, and he'd reappear a few months later, more chipper than a lark in spring. "Hey, Darling. How's my Dallas Cowboy's Cheerleader?" He called the two of us his "aces," and the way she smiled when the three of us drove down to Mexico Beach with their dog Germia told me everything would be fine, *just fine* this time. He wouldn't get drunk again. He promised.

2. Revise by taking the following scene outline and making it a dramatic scene. Make us feel what Brooke feels (obviously, you'll have to invent your own "story" details).

 Sitting on the dock, staring across the lake, Brooke felt helpless. She watched the ripples blow across the lake. They continued into her head where they disrupted her already jumbled thoughts. She knew she was killing herself here [in this town]. She knew she was living a dangerous life. Somehow it didn't matter to her.

 It's hopeless.

3. Revise the following paragraph to make the language clear and logical while retaining the writer's passion for her topic.

 My special mother attempted to buy me designer outfits, because they carried larger sizes, so that I wouldn't feel shabby if I didn't fit into the teen department. My obsession with looking good did weigh heavily on how I viewed myself in comparison to others. It is very difficult to compare the physical attributes you possess to those embracing a tight ass gracing the glossy covers with their perky breasts and hipbones showing through their white spandex tube dress.

4. If you can, rewrite this paragraph in 50 percent or fewer words.

 We couldn't get by an entire family meal without arguing. The proud parents of five. When it came time for designating chores for cleaning up afterwards, Jay would always get off easiest. We hated him for it. He would get the easiest job of sweeping the kitchen floor while the rest of us had to hand wash pots and pans, put up the leftovers, or load the dishwasher. He would sit around the television with his big goofy pre-teen smirk until we had finished all the hardest work. Sometimes he would end up sweeping up pulled out hair or broken nails from the jealous-driven fight one of us would start with him. We thought for sure there was some sort of favoritism going on directed towards Jay because he was the only boy. Mom and dad sometimes would leave the house to get away from all the yelling and arguing. We just wouldn't get along. They always told us, *we should be nice to one another for the simple fact that we were family.*

5. Recast this transition paragraph in at least two different ways, attempting both to eliminate the number of *I* and *me/mys* and to reduce wordiness in general.

   After I had learned the minimum amount of information necessary for flats fishing, I decided to try my luck at the sport. I began to venture out onto the flats with Hutch once in a while, just to get a taste of the hobby. At first, I found the fishing trips to be tedious, and uneventful on my part, but I continued to stick it out in hopes that some miracle would occur and change my way of thinking. Just as I began to lose all hope, my prayers were answered. In one brief moment I developed the utmost respect, and undying obsession with the sport of flats fishing. In a manner of minutes I was converted from anti-angler to passionate fisherman. My story of this miracle goes as follows as my journey takes place on the outskirts of Tallahassee.

6. Revise to all first-person, continuous present tense and, if possible, avoid "to be" verbs:

   Even though I was in a swimming pool with no hope of seeing any marine life, unless you count the cockroach and clumps of hair that I saw, it was still exhilarating to feel the weight of the water pushing down on my body yet I could breathe comfortably.

7. Analyze the strengths and weaknesses of the following paragraph. Revise to eliminate the weaknesses *and* to increase the effectiveness of the strengths.

   We boarded the Little Neddy II docked at the port at Boynton Beach, Florida. We were ten beginner divers ready to set our eyes on a brand new underwater landscape. As we set out for our dive spot, which was located twenty-five minutes off shore, we received our pre-dive briefing. We would be jumping off the end of the dive boat and grouping together to ready for our decent. I pulled on my neoprene composite wet suit and put on my booties. Then, as the boat began to rock violently as each wave crashed into its side, sending a powerful spray of salt water all over my face, I strapped my black fins complete with water channels and ribs, allowing for ease of movement, on to my feet. After I got my buoyancy control device with the tank attached and my mask on I then placed the regulator in my mouth. I took a few slow, deep breaths off the regulator to make sure that it was indeed supplying me with the dry compressed air that I needed. Inching my way to the very edge of the dive platform I was a little hesitant about the sixty feet we would be descending. Not to mention the warning about the possible presence of Nurse Sharks that our Dive Master had given us in our pre-dive briefing.

8. Revise for clarity. Make sure that references are clear and comparisons are parallel. Consider using active verbs in place of "to be" verbs and using specific referents/references for words like "it" and "they" and so on.

    I have done a great deal of research on both the Republican and Democratic Parties, and I have come to the conclusion that neither is flawless. In fact, neither is close. However, I have recently discovered much about the Democrats that troubles me, and I am stunned that it doesn't concern more people than it does. The self proclaimed "Party of the little guy" is a hypocritical wing of government, and various recent events have indicated to me that they want anything but what is best, not to mention fair, for America. Whether it be issues such as tax cuts, oil supply, and education, or admired leaders such as John F. Kennedy and Bill Clinton, the Democratic Party exudes hypocrisy.

9. Rewrite to reorder sentences. Eliminate repetition to clarify, and eliminate "I" when possible.

    Some people are lucky to have their first love stay with them forever and grow to a lifelong love. It remains constant and stable for as long as time will allow. Mine was no such love and as a result I had to let it go. But that isn't to say that I am not thankful everyday for what I was able to learn, grow, and experience from my relationship with Mr. Catch 22. He will still be my love, my first love. I may not feel the same as I did but I am lucky enough to say that I grew up because of him and am able to call him my friend now because of the mutual acknowledgement of what we both did wrong to each other. I knew what I wanted and didn't want in love because of him.

10. Rewrite to avoid the word "it." Try to match the rhythm and clarity of the opening sentence, but break down longer sentences and seek a more conversational vocabulary.

    I am not a brilliant philosopher. My IQ rests at a reputable height not scorned by the mediocre population, yet it can be smiled upon with slight condescending by those who uphold the level of genius beyond my ability. Despite my unbrilliance, I let my mind wander through mysteries and puzzles and common observances that prick my awareness in their simplistic enigma. I question the genesis, the exodus, the rules and customs of numbers with fascination; however, in my own limited comprehension I strive for a higher understanding than is offered by mere experience. Some call it enlightenment, transcendence, or the wisdom of the ages. I call it a daily struggle of the learning and relearning, of the absorption and regurgitation of information swirling its stimuli around my head in a constant buzz.

KURT VONNEGUT, JR. (b. 1922)

How to Write with Style

CONSIDER THIS:

Before reading, think about your own best advice on style. What eight pieces of advice about writing with style would you give a friend who came to you for such advice? As you read Kurt Vonnegut's essay, see if you have offered any of the same advice. Consider as you read whether he seems to follow his own advice.

Kurt Vonnegut was born in Indianapolis and earned an M.A. from the University of Chicago. He's been a newspaper editor and a journalist, and he worked in public relations for General Electric for a time. Vonnegut has also taught at the University of Iowa, Harvard University, and the City College of New York. He is widely celebrated as the iconoclastic author of 17 novels (including *Slaughter House Five* and *Breakfast of Champions*), a number of which have been made into movies.

Vonnegut's views about teaching writing have evolved over the years. Resistant for some years to the idea of writing instruction being offered in the schools, by 1999, an apparent sea change had taken place. "The primary benefit of practicing any art, whether well or badly, is that it enables one's soul to grow. So the proliferation of creative writing courses is surely a good thing," he explained. Here's Vonnegut's teaching philosophy: "When I taught at Iowa, then Harvard, then City College, here is what I tried to get away with, only in effect, not actually: I asked each student to open his or her mouth as wide as possible. I reached in with a thumb and forefinger to a point directly beneath his or her epiglottis. There is the free end of a spool of tape there. I pinched it, then pulled it out gradually, gently, so as not to make the student gag. When I got several feet of it out where we could see it, the student and I read what was written there."

Newspaper reporters and technical writers are trained to reveal almost nothing about themselves in their writings. This makes them freaks in the world of writers, since almost all of the other ink-stained wretches in that world reveal a lot about themselves to readers. We call these revelations accidental and intentional, elements of style.

These revelations tell us as readers what sort of person it is with whom we are spending time. Does the writer sound ignorant or informed, stupid or bright, crooked or honest, humorless or playful—? And on and on.

Why should you examine your writing style with the idea of improving it? Do so as a mark of respect for your readers, whatever you're writing. If you scribble your thoughts any which way, your readers will surely feel that you care nothing about them. They will mark you down as an egomaniac or a chowder head—or worse, they will stop reading you.

The most damning revelation you can make about yourself is that you do not know what is interesting and what is not. Don't you yourself like or dislike writers mainly for what they choose to show you or make you think about? Did you ever admire an empty-headed writer for his or her mastery of the language? No.

1. FIND A SUBJECT YOU CARE ABOUT

Find a subject you care about and which you in your heart feel others should care about. It is this genuine caring, and not your games with language, which will be the most compelling and seductive element in your style.

I am not urging you to write a novel, by the way—although I would not be sorry if you wrote one, provided you genuinely cared about something. A petition to the mayor about a pothole in front of your house or a love letter to the girl next door will do.

2. DO NOT RAMBLE, THOUGH

I won't ramble on about that.

3. KEEP IT SIMPLE

As for your use of language: Remember that two great masters of language, William Shakespeare and James Joyce, wrote sentences which were almost childlike when their subjects were most profound. "To be or not to be?" asks Shakespeare's Hamlet. The longest word is three letters long. Joyce, when he was frisky, could put together a sentence as intricate and as glittering as a necklace for Cleopatra, but my favorite sentence in his short story "Eveline" is this one: "She was tired." At that point in the story, no other words could break the heart of a reader as those three words do.

Simplicity of language is not only reputable, but perhaps even sacred. The *Bible* opens with a sentence well within the writing skills of a lively fourteen-year-old: "In the beginning God created the heaven and the earth."

4. HAVE THE GUTS TO CUT

It may be that you, too, are capable of making necklaces for Cleopatra, so to speak. But your eloquence should be the servant of the ideas in your head. Your rule might be this: If a sentence, no matter how excellent, does not illuminate your subject in some new and useful way, scratch it out.

5. SOUND LIKE YOURSELF

The writing style which is most natural for you is bound to echo the speech you heard when a child. English was the novelist Joseph Conrad's third language, and much that seems piquant in his use of English was no doubt colored by his first language, which was Polish. And here indeed is the writer who has grown up in Ireland, for the English spoken there is so amusing and musical. I myself grew up in Indianapolis, where common speech sounds like a band saw cutting galvanized and employees a vocabulary as unornamental as a monkey wrench.

In some of the more remote hollows of Appalachia, children grow up hearing songs and locutions of Elizabethan times. Yes, many Americans grow up hearing a language other than English, English dialect a majority of Americans cannot understand.

All these varieties of speech are beautiful, just as the varieties of butterflies are beautiful. No matter what your first language, you should sure it all your life. If it happens not to be standard English, and shows itself when your write standard English, the result is usually delightful, like a very pretty girl with one eye that is green and one that is blue.

I myself find that I trust my own writing most, and others seem to trust it most, too, when I sound most like a person from Indianapolis, which is what I am. What alternatives do I have? The style most vehemently recommended by teachers has no doubt been pressed on you as well: to write like cultivated Englishmen of a century or more ago.

6. SAY WHAT YOU MEAN TO SAY

I used to be exasperated by such teachers, but am no more. I understand now that all those antique essays and stories with which I was to compare my own work were not magnificent for their datedness or foreignness, but for saying precisely what their authors meant them to say. My teachers wished me to write accurately, always selecting the most effective words, and relating the words to one another unambiguously, rigidly, like parts of a machine. The teachers did not want to turn me into an Englishman after all. They hoped that I would become understandable—and therefore understood. And there went my dream of doing with words what Pablo Picasso did with paint or what any number of jazz idols did with music. If I broke all the rules of punctuation, had words mean whatever I wanted them to mean, and strung them together higgledy-piggledy, I would simply not be understood. So you, too, had better avoid Picasso-style or jazz-style-writing, if you have something worth saying and wish to be understood.

Readers want our pages to look very much like pages they have seen before. Why? This is because they themselves have a tough job to do, and they need all the help they can get from us.

7. PITY THE READERS

They have to identify thousands of little marks on pages and make sense of them immediately. people don't really master it even after having studied it all through grade school and high school—twelve long years.

So this discussion must finally acknowledge that our stylistic options as writers are neither numerous nor glamorous, since our readers are bound to be such imperfect artists. Our audience requires us to be sympathetic and patient teachers, even willing to simplify and clarify—whereas we would rather soar high above the crowd, singing like nightingales.

That is the bad news. The good news is that we Americans are governed under a unique Constitution, which allows us to write whatever we please without fear of punishment. So the most meaningful aspect of our styles, which is what we choose to write about, is utterly unlimited.

8. FOR REALLY DETAILED ADVICE

For a discussion of literary style in a narrower sense, in a more technical sense, I commend to your attention *The Elements of Style*, by William Strunk, Jr., and E. B. White (Macmillan, 1979). E. B. White is, of course, one of the most admirable literary stylists this country has so far produced.

You should realize, too, that no one would care how well or badly Mr. White expressed himself, if he did not have perfectly enchanting things to say.

PICO IYER (b. 1957)

In Praise of the Humble Comma

CONSIDER THIS:

Pico Iyer was born in Oxford, England, son to two professors from India. Iyer was raised in England and California. He has been a writer for *Time* magazine since 1982. In an *Insight & Outlook* radio interview, Iyer explained his early writing days as such: "I was a travel writer in the sense that many of us are: just writing about my holidays. Then, when I went to college in England, I suddenly realized that living in California was exotic and that I could just write about California—my home, sort of—and be counted as a travel writer in England." "People are traveling even if they've never left their home town," Iyer said in an interview for Powells.com. "All of us, whether we move or not, are having to deal with this crossing of cultures." Iyer sees writing as a major part of this globalization. "These writers from four corners of the universe who are working within English Literature are flooding it with alien smells and curious words, different customs, and utterly unprecedented rhythms."

You may not have expected that any writer would care to write an essay on a single mark of punctuation. But, for fun, before you begin reading, decide what mark of punctuation you use the most, think is the most crucial, which might be at the center of your essay of the same type. Can you list 10 reasons why you think that punctuation matters? As you read Iyer's work, consider the tone of the essay.

To what degree is he making fun of writing rules, and to what degree is his essay a serious examination of the possibilities of the comma?

The gods, they say, give breath, and they take it away. But the same could be said—could it not?—of the humble comma. Add it to the present clause, and, all of a sudden, the mind is, quite literally, given pause to think; take it out if you wish or forget it and the mind is deprived of a resting place. Yet still the comma gets no respect. It seems just a slip of a thing, a pedant's tick, a blip on the edge of our consciousness, a kind of printer's smudge almost. Small, we claim, is beautiful (especially in the age of the microchip). Yet what is so often used, and so rarely recalled, as, the comma—unless it be breath itself?

Punctuation, one is taught, has a point: to keep up law and order. Punctuation marks are the road signs placed along the highway of our communications—to control speeds, provide directions and prevent head-on collisions. A period has the unblinking finality of a red light; the comma is a flashing yellow light that asks us only to slow down; and the semicolon is a stop sign that tells us to ease gradually to a halt, before gradually starting up again. By establishing the relations between words, punctuation establishes the relations between the people using words. That may be one reason why schoolteachers exalt it and lovers defy it ("We love each other and belong to each other let's don't ever hurt each other Nicole let's don't ever hurt each other," wrote Gary Gilmore to his girlfriend). A comma, he must have known, "separates inseparables," in the clinching words of H. W. Fowler, King of English Usage.

Punctuation, then, is a civic prop, a pillar that holds society upright. (A run-on sentence, its phrases piling up without division, is as unsightly as a sink piled high with dirty dishes.) Small wonder, then, that punctuation was one of the first proprieties of the Victorian age, the age of the corset, that the modernists threw off: the sexual revolution might be said to have begun when Joyce's Molly Bloom spilled out all her private thoughts in 36 pages of unbridled, almost unperioded and officially censored prose; and another rebellion was surely marked when E. E. Cummings first felt free to commit "God" to the lower case.

Punctuation thus becomes the signature of cultures. The hot-blooded Spaniard seems to be revealed in the passion and urgency of his doubled exclamation points and question marks ("*¡Caramba! ¿Quien sabe?*"), while the impassive Chinese traditionally added to his so-called inscrutability by omitting directions from his ideograms. The anarchy and commotion of the '60s were given voice in the exploding exclamation marks, riotous capital letters and Day-Glo italics of Tom Wolfe's spray-paint prose; and in Communist societies, where the State is absolute, the dignity—and divinity—of capital letters is reserved for Ministries, Sub-Committees and Secretariats.

Yet punctuation is something more than a culture's birthmark; it scores the music in our minds, gets our thoughts moving to the rhythm of our hearts. Punctuation is the notation in the sheet music of our words, telling us where to rest, or when to raise our voices; it acknowledges that the meaning of our discourse, as of any symphonic composition, lies not in the units but in the pauses, the pacing and the phrasing. Punctuation is the way one bats one's eyes, lowers one's voice or blushes demurely. Punctuation adjusts the tone and color and volume till the feeling comes into perfect focus, not disgust exactly, but distaste; not lust, or like, but love.

Punctuation, in short, gives us the human voice, and all the meanings that lie between the words. "You aren't young, are you?" loses its innocence when it loses the question mark. Every child knows the menace of a dropped apostrophe (the parent's "Don't do that" shifting into the more slowly enunciated "Do not do that"), and every believer, the ignominy of having his faith reduced to "faith." Add an exclamation point to "To be or not to be . . ." and the gloomy Dane has all the resolve he needs; add a comma, and the noble sobriety of "God save the Queen" becomes a cry of desperation bordering on double sacrilege.

Sometimes, of course, our markings may be simply a matter of aesthetics. Popping in a comma can be like slipping on the necklace that gives an outfit quiet elegance, or like catching the sound of running water that complements, as it completes, the silence of a Japanese landscape. When V. S. Naipaul, in his latest novel, writes, "He was a middle-aged man, with glasses," the first comma can seem a little precious. Yet it gives the description a spin, as well as a subtlety, that it otherwise lacks, and it shows that the glasses are not part of the middle-agedness, but something else.

Thus all these tiny scratches give us breadth and heft and depth. A world that has only periods is a world without inflections. It is a world without shade. It has a music without sharps and flats. It is a martial music. It has a jackboot rhythm. Words cannot bend and curve. A comma, by comparison, catches the gentle drift of the mind in thought, turning in on itself and back on itself, reversing, redoubling and returning along the course of its own sweet river music; while the semicolon brings clauses and thoughts together with all the silent discretion of a hostess arranging guests around her dinner table.

Punctuation, then, is a matter of care. Care for words, yes, but also, and more important, for what the words imply. Only a lover notices the small things: the way the afternoon light catches the nape of a neck, or how a strand of hair slips out from behind an ear, or the way a finger curls around a cup. And no one scans a letter so closely as a lover, searching for its small print, straining to hear its nuances, its gasps, its sighs and hesitations, poring over the secret messages that lie in every cadence. The difference between "Jane (whom I adore)" and "Jane, whom I adore," and the difference between them both and "Jane—whom I adore—"marks all the distance between ecstasy and heartache. "No iron can pierce the heart with such force as a period put at just the right place," in Isaac Babel's lovely words: a comma can let us hear a voice break, or a heart. Punctuation, in fact, is a labor of love. Which brings us back, in a way, to gods.

Classroom Authors

SARAH ANDRAE

Self-analysis of Style

CONSIDER THIS:

Sarah Andrae completed her informal self-analysis as the final exercise in a summer undergraduate writing course. To think about herself as a stylist, she reread her course writings and commented on them. In that sense, this writing is a global yet focused (on style) writing process narrative. Summarize what Andrae appears to have learned about her own writing style in a six-week writing course. What else do you wish she had shared with you about her writing style, particularly in light of the readings on style you completed in this chapter?

Listing. Repetition. Fragments. I have never used these styles in my writing, until I got to this class. I like to read various genres of material—crime novels, fashion magazines, collections of short stories. I would often find authors utilizing styles like listing and fragments. I always wanted to integrate those types of things into my own writing, but I never felt bold enough to do so. I ventured out on a limb with the start of this class.

When I started to draft my first essay, the beginning was the only thing that excited me. I knew I wanted it to be different and radical, yet I had no idea how to accomplish that. Then the light bulb clicked. Lists! I will do a list of adjectives/synonyms in the first paragraph. I used a thesaurus and wrote an exhaustive list. I did not use all of them, but I had a purpose now. As the paper progressed, I began repeating some of the words from the list. I also gave them an internal voice by using italics. I wanted my feelings and emotions to carry more weight in the essay, and I felt that my new style would get that point across.

Along with my fragmented sentences of fat adjectives, I transformed my essay into a letter. The thought of using this technique would not have entered my mind had it not been for Wendy's suggestion. At first, the idea did not appeal to me simply because I was afraid to shift gears. I was more comfortable with creating descriptive scenes with plenty of dialogue. I did not have the first clue on writing an open letter as an academic paper. It would also be a change in regards to how I wrote about my grandmother. I have written two papers about my relationship with her, but I have never addressed her personally.

I wasn't sure where to start. How would I restructure? The one thing I did not want to lose was that beginning paragraph. I had grown so attached to those adjectives. I had to find a way to let them stay. *Vinegar and Oil* taught me a lot about utilizing alternate styles in my writing. There were many firsts. Repetitive Lists. Fragmented sentences and thoughts. The letter format. Yet, they all helped in shaping a beautiful emotional piece about my grandmother and myself.

The premise for the second and third essay worried me. First, I had no clue about a topic. Write about an object? Any object. There are thousands of things out there that interest me, but I could not choose one. Finally, I settled on brassieres. I did not think there would be that much information, but I was definitely surprised. I did not want my historical essay to be boring, but I did want it to be informative. I decided to use subtitles much like Ricky Jay did in his essay titled *The Story of Dice.* I wanted the headings to be catchy and even comical.

I tried to have a chronological history of the bra, beginning with the corset. I have always been taught "never use I or you in a research paper." Well, I had to break that rule. In order to give the paper some zing, I added my own voice, along with plenty of humorous lines. Fragments also entered into this essay. Amanda pointed out that I had a tendency to use fragments, and they worked well in my writing. In my second essay, it seemed that more fragments and listing were just waiting to come out of hiding. So, in a subsequent draft I took her advice and went back to my roots. I am still new to this new style, but I am starting to get the hang of it. However, I am worried that it will get redundant and pointless. That's why I have to reread my essays several times with and without the lists/repetition/fragments. I want to know if the power of my voice is there. Could be overkill though. Hopefully, my readers get it.

I enjoyed working with the "traditional" version of paper two, and I could not quite make the leap to the "radical" version. I had this feeling that I had somehow combined both of them together. I tried to get some ideas from my small workshop group and then from the whole class. Everyone seemed to have great advice, but uncertainty still lingered.

Humor. I had to have it. There was no doubt in my mind. I wanted to look at another perspective on the bra issue. Another point-of-view if you will. What do guys think about bras? Modern guys, that is. Some men do not even want to go into places like Victoria's Secret or even the lingerie department at Sears. Why? What's the big deal? I tried to look at things through my boyfriend's eyes. He hates even thinking about passing by one of these stores. I have to look around alone, while I see other women with their significant others. The second version of my essay on bras would be radical in the sense that I would not do most of the talking. I would have a guy speak his opinion. I just hope it came across that way.

AMANDA FLEMING

Style Analysis

CONSIDER THIS:

When she completed this informal style analysis, Amanda Fleming was a graduate student enrolled in the undergraduate course that Sarah was taking, but she was gaining graduate credit by completing additional writing assignments outside of the classroom. Fleming chose to focus on several elements that were typically atypical in her writing style and to illustrate these with quotes from her writing portfolio drafts. Again, ask yourself what more you'd like to learn about the author as stylist.

I suppose you could say I write in the same manner I keep my room.

Rule of Order:

I have my tapes and CDs and books in alphabetical order.

I try to keep the bed made, t-shirts folded, and my socks in some arrangement.

I make attempts to keep a common color throughout the room.

I thrive on themes, like "coastal" or "French provincial."

The alarm goes off at the same time everyday, and it's the only way I wake up.

Food never stays in the room over night.

Dogs are not allowed, unless they are mine.

Spiders are never allowed.

Feng Shui tried to work once, and there seems to be logic in the bed running N-S.

Pencils have a cup. Pens have a glass. Jewelry has a dish. Shoes have cubbyholes.

Rule of the Senses:

My eyes like pictures on the walls.

My nose likes the smell of magnolia-scented candles.

My ears like good music, like the Cowboy Junkies.

My mouth likes it when I have food near the computer.

Rule of Chaos:

If I like it, it stays, even if it does not match. (Most of the time it does.)

It's ok to use various hues of the color blue, but it must flow.

It's ok to spend a fortune on something you really, really, really like.

A bizarre photograph or sculpture looks better off by itself. Isolation creates attention.

Have a collection of something unpractical. Sand pails. Loose neck fruit animals.

*****Repetition** allows the poet in me to step forward, create echoes of important phrases and ideas, and give a musical quality to my piece. I think I use it to squeeze the juice from the orange. I like repeating patterns because it shows consistency in thought.

EXAMPLES:
She wore her hair one length, with sumptuous large roller curls spilling a la ***Rita Hayworth*** *in Gilda. And she weighed less than the cigarette balanced between her two slim fingers. With her lips parted in a smile, her cheekbones put* ***Rita to shame. To absolute shame.***

When the sun set, my grandmother stared out toward the gulf, ***listening.*** *We'd lay in bed because we had nothing to do in the dark, and we'd listen together. We'd talk and look at the moonlit ceiling, the salt crusty nets on the wall, smell the air and* ***listen.***

You imagine your grandmother among her statues of pelicans, her bottles of medicine, her tape player you bought her so she could ***listen*** *to music as she died slowly. You imagine her dying there, beside the ocean, where she wanted to live, and die (not in the intensive care unit taking heavy breaths as she would end up doing two days before Christmas). She* ***listens*** *to the waves collapsing on the shore . . . .*

The doctor explains to your mother how her bones are brittle, how they aren't ***strong. Strong like*** *when she leaned against fences at neighborhood swimming pools.* ***Strong like*** *when she forged a stream across several exposed rocks . . . .*

I won't lie . . . I won't lie. I didn't just think about it. . . . I won't lie. It has crossed my mind. It still does.

I knew *when I fired the recoil would make me jump.* ***I'd miss*** *the target.* ***I'd drop*** *the gun.* ***I'd ruin*** *the gun. Now that I was closer to the chamber,* ***it would*** *hurt my ears.* ***It would*** *make me jump. I took aim,* ***because*** *I was always a tomboy.* ***Because*** *I was always the one leading the other tent mates into the dark tent at Girl Scout camp, the one to not turn down the dare of eating an entire jalapeno pepper. But I could not pull the trigger.*

******Fragments.** The writer in me wants emphasis brought on by neon signs and flying banners, arrows, dashes to point toward specific words and phrases. Perhaps I overuse this one, but so far no one has stopped me. Ever. I use it when I talk, and I extend it to placing my bed in a room without any other furniture, wearing simple black and a silver necklace with that special charm, and parking way out in the parking lot just so I'll know where I left my car. Isolating words and ideas and furniture is a groovy thing, and perhaps it stems from some Grammar A victim who is silently rebelling because *now that she knows the rule she's going to break it.* The attention to the isolated words is the attraction here.

Also, there's an underlying force when I write to make my writing as smooth as possible. Thus, I tend to write as I would speak.

EXAMPLES:
I expected the island to always be that way. ***Quiet. Salty. Secluded.***

. . . and you fly on toward Atlanta, marking every point along the way on your map provided by Delta. ***Ono Island. Houston. Lake Charles.***

Remember, you may handle your mount 30 times before he ever gets to your living room wall. ***Skinning. Cleaning. Preserving. Gluing. Drying. Brushing. Gelling. Drying some more.***

I must have lay there, staring over toward the glass window criss-crossed with masking tape most of the night. Flakes of hail tapped the glass. There could be the sound of a locomotive at any moment, bouncing like a spring across the water. Each time I thought I might fall asleep I'd wake to define a sound, to slow my heart down. ***I'd listen for Tasha's breathing. The synchronized pattern the twins made. A subtle drunken snore from Eaton in some other room. Thunder near Devil's Swamp. The Visqueen sealing off each of the windows, inhaling each time the wind subsided, taking a deep breath with each burst of wind. Riding it out, just like Jim would.***

He should have caught the hint when I left each of his potted plants on the top step in full sunlight without water. ***Yellow mums wrapped in cellophane. Petunias planted in a tin bucket. A coffee mug of Johnny Jump Up's.***

For the ten years following my royal march across that flat bed trailer I volleyed men like tennis balls. ***Good men. Rich men. Never marrying one of them, because when you live on an island the good ones get married or move away.*** *A woman who wants to be sexually active has to be brave.* ***Take chances. Compromise her standards.***

"You 're overreacting. So I'm single. So I lose focus. Can't a woman let her guard down for one lousy night? Does she have to be become instant stalker material or be persecuted by a nonprofit organization? ***The recipient of potted plants? Her hedge shaped like a character at the Disney Park?"***

****Lists.** One thing I noticed was that I tended to use lists that echoed a repetition. My isolated (in boxes or literal, down the page) lists usually tend to fall flat, remain unexciting, by simply cataloging rather than producing an exciting palette of information. Lorrie Moore uses lists on one of her short stories in Self Help. The main character is a list person, and she's always writing and making mental lists of things to do. After a scene with her boyfriend she may be making a list, and in that list may be something along the lines of: "Find a new boyfriend." This pushes the text forward. I once had a teacher who called the repetition of words or ideas "dead raccoons." That's real catchy. But the idea is that if you saw a bunch of dead raccoons on a trip, say, every mile or so, you might think, "How about that. There's something killing those raccoons." In the last two papers I found myself wanting to list everything. When I looked back at my earlier writing before this class, I noticed I listed more than I thought I did, and I also tended to use repetition within the list:

EXAMPLES:
Crab Scallop Strawberry Top Shell Cone Shell Sea Horse Pancake Sand Dollar Coquina Sea Urchin Spine Arrowhead Sand Dollar

Item #1: Turkey.

22 Flavors: American Elk (or, Wapiti)/Axis/Antelope

We unpacked jumbo-sized bottles of deer urine. Scent-A-Way. Wild hog's teeth. Four pair of boots. Three boxes of t-shirts (exclusively for hunting and fishing). Three tackle boxes.

Venison—365 Days A Year

Itemized List of Hunting Supplies

Variation of a list:
"Does she have to ***become instant stalker material or be persecuted by a non-profit organization? The recipient of potted plants? Her hedge shaped like a character at the Disney Park?"***

****Fractured narratives,** *ugh* can work really well if there is some balance. Have I found that balance yet? *Balance is stability. Stability is constancy. I do nothing the same way twice.* I tried so much in the last paper (Version A) to weave some articles, price lists, and lists of various kinds of deer, into the text, to move the text along in a new way without diverting from the main body. *Axis Deer, Whitetail Deer, Black-Tail Deer, Moose, Antelope.* I attempted a piece early this semester that took a short story I wrote this summer about a mother whose daughter has chosen to go live with her father in another state. The mother blames herself that her daughter is headed for disappointment (dad is a jerk) and she remembers the boy who kissed her in the back of the library, who was a little too passionate. She wishes she had married him, then her daughter would have spirit. I took it, broke it open, and weaved the lyrics to the Indigo Girls "History of Us."

(i went all the way to paris to forget your face/captured in stained glass, young lives long since passed/statues of lovers every place/i went all across the continent to relieve this restless love/i walked through the ruins, icons of glory/smashed by the bombs from above)

Surprisingly, it added a new dimension. The song is also an echo (of sorts) of a lost (passionate) love. Although the two texts tell different stories, they work by moving toward a common theme.

EXAMPLES:
"You wouldn't hear a Redneck say deer heads detract from the decor. "(Jeff Foxworthy)

Mental Note: One thing you'll always hear from behind you as you stare up toward someone's dusty deer head: "Yep, there's a long story behind that." Prepare yourself.

On top of the television lay two rattles ***(one from a diamondback rattlesnake)****, a deer skull positioned comically atop a wild boar jaw* ***(a wild mental image if you were trying to figure out what animal it was alive)****, and an assortment of tortoise shells.*

He packed a good argument, that deer wasn't considered red meat, and it was healthier than most kinds of meat because it has less fat. ***I know a guy who had a heart attack last year and now eats deer meat because his doctor recommended it.***

***Run-On/Labyrinthine** sentences create immediacy and consistency in thought in some of my pieces. Although this is the hardest style for me to play with, I find it exciting to create lengthy passages for effect.

EXAMPLES:
You may schedule a lunch at the Cheese Barn on Grace Avenue, meet after work, talk and connect about old times, laugh, promise when you get that convertible you want you're going to take her for a drive, going to take her parasailing because she's always wanted to go, and you decide to get together more often, you say you'll call her, you say you love her, and when you hug her you can feel how osteoporosis has set in with a rage for you can't hug her around her shoulders but must hug her around her waist and her white hair falls in your face and it's thin thin thin, then she hobbles over to her car, gets in, and before you can get yours cranked she 's shot out of the lot, the little speed demon, and headed for her empty apartment on the bayou.

I spent $300 on a Minolta 100-300 zoom lens to see if that would get me into the woods both to find out for myself and to satisfy some craving of my lonely hunter, who wanted his beloved to share in the experience of being quiet enough ***("Don't you cough, or sneeze, or whack at any mosquitoes.")****, patient enough* ***("You better bring one of your books.")****, and lucky enough see a deer in the wild come into view.*

CONNECTING TO READING

A. In your journal, to prepare for class discussion, make a list of productive rules that you use as a writer. Where did they come from and how did you know to keep these rules handy?

B. In a class discussion group, consider the ways you and your friends manage to avoid or to work around writer's block. Can you discover the rules that may be contributing to blocked writing for you as Mike Rose was able to discover rules behind the habits of the students he studied? In general, do you see yourselves as flexible or inflexible writers (using set or flexible rules)? Explore why and be prepared to share your observations in a class discussion.

C. In a class discussion, using both Richard Marius's and Kurt Vonnegut's essays, make a composite set of advice for writing with style. In a follow-up journal entry after this in-class exercise, discuss when your class's advice might be useful and when it might be dangerous for a writer (for you as a writer).

D. In an e-mail to a writing partner, discuss the way individuals are judged by their language use. Explore in more depth why this happens. What's at stake when we conform to community or cultural expectations of language use? What pressures have you felt to conform to? What has been disturbing or harmful about such pressure? Be specific and tell stories (that you feel comfortable telling). Explore instances when you felt you were part of a larger, politically charged discussion; for instance, you may speak a minority dialect and believe that you have been unfairly judged by those who assume that dialect reflects certain things about you and your community. Or you may have attended a school where bicultural education was advocated or avoided. On the other hand, you may have experienced these discussions on a smaller scale, feeling classroom pressures to conform via pressures that you have "good language etiquette," that you "clean up" your language so as not to offend. What does it mean to you—to any writer—to resist or give in to such pressures? Several essayists in Chapter 2 address such issues. Respond fully to the writing your partner sends to you, store this dialogue in your journal, and use it as speaking notes for a full class discussion.

E. In an entry on a class discussion board, agree or disagree with my contention, shared in the introduction to this textbook and throughout this chapter, that language matters. Agree or disagree, but be sure to support and illustrate your position. Then respond to two other peer postings on this topic.

CONNECTING TO WRITING

A. As a two-part journal entry, draft a preliminary style self analysis in two versions. (1) Who were (are) you as a stylist as your writing course begins? Feel free to use illustrative details, including quotes from writing before this course. (2) Who are you as a stylist at this point in the term? The same or different and why? Illustrate with style examples from your most recent course essay.

B. In a journal entry that you revise into an informal, one-page position paper, suitable for sharing with a small group or the entire class, investigate whose language matters and what it means to write in a multicultural, multilingual country like ours. To do this, choose a quote from one of the authors in this chapter or from those found in Chapter 2 and use that to let you explore your attitudes. For instance, if you know more than one language, can you—and should you ever even try to—forget the first-language or the community dialect that shaped you as you write in your second language?

C. Prepare the following journal entry for a small group discussion. Choose a piece of representative writing of your own and analyze it, pointing out to your readers what characteristic stylistic moves mark it as all yours. What is your preferred writing style? How does someone (how do you) know that a piece of writing is yours? To get ideas for this activity, read Amanda Fleming's self analysis in this chapter and then return to her essays in Chapter 4 and see if you agree with her observations regarding her writing style.

D. In an open letter to a high school student writer, extend the discussion you find in Richard Marius's essay: Identify two rules you find false and examine them for possible truths.

E. For a group discussion on sentence style, collect some sentences you like from published writings you generally read (newspapers, books, magazines you have around the house). As a group, discuss them, imitate them (have each member nominate one sentence for the entire group to imitate), and then analyze them. What makes them work? Share your findings with another group that is completing this activity based on its own collected set of sentences.

WRITING PROJECTS

1. Write an essay about the importance of language in your life, considering especially issues of authority. The following prompts might help you come up with a topic:

- What languages do you speak? When do you speak them and to whom?
- Under what circumstances does your dialect change? Tell a story about this.
- Have you ever traveled and not known the language? Where, when, how did you feel, what did you do? Did you try to learn the language? Did you enjoy not knowing?
- When do you feel silenced, without language?
- Do you share a private language with anyone or anything? (Did you have a secret language as a child? Are you a twin or close to a sibling with whom you share a language?)
- Do you think differently in different languages? If you know two languages, how are dreams different in the two? Is one language better for talking about certain subjects?
- Tell a story about youself and language.
- Tell a story about your family and language.
- Have you lost a language? Where, how, why?
- Is there a professional language you wish you knew? Sports, politics, music, science, or anything else?

2. Write an essay about an issue of language that is important to your culture-at-large. The following prompts might help you come up with a topic:

- Do you have a peer group that uses a certain language? Give examples.

- Do you or someone you know work in a profession with its own language? For instance, what is the language of school? What is the language of therapy? What is advertising language?
- Do animals have languages? If they do, explain why you think so. If you don't think so, explain why you don't believe they do.
- Do you think we should all know several languages? Why or why not? Do you want your children to know more than one language?
- What—if anything—will be lost when/if we all speak the same language (as when Europe moved to the eurodollar)? What will be gained?
- How important is a language to a culture?
- Well into this century, some cultures had only spoken and not written languages. What would be the benefits of this? The drawbacks? The implications?
- What is your acquaintance/relationship to braille, to American Sign Language, to Esperanto, to computer languages. Are these true languages? What do we mean by the idea/concept of *true* language?

3. Write an essay about another writer's style. Choose three authors in this book whose style you enjoy. Explore what makes them similar and different as well as what it is about their writing style in particular that appeals to you as a writer. Compare, if you wish, your own style to theirs. Use illustrative quotes when useful.
4. In your persuasive essay, make a strong argument for learning conventions, mastering the basics, knowing the essential tools of your craft. What should writers learn about grammar and usage? when and why? What are the joys and pleasures of knowing these things about (your) writing?
5. Following the lead of Ken Autrey, Julia Alvarez, and Allison Joseph, write a poem about language. Poets are especially attuned to the way a single word choice may make a difference in their meaning. I suspect that's why so many write poems about language. Then, write a commentary that speaks to the issues addressed in the poem. Think of this as your mini-essay on "How and Why I Wrote [title of your poem]."
6. Write an open letter to a writer who is having difficulty with a school assignment. Using what you've learned in this chapter in particular but in all your time as a writer, provide this fellow writer with your best advice for developing a better relationship to writing rules and/or for avoiding and working through writing blocks.
7. Write a "how to" essay for writers like you. That is, if you are interested in writing for newspapers, offer advice—in the manner of Kurt Vonnegut—on how—as a newspaper columnist—to write with style. If you're hoping to be a technical writer, a nonfiction author, or more simply a writer who does well in school, offer advice and discussions about style tailored to that audience and that writer's typical writing genre.
8. Write an essay that attempts to characterize and analyze a writer's voice/style. Choose a writer whose work you admire and analyze his or her

writing style, particularly sentence style, using, perhaps, the discussion in my essay in this chapter to help you. Show your readers exactly how this author makes a text sound like his or her own. As an alternate option, examine your own evolving writing style by sharing papers written during various periods of your life. What, if anything, remains consistent; what, if anything, has changed? What lessons can you draw about your development as a stylist?

9. In your persuasive essay, argue for stylistic anarchy and/or experimentation. When is it important for a writer to take risks, to explore, to experiment, to break the rules? What are the benefits and consequences of doing so? Along the way, explain why you are conducting your argument in conventional prose (if you are) and how you know when you've gotten better as a writer if and when you put experimentation at the center of your writing process.

10. Imitation is a form of flattery. Flatter Pico Iyer by writing an essay about one of your favorite marks of punctuation. As he does, illustrate your definition by deploying that type of punctuation to its fullest.

* * * *

As a teacher you try to make them [students] see things on their own. Once they see it on their own they can move on—they can revise and see their work without the teacher's help. I try to get them to look hard at what they're saying. I've been teaching seven years. After that long, I know that what I really want is to get them to question: Why am I using that word? Is it right, or was it just easy—did it just come to me because I can spell it? It's the same reason you put the same sweater on every day: it's not dirty, but it's not clean—you woke up late again. But if you want to look a little better you're going to have to work a little harder.

—Nikki Giovanni

Credits

DIANE ACKERMAN, "Mute Dancers: How to Watch a Hummingbird." Copyright © 1994 by Diane Ackerman. Reprinted by permission of William Morris Agency, Inc., on behalf of the Author.

JOHN AGARD, "Listen Mr. Oxford Dan." By kind permission of John Agard, c/o Caroline Sheldon Literary Agency from *Mangoes & Bullets* (Serpent's Tail, 1990).

SHERMAN ALEXIE, "White Men Can't Drum." Used by permission of the author.

JULIA ALVAREZ, "Bilingual Sestina" from *The Other Side/El Otro Lado.* Copyright © 1995 by Julia Alvarez. Published by Dutton, a division of Penguin USA. Originally published in *The George Washington Review.* Reprinted by permission of Susan Bergholz Literary Services, New York. All rights reserved.

KEN AUTREY, "Prepositions in Alabama." Reprinted by permission of the author.

WENDY BISHOP, "Its Not the Heat, It's the Humidity—It's Not the Cold, It's the Darkness" from *When We Say We're Home: A Quartet of Place and Memory,* edited by W. Scott Olsen. Reprinted courtesy of The University of Utah Press; "Reading, Stealing and Writing Like a Writer," reprinted from *Elements of Alternative Style: Essays on Writing and Revision,* edited by Wendy Bishop. Copyright © 1997 by Boynton/Cook Publishers, Inc. Published by Boynton/Cook Publishers, a subsidiary of Reed Elsevier, Inc., Portsmouth, NH. Reprinted by permission of the publisher; "Try This" was originally published as "What We (Might) Write About When We Write (Autobiographical) Nonfiction" from *Teaching Lives: Essays and Stories.* Copyright © 1997 Utah State University Press. Reprinted by permission.

CHRISTY BROWN, "The Letter A" from *My Left Foot,* Secker & Warburg, 1954. Used by permission of The Random House Group Limited.

RAYMOND CARVER, "Sunday Night" from *Where Water Comes Together with Other Water.* Copyright © 1984, 1985 by Raymond Carver. Used by permission of Random House, Inc.

EDWARD CORBETT AND ROBERT CONNERS, "A Brief Explanation of Classical Rhetoric" and "Formulating a Thesis" from *Classical Rhetoric for the Modern Student,* Fourth Edition. Copyright © 1965, 1971, 1990, 1999 by Oxford University Press, Inc. Used by permission of Oxford University Press, Inc.

GAY LYNN CROSSLEY, "Making Peace with the Research Essay—One Teacher's History." Reprinted by permission from *The Subject is Reading: Essays by Teachers and Students,* edited by Wendy Bishop. Copyright © 2000 by Boynton/Cook Publishers, Inc.

Published by Boynton/Cook Publishers, Inc., a subsidiary of Reed Elsevier, Inc., Portsmouth, NH.

DOMITILA DE CHUNGARA, "Let Me Speak!" from *Let Me Speak!* by Domitila Barrios de Chungara with Moema Viezzer. Copyright © 1979 by *Monthly Review Press.* Reprinted by permission of Monthly Review Foundation.

ANNIE DILLARD, "Transfiguration" and "How I Wrote the Moth Essay—and Why." Used by permission of the author and Blanche C. Gregory, Inc.

RITA DOVE, "To Make a Prairie." First published in the Phi Beta Kappa magazine *The Key Reporter.* Copyright © 1993 by Rita Dove. Reprinted by permission of the author.

PETER ELBOW AND PAT BELANOFF, "Summary of Ways of Responding" and "Writing a Research Paper" from *A Community of Writers,* 3/e. Copyright © 1999 The McGraw-Hill Companies, Inc. Used by permission.

TOBY FULWILER, "A Lesson in Revision." Reprinted by permission from *The Subject is Writing: Essays by Teachers and Students,* Second Edition, edited by Wendy Bishop. Copyright © 1999 by Boynton/Cook Publishers, Inc. Published by Boynton/Cook Publishers, Inc., a subsidiary of Reed Elsevier, Inc., Portsmouth, NH; "The Role of Audiences" from *College Writing,* 1/e. Copyright © 1991. Used by permission of the author.

GAIL GODWIN, "The Watcher at the Gates" from *The New York Times Book Review,* January 9, 1977. Copyright © 1977 by The New York Times Co. Reprinted with permission.

MELISSA GOLDWAITE, "This, Too, Is Research." Reprinted by permission from *The Subject is Research: Process and Practices,* edited by Wendy Bishop and Pavel Zemliansky. Copyright © 2001 by Boynton/Cook Publishers, Inc. Published by Boynton/Cook Publishers, Inc., a subsidiary of Reed Elsevier, Inc., Portsmouth, NH.

GERALD GRAFF, "Hidden Meaning, or Disliking Books at an Early Age" from *Beyond the Culture Wars: How Teaching The Conflicts Can Revitalize American Education.* Copyright © 1992 by Gerald Graff. Used by permission of W. W. Norton & Company, Inc.

STUART GREENE, "Argument as Conversation: The Role of Inquiry in Writing a Research Argument." Reprinted by permission from *The Subject is Research: Process and Practices,* edited by Wendy Bishop and Pavel Zemliansky. Copyright © 2001 by Boynton/Cook Publishers, Inc. Published by Boynton/Cook Publishers, Inc., a subsidiary of Reed Elsevier, Inc., Portsmouth, NH.

KATHERINE HAAKE. "Exercise I: Beyond the End of Writing" from *What Our Speech Disrupts.* Copyright © 2000 by the National Council of Teachers of English. Reprinted with permission.

PATRICIA HAMPL, "Memory and Imagination." Originally published as "Grandmother's Sunday Dinner" from *A Romantic Education.* Copyright © 1981 by Patricia Hampl. Used by permission of W. W. Norton & Company, Inc.

EVANS D. HOPKINS, "Letter from Prison. Lockdown. Life Inside is Getting Harder" from *The New Yorker,* February 24/March 3, 1997. Used by permission of the author.

LANGSTON HUGHES, "Theme for English B" from *The Collected Poems of Langston Hughes.* Copyright © 1994 by The Estate of Langston Hughes. Used by permission of Alfred A. Knopf, a division of Random House, Inc.

PICO IYER, "In Praise of the Humble Comma" from *Time Magazine.* Copyright © 1988 TIME Inc. Reprinted by permission.

ALLISON JOSEPH, "Rules of Conduct: Colored Elementary School, 1943" reprinted from *In Praise of Pedagogy,* edited by Wendy Bishop and David Starkey. Copyright © 2000 by Allison Joseph. Reprinted by permission of the author.

JAMAICA KINCAID, from *A Small Place.* Copyright © 1988 by Jamaica Kincaid. Reprinted by permission of Farrar, Straus and Giroux, LLC.

BARBARA KINGSOLVER, "In Case You Ever Want To Go Home Again" from *High Tide in Tucson: Essays from Now or Never*. Copyright © 1995 by Barbara Kingsolver. Reprinted by permission of HarperCollins Publishers, Inc.

ANNE LAMOTT, "Index Cards" and "Shitty First Drafts" from *Bird By Bird*. Copyright © 1994 by Anne Lamott. Used by permission of Pantheon Books, a division of Random House, Inc.

SPIKE LEE, "Journal Entries: Do the Right Thing." Excerpted with permission of Simon & Schuster Adult Publishing Group from *Do The Right Thing* by Spike Lee with Lisa Jones. Copyright © 1989 by Spike Lee.

GERALD LOCKLIN, "Amphibians Have Feelings Too" from *The Firebird Poems*. Copyright © 1992 by Gerald Locklin. Used by permission of the author.

BARRY LOPEZ, "My Horse." Republished with permission of Barry Lopez. Permission conveyed through Copyright Clearance Center, Inc.

RICHARD MARIUS, "False Rules and What is True About Them" from *A Writer's Companion*. Copyright © 1999 The McGraw-Hill Companies, Inc. Used by permission.

PAULE MARSHALL, "The Poets in the Kitchen" from *Reena and Other Stories* by Paule Marshall. Copyright © 1983 by Paule Marshall. Used by permission of The Feminist Press at The City University of New York, www.feministpress.org.

BARBARA MELLIX, "From Outside, In" originally appeared in *The Georgia Review*, Volume XLI, No. 2 (Summer 1987). Copyright © 1987 by The University of Georgia and Copyright © 1987 by Barbara Mellix. Reprinted by permission of Barbara Mellix and *The Georgia Review*.

LORRIE MOORE, "How to Become A Writer" from *Self-Help*. Copyright © 1985 by M. L. Moore. Used by permission of Alfred A. Knopf, a division of Random House, Inc.

DONALD MURRAY, "Trying on the Essay" from *Crafting a Life*. Used by permission of the author, Donald Murray, Professor Emeritus of English, University of New Hampshire.

DEAN NEWMAN, "Becky's Mirror." Used with permission of the author.

CHRIS OLSON, "Learning to Read: For Me It's Been the Struggle of a Lifetime." Reprinted by permission from *The Subject is Reading: Essays by Teachers and Students*, edited by Wendy Bishop. Copyright © 2000 by Boynton/Cook Publishers, Inc. Published by Boynton/Cook Publishers, Inc., a subsidiary of Reed Elsevier, Inc., Portsmouth, NH.

LINDA PASTAN, "Marks" from *Five Stages of Grief*. Copyright © 1978 by Linda Pastan. Used by permission of W. W. Norton & Company, Inc.

RICHARD RODRIGUEZ, "Going Home Again." Copyright © 1974 by Richard Rodriguez. Reprinted by permission of Georges Borchardt, Inc., for the author.

MIKE ROSE, "The Discourse of Academics." Reprinted with the permission of The Free Press, a Division of Simon & Schuster Adult Publishing Group, from *Lives on the Boundary: The Struggles and Achievements of America's Underprepared* by Mike Rose. Copyright © 1989 by Mike Rose; "Writing Around Rules." Copyright by Mike Rose. Originally published in *Patterns In Action*, by Robert Schwegler. Reprinted by permission of the author.

SCOTT RUSSELL SANDERS, "The Most Human Art: Ten Reasons Why We'll Always Need a Good Story." Reprinted as it appeared in *The Utne Reader*, and excerpted from "The Power of Stories" which was originally published in *The Georgia Review*. Copyright © 1997 by Scott Russell Sanders. Reprinted by permission of the author.

FAN SHEN, "The Classroom and the Wider Culture: Identity as a Key to Learning English Composition." Copyright © 1989 by the National Council of Teachers of English. Reprinted with permission.

EILEEN SIMPSON, "Dyslexia" from *Reversals*. Copyright © 1979, 1991 by Eileen Simpson. Reprinted by permission of Georges Borchardt, Inc.

LEONORA SMITH, "The Five Paragraph Essay." Reprinted with permission from *Spatial Relations*. East Lansing: Michigan State University Press, 2002.

BRENT STAPLES, "Just Walk On By: A Black Man Ponders His Power to Alter Public Space." Used by permission of the author.

DONNA STEINER, "Sleeping with Alcohol." Reprinted with permission of the author and the *Bellingham Review*

RICHARD STRAUB, "Responding, Really Responding, to Other Students' Writing." Reprinted by permission from *The Subject is Writing: Essays by Teachers and Students*, Second Edition, edited by Wendy Bishop. Copyright © 1999 by Boynton/Cook Publishers, Inc. Published by Boynton/Cook Publishers, Inc., a subsidiary of Reed Elsevier, Inc., Portsmouth, NH.

AMY TAN, "Mother Tongue." Copyright © 1990 by Amy Tan. First appeared in *The Threepenny Review*. Reprinted by permission of the author and the Sandra Dijkstra Literary Agency.

DEBORAH COXWELL TEAGUE, "Making Meaning—Your Own Meaning—When You Read." Reprinted by permission from *The Subject is Reading: Essays by Teachers and Students*, edited by Wendy Bishop. Copyright © 2000 by Boynton/Cook Publishers, Inc. Published by Boynton/Cook Publishers, Inc., a subsidiary of Reed Elsevier, Inc., Portsmouth, NH.

HAUNANI-KAY TRASK, "Tourist, Stay Home" from *The Progressive*, July 1993. Reprinted by permission from *The Progressive*, 409 East Main Street, Madison, WI 53703.

KURT VONNEGUT, Jr., "How to Write with Style." Reprinted with permission from Jacob, Medinger and Finnegan, agents for the author.

CATHERINE WALD, "Research and the Fiction Writer: Perils, Pleasures, and Pitfalls" from *Poets and Writers Magazine*, September-October, 2000. Reprinted by permission of the author.

WINSTON WEATHERS, "The Winston Weathers Writing Way: A Self-Examination" from *Writers on Writing*, edited by Tom Waldrep. Reprinted by permission of Tom Waldrep, Director, The Writing Center and Director, The Center for Academic Excellence, Medical University of South Carolina, Charleston, SC.

RICHARD WILBUR, "The Writer" from *The Mind-Reader*. Copyright © 1971 by Richard Wilbur. Reprinted by permission of Harcourt, Inc.

LYNNA WILLIAMS, "We Told You This, Didn't We?" from *The Chattahoochee Review*. Used by permission of the author.

TERRY TEMPEST WILLIAMS, "Why I Write" published as "A Letter to Deb Clow" from *Red: Passion and Patience in the Desert*. Originally appeared in *Northern Lights* magazine, summer 1998 edition. Copyright © 1998 by Terry Tempest Williams. Reprinted by permission of Brandt & Hochman Literary Agents, Inc.

STANLEY L. WITKIN, "Writing Social Work" from *Social Work*, Volume 45, No. 5. Copyright © 2000 National Association of Social Workers, Inc., Social Work. Reprinted with permission.

RICHARD WRIGHT, "The Library Card" from *Black Boy* by Richard Wright. Copyright © 1937, 1942, 1944, 1945 by Richard Wright. Copyright renewed 1973 by Ellen Wright. Reprinted by permission of HarperCollins Publishers, Inc.

JANE YOLEN, from *How Writers Write*, edited by Pamela Lloyd. Copyright © 1987. Reproduced courtesy of the author.

Definitions of "nature," "naturalist," "natural science," and "natural history" from *Webster's New World™ Dictionary, 2nd College Edition*. Copyright © 1976 by Wiley Publishing, Inc. All rights reserved. Reproduced here by permission of the publisher.

Index